African-American Heroes

Colin Powell

Stephen Feinstein

Enslow Elementary
an imprint of
Enslow Publishers, Inc.
40 Industrial Road
Box 398
Berkeley Heights, NJ 07922
USA
http://www.enslow.com

Words to Know

adviser (ad-VIE-zer)—A person who gives other people advice on how to solve problems or what to do.

career—The job that a person does through life.

Joint Chiefs of Staff—The highest military advisory group in the United States.

lieutenant (loo-TEN-ent)—A type of officer in the armed forces.

military (MIL-uh-te-ree)—Having to do with soldiers and war.

National Security Adviser—Someone who tells the President of the United States what can be done to keep our country safe.

promoted—Given a more important job.

ROTC—A college program that trains students to become officers in the U.S. military. It stands for Reserve Officer's Training Corps.

Enslow Elementary, an imprint of Enslow Publishers, Inc.

Enslow Elementary® is a registered trademark of Enslow Publishers, Inc.

Library of Congress Cataloging-in-Publication Data

Feinstein, Stephen.

   Colin Powell / Stephen Feinstein.

     p. cm.

   Includes bibliographical references and index.

   Audience: Grades K-3.

   ISBN-13: 978-0-7660-2761-9

   ISBN-10: 0-7660-2761-9

   1. Powell, Colin L.—Juvenile literature. 2. Statesmen—United States—Biography—Juvenile literature. 3. Cabinet officers—United States—Biography—Juvenile literature. 4. African American generals—Biography—Juvenile literature. 5. Generals—United States—Biography—Juvenile literature. 6. United States. Army—Biography—Juvenile literature. I. Title.

E840.8.P64F45 2007

355.0092—dc22

[B]   2006026899

Printed in the United States of America

10 9 8 7 6 5 4 3 2

Enslow Publishers, Inc., is committed to printing our books on recycled paper. The paper in every book contains 10% to 30% post-consumer waste (PCW). The cover board on the outside of each book contains 100% PCW. Our goal is to do our part to help young people and the environment too!

Illustration Credits: AP/Wide World, pp. 1, 3, 9, 14 (top), 17, 18, 20, 21; Artville, LLC, p. 19; Archives, The City College of New York, CUNY, p. 11; Library of Congress, p. 5; collection of Colin L. Powell, pp. 3, 6, 10, 12, 14 (bottom); U.S. Department of Defense, p. 16.

Cover Illustration: AP/Wide World.

Contents

Chapter 1

The Boy Who Liked to Sleep Late

Colin Luther Powell was born on April 5, 1937, in Harlem in New York City. When he was three years old, his family moved to the South Bronx, another part of the city. They lived in a poor neighborhood.

Colin's mother was named Maud Ariel, known as Arie. His father was named Luther. They had come to the United States from the island of Jamaica.

Both of Colin's parents worked hard at their jobs. They wanted a better life for Colin and his older sister Marilyn.

Colin L. Powell has served our country in many ways.

In this picture, Colin is about nine years old.

Colin liked to spend time with his neighborhood friends. In this picture, he is second from the right.

Maud and Luther believed that the way to a better life was through hard work and education. But Colin did not try very hard in school, so his grades were not very good. Colin was not interested in the subjects taught in school. He wanted to know how things worked. He liked to take things apart and put them back together.

Colin liked to sleep late on Saturday mornings. But his parents did not want him to waste time. One day Colin's mother told his cousin Victor to pour a glass of water on Colin's head. This woke Colin up.

Colin's parents wanted him to be the best that he could be. So he promised them that he would study enough so that he could graduate from high school.

Chapter 2

Colin Joins ROTC

In 1954, Colin entered the City College of New York. The next year Colin joined the **ROTC**. At the time he was not planning a career as a solider. But Colin liked the ROTC. While in military training, Colin showed that he could become a good leader. He studied hard in his ROTC classes. He got straight As in all of them.

Colin graduated from college in 1958 at the top of his ROTC class. He went straight into the U.S. Army as a second **lieutenant**.

Colin's parents were pleased that Colin was in the Army. In those days, African Americans were treated more fairly in the Army than in many other jobs.

These college students are in ROTC, just like Colin was.

Colin went to an ROTC summer camp in North Carolina. It was hard work, but Colin had time to relax for this picture.

After learning to be a soldier in Georgia, Colin was sent to Germany. There he was a platoon leader in charge of forty men. Then the Army sent Colin to Massachusetts.

One day in 1960, Colin went on a blind date with a woman named Alma Vivian Johnson. Two

This is Colin's college graduation photo. He went straight into the army after college.

years later, Colin and Alma were married, on August 24, 1962. Later, they had three children: Michael, Linda, and Annemarie.

Colin Powell and Alma Johnson were married in 1962.

Colin Goes to Vietnam

Chapter 3

In December 1962, Colin was a captain. The Army sent him to Vietnam. Colin helped the South Vietnamese army in a war against the North Vietnamese.

One day Colin was badly hurt while in the jungle. He stepped on a trap, a sharp stick in the ground that stuck into his foot. Colin was awarded a Purple Heart medal for his bravery. Colin returned home in 1963. He was proud that he had risked his life for his country.

In 1968, Colin was sent back to Vietnam. By this time he had become a major in the Army.

The Purple Heart medal is given to American soldiers who are wounded.

Captain Colin Powell, left, with two of his soldiers in Vietnam.

One day the helicopter in which Colin was flying crashed. It burst into flames. Colin, who was thrown clear, was not hurt. He rushed back into the burning helicopter. He pulled several injured soldiers to safety.

Colin came home from Vietnam the next year with more medals. He had fought bravely. But in 1975 the war ended with a North Vietnamese victory. Colin felt that the United States must never again go to war without without having enough soldiers to win.

Chapter 4

Colin Rises Through the Ranks

As the years went by, Colin was **promoted** again and again. From 1987 to 1989 he served as **National Security Adviser** for President Ronald Reagan. In 1989 Colin became a four-star general.

The Pentagon is a five-sided building in Washington, D.C. Colin worked there with other American military leaders.

A general is the highest rank in the U.S. Army.

On April 4, 1989, President George H.W. Bush asked Colin Powell to be Chairman of the **Joint Chiefs of Staff**. This is America's most important military job.

In this picture, the first President Bush is saying that he has chosen Colin Powell to be Chairman of the Joint Chiefs of Staff.

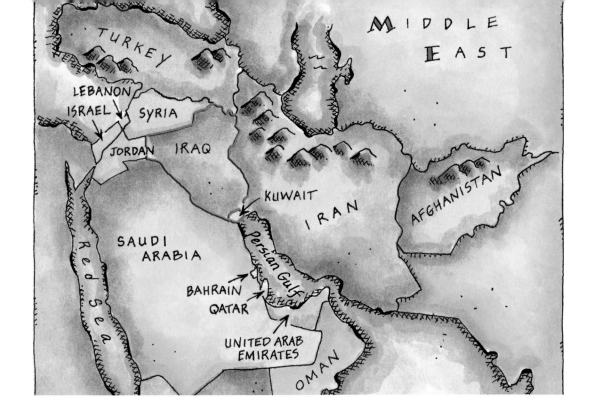

In August 1990, Iraq, a country in the Middle East, attacked the much smaller country of Kuwait. In January 1991, the United States went to war to free Kuwait.

General Colin Powell made sure there were enough soldiers to get the job done. America and its friends won the war in just a few weeks. The American soldiers were welcomed home as heroes.

In 1993, Colin left the Army after thirty-five years. In January 2001, he was made Secretary of State by President George W. Bush. Colin became the first African American to hold such a high job in the U.S. government.

President George W. Bush and his wife, Laura, visit Colin and Alma Powell for dinner. President Bush chose Colin to be his Secretary of State, a very important job.

Colin's Own Words

"A dream doesn't become reality through magic; it takes sweat, determination and hard work."

Colin Powell left the government in 2004. Today he visits schools to speak to the students. He tells young people to work hard and make the most of their lives.

Timeline

1937 Colin is born in New York City on April 5.

1958 Colin graduates from college and joins the U.S. Army as a second lieutenant.

1962–1963, 1968 Colin serves in the U.S. Army in Vietnam.

1973–1974 Colin is a battalion commander at Camp Casey in South Korea.

1987–1989 Colin serves as National Security Adviser for President Ronald Reagan.

1989 Colin is named Chairman of the Joint Chiefs of Staff.

1990–1991 Colin oversees the successful operation of the Persian Gulf War.

1993 Colin retires from the U.S. Army.

2001–2004 Colin serves as Secretary of State for President George W. Bush.

Learn More

Books

Passaro, John. *Colin Powell*. Chanhassan, Minn.: Child's World, 2000.

Sievert, Terri. *U.S. Army at War*. Mankato, Minn.: Capstone, 2002.

Steins, Richard. *Colin Powell: A Biography*. New York: Greenwood Press, 2003.

Strong, Mike. *Colin Powell: It Can Be Done!* Mankato, Minn.: Capstone, 2003.

Web Sites

Academy of Achievement: Colin L. Powell
<http://www.achievement.org/>
Go to "Select Achiever," then click on "Powell, Colin L."

"Colin Powell"
<http://www.factmonster.com>
Go to "Search" and type in "Colin Powell."

Index

Preface

In this third edition we have retained the goal proclaimed in previous editions: to supply an exposition of international economics that is serious in its theoretical underpinnings and yet connected to current economic events. The current economic events are not in short supply. Nor are advances in some areas of international economic theory, particularly the macroeconomic and monetary area. The late comic Fred Allen once ad libbed, as a joke fell flat, "When we warmed up the audience before the show, we must have cremated them." The trick is to adapt a textbook to the pace of events and intellectual development without losing the student in the resulting turbulence.

We retain in the third edition the five-part organization that appeared with the second edition, although with two new chapters added to Part 4. We have also stuck to the second edition's level of difficulty, restricting the text to material that requires only the background in micro and macro theory provided by the standard course on principles of economics. To make the book adaptable for instructors wishing a more advanced approach, we have retained the mathematical supplements presented at the back of previous editions and also expanded the use of appendices at the ends of chapters. The appendices typically offer geometrical constructions that some instructors favor but others wish to avoid. The conclusions reached in the appendices always receive self-sufficient coverage in the text, although with less weighty or less general analytical underpinning.

The real-variables part of the book (Parts 1–3) retains the organization of the second edition, although with many minor changes to clarify and enliven the exposition. We have, for example, been concerned to show the student how our models can explain what happens when the economy is buffeted by some large disturbance. An example is the "Dutch disease" that sets in when one sector's comparative advantage is greatly enlarged, putting competitive pressure on the factors of production employed in other sectors. Another is the application of the factor-proportions model to explain the rapid expansion of the share of world exports of manufactures coming from the Newly Industrializing Countries.

The most drastic changes in the volume come in Part 4, impelled by the unsettled state of macroeconomic theory in general and the rapid development in the 1970s of the financial-asset approach to the foreign exchange rate. The chapter on the balance of payments account (Chapter 15) has been placed at the front of Part 4 and somewhat reoriented to provide an introduction and overview for the section. Parallel expositions of the simple Keynesian and monetarist approaches are retained from previous editions (Chapters 16 and 17). However, the role of financial assets and international capital movements is developed more fully than in previous editions, with simple partial approaches sprouting in Chapters 16 and 17, to blossom into a full theoretical and empirical treatment in Chapters 19 and 20. The analysis of exchange-rate flexibility makes its appearance in Chapter 18, which addresses the effects of exchange-rate changes; Chapter 19 symmetrically considers the determinants of the equilibrium exchange rate, leading up to the financial-asset approach. Part 4 closes with a new chapter on the problem of inflation, designed to apply tools presented in the preceding chapters to an urgent contemporary problem.

Throughout the book we have tried to reinforce the student's sense of the usefulness of theory by showing that parameters can be measured and hypotheses tested against data and experience. In Chapter 8 we retain and update the review of research on the Heckscher-Ohlin theorem and other propositions about the determinants of actual patterns of commodity trade. Chapter 19 offers an analysis of the recent behavior of effective and real exchange rates for a few countries, and Chapter 24 closely explores evidence on the performance of floating exchange rates.

The book covers a conventional full line of topics and with some additional material can serve as the basis for a full-year course at the undergraduate level, or for separate semester courses on the real and financial aspects of international trade. However, we have paid careful attention to the needs of one-semester courses. In particular, we view the chapters in Part 1 and the first three chapters of Part 4 as the nucleus of a one-semester course that attempts to cover both the core of the real theory (with applications) and elements of balance of payments adjustment. Many of the chapters outside this core are at least somewhat independent of each other, and so can be selected to round out the course, with an emphasis depending on what topics the instructor wishes to emphasize.

Authors whose textbook reaches its second revision have acquired a string of debts to colleagues, students, and various helpers that stretches the bounds of memory, let alone explicit acknowledgment. Like other hard-pressed debtors we make only the most urgent payoffs. Richard Brecher, Liam Ebrill, and Judith Cox provided valuable critiques. David G. Hartman and Refik Erzan assisted with important problems. A textbook revision quickly becomes a thousand-piece jigsaw puzzle (without diagram) for a secretary, and Marjorie Adams and Jacqueline McManus solved this one efficiently.

Contents

WORLD
TRADE
AND
PAYMENTS

1

Introduction

Unique among the concerns of economics, international trade has always carried a note of romance — the lure of the exotic, the hint of danger. Traders' dreams of bartering for the riches of the Orient spurred the European voyages of discovery that began in the fifteenth century. Today, supertankers move hundreds of thousands of tons of crude oil at a time from producing to consuming lands at strikingly low cost — and have been known to pollute hundreds of miles of shoreline when they have broken up at sea.

The romance of international commerce surges through its contact with public policy. British restrictions on colonial trade helped to fuel the American Revolution. After World War II the nations of Western Europe, sickened of the recurrent wars spawned by modern nationalism, sought permanent reconciliation and peace through a trade treaty — removing barriers to commerce through the European Common Market.

In this book we try to provide an understanding of the economic causes and consequences of international exchange. Any branch of economics rests on theoretical concepts and models. The scholar's job is to bring systematic observation and explanation to the chaotic diversity of the world he observes. The Census Bureau records data on about 14,000 classifications of commodities entering into the foreign trade of the United States — about 4,000 for exports and 10,000 for imports. Do we need 14,000 explanations for these trade flows? Could we find one that would cover every bundle of merchandise? Our quest is for the simplest model, or the smallest family of models, capable of answering what seem to be the important questions about patterns of trade, and how public policy should deal with them.

3

The foreign commerce of nations is one of the oldest branches of economics, and has drawn the attention of some of the greatest economists. Indeed, many of the ideas you will meet in this book can boast of famous ancestors. We owe much of our understanding of money in international trade to the philosopher David Hume (Chapter 17). One of our principal models of international trade and production (Chapter 5) derives from David Ricardo, an English stockbroker with a powerful analytical mind. Yet much of present-day international economics is quite new. A most fruitful model relating trade to factors of production comes from two twentieth-century Swedish economists, Eli F. Heckscher and Bertil Ohlin (Chapter 7). And our understanding of how trade relates to employment, and how policy can deal properly with both, is a late fallout of the Keynesian Revolution of the late 1930's (Chapter 16).

1.1 THE SUBJECT OF INTERNATIONAL ECONOMICS

International economics is somewhat curiously related to the other conventional branches of economics. Public finance, money and banking, or labor economics selects a neatly distinguished group of transactors or markets in the economy for special study. "But," you may ask, "doesn't international economics similarly deal with international markets?" It does, and these markets are capable of exact *legal* definition. Sovereign states are ubiquitous; therefore, we can always tell whether the two parties to a transaction are citizens of different countries.

But are international transactions economically unique and readily separated from transactions within nations? Does the Kansas wheat farmer know or care whether the bushel of wheat he sells will be exported? When you buy a handkerchief, do you inspect it closely for a label indicating manufacture abroad? International transactions are of a piece with domestic markets. Ultimately our explanation of international trade must be part of an explanation of each national market.

This intertwining of international and national markets runs through all of international economics. If India decides to train more physicians, the supply of physicians in Britain is apt to increase (through emigration). If the United States raises government spending to increase employment, employment in Canada is almost sure to increase. Hence you should not be surprised that international economics can easily (and usefully) be viewed as "international aspects of supply and demand," or "international aspects of money and finance," or "international aspects of taxation."

Nonetheless, there are good reasons for treating international trade and payments as a separate field of study. Here are two reasons that we think are most important:

1. The models we find useful for explaining international trade are simple, but strong and general. They not only explain patterns of international trade, but they also tell much about patterns of production, income distribution, etc., within countries.
2. The policy questions that arise in international exchange differ from those typically discussed within nation-states, and they require a special analytical apparatus. Yet we contend that the *principles* of policy-making should be the same at home and abroad. International economics can at once attack the special questions of international economic policy and show how to couple foreign and domestic policies correctly.

What, indeed, is the simplest possible way to model the international economy? The central questions about international trade deal solely with *exchange* between traders in two national markets. We shall argue that the sparest and clearest explanation of trade between nations, and the gains nations derive from trade, requires only a description of the exchange of fixed endowments of goods. The simplification we make, by concentrating first on exchange, is to put aside the details of how goods are produced. We can then explain, for example, what happened in 1973 when the exporting nations quadrupled the price of oil. Having set the essentials, we then can expand the basic model of trade to explore details of how bundles of goods are produced.

Why should we employ separate models to explain international trade and domestic trade? The traditional answer has been that factors of production — labor and capital — in the long run move freely within the national economy, but their mobility between countries is sharply limited. We suppose that labor and capital move freely between New York and California, whenever workers or lenders feel that such a shift will improve their real incomes. If that assumption is correct, the goods traded between the two states, and the effect of that trade on their "native" factor endowments will be less interesting. (California has no natives.) On the other hand, if little movement of labor and capital takes place between, say, Mexico and France, the commodities they trade and their benefit from the exchange become both interesting and important.

The assumption that factors of production are perfectly mobile within countries and perfectly immobile between them is obviously not completely true. Think of the international migrations of the nineteenth century, the outflow of long-term capital from the United States in the last three decades — and the immobility of low-paid labor out of America's Appalachia or Italy's Mezzogiorno! However, probably no assumption used by economists is completely true. We start out by supposing that the assumption is true, but we then relax that assumption in two ways. We introduce a form of immobility in the domestic economy by assuming that one factor of production used by each industry is tied to that industry and cannot find employment elsewhere, no matter what happens to its wage. We also relax the assumption that factors are immobile between countries; after we learn how trade affects the incentive for factors to migrate internationally, we can show more easily what happens when some factors seize the opportunity.

We mentioned above a second reason for studying international economics separately: Special questions of policy arise in the international economy. Trade takes place between sovereign nations — between us and them. Two governments, with potentially clashing objectives, can apply their policies to the flow of trade between them — and against each other's interests. More profoundly, because of the fear and suspicion of outsiders felt by even the most saintly mortal, we chronically ask whether or not the nation benefits from trading with foreigners. No one asks whether Vermont gains from trading with New Hampshire, or Minneapolis with St. Paul. But the proposition that the United States and France both gain from trading with each other might not win a majority vote — in either country. Rich countries fear that they will suffer from importing the products of low-wage foreign labor. Poor countries dread imports created by foreign high-level technology. A critical role for the theory of international trade, then, is to identify exactly the gains from trade and their indications for economic policy. Our first approach to trade through a simple model of exchange proves particularly helpful for pinning down the gains from trade.

Picking the best (or the best available) economic policy is the job of welfare economics — the branch of our subject that seeks maximum economic welfare. The odor of value judgments always lurks around welfare economics, especially when we ask, "Whose welfare?" International economics takes a flexible approach to this question. Following the tradition of general economics, we often concentrate on the welfare — the maximum real income — of a country's citizens. But our welfare analysis can serve other goals as well. Finding clashes and harmonies between national and world welfare is an important task of this book. We shall also glance at the welfare of groups of countries (such as the European Common Market) and at the welfare of groups of income recipients within a country. Changes in the international economy or in policies toward trade almost always change the distribution of a country's income as well as its level. Only by understanding the relation between trade and income distribution can we discover why American labor is opposed to foreign investment by U.S. companies, or why the South once opposed but now favors high tariffs.

A great deal of economic policy-making is concerned with the short run, and with such objectives as full employment and price stability. Especially in a large economy like that of the United States, where a small share of output is traded abroad, officials often pick solutions for these problems as if the foreign sector mattered not at all. This practice has grown less and less tenable. Bursts of inflation in the 1970's were often unleashed by so-called supply shocks in international prices. And countries have learned that movements of their exchange rates can lower or raise the domestic prices of internationally traded goods and thus help or hinder their campaigns against inflation. The proliferating problems of macroeconomic policy in the open economy have bestirred economists to investigate how a country might solve them. We shall find that a nation with enough policy instruments, and enough information about their effects, can solve the problem of its balance of payments and achieve its internal objectives as well. We saw before that international transactions intertwine with domestic ones. Thus policies must deal with domestic and international short-term problems together.

Countries' interests can clash over short-term policy issues. In 1971 the United States seemed to create an international crisis by refusing to exchange its gold stock for dollars acquired by foreign central banks. This seeming act of aggression was in fact an act of defense. It bore on the problem of how countries share the righting of imbalance in their international transactions. Thus, another task for our models of international economic policy is to expose the sources of harmony and conflict among countries. We shall find that the positions countries take on the exotic question of international reserves become clear once we understand that these positions relate to this problem of sharing the burden of adjustment.

1.2 THE ORGANIZATION OF THIS BOOK

We have seen that international economics builds models to explain the links between national economic systems ("inter-national economics," indeed) and to show how nations' policies can yield maximum welfare and stability. Our purpose in this book is to explain those models simply but comprehensively and to show how they can be used. We shall apply those models liberally to present-day issues of international economic policy — not from a delusion that those problems will look the same tomorrow as they do today, but because they provide a handy proving ground to turn theoretical concepts and models into an "active vocabulary" for understanding new issues as they arise.

We promised to begin with the simplest model of trade between nations, and that is the focus of Part 1. In Chapter 2 we shall investigate exchange between the citizens of two countries who hold arbitrary stocks of goods that they can barter with one another. In Chapter 3 we shall examine the nation's productive apparatus to show how the production capabilities of trading countries affect their international trade. And in Chapter 4 we shall illustrate some uses of this basic apparatus for analyzing changes in the terms of trade (for example, the oil price increase), the growth of productive capacity (can our economy's growth make us worse off?), and flows of capital from one country to another.

In Part 2 we shall build into this simple model various explanations of the nation's production apparatus. We first describe production processes in the fashion of David Ricardo, with a unit of each output requiring inputs of only a certain number of man-hours (Chapter 5). Or each output can be assumed to require labor plus units of a factor of production used only in that sector (Chapter 6). Or each output can require both capital and labor, but in different proportions (Chapter 7). Each model will tell its own story about how trade interacts with the domestic pattern of production and affects the distribution of income. In the remainder of Part 2 we shall develop other aspects of exchange between countries. The empirical structure of international trade and its long-run changes will be examined. The assumption of perfect competition in markets will be removed in order to understand international cartels and commodity agreements and oligopolistic industrial markets. International factor movements and the activities of the multinational company will be added to the roster of transactions.

In Part 3 we shall take up tariffs and other controls on trade, identifying their effects and asking in what circumstances they might be desirable from the nation's point of view. We shall find a major clash of interests — in that the welfare of all countries together would generally be raised by removing all restrictions on international trade, but that one country acting alone can sometimes improve its own welfare by maintaining or increasing restrictions. Chapters 11 and 12 are concerned with the theory of controls on trade, and Chapters 13 and 14 apply this theory to present-day tariff policies and the problem of economic integration.

In Part 4 we shall turn to models of short-run disequilibrium and adjustment in order to understand what happens when income and expenditure are not equal to one another or money prices are sticky. In Chapter 15 we introduce the foreign-exchange rate and explain the balance of payments accounts. Since 1973 the major industrial countries' exchange rates have been determined largely by market forces, with major effects on the operation of the economic system. Chapters 16 and 17 present two polar models of income and monetary disturbances in the open economy — one assuming all money prices are flexible (except the exchange rate), the other keeping prices rigid and allowing the economy to depart from full employment and utilization of capacity. In Chapters 18 and 19 we explore the interdependence of the exchange rate with levels of income and prices in the national economy: how the exchange rate affects the national economy, and how prices and asset yields in the national economy affect the exchange rate. A theme running throughout Part 4 is the pervasive importance of international capital movements and adjustments in financial portfolios for equilibrium and adjustment in the international economy. The full version of this story emerges in Chapters 19 and 20. In Chapter 21 we draw upon the full tool kit developed in Part 4 to address the most urgent policy problem of the 1980's — international inflation.

In Part 5 we shall consider economic policy in the open economy, starting with the methods a country can use to achieve its domestic goals of full employment and price stability and its goal for its balance of international payments. The demand and supply of international reserves will be analyzed to determine how countries finance disequilibria in their balances of payments when they do not want the exchange rate to do all the adjusting. Finally, we shall consider the different ways in which countries can manage their international payments and their implications for the system of international economic relations. During the 1970's the industrial countries left their exchange rates to be determined largely by market forces, whereas between 1945 and 1971 they solemnly swore to hold them at fixed values. We seek to determine which policy system works best.

After the final chapter we have placed a group of supplements to the principal theoretical chapters of the book. We made the basic decision to keep the chapter texts completely free of any formal mathematics other than a sprinkling of high-school algebra, using simple diagrams and verbal reasoning instead. To satisfy the members of the reading audience who seek a more formal approach, we have added supplements that demand some mathematical sophistication; that is, a basic knowledge of differential calculus. The supplements are designed to be read with the text, but the text is, of course, independent of the supplements.

SUGGESTIONS FOR FURTHER READING

Following each chapter of this book is a brief list of suggestions for further reading. We have in mind principally the instructor who wishes to assign fuller accounts of some points developed in the chapter and the student who seeks further enlightenment — or a term-paper topic. Sometimes we shall refer to classic expositions of important ideas in the chapter. In other cases we shall mention fuller contemporary accounts. Many references deal with applications of international economics to empirical explanation and policy-making. To each reference we have appended a few words to explain its content. What follows is a list of volumes of readings or collected material relevant to many aspects of international economics.

Baldwin, Robert E., and J. David Richardson, eds. *International Trade and Finance: Readings*. 2nd ed. Boston: Little, Brown and Co., 1981. Many readings useful to undergraduate students.

Bhagwati, Jagdish, ed. *International Trade: Selected Readings*. Harmonds-worth, England: Penguin, 1969. Collection of scholarly papers.

Caves, Richard E., and Harry G. Johnson, eds. *Readings in International Economics*. Homewood, Ill.: Richard E. Irwin, Inc., 1968. A collection of classic articles, mostly on the theory of international economics.

Cooper, R. N., ed. *International Finance: Selected Readings*. Harmonds-worth, England: Penguin, 1969. Companion to Bhagwati's volume, listed above.

Dornbusch, Rudiger, and Jacob A. Frenkel, eds. *International Economic Policy: Theory and Evidence*. Baltimore: Johns Hopkins University Press, 1979. Up-to-date papers surveying the major aspects of international economics; some are addressed to the professional economist, others are less technical.

Ohlin, Bertil, Per-Ove Hesselborn, and Per Magnus Wijkman, eds. *The International Allocation of Economic Activity: Proceedings of a Nobel Symposium Held at Stockholm*. London: Macmillan, 1977. Reflections by leading scholars on the current state of international economics.

I

THE BASIC TRADE
MODEL

2

The International Exchange of Commodities

Some patterns of trade need almost no explanation. If you live in the United States and have a taste for coffee, you have your coffee imported from Brazil or some other coffee-growing country because it is not produced at home. If you live in Germany or Italy, you depend on foreign sources to supply fuel and lubricants for your sports car. If such imports were cut off, your level of well-being or "real income" would surely be reduced. If all trade were of this kind — with each country producing commodities desired by all countries but available only locally — there would be little need for the economist either to expound on the virtues of trade or to explain the pattern of trade. These would be almost self-evident. Indeed, millions of dollars in world trade are spent each year on coffee, chromium, copper, tea, oil, sugar, and other items that nature has placed in some communities but not in others.

Many items in international commerce, however, cannot be described or explained this way. Automobiles, steel, textiles, processed foods, and myriads of other items are produced in a number of countries. What are the reasons for the large volume of international trade in these goods? In searching for an explanation we naturally inquire about costs. Transistor radios are produced and exported from Taiwan and Korea, wool comes from Australia, and butter from New Zealand. In countless examples we can find the source of trade to be the country with the relatively low cost of production. But, as we shall see in this chapter, cost differences need not represent the ultimate rationale for trade.

Our strategy in this opening part of the book is to describe what we call "the basic trade model," characterized by two types of simplification. First, we restrict the number of countries participating in trade to two and, as well, assume that only two basic commodities are produced or consumed (we call them food and clothing). If the basis for mutual gains from trade can be established in such a simple, stripped-down model, all the more reason to expect flourishing trade in a world of many countries and many commodities. Second, we postpone until Part 2 a consideration of the *details* concerning production — how technology helps determine the way in which productive factors combine to produce commodities.

In the present chapter we simplify matters even further. Commodities only exist in nature. It is impossible to identify costs of producing commodities and thus to connect trade patterns to underlying cost differentials. Each country is literally *endowed* with certain amounts of food and clothing, and there is no way in which the quantities in the "endowment bundle" can be varied in response to changes in price. Our motivation in making such a patently unrealistic assumption is twofold: (1) Such a simple trading world is easier to describe than one in which resources can be pulled out of one sector and attracted to another by the signal of a rise in price; and (2) The ultimate rationale for mutually beneficial trade can be seen to rest on deeper considerations than the existence of cost differentials between countries.

In the next two chapters we see how more obvious sources of trade gains — for example, being able to concentrate one's resources on those activities one does best — serve to enhance and enrich the description of the possibilities for gain already established in this chapter's austere model of commodity exchange.

2.1 THE GAINS FROM TRADE

The result we establish in this section is absolutely basic:

> *If in the absence of trade relative prices of commodities differ between countries, countries can gain by exchanging commodities at intermediate price ratios.*

Relative Prices and the Budget Line

The concept of "relative" price arises naturally in this simplified two-commodity trading world. Clothing's relative price is the amount of food that must be surrendered in a market exchange for one unit of clothing. You are more used to prices being quoted in money terms — dollars in the United States, escudos in Portugal, and yen in Japan. If you know money prices, you can compute relative prices; if clothing costs $5 a yard and food $10 a bushel, the relative price of clothing is $\frac{1}{2}$, measured in bushels (of food) per yard (of clothing).

The reason we wish to concentrate here on relative prices instead of absolute (currency) prices is that we are making an extremely simple assumption about the link between people's expenditures and the "incomes" represented by their endowment bundles of clothing and food. In general we would expect the aggregate value of expenditures to be closely related to the aggregate value of income, with any excess of spending over income coming out of cash balances, sales of assets, or accumulation of debt. Similarly, expenditures could be cut below income levels to augment an individual's stock of assets. Our simple assumption is that individuals (and nations) spend exactly the value of their incomes.

Such an assumption, which we refer to as the "classical" form of budget constraint, greatly eases our task in the first three parts of this book because it allows us to postpone (until Part 4) those issues having to do with exchange-rate crises, the international monetary system, and a nation's balance-of-payments adjustment problems. We take for granted the advantages that a monetary system conveys in easing transactions. We only require that any market purchases of food be matched exactly by a sale of clothing of equivalent value. Because of this restriction on spending behavior, it becomes important to pierce the "monetary veil" of currency prices to know how much clothing must be exchanged per unit of food or how much food has to be surrendered to purchase one clothing unit.

Figure 2.1 illustrates the consumption choices available to an individual who possesses endowment bundle E (OG units of clothing and OF units of food) but who is capable of trading food for clothing (or vice versa) at some specified market prices. Given these prices, the individual can compute all the combinations of food and clothing that have the *same value* as does his endowment point, E. These combinations are shown in Figure 2.1 by a downward sloping line through E, the budget line BEA. For example, suppose the individual wishes to consume the commodity bundle shown by point H on this line. Let food and clothing prices be denoted by p_F and p_C respectively. Since H has the same value as endowment point E, the value of purchases of food (p_F times amount HJ) must equal the value of clothing given up in exchange (p_C times amount JE). That is, clothing's relative price, p_C/p_F, is shown by the absolute value of the *slope* of the budget line, HJ/JE.

The slope of the budget line indicates how much of one commodity must be given up to obtain one unit of the other. If commodity prices change but the individual's endowment point (E in Figure 2.1) does not, the budget line changes slope but must still pass through the production or endowment point. Suppose that food's relative price rises. Would this be shown by rotating budget line BEA around point E in a clockwise or counterclockwise direction? This is a simple question, but experience reveals that it is well worth thinking through. A higher rela-

---

FIGURE 2.1   The Budget Line

The slope of the budget line, *BEA*, which is *HJ/JE*, shows the relative price of clothing. Its inverse, *JE/HJ*, is the relative price of food.

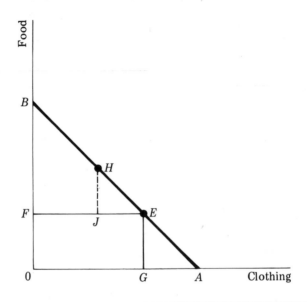

---

tive food price than is shown by line *BEA* in Figure 2.1 would be shown by a *flatter* line through *E* — more clothing would have to be given up in exchange for one unit of food.

The budget line through the endowment point shows only what food and clothing bundles *could* be purchased; it does not specify which point *would* be demanded. To determine consumption choices, we must have information about taste patterns or preferences as well as about endowments and relative prices.

Indifference Curves

Indifference curves, expressing our individual's preferences or tastes concerning food and clothing, are illustrated in Figure 2.2. Start by considering the bundle of food and clothing shown by point *E* (quantity *OD* of clothing and *OF* of food). As long as both commodities yield satisfaction, any consumption bundle northeast of *E*, such as *H*, must be preferred to *E*, and any bundle with less of both commodities than *E*, such as *I*, must be less desirable than *E*. To proceed, suppose one unit of clothing is added to the consumption basket at *E*, which leads to the higher level of satisfaction that would be obtained from bundle *J*. Then ask how much food must be taken away from the individual so that his welfare is reduced back to exactly what it was at *E*. Suppose this quantity is *JB*. If so, the individual is indifferent to the choice of consuming bundle *E* or bundle *B*. *E* and *B* lie on the same indifference curve, labeled y_0 in Figure 2.2. (Throughout the book the symbol "*y*" indicates "real income," "utility," or "satisfaction.")

The foregoing remarks establish that indifference curves are negatively sloped: A sacrifice in the quantity of one commodity consumed must be balanced by the appropriate increment in the quantity of the other commodity. The indifference curves in Figure 2.2 are also bowed in toward the origin, reflecting the common assumption that the marginal rate at which individuals are willing to substitute more of one commodity for less of another changes along an indifference curve. The ratio *JB* to *EJ* in Figure 2.2 shows the *marginal rate of substitution* between food and

---

FIGURE 2.2   Indifference Curves

The bowed-in shape reflects diminishing marginal rates of substitution. All points on indifference curve y_1 are preferred to any point on indifference curve y_0.

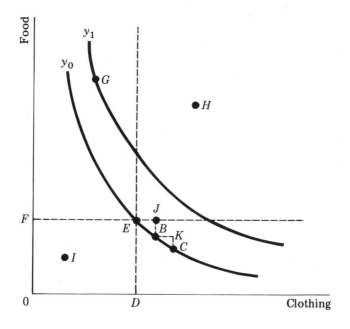

clothing in moving from E to B. The ratio KC to BK is smaller, showing that the further sacrifice of food involved in moving from B to C (C has one more unit of clothing than does B) can be smaller while still keeping the individual on indifference curve y_0. As the consumer has less and less food, each unit has greater value to him, whereas each additional unit increment of clothing will raise his satisfaction less the more clothing he possesses. That is, the *marginal rate of substitution*, as indicated by the slope of the indifference curve, diminishes along the curve y_0 as more clothing is substituted for food.

The indifference curve y_0 is one of many that could be drawn. Indeed, the "commodity space" is filled with these curves. Another is curve y_1, which is further out from the origin and, therefore, indicates a higher level of real income than does curve y_0. For example, point G is preferred to point E. If the individual initially possessed the bundle of food and clothing indicated by point E, and he were allowed to exchange some clothing for food so that he could consume point G, he would clearly improve his well-being. As we shall illustrate, trade can bring about precisely this kind of gain.

Trade Benefits Both Countries

Let us reinterpret Figure 2.2 now as a set of indifference curves for the home country, and E as the aggregate bundle of food and clothing available to that community in the absence of any possibility of exchanging goods with other nations.[1] These indifference curves, along with endowment point E, are redrawn in Figure 2.3. Two budget lines are drawn through E: line CED and line AEB. They each represent a different set of relative prices, with food being relatively cheaper (and clothing relatively more expensive) along CED than along AEB. For each relative price (and associated budget line) there is a most preferred consumption point if the community can exchange commodities at those prices. For example, point F is the best consumption point along line CED — all other points would lie on lower indifference curves. Note that point F could *not* be consumed if the community were not allowed to trade with other nations, for it would then be forced to consume food and clothing precisely in the amounts locally available (as shown by E). The slope of line AEB thus shows the relative price of clothing that must exist if trade is disallowed. At no other price would the community be content to consume food and clothing in the proportions indicated by point E.

[1] Some of the problems involved in aggregating indifference curves of individuals in order to talk about the welfare of the community are discussed in Section 2.4. The basic reference to the issue of drawing indifference curves for a community is P. A. Samuelson, "Social Indifference Curves," *Quarterly Journal of Economics,* 70 (February 1956): 1–22.

FIGURE 2.3 The Trade Triangle for the Home Country

The home country originally consumes its endowment bundle, E, at relative prices shown by line AB. If it could trade at prices shown by line CD, it could export GE units of clothing to obtain FG units of food, thus consuming the bundle shown by F and improving its real income to the level shown by the y_1 indifference curve.

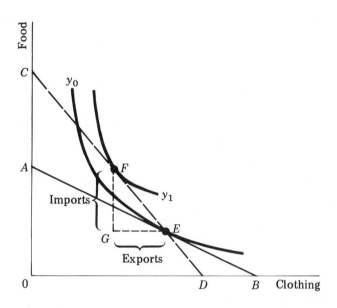

Line CED in Figure 2.3 thus illustrates the possibilities open to this community to trade at relative prices *different* from those prevailing before trade. It could then offer to export GE units of clothing, which have the same value as FG units of food. Such trade would allow the community to consume the bundle, F, on the indifference curve y_1 This indifference curve is higher than the original curve, y_0, passing through the endowment bundle. In such a manner we can prove that the opportunity to trade at relative prices that differ from those in isolation at home must improve real incomes at home.[2]

But is such trade feasible? Could the home country obtain the desired

[2] Here we only consider the case in which the relative price of food offered to the home country is lower than the price shown by AEB. However, the symmetry of the case should convince you that if the home country were offered a relative clothing price lower than line AEB (shown by a line through E flatter than AEB), it could also reach a higher indifference curve than y_0.

food imports from abroad? Figure 2.4 illustrates a case in which the foreign country would, at the same price ratio as shown by line CED in Figure 2.3, be willing to export amount FG of food to the home country. In Figure 2.4 the foreign country's endowment point is E^*, and through that point line $C^*E^*D^*$ has been drawn with the same slope as line CED in Figure 2.3, thereby showing the same relative commodity prices. Along budget line $C^*E^*D^*$ the foreign country's most desired consumption point is F^*. It would be willing to export E^*G^* of food (equal to FG in

---

FIGURE 2.4 The Trade Triangle for the Foreign Country

The foreign country originally consumes its endowment bundle, E^*, at relative prices shown by line A^*B^*. If it could trade at prices shown by line C^*D^*, it could export E^*G^* units of food to obtain G^*F^* units of clothing, thus consuming the bundle shown by F^* and improving its real income to the level shown by the y_1^* indifference curve.

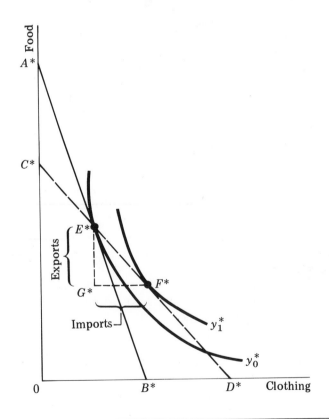

Figure 2.3) in exchange for G^*F^* imports of clothing. Note that if the foreign country could not engage in trade, it would evaluate food and clothing by its marginal rate of substitution at E^*, shown by the slope of line $A^*E^*B^*$. But this slope is different from the slope of AEB in Figure 2.3. The relative price of food and clothing that is illustrated in Figure 2.3 by CED and in Figure 2.4 by line $C^*E^*D^*$ lies intermediate between the low price of clothing in the home country before trade (shown by the slope of AEB in Figure 2.3) and the high price of clothing in the pretrade situation in the foreign country (shown by the slope of $A^*E^*B^*$ in Figure 2.4). This justifies the basic result that we stated at the beginning of this section: A divergence in the relative price of commodities in the two countries before trade indicates a mutual potential gain from trade for *both* countries at a common intermediate price ratio. No "exploitation" is involved. Although world total supplies of food and clothing are unaltered throughout (by the fixed-endowment assumption), a redistribution of each commodity from the country in which it is cheaper to the country in which it is valued more highly increases the welfare of both countries.

2.2 FREE-TRADE EQUILIBRIUM

The common price ratio allowing mutually beneficial trade in Figures 2.3 and 2.4 is an example of a *free-trade equilibrium*. The most basic tools in economics, demand and supply curves, can be used to establish that such an equilibrium can be obtained.

Consider each country in turn. Figure 2.3 illustrated two price ratios for the home country. At each price ratio the total quantity of food made available (or supplied) was a fixed constant — the vertical distance to the endowment point E. Total food demand at home depended on price, rising from amounts shown by E at prices AEB to the vertical distance to point F at lower food prices shown by line CED. In the foreign country (Figure 2.4), it is also possible to trace out demand for food as it varies with price. Total foreign supply, of course, remains fixed at point E^*.

Free trade implies that there is one world market in which a common price is established. Figure 2.5 adds together home and foreign food-demand curves on the one hand, and home and foreign supplies of food on the other. At relative price for food, OT, the world market is cleared. This price corresponds to the parallel lines CED (Figure 2.3) and $C^*E^*D^*$ (Figure 2.4).[3] In Figure 2.5 two other relative food prices are

---

[3] As discussed in Chapter 3, the world supply curve would normally be positively sloped when commodities are produced, whereas the demand curve may, for high prices, become positively sloped. These complications are ignored here.

FIGURE 2.5   World Demand and Supply

The terms of trade, OT, are determined by the equilibrium between the world's demand for food $(D_F + D_F^*)$ and the supply of food $(S_F + S_F^*)$.

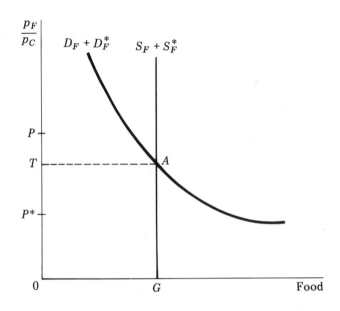

indicated on the vertical axis. High price OP indicates the food price at which the home market would be cleared if the home country could not trade. This is shown by line AEB in Figure 2.3. By contrast, the food price that would rule in isolation abroad is lower, OP^* (corresponding to line $A^*E^*B^*$ in Figure 2.4). The world market with free trade is cleared at the intermediate price, OT. Of course, with world demand and supply for food equated at OT, so must world demand and supply for clothing be equated.[4]

Thinking of the world as a single market in which total world demands and supplies are compared provides us with one way of illustrating free-trade equilibrium. An alternative diagram, showing the same forces determining the free-trade equilibrium price ratio of clothing to food, focuses on each country's *excess* demand or supply for one of the commodities. Figure 2.6 shows a downward-sloping home import demand

[4] At price ratio OT home excess demand for food has the same *value* as foreign excess demand for clothing.

FIGURE 2.6   Excess Demand and Supply

Equilibrium quantity *OA* shows free-trade imports of food by the home country at the equilibrium price ratio, *OT*.

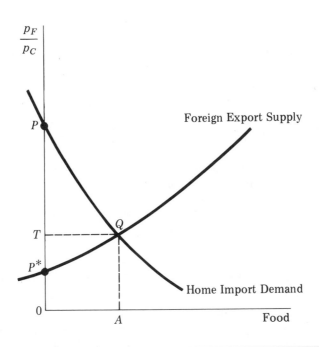

curve for food together with an upward-sloping foreign export supply curve for food. The relative food price, *OP*, corresponds to the no-trade price ratio for the home country illustrated in Figure 2.3 by line *AEB*. For higher prices of food the home country would attempt to export food, while for lower prices its demand for food exceeds the quantity available in its endowment bundle. The foreign country's demand for food is brought into balance with its own supplies at the lower price ratio, *OP**. Higher prices bring forth excess supplies for export. At the free-trade equilibrium price ratio, *OT*, home import demand balances foreign export supply.[5]

[5] Economists frequently illustrate free-trade equilibrium positions by using the concept of an "offer curve." This is discussed in the appendix to Chapter 3. Also analyzed in Chapter 3 (and the appendix) is the *possibility* that the foreign export supply curve becomes backward bending at a sufficiently high price.

2.3 A CASE FOR FREE TRADE

We are now in a position to present a basic plank in the free-trade case: Free trade leads to a world distribution of consumption that cannot be altered in any way so as to improve the welfare of *all* trading participants. In this sense, free trade is *efficient*.

Before turning to a diagram, let us consider the logic of the argument. Dismantling all possible barriers to exports and imports (and ignoring costs of transportation) implies that individuals in both countries face the same commodity prices with free trade. Each individual picks his most preferred point on his budget line, and (as Figures 2.3 and 2.4 illustrate) at such a point his marginal rate of substitution is equated to the commodity price ratio — the same price ratio faced by all other individuals. Thus with free trade each individual faces the same "trade-off" at the margin between food and clothing as does every other. In Section 2.1 we established the mutual gains from trade that are available if marginal rates of substitution (or price ratios) *differ* between countries. The matching up of price ratios between countries with free trade signals that all such mutual gains have already been achieved.

The Box Diagram and the Contract Curve

Economists have devised the "box diagram" to illustrate welfare propositions in those cases in which the distribution between participants of fixed total bundles of commodities is at issue. This matches the assumption in this chapter that each country's endowment bundle is fixed, making world total supplies of food and clothing also given.[6] It is these fixed total supplies that provide the dimensions of the box.

In Figure 2.7 any point within the box can represent a division of the fixed world totals of food and clothing between the two nations. For example, point $E(E^*)$ can show the original endowment allocation. We shall measure quantities belonging to the home country with respect to the southwest "O" origin and those belonging to the foreign country with respect to the northeast "O^*" origin. A pair of indifference curves has been drawn through endowment point $E(E^*)$. The curve y_0 for the home country illustrates that a consumption bundle such as A would be valued exactly as highly by the home country as would endowment point E. The shape of the foreign indifference curve y_0^* through E^* is explained by the measurement of foreign clothing consumption leftward from O^* and foreign food consumption downward from O^*. Point B means as

---

[6] One reason for studying a model of fixed endowments first is that it reveals the basic nature of the gains from trade independently of any additional gains that can be obtained if trade causes resources to be reallocated so as to increase world outputs.

FIGURE 2.7   The Box Diagram and the Contract Curve

The CC' curve is the contract curve — the locus of all points where an indifference curve of the home country is tangent to an indifference curve of the foreign country. Point Q represents free trade equilibrium.

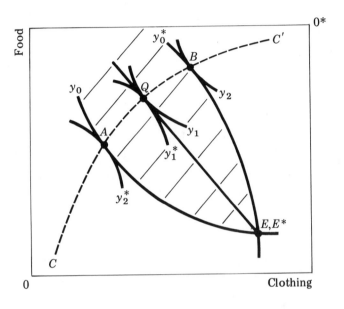

much to foreigners as does endowment point E^* — they both lie on curve y_0^*. Note that *any* redistribution of the world totals between countries that lies in the shaded area between curves y_0 and y_0^* represents an improvement in welfare for both. Free trade leads to one such point.

   The CC' curve is the locus of all distributions that equate marginal rates of substitution between countries. That is, move along any indifference curve for the home country (say y_0) until you find a point where a foreign indifference curve is tangent to it (point A has foreign curve y_2^* tangent to home curve y_0). This point has special significance: It shows the redistribution that obtains the maximum welfare abroad possible without altering welfare at home. The *contract curve*, CC', collects all such points. From any point *off* the contract curve (say E) it would be possible to redistribute commodities and improve welfare in both countries. (Anywhere in the shaded area would do.) From any point *on* the contract curve it is still possible to make one country better off, but *not* without inflicting harm on the other. All points on the contract curve thus pass the "efficiency" test.

Free trade leads to a world consumption at which marginal rates of substitution in each country are equated to a common price ratio, line QE in Figure 2.7. The free-trade point is on the contract curve. It raises the welfare of both participants and leaves the world at a point from which *further mutual* gains are not possible. But free-trade advocates cannot go further. The free-trade point cannot be compared with other points on the contract curve — not without making some intercountry comparisons of worthiness. Economists typically shy away from such comparisons.

2.4 DISAGREEMENTS OVER FREE TRADE

Although free trade has long had its vocal adherents, arrayed against them are "protectionists" of various types who argue that it is in someone's interest (a local group, a nation, a group of nations) to cut back the volume of trade by means of tariffs, quotas, or other devices (which we shall analyze in Part 3). Without delving too deeply into these questions at this stage, it is possible to suggest why individuals may be hurt by free trade and why a country may not wish to accept the trading patterns suggested by a free-trade equilibrium.

The Individual in International Trade

Do individuals gain from trade? In some broad sense of the word the answer must be yes, unless existence as a jack-of-all-trades is deemed superior to the degree of specialization and division of labor indulged in by most. But within the austere confines of the two-commodity food and clothing model presented in this chapter, does trade benefit the individual? Our demonstration in section 2.1 that trade is beneficial if the relative prices offered in trade *differ* from those at home is most applicable to individuals. For the individual, therefore, international trade is to be preferred to a state of isolation.

Suppose a community is not made up of identical individuals. Then some people may be hurt by opening the country up to international trade. Perhaps images come to mind of skilled American artisans undercut by cheaper foreign labor or nineteenth-century British landlords seeing their rents suffer as low-cost sources of food are opened up abroad. An examination of the impact of trade on wages, rents, and other factor returns must be postponed until Part 2, but the point that some individuals may be hurt by trade can be made at this time.

Take a close look at what happens in most communities before they engage in trade with other countries: Individuals at home will be trading with each other. Some equilibrium price ratio will be established at which all those net sellers of clothing find purchasers who are willing to give up an equivalent value of food in exchange. Now suppose the community has an opportunity to trade in food and clothing with the outside world, and suppose that food is relatively cheap abroad (and clothing relatively expensive). Not everyone at home need gain by this new trading opportunity. Indeed, the potential losers are easy to identify — all the individuals who were net sellers of food at home.

The situation for one of these individuals is shown in Figure 2.8. He owns the bundle of food and clothing shown by E and is "exporting" EA units of food (to others of his countrymen) in order to purchase AG units of clothing. International trade lowers the relative price of food; this individual's budget line rotates from "1" to "2" (around his endowment point, E). His consumption is reduced from G to H, and he is unquestionably worse off.

If some individuals gain from opening up their country to international trade while others lose, what can be said about the community as a whole? This is an issue typically faced in the political realm where decisions (here trade policy) almost always entail some groups being hurt and others gaining. Although the typical result in such cases is that some groups *do* get hurt while others gain, the economist is tempted to ask about the possibility of compensation so that all parties can gain by the move.

This line of argument is worth pursuing because it *is* possible to design a scheme whereby *all* individuals who would lose by a move from no international trade to free international trade can be compensated by those individuals who stand to gain by such a move, so that the latter group would still gain after payment of the compensation. First, examine what each individual would consume if trade is limited to the local community. Whatever the consumption bundle (e.g., point G for the individual shown in Figure 2.8), that individual has gained if he trades from his endowment bundle to obtain his new consumption bundle. The redistribution scheme is to switch endowment points among individuals so that each consumption point becomes the endowment point (point G becomes the new endowment point for the individual in Figure 2.8). Are there enough supplies of food and clothing to go around? Yes, since the local market was originally cleared. Now open the community to international trade. With prices different in the world market, every individual can gain by a move from his new, "compensated" endowment point. Free trade, with compensation, has benefited everyone.[7]

---

[7] For the individual in Figure 2.8, the budget line appropriate to world prices now passes through G, with the same slope as line 2. Trade would now clearly benefit such a person. Of course, those who were originally clothing exporters do not gain by international trade as much as they would if there had been no compensation.

FIGURE 2.8   International Trade Can Hurt

This individual was a net seller of food (amount EA) at home, with home prices shown by line 1. With food relatively cheaper on world markets (line 2), the individual's consumption is reduced from G to H. He is hurt by international trade.

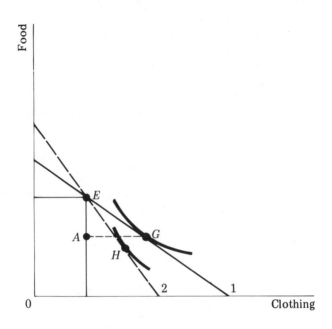

To summarize, everyone stands to gain from trade as such, even in this simple model that ignores more obvious sources of gain (being able to consume goods not available locally at all; being able to reallocate productive resources). The move from local trade to more extended international trade could also be defended if one ignores the local redistribution of income or makes appropriate compensations. But it is precisely this redistribution that often causes such controversy over new initiatives in the trade area. We seldom witness a country debating whether to engage at all in trade with other countries (nineteenth-century Japan aside). But we have witnessed Britain's agony in deciding whether to enter the European Common Market, or special interest groups lobbying in the U.S. Congress for tariff protection. Even sharp changes in international prices that are described in "crisis" terms are not harmful to all. How should an American shareholder in a major oil company have felt about the energy crisis as it erupted in the 1970's? He and his nonstockholding neighbor might have different views.

Self-Sufficiency versus International Dependence

The decade of the 1970's was characterized by severe swings in the relative prices of some internationally traded commodities. It was changes in the price of oil and related energy products that caused the greatest concern. In the United States many voices were raised to suggest that the country was "too dependent" on imports of oil from abroad.

In our basic explanation of the gains from trade earlier in this chapter, there was no limitation on welfare inherent in a large volume of trade. A country gains from trade only to the extent that its pattern of consumption is allowed to differ from its pattern of production. To be self-sufficient in every item is to throw away the benefits that are associated with international trade.

Governments often seem to be concerned not only with the gains that may be achieved by allowing their nationals to establish trading relationships with foreign nationals, but also with the extent to which such trade establishes a dependency upon foreign sources of supply. An *increase* in the relative price of a commodity that is imported hurts. So why not avoid that hurt by ceasing to import the commodity? Such a move to self-sufficiency would of its own serve to raise the price of the formerly imported items — thus bringing about the very damage it was intended to avoid.

A defense for a policy of limiting trade can be mounted, however, by considering the costs of adjusting to sudden changes in prices and/or foreign supplies. No nation wishes to be completely dependent upon others for foodstuffs, military equipment, or other items deemed essential for survival, because crucial time may be required to establish local sources of supply. This issue, of course, raises questions taking us beyond the framework of this chapter's model of commodity exchange. But it may help to explain why the search for gains from trade is moderated by the realization that changes in the terms on which trade is conducted can cause severe changes in welfare for an economy heavily dependent upon trade.

SUGGESTION FOR FURTHER READING

Meade, James. *The Stationary Economy*. London: Allen and Unwin, 1965.
    Chapters 1–4 present the exchange model.

3

Production and the Demand for Imports

The crudest assumption about a country's production patterns was adopted in the preceding chapter. Each period, the community is endowed with quantities of commodities that are inexorably fixed. No change of prices or new trading opportunities could divert resources to higher priced industries. Assumptions as stark as this are made for a reason. In this case it was to reveal that the gains from trade are so universal that they will appear even without production changes. Now we shall alter this assumption in order to capture the richer flavor of international trade — encouraging countries to concentrate their resources on those activities they do "best."

3.1 THE PRODUCTION-POSSIBILITIES SCHEDULE

Economics would become superfluous, and therefore totally uninteresting, if a community could produce as much as it desired of all goods and services. That it cannot do so reflects both the basic limitation of resources, natural and man-made, and the quality of technological knowledge that guides the transformation of resources into final commodities. The production-possibilities schedule (or "transformation" schedule as it will sometimes be called) shows the maximum amount of one commodity that can be produced given the quantities of all other commodities produced. An illustration of such a schedule is the TT' curve, in Figure 3.1, for a simple economy capable of producing only two commodities, which we again call food and clothing. For example, if clothing output is distance OG, the maximum amount of food that can be produced is AG.

Figure 3.1 illustrates several properties of production. First, some

30

points of production (e.g., *D*) are beyond the productive capacity of this community. If the resource base should expand with time, or if better techniques of production are developed, then point *D* could eventually be produced. Second, and closely related, is the negative slope of the *TT'* schedule. To produce more food than is shown by point *A*, some current production of clothing must be sacrificed to release resources from clothing into the food industry. Third, note that the community *can* produce at point *C*. Such a point, of course, would be inefficient in the sense that the *TT'* schedule shows that more of both commodities can be produced than at *C*. If the community does not use all of its available resources, a point such as *C* is quite possible. For example, during the depression in the early 1930's most industrial countries faced severe unemployment of labor and capital equipment. Perhaps less obvious is the possibility of the combination of production shown by *C* even *with* full employment of all resources. Point *C* might represent the out-

---

FIGURE 3.1 The Production-Possibilities Schedule

The bowed-out curve *TT'* shows the maximum amount of food that can be produced for each amount of clothing, subject to the constraints of technological knowledge and a fixed resource base. The slope shows the opportunity costs of producing clothing, which increase as more clothing is produced.

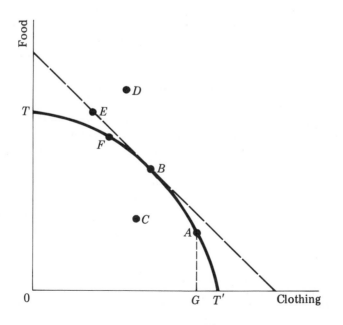

come of an arbitrary across-the-board decision to employ exactly 62 percent of every factor of production in the clothing industry, with the remaining 38 percent producing food. Such a decision would take no account of the fact that some resources are especially productive in one sector and not in the other, or, more generally, of the fact that techniques of producing clothing are qualitatively different from those used in food production. An economic answer lurks behind the question of allocating the community's resources most efficiently. As will be explained in the next section of this chapter, the forces of competition ensure that society's production of commodities is efficient, in the sense of lying along the production-possibilities curve.

The TT' schedule has been drawn bowed out from the origin, reflecting the so-called law of increasing costs. This shape embodies the assumption that the *opportunity costs* of obtaining an additional unit of a commodity increase as more of that commodity is produced. Consider clothing production, as shown initially at point F. The slope of the TT' curve at F shows the sacrifice in food production that is required to produce an additional unit of clothing. This is clothing's opportunity cost — the cost of an extra unit of clothing, *not* in dollars, *not* in labor or material costs, but in terms of the quantity of the other desired final commodity, food, that must be foregone in order to release the resources required by the unit expansion in the clothing industry. Note how this opportunity cost of producing clothing has risen when production of clothing expands to the level shown at B. That is, TT' at B is steeper than at F.

What accounts for this general relationship whereby the opportunity cost of any commodity rises as its output increases? Some factors, e.g., highly skilled labor especially trained to produce clothing, may be employed already in clothing production at F and cannot be obtained from further reductions in food output to reach point B. Alternatively, the supply of the best grade of fertile land may increasingly be used up by the time B is reached, necessitating the use of poorer land for food production in moving to F. Elements of this phenomenon — the variability in the aptitude of factors in each occupation — are almost always present in the real world to help account for increasing costs. (A particularly simple case in which some resources cannot be transferred from one occupation to another forms the setting for Chapter 6.) Even if each factor has the same potential skills in one occupation as in another, the fact that the two industries may require, for example, labor and capital in different proportions is sufficient to generate increasing costs. (This more subtle point is picked up in Chapter 7.)[1]

---

[1] Some texts treat symmetrically the case of *decreasing* opportunity costs — the transformation curve is (at least for a range) bowed *in* toward the origin. We have decided to ignore this case at this time, assuming that country size is sufficient that production typically hits the stage of increasing cost.

If an economy cannot engage in trade with other communities, the production-possibilities schedule in Figure 3.1 also serves as a "consumption-possibilities" schedule; the community can only consume what it produces. The opportunity to trade commodities at fixed world prices, however, opens a new range of consumption possibilities. For example, if the world terms of trade are shown by the slope of the dashed line (literally the relative price of clothing is given by the negative of the slope of line *EB*), the country would maximize its income by allocating resources so as to produce at point *B*. That is, a line with the same slope through any other production point, such as *A* or *F*, would lie below the line through *E* and *B*. If trade is possible at these world prices, the dashed line in Figure 3.1 becomes the community's consumption-possibilities schedule, which is clearly superior to curve *TT'*. For example, point *E* could be consumed at these prices, and this is a consumption bundle lying outside the possibility of consuming along *TT'*.

Before continuing this discussion of the gains from trade when production can be varied, we detour in order to establish two properties of competitive markets: (1) production takes place *on* (rather than below) the production-possibilities schedule, and (2) market prices determine *where* the community produces along the production-possibilities curve. At the point of production, the opportunity cost of producing a commodity is brought into line with its relative market price. This is illustrated in Figure 3.1 by the tangency between price line *EB* and the *TT'* curve at production point *B*.

3.2 THE EFFICIENCY OF COMPETITION

To understand how competition favors the efficient allocation of resources we must investigate the requirements for the community's bundle of outputs to lie on the production-possibilities schedule instead of below it. For this purpose we must review some basic principles of production theory. Again, a simplified model in which only two commodities, food and clothing, are produced will be useful. We shall also simplify by assuming that each commodity can be produced with only two factors, say, labor and capital, and that these are the same factors for each industry.

Figure 3.2 shows two arbitrarily chosen *isoquants* for the food industry. An isoquant is a locus of input bundles, all of which yield the same level of output. Each point in the diagram represents a quantity of labor and capital employed in producing food. Associated with each such bundle of inputs is the technologically determined, corresponding level of food production, F. Thus both points A and B in Figure 3.2 are associated with the level of food output, $\overline{F}_2$. A lower level of production, $\overline{F}_1$,

FIGURE 3.2 Isoquants

Two isoquants for the food industry are shown, each illustrating all combinations of labor and capital inputs that can produce a given quantity of food.

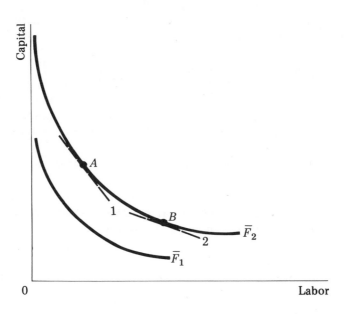

can be obtained with correspondingly smaller inputs of labor and capital, as shown by the $\overline{F}_1$ curve.

You will no doubt note that the isoquants resemble in appearance the indifference curves shown in Chapter 2. (An indifference curve shows the collection of commodity outputs, all of which yield the same level of satisfaction. An isoquant shows factor input combinations, all of which produce the same level of output.)[2] Both types of curve are bowed in toward the origin. The curvature of indifference curves reflects the diminishing marginal rate at which one commodity can be substituted for another in keeping constant the level of consumer satisfaction. Similarly, along an isoquant the rate at which labor can be substituted for capital with no sacrifice in output changes as more labor-intensive techniques are employed. The slope of the $\overline{F}_2$ isoquant at A, for example, shows how much

[2] There is an important difference between indifference curves and isoquants. We can measure the actual level of output along an isoquant, whereas with indifference curves we make no claim to measuring the absolute value of satisfaction.

capital can be removed from F production when one additional unit of labor is employed and output is kept constant. The slope of the $\overline{F}_2$ isoquant at B shows that as this substitution of labor for capital proceeds, labor becomes less productive in the sense that less capital can be taken off the job when another unit of labor is added. The law of diminishing marginal rate of substitution between factors in production is illustrated by the fact that isoquant $\overline{F}_2$ at B is flatter than at A.

These remarks about the meaning and properties of isoquants in the food industry carry over, of course, to properties of technology in clothing. Figure 3.3 is designed to illustrate the extra conditions required for resources to be allocated efficiently between the two sectors.

Points A and B in Figure 3.3 represent an *arbitrary allocation* of labor and capital to food and clothing, an allocation that disregards any tendency for clothing producers to prefer more labor-intensive techniques than would food producers. If the two industries could somehow "swap" resources in such a way that food output *and* clothing output could be

---

FIGURE 3.3   An Inefficient Allocation of Resources

Allocating the labor-capital bundle A to clothing and B to food is inefficient. A transfer of labor to clothing and capital to food (shown by arrows AC and BD, of equal length) would serve to raise outputs in *both* industries.

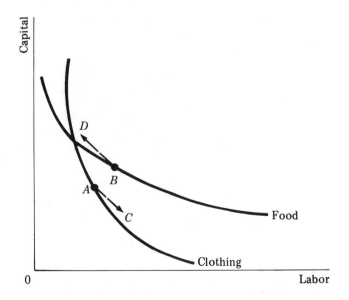

increased, the (A, B) allocation shown in Figure 3.3 would be proved inefficient. Try it. Suppose that the clothing industry takes some labor from the food industry and gives it some capital — arrow AC reflects this change. Arrow BD, equal in length and precisely opposite in direction, shows the food industry now using more capital (that given up by clothing) and releasing the extra labor required by clothing. The economy's total resource use is the same. But point C lies above the clothing isoquant through initial point A, and point D lies above the food isoquant through initial point B. Therefore, that initial allocation of labor and capital was inefficient. The clue to this inefficiency is found in the fact that the slopes of the isoquants at A and B are unequal.

Why does competition ensure that resources will be allocated efficiently so that at the production point each isoquant has the same slope? Because in each industry the choice of technique is guided by commonly faced prices that must be paid to hire capital and labor. Firms in each sector are attempting to minimize costs. Just as a consumer minimizes the cost of obtaining a given level of real income by choosing a point at which his indifference curve is tangent to his budget line, so does a cost-minimizing firm select its most economical input bundle by going to the point of tangency between an isoquant and a constant-factor-cost line. For example, suppose that the slope of line 1 in Figure 3.2 is chosen to reflect the ratio of the wage rate to the rental on capital equipment. Then the best (cheapest) way of producing $\bar{F}_2$ units of food is to pick point A. Any other point, such as B, would entail higher costs; a line parallel to line 1 (to show the same factor prices) but passing through B lies above line 1. Point B would only be chosen if the wage/rental ratio falls to the slope of line 2.

If firms in both industries face the same wage rate for labor and the same rental on capital equipment, as they do in competitive markets, the marginal rate of substitution between labor and capital in each industry is set equal to the common wage/rental ratio, and the two are therefore equal. In such a manner does competition in a nation's factor markets ensure that the conditions for an efficient allocation of resources are met, so that the community's production point does lie along the efficient production-possibilities locus.[3]

But does competition also require the "best" point to be chosen along the transformation curve? Yes — as you can see in Figure 3.4, which

---

[3] The parallel between producer behavior in choosing inputs and consumer behavior in making a consumption choice suggests the following exercise: Construct a "production box" diagram for a country with fixed labor and capital resources as an analogy to the "consumption box" diagram in Figure 2.7. Show that the "contract curve" of Figure 2.7 has its analog in the set of capital-labor allocations that are *efficient* in the sense described above. More details are provided in the appendix to Chapter 7.

FIGURE 3.4   The Optimal Production Point for a Closed Economy

An economy not engaged in trade can produce and consume anywhere along TT'. Point A, where an indifference curve is tangent to the transformation curve, represents a higher level of welfare than any other point (e.g., B). The slope of the common tangent at A shows the relative price of clothing.

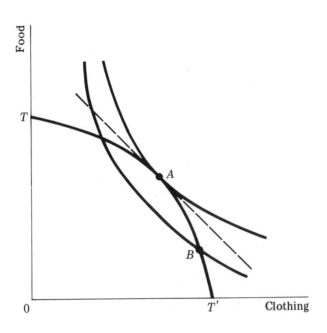

illustrates a competitive equilibrium for a community not engaged in trade, whose taste patterns can be displayed by a series of community indifference curves. Competition in factor markets has been shown to ensure production somewhere along TT'. Two indifference curves have been illustrated in Figure 3.4. Satisfaction is clearly maximized (in the absence of trade) by producing at point A. Any other production point along TT', such as B, yields less real income. Consider the slope of the dashed line tangent to both the indifference curve and transformation schedule at A. Our previous account of the exchange model in Chapter 2 showed that the marginal rate of substitution in consumption is set equal to the ratio of commodity prices. The slope of the dashed line in Figure 3.4 shows the ratio of the price of clothing to the price of food. But what about production? Recall that the marginal cost for a competitive firm is, in equilibrium, set equal to the market price of the commodity produced by the firm. This equality holds for clothing and food producers alike. Therefore the ratio of the price of clothing to the price of food is equal, in competitive markets, to the ratio of their marginal costs of production. The slope of the transformation curve equals the ratio of marginal costs in the two industries. It shows the amount of food that must be sacrificed in order to release sufficient capital and labor to produce an extra unit of clothing.

3.3 PRODUCTION AND FREE-TRADE EQUILIBRIUM

Patterns of production in all countries have been significantly affected by international trade. Some countries have taken advantage of trade to pour a relatively large volume of resources into activities for which there is little local demand — Zambian copper, Saudi Arabian oil, Greek shipping services. Other countries, such as the United States, have a more balanced productive base; yet certain sectors feel heavily dependent upon the export trade, as witnessed by Japanese purchases of American soybeans and lumber, or the occasional large wheat sales to the Soviet Union.

These production patterns lead to gains from trade that go beyond the consumption gains described in the preceding chapter. They can be illustrated for a country again assumed to be capable of producing only two commodities, food and clothing.

Consider Figure 3.5, which shows the consequence of trade for the home country. If the home country is not allowed to engage in international trade, its consumption possibilities are restricted to points on its TT' schedule, and of these the best is shown by point E where indifference curve y_0 is tangent to TT'. The pretrade relative price of clothing that clears the local market is shown by the slope of line 1. Suppose that, with the opening of trade, world prices are shown by the slope of line 2. Because clothing is relatively expensive abroad, free trade encourages resources to flow from food production into the clothing industry until local marginal costs equal world prices, at A. Line 2 shows the new expanded locus of consumption possibilities, and the most desired consumption bundle is point B. At these prices the community desires to export DA of its clothing output in exchange for BD imports of food. BDA represents the trade triangle.

The gains from trade are shown by the increase in real income in moving from curve y_0 to the higher curve, y_1. If resources had been frozen into their occupations at point E the country would still have gained from trade — the consumption point moving from E to F on curve y_2. The movement from F on y_2 to B on y_1 shows the extra gains to be had from trade when production is allowed to change from E to A. That is, the

FIGURE 3.5 The Trade Triangle in the Home Country

With free-trade prices shown by the slope of line 2, production at home takes place at A and consumption at B. BDA is the trade triangle — the community exports DA units of clothing in exchange for imports of BD units of food.

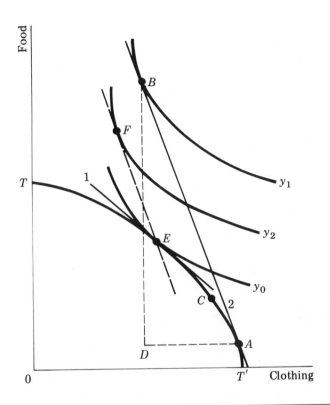

total gain from trade can be decomposed into (1) the gain attributable to consuming at prices different from original home prices — the movement from E to F in consumption, and (2) the gain attributable to the shift of resources that moves production from E to A, thus raising incomes and allowing consumption to expand from F to B.

World prices are determined by supply and demand in both countries. In a free-trade equilibrium the home country's import demand for food must be matched by the foreign country's willingness to export the same quantity of food. If the price line 2 in Figure 3.5 is to reflect an *equilibrium* price ratio, the trade triangle, BDA, must have its mirror image in the foreign country. That is, production and consumption decisions abroad must be as shown in Figure 3.6. The foreign country also has gained from trade — the movement from E^* to B^* entailing a rise in real incomes abroad from level y_0^* to y_1^*. Foreign exports of A^*D^* of food match home imports of BD. The slope of A^*B^* is, of course, the same as the slope of BA in Figure 3.5.

As in the preceding chapter, there are two alternative, but equivalent ways of illustrating which price ratio will clear world markets. One sweeps countries together to illustrate world demand and supply curves, the other matches one country's excess demand with the other's excess supply.

Constructing world demand and supply curves in Figure 3.7 requires very little more than already established in Figure 2.5, in Chapter 2. Consider any price ratio, whether or not it is an equilibrium ratio. For each country find the optimal (or competitive) production point by locating where the opportunity cost of producing food (reflected in the slope of the transformation schedule) matches that price ratio. For example, point A in Figure 3.5 is the production point corresponding to the price ratio shown by line 2. Note that production of food is encouraged by a rise in food's relative price — thus the upward-sloping world supply schedule $(S_F + S_F^*)$ in Figure 3.7. The demand curve is constructed as before: With the price ratio determining the production point, each price ratio corresponds to a unique budget line (tangent to the transformation schedule at the production point), and there is a "best" consumption choice made for that budget line. As food becomes relatively cheaper in world markets, the quantity of food demanded in the world is shown to increase in Figure 3.7. Equilibrium is established when the world market clears, at relative price for food, OA in Figure 3.7.

Excess demand and supply curves would look much as in Figure 2.6, and need not be redrawn here. Although in Chapter 2's model of commodity exchange the foreign country's total supply of food was fixed, its excess supply of food, the quantity it was willing to export to the home country, did respond to changes in prices. With production variable along the transformation curve, as in this chapter, both home import demand for food and foreign export supply will be more responsive to price changes than in the exchange model.

3.4 COMPARATIVE ADVANTAGE AND THE PATTERN OF TRADE

In this example of free-trade equilibrium we have illustrated the case in which the home country exports clothing and imports food. Such a pattern of trade corresponds to the comparison of *relative* commodity prices before trade; clothing was relatively cheaper at home (at E in Figure

FIGURE 3.6 The Trade Triangle in the Foreign Country

The slope of line 2 is the same as in Figure 3.5. Trade is balanced as the foreign country's trade triangle, $A^*D^*B^*$, matches the home country's BDA in Figure 3.5.

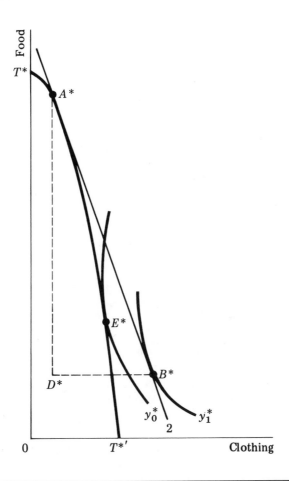

3.5) than abroad (at E^* in Figure 3.6). Since relative pretrade prices depend upon local supply and demand in each country, so does the pattern of trade. The home country is said to have a *comparative advantage* in clothing if clothing's relative price is lower at home before trade.

In general, positions of comparative advantage depend both upon the relationship between taste patterns in the two countries and between conditions of production, as expressed in the transformation curves. Fig-

---

FIGURE 3.7   World Demand and Supply

The equilibrium relative price of food, *OA*, clears the world market.

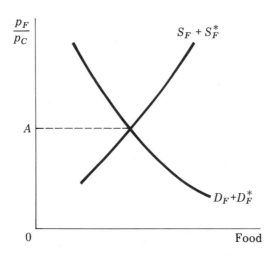

ure 3.8 illustrates this comparison between tastes, on the one hand, and supply, on the other. By showing quantities of food *relative* to quantities of clothing we can ignore sheer differences in size of countries as a determinant of pretrade relative prices.[4] Consistent with Figures 3.5 and 3.6, Figure 3.8 shows that food is relatively expensive at home before trade at *OA* (compared with price ratio *OA**) both because demand at home is biased toward food and because supply at home is biased away from food. Of course these biases need not both work in the same direction in establishing positions of comparative advantage. If the two countries' taste patterns had been reversed, the foreign country would still have retained its comparative advantage in producing food (*E* shows a relatively lower p_F/p_C than does *B*); the supply bias in Figure 3.8 has been assumed to dominate. Of crucial importance in determining the trade pattern is a comparison of cost ratios at home and abroad before trade. Such a comparison depends not only on general conditions of supply and cost (as captured by the shape of the transformation curve), but also on how local demand keeps costs low if weak or drives costs up if relatively strong.

---

[4] Here we assume that indifference curves are radial blowups of each other in each country (the technical term is that they are *homothetic*) so that only relative price, and not income, determines the *ratio* of goods demanded.

FIGURE 3.8   Relative Demands and Supplies

Relatively strong demand and relatively weak supply conspire to make food relatively expensive at home.

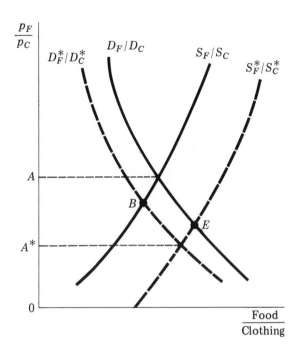

3.5 THE ELASTICITY OF IMPORT DEMAND

A country immersed in trade often faces disturbances in the terms of trade — that is, increases or decreases in the relative price of what it imports. Let us focus now on the following question: How sensitive is the demand for imports to a price change? In part, the answer should be obvious. If the home country imports food and if the price of food rises, we would expect both production of food to rise (a movement along the transformation schedule) and consumption to fall; therefore the discrepancy between the two (imports equal consumption minus production) would fall as well.

The extent of the response in production would depend on all those factors determining the degree to which the transformation schedule is bowed out. Similarly, the consumption response would depend in part on the shape of indifference curves. If these are sharply bowed in, any given rise in food's price causes the consumer to purchase less food, but little movement along an indifference curve is required to adjust the marginal rate of substitution (slope of the indifference curve) to the new price. But more is involved, and this is the tricky part: Any price change affects the *real income* of a trading community and, through this effect, the demand for all commodities as well. When analyzing the effect of price changes on demand, it is important to isolate the *substitution effect* (movements along a given indifference curve) from the *income effect* (movements from one indifference curve to another).

There are two important aspects of the income effect on demand when price changes: (1) determining how real income has been affected by the price change, and (2) determining what the impact on demand for importables of a given change in real income is. The second reflects only the consumer-preference pattern. Revert, for the moment, to the practice of quoting incomes and prices in dollar units. If incomes rise by $100 and if spending on food (the good being imported) rises by $40, we speak of the *marginal propensity to import* (food) of 0.4. The answer to (1) depends intimately on the extent of trade. The greater the quantity of food currently imported, the more severely will real incomes be hit by a rise in food's relative price.

These points can be illustrated in Figure 3.9. Suppose that production is rigidly given by point E and that initially the home country imports food at the price ratio shown by line 1, consuming at A. We illustrate a price *reduction* for imports, the new terms of trade shown by the slope of a steeper line (2 or 3, which are parallel). With the budget line rotating around the production point (E), consumption of food rises (from A to B). This demand change can be decomposed into two parts: (1) the move from A to C. This is the *substitution effect* — the change in demand if consumption is restricted to the same indifference curve. (2) The move from C to B. This is the *income effect*. A fall in import prices raises real income (from curve y_1 to curve y_2). The income effect shows how such an increase in real income would spill *at constant prices* into increased demand for both commodities.

We emphasized that the income effect depends sensitively on the extent (and direction) of trade. Consider the following exercise: In Figure 3.9 suppose the production point was point G instead of point E. That is, suppose imports of food were roughly twice the amount illustrated initially (distance AG is roughly twice distance AE). Then show by drawing the new budget line through G that the drop in food price raises real income by more than previously (indeed, by roughly twice as much). As a second exercise, suppose that this country initially *exported* food, as it would with exactly the same taste pattern if initially

FIGURE 3.9   Substitution and Income Effects

With point *E* the production point, consumption is initially at *A* at terms-of-trade line 1. A fall in food's import price is shown by steeper lines, 2 or 3. The substitution effect is the move from *A* to *C* along the initial indifference curve. The income effect is the move from *C* to *B*.

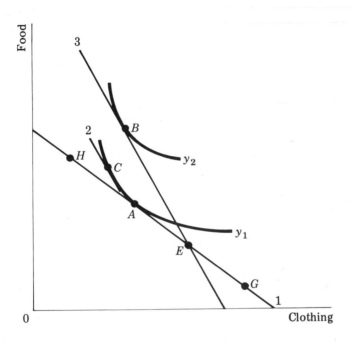

the production point was at *H*. Show how with the same fall in food's price real income now falls. (Draw the new budget line through *H*).

This discussion illustrates a general point worth emphasizing: For a country engaged in trade any price change affects real income. If the price of a commodity rises, real income at home goes up if that commodity is exported and falls if it is imported. Furthermore, the extent of the impact on real income is proportional both to the extent of the price change and to the volume of trade. These basic points find countless applications throughout this book, including the next chapter, where we shall discuss both the cases of export growth and the oil crisis.

If the *price of imports rises*, we can now collect the *three* ingredients that contribute to a reduction in import demand: (1) A substitution effect in consumption — less will be demanded (along an indifference curve); (2) An income effect — the increase in the price of imports lowers real incomes (pushes consumers onto lower indifference curves) and thus lowers import demand; and (3) The production effect — the rise in import price serves to attract resources from other industries. Production of importables rises.

The *elasticity* of import demand relates the relative extent of import reduction to the initiating price rise. Suppose food import prices rise by 10 percent. By how much will these ingredients conspire to reduce import demand? If the answer is greater than 10 percent, import demand is said to be *elastic;* if less than 10 percent, it is *inelastic.* These are purely matters of definition, but the distinction between elastic import demand and inelastic import demand is intimately rooted in the question of what happens to the aggregate volume of exports supplied.

Take the elastic case first. Suppose a 10 percent rise in import price causes a cut of 15 percent in the quantity of imports demanded. Is more or less being paid for imports? Per unit, more — which is what price reflects. But payment equals price times quantity, and in the case of elastic import demand the quantity falls relatively more than price rises. Therefore payments fall as price rises. But how are payments expressed? Recall the budget constraint: Exports must pay for imports. The *volume* of the good being exported must fall as the relative price of imports rises if the demand for imports is elastic.

The case of *inelastic* demand for imports reverses this conclusion. If the relative price of food imports rises by 10 percent and quantity of imports demanded falls by only 5 percent, the country must face a higher overall import bill. That is, the volume of exports required to finance imports at the higher price has gone up.

You may notice something odd about the behavior of export supply for an economy in which import demand is inelastic. For example, an inelastic import demand for clothing in the foreign country must imply that a fall in clothing's relative price lowers the quantity of food that must be given up as exports by foreigners. That is, the foreign supply of exports of food would fall as the relative price of food *rises.* In Figure 2.6 this would be shown by a stretch of the foreign export supply function that is *negatively sloped* (or backward-bending).

Just as with import demand, a three-part analysis can be used to reveal how export supply changes with price: (1) A rise in food's relative price causes resources to be shifted into food production abroad — this by itself would tend to raise exports of food; (2) The substitution effect in consumption abroad points to reduced foreign demand for food as food becomes more expensive — this effect supports a rise in food exports from abroad as well; (3) The income effect abroad runs counter to these two forces and must outweigh them if foreign import demand for clothing is inelastic. As food's relative price rises, foreigners as a group find their real incomes increased since the nation exports food.

Part of the increase in real income would be channeled into extra food consumption, and this, by itself, would tend to lower the quantity of food available for export.

This concern with demand behavior on the part of *exporters* of a commodity is, in a sense, unique to international trade theory. Usually when students are first introduced to demand theory the question is posed as follows: Suppose the price of some commodity (apples) rises — what happens to the quantity of apples demanded assuming all other prices are constant and *money income* is constant? In effect, questions about demand behavior are asked in the context in which individuals are always net buyers (of apples or whatever commodity is being discussed), so that a price rise reduces real income. In such a case, substitution and income effects go hand in hand to help reduce quantity demanded whenever price rises.

When the price of oil went up dramatically in the 1970's, what happened to the demand for gasoline by oil-exporting countries? Traffic jams in Carácas, Lagos, and Teheran increased. Perhaps Venezuela, Nigeria, and Iran sound special because they were made better off by the rise in oil prices. But this stance — of being an exporter of a commodity that has gone up in price — is one generally shared by *half the market!* The volume of purchases must be matched by the volume of sales. When demand behavior in a context of international trade is studied, it is inappropriate to disregard the fact that any price rise makes exporters better off even if it worsens the lot of importers.[5]

Suppose we relax the assumption that only two commodities (food and clothing) are involved in trade. Instead, suppose a country exports many commodities and that the price of *one* of them rises. What happens to *other* export sectors whose prices have not risen? They are squeezed. They probably lose resources to the sector that has benefited from a rise in price. As well, with home real incomes improved, increased home demand would cut into supplies available for export from these other sectors. This kind of general interdependence among export sectors — sometimes labeled the "Dutch Disease" — we explore more fully in Part 2 of this book. Here we stress that an aggregate *index* of export volume in a many-commodity world might shrink when an *index* of export prices

[5] The field of labor economics provides another example in which income effects might dominate substitution effects for exporters. If the wage rate rises, will more or less labor be supplied by households? Hours of labor worked represent exports of individuals with a given stock (24 hours per day) and an alternative usage — leisure. An increase in the wage rate implies both a substitution effect (less higher priced leisure purchased) and an income effect (workers are better off at a higher wage and thus consume more leisure). If the income effect dominates, less labor is supplied (exported) at the higher wage. Countries such as Malawi and Lesotho typically export large quantities of workers to Zambia and South Africa. Perhaps less labor would work in foreign mines if wage rates were higher.

rises, even though the volume of the particular export that has gone up in price may expand.[6]

3.6 SUMMARY

Both this chapter and the preceding one have been designed primarily to identify the sources of gain from engaging in trade. A simple model — what we call the *basic trade model* — has been developed to illustrate the nature of the gains from trade and how these gains are enhanced if a nation's production patterns can also be realigned to take advantage of trading opportunities. In this chapter we have also examined more carefully the ways in which an economy responds to a change in the terms of trade. In particular, price changes cause production to respond along the production-possibilities curve and consumers to substitute against commodities that have risen in price. The essence of any trading situation is that price changes reallocate real incomes, causing them to fall in the country importing the commodity that has risen in price and to rise in the exporting country. These income changes are both important in their own right, and they feed back to affect demand for importables and exportables.

The stage is now set for applications of this basic trade model that lead to an understanding of the way in which a nation is affected by changes both at home and abroad. Before proceeding, it is important to highlight some fundamental assumptions that will be carried through in these applications.

We continue to assume that markets are competitive. This means that producers and consumers in each country make decisions on the basis of market prices that each feels he cannot influence by his own actions. Relative prices are flexible and adjust so as to clear the market. The specter of unemployment is banished (until later), and the efficiency properties of competition assumed so that production takes place along the production-possibilities schedule and prices reflect local opportunity costs.

Finally, a word about the budget constraint is in order. The classical version, which we continue to use, is that each nation's demand is restrained by its ability to produce commodities. Literally, the aggregate value of consumption equals the aggregate value of production. International trade is the means whereby the *composition* of consumption can differ radically from the composition of production. In no way is

---

[6] The distinction between aggregate export behavior and individual export performance is discussed in R. W. Jones and E. Berglas, "Import Demand and Export Supply: An Aggregation Theorem," *American Economic Review*, March 1977.

this classical form of the budget constraint defended as being realistic. Indeed, Part 4 of this book deals explicitly with a world in which international adjustments are required in order to accommodate the desire of individual nations to overspend (and run deficits) or to underspend (and run surpluses). But these are different issues, and they will be considered in due course.

SUGGESTIONS FOR FURTHER READING

Jones, Ronald W. "Stability Conditions in International Trade: A General Equilibrium Analysis," *International Economic Review*, 2 (May 1961): 199–209. The first part of the article discusses the breakdown of consumption and production changes when the terms of trade change.

Leontief, Wassily. "The Use of Indifference Curves in the Analysis of Foreign Trade," *Quarterly Journal of Economics*, 47 (May 1933): 493–503; reprinted in American Economic Association, *Readings in the Theory of International Trade*. Philadelphia: Blakiston, 1949, chap. 10. An early exposition showing how to combine transformation schedules and indifference curves to illustrate equilibrium with trade.

Meade, James. *The Stationary Economy*. London: Allen and Unwin, 1965. Chap. 4 gives some simple exercises.

APPENDIX:
THE OFFER-CURVE DIAGRAM

All the diagrams we have used to show free-trade equilibrium and the pattern of trade have illustrated directly how quantities demanded and supplied respond to relative prices. An alternative diagrammatic apparatus, in use in the literature in international trade for more than a century,[1] contrasts directly the quantity of one commodity a country wishes to import against the quantity of the other commodity *offered* in exchange as exports. Retaining the assumption that the home country is an exporter of clothing in a free-trade equilibrium, Figure 3.A.1 illustrates the *offer curves* for the two countries.

Relative prices are shown in this diagram by the slopes of rays from the origin. Consider the home country's response to world relative price of clothing shown by the slope of ray *OA*. At this relative price the home country chooses to demand quantity *AF* of food over and above its local production. In order to obtain this by imports, it must be prepared to export *OF* units of clothing, which have equivalent value. Should the relative price of

---

[1] Offer curves, or "reciprocal demand-and-supply" curves, were extensively used by Alfred Marshall in his *Pure Theory of Foreign Trade* (London School of Economics and Political Science, 1930), first published in 1879.

FIGURE 3.A.1 Offer Curves

Free-trade equilibrium is shown by point Q, with the equilibrium terms of trade equal to the slope of ray OQ.

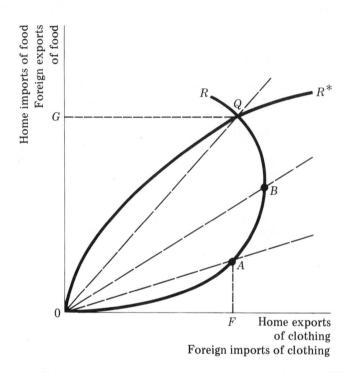

food fall to the level shown by ray OB, home demand for imports of food rises. In this range home import demand is elastic since the quantity of clothing exports it is willing to give up increases from A to B. By contrast, a further reduction in food's relative price to the ray OQ shows a reduction in clothing exports. More food imports are demanded at Q than at B, but the fall in food's relative price has been more severe so that total outlay (as measured by clothing exports) has fallen. This inelasticity in import demand reflects a behind-the-scenes conflict between greater production of clothing at Q than at B (since clothing's relative price has risen) and lower local demand for clothing via the substitution effect, on the one hand, and a stimulus to local demand for clothing via the income effect, on the other. (The rise in clothing's relative price from B to Q raises real incomes for the home clothing-exporting country.) This conflict is won by the income effect in the move from B to Q, and by the substitution effects in production and consumption in the move from A to B.

The foreign offer curve (OR^*) is elastic throughout the portion drawn. Decreases in the relative price of the commodity imported abroad (clothing) correspond to steadily rising import demand and export supply as clockwise-moving rays from the origin sweep the curve OR^*. Equilibrium is attained at a price ratio (shown by ray OQ) at which home demand for imports of food matches foreign supply. This equilibrium point, Q, also reveals that foreign demand for clothing imports matches home export supply. With reference to Figure 2.6, the quantity of food entering trade (OG in Figure 3.A.1) would correspond to OA, while the quantity of clothing imported abroad (GQ in Figure 3.A.1) would be shown in Figure 2.6 by the *area OTQA*. With reference to Figure 3.5, home clothing exports (DA in Figure 3.5) are shown by GQ in Figure 3.A.1, while the slope of OQ in the offer curve diagram, the equilibrium relative price of clothing, is shown in Figure 3.5 by the (absolute value of) the slope of line AB.

4

Applications of the Basic Trade Model

If Brazil has a bumper coffee crop, what happens to the world price of coffee? To real incomes in France? To welfare in Brazil? If oil supplies from the Middle East are restricted, how does the impact on Japan compare with that on the United States? These are examples of questions that can be put to the basic trade model outlined in the preceding two chapters.

4.1 A PRELIMINARY ASSUMPTION: MARKET STABILITY

Before proceeding with applications of this type, the economist must assume that the free-trade equilibria he is describing are *stable*.

Suppose that discrepancies between world demand and supply force relative prices to change so that the commodity found in excess supply has its relative price bid down. Then if world demand and supply curves have the shapes illustrated in Figure 4.1, the market equilibrium (at Q) is stable. For example, suppose food's relative price is distance OB. The excess world supply of food at that price (EG) forces food's price down toward its equilibrium value, OA. (Note that the world demand curve for food need not be downward-sloping everywhere, since an increase in food's relative price may cause exporters of food, who are made better off by such a price rise, to increase their demands by more than net importers have reduced theirs.)

Is it possible to illustrate *un*stable market equilibria, or would this violate some postulate of behavior we have already made for consumers or producers? Yes, unstable equilibria are possible. The appendix to this

FIGURE 4.1   A Stable Free-Trade Equilibrium

At price *OB* excess world supply of food forces relative price toward equilibrium point *Q*.

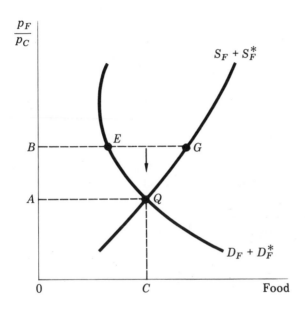

chapter gives an illustration and describes its implications. Here, however, we shall proceed with applications of the model that assume the market is stable.

4.2 FOREIGN SOURCES OF CHANGE

If a country engages in trade with other nations, it must be prepared for changes in foreign markets to affect conditions at home. It used to be said that if America sneezes, Europe catches pneumonia — a reference to the contagion of recession in the United States on other countries' employment levels. That particular phenomenon, the international transmission of business cycles, is out of bounds in our present flexible-prices, full-employment model (it will be picked up in Part 4). However, other ways in which the home country can be affected by changes abroad are easily handled. Let's consider two of them.

Changes in Foreign Demand

Suppose patterns of foreign taste change, such that out of any given income abroad a greater fraction would be spent on the home country's export commodity, clothing, than previously. Figure 4.2 illustrates this change of tastes abroad by the shift in the foreign excess demand curve from M^* to $M^{*'}$.

Two alternative export supply functions for the home country are drawn: X_1 and X_2. With either one the initial equilibrium position is shown by point Q. When foreign demand for home clothing exports shifts outward from curve M^* to curve $M^{*'}$, the relative price of clothing must be driven upward, either to point A or point B, depending on home supply response. If home exports respond positively to price, as with curve X_1, the increase in foreign demand for clothing results in greater foreign imports of clothing (point A). But we have already noted that for the home country an increase in clothing's relative price implies an increase in real incomes, part of which spills over into increased demand

FIGURE 4.2   An Outward Shift in Foreign Demand

An outward shift in foreign demand for home exports of clothing raises clothing's price, but may or may not increase home exports of clothing.

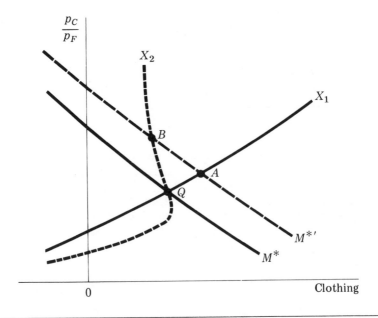

for clothing. If this outweighs the substitution effect in demand at home as well as any increased production of clothing (triggered by the price rise), the home export supply curve is backward-bending as with curve X_2.[1] An outward shift in foreign demand for home clothing would cause home exports to fall (compare Q and B). Foreigners are willing to buy more at any given price, but such a change in foreign tastes has so driven up price that they end up importing less.

The Oil Crisis

Changes of supply abroad can affect prices and home real incomes even more dramatically than shifts in foreign taste patterns. Few commodity markets have changed as much or received as much attention as the market in oil (and related energy sources). Given the rapid growth in world demand for energy in the late 1960's and early 1970's, some tightening of oil prices was starting to occur even before the politically inspired decision of Arab oil producers in October of 1973 to cut production and raise prices. The success of the Organization of Petroleum Exporting Countries (OPEC) in finally forming an effective cartel is a story that we shall pick up later (Chapter 9). We shall concentrate now on the impact of an increase in oil prices on oil-importing nations.

The price rise was dramatic. For a complete decade (1960–1970) the posted price of Arabian light crude oil remained a constant $1.80 per barrel. (Actual prices differed a little from the posted price). By October 1, 1973, this had increased to $3.01, but a scarce three months later the posted price had experienced almost a fourfold further increase (to $11.65 per barrel).[2] Although in the succeeding four years the nominal price of oil rose, in real terms (i.e., relative to other prices) it fell slightly until the next round of sizable increases in 1979.

Some estimates can be made of the magnitude of the terms-of-trade effect on real incomes. Imports of petroleum products into the United States rose from $7.6 billion in 1973 to a figure of $24.3 billion in 1974 — the value more than tripled. Quantity figures remained roughly constant (imports of crude products up slightly, of refined products down around 10 percent), so that as a first order of magnitude the rise in oil prices entailed a real income loss of roughly $16.7 billion (the increased cost of purchasing the same quantity of imports).

U.S. dependence on imports of oil had been steadily increasing up to 1974 (around 35 percent of U.S. requirements were imported in 1973,

---

[1] When curve X_2 is backward-bending, home import demand for food is inelastic.
[2] These figures are cited in *Energy and Prices 1960–73*, prepared by Foster Assoc. Ballinger, 1974.

with this figure approaching 50 percent at decade's end). But a country like Japan depends far more heavily on foreign sources. Japan imports over 99 percent of the crude oil it consumes. Between 1973 and 1974 the quantity of imports (of crude and partly refined petroleum) dropped around 4 percent but the *value* of imports rose by an estimated $12.9 billion.[3] Relative to income and size, the terms-of-trade impact on Japan was more severe than for the United States.

Of course the prices of other traded goods were also changing in this period. Suppose we let the "unit value of imports" (a price index) to the United States have a value of 100 in 1973. Then one year later this had jumped to 150, but the unit value of export prices had risen somewhat, to 127. Thus the terms of trade (the ratio of export to import prices) deteriorated for the United States from 1973 to 1974 from an index of 100 to 85. Four years later (1978) inflationary forces had raised both import and export prices, but left the terms of trade virtually unchanged. However, the further price rises in the energy field in 1979 drove the U.S. terms of trade down to around 79.[4] By contrast, Japan's terms of trade fell from 100 in 1973 to 74 in 1974. The strengthening value of the yen in subsequent years helped keep import prices down so that by 1978 the terms of trade stood at 81. But the rise in oil prices and Japan's heavy dependence upon imports helped push this figure down almost 10 points one year later.[5]

4.3 CHANGES ORIGINATING AT HOME

It goes without saying that any alteration in conditions at home will in general affect incomes and prices at home. The issue we wish to consider here is how the impact of changes at home on home incomes and growth is moderated or exacerbated by trading links with the rest of the world. Two broad classes of disturbances are considered: (1) a change in home composition of outputs that does not disturb incomes initially and (2) growth in production possibilities at home.

---

[3] Bank of Japan, *Economic Statistics Monthly*.

[4] These figures are calculated from the U.S. *Survey of Current Business*.

[5] See the Bank of Japan, *Economic Statistics Monthly*. Some countries are heavily dependent both on the import and the export side on a few primary products. For example, in Zambia when oil prices rose from 1973 to 1974 the unit value of imports (price index) rose 30 percent, but the rise in world copper prices raised the unit value of exports by 20 percent. The following year (1975) import prices continued to rise but copper prices crashed. With 1973 as a base year of 100, Zambia's terms of trade deteriorated only to 92 in 1974, but fell to 47 one year later. (These figures are computed from the International Monetary Fund, *International Financial Statistics*.)

The Composition of Outputs

The problem discussed here could be presented in the general setting in which resources can smoothly be transferred from sector to sector, with generalized increasing opportunity costs reflected by the bowed-out transformation schedule in Chapter 3. But it simplifies matters to revert to the more stark assumption in Chapter 2 that the economy's production bundle is unresponsive to any change in prices; the production-possibilities schedule is like the right-angled shape of Figure 2.1 (*FEG*). Even so, suppose that the economy's production point shifts in such a fashion that at the original world prices the *value* of incomes produced is not altered. To be explicit, reconsider Figure 2.1 and assume that the initial world price ratio for clothing is given by the slope of line *BEA* and that the corner of the transformation schedule shifts from *E* to *H*. Assume, furthermore, that the home country exports clothing and imports food both before and after this assumed change in production.

What difference would such a change make? At initial prices, none — at least to real incomes and the consumption pattern. (The country, of course, would export less clothing and import less food.) But if these production changes at home are significant enough to disturb world markets, the terms of trade must adjust, and this price change affects real income and consumption at home. And it is clear in which direction price changes. With clothing production reduced and food production expanded, the relative price of food falls. Such a production change at home, in favor of import-competing food, must improve the home country's terms of trade.

This example is chosen for a reason. Suppose we revert to the more general stance regarding production — that production possibilities are described by a smoothly bowed-out curve such as that shown in Figure 3.1. Initially, production is at *B* with world prices depicted by the slope of the dashed line tangent to *B*, and the home country is again an importer of food. Instead of assuming some arbitrary shift in the entire transformation schedule (as we did previously), suppose only that production is forced to move from *B* to *F* — resources are dragged away from clothing and put into food. It is not quite true that at initial world prices the value of production is unchanged; point *F* lies a bit below the dashed initial world price line. But once again we must conclude that if world markets are disrupted by this production change, the terms of trade improve, and thus the relative price of food imports will fall.

This argument serves as the opening wedge in the case for tariffs. If the government at home can somehow divorce domestic prices from world prices it might encourage greater production of the commodity being imported by raising its relative domestic price. And (at least up to a point) this may increase welfare at home by causing world prices to change. The composition of outputs is important for welfare because it is important for the terms of trade.

The Growth of Outputs

Is a community necessarily made better off by producing more? The wary reader may wonder about the quality of life as it is affected by the extra production. Is growth beneficial if it leads to increased congestion, pollution, and crime in urban areas? In a different vein, is aggregate growth desirable if it reflects a population explosion that threatens to lower *per capita* income? These arguments against growth are both popular and easily understood. But there is a less obvious question: Can an outward shift of a community's production-possibility schedule with a constant population — with food and clothing "goods" instead of "bads" — ever lead to a lowering of real incomes at home? In a context of international trade, the answer is "perhaps."

The preceding discussion of the way in which changing the composition of output can alter the terms of trade and, therefore, real income should serve as the key to the possibility that these terms-of-trade changes might even outweigh the directly beneficial effect of growth. Consider a country like Brazil, heavily committed to an export crop like coffee for which world demand might be highly inelastic. Suppose it is a good season, or for some other reason Brazil's transformation schedule shifts out primarily in the direction of coffee production. The world price of coffee might fall so much that Brazil loses real income as a consequence of the good crop. The argument has validity as well for groups within a country. Agriculture provides the prime example. Many nations attempt, on behalf of their farmers, to encourage crop restriction programs to keep farm prices from falling in the face of inelasticity in demand.

This possibility — that growth could lower real incomes by being concentrated in a nation's export sector and by significantly worsening the country's terms of trade — is illustrated in Figure 4.3. It is known as a case of *immiserizing growth*. Initially, the terms of trade are given by the slope of line 1, with the home country's production at A and consumption at B. Growth in some form that favors the nation's export industry, clothing, shifts the transformation schedule outward from TT to $T'T'$. As a consequence we assume that the relative price of clothing in world markets drops to the level shown by the slope of line 2. The home country adjusts its production to point C and, at the new terms of trade, maximizes its real income by consuming at point D. But its real income after growth, as indicated by the y_1 indifference curve, is lower

FIGURE 4.3 Immiserizing Growth

Growth biased toward the nation's export industry (clothing) can reduce real income by so worsening the terms of trade (from line 1 to line 2) that consumption (at D) ends up on a lower indifference curve than initially (at B).

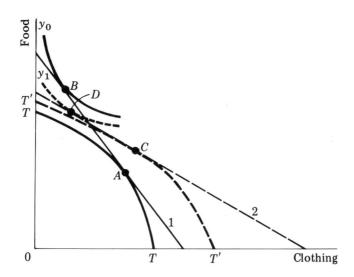

than the original real income shown by indifference curve y_0. Economic growth has made the country worse off.

Two basic factors could contribute to produce this result. (1) Growth primarily increases capacity and output in a nation's export industries. (2) Demand elasticities throughout the world for the country's export commodity are quite low. The first factor ensures that the major effect of growth in world markets is the increased supply of the nation's exports, whereas the second suggests that the terms of trade must deteriorate sharply to raise world demand enough to clear commodity markets. Figure 4.4 illustrates these two factors. The home country experiences growth, and at initial prices (OA) this growth is concentrated in its clothing export sector. This is shown by the rightward shift in the world supply schedule. The world demand curve also shifts to the right since at home a fraction of the extra incomes earned in the clothing sector spills over into extra clothing demand. The relative price of clothing is driven down to OB, and such a drop is more severe the less elastic is

FIGURE 4.4   Output Growth and Terms-of-Trade Deterioration

Growth concentrated in the home country's clothing export sector shifts
the world supply curve to the right by more than the world demand curve.
The deterioration in the terms of trade $(OA$ to $OB)$ is more severe the
less elastic is world demand.

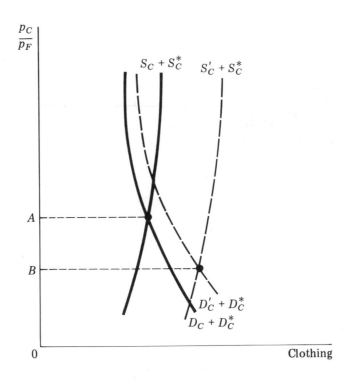

world demand. This inelasticity in demand is a condition feared by
many agricultural communities.

This discussion perhaps casts too pessimistic a pall over the prospects of growth for a country engaged in trade. For a small country, little change in world markets could be expected as a consequence of
growth, so that the feedback on home real incomes through a terms-of-
trade effect could safely be ignored. And, for a larger country, growth
might improve the terms of trade if it were concentrated in a country's
import-competing sector. Clearly the assumed *composition* of output
changes has much to do with the terms-of-trade effect. But is it possible

to isolate the effect of growth per se on real income in a trading economy? Yes, by considering the following case.

Figure 4.5 is designed to illustrate the initial effect (at constant world prices) of *neutral* or *uniform* or *balanced* growth on production and consumption. At terms of trade given by the slope of line 1, production takes place along *TT* at point *A*. Line 1 is the budget line, allowing consumption at point *B*, with imports of food equal in value to exports of clothing. Balanced growth is represented by the uniform expansion of the transformation curve to *T'T'*, so that at the initial terms of trade, shown also by the slope of line 2, production would expand proportionally from *A* to *C*. If the higher incomes result in a uniform expansion in demand (from *B* to *D*), distance *DC* must exceed distance *BA*. The *structure* of the home country's economy is identical before and

---

FIGURE 4.5   Uniform Growth at Given Terms of Trade

If the transformation schedule shifts uniformly outward, and if all demands expand uniformly at constant prices, growth must worsen the terms of trade by increasing the demand for imports.

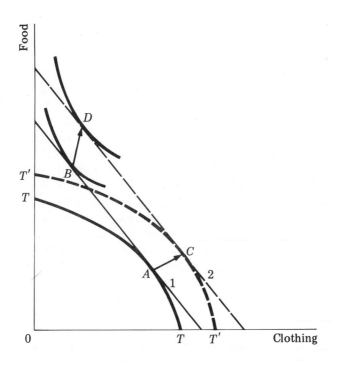

after growth, but the increase in size spills over to increase the absolute quantity of food demanded as imports and clothing offered as exports. If the rest of the world is not experiencing growth (at least at this rate), there is pressure set up for the home country's terms of trade to deteriorate. *The sheer act of growing more than other countries will increase the demand for imports and thus induce a deterioration in the terms of trade that to some extent may erode the gains from growth.*[6]

4.4 CHANGES IN BOTH COUNTRIES: THE TRANSFER PROBLEM

It is not difficult to think of changes in the factors governing world trade that would initially affect both (all) countries: Too much rainfall over a wide area can simultaneously cut crop yields in a number of countries; multilateral tariff negotiations can alter market prospects for all trading participants. In this section we shall consider a different kind of change — a transfer from one country to another of purchasing power and/or basic command over resources, which is a problem that has engaged economists for decades if not centuries.

The Transfer Problem: Purchasing Power

Consider the following case. The home country is obligated to make a gift or reparations payment to the foreign country. It could be France after the Franco-Prussian War in 1870–71, or Germany after World War I. To broaden the possible categories we could consider a different kind of "gift" — the Marshall Plan, whereby the United States sent aid to Europe after World War II. For analytic purposes we should also include international lending and borrowing, but we shall ignore the future problems of repaying loans (a reverse transfer). A recent example concerns the "recycling" of surpluses earned by oil-exporting countries into loans to Western Europe. All these cases have something in common: One country transfers purchasing power to another.

The easiest way to prepare the basic trade model to handle this problem is to let the home country cut the aggregate value of its spending below the current value of its produced income by precisely the same amount that the foreign country expands its spending above its current aggregate production level. (Only in this way can *world* expenditure balance *world* production.) This amount is called the *transfer*.

---

[6] You may wonder if in this case of neutral growth the terms of trade could deteriorate to such an extent that growth becomes immiserizing. The answer is yes, if elasticities are sufficiently low. The supplement provides the details.

How does such a transfer affect the terms of trade? We can answer this by asking what the transfer does to world demand and supply for one of the traded commodities, e.g., food. A transfer of purchasing power would leave the world supply schedule in place but might cause the world demand curve to shift. At any given price ratio the home, transferring, country can be expected to cut back its spending on all normal commodities such as food. Abroad, the receipts of the transfer are in general disbursed over all commodities, including food. That is, the home demand curve for food shifts leftward, the foreign curve shifts rightward, and depending on the differences in the two countries' taste patterns, the world demand curve could shift in either direction.

The first conclusion, then, is that transfer can move the terms of trade either up or down. To probe more formally, let m and m^* denote home and foreign *marginal propensities to import.* These propensities indicate, for each country, the fraction of a unit extra total spending that would be allocated to the consumption of importables at initial prices. Thus if T denotes the transfer, the home country, at initial prices, would cut its spending on food by $m \cdot T$. The foreign country imports clothing, so that it allocates $(1 - m^*)$ times the transfer to extra food consumption. We conclude that the world demand curve for food shifts to the right if and only if $(1 - m^*) \cdot T$ exceeds the home cut, $m \cdot T$. That is, the terms of trade turn against the transferor (food's relative price rises when the home country makes a transfer) if and only if the sum of the two countries' marginal propensities to import falls short of unity.

If the sum of the marginal propensities to import is less than unity, we speak of the "secondary burden" of the transfer in acknowledgment of the fact that price changes create an international redistribution of income additional to the initial loan or grant. Between the two world wars a number of eminent economists were concerned with the practical importance of this issue. John Maynard Keynes eloquently argued that the reparations payments imposed by the Allies on Germany after World War I underestimated the true payment that Germany would be called upon to make.[7] According to Keynes, Germany's export prices would have to fall considerably, coupled perhaps with a rise in its import prices, in order for Germany to create the export surplus that is the counterpart of the financial transfer. In reply to Keynes, Bertil Ohlin proposed that the transfer itself, by lowering spending in Germany and raising spending in the recipient country, could bring about the required export surplus without requiring a change in the terms of trade. Ohlin's reasoning is closer to our analysis, which suggests that there is no ne-

[7] John Maynard Keynes, *The Economic Consequences of the Peace.* New York: Harcourt, Brace and Howe, 1920.

cessity for the terms of trade to change one way or the other.[8] In any event, tracing the adjustments that the German reparations required is difficult, for this period was characterized by an additional reverse transfer in the form of private loans and capital movements from the United States to Europe.

The transfer criterion tells us that the terms of trade move in favor of the country making the transfer if the sum of import propensities exceeds unity. How far in favor can the terms of trade go? The discussion of the possibility of immiserizing growth, in the last section, should alert you to the analogous possibility that the home country, by giving away purchasing power, might so improve its terms of trade that it ends up with improved welfare. This, however, cannot happen here — "it is never better to give than to receive." Figure 4.6 helps explain the limits to any "secondary blessing" of the transfer.

The initial world equilibrium in the food market is shown by a relative price for food, OA, and quantities produced and consumed, OF. If the home country makes a transfer, its real income is reduced. On the other hand, if its terms of trade improve (food's price falls), this loss will not be as severe. Let price OB represent exactly the improvement in the terms of trade (compared with OA) required to compensate the home country for the transfer. That is, *if* the price of food could fall to level OB, neither country's welfare would be altered from its pretransfer level. The question boils down to the following: Can the transfer shift world demand to the left sufficiently to reduce food's price to OB or lower? The answer is no, because after the transfer *if* the price were OB, world demand for food would have to exceed its initial value, OF. The reason follows from looking at income and substitution effects. By assumption, net real income in neither country is changed if food's price falls to OB; therefore, there is no income effect. Substitution effects in both countries call for greater food demand at a lower price. Therefore, even if the transfer shifts the world demand schedule to the left, it must be to some position such as $(D_F + D_F^*)'$, with a new relative price for food (OG) above OB.

Brazil might improve its position by burning part of a bumper coffee crop. It cannot improve its position by giving that coffee away. Growth (or the reverse) shifts the world supply curve; a transfer of purchasing power does not. Without a change in supply, price changes can never outweigh the direct effect of the transfer.

[8] See the exchange between Keynes and Ohlin: Keynes, "The German Transfer Problem," *Economic Journal*, 39 (March 1929): 1–7 and B. Ohlin, "The Reparation Problem: A Discussion," *Economic Journal*, 39 (June 1929): 172–73. Both are reprinted in American Economic Association, *Readings in the Theory of International Trade*.

FIGURE 4.6 Transfer and the Terms of Trade

A transfer may improve the terms of trade of the transferor, as shown by the drop in food's relative price from *OA* to *OG* when the home country (the importer of food) makes a transfer. *OB* represents such an improvement in the home country's terms of trade that its real income would be unaffected by the payment. Therefore, at price *OB* world demand must exceed world supply, because only substitution effects are involved in demand.

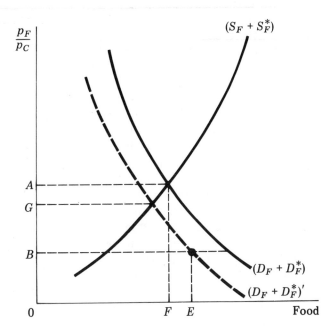

The Transfer Problem: Real Resources

A transfer in the form of a gift, a loan, or reparations often involves more than a redistribution of purchasing power. Real resources may be moved from one country to another. This movement may be direct, such as in the stripping of German capital equipment at the end of World War II and its relocation in Eastern Europe and the Soviet Union. Or the process may be more indirect: A country such as Canada may borrow on the New York market, causing a greater investment in new capital equipment in Canada and perhaps less new capital equipment in the United States. In this section we shall investigate the possible repercussions on the terms of trade and real incomes of a transfer of real capital from one country to another.

To analyze the effect of such a real transfer on the terms of trade we should reconsider the logic used in the previous section. In a stable market the relative price of a commodity will rise only if the transfer creates an excess world demand for that commodity at the original price. The world supply schedule in our previous analysis was unaffected by transfer. But if productive resources are involved in the transfer, the world supply curve, as well as the demand curve, may shift.

How much might world supply change? Obviously much depends on how the resources are used in each country. At one extreme the pattern of output reduction in the transferor might exactly match the output expansion made possible in the receiving country. In such a case no changes in world output take place — it is as if only purchasing power were transferred. At the other extreme the output changes in each country might involve completely different commodities. For example, each country might produce only one commodity, and exchange it in trade for the other country's commodity. The home country transfers resources out of clothing (its only produced commodity in this example) and into the foreign country, where they are devoted to food production. Such extreme output changes lead to definite conclusions as to movements in the terms of trade: The transferor's real income loss is partly mitigated by a terms-of-trade improvement. The transfer has increased world food output (and lowered clothing output) and lowered food's relative price.[9]

Figure 4.7 illustrates a less extreme example, one in which outputs and demands fall uniformly in the transferor and expand uniformly in the receiving country. Is there any presumption as to the terms-of-trade movement in such a case? Yes, but it is more than a presumption. The terms of trade *must* move in favor of the transferor. Segment AB in the paying country matches segment A^*B^* in the receiving country — the diagonals of each country's trade triangle before the transfer. With the resource transfer the home country's transformation curve uniformly shrinks to $T'T'$ (and the receiving country's curve uniformly shifts outward to $T^{*'}T^{*'}$), by assumption. Segment DC must be shorter than D^*C^* so that there must be excess world demand for clothing (and supply of food) at the initial prices. The relative price of clothing must rise.

This result should remind you of the case of balanced growth in one country, illustrated in Figure 4.5. A transfer of resources in the neutral case is similar to having balanced growth in one country (the receiving country) *and* balanced contraction in the other (the transferor). On both counts you would expect the terms of trade to turn against the

---

[9] The transferor could actually have its real income increased by such a supply change.

FIGURE 4.7 Transfer of Resources: The Neutral Case

If a transfer of resources shrinks production and consumption uniformly toward the origin in the paying country and outward in the receiving country, the terms of trade must improve for the paying country.

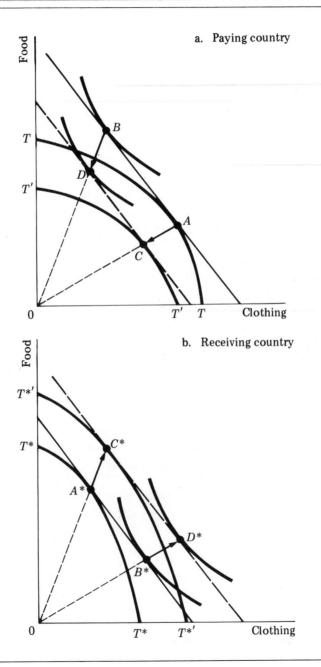

a. Paying country

b. Receiving country

receiving (or growing) country. The logic is identical to the growth case, except that it is fortified by the other country's decline as well.

4.5 SUMMARY

Three basic applications have been discussed:

1. Cases in which foreign disturbances are transmitted to the home country. Generally speaking, any source of disturbance abroad that causes world markets to settle at new prices has its effect on the home country. A change in foreign tastes or in foreign supplies each involves a terms-of-trade impact for the home country. And this impact may be sizable, as our discussion of the oil crisis suggested.

2. Cases in which disturbances at home are transmitted abroad, with consequent reverberations at home. Any change in the composition of outputs at home could affect world prices. A growing community finds that repercussions of its growth are reflected in its terms of trade. We argued that on balance the benefits of growth in one country would spill over to affect other countries favorably through cheapening the growing country's exports. We even considered extreme cases in which growth might leave a country in a worse position. Agriculture supplies many examples in which crop restriction (the opposite of growth) might benefit farmers.

3. Some disturbances may affect both countries in opposite directions. The transfer process, wherein a gift or a loan is made between countries, provides the classic example. If only purchasing power is transferred, the crucial consideration involves how tastes differ between payer and receiver. But this is an older theme: The elements of the transfer problem are embedded in *any* price change in a trading community. When the relative price of food rises, real incomes of food importers are damaged and those of food exporters are enhanced. The classical transfer problem seems to turn things around: First, the transfer is made and *then* we ask what happens to the terms of trade. Any required price adjustment involves a "secondary" transfer of real income. If resources are transferred as well, the problem becomes much like the growth (and decline) exercise.

"Every exit is an entrance to another stage." And the completion of this survey of the basic trade model is a prerequisite for investigating what lies behind nations' productive structures (Part 2), what devices they might profitably and selfishly employ in disturbing trade patterns through commercial policy (Part 3), and what kind of problems nations encounter in the process of mutual adjustment to changing trade and payments situations (Part 4).

SUGGESTIONS FOR FURTHER READING

Bhagwati, Jagdish. "Immiserizing Growth: A Geometrical Note," *Review of Economic Studies,* 25 (3) (June 1958): 201–05. An early treatment of the possibility that growth can harm a country.

Samuelson, Paul A. "The Transfer Problem and Transport Costs: The Terms of Trade When Impediments Are Absent," *Economic Journal,* 62 (June 1952): 278–304. A thorough analysis of the classical transfer theory.

APPENDIX:
INSTABILITY AND MULTIPLE EQUILIBRIA

The counterpart to Figure 4.1's illustration of a stable free-trade equilibrium is Figure 4.A.1's depiction of multiple possible free-trade equilibria. Point C in Figure 4.A.1a shows world demand and supply for food in balance, but the equilibrium point is unstable. If the price of food were slightly higher, at (2), world demand for food would exceed world supply by distance AB. Such an excess demand would drive food's price upward, away from point C. (Similarly, for a price of food lower than (1), world excess supply would drive food's price lower, toward stable equilibrium point E.)

Figure 4.A.1b illustrates this instability in an offer-curve diagram. At disequilibrum terms of trade (2), TV indicates the excess of the home country's import demand for food (given by point W along home offer curve $OIWQHR$) over foreign export supplies (given by point V along foreign offer curve $OHQVIR^*$). Food's price will rise, rotating price line (2) clockwise toward stable intersection point I and away from unstable point Q. Point Q in 4.A.1b corresponds to point C in 4.A.1a.

Each diagram helps reveal the ingredients that conspire to make an equilibrium unstable. As point Q in the lower panel indicates, instability requires a high degree of inelasticity in *both* countries' offer curves.[1] The upper panel shows that for instability the aggregate world demand curve in the neighborhood of equilibrium must be positively sloped — and even flatter than the world supply curve.

How can the world demand curve be positively sloped? Only if at least one country's demand curve has a positive slope in the neighborhood of a free-trade equilibrium. Consider, first, the importer of food — the home country. As food's price rises from (1), substitution effects suggest less food is demanded. Furthermore, real income falls so that, assuming food is a "normal" commodity, both income and substitution effects conspire to reduce the home country's demand for food. Thus, instability must stem from the demand behavior of the exporter. For foreign exporters of food, income and substitution effects run counter to each other. As the price of food rises, so does foreign real income, and this tends to make the foreign demand curve for food positively sloped. In order for the *world's* demand curve to be positively sloped,

---

[1] As the supplement to Chapter 4 proves, the criterion for stability is that the *sum* of the two countries' elasticities of demand for imports exceeds unity.

FIGURE 4.A.1 Multiple Equilibria

There may be multiple free-trade equilibria. The middle equilibrium point (C in a, or Q in b) is unstable, flanked by a pair of stable equilibria.

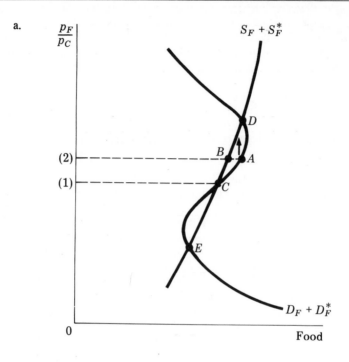

a.

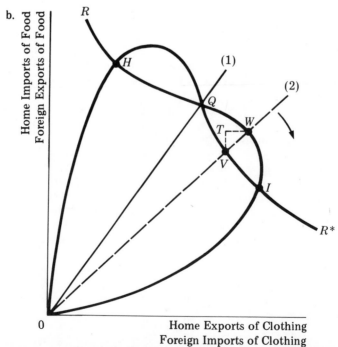

b.

the exporter's income effect must outweigh the income effect of the importer as well as *both* countries' substitution effects. In order for the market to be unstable, the exporter's income effect must *in addition* outweigh any positive production response of food producers at home and abroad.

There is nothing automatic in the relationship between income and substitution effects to guarantee market stability. Therefore, an additional assumption must be made that the market is stable. Little interest attaches to equilibria that are unstable because prices will tend to run away from such equilibria. The applications of the basic trade model considered in Chapter 4 involve comparing one equilibrium with another, under the assumption that prices do approach the second equilibrium after the market is disturbed (by growth, or taste changes, or transfers). Such a procedure makes sense only if we assume the market is stable. The supplement to Chapter 4 probes more deeply into the analytics of this issue.

II

PRODUCTION, INCOME DISTRIBUTION, AND TRADE PATTERNS

5

The Ricardian
Trade Model

Twin themes run through the next several chapters. We shall explore more thoroughly the production structure of economies in order to reveal: (1) how the pattern of trade is influenced by differences in countries' technology and availabilities of basic factors of production, and (2) how trade serves to redistribute factor returns within a country in an uneven fashion — some factors gain from trade whereas others may lose.

David Ricardo's name is associated with the earliest model of trade.[1] We have already demonstrated, in Chapter 2, the basic result concerning gains from trade: Countries can mutually benefit from trade if the *relative* prices of commodities differ between countries in the absence of trade. Ricardo is credited with establishing this result in a simple model in which a country's relative prices must reflect the ratio of labor costs of production. Thus the trade pattern in a Ricardian world is determined by differences in labor productivities between countries.

5.1 THE RICARDIAN MODEL FOR A CLOSED ECONOMY

Ricardo adopted the "labor theory of value" in describing the ratio in which commodities are exchanged for each other in an economy closed

---

[1] A recent edition is David Ricardo, *The Principles of Political Economy and Taxation*. New York: Penguin, 1971, chap. 7. This work was first published in 1817.

to the possibility of foreign trade. According to a strict version of the labor theory of value:

1. Labor is the only factor of production that gets a remuneration.
2. All labor is homogeneous and occupations all pay the same wage.
3. In any occupation the number of man-hours required per unit of output neither rises nor falls as output expands. Real cost per unit remains constant.

Suppose we return to a simplified economy in which only two commodities, food and clothing, can be produced or consumed. Let a_{LC} and a_{LF} each represent the invariant real labor costs per unit of output in the clothing and food industries, respectively. If, say, twice as many man-hours are needed to produce a unit of food as to produce a unit of clothing, the price of food must be double that of clothing; prices are proportional to labor costs. If output levels are designated by x_C and x_F (for clothing and food outputs, respectively), the total quantity of labor allocated to clothing production would be given by the product $a_{LC}x_C$ (and to food by $a_{LF}x_F$).

The production-possibilities schedule for a Ricardian model does not exhibit the traditional bowed-out shape. Instead, it is a downward-sloping straight line, whose constant slope reflects the ratio of labor costs (and prices). One way of seeing this is to consider the sum of the total labor force allocated to clothing ($a_{LC}x_C$) and to food ($a_{LF}x_F$). In a fully employed economy this sum adds up to the total labor force available (L), which we assume constant. (Recall that the production-possibilities schedule shows the maximum combination of outputs that can be obtained from a given resource base.) This full-employment relationship is shown in equation 5.1:

$$a_{LC}x_C + a_{LF}x_F = L. \tag{5.1}$$

With fixed labor requirements per unit of output, this equation describes the straight-line transformation schedule illustrated in Figure 5.1. The endpoints each show the maximum quantity of each commodity that could be produced if that activity absorbed the entire labor force.[2] The slope is easily calculated to be (minus) the constant ratio, a_{LC}/a_{LF}.

For further understanding, we ask how much extra food could be produced if clothing output is reduced by one unit. This reduction would release a_{LC} units of labor. Since a_{LF} man-hours are required per food unit, a_{LC}/a_{LF} extra food units could be produced. This figure must, in a closed economy, represent the relative price of clothing — measured in

---

[2] As an example suppose it takes 20 man-hours to produce a unit of food and 10 man-hours per unit of clothing. An economy that possessed a thousand man-hours of labor supply could produce a maximum of 50 units of food or 100 units of clothing, or any linear combination of the two.

units of food that must be surrendered to purchase one unit of clothing.

A closed economy must rely on its own production to satisfy its consumption needs. Therefore relative prices in such an economy are shown by the constant slope of the transformation schedule. The pretrade consumption (and production) pattern would be illustrated in Figure 5.1 by the point at which an indifference curve (not drawn) is tangent to the straight-line transformation schedule. And this easily generalizes to a closed economy with any number of commodities. Relative prices are all technologically determined by the invariant labor productivities. As will soon become clear, this view of the determinants of price is no longer applicable once the economy is opened to trade.

5.2 COMPARATIVE COSTS AND THE PATTERN OF TRADE

Trade patterns reflect a comparison of relative prices between countries in the pretrade state. Once again it becomes useful to consider diagrams in which relative outputs are related to relative prices.

FIGURE 5.1 The Ricardian Production-Possibilities Schedule

The opportunity cost of producing clothing is shown by the slope of the straight-line transformation schedule, which is the ratio of labor coefficients a_{LC}/a_{LF}.

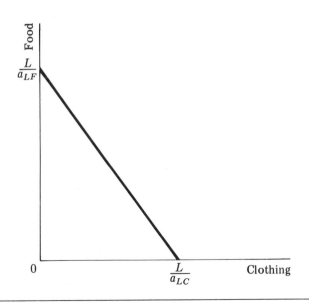

The relative supply curve in a Ricardian world is *horizontal:* If both food and clothing are to be produced, the relative price of food must reflect the (constant) ratio of labor costs in food to labor costs in clothing. The straight-line transformation schedule of Figure 5.1 supports the horizontal relative supply curve of Figure 5.2. This implies that demand has *no* role in determining pretrade prices, and this is indeed a peculiarity of the Ricardian model. The pattern of trade is completely determined by the technological differences between countries. The foreign country emerges as a food exporter if and only if its relative supply curve is lower than the home country's. Put more generally, the foreign country has a comparative advantage in food (and exports food) only if

$$\frac{a_{LF}^*}{a_{LC}^*} < \frac{a_{LF}}{a_{LC}}. \tag{5.2}$$

We suppose this to be the case. The Ricardian model is the extreme case in which trade patterns are determined solely by differences in rela-

---

FIGURE 5.2   Relative Demands and Supplies in a Ricardian Model

The Ricardian relative supply curve is horizontal. The pretrade relative price of food is the invariant labor cost ratio, a_{LF}/a_{LC}.

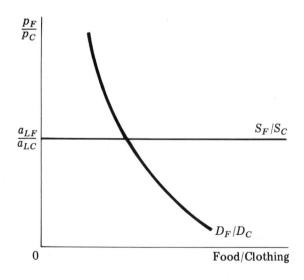

tive costs and these cost differences are independent of the production pattern.[3]

Ricardo discussed his theory of comparative costs in the context of a numerical example in which one country (England in his case) had higher labor costs per unit of production than the other country (Portugal) in all (both) commodities. Why should Portugal import anything from England? Because, although English labor was at an absolute disadvantage in both commodities (wine and cloth), its disadvantage was assumed by Ricardo to be relatively less in one of the goods (cloth). Criterion (5.2) illustrates that *comparative* costs provide the key to trade patterns. As we shall see in section 5.4, if Portugal has an absolute cost superiority in both goods, the Portuguese wage rate must be higher than that of the English. Suppose this advantage is a consequence of superior Portuguese technology (or, in the case of wine, superior climate). Then English labor might be tempted to migrate south. Ricardo assumed that national borders kept labor (or any other productive factor) at home. Thus trade in commodities is a substitute for international mobility of factors. Commodities enjoy a world market, but factors of production compete with each other only within national boundaries. This assumption underlies much, but not all, of the theory of trade that we will discuss. Although this assumption is not strictly realistic, there is little doubt that national differences in languages, customs, and laws severely inhibit permanent flows of factors internationally. We shall subsequently examine explicitly the consequences of allowing for international movements of capital and labor.

5.3 INTERNATIONAL PRICES AND THE GAINS FROM TRADE

We have assumed, in equation 5.2, that comparative cost ratios differ between countries. This implies that in the Ricardian model once trade is established the common relative price cannot equal the cost ratio in both countries, since these cost ratios stay a constant distance apart. Indeed, the typical classical representation in such a case had international prices distinctly different from the cost ratio in either country. This led to the conclusion that the labor theory of value, so useful in explaining domestic price ratios for a closed economy, would be rendered useless as an explanation of international values.

---

[3] Compare with the case of vertical relative supply curves, which is the model of exchange introduced in Chapter 2. In that case pretrade price ratios are determined by supply *and* demand (as in the general case), but demand has no influence on quantities produced. The exchange model and the Ricardian model represent the two extreme cases.

The problem with asserting that relative prices reflect relative (labor) costs is that a country may be forced by international competition to give up some line of production completely. If so, it is precisely because the international price of some commodity falls short of the costs required to produce the commodity at home that no production can take place. Figure 5.3 illustrates a free-trade equilibrium in which the home country specializes in the production of clothing in which it has (by virtue of inequality 5.2) a comparative advantage, and the foreign country's labor force is entirely devoted to food production. A market-clearing free-trade price ratio is established — the same ratio for each country (dotted line BE has the same slope as E^*B^*) — with home exports of clothing (CE) matched by foreign imports of clothing (C^*B^*). The rationale for the gains from trade is similar to that described for the basic trade model in Part 1. What is special about the Ricardian model is the potentially drastic consequence of trade for patterns of production. In each country not only are *some* resources attracted to the export sector but *all* resources flow there. Clearly this reflects the assumption of constant opportunity costs as opposed to increasing opportunity costs (along a bowed-out production-possibilities curve). Each country gains from trade, with free-trade consumption points $(B$ and $B^*)$ lying on higher indifference curves than pretrade consumption bundles $(A$ and $A^*)$.

Does the assumption of constant (labor) costs necessarily require each country to be completely specialized with trade? No. The international terms of trade must lie somewhere between the cost ratios in each country — but not necessarily *strictly* between. For example, if one country is much larger than the other, the world terms of trade could settle at the cost ratio of the large country. If the world is made up of the United States and Costa Rica, it may be impossible for Costa Rica, with a presumed comparative advantage in sugar, to supply the entire American market. In such a case, world prices would have to reflect American costs so that some American sugar production would also take place.

This kind of possibility is shown more generally in a diagram designed primarily to show the trade gains from a *world* point of view — gains from the reallocation of labor resources that are over and above the consumption gains described in the model of exchange in Chapter 2. Recall that in Chapter 2 we demonstrated that both parties could gain even though world production remained constant. Figure 5.4 is designed to illustrate the extra gains that arise when trade encourages larger world production.

The concept of a transformation schedule, or production-possibilities schedule, is familiar as applied to an individual country. What we propose here is somehow to *add* the two countries' transformation curves to show the production possibilities with free trade for the world as a

FIGURE 5.3   Free-Trade Equilibrium

Pretrade equilibrium at home is shown by point *A* in the upper diagram;
abroad it is shown by *A** in the lower diagram. Equilibrium terms of trade are
illustrated by the slope of the dashed line for each country. The home country
produces at *E* and consumes at *B*; the foreign country produces at *E** and
consumes at *B**.

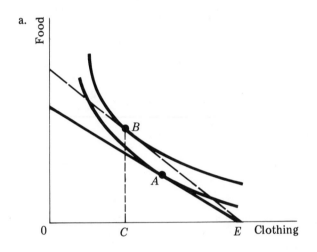

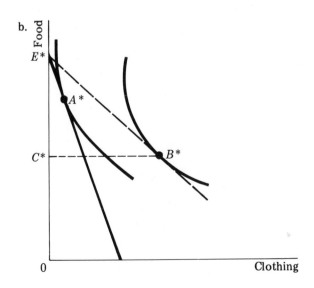

whole. This is shown by the solid line in Figure 5.4, *ABC*, with the stretch *AB* depicting the home country's transformation schedule and *BC* showing the foreign country's transformation schedule. To trace out the world production-possibilities locus consider all conceivable world terms of trade. For very high food prices, both countries would specialize in food. Thus *OA* in Figure 5.4 is the sum of the two countries' vertical intercepts in Figure 5.3. As p_F/p_C is reduced, it eventually reaches the home country's cost ratio, given by a_{LF}/a_{LC}. For such a price ratio the foreign country must remain specialized in food, but the home country can produce anywhere along its own transformation schedule. In Figure 5.4 point *B* represents the world output combination when the home country specializes in clothing and the foreign country in food. World production would be fixed at point *B* for any lower values for p_F/p_C until this price ratio reaches the cost ratio for the foreign country a_{LF}^*/a_{LC}^*. At such a price ratio the foreign country can commence production of clothing. The distance *OC* in Figure 5.4 corresponds to maximal world production of clothing.

FIGURE 5.4   The World Transformation Schedule

The locus *AJBC* shows the maximal world outputs of food and clothing that can be obtained with free trade. With no trade allowed, world outputs would lie somewhere in the shaded area.

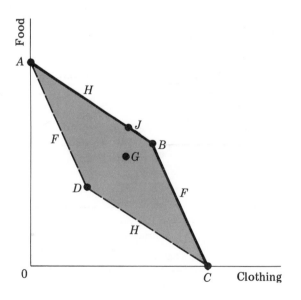

From the world point of view, schedule ABC in Figure 5.4 represents the best locus of production that can be obtained. What is the worst? Clearly if unemployment is allowed in each country, or if the best techniques available for production in each country are ignored, *any* point within $OABC$ is possible. But suppose production in each country is constrained to lie on that country's transformation schedule. From the world point of view the worst pattern of production would assign the foreign country production of clothing, in which it has a comparative *dis*advantage, before the home country is allowed to produce any. Thus the dashed line ADC in Figure 5.4 shows the inner locus of possible world production. For example, at point D the home country specializes in food and the foreign country in clothing. In general, the requirement that each country fully utilizes its resources given its own technology only ensures that world production lies somewhere in the shaded area in Figure 5.4. The discipline of free trade ensures that world production lies on the outer locus ABC. By contrast, if no trade took place and each country produced at A and A^* in isolation in Figure 5.3, world production would be shown by an interior point such as G in Figure 5.4.

Point B in Figure 5.4 shows world output when each country specializes completely in producing the commodity in which it has a comparative advantage. Point B will in fact represent production if demand conditions yield a free-trade equilibrium price ratio strictly between the cost ratios in each country. But this need not be the outcome. Fairly strong world demand for food could result in point J as the world production point, with food's relative price driven up to the relative labor cost (for food) in the home country. As we have already hinted, such a result is more likely if the home country is substantially larger than the foreign country (so that line segment AB is much longer than BC).

The interplay of demand and supply with free trade can be seen in the depiction of the world food market in Figure 5.5. The supply curve is derived from the world transformation schedule in Figure 5.4. Distance OA represents the maximal output of food in the foreign country, and length AB shows how much food could be produced at home if all labor were devoted to raising food. The kind of equilibrium illustrated earlier in Figure 5.3, in which world prices settled strictly between the cost ratios in each country (with the home country specialized in clothing and the foreign country in food), is also shown in Figure 5.5; the world demand curve cuts the world supply curve at an intermediate price. To construct the world demand curve, just add, for each price, the quantity that would show optimal consumption of food for each country separately along that country's budget line. Clearly, a different set of tastes could lead to an equilibrium world output of food less than OA or (as at point J in Figure 5.4) greater than OA. But at least one country must be completely specialized.

FIGURE 5.5   The World Market for Food

The world supply curve is composed of two horizontal steps, each at the price corresponding to a country's relative labor cost of food, and the vertical section at output A.

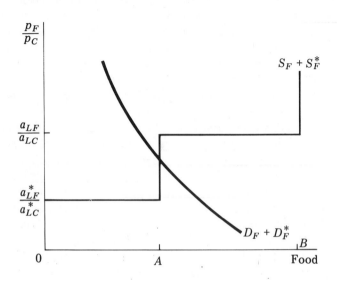

5.4 WAGE COMPARISONS, PRODUCTIVITIES, AND THE TERMS OF TRADE

Although commodities move freely from country to country with trade, labor does not. There is no reason why home wages should match up with foreign wages. What determines the wage rate in a Ricardian model, and how is the comparison between home and foreign wages dependent on the commodity terms of trade?

In any economy wage rates are closely linked to productivity. This relationship is exact in a model in which we assume that competition exists. Begin the argument by considering the general relationship between costs and prices in the home country. In a competitive equilibrium the unit costs of producing any commodity cannot fall short of that commodity's market price. The reason is simple: If unit costs in food production, say, were less than the price of food, the consequent profits would signal new entrants into the food industry. By enlarging food output, we would drive down the price of food; increasing the demand for labor would cause the wage rate to be bid up. This process, whereby new firms are attracted to the food industry, would continue until unit costs are raised enough to equal price. Unit costs can, however, exceed price, even in a competitive equilibrium. You may wonder what entrepreneur in his right mind would continue producing food if it is priced lower than the labor costs of production. In our competitive model the answer is "none." Therefore, local food production would be zero. For an economy engaged in trade, food can be obtained from abroad instead of being produced at home. Indeed, in many of our illustrations in this chapter world terms of trade were established at which the home country produced no food and the foreign country no clothing.

When speaking of "prices" we have most often had in mind "relative price" — the quantity of one commodity that must be given up in exchange for one unit of the other. In analyzing production and factor returns it is frequently more convenient to refer to absolute prices in terms of a common unit of account or money. For example, we shall refer to the wage rate at home as w, and by this mean dollars, say, per man-hour. An expression like w/p_F would get rid of the nominal currency unit of account and denote food units per man-hour. With this in mind consider the *competitive profit conditions* shown in equations 5.3 and 5.4:

$$a_{LC}w \geqq p_C \qquad (5.3)$$

$$a_{LF}w \geqq p_F. \qquad (5.4)$$

These equations state formally our argument in the preceding paragraph. A competitive equilibrium must be characterized by an equality between unit cost and price if production is carried on. Unit cost can never be less than price in a competitive equilibrium. Unit costs may exceed price, but only if all producers leave the industry. A similar set of conditions would, of course, apply to the foreign country, except that the wage rate abroad, denoted by w^*, need not be the same as at home, although with trade the price of either commodity will be identical in the two countries.

Labor's physical "productivity" is measured in each industry by the inverse of the labor coefficient. For example, $1/a_{LC}$ is the number of units of clothing that can be produced with an input of one man-hour.[4] If this is multiplied by the price of clothing, to obtain $p_C \cdot 1/a_{LC}$, a measure is derived of the "value" of labor's productivity in clothing. Thus equations 5.3 and 5.4 can be reinterpreted as saying that the wage rate must equal the value of labor's productivity in any industry in which labor is employed, and be equal to or exceed the value of its productivity in any industry that must shut down.

---

[4] Because the input coefficients, a_{LC} and a_{LF}, are assumed to be constant, $(1/a_{LC})$ denotes both labor's "average product" and "marginal product."

These remarks suggest that wage rates are linked both to commodity prices and to physical productivities. Therefore, a comparison between home and foreign wage rates must as well involve a comparison in labor productivities in the two countries and the commodity terms of trade. Suppose a free-trade equilibrium is attained at terms of trade lying strictly between the cost ratios of the two countries so that the home country specializes in clothing production and the foreign country in food. Then at home,

$$a_{LC}w = p_C,$$

while abroad,

$$a_{LF}^* w^* = p_F.$$

Dividing these two we obtain equation 5.5:

$$\frac{w}{w^*} = \frac{(1/a_{LC})}{(1/a_{LF}^*)} \cdot \frac{p_C}{p_F}. \tag{5.5}$$

The ratio of home to foreign wage rates depends both on the ratio of home to foreign labor productivities in the single commodity produced by that country — clothing at home and food abroad — and on the relative prices of these two commodities. The basic trade model in Part 1 illustrated that home real incomes would rise (and foreign real incomes fall) if the relative price of home exports improved. With labor the only recipient of a nation's income, the same kind of result must link home and foreign wage rates: w/w^* must rise as (p_C/p_F) goes up. Without consulting commodity prices there is no way of comparing home productivity in clothing $(1/a_{LC})$ with foreign productivity in food $(1/a_{LF}^*)$.

If the comparison of wage rates internationally depends on commodity prices as well as productivities, are there any upper or lower limits to the ratio (w/w^*)? Yes. The extreme cases are those in which either the home or foreign country can produce both commodities, as shown by the flat stretches in the world transformation schedule in Figure 5.4. If world demand for clothing grows sufficiently, the relative price of clothing will reach such a level that the foreign country (which has a comparative *dis*advantage in clothing production) will be able to produce clothing as well as food. But with both countries producing clothing, their wage rates are tied solely to their labor productivities in clothing. More formally, with clothing price high enough that both produce clothing,

$$a_{LC}w = p_C$$

and

$$a_{LC}^* w^* = p_C.$$

Dividing shows that

$$\frac{w}{w^*} = \frac{(1/a_{LC})}{(1/a_{LC}^*)}. \tag{5.6}$$

If, say, the home country's labor is twice as efficient as foreign labor in clothing production, home wages could be double the foreign wage rate. But that is the maximum. The lower limit is provided by a comparison between home and foreign labor productivity in food.

If each country has an absolute advantage in one commodity (say a_{LC} is lower than a_{LC}^* but a_{LF} is higher than a_{LF}^*), it is not at all surprising that with trade each country should concentrate production (perhaps exclusively) in the activity in which it excels. It was Ricardo's contribution to demonstrate that mutually profitable trade depends only on *relative* cost differences. Suppose the home country is more efficient than the foreign country in *every* line — although relatively even more efficient in clothing than in food (inequality 5.2). Then with trade the home country imports food from abroad. Does this mean residents at home are purchasing food from a more expensive (foreign) source than locally available? No. Despite the fact that a_{LF}^* is (by assumption) higher than a_{LF}, this is compensated for by the fact that foreign wages must be lower than those at home. Our discussion of the limits to the wage rate comparison shows that an absolute advantage in every occupation must be reflected in a higher wage rate.

5.5 MANY COMMODITIES AND MANY COUNTRIES

The Ricardian model of trade is sufficiently simple to allow us to break out of the confines of discussing trade with only two countries involved and only two commodities.[5]

Consider, first, the position of some small country previously isolated from an already flourishing world economy. This small country has had to rely on its own technology, as summarized by a set of labor input coefficients for all the commodities it consumes. Following Ricardo, we assume that the country's technology is determined by local conditions and need bear no resemblance to technology being utilized in other countries. We have assumed the country is "small" so that we may suppose that once this nation is allowed to trade, preexisting *world* prices

[5] More details on this subject can be found in R. W. Jones, "Comparative Advantage and the Theory of Tariffs: A Multi-Country, Multi-Commodity Model," *Review of Economic Studies,* 28 (June 1961): 161–75, reprinted in R. W. Jones, *International Trade: Essays in Theory.* Amsterdam: North-Holland, 1979, and in the supplement to Chapter 5.

are not disturbed — the small country is a "price-taker," much like an individual or firm in a competitive market.

What will the country produce and trade when contact is made with the world economy? Suppose the new trading country adopts the same currency as does the rest of the world.[6] How do local costs of production compare with world prices? Given local technology, much depends on the wage rate. If the wage rate is ridiculously low, the new country might find it could produce all, or almost all, commodities at a cost lower than world price. This could not represent an equilibrium, for the wage rate would be bid up. Suppose the wage rate is so high that costs locally exceed world prices for all commodities. This would clearly not represent equilibrium either. Do we split the difference and argue that the wage rate will probably settle at a level allowing the country an edge in monetary costs in, say, half the commodities, while for the other half world prices are below local costs? No. If local technology is really unrelated to that in the rest of the world, this small country will likely produce only *one* commodity, and its wage rate will be determined by labor productivity in the single commodity in which this country has the greatest comparative advantage.

To see why this must be, calculate for each commodity, i, the ratio between the world price, p_i, and the technical man-hours of labor required in this country to produce one unit of commodity i, a_{Li}. This ratio, p_i/a_{Li}, shows the quantity of dollars obtainable per man-hour if labor is used to produce i and the output is sold at world prices. Clearly, the commodity with the highest p_i/a_{Li} ratio is the most attractive. The forces of competition ensure that this ratio is precisely the wage rate. For, if the wage were lower than this, entrepreneurs would rush to employ all the labor they could to produce i, which would yield a positive profit over and above payments to labor. Such competition would drive up the wage. Could the wage be higher than the highest p_i/a_{Li}? No, because then to produce any i would involve losses. And, if the wage exactly equals the highest p_i/a_{Li}, it would exceed such a ratio for any other commodity. The only exception would be a tie — where, accidentally, the country's technology has the ratio between a_{Li} and the labor cost figure for some other commodity, a_{Lj}, exactly equal to the world price ratio, p_i/p_j.

We have pursued this example in some detail because it throws into stark relief a major feature of Ricardian models: that trade forces an extremely high degree of specialization in production. Two assumptions of the Ricardian model help contribute to this result: (1) labor

---

[6] This is not the place to launch into a discussion of different currencies and the exchange rates that link them together (see Part 4). It will become clear, however, that a country could change its exchange rate as it pleases so long as the wage rate is changed proportionately.

costs are not driven up as the country responds to trading opportunities — the a_{Li} do not depend on output levels, and (2) labor is mobile from occupation to occupation, helping to guarantee a uniform wage for all. These themes are further developed in subsequent chapters. But these assumptions can be changed without altering the general notion that the existence of trade itself allows a great degree of specialization in production. Countries typically consume a much wider variety of commodities than they produce at home.

5.6 TECHNICAL PROGRESS AND WORLD MARKET SPILLOVER

In our preceding discussion of two-country, two-commodity trade we have pointed out that the terms of trade could settle at the cost ratio of one of the countries. In such a case, that country could produce both commodities. The point is that for a large country international prices are not independent of its own relative production costs. To illustrate this, let us suppose once again that there are many commodities, but only two countries. Assuming all commodities are produced somewhere, it is clear that either nation may produce quite a few. In this case world prices must adjust to local costs. Suppose the home country produces commodities 1, 2, and 3, and the foreign country produces the remainder. Then the prices of the first three commodities must be in proportion to home labor costs; the prices of the remaining commodities are all proportional to foreign labor costs. If there were a commodity produced by both countries, the cost structure of the two countries would be linked by the technology of producing that commodity. (For example, equation 5.6 shows how home and foreign wage rates are linked if both produce clothing.) But suppose they are not. Then demand patterns help determine the relationship between home and foreign wage rates and therefore the relationship between all home prices and all foreign prices.

This kind of link allows us to analyze the impact on prices, wages, and real incomes of an improvement in technology in the home country in producing one of the commodities (say commodity 1) in which it has a clear comparative advantage. The relationship between home wages and all other commodities produced remains unchanged. Therefore let these other prices (p_2, p_3) and the home wage, w, remain constant in absolute terms. The price of commodity 1 must then fall by the extent of the technical change.

How are foreign prices and wages affected by such a change? If nominal prices and the wage rate abroad were unaffected, the foreign real wage and real income would rise, since one of the commodities consumed abroad (commodity 1) has gone down in price. In such a case home workers also gain in real terms to the extent that they consume the first commodity. Technical progress must increase world incomes. But the distribution between countries may not be as balanced as this example illustrates.

The possibility of immiserizing growth was discussed in Chapter 4. Growth in one country could so deteriorate its terms of trade that the country loses in real terms. The same phenomenon is possible here. When commodity 1 becomes cheaper, consumers throughout the world will tend to substitute away from other commodities toward commodity 1. But suppose this tendency is weak (so that demands generally are rather *inelastic*). The improvement in world real income represented by the technical progress may primarily be spent on the commodities produced by the foreign country. If so, all foreign prices would rise relative to all home prices. If this rise is sufficiently large, the home country might lose as a consequence of technical progress.

The distribution of world gains could be skewed in the opposite direction to such an extent that the foreign country actually loses. This perhaps sounds paradoxical, for initially foreign consumers benefit from the fall in the price of a commodity (1) that they consume but do not produce. But if commodity 1 is a particularly good substitute in consumers' taste patterns (throughout the world) for the range of commodities produced by the foreign country, the fall in p_1 may so drain world demand away from foreign-produced goods that the foreign price level and wage rate fall. At issue is the conflict between substitution effects (switching demand away from foreign goods) and world income effects (supporting demand for foreign goods). If the former are particularly strong and biased, technical progress in some commodity at home could actually harm the rest of the world. The Ricardian model allows a fairly simple analysis of this case despite our assumption that many commodities are produced, because in each country labor coefficients bind relative prices of goods locally produced. World markets have only one price ratio to determine — that between the range of commodities produced at home and the range of commodities produced abroad.[7]

5.7 NONTRADED COMMODITIES

We have thus far neglected the costs involved in transporting commodities from one location to another as well as man-made impediments (tariffs, quotas) to international trade. Realistically, no commodity can

[7] Alternatively, world market forces determine the *factoral* terms of trade — the ratio between home and foreign wage rates. More details are found in R. W. Jones, *International Trade: Essays in Theory* (North-Holland, 1979), chap. 17.

be freely shipped from one country to another. Theory abstracts from many aspects of reality, however, and trade theory often neglects costs of transport and the discrepancy they create between prices of traded commodities in different locales. But for some purposes it is convenient to consider those commodities for which transport costs are so high that no international trade can take place. The Ricardian model has such a simple production structure that adding commodities whose markets are purely local is a relatively easy task.

Consider again the case of a country too small to be able to influence world prices. If these world prices do not reflect the small country's own technology, that country will pick the best of the traded goods to produce, the one with the highest p_j/a_{Lj} ratio. And, as we discussed already, the wage rate will be set equal to this maximum figure for dollars (say) per man-hour in producing tradables. Suppose there is also some commodity (call it N) that cannot be obtained from the rest of the world (for example, personal services supplied by local labor — opera singers, doctors, etc.), but for which there is local demand. Let a_{LN} represent the (constant) labor cost of obtaining one unit of the nontraded commodity. Then N must be priced such that

$$p_N = wa_{LN}. \tag{5.7}$$

That is, the price of the nontraded good is determined by local technology and prices of traded goods (which determine the wage rate).

Suppose world prices for all the commodities that can enter trade are fixed. Then it is possible to think of a *composite* traded commodity, and the demand for such a composite will behave in the same regular way as the demand for any single commodity. Since all tradables are assumed to have a fixed price relationship with each other, any arbitrary unit of "output" of the composite can be adopted. In particular we can take the dollar *value* as a unit. Consider the transformation schedule, FAG, in Figure 5.6. Distance OF measures the maximum dollar value of tradables that can be *produced* if all labor is devoted to producing the tradable item, call it j, which maximizes the number of dollars that can be earned per man-hour. If, instead, the entire labor force had produced the nontradable commodity, quantity OG (in natural physical units) of commodity N could be produced. With Ricardian technology, the transformation schedule must be a straight line, whose slope is the dollar price of the nontradable. Figure 5.6 also shows an indifference curve tangent to FAG at point A. Point A represents the free-trade equilibrium for this small country.

Figure 5.6's depiction of an equilibrium where an indifference curve is tangent to the transformation curve may remind you of the way in which equilibrium for a *closed economy* is described. The reason for this is that the details of the *composition* of trade are suppressed in the

FIGURE 5.6   Nontradables and Tradables

A composite traded good can be formed if world prices of tradables are constant. Equilibrium production and consumption response for nontradables can be shown by the tangency of transformation schedules and indifference curves.

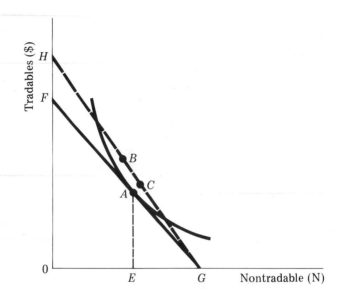

diagram. Distance OE represents the quantity of nontradable, N, that is produced. It also shows how much N is consumed in equilibrium — these must balance. Distance AE shows two things. On one side it shows the dollar value of production of tradable commodity j, the good reflecting the optimal use of labor among the set of all tradables. This same amount, AE, shows the aggregate value of consumption of all tradables. Hidden from view is the allocation of this amount over all the commodities purchasable on world markets. Figure 5.6 does not deny trade; instead, point A shows a position of *balanced trade.* It shows that the aggregate value of consumption of all tradables (spread out over many commodities) equals the aggregate value of production of all tradables (concentrated on one product, commodity j).

Suppose, now, that conditions of production at home change, with no change in world prices. In particular, suppose that some new process is discovered whereby the quantity of labor required to produce a unit of commodity i is reduced — so much so that p_i/a_{Li} now exceeds p_j/a_{Lj}.

With Ricardian-type technology, the impact on this economy is simple but drastic. It is drastic in the sense that local production of commodity j is wiped out. The new method of producing commodity i establishes it as the new best way of earning dollars on the world market — at the expense of the previous best traded industry, j. But an asymmetry now becomes apparent: The nontradable sector is not competed away. In Figure 5.6 the change in technology leads to the new schedule $HBCG$. If all labor were devoted to tradables, around 20 percent greater value could be produced in i than used to be the case in j. The wage rate is driven up by this amount, as is the dollar price of nontradables. The N sector can pass on its higher costs to consumers; the j sector, competing at given world prices for j, cannot.

The rise in p_N may cause consumption and production of nontradables to fall — such as the move from A to B in Figure 5.6. This indeed would be the case if demand for tradables as a group were elastic. But the new indifference curve could be tangent at C; substitution effects might be weak and newly created incomes might spill over primarily in the direction of nontradables. That is, despite the wage-provoked increase in wages and price of the nontradable, this sector of the economy may actually expand.

The kind of reaction described here, in which progress in one tradable sector spells trouble for another, may come about by changes in world prices instead of technical progress. Such a case could also be analyzed, but care must be taken with the concept of a composite tradable since consumers are faced with a relative price change within the composite. In the following chapter we return to this kind of question in a model in which nonlabor resources are also required for production.

5.8 SUMMARY

The Ricardian model is both the oldest and the simplest model of trade in which the details of production are fully incorporated. In summarizing its content, we shall point out its peculiar features, which illuminate some truths about world trade and which will require modifications in the next two chapters.

1. The pattern of trade is dictated solely by the "supply side." In particular, in our two-commodity case the home country must export clothing and import food if the invariant labor productivity in clothing in the home country is relatively higher than that abroad. This assumption was embodied in inequality 5.2. In more general models both supply and demand differences contribute to the relationship between pretrade commodity price ratios in the two countries and, therefore, to the pattern of trade.

2. If the world terms of trade lie strictly between the cost ratios in the two countries, each will specialize completely in the production of one commodity (clothing in the home country and food abroad). This severe shift of resources is not characteristic of the models of trade to be considered next, in which a country might engage in trade while supporting an import-competing industry.

3. The Ricardian model puts extreme emphasis on differences in technology between countries, without explaining *why* methods of production should differ. Subsequent models incorporate the influence of nonlabor factors of production in affecting labor productivities and allow a distinction between similarity in technical knowledge and similarity in techniques of production actually adopted. (Rice in Thailand may be grown differently than in Louisiana, even though no technological secrets may be guarded.)

4. The spillover effects of technical change in one country on real incomes at home and abroad are simple to analyze in a Ricardian model because within a country technology firmly binds relative costs. Progress in one country may benefit all. Alternatively, the home country may lose (the case of immiserizing growth) or foreigners may lose (if the markets for their products are strongly disrupted by the lowering of costs at home).

5. Some commodities do not enter international trade because of high transport costs. In a world in which technology and/or prices for some traded commodities change, nontraded commodities are not subject to as intense competitive pressure as tradables. In the Ricardian model for a small country, progress in one tradable sector may completely wipe out another. These extremes are moderated in future models.

6. Finally, note that the Ricardian model is not wedded to a theory of *labor* productivity. Rather, it is a model of production that severely aggregates all of a nation's productive factors into a single "lump," presumed to be of the same quality and composition for each industry. The trade models to be examined in the next two chapters have been developed primarily to relax this assumption and to reveal how differences in countries' resource endowments affect the trade pattern and how trade reacts unevenly on local distribution of income among factors.

SUGGESTIONS FOR FURTHER READING

Elliott, G. A. "The Theory of International Values," *Journal of Political Economy,* 58 (February 1950): 16–29. Discusses the two-country, many-commodity case.

Graham, Frank. *The Theory of International Values.* Princeton: Princeton University Press, 1948. Many numerical examples of the many-commodity Ricardian case.

Jones, Ronald W. "Comparative Advantage and the Theory of Tariffs: A Multi-Country, Multi-Commodity Model," *Review of Economic Studies,* 28 (June 1961): 161–75. The extension of Ricardian theory to higher dimensional cases.

———, "Technical Progress and Real Incomes in a Ricardian Trade Model," chapter 17 in *International Trade: Essays in Theory.* Amsterdam: North-Holland, 1979.

Ricardo, David. *The Principles of Political Economy and Taxation.* New York: Penguin, 1971. Chapter 7 is the classic source, with the example of England and Portugal producing wine and cloth cited in most textbooks.

6

Increasing Costs, Specific Factors, and Trade

The Ricardian model is characterized by extreme degrees of specialization. In contrast to this model, we often witness a country importing large quantities of particular commodities without entirely giving up its local production of these items. Britain for years has been extremely dependent on other countries for supplies of foodstuffs, yet retains some local agriculture. Reliance on the one-factor Ricardian model also serves to hide the reasons for the strong internal disagreements within a nation that often accompany trade policies. Explicitly allowing for more productive factors helps to reveal how changes in the terms of trade create real gains for some income groups and real losses for others.

6.1 THE TRADE MODEL WITH INCREASING COSTS

In the Ricardian trade model an industry could expand by hiring more labor without driving up average costs. Increasing costs of production can be introduced by assuming that in each industry there is some non-labor factor also required in the production process — a factor that is used specifically in that industry and not in others and is available only in limited supply. Return to our two-commodity (food and clothing) example, and assume now that food production requires land as well as labor and that clothing output combines labor with capital.[1] The econ-

---

[1] Economists recognize many difficulties in the concept of "capital" — its homogeneity, the difficulties of measurement, etc. Here we ignore these problems and assume capital is in the form of homogeneous machines useful in producing clothing. Similarly, we assume all labor is homogeneous. Chapter 8 introduces notions of different labor skills and "human capital."

omy possesses three distinct productive factors: labor, land, and capital. Whereas labor is used in both industries, land and capital are each tied exclusively to one industry. The phenomenon of increasing costs is a direct outgrowth of the *law of diminishing returns:* Increments of output fall as more labor is applied to given land (in the food industry) or given capital (in the clothing sector).

The concepts of diminishing returns and constant returns to scale should be carefully distinguished, for both are being assumed in this economy. "Constant returns to scale" are said to prevail if, when *all* productive factors employed in an industry are expanded in proportion to one another, total output expands in the same proportion. Diminishing returns are perfectly consistent with this; if the quantity of labor employed to produce food is doubled, but the quantity of cooperating land is held constant, output cannot double. Food production rises, but not in proportion to labor input. The returns to increased labor input are said to be "diminishing."

These basic ideas find geometric expression in Figure 6.1. The relationships shown in quadrants II, III, and IV support the bowed-out production-possibilities schedule in quadrant I:

1. Quadrant III shows a downward-sloping 45° line to illustrate the full employment of the economy's total (fixed) labor resources either to produce food (shown leftward from the origin) or to produce clothing (measured downward from the origin).
2. The labor productivity curves for the two industries (quadrants II and IV) illustrate diminishing returns to labor as more is applied to the fixed amount of the cooperating factor (land in food and capital in clothing).

The production-possibilities schedule in quadrant I reflects increasing opportunity costs. Endpoint *D* shows the maximum amount of food that could be produced if all the economy's labor force were employed in food. (*OD* is also shown by *AC* in quadrant II.) Similarly, endpoint *F* is the maximum clothing output, obtainable if labor force *OB* is used to produce *BE* units of clothing (quadrant IV). Any intermediate allocation, such as *G* in quadrant III, results in food output (*HJ*, quadrant II) *and* in clothing output (*IK*, quadrant IV), which is shown as point *N* on the transformation schedule (quadrant I). Other points can be derived in similar fashion (e.g., labor allocation *G'* yields output bundle *N'* — by completing the rectangle). Consider the movement from *N* to *N'* that accompanies the labor reallocation from *G* to *G'*. As extra labor is poured into the clothing sector, diminishing returns decrease labor's productivity at the margin. Meanwhile, the departure of labor from the food industry has served to raise the productivity of remaining workers in food. On both counts the relative cost of producing clothing rises —

FIGURE 6.1   Production Possibilities with Diminishing
Returns and Increasing Opportunity Costs

The production-possibilities curve in quadrant I is derived by picking a
labor allocation along the full-employment line (quadrant III) and displaying
the outputs of food (quadrant II) and clothing (quadrant IV) obtainable
in quadrant I. Diminishing returns lead to increasing opportunity costs.

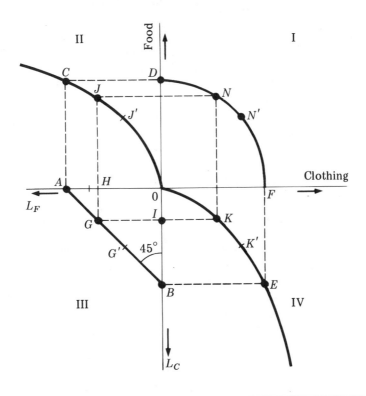

the transformation schedule is bowed out because labor is subject to
diminishing returns in each sector.

6.2 THE TERMS OF TRADE AND
THE DISTRIBUTION OF INCOME

Figure 6.1 is basic to much of our discussion. Although it explicitly
shows *quantities* of commodities and labor, the slopes of the schedules
reflect relative *prices* in a competitive economy. Thus this diagram can

be used to analyze how the internal distribution of income responds to changes in relative commodity prices.

Suppose the economy allocates labor as at point G. Then labor's *marginal physical product* in producing food (MPP_L^F) is shown by the slope of the total product schedule at point J (quadrant II). If one more unit of labor is added (from point J), food output rises, by an amount shown by the slope at J. Similarly, for this same labor allocation (shown by G), OI units of labor are combined with a fixed amount of capital to produce IK units of clothing. The slope of the curve at K (measured now as horizontal output divided by vertical labor in quadrant IV) indicates labor's marginal physical product in clothing (MPP_L^C). In a competitive economy, a factor earns a reward equal to the *value* of its marginal product. Letting p_C and p_F denote commodity prices, and w the wage rate, production of both food and clothing thus requires:

$$w = p_C \cdot MPP_L^C$$
$$w = p_F \cdot MPP_L^F. \tag{6.1}$$

With labor earning the same return in both industries, this relationship illustrates that the commodity price ratio, p_C/p_F, is related to the ratio of labor productivities. Indeed, equation 6.2 reveals the precise nature of this link. Note that clothing is relatively cheap if, at the margin, labor is relatively productive in producing clothing.

$$\frac{p_C}{p_F} = \frac{MPP_L^F}{MPP_L^C}. \tag{6.2}$$

In our earlier discussion of an economy's output possibilities we observed that the slope of the transformation schedule reflects the commodity price ratio in a competitive economy. From point N consider the effect on food output of employing another unit of labor:

$$\Delta X_F = MPP_L^F \cdot \Delta L_F.$$

Alternatively, if another unit of labor were used in clothing,

$$\Delta X_C = MPP_L^C \cdot \Delta L_C.$$

Suppose the labor added to food (ΔL_F) must come from the clothing sector (i.e., equals $-\Delta L_C$). Then dividing these two expressions reveals that

$$\frac{\Delta X_F}{\Delta X_C} = -\frac{MPP_L^F}{MPP_L^C}.$$

That is, the slope of the transformation curve is given by the ratio of labor's marginal products, confirming equation 6.2.

We have said nothing about what determines the commodity price ratio. In a closed economy we could show equilibrium outputs (and prices) in Figure 6.1 by drawing in the set of community indifference curves and locating the point of tangency with the transformation curve. If the economy is engaged in trade, foreign demands and supplies also help determine prices. If this community is "small," it is a price taker, too insignificant to affect world prices by its own actions. In any of these cases we are now in position to answer the following questions: Suppose the terms of trade change. How is the internal distribution of income altered as among laborers, capitalists, and landlords? If clothing's relative price rises on world markets, are capitalists pleased? Do workers complain? — or is it impossible to tell without knowing how laborers spend their incomes?

Suppose production is initially at N in Figure 6.1 and let the relative price of clothing rise, encouraging labor to shift out of food and into clothing until point N' is reached. The new (higher) relative price of clothing corresponds to the steeper slope at N'. Owners of capital are delighted by the price change. More workers are now employed per unit of capital. (In quadrant IV the production point has moved from K to K'.) The law of diminishing returns tells us that this lowers labor's marginal physical product in clothing. But this same law has capital's marginal physical product (MPP_K^C) rising. Let r_K denote the rental that must be paid to hire a unit of capital. This rental must match the value of capital's marginal product:

$$r_K = p_C \cdot MPP_K^C. \tag{6.3}$$

Capitalists have unambiguously gained by this price change: r_K/p_C, the value in clothing units of the return to capital, has risen because MPP_K^C goes up as more laborers are added to a fixed number of machines. Since p_C rises relative to p_F (clothing's relative price has risen by assumption), r_K/p_F would also have to rise. That is, the real income of capitalists must go up.

Landlords unambiguously lose by this price change. With land trapped in food production, and with food's relative price falling, some labor is driven off the land to enter clothing production (the move from J to J' in quadrant II of Figure 6.1). This raises labor's marginal physical product in food, but lowers that of land. With land rents (r_T) tied to the value of land's marginal product (as in equation 6.4), rents in food units, (r_T/p_F),

$$r_T = p_F \cdot MPP_T^F \tag{6.4}$$

must decline. Since clothing's price has risen relative to food's price, r_T divided by p_C must fall by an even greater amount. Landlords find their real income lowered by the fall in food's relative price.

The fate of workers is not so extreme, and this reflects the fact that labor is used in both industries and is mobile between them. Appeal to the behavior of labor's marginal physical product seems to lead to mixed results: The increase in clothing production from N to N' has lowered labor's marginal physical product in clothing (from the slope at K to the slope at K'), but raised it in food (compare the slope at J' with that at J). Does this mean that workers will receive a different wage in the two industries? No. The movement of labor from food to clothing, and the consequent drop in MPP_L^C and rise in MPP_L^F is created precisely to keep wage rates the same in both sectors. By equation 6.1, the rise in p_C relative to p_F necessitates a fall in MPP_L^C relative to MPP_L^F. But what happens to this common wage? From equation 6.1 the answer is that it rises relative to food's price, but falls relative to clothing's price. Whether any individual laborer welcomes this move would depend in large part on his taste pattern. His *real* wage would tend to rise if food bulks large in his budget, but fall if he is a heavy clothing consumer.[2]

Changes in commodity prices thus have an uneven impact on the various categories of productive factors. Those factors of production (labor in this model) that have opportunities for employment in all sectors of the economy and are highly mobile may find their real position not significantly altered by changes in the terms of trade. However, specific factors (land and capital in our model) are severely affected. Those used only in the industries suffering from a fall in relative price have no other outlet for employment. Their low mobility ensures that real rentals fall. By contrast, those specific factors in the favored industry (owners of capital in the clothing industry) find their rentals unambiguously raised. They are sheltered from increased competition from similar factors in other industries (no textile machines are available in the food industry) and benefit from the arrival of newly attracted other factors (labor) that serve to raise productivity via the law of diminishing returns. Any government policy — for example, tariff changes — that serves to affect relative commodity prices can thus be expected to be favored strongly by some, opposed by others, and not be a matter of particular concern for still other groups. Very few policies that have an impact primarily on commodity prices can be expected to have widespread approval.

The fact that the impact of a commodity price change on the distribution of income is so strong for some factors reflects a feature of the

[2] Suppose laborers have taste patterns similar to those of landlords and capitalists. Then much can be gleaned from the community's trade pattern. If the community is a food importer, demand for food is relatively strong compared with production. A rise in the relative price of clothing represents an improvement in the community's terms of trade. As argued elsewhere, this lends a presumption that the real wage rises. See R. Ruffin and R. Jones, "Real Wages and Protection: The Neo-Classical Ambiguity," *Journal of Economic Theory*, April 1977.

model that is basic: More than one factor is used in each sector, and each sector produces just one output. Consider what this means for a competitive economy in which prices reflect unit costs and costs reflect the separate wage and rental components. Suppose the wage rate goes up 10 percent and the rental on land rises by 20 percent. What conceivably could happen to the cost of producing a unit of food? It cannot fall; it must rise by at least 10 percent, but it cannot rise by more than 20 percent. Because unit cost brings together the separate wage and rental components, any changes in wages and rents must, between them, trap the unit cost change. Changes in costs per unit (and thus commodity prices) must be an average of underlying changes in relative factor costs.[3] Put this into reverse and suppose the price of food rises 15 percent, and the price of clothing remains unchanged. We have argued that land rentals must unambiguously rise in real terms (that is, the rise in r_T must exceed 15 percent) and the return to capital must fall (i.e., rise by *less* than clothing's price, which by assumption is constant). But 15 percent must be an average of land rents (up over 15 percent) and wages. Therefore, wages cannot rise by as much as 15 percent. And the unchanged price of clothing must average out the fall in the return to capital and the change in wages. The wage rate must therefore rise. It is trapped between zero and 15 percent. The underlying rationale is that each commodity price change is trapped between the changes in the returns to the two factors used in that industry.

6.3 GROWTH IN A SMALL TRADING COMMUNITY

Whereas in the preceding section we examined an economy with a fixed resource base adjusting to a change in relative commodity prices, we now ask how an economy facing fixed commodity prices adjusts to a change in its factor endowments. This question fits the case of a country that is experiencing growth but is too insignificant to have its own growth disturb world prices. This question also serves as a prelude to the discussion of the pattern of trade in the next section.

Clearly, the response of outputs to growth at constant prices greatly depends on the type of growth being experienced. Not surprisingly, a balanced expansion in *all* productive factors would serve to shift the transformation schedule outward in a uniform fashion — at constant prices all outputs would expand in the same proportion as all factors. The more interesting cases involve asymmetric growth.

Suppose, first, that growth is confined to one of the specific factors. To be precise let us consider for this small trading community the con-

---

[3] This argument is made explicit and formal in the supplement to Chapter 6.

sequence of a 50 percent increase in the quantity of land available. The primary impact of such a change is to increase labor's productivity in producing food. At constant commodity prices this will entail a shift of labor resources and bring in its wake a change in all factor returns and an outward shift in the community's production-possibilities curve.

Figure 6.2 reproduces labor's productivity in food schedule from quadrant II of Figure 6.1. The new dashed curve shows the impact on labor's productivity of a 50 percent increase in the quantity of land available for producing food. Suppose that initially *OH* units of labor are employed, with output *HJ*. With more land available this given quantity of labor could produce a greater output — *HJ'* instead of *HJ*. Furthermore, the slope at *J'* must be greater than at *J* — a higher land/labor ratio pushes up labor's marginal physical product. This is a signal for labor to be attracted from the clothing sector. But first ask: Has labor's productivity increased by 50 percent (in the sense of *J'J* representing 50 percent of *HJ*)? No. Constant returns to *scale* ensure that food out-

---

FIGURE 6.2   An Increase in Land Shifts Labor's Productivity Curve

An increase of land by 50 percent shifts labor's productivity curve radially outward by 50 percent (*QJ* is 50 percent of *OJ*). The slopes at *J* and *Q* are the same.

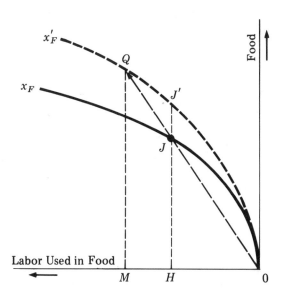

put would increase by 50 percent if land *and labor* inputs each rose by 50 percent. Let *MH* be 50 percent of *HO*. Then output *MQ* will be 50 percent higher than *JH*. In short, the impact of a 50 percent increase in land's endowment is to shift labor's productivity schedule radially outward from the origin by 50 percent.

This shift in the labor productivity schedule in quadrant II gets translated into an outward shift in quadrant I's production-possibilities curve. Clearly, for any given labor allocation the same quantity of clothing would be produced, but more food (e.g., *HJ'* instead of *HJ* for allocation *OH* of labor to food in Figure 6.2). The new production-possibilities curve is shown by the dashed curve in Figure 6.3. Consider its properties:

1. The new schedule lies everywhere outside the old curve except for point *D* showing complete specialization in clothing.

2. If point *A* represents the initial point on the old transformation schedule, then the point (*B*) on the new one at which the slope is the same as at *A* lies northwest of *A*. To see this, ask what the slope at *C*

FIGURE 6.3   An Increase of Land Shifts the Production-Possibilities Schedule Upward

An increase in land, used only in food, causes more food (and less clothing) to be produced at given terms of trade.

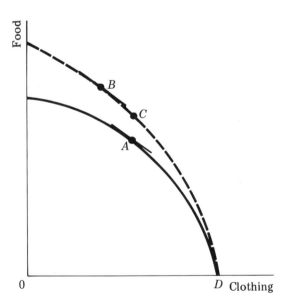

must be, where *C* lies directly above *A*. At point *C* the same quantity of labor is used to produce clothing as at *A* (clothing output is the same). Therefore, labor's marginal physical product in clothing at *A* and at *C* is the same. But at *C*, labor's marginal productivity in food has been increased because the land/labor ratio has risen. That is, the relative cost of producing food at *C* must be lower than at *A*; the new curve at *C* must be steeper than the old at *A*. The new curve lies above the old, but at comparable clothing/food prices *less* clothing (and *more* food) would be produced in the new situation.

This shows that growth in one factor in a small community facing given terms of trade leads to a radical change in the composition of outputs. Clothing output must actually decline. With more land, the community will opt to produce more food. It will do so in part by taking some labor away from the clothing sector, which must, as a consequence, decline.[4]

Labor growth leads to a more balanced expansion of both outputs because the use of labor is not confined to any one sector of the economy. Figure 6.1 is once again of use in detecting the effect of this kind of change. The 45° line in quadrant III shifts to the southwest, and the construction clearly shows that this would shift the production-possibilities curve outward. But the outward shift need not be uniform, for much depends on the relative shapes of the labor productivity curves in the two sectors (quadrants II and IV). More specifically, the rate at which labor's marginal product would fall in each sector as more labor is added helps determine which sector attracts more labor. But both sectors expand to some extent.[5]

Even though the terms of trade are kept constant for this small community, factor growth affects the distribution of income unevenly. Not surprisingly, in the case in which the quantity of productive land expands 50 percent, land rents per acre are driven down. (The labor/land ratio declines, driving down land's marginal product.) Also, again perhaps not surprisingly, labor must benefit. Labor's marginal product rises in both sectors (recall that some labor is drawn away from clothing, serving to raise the capital/labor ratio in that sector). With both commodity prices constant the real wage unambiguously rises with the expansion in land.

How about capitalists? It may come as a surprise that one can be quite definite as to the impact of land growth on the return to capital —

---

[4] You may wonder whether the output of food rises by more than 50 percent in going from *A* to *B*. The answer is in the negative — output of food could rise by 50 percent only if the food industry attracted 50 percent more labor (thus leaving the land/labor ratio in food unchanged). The rise in wages relative to rents forces the expanding food sector to economize, relatively, on labor so that labor input cannot rise 50 percent if land does.

[5] Details are provided in the supplement to Chapter 6.

it must *fall*. Capitalists do not benefit at all from the greater availability of the other specific resource (land). The reason? The wage rate has been bid up and, with a fixed price of clothing, capitalists are squeezed since less is available as a return to capital.

The same kind of distributional story results from capital growth unaccompanied by labor or land endowment changes. Workers would benefit, at the expense of both landlords and capitalists. But these roles do get reversed in the case of population (labor) growth unmatched by expansion in capital or land. As we have seen, both sectors would expand. Labor is used more intensively everywhere, and this drives down the wage. At constant commodity prices the drop in wages allows returns to both landlords and capitalists to get driven up.

These remarks, coupled with the analysis of terms-of-trade changes in the previous section, lead to the following generalizations:

1. If commodity prices remain constant but factor endowments change, the fortunes of the specific factors (land and capital) rise or fall together and are opposed to those of the mobile factor (labor).

2. If endowments remain constant but commodity price ratios change, the returns to the specific factors are driven widely apart, whereas the return to mobile labor is relatively unaffected. If the relative price of clothing rises, capitalists unambiguously gain and landlords lose.

These are important properties of this model, and we shall make use of them in subsequent policy discussions. Consider, here, some basic political considerations. The first generality suggests a natural political alliance between landlords and capitalists in small but growing communities immersed in a world market for sales and purchases. One would expect a mutual interest of landlords and capitalists in legislation designed to encourage immigration of labor, whereas workers already in the country might oppose immigration. In the 1920's the United States imposed tight immigration restrictions, largely because of pressure from the unions. The second generality suggests that if the legislation being considered concerns relative commodity prices, landlords and capitalists would be diametrically opposed. The so-called Corn Laws in nineteenth-century Britain provide an important example. Parliamentary over-representation by the landed gentry allowed laws that prevented the importation of cheap grains. After 1832 and the Reform Bill, parliamentary representation of industrialists (and labor) was expanded. By 1846 the movement to freer trade was in full swing. The interests of capitalists were clear: Lower food prices would drive workers off the land and serve to lower the industrial wage, thus leading to greater profits.[6]

---

[6] The wage would not fall as much as the price of food.

6.4 FACTOR ENDOWMENTS AND THE PATTERN OF TRADE

The preceding discussion of the impact of factor growth on a small trading country's productive structure is of direct relevance to a different question: What determines the pattern of trade? The reason these two issues are linked is that trade patterns depend on supply and demand differences between countries, and differences in factor endowments are key determinants of supply. As already discussed, trade patterns are discernible from an international comparison of pretrade commodity price ratios, and these are determined by the equality within each country of *relative* demand and *relative* supply. Figure 6.4 illustrates how the pretrade relative price of clothing at home, *OA*, is determined. Note that the relative supply curve is rising — consistent with a production-possibilities curve showing increasing costs.

If Figure 6.4 shows the pretrade situation at home, how can the situation differ abroad:

FIGURE 6.4 Relative Demand and Supply

Pretrade price ratio, *OA*, is determined by relative demands and supplies. The supply schedule lies farther to the right the greater the community's capital endowment and/or the smaller its land base.

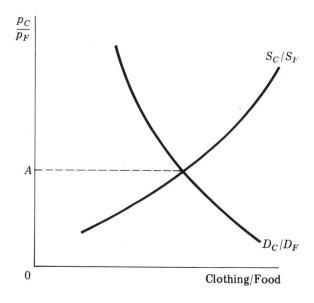

1. Foreign tastes may differ. Compared with home demand foreigners may, for comparable price ratios, consume a larger clothing/food ratio. If so, this would by itself tend to make clothing more expensive abroad and, with the opening of trade, lead foreigners to import clothing.

2. Foreign technology may differ. This was the source of trade in the Ricardian model. Suppose both countries were to produce clothing and food in identical proportions. The height of the relative supply curve would indicate marginal cost ratios of clothing to food in each country. This ratio could be higher abroad if the home country has a *relative* technological superiority in producing clothing.

3. Factor endowment proportions could be different abroad. This is the feature we wish to highlight. Suppose, first, that foreigners have a roughly comparable labor force and land supplies but much more capital. With capital used only in the clothing sector (by assumption), the capital-rich foreign country would have an advantage in producing clothing. Its relative supply curve would lie to the right of the home country's. Indeed, our discussion of growth in the previous section reveals that at comparable prices the foreign country (with more capital) would produce more clothing and *less* food than would the home country. If, instead, foreigners differed only in having more land, the foreign relative supply curve of clothing would lie to the left of the home curve, tending to support an eventual trade pattern in which foreigners import clothing. Finally, if foreign and home endowments of capital and land are each roughly comparable, but the foreign country has a larger labor force, the consequence for the trade pattern is less clear. Foreigners would have a comparative advantage either in food or clothing, depending on the shapes of labor productivity schedules (in quadrants II and IV of Figure 6.1). What is clear is that wages would tend to be lower in the labor-abundant foreign community.

6.5 RADICAL INTERDEPENDENCE AND "THE DUTCH DISEASE"

The energy crisis of the 1970's and early 1980's and associated wide swings in the prices of some world-traded products and resources have led to radical internal stresses for those economic sectors producing commodities whose world prices have been somewhat stable. In Europe this kind of phenomenon came to be called "the Dutch Disease." The name referred specifically to the rapid development in the Netherlands of the sector producing natural gas and the resulting squeeze put on other traditional export sectors of the Dutch economy. Similarly, in Norway and Great Britain rapid exploration of North Sea oil deposits created severe hardships for manufacturing sectors in these countries competing in world markets. Much less disruption is brought about in those economic sectors servicing purely local markets — the "nontraded" sector.[7]

The simple model developed in this chapter can be utilized to reveal strategic features of this phenomenon. Suppose there are a number of industries producing for the world market, and in each one of these labor is drawn from a common pool (labor is the "mobile" factor) and combined with another factor specific to that sector and in fixed supply. Previously the broad categories "land" and "capital" have been used for specific factors. But now let each sector have its own supply of capital equipment (and managerial expertise) that is uniquely designed for use just in that sector; some time would have to elapse before such capital could be transferred to other sectors (say through depreciation and replacement).

Now let the world price of the output in one of these sectors rise. The main features of our food-clothing model generalize readily to this multisector case.[8] In particular, returns to factors specifically used in the favored (booming) traded sector rise by more than price. More crucially, the wage rate is bid up, and this increase in wages will squeeze all the other traded sectors that have not experienced a rise in price. In a Ricardian model with fixed labor coefficients (Chapter 5) a wage rise would cause any traded sector facing fixed world prices completely to collapse. Here the industry may survive, but only as long as lower returns are accepted by specific factors. Higher wage rates triggered by the rise in price in the booming sector put the squeeze on "profits" (or return to specific capital and management) in any other traded sector.

Figure 6.5 illustrates such a case of the Dutch Disease. A typical traditional export sector facing a constant price, $\bar{P}$, on world markets has an upward-sloping supply curve, S, as increases in output are achieved by combining more labor with a fixed quantity of capital. The presumed boom in another export sector pushes up the wage rate and, through this connection, affects costs throughout the rest of the economy. For this traditional export sector the returns to the specific factor are squeezed and output is lowered from OA to OD if the sector does not benefit from a rise in price.

In concluding our discussion of the Ricardian model, we introduced the concept of a nontraded sector, an industry producing a commodity that can neither be exported nor imported because of high costs of transport. Suppose we add such a sector here. When one export sector ex-

---

[7] An analytic treatment of some aspects of this issue is found in W. M. Corden and J. Peter Neary, "Booming Sector and De-Industrialisation in a Small Open Economy," unpublished.

[8] Formal extensions are found in R. W. Jones, "Income Distribution and Effective Protection in a Multi-Commodity Trade Model," *Journal of Economic Theory*, August 1975, pp. 1–15.

FIGURE 6.5 "The Dutch Disease"

A boom in a new export sector raises wages, which shifts costs upward for a traditional export sector. Returns to capital get squeezed and output falls.

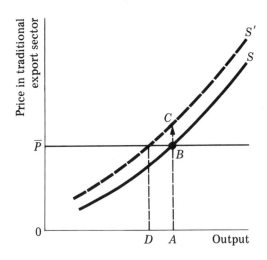

pands, raising wage rates, the nontraded sector also experiences a rise in costs. However, the price to consumers can be raised. Figure 6.6 illustrates the supply curve for nontradables pushed upward from S_N to S'_N by the wage rise. If there were no shift in demand, these cost increases could partially be passed on to consumers, with output and price changing from A to C. In this fashion the feedback effect on nontraded sectors of the economy when an export sector experiences boom conditions is less adverse than for other traded sectors tied into world markets and thus unable to pass on costs to consumers. Further to alleviate the situation for nontradables, the demand curve may shift to the right. With an export boom caused by a price rise, the community's real income expands with the favorable movement in the terms of trade. This will partly spill over to increase demand in the nontradable sector. In addition, local demand might increase as a consequence of a direct substitution effect away from the exportable that has risen in price toward other markets. Figure 6.6 shows an extreme case in which the shift from D_N to D'_N is sufficient to raise price (from OB to OD) by *more* than the original cost push (distance AF). In such a case output would actually expand and the return to the factors specific to nontradables would also expand.

Much the same story can be told if, instead of a price rise in one traded goods sector, there is technical progress (as illustrated in Chapter 5 for

FIGURE 6.6 Cost and Price Changes for Nontraded Goods

A boom in a new export sector raises wages, which shifts costs upward for the nontraded sector. But price can rise to some extent, perhaps significantly if the increase in real incomes shifts demand from D_N to D_N'.

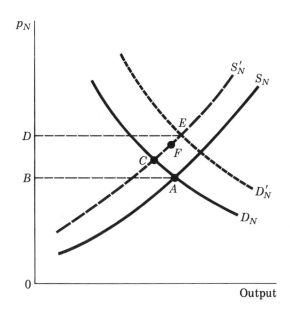

the Ricardian model), or there are new discoveries (such as North Sea oil).

The role of the doctrine of *comparative* advantage is crucial in understanding the phenomenon of the Dutch Disease. A country exports those commodities in which it possesses a *comparative* advantage, and it may lose such an advantage in some commodities even if its technology is unchanged if, in other sectors, its technology (or price) improves. In the present model the route through which traditional sectors get squeezed is via a rise in the wage rate. Although our model is not explicitly geared to handle the phenomenon at this stage, another avenue through which traditional traded sectors can be affected is the exchange rate. British manufacturers of commodities enjoying an export market were hit at the end of the 1970's by a strengthening of the British pound, caused in part by anticipation of future oil revenues as North Sea discoveries tantalized the British with visions of sitting on the same side of the bargaining table as Arab OPEC producers.

6.6 SUMMARY

In this chapter we have presented one of the classic models of production — a model in which diminishing returns describe the attempt of any sector to increase output by applying more labor to a fixed quantity of another factor specific to that sector. Commodities thus differ in their factor demands (clothing makes no use of land and food does not require capital) and factors of production differ in their degree of mobility (labor is costlessly transferable from sector to sector at a common wage whereas land and capital are each specific).

This description of an economy is rich in its conclusions for a community engaged in trade:

1. The internal distribution of income is vitally affected by any change in relative commodity prices. A productive factor specifically tied to some occupation (e.g., land in the production of food) unambiguously gains by an increase in the relative price of the commodity in whose production it is employed. This price rise will cause other specific factor(s) to lose in real terms. The mobile factor, labor, is less affected by these commodity price changes since it can move from sector to sector. This feature of the model by itself predicts that any political decision within a community that threatens to affect commodity prices (such as tariff legislation — see Part 3) will arouse ardent support on the part of some, strong opposition from others, as well as fairly widespread apathy from groups not vitally affected. This discrepancy in interests can be read in the historical record of almost any significant move toward, or away from, free trade. Changes in trade policy are apt to prove divisive, and in this chapter we traced the lines of division along the characteristics that distinguish one productive factor from another.

2. Income distribution is also affected by growth. Not surprisingly, greater supplies of a factor tend to depress its return. If commodity prices are largely determined by world markets, there is a natural alliance among specific factors (landlords and capitalists) to raise their own returns by encouraging immigration of nonspecific labor.

3. The composition of outputs is quite sensitive to changes in a community's underlying factor endowment base. This is especially true for changes in specific factors. A community relatively heavily endowed with land (capital) will tend to have a comparative advantage in producing land-using food (capital-intensive clothing). The pattern of world trade is closely linked to wide differences in resource endowments.

4. Trade encourages resources to move into sectors in which an economy has a comparative advantage. But, unlike the Ricardian model of Chapter 5, a country may nonetheless still support import-competing industries. The law of diminishing returns helps explain how a small amount of production may prove competitive even though the commu-

nity relies on imports to provide the bulk of its consumption of some items.

5. All the essential features of the two-commodity model remain for economies characterized by a wide variety of productive activities if, in each, use is made of some factor of production available in nation-wide markets (e.g., labor) as well as other productive factors specifically tied to each industry. In particular any change in relative prices of traded commodities, or changes in technology, or discoveries of new resources, are apt to have radical repercussions on various sectors of the economy. The "Dutch Disease" describes how a favorable change in conditions affecting one tradable sector can adversely affect other tradable sectors by squeezing their profits (or returns to specific factors). For a small open economy, cost increases may successfully be passed on to consumers in sectors protected from foreign competition by high costs of transport, even though such relief is not available in traditional export or import-competing sectors.

SUGGESTIONS FOR FURTHER READING

Jones, Ronald W. "A Three Factor Model in Theory, Trade and History," chap. 1 in Bhagwati, Jones, Mundell, and Vanek, eds., *Trade, Balance of Payments, and Growth*. Amsterdam: North-Holland, 1971, reprinted in R. W. Jones, *International Trade: Essays in Theory*. Amsterdam: North-Holland, 1979. Sets out the basic model and explores some applications to trade and economic history.

Mayer, Wolfgang, "Short-Run and Long-Run Equilibrium for a Small Open Economy," *Journal of Political Economy,* 82 (September/October 1974): 955–68. Interpretation of the specific-factors model as a short-run version of the Heckscher-Ohlin model in Chapter 7.

O.E.C.D. Economic Surveys, *Netherlands.* The March 1979 issue surveys recent developments in the Netherlands and fills in the details on the rise in wages and the exchange rate along with the huge expansion in the natural gas sector.

7

Factor Endowments and Heckscher-Ohlin Theory

A theory of international trade that highlights the variations among countries of supplies of broad categories of productive factors — labor, capital, and land, none of which may be specific to any one sector — was developed earlier in this century by two Swedish economists, Eli Heckscher and Bertil Ohlin.[1] Their model subsequently has been developed and extended in scores of journal articles and treatises. Some of the new results were startling: Two countries that share the same general technology but differ in their endowment of the basic factors of production may nonetheless find that free trade in commodities forces wage rates in the two countries into absolute equality. Advocates of protection seemed to find support in another proposition: Even a broad-based factor such as labor may unambiguously gain by the imposition of tariffs.

Most of these propositions were carefully proven and adequately qualified primarily in a simple form of the theory — the "two-by-two" model, so called because it analyzed an economy producing two commodities with the use of only two productive factors. This model has proved to be immensely popular not only in the area of international trade but also in other fields such as public finance and economic growth. Our strategy in this chapter is to discuss some of its properties in relation to the Ricardian and diminishing-returns models described in the preceding two chapters. The appendix to this chapter introduces some

[1] E. Heckscher, "The Effect of Foreign Trade on the Distribution of Income," *Ekonomisk Tidskrift,* 21 (1919): 497–512, reprinted in American Economic Association, *Readings in the Theory of International Trade.* Philadelphia: Blakiston, 1949, chap. 13. B. Ohlin, *Interregional and International Trade.* Cambridge: Harvard University Press, 1933. In 1977 Ohlin shared the Nobel Prize in economics for his early work in trade theory.

geometrical tools appropriate to the analysis of the two-by-two model, whereas the supplement provides a more complete, formal account of the Heckscher-Ohlin propositions. Our concern here is to concentrate on some basic properties as a prelude to a discussion of trade patterns in a world populated by many countries and many commodities.

7.1 HECKSCHER-OHLIN THEORY: THE BASIC ELEMENTS

The Heckscher-Ohlin theory attempts to describe trading patterns and to analyze the consequence of trade for a nation's distribution of income. Its two principal propositions can be stated at the outset.

1. *Countries export commodities whose production requires relatively intensive use of productive factors found locally in relative abundance.*
2. *Commodity trade tends generally (if only partially) to eradicate international discrepancies in wages, rents, and other factor returns.*

Neither of these propositions is universally true. By the end of this chapter we shall appraise their claim to validity in a world of many countries and commodities. But first it proves useful to concentrate on those basic features of production within a country that are largely similar to the diminishing-returns model we analyzed in Chapter 6. Throughout this discussion we assume each community is capable of producing two commodities (food and clothing) by combining in each the services of two productive factors (labor and capital). We assume these factors are each homogeneous and mobile between sectors; for example, machines are equally adept at producing either food or clothing and can costlessly be reallocated from one sector to another.

Increasing Costs

If commodities differ from one another in the relative intensity with which they employ productive factors, an attempt to increase the production of either commodity serves to drive up the relative cost of producing that commodity because upward pressure is put on the price of the factor intensively used in its production. Since relative commodity costs (and prices) are reflected in the slope of the transformation schedule, this schedule must be bowed out from the origin.

To see why factor intensities are so crucial, let us suppose that food and clothing always used factors in identical proportions — say two operators per machine. Then if the clothing industry expands, it can obtain its required inputs (at a 2:1 ratio) from the food sector without either sector having to change the ratio in which it uses capital and labor. This case is just like the Ricardian example in Chapter 5, except that now it is a "2-men and 1-machine" theory of value instead of a "labor" theory of value. Transformation curves would be straight lines, whose slopes would indicate the ratio of bundles of "2-men plus 1-machine" required per unit output of food and clothing.

Suppose, instead, that food is capital-intensive relative to clothing. By this we mean that when both food and clothing producers select the least-cost techniques of production,[2] a choice made with reference to prevailing wages and costs of hiring capital (rentals), the capital/labor combination adopted for food always exceeds that chosen for clothing.[3] As clothing expands, resources cannot be released from the food industry and employed in clothing without the relative wage rate being driven upward. Clothing producers require relatively heavy doses of labor as contrasted to capital — heavy compared with the ratio in which labor and capital are being released from the capital-intensive food sector. Thus the attempt of clothing producers to expand puts pressure on the labor market — wages are driven up relative to rentals. The expanding sector forces up the relative return to the factor it uses intensively.[4]

This change of factor prices is what is required to clear factor markets. With wages driven upward, both industries will switch to less labor-intensive techniques of production, thus easing the pressure on the community's fixed supply of labor. But it is precisely this change in factor prices that causes relative commodity prices to change. A rise in wages relative to rents affects costs in both industries, but raises them primarily in the labor-intensive clothing sector. Thus the law of increasing costs indeed prevails in the Heckscher-Ohlin model and the transformation schedule is bowed out.

Commodity Prices and the Distribution of Income

Whereas this description of movements along a transformation schedule concentrates on the effects of factor price changes on costs and relative commodity prices, often in trade the question is posed the other way.

[2] Recall the discussion in Chapter 3 whereby least-cost techniques are shown by a tangency between an isoquant and a line whose slope indicates the ratio of factor prices.
[3] This is not a universal property of production. As the controversy surrounding the study of American trade patterns showed, a commodity such as food might be capital intensive in some countries but labor intensive in others. See Chapter 8.
[4] You may notice the analogy here to our earlier discussion (Chapter 4) of the transfer problem. A transfer of real income from home to foreign country usually forces a change in relative commodity prices: The relative price of the commodity consumed intensively abroad rises. A comparison of marginal propensities to consume between countries in Chapter 4 is analogous to our current comparison of factor intensities between industries.

Any change in a community's terms of trade will have striking distributional consequences for laborers and capitalists in this Heckscher-Ohlin model. *A rise in the relative price of labor-intensive clothing must unambiguously raise real wages (and just as unambiguously lower the real return to capital).*[5] The reasoning is identical with that provided for specific factors in the diminishing-returns model (Chapter 6). It rests upon the asymmetry in our assumptions about technology: It takes two factors (labor and capital) to produce each commodity.[6]

To review the argument, let us suppose that wages rise by 15 percent and the rental on capital by 5 percent. What can happen to unit costs (and prices) in the clothing sector? They must rise by at least 5 percent, but cannot rise by over 15 percent. Of course, the cost of producing food also rises — by between 5 percent and 15 percent. As we have just argued, the cost of producing labor-intensive clothing will be pushed up more than food since wages have risen relative to rents. Therefore, we have the following relationship among commodity and factor prices: The price of labor-intensive clothing rises relatively more than that of capital-intensive food. And the factor price changes are magnified reflections of the commodity price changes: The percentage rise in wages is greater than the rise in all commodity prices, and the return to capital rises relatively less than all commodity prices. Commodity price changes must be trapped between the factor price changes.

These wide swings in factor prices characterized the returns to specific factors in the model of Chapter 6. Recall that in that model labor was the only mobile factor, and this mobility ensured that real wages would *not* change radically when commodity prices changed. But changes in *some* factor returns must be more extreme than all commodity price changes because, as we have argued, changes in unit costs and prices must average out underlying factor price changes. In the simple Heckscher-Ohlin model there are only two factors — mobile labor and mobile capital — and, therefore, each must always adopt an "extreme" position in the ranking of factor and commodity price changes.[7]

---

[5] This relationship is known as the *Stolper-Samuelson Theorem,* from its initial use in describing the impact of tariff protection if imports are labor intensive. See W. F. Stolper and Paul A. Samuelson, "Protection and Real Wages," *Review of Economic Studies,* 9 (November 1941): 58–73; reprinted in American Economic Association, *Readings in the Theory of International Trade.* Philadelphia: Blakiston, 1949, chap. 15.

[6] A counter-example, with the asymmetry running the other way, would be provided by a joint production activity such as raising sheep: One sheep (input) yields both mutton and wool (outputs).

[7] This conclusion can be moderated just by adding one more factor and commodity. Even if all factors are mobile, some factor price change could be trapped between the commodity price changes. Issues of this type are discussed in R. W. Jones and J. Scheinkman, "The Relevance of the Two-Sector Production Model in Trade Theory," *Journal of Political Economy,* October 1977, pp. 909–35.

The relationship between factor and commodity prices in the Heckscher-Ohlin model supports two basic contentions. The first has to do with the direction of trade. Suppose both countries share a common technology. This does not necessarily mean that they must adopt the same actual capital/labor ratios in, say, food production; that would depend on whether wages and rents were the same internationally. But to the extent that factor prices differ between countries prior to trade, there is a systematic difference implied for commodity cost ratios as well: The country with relatively low wages before trade will also be the country in which costs of producing labor-intensive clothing are low. When trade is opened up, this country will export clothing. This is a version of what is known as the *Heckscher-Ohlin theorem:* Countries will export commodities making relatively intensive use of the factor of production that is relatively cheap before trade.

The second contention is that, as a consequence of trade, factor prices in the two countries are driven closer together. Suppose the home country initially paid its labor relatively little. Trade affords the home country the opportunity to export labor-intensive clothing and relieve local pressure on expensive capital by importing capital-intensive food. The relative price of clothing rises at home as clothing production expands to satisfy world demand and as production of food is cut back (with consumption of food partly provided by imports). These commodity price changes in turn cause the wage rate to be bid up at home (and down abroad) while rentals on scarce capital fall.

Both these contentions follow from the technological relationship between cost ratios and factor price ratios discussed above and visually represented in Figure 7.1.[8] If both countries produce both clothing and food and share the same technology, their pretrade points must lie on the same curve. We have supposed the home country to be initially the cheap-labor country. The wage/rent ratio at home prior to trade is OA, and abroad OA^*. Therefore, clothing is initially relatively cheap at home (OP versus OP^*). In the absence of any transport costs for commodities (or man-made interferences such as tariffs), free-trade commodity prices settle at some intermediate level such as OT. But this means relative wages have risen at home and fallen abroad — so much so that after trade the wage/rent ratio for both countries is the same value (OB). Free trade has caused factor prices to be equalized across countries

---

[8] The curve in Figure 7.1 is positively sloped since clothing is labor intensive. A ray from the origin to any point on the curve cuts the curve from the bottom; this reflects the magnified influence of commodity price changes on factor prices.

FIGURE 7.1 Factor Prices and Commodity Prices

The Heckscher-Ohlin technology determines that an increase in the relative price of labor-intensive clothing has a magnified effect on the wage/rent ratio. If countries share the same technology, and if before trade the home country is the low-wage country (*OA* versus *OA** abroad), clothing must be relatively cheap at home (*OP* versus *OP**). With free trade the home country exports clothing, and factor prices are equalized at *OB* if terms of trade settle at *OT*.

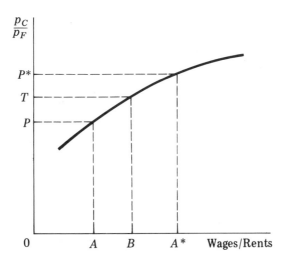

despite our assumption that factors are not mobile internationally.[9] Later in this chapter we shall review the strength of this argument that trade leads to factor price equalization between nations.

Factor Endowments and Outputs

Changes in a country's underlying factor-endowment proportions can be expected to alter the composition of outputs. This was true for the specific-factors model in Chapter 6 and is also a feature of the Heckscher-Ohlin model.

---

[9] Note that wages and rents are separately equalized. Figure 7.1 shows the ratio brought to equality at *OB*. But this ratio determines techniques, which will be the same internationally (since the same technology was assumed). With techniques and commodity prices the same, individual factor prices must also be the same.

Suppose a country's capital stock increases with no growth in population or (more accurately) in its labor supply. How does this affect full-employment levels of clothing and food output? In particular, how would outputs be changed if commodity prices were unaltered? Capital-intensive food output must expand, and output of labor-intensive clothing not only does not expand as much, it must decline. The reasoning is straight-forward. If commodity prices are held constant, so also are factor prices and, therefore, techniques of production. This is crucial, for as food output expands to absorb the extra capital stock, more labor input is required as well (to keep factor proportions in food constant). Where does the labor come from? It is released from the clothing sector (which also releases some of its capital in order to keep factor proportions in clothing unchanged). The impact of growth in one factor of production on outputs at constant prices is severe — one output actually declines.[10]

This result can be generalized in terms of proportions to the following two *equivalent* propositions concerning production patterns in two countries sharing the same technology.

1. *If countries face the same commodity prices, the relatively labor-abundant country (higher labor/capital endowment ratio) must produce relatively larger quantities of the labor-intensive commodity.*
2. *If countries attempt to produce outputs in the same proportion, the relative cost of producing capital-intensive food is lower in the relatively capital-abundant country.*

These propositions are illustrated in Figure 7.2 in the positioning of the home country's relative supply curve (1) to the right and (2) below the foreign country's relative supply curve, because the home country is assumed to be relatively labor abundant and clothing to be the relatively labor-intensive commodity. The single relative demand curve in Figure 7.2 illustrates that if demand conditions are similar in the two countries clothing must be the relatively low-cost item at home prior to trade so that with trade the labor-abundant country exports labor-intensive clothing. However, if home and foreign tastes differ sufficiently, such a trade pattern could be reversed. Figure 7.2 would illustrate this if the foreign relative demand curve cut the foreign relative supply curve at point C instead of B. Prior to trade clothing would be relatively cheap abroad because foreign tastes are biased away from clothing, thus reducing pretrade output and, therefore, price even below the level ruling

---

[10] This is known in the literature as the *Rybczynski theorem.* See T. M. Rybczynski, "Factor Endowment and Relative Commodity Prices," *Economica,* N.S. 22 (November 1955): 366–41. See also R. W. Jones, "Factor Proportions and the Heckscher-Ohlin Theorem," *Review of Economic Studies,* 24 (October 1956): 1–10, reprinted in R. W. Jones, *International Trade: Essays in Theory,* Amsterdam: North-Holland, 1979.

FIGURE 7.2   Relative Demands and Supplies

The labor-abundant home country's relative supply curve for labor-intensive clothing lies below and to the right of the foreign country's supply curve. If tastes are identical between countries, pretrade clothing prices are shown by point *A* at home and by *B* abroad.

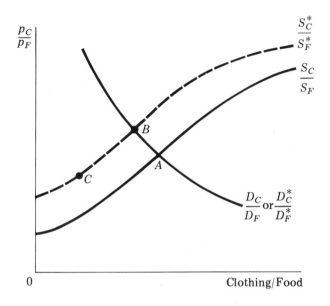

in the labor-abundant home country. Once again we observe the same phenomenon: Pretrade price differences between countries depend on supply *and* demand differences.[11]

Factor Endowments and Factor Prices

Embedded in our previous discussion is a curious result: If two countries have the same technology, and both produce food and clothing in a free-trade setting in which they face the same prices for clothing and food, factor prices are equalized between countries. What makes this result curious is that the countries by assumption differ in factor supplies. One might suppose that in general a country possessing relatively large supplies of capital would also be a country in which wages are high

---

[11] Only in the Ricardian model did supply differences (labor-cost differences) completely determine the pattern of trade.

and returns to capital low. And yet with free trade this supply influence on factor prices seems to disappear.

The influence of factor endowments on factor prices is clear for an economy not engaged in trade. As illustrated in Figure 7.2, the labor-abundant country would tend to produce relatively more labor-intensive clothing. And this leads to a presumption that the relative price of clothing is lower at home. Thus in a closed economy factor endowments can influence factor prices *through* their influence on commodity prices. Figure 7.1 depicts the way in which factor prices are locked into commodity prices, with no room left for factor endowments to play an independent role. Free trade serves to make all countries face similar commodity prices, allowing factor-endowment differences only to influence volumes of production. Indeed, Figure 7.2 shows that at comparable prices the labor-abundant home country produces relatively large quantities of labor-intensive clothing. With trade, this large production can be sold in world markets, without forcing home prices to adjust and, with them, wages and rents.

However, this discussion obscures the possibility that factor endowments can influence *which* commodities are produced as well as the relative volumes of each. The two-commodity model severely inhibits us in revealing this important role for factor endowments, and so we turn now to a discussion of production and trade patterns in a many-commodity world.

7.2 TRADE PATTERNS IN A MULTILATERAL WORLD

Our strategy in this section parallels the one we chose in discussing many-commodity trade and production patterns in a Ricardian world. We ask how a small country with a given technology and fixed factor supplies reacts when trade is made possible with an outside world that produces many commodities but does not necessarily share the same technology. We assume the small country does not influence the given levels of world commodity prices. We then proceed to ask how this country's production and trade patterns would differ from those of *another* small country that does share an identical technology but has a higher relative endowment of capital.[12]

To identify the production pattern in the small country several ingredients must be known: (1) the small country's technology, in the

[12] This section rests heavily on the discussion in R. W. Jones, "The Small Country in a Many-Commodity World," *Australian Economic Papers* (December 1974): 225–36, reprinted in R. W. Jones, *International Trade: Essays in Theory.* Amsterdam: North-Holland, 1979.

sense of isoquants showing combinations of its labor and capital that can produce a given quantity of each commodity, (2) world prices for all these commodities, and (3) the country's factor-endowment base. Information about these ingredients can be displayed in a diagram (Figure 7.3) showing *unit-value* isoquants for all commodities. Here we assume there are five possible commodities. Each unit-value isoquant shows all combinations of capital and labor that can produce $1 worth of output of that particular good. The shape of each unit-value isoquant should be familiar, for at a *given* world price for the commodity the *quantity* of the commodity that yields exactly $1 on world markets is a given constant. But the position of the curve obviously depends on world prices: A doubling of commodity 3's price, for example, would contract the unit-value isoquant for commodity 3 uniformly halfway toward the origin. Exactly half the bundles of inputs that produced $1 worth of x_3 before can now yield $1 since p_3 has doubled.

Figure 7.3 reveals the following information about possible production patterns for this small country:

1. Some commodities will never be produced by this country because its technology in these commodities is inferior to that prevailing somewhere in the rest of the world. This is illustrated by commodity 5. Regardless of how the small country might choose to produce the fifth commodity, there are better uses for its labor and capital — "better" in the sense that production of some other commodity could earn $1 on world markets with less labor and less capital. Commodity 5 in this sense is "dominated" by the group of the other commodities.

2. Certain techniques for producing some commodities will never be observed, regardless of the community's endowment base. Consider point *G*, showing the bundle of capital and labor that, if used to produce commodity 2, would yield output worth $1 on world markets. The country would be better served by producing commodity 3 with techniques shown, say, by point *D*. A dollar earned this way would cost less in inputs of labor and capital.

What is less obvious is that other techniques of production — say, input bundle *H* to produce commodity 1 — may never be observed *despite* the fact that there is no single unit-value isoquant lying closer to the origin than *H*. This point is crucial. Although *H* is not dominated by some other single production point (as was *G* by *D*), it *is* dominated by a *blend* of production of commodities 1 and 2. Consider point *I*, lying, say, 60 percent of the way from *B* to *A*. Suppose the community produces the first commodity by using the factor proportions shown by *A*, but with only 60 percent of the scale indicated by *A*. In addition, suppose the economy devotes capital and labor to producing the second commodity by using the proportions at *B*, but with only 40 percent of the scale shown by *B*. This output combination (60 cents worth of the

FIGURE 7.3   Unit-Value Isoquants

With given world prices the home country's technology determines for each
commodity quantities of labor and capital that produce $1 worth of output.
Production takes place on the inner frontier *ABCDEF* (extended).

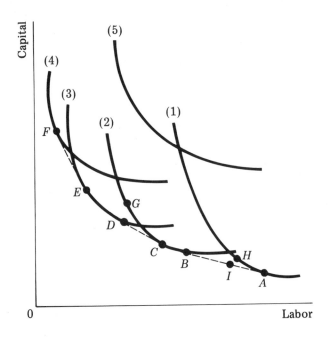

first commodity and 40 cents worth of the second) uses a total bundle of
inputs shown by point *I*, the point 60 percent of the way to *A* on the
chord joining *B* and *A*. In a similar fashion, it is necessary to draw in
the tangent chords *CD* and *EF*. Curve *ABCDEF* (extended at each end
to follow isoquants 1 and 4) shows the best assortment of inputs of capital and labor that will allow this country to produce and sell exactly $1
worth of output(s) at world market prices.

So far we have talked only about the possibilities of production. Actual production patterns depend on further information: What are factor endowments? With respect to Figure 7.3 there is, of course, no reason why the community's factor-endowment bundle will lie *on* the inner
locus *ABCDEF* (extended). That would only mean that total national
product would add up to exactly $1. What is relevant is not scale but
proportions. For example, suppose the ray from the origin whose slope
shows the economy's endowment capital/labor ratio cuts this locus be-

tween points *D* and *E*. Then with trade this community would devote *all* its resources to producing commodity 3, and export this good to satisfy its demands for all other commodities. On the other hand, if the economy had a slightly higher endowment proportion of capital, so that a ray from the origin to the endowment point cuts the locus on the dashed line between *E* and *F*, the country would produce *both* commodities 3 and 4, although it would not produce any of commodities 1, 2, and 5. The *pattern* of production depends very much on factor endowments.

Turn, now, to the question of factor prices. Figure 7.3 can be used to illustrate the wage/rental ratio that would correspond to any factor-endowment proportions. The factor price ratio is shown by the *slope* of the inner locus *ABCDEF* (extended) at the point where it crosses the factor-endowment ray. Figure 7.4 traces out the relationship between factor endowments and factor prices for the assumed set of given world prices. Start by having the country so labor abundant that wages are extremely low — the wage/rent ratio shown by slopes along the first unit-value isoquant to the right of *A* in Figure 7.3. Specialization in the

---

FIGURE 7.4   Factor Endowments and Factor Prices

Generally, the greater the capital/labor endowment ratio the higher the wage/rent ratio for countries facing fixed world commodity prices. However, there are plateaus of incomplete specialization where factor prices are uniquely determined by world commodity prices.

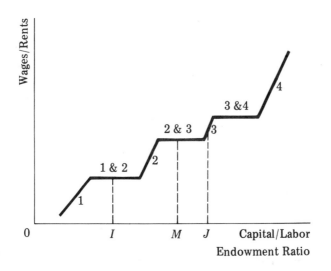

first commodity would be complete. The country could not successfully compete in any other commodity because its capital requirements are too severe in relation to the relatively high premium that capital earns at home. If we imagine this country's capital/labor endowment ratio steadily growing, it eventually produces both commodities 2 and 1 (say, in proportions shown by point I). For local variations of the capital/labor ratio near this production point the country remains incompletely specialized in 2 and 1, and *factor prices are frozen* at the level shown by the slope of chord AB. This is the kind of result shown earlier in the two-commodity example in which a country produced both food and clothing and the wage/rent ratio was locked into the world commodity price ratio.

Figure 7.4 shows this pattern of alternately being completely specialized and then incompletely specialized as greater capital/labor endowment ratios are considered. For example, point I in Figure 7.3 corresponds to point I in Figure 7.4. A country with this factor-endowment ratio would be incompletely specialized.

Now suppose we consider two small countries facing the same set of world prices and sharing the same technological knowledge. Must their wage rates be the same? their capital rentals? Not necessarily. Obviously, much depends on factor endowments. Suppose the home country is labor abundant compared with the other country sharing its technology — for example, let OI at home and OJ in the other country (Figure 7.4) depict factor-endowment proportions. With free trade the wage rate is higher abroad. Even if the other country's endowment proportions allowed it to be incompletely specialized (say, its ratio is now OM, with both countries producing commodity 2 in common), foreign abundance in capital will still be reflected in a higher wage rate abroad.

The factor price equalization theorem — that free trade causes different nations' factor prices to be brought into equality — is a strong result and one not apparently supported by the evidence. Even casual observation reveals that U.S. wages exceed those in Korea or Brazil. If countries do not share the same technological knowledge, then any presumption of factor price equalization disappears, just as in a Ricardian world. But as Figure 7.4 illustrates, even *with* the assumption that two countries have access to the same technology, factor prices need not be equalized. In a world of many commodities the factor-endowment proportions must be rather similar between countries in order that factor prices *could* be equalized. (Countries would have to lie on the same plateau in Figure 7.4.)[13] And note that techniques of

[13] Consider what happens as the number of tradable commodities is increased: It becomes less likely that two countries with identical technologies but different factor endowments will lie on the same plateau (i.e., have identical factor prices).

production can differ between countries even when they share the same technological knowledge. If the home country's endowment proportions are *OI* in Figure 7.4 and a foreign country's are *OM*, they both produce commodity 2. But the foreign country adopts more capital-intensive techniques of production than does the home country. Why? Because foreign wage rates are relatively higher, a consequence of a greater capital endowment per man. In this broader context of many commodities, the Heckscher-Ohlin theory does not impose the assumption that techniques of production must be identical throughout the world. Instead, it is capable of explaining *why* techniques and productivities *differ* systematically between countries. They do so in part because countries differ in their supplies of productive factors.

So far we have concentrated on comparisons between two countries that share a common technology and face given world prices. But Figures 7.3 and 7.4 can also be used to describe shifting patterns of production and income distribution in a country accumulating capital. Suppose world commodity prices remain reasonably constant while growth increases a country's capital/labor ratio. These diagrams then reveal that the growing country will continuously be breaking into new markets and being dispossessed in others; its resources will steadily shift into sectors requiring more capital-intensive means of production. Associated with the process is an increase in the wage rate. Countries such as Japan can no longer be considered low-wage countries. Growth and higher wages in Japan have gone hand in hand with the Japanese losing their comparative advantage in labor-intensive occupations such as textiles or shipbuilding to countries such as South Korea or Taiwan. These latter countries, called the Newly Industrializing Countries (NICs), will eventually lose their comparative advantage in more labor-intensive activities to countries further behind in the growth process.

Concentration in Production

Trade patterns in this many-commodity world reflect the tendency of countries to concentrate production rather severely. Returning to Figure 7.4, consider the trading pattern of a country with some "intermediate" capital/labor endowment ratio, say *OM*. It produces only commodities 2 and 3. It may export either good 2 or good 3 or both. But look at its imports. It relies on the rest of the world for commodity 1 (more labor-intensive than either of the goods it might export), for commodity 4 (more capital-intensive than either 2 or 3), as well as for commodity 5 (which, by assumption in Figure 7.3, it cannot produce competitively because of inferior technology even though 5's capital/labor requirements are close to those of 2 and 3).

The trade pattern revealed by this example suggests that a country may not export all commodities with a capital/labor ratio higher than some crucial value and, in turn, import all commodities with lower capital/labor ratios. Such a view of trading patterns is inappropriate for a world that consists of many countries and many commodities. Trade allows countries greatly to *concentrate* their productive activities on a few traded commodities whose factor requirements closely mirror the particular capital/labor proportions found locally, and to satisfy their demands by importing a variety of commodities whose factor requirements (if they were to be produced at home) would range the entire spectrum from very low to very high capital/labor ratios.

Although this Heckscher-Ohlin model predicts that trade will enforce a high degree of concentration in a country's productive activities, a glance at actual production patterns suggests that this conclusion is partially blunted in practice. Consider some of the reasons.

Transportation Costs. We have been abstracting completely from the fact that commodities cannot be moved from one location to another without incurring costs of transport, e.g., shipping charges, insurance costs, and the real costs involved in time required to transport goods. The impact of transport costs for patterns of trade is that they provide a natural protective umbrella for local production. For some items transport costs would bulk large relative to production costs; thus most localities produce their own bricks, pour their own cement. The introduction of refrigeration in trains and ships allowed much greater worldwide concentration in meat packing, vegetable farms, and the like.

If transport costs are greater than the cost spread between countries, that commodity does not enter trade. In this case we speak of *nontraded goods*. The distinction between traded and nontraded goods is especially important for small trading communities. Local prices of nontraded goods are determined by local conditions affecting demand and supply. Local prices of traded goods (whether exportables or importables) are determined for this country by conditions in the rest of the world. Through policy changes, the home country can affect local prices of nontraded goods, but it cannot affect prices of traded goods.[14] In any case, a country produces all its nontraded goods as well as whatever exportables are suggested by comparative advantage and importables that prove competitive with world prices augmented by the relevant transport costs.

Protection of Local Industries. Whereas transport costs represent nature's way of providing protection for local industries, import duties and discriminatory taxes are man's way of artificially achieving the same end. Part 3 of this text deals extensively with commercial policy. Here

---

[14] This distinction has been discussed in Chapter 5 and is also important in such questions as the effect of exchange-rate changes for a small country. See Part 4.

we just note that one consequence of protective policy is that a nation will engage in a wider variety of productive activities than could be sustained in the brisk climate of free trade. One question that obviously comes up is what costs (or benefits) a nation incurs by stimulating this wider productive base.

Specific Factors: Short Run and Long Run. The Heckscher-Ohlin account of trade has often been referred to as *long-run* theory.[15] It implicitly assumes that sufficient time is allowed to elapse so that factors of production such as skilled labor, various kinds of capital goods, and entrepreneurs are neither trapped in depressed industries if possible returns elsewhere in the economy are superior nor can successfully beat off competition from new entrants of productive factors with similar skills. Factors are mobile from industry to industry.

Chapter 6 provides an illustration of *short-run* theory if what were referred to there as "capital" and "land" in reality represent productive factors that are specifically tied to their occupations in the short run but can be transformed to compete with each other in the long run. Examples abound of workers who can be retrained with new skills to enter new occupations only after a number of months or years, or of textile machines that must be scrapped or allowed to depreciate before they can figuratively be beaten into tractors or lathes.

Consider the case of a textile manufacturer and mill owner being offered a price increase (say, through tariff protection). Suppose textiles are labor intensive. Long-run Stolper-Samuelson theory suggests that if capital is mobile into and out of the textile industry such an increase in textiles' price will push real wages up and *lower* the return to capital. Should the textile manufacturer heed the implied advice to oppose such protection? Not if he pays more attention to the possibility that in the short run he stands to gain, perhaps considerably, by the magnified *increase* in returns (or rents) to himself and his mill as specific factors employing relatively mobile labor. Unless individuals are particularly longsighted, one could argue that the "short-run" type of model developed in Chapter 6 may have more relevance for policy questions (e.g., tariffs) concerned largely with changes in the distribution of income.

Both short- and long-run models have a simultaneous role in describing a nation's trade patterns. Some factors of production are genuinely specific both in the short and long run — natural resources provide the obvious examples. (However, a nation's position can change over time

[15] For example, see Wolfgang Mayer, "Short-Run and Long-Run Equilibrium for a Small Open Economy," *Journal of Political Economy,* 82 (September/October 1974): 955–68 and Michael Mussa, "Tariffs and the Distribution of Income: The Importance of Factor Specificity, Substitutability, and Intensity in the Short and Long Run," *Journal of Political Economy,* 82 (November/December 1974): 1191–1204.

from net exporter to net importer as reserves or supplies become more scarce and local incomes and demands grow. Oil and iron ore used to be exported from the United States.) Although the strict Heckscher-Ohlin setting with mobile capital and labor suggests only one or two traded goods produced (ignoring transport costs and tariff protection), a wider variety of production can obviously be supported by the existence of natural resources.[16]

Aside from natural resources, there is another way in which considerations relevant to the specific factors model can help explain why a nation produces more traded goods than the small number suggested by the Heckscher-Ohlin theory. Return to Figure 7.3. Assume that the current capital/labor endowment ratio cuts the $ABCDE$ (extended) inner locus between E and D, so that the Heckscher-Ohlin solution for this country would (in the absence of transport costs) suggest production only of tradable good 3. However, suppose that in the recent past the prices of both goods 2 and 4 had been somewhat higher — enough to have made them at one time the recipients of capital investment — just as good 3 is currently the favored industry. If real capital were literally mobile, machines in industries 2 and 4 would shift into 3 as soon as prices of 2 and 4 fell. In reality, however, capital in 2 and 4 can be "trapped" in the short run, with production of goods 2 and 4 simultaneously being carried on with 3. Something has to give, and that would be the rate of return to capital and entrepreneurs in industries 2 and 4. The appendix to this chapter pursues the geometry of this case as well as the general relationship between short-run production patterns and Heckscher-Ohlin theory.

A stylized picture emerges from this example. A factor such as capital is not instantaneously shiftable. At any time there are some traded activities that earn higher returns to capital in place than do others. Variations over time in world commodity prices and/or a country's own technology help account for the presence of production in sectors of the economy whose rationale for existence lies in the past. With the passage of time certain industries are disappearing from the scene just as new ones emerge. The specificity of factors such as capital in the short run, and the consequent possible variety in rates of return, help blunt the stark long-run suggestion that only one or two traded industries can survive. Every period carries with it echoes of the past. But the *range* of such activities could be expected to be different in generally capital-rich countries from those abundant primarily (say), in unskilled labor.

---

[16] The existence of resources is obviously not sufficient for active production. Recent rises in prices of coal and gold, for example, have caused long-closed mines in the United States and South Africa again to become profitable.

7.3 SUMMARY

This chapter has built upon some propositions of the basic Heckscher-Ohlin theory for a trading world consisting of only two countries, two commodities, and two completely mobile productive factors in order to discuss trading and production patterns in a world of many commodities and many countries. As contrasted to the discussion in Chapter 6 of production in which output in each sector is obtained by combining labor drawn from a national market with a factor specifically tied to that industry, the Heckscher-Ohlin theory assumes no factor is specific. Labor and capital are costlessly transferable from sector to sector.

Some of the Heckscher-Ohlin properties are similar to those encountered in the previous chapter.

1. Output in any industry cannot be expanded without driving up relative costs. Costs are bid up because the factor used relatively intensively in that industry has its return bid up by a magnified amount.

2. Any change in a country's terms of trade is accompanied by a relatively more profound redistribution of factor incomes. Even a broad-based factor such as labor would unambiguously gain if the relative price of labor-intensive goods should rise. This particular result contrasts sharply with the conclusion in Chapter 6 that a mobile factor such as labor cannot significantly alter its real wage through changes in commodity prices, although certain specific factors definitely could. We argued that the Heckscher-Ohlin model is less applicable to questions of short-run impact of policy changes on income distribution than is the specific-factors model of Chapter 6.

3. Differences in factor endowments influence the direction of trade. A relatively ample endowment of capital would lead to exports that intensively require capital.

Perhaps the most striking conclusion of the simple Heckscher-Ohlin model is one not shared by the specific-factors model. This is that free trade in commodities can completely substitute for international mobility of capital and labor in the sense of driving wages and rents to equality for countries sharing the same technology. The sharp contrast between this factor price equalization result and observed international comparisons of wage rates and returns to capital has done much to discredit Heckscher-Ohlin propositions as a whole. In defense of the Heckscher-Ohlin theory, the following can be pointed out:

1. If countries differ in technological knowledge (or climate and other influences on the relationship between inputs and outputs) any presumption for free trade bringing about absolute factor price equalization disappears.

2. Even if countries differ in technological knowledge, many propo-

sitions of the Heckscher-Ohlin theory are unaffected. For example, the impact of a tariff on real wages at home depends only on home technology and not at all on how commodities are produced abroad.

3. When viewed in a multicountry, multicommodity setting, factor price equalization is less likely to occur even between countries sharing the same technology. Instead, any significant difference between countries in basic capital/labor endowment proportions would be reflected in countries producing different sets of commodities. If they were to produce a commodity in common, the capital-rich country was apt to adopt more capital-intensive techniques precisely because its labor force was more productive and better paid.

The pattern of trade in a Heckscher-Ohlin world of many countries and many commodities shares much in common with a Ricardian world. Countries concentrate their productive activities around a few commodities whose demands for factors closely reflect total factor availability. More capital-abundant countries would produce more capital-intensive commodities. If taste patterns are roughly comparable among nations, most will import commodities representing a wide dispersion in factor requirements (if produced at home) compared with those adopted in the export sectors. Factor intensities in a nation's aggregate *output* bundle reflect that country's factor endowment proportions. Factor intensities in a nation's aggregate *consumption* bundle reflect average world factor endowments if countries have similar tastes. Trade flows represent the difference between output and consumption, so that relatively capital-abundant countries on the average import relatively labor-intensive commodities. But this is an *average* result — the wide dispersion in imports still remains.

Transport costs and tariffs serve to widen the range of productive activities any one nation can enter. Resources specific to certain activities also convey a comparative advantage not captured solely by capital/labor rankings. And in the short run, many types of capital (and perhaps skilled labor) are not mobile between sectors, and this will tend to lessen the concentration of production. But the spirit of the Heckscher-Ohlin theory still remains to suggest that differences between countries in the endowment of broad classes of productive factors such as capital and labor will be reflected in differences in patterns of production and trade.

SUGGESTIONS FOR FURTHER READING

Heckscher, Eli. "The Effect of Foreign Trade on the Distribution of Income." Reprinted in American Economic Association, *Readings in the Theory of International Trade*. Philadelphia: Blakiston, 1949, chap. 13. This article originally appeared in Swedish: *Ekonomisk Tidskrift,* 21 (1919): 497–512. It discusses the effect of trade on factor prices in a nonmathematical, nongeometric format.

Johnson, Harry G. "Factor Endowments, International Trade and Factor Prices," *The Manchester School of Economic and Social Studies,* 25 (September 1957): 270–83; reprinted in *International Trade and Economic Growth.* Cambridge: Harvard University Press, 1958, chap. 1. Discusses the Heckscher-Ohlin model.

Jones, Ronald W. "Factor Proportions and the Heckscher-Ohlin Theorem," *Review of Economic Studies,* 24 (October 1956): 1–10; reprinted as chap. 1 in *International Trade: Essays in Theory.* Amsterdam: North-Holland, 1979. Emphasizes alternative definitions of factor abundance and comments on the meaning of the Heckscher-Ohlin theorem.

————. "The Small Country in a Many-Commodity World," *Australian Economic Papers* (December 1974): 225–36; reprinted as chap. 2 in *International Trade: Essays in Theory.* Amsterdam: North-Holland, 1979. A more general treatment of the material in section 7.2.

Ohlin, Bertil. *Interregional and International Trade.* Cambridge, Mass.: Harvard University Press, 1933. Together with the Heckscher article this book forms the basis for the modern theory of trade.

Rybczynski, T. M. "Factor Endowment and Relative Commodity Prices," *Economica,* N.S. 22 (November 1955): 336–41. A statement and proof of the Rybczynski theorem, using production box diagrams.

Samuelson, Paul A. "International Factor-Price Equalization Once Again," *Economic Journal,* 59 (June 1949): 181–97; reprinted in Stiglitz, ed., *The Collected Scientific Papers of Paul A. Samuelson,* vol. 2. Cambridge, Mass.: MIT Press, 1966, chap. 68. A restatement of Samuelson's factor price equalization theorem.

Stolper, W. F., and P. A. Samuelson. "Protection and Real Wages," *Review of Economic Studies,* 9 (November 1941): 58–73; reprinted in Stiglitz, ed., *The Collected Scientific Papers of Paul A. Samuelson,* vol. 2, Cambridge, Mass.: MIT Press, 1966, chap. 66. The original statement of the Stolper-Samuelson theorem.

APPENDIX:
THE GEOMETRY OF THE TWO-SECTOR MODEL

Probably no body of theory in economics has been prodded and poked in so many different ways as the two-sector model of production and trade that provides the core of simple Heckscher-Ohlin theory. In the text we relied primarily on a verbal account. In the supplement to this chapter we shall explore the analytical structure of the model with algebraic techniques. In this appendix we provide a brief guide to several geometric constructions of the two-sector model.

The setting is that described in the first part of the chapter. Consider the production relationships within a country possessing a fixed endowment of capital (K) and labor (L). In basic Heckscher-Ohlin theory capital is ho-mogeneous and can costlessly be reallocated from the clothing sector to the food sector. Likewise, labor is mobile between sectors and earns the same wage in each. The *production box diagram* in Figure 7.A.1 shows possible interindustry allocations of labor and capital from fixed national totals (shown by the dimensions of the box). For example, point C represents a possible allocation; the quantity of capital and labor allotted to food at C is shown by the vertical and horizontal distances, respectively, to the southwest food origin, while the remaining supplies of capital and labor are allotted to the clothing sector.

Although a point such as C represents a possible allocation that would preserve full employment, it is not an *optimal* allocation. As discussed in Chapter 3 (and illustrated for a *consumption* box diagram in Chapter 2), optimal allocations require that for any given amount of food production, clothing production is maximized; such points are shown by the *contract curve*, $O_F ABO_C$, in Figure 7.A.1. For example, at points A or B an isoquant for the food industry is tangent to an isoquant for the clothing industry. Competitive markets ensure that each sector hires factors until ratios of

---

FIGURE 7.A.1 The Production Box Diagram

Points on the contract curve $O_F ABO_C$ show efficient, competitive allocations of the economy's fixed overall endowments of labor and capital.

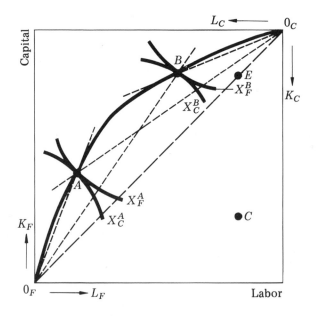

marginal products are equated to the ratio of factor prices (wages to rentals), and factor mobility between sectors ensures that this ratio is common to both industries. At any point on the contract curve the common slope of the iso-quants precisely reflects the wage/rental ratio.

Suppose the economy is initially in full production equilibrium at point A on the contract curve, and that a rise in food's price encourages the food industry to expand by taking capital and labor from the clothing sector so as to move to point B on the contract curve. We have assumed that food is produced by capital-intensive techniques at A, relative to clothing: Ray $O_F A$ is steeper than ray $O_C A$. Then the move from A to B must *lower* the capital/labor ratio in both sectors, and the common slope at B reflects a lower wage/rent ratio than at A. The reasoning is simple: If factor prices did not change, the expansion in food production would create a greater demand for capital per unit labor demanded than would be released by the clothing sector. Factor markets can be brought into balance only by having wage rates fall relative to rentals on capital, and such a factor price change will encourage *both* industries to adopt more labor-intensive techniques.

Underlying this argument is the assumption about technology made in this and the previous two chapters, namely, that production exhibits constant returns to scale. This implies that the kind of technique adopted (capital/labor ratio) depends only upon factor prices and not upon scale of output. One consequence of this assumption is that the contract curve in Figure 7.A.1 cannot cross the diagonal of the box. The reason? The slopes of all food isoquants along any ray from the food origin are the same since capital/labor ratios along the ray are constant and scale does not matter. Similarly, the slopes of the clothing isoquants are invariant to scale changes along a ray from the *clothing* origin. The diagonal of the production box, $O_F E O_C$, is a ray from *both* origins simultaneously. Therefore if the contract curve ever crossed the diagonal at a point (such as E), the contract curve would have to *be* the diagonal. If food is capital intensive for some scale of output, it must be capital intensive for all.[1]

Each point along Figure 7.A.1's contract curve, $O_F A B O_C$, shows explicitly the allocation of labor and capital to each sector, and also reveals output combinations along the community's transformation schedule. Point B in Figure 7.A.1 corresponds to point B' on Figure 7.A.2's transformation curve. The pair of straight lines through point B', L_B and K_B, represents the con-straints each factor would *separately* impose upon outputs if techniques were frozen at the levels indicated by point B in Figure 7.A.1. For example, the labor constraint (L_B) is similar to that shown for a Ricardian model in Figure 5.1 and written explicitly in equation 5.1. The capital constraint (K_B) is flatter, since clothing is assumed to be produced by labor-inten-sive techniques. That is, the slope of the capital constraint line (equal to $-a_{KC}/a_{KF}$, where a_{KC} and a_{KF} are the required inputs of capital per unit of clothing and food respectively) indicates what clothing's relative price would

[1] However, at a different ratio of endowments, food might switch over and become the labor-intensive commodity. See the discussion of factor-intensity reversals in Chapter 8.

FIGURE 7.A.2   The Transformation Curve

At all points along TT there is full employment of labor and capital — an intersection of factor constraint lines.

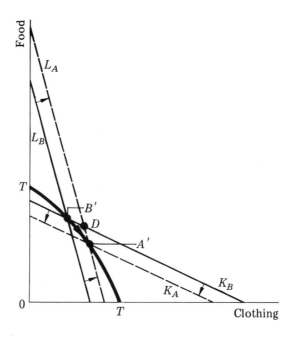

be if capital were the only factor of production that need be paid. This price of clothing would be lower than if, instead, labor were the only factor that need be paid, since clothing is labor intensive. Of course both factors require remuneration, so that the slope of the transformation schedule at B' (representing clothing's relative price at that point) must lie between the slopes of L_B and K_B.

The move from B to A in the box diagram corresponds to the expansion in clothing output from B' to A' along Figure 7.A.2's transformation schedule. The shift of resources toward labor-intensive clothing must put upward pressure on the wage/rental ratio (the isoquants at A in Figure 7.A.1 are steeper than at B). This causes *both* sectors to economize on the use of labor per unit output. Such a lowering of the a_{Lj} coefficients means that the given overall labor endowment can support a larger volume of output; this potential expansion is shown by the outward shift of the labor constraint line from L_B to L_A in Figure 7.A.2. By contrast, the more intensive use of capital in the two sectors causes the capital constraint line to shift in from K_B to K_A. At the intersection point of K_A and L_A, point A', both capital and labor are fully employed. Furthermore, clothing's relative price at A' must exceed its value at B'; the increase in the wage/rental ratio has driven up the relative cost of producing labor-intensive clothing.[2]

In the text we have already noted that the "triangular" structure of production, whereby each single commodity is produced with *two* productive factors, requires a *magnified* response of factor prices to a change in commodity prices. Thus if the price of clothing rises and the price of food is kept constant, the return to the factor used intensively in producing clothing (labor) must rise by a greater percentage than the price of clothing and the return to the other factor (capital) must rise by less than the price of food (i.e., it must fall).[3] The reason? Each commodity price change must lie between changes in the returns to the two factors used to produce the commodity. In the example cited, labor's *real* wage unambiguously rises. An analogous (or *dual*) *magnification* result links the changes in the composition of food and clothing outputs should the endowment of *one* factor rise and the other be kept constant, assuming that commodity prices are kept constant.[4] For example, suppose the labor endowment expands while aggregate capital supply is kept constant. In Figure 7.A.2 the labor constraint line shifts outward from L_B to, say, the L_A position. Note where it intersects the unchanged K_B capital constraint line (at point D). Labor-intensive clothing production has expanded while food production actually *falls*. If techniques are unchanged, clothing cannot absorb the newly available labor supply without also using more capital. And the only place the extra capital can be obtained is from the capital-intensive food sector. Thus clothing expands by using all the new labor supply *plus* both labor and capital released by the food sector. If the aggregate labor force has expanded by 10 percent, the supply of clothing at constant prices will have risen by greater than 10 percent (i.e., by a magnified amount).[5]

Temporal Adjustment from Sector-Specific to Heckscher-Ohlin Models

The two-sector Heckscher-Ohlin model has often been called a long-run model because of its assumption that both productive factors are mobile between occupations and earn the same return in each. By contrast, the sector-specific model described in Chapter 6 assigns to each industry a factor of production used nowhere else in the economy, although each industry also draws labor from a common pool. One interpretation of the specific-factor model con-

---

[2] As factor prices change in moving from B' to A' in Figure 7.A.2, the factor constraint lines need not shift in a strictly parallel fashion, depending upon other features of the technology, such as elasticities of substitution between capital and labor.

[3] This relationship was termed the Stolper-Samuelson result in the text.

[4] If commodity prices are kept constant, so also will be factor prices and therefore production techniques. Thus the endowment changes must be absorbed completely at the *extensive* margin (i.e., by output changes) rather than at the *intensive* margin (i.e., by changes in factor proportions).

[5] Formal details are provided in the supplement to Chapter 7.

siders each industry to use labor and a type of capital equipment which is fixed in supply to that sector in the short run, but over time can be converted into the kind of capital used in the other sector. (This process can perhaps more easily be visualized if capital in one sector is allowed to depreciate and not be replaced and new capital directed toward the other sector.)

Figure 7.A.3 shows, in the upper panel, the production box diagram (similar to Figure 7.A.1) and, in the lower panel, a diagram whose curves show the value of labor's marginal physical product for given prices of food and clothing and given allocations of capital. Initially full short- and long-run equilibrium is at point A in the upper panel. The horizontal line through A indicates the initial division of the economy's capital stock between sectors. In the lower panel the L_F curve shows the value of labor's marginal product in producing food — the given price of food times the marginal physical product of labor in producing food for various combinations of labor devoted to food production (measured rightward from the O_F origin) and the given initial capital assignment to the food sector. For given price of food and capital stock, labor's marginal product is driven downward by any increase in labor use. (This diminishing marginal physical product of labor was shown by changes in the slope of the total productivity curve in Figure 6.2.) The L_C curve shows the value of labor's marginal product in the clothing sector, where inputs of labor are measured leftward from the O_C origin. Intersection point D shows the original wage rate (see equation 6.1) and the original equilibrium allocation of labor between sectors — the same allocation as shown in the upper panel by point A.

Suppose the price of food rises by around one-third and the price of clothing remains constant. This price rise acts as a stimulus to the sector producing food, but in the short run we assume that only labor can be attracted to the food sector. The lower panel shows how the value of labor's marginal product is shifted upward to L_F' — uniformly by about one-third. That is, distance DE is approximately one-third of the existing wage rate. However, the wage rate does not rise by this amount. Instead, higher potential wages in the food sector attract labor from the clothing sector; short-run equilibrium is restored at point G. The wage rate rises, but by less, relatively, than the price of food. Point C in the upper panel lies directly above point G and thus shows the new short-run labor allocation together with the fixed (in the short run) allocation of capital.

Figure 7.A.3 also traces through the process of adjustment over time as capital as well as labor becomes mobile. In the short-run situation at C the return to capital in the food sector was driven up by the price rise and the greater labor/capital ratio adopted at C. (That is, the rental on capital went up relatively more than the price of food.) By contrast, point C reveals that less labor is used per unit of capital in clothing, thus lowering the return to capital in the clothing industry. This discrepancy in rates of return provides the incentive for a reallocation of capital over time to the food sector. In the top panel this reallocation (of capital and additional labor) is shown by the path from C to B. At point B the rates of return are brought back to equality with each other in the new long-run equilibrium. In the lower panel the value of the marginal product of labor schedule in the food sector shifts propor-

FIGURE 7.A.3   Short-run and Long-run Response to Price Changes

A rise in food's price attracts labor but no capital can move in the short run — from A to C. Long-run adjustment is from C to B. The bottom diagram has wages rise in the short run (from D to G), but fall in the long run (to H).

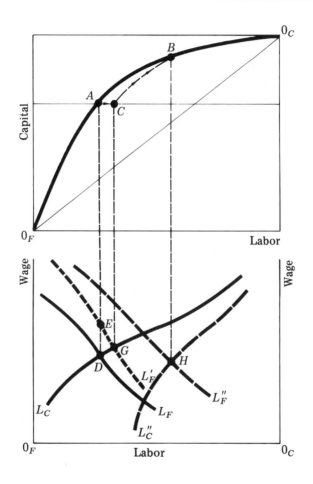

tionately to the right as the capital supply in food expands (in the movement from C to B in the upper panel). That is, the L'_F curve shifts to the L''_F position. In the clothing sector the loss of capital shifts the value of labor's marginal product curve in from L_C to L''_C. The intersection point, H, shows a labor allocation that corresponds to point B in the upper panel.

Note the reversal of labor's fortunes in moving from the short-run equilib-

FIGURE 7.A.4   Short-run and Long-run Transformation Curves

The long-run transformation curve, TT, is the outer envelope of short-run transformation curves, such as $t_A t_A$ and $t_B t_B$. The allocation of capital between sectors is fixed along a short-run curve.

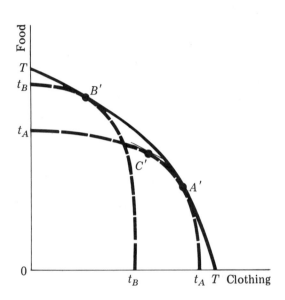

rium at C (upper panel) to the long-run equilibrium at B. The wage rate has fallen from G to H (lower panel). Although the rise in food's price in the short run was shared to some extent by a rise in wages (the move from D to G), the subsequent movement of resources to the capital-intensive food sector serves to depress the wage rate. And the wage rate must fall below its initial long-run value at D; in the Heckscher-Ohlin model a rise in the price of the capital-intensive commodity (food) must lower the wage rate.

Figure 7.A.4 relates the transformation schedule, TT, that is supported in the long run by points on the contract curve to the series of short-run transformation schedules that correspond to a fixed allocation of capital.[6] Point

[6] This construction is described in W. Mayer, "Short-Run and Long-Run Equilibrium for a Small Open Economy," *Journal of Political Economy*, September/October 1974, pp. 955–68. The adjustment process from short run to long run is described also in M. Mussa, "Tariffs and the Distribution of Income: the Importance of Factor Specificity, Substitutability, and Intensity in the Short and Long Run," *Journal of Political Economy*, December 1974, pp. 1191–1204, and R. W. Jones, "Income Distribution and Effective Protection in a Multi-Commodity Trade Model," *Journal of Economic Theory*, August 1975, pp. 1–15. The diagrammatic linkage between the production box diagram and the value of labor's marginal

A' corresponds to initial full equilibrium at point A in Figure 7.A.3. The short-run transformation schedule $t_A t_A$ shows maximal output combinations when the capital stock is kept allocated in the same manner as shown by the horizontal line through A and C in Figure 7.A.3. Only point A along this line is a point on the contract curve. All other points must thus lead to output combinations along Figure 7.A.4's $t_A t_A$ curve that are inferior to some points on the long-run TT locus. The rise in food's price that moves labor's allocation in Figure 7.A.3 from A to C in the short run is captured in Figure 7.A.4 by the move from A' to C'. The transition to the new long-run equilibrium at these prices involves a reallocation of capital and a shift to a new short-run locus. Final equilibrium is reached at point B in Figure 7.A.3, corresponding to point B' in Figure 7.A.4. The short-run transformation curve $t_B t_B$ has a fixed capital allocation appropriate to point B on the contract curve. The slope of TT at B' equals the slope of $t_A t_A$ at C'; the movement of capital (and labor) from C to B in Figure 7.A.3 is undertaken at constant prices in response to a (short-run) differential in rates of return to capital in the two sectors.

Technical Progress and Short-run Profit Squeeze

Section 7.2 of the text discussed the situation of an open economy, too small to affect world prices of tradable commodities, and with a Heckscher-Ohlin two-factor technology. Figure 7.3 introduced the concept of the *unit-value isoquant* in order to show how the country's factor-endowment proportions either lead the country to specialize in producing one traded commodity (for example, if the endowment ray cut the unit-value isoquant between points D and E only commodity 3 would be produced) or to produce two commodities (if the endowment ray passed through point I, commodities 1 and 2 would both be produced). Figure 7.A.5 shows, in its upper panel, this kind of situation where the ray through point I shows the economy's capital/labor endowment ratio and the economy produces both commodities 1 and 2. The unit-value isoquant for commodity 3 shows that at initial world prices and the level of this country's technology, no production of commodity 3 takes place.

The slope of AB in the upper panel of Figure 7.A.5 reflects the economy's wage/rental ratio in the initial long-run equilibrium. But more can be said: Horizontal distance OA is the reciprocal of the wage rate and vertical distance OB equals the reciprocal of the return on capital in industries 1 and 2. All points on line AB show values of capital and labor that, at given world prices for commodities 1 and 2 and the determined wage and rental, add up exactly to \$1. In particular, OA units of labor would cost \$1 to hire, which is only possible if distance OA equals $1/w$. Alternatively OB units of capital can be

product curves, Figure 7.A.3, is presented in J. P. Neary, "Short-Run Capital Specificity and the Pure Theory of International Trade," *Economic Journal,* September 1978, pp. 1–23.

FIGURE 7.A.5   Unit-Value Isoquants

In the top panel long-run equilibrium has industries 1 and 2 coexisting at point I. The inverse of OA is the wage rate. In the bottom panel technical progress in sector 3 causes it to be the sole sector surviving in a long-run equilibrium, although industries 1 and 2 can subsist in the short run with lower returns to sector-specific capital.

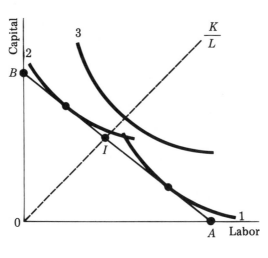

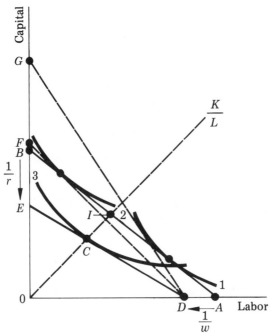

rented for $1, which implies that the inverse of the common rental on capital, $1/r$, equals distance OB.

The lower panel of Figure 7.A.5 illustrates how the equilibrium is altered if at the same set of world prices the home country's techniques in producing commodity 3 improve so that it becomes *in the new long-run equilibrium* the sole commodity produced at home. The new wage/rental ratio is shown by the tangency at point C. As drawn, the technical progress has lowered the wage/rental ratio, but has raised the wage rate (from the reciprocal of OA to the reciprocal of OD). Relatively, it has raised the long-run return to capital by more (from the reciprocal of OB to the reciprocal of OE).

This diagram can also be used to illustrate the short-run equilibrium situation before industries 1 and 2 are phased out of business. We assume again that in the short run capital is specifically tied to each sector (and that some capital is available at the new techniques to produce commodity 3) so that returns to capital can differ from industry to industry but that labor is mobile and earns a common wage. As indicated by point D, the common value of the wage rate has been bid up.[7] Line DF has been drawn tangent to the unchanged unit-value isoquant for the second industry while line DG is tangent to the unit-value isoquant for the first industry. In each of these industries the return to capital has fallen: From the inverse of OB to the inverse of OF for sector 2 and to the inverse of OG for sector 1. More especially, capital cannot earn a return in either sector 1 or 2 to compare to its return in sector 3.[8] Industries 1 and 2 can coexist in the short run with industry 3, but sector-specific capital will be hurt and these industries will gradually phase out. At any instant of time an economy may support a wide variety of industries with differing rates of return, as determined by the sector-specific model of Chapter 6. The long-run Heckscher-Ohlin model of Chapter 7 indicates the sector(s) that local technology, world prices, and factor endowments single out for eventual success in competing in world markets.

[7] Point D shows the wage rate in the new *long-run* equilibrium. Here we have abstracted from the fact that capital must be reallocated over time from sectors 1 and 2 to sector 3 and that such a capital movement affects the wage rate. The lower panel in Figure 7.A.5 shows by points F and G what the returns to capital would be in sectors 1 and 2 once the wage rate has reached the value (the inverse of OD) it obtains *after* capital has been reallocated to sector 3.

[8] Technical progress that results in industry 3 becoming the only sector to be producing in long-run equilibrium might actually *lower* the wage rate. (If ED were flat enough, point D could be to the right of point A.) In such a case rates of return to capital in sectors 1 and 2 would rise, but sector 3 nonetheless shows a higher rate of return.

8

Patterns of Trade and Economic Change

In this chapter we put to use our models of how factor endowments and production technologies of nations can affect their international trade. The productive apparatus of a country is a major factor explaining the pattern of trade that passes through its ports. And the long-run changes in trade reflect changes in factor endowments and technologies.

8.1 U.S. TRADE AND ECONOMIC STRUCTURE

The United States is a major exporter of grain and high-technology machine tools and a major importer of coffee and simple manufactured goods. How can we explain these facts, among the myriad other details of America's pattern of commodity trade? Economists have seized on many hypotheses presented in the preceding chapters, as well as a few new ones.

Leontief's Paradox

Much of the research done on America's trade structure flows from an attempt by W. W. Leontief to test the Heckscher-Ohlin theorem: a country exports goods that make intensive use of its relatively abundant factor of production. Leontief calculated the capital and labor required to produce a million dollars' worth of U.S. exports and a million dollars' worth of goods directly competitive with U.S. imports. For each industry, such as automobiles, he measured the capital and labor re-

144

quired per unit of output — not just in the auto assembly process itself, but also in the steel, rubber, glass, etc., industries that supply inputs to the automobile industry. Noting the average composition of U.S. exports in 1947, he then computed the capital and labor needed to produce a million-dollar bundle of typical exportable goods. From the composition of U.S. imports that year (excluding items not produced in the country such as coffee and bananas), he estimated the capital and labor required to produce a million dollars' worth of replacements for these imports at home.

The United States seems obviously endowed with more capital per worker than any other country. Therefore, Leontief reasoned, the Heckscher-Ohlin theorem predicts that U.S. exports will require more capital per worker than do U.S. import-competing goods. But his figures showed that import replacements demand 30 percent *more* capital per worker than exports; the U.S. trade pattern is that of a labor-rich country! (His results appear in Table 8.1.) Concerned that his findings might simply stem from distortions in the U.S. trade pattern just after World War II, he repeated the calculation using the average composition of exports and imports in 1951. As section 2 of the table shows, the greater capital-intensity of import-competing goods was reduced substantially but still remained. A repeat of the test for 1962 (section 3 of Table 8.1) again yielded the paradoxical result, almost as strong as ever.

This curious disease proved contagious. Similar calculations for Japan, to all appearances the most labor-rich industrial country, revealed its exports to be more capital-intensive than its import replacements. India's exports to the world at large proved relatively labor-intensive, but her exports to the United States proved more capital-intensive than goods competing with imports from America. Canada provided relief by being more capital-intensive in her exports than in her import-competing goods — Canada would appear to be a relatively capital-rich country — but the same capital-intensity marked Canada's bilateral exports to the apparently capital-richer United States.[1] Paradoxes abounded!

These failures to confirm a simple and highly plausible hypothesis sent economists scurrying — both back to the theoretical model and forth to the statistical evidence. Here we review some of the principal qualifications and subsidiary tests.

[1] The conclusions drawn from bilateral trade patterns here and in the balance of this chapter depend on certain assumptions. Broadly speaking, they follow if each country's output of one class of goods is not identical to outputs of similar goods produced elsewhere. This assumption makes sense for industrial goods. A recent statistical study reaffirms the pervasiveness of these paradoxes; see Robert E. Baldwin, "Determinants of Trade and Foreign Investment: Further Evidence," *Review of Economics and Statistics*, 61 (February 1979): 40–48.

TABLE 8.1 Domestic Capital and Labor Requirements
per Million Dollars of United States Exports
and Competitive Import Replacements

Factor	Exports	Competitive imports	Ratio of imports to exports
1. U.S. production structure in 1947 and average composition of trade in 1947:			
Capital	$2,550,780	$3,091,339	
Labor	182	170	
Capital per man-year	$14,010	$18,180	1.30
2. U.S. production structure in 1947 and average composition of trade in 1951:			
Capital	$2,256,800	$2,303,400	
Labor	174	168	
Capital per man-year	$12,977	$13,726	1.06
3. U.S. production structure in 1958 and average composition of trade in 1962:			
Capital	$1,876,000	$2,132,000	
Labor	131	119	
Capital per man-year	$14,200	$18,000	1.27

Sources: W. W. Leontief, "Factor Proportions and the Structure of American Trade: Further Theoretical and Empirical Analysis," *Review of Economics and Statistics,* 38 (November 1956): 392, 397; Robert E. Baldwin, "Determinants of the Commodity Structure of U.S. Trade," *American Economic Review,* 61 (March 1971): 134.

Effectiveness of U.S. Labor

Leontief himself suggested that the explanation of his results might lie in the superior efficiency of American labor. Perhaps U.S. workers were three times as effective as foreign labor, in the sense that *with the same amount of capital* they could turn out three times as much. The apparent abundance of capital per worker in the United States could then be an illusion, in that the *effective* U.S. labor force would be thrice the number of workers actually employed. Of the possible explanations for this alleged superiority, Leontief believed that superior American entrepreneurship and economic organization increased effectiveness of labor.

This explanation has found few takers. It is dubious as theory, because it seeks to make the Heckscher-Ohlin theorem run backward: Leontief predicts the state of the U.S. factor endowment from the factor-proportions pattern in U.S. trade, whereas the theorem addresses the opposite relation. Leontief's hypothesis is not easily tested empirically, but the evidence we have fails to support it.[2] American entrepreneurship may indeed excel, but why should it be much more adroit at coaxing extra output from labor than from capital? If organizational superiority simply made *all* American factors more productive than their foreign counterparts, the effective capital-richness of the U.S. economy should be unaffected. We would still expect, following Heckscher-Ohlin, that U.S. exports should be capital-intensive relative to import replacements.

Labor Skills

Many critics of Leontief's results worried about the fact that he grouped all labor together as a single factor of production and neglected the fact that educated and trained labor itself embodies a great deal of capital. That is, a society can create productive capital by using its current productive resources to create durable machines or to enlarge human abilities and skills. In each case the result is a durable, productive asset that yields up its services over future years. The one is capital just as much as the other. The rich stock of industrial crafts and skills found in the United States and the country's heavy investment in postsecondary education both suggest that the nation is very well endowed with human capital in comparison to other nations.

It was soon established that U.S. export industries require large proportions of skilled and educated labor — whether skilled craftsmen on the production lines or persons with advanced training in nonproduction activities.[3] The invisible capital bound up in these human resources was not counted by Leontief when he assessed the capital-intensity of U.S. exports and import replacements. What would happen if we redid Leontief's calculation including in the capital figure the value of each industry's human capital as well as its physical capital? Of course, human capital cannot be valued directly, like the machines and buildings owned by a manufacturer, because skilled workers are not bought and sold —

[2] Mordechai E. Kreinin tried to test Leontief's conjecture by asking multinational companies to compare the labor time required per unit of output in their United States factories with that in their European plants. From their replies he concluded: "A realistic factor by which to multiply the number of United States workers in order to allow for the difference in effectiveness is 1⅕ or at most 1¼, but not 2 or 3." See his "Comparative Labor Effectiveness and the Leontief Scarce-Factor Paradox," *American Economic Review*, 55 (March 1965): 131–40.

[3] See Robert E. Baldwin, "Determinants of the Commodity Structure of U.S. Trade," *American Economic Review*, 61 (March 1971): 126–46.

only their services. But if we value labor skills indirectly by capitalizing the extra income they yield to the skilled worker over the wages of the unskilled, this component of capital indeed suffices to reverse Leontief's paradox.[4]

That still leaves us curious, though, why Leontief got his result in the first place. If capital is cheap and abundant in the United States compared to other countries, why should American exports not utilize it heavily in both its human and physical forms? It may be that human and physical capital are alternatives to each other in the nation's production, in the sense that industries making heavy use of human capital need rather little physical capital and vice versa. We know that the larger the net exports of American manufacturing industries, the greater is their use of human capital and the less is their use of both physical capital and "raw" labor.[5]

Research and Development

Somewhat related to the role of skilled labor is the influence of research and development in U.S. exports. "Research" itself demands much skilled labor. We know that industries that carry on significant amounts of research in the United States tend strongly to be net exporters, and so typical U.S. exports are much more "research intensive" than the typical goods competing with imports. Hence, the role of research in the exporting activities in part explains the intensive use made of skilled labor in export production.[6] It confirms our previous finding that the United States exports products intensive in skilled labor and imports products that (if produced at home) would demand large quantities of scarce unskilled labor (and perhaps scarce capital).

Natural Resources

Natural resources pose a problem for Leontief's original test similar to that raised by labor skills. Resources are part of society's capital — in

[4] Peter B. Kenen, "Nature, Capital, and Trade," *Journal of Political Economy,* 73 (October 1965): 437–60.

[5] William H. Branson and Nikolaos Monoyios, "Factor Inputs in U.S. Trade," *Journal of International Economics,* 7 (May 1977): 111–31.

[6] Donald Keesing, "The Impact of Research and Development on United States Trade," *The Open Economy: Essays on International Trade,* ed. P. B. Kenen and R. Lawrence. New York: Columbia University Press, 1968, 175–89. It is also possible to view research, like skills, as creating a form of capital — knowledge — which Leontief failed to value in totaling up the capital requirements of various industries. If this intangible capital belonging to each industry were valued by capitalizing the extra profits it generates, the capital-intensity of the exporting industries would be significantly increased. Note that using research resources to create knowledge does not differ in principle from creating capital by using them to build machines or to instill labor skills.

this case a gift of nature rather than an asset stored up through human effort. The United States has come to be a heavy importer of raw materials (see section 8.3). We may predominantly import goods that are intensive in natural resources, paying for them with exports of our relatively abundant capital *and* labor. The proposition is quite similar to the one suggested concerning labor skills: the United States is abundantly equipped with human capital, and exports goods requiring lots of human capital while importing goods that (if produced at home) would demand much physical capital and unskilled labor — *and* natural resources.

Of course, most natural resources are converted into useful forms only through the application of heavy doses of other factors of production — physical capital in particular. One reason why natural resources may offer a key to unlocking Leontief's paradox is the casual observation that many processes using natural resources — whether coal mining or farming — also seem to demand a lot of physical capital. Thus the U.S. dependence on imports of many natural resources might help explain the import-competing industries' appetite for physical capital.[7]

The evidence definitely supports these conjectures. Several studies have separated U.S. industries involved in extracting natural resources from the rest. For industries not heavily involved with resources, capital-intensity is positively associated with export status, contrary to Leontief's negative relation. And the U.S. natural-resource industries indeed do turn out to be import-competing.[8]

Tariffs

Several critics have urged that Leontief's findings are distorted by the influence of U.S. and perhaps foreign tariffs. Recall the way in which Leontief calculated his typical bundle of import-competing products: by taking the actual composition of U.S. imports and using these percentages to assign importance to the individual lines of import-competing production. Suppose that the U.S. tariff were systematically designed to protect domestic industries requiring large quantities of unskilled labor. High tariff rates on such products would preclude most imports of such goods, and labor-intensive industries would hence carry very small weights in determining the average capital-labor requirements of import-competing production. The Heckscher-Ohlin theorem predicts trade pat-

---

[7] W. P. Travis and others have pointed out that this argument would fail if factor prices were in fact equalized between countries. The evidence that the factor price equalization theorem fails in practice seems compelling, however. For discussion, see Baldwin, "Determinants of the Commodity Structure of U.S. Trade," pp. 128–29.

[8] Jon Harkness and John F. Kyle, "Factors Influencing United States Comparative Advantage," *Journal of International Economics,* 5 (May 1975): 153–65.

terns from factor endowments only on the assumption that market forces are given free play and are not blocked by tariffs or other impediments. Therefore, we cannot fairly test it without allowing for their influence.

Some evidence indeed suggests that the U.S. tariff most heavily protects industries requiring large quantities of labor, especially unskilled. If we identify and weight the import-competing industries not by actual flows of imports but by the mix of imports that the United States would purchase if these tariffs were removed, the average capital-intensity of import-competing production falls.[9] Hence the tendency of American tariffs to conceal the import-competing character of labor-intensive industries helps to explain Leontief's paradox.

Factor-Intensity Reversals

An exotic but important problem with Leontief's test lies in the possibility that a theoretical assumption essential to the Heckscher-Ohlin theorem may be violated in practice. This assumption, mentioned in Chapter 7, is that one (of two) commodities would be produced by labor-intensive methods, compared with the other, for any common ratio of factor prices. That is, factor-intensity rankings never reverse when factor prices change. There is no a priori reason for this assumption to be valid, yet the model's conclusions change greatly if it fails to hold.

The assumption would fail in a situation where we can find one wage/rent ratio at which commodity 1 is labor-intensive relative to commodity 2, but others at which its efficient production is capital-intensive. Where such a reversal has occurred, the Heckscher-Ohlin theorem no longer holds. When we hypothesize that the labor-rich country enjoys a comparative advantage in the labor-intensive commodity, the capital-rich country in the capital-intensive commodity, we quickly realize that when a factor-intensity reversal has occurred *these are the same commodity*. In a two-country model both countries cannot export the same good. Hence, where a factor-intensity reversal has occurred, one of the two countries must show a "Leontief paradox."

What can we make in practice of the possibility of factor-intensity reversals? A reversal could potentially explain a paradoxical result for the United States — or for Japan. But, with an embarrassment of riches, we have both! One can only examine the evidence directly to see if intensity reversals seem to afflict an important group of internationally traded commodities. Economists differ on the answer to this question, and one can say only that substantial reversals are possible. For example, Michael Hodd found a reversal in the trade flows between Britain and

[9] Baldwin, "Determinants of the Commodity Structure of U.S. Trade," pp. 130, 139.

the United States: Each country exports capital-intensive goods to the other.[10]

Agriculture is an activity that seems particularly prone to factor-intensity reversals. Rice is raised in the United States using elaborate mechanical equipment, in the Far East with large quantities of hand labor. That fact does not explain the Leontief paradox for the United States, because capital-intensive agriculture is an export industry and thus supports our normal expectation that U.S. exports would be capital-intensive. However, Japan's heavy imports of foodstuffs that would be produced with labor-intensive technology by the Japanese may explain why the exports that pay for the country's food imports appear capital-intensive.[11]

8.2. DEVELOPING COUNTRIES' EXPORTS

Economists have wondered whether the Heckscher-Ohlin theorem provides useful predictions about the composition of less-developed countries' (LDCs) rapidly growing exports of manufactured goods. These shipments, which have been increasing in volume by more than 10 percent annually, raise many questions of policy for both the LDCs and the industrialized countries. The LDCs are concerned with what export industries will make the best use of their factor endowments, the industrial countries with which of their industries may contract as manufactures trade with the LDCs expands.

Hal B. Lary proposed a simple measurement to flag the products most likely to appear among the expanding exports of the LDCs.[12] The lower an industry's value added per worker in the United States, the more likely are the developing countries to be its exporters. Value added per worker is the sum of an industry's payments to all primary factors of production divided by its number of employees. Value added per worker can be high because the industry incurs user costs of a large amount of physical capital or pays rents for the use of natural resources. It can be high because the industry's workers are highly paid. Among industries differences in average pay are closely associated with the average amount of human capital and skills possessed by its employees. Therefore value added per worker is a respectable summary indicator of how much capital (of all sorts) the industry requires. Furthermore, if there

[10] Michael Hodd, "An Empirical Investigation of the Heckscher-Ohlin Theory," *Economica,* 34 (February 1967): 20–29.
[11] Seiji Naya, "Natural Resources, Factor Mix, and Factor Reversal in International Trade," *American Economic Review,* 57 (May 1967): 561–70.
[12] Hal B. Lary, *Imports of Manufactures from Less-Developed Countries,* New York: National Bureau of Economic Research, 1968.

are no factor-intensity reversals, an industry that is capital-intensive in the United States can only be carried on with relatively capital-intensive technology in other nations, even if all industrial technologies offer some possibilities for using relatively more labor in countries where wages are low.

Lary's investigations suggested that factor-intensity reversals are not an important problem among manufacturing industries. Later studies have confirmed Lary's conjecture about LDCs' factor endowments and export patterns. The less capital (both physical and human) a country possesses, the more labor-intensive are its exports (that is, the lower is value added per worker in the corresponding industry in the United States).[13]

8.3 LONG-RUN CHANGES IN TRADE PATTERNS

The controversy over the Leontief paradox illustrates the uses of our models of production and trade. The Heckscher-Ohlin theorem sheds light on trade patterns — although only after an interpretive struggle and some help from the concept of specific factors of production. The models of production and trade also aid in the analysis of historical patterns and their changes. Consider an important trend in the trade of the United States. A century ago, the United States was, compared to its principal trading partners, rich in natural resources. Over the years some American natural resources — forests, metallic ores — have been partially depleted, and other nations have been drawn into world trade to supply these primary products. These facts would lead us to expect that "land" — natural resources in general — has gone from being the abundant to being the scarce factor in the U.S. endowment, and that American trade has switched from predominantly exporting resource-intensive products to principally importing them.

Some calculations by Jaroslav Vanek confirm this trend. How is the natural-resources content of trade flows measured? This cannot be done directly. Agricultural land varies too much in topography, climate, etc., to be measured by total acreage. And the natural resources available to produce metals and minerals can hardly be tallied except by the outputs themselves. Therefore Vanek proceeded indirectly by measuring for

[13] Bela Balassa, "The Changing Pattern of Comparative Advantage in Manufactured Goods," *Review of Economics and Statistics,* 61 (May 1979): 259–66; Mario I. Blejer, "Income Per Capita and the Structure of Industrial Exports: An Empirical Study," *Review of Economics and Statistics,* 60 (November 1978): 555–61. Blejer found that he had to sort out the natural-resource-intensive industries to make his results stand out clearly, as we did in assessing the factor content of United States trade.

various years the value of the products of natural resources embodied in U.S. exports and in the goods produced in the United States in competition with imports. Sure enough, the value of resource products embodied in the typical bundle of U.S. exports fell from nearly twice that required (at home) for the production of goods competing with our imports, in 1870, to a level about three-fourths of the requirements for imports in 1955.[14] One can say that the U.S. trade pattern has changed toward the export of products using factors other than natural resources intensively and toward the import of resource-intensive products.

Bilateral Balances of Trade

Historical inquiries have prompted the development of enriched versions of our theoretical models. A case in point is the analysis of more than two countries and factors of production. Nature persistently presents us with at least three factors and many more commodities and countries. The formal theory grows very complicated when we allow for many entities, but we still need some feeling for its application in these complex situations. One such application concerns not the pattern of trade but the bilateral balances of trade that might develop between pairs of countries.

Consider the problem first as purely theoretical. Suppose that we can rank three regions in the trading world by their endowments of land, labor, and capital in the following fashion:

Relative factor supply	Region A	Region B	Region C
Ample	Labor	Land	Capital
Moderate	Land	Capital	Labor
Scarce	Capital	Labor	Land

Each region trades numerous commodities with the others under purely competitive conditions. These patterns of factor abundance imply something about bilateral trade balances among these countries. Region *A* is rich in labor but *B* is poor. Thus *B*'s demand for imports of the goods in which *A* specializes will be strong, the comparative disadvantage of

[14] Jaroslav Vanek, "The Natural Resource Content of Foreign Trade, 1870–1955, and the Relative Abundance of Natural Resources in the United States," *Review of Economics and Statistics,* 41 (May 1959): 146–53.

their domestic production being great. But the converse should not hold: A's maximum disadvantage lies in capital-intensive goods, but B is only moderately well endowed with capital. Hence, other things equal, A is likely to have a trade surplus with B. The situation for bilateral trade between A and C is the reverse: C's endowment is suitable for specialization in the capital-intensive goods A is most likely to import, yet C is moderately well endowed with labor and hence may not be equally receptive to A's exports. A is likely to have a trade deficit with C. Note that A's predicted surplus with B and deficit with C is consistent with overall balance for A, its total exports equaling total imports. When we find, by the same reasoning, that B is likely to run a surplus on bilateral trade with C, it is clear that this model is also consistent with overall trade balance for B and C as well.

Karl-Erik Hansson, who set forth this schema, proposed that it explains rather well the pattern of bilateral trade balances observed among major trading areas, up to World War I. Equate region A with the tropics, well suited to export resource-intensive products requiring unskilled labor but relatively little capital. Equate region B with the United States and the other temperate regions settled by European emigrants. Equate region C with the European countries. Trade balances between these regions were relatively stable and agreed closely with the theoretical prediction.[15] This is a casual "test" of the theory, but it does illustrate the richness of the Heckscher-Ohlin theory for explaining historical patterns.

8.4 TECHNOLOGY AND CHANGING TRADE PATTERNS

Nations' changes in stocks of factors of production have apparently been potent determinants of their changing structures of trade. But factor endowments are far from the only sources of change. Technological innovations have repeatedly transformed trade patterns, threatening the markets for traditional products (for example, natural rubber) or adding new products to the export lists. Yet what country comes to produce a new good for export — even what country makes the innovation — can be explained in part by structures of production.

Innovation and Technological Gap

A new product is developed, or a new production process is embodied in a novel kind of capital equipment. The innovating firm tests its discov-

[15] Karl-Erik Hansson, "A General Theory of the System of Multilateral Trade," *American Economic Review,* 42 (March 1952): 58–68.

eries on the market — presumably the market closest and best known to it. This is generally its home or local market. If the innovation proves profitable, the firm looks for wider markets, perhaps in foreign lands. The country's exports grow. If the innovation's success is repeated abroad, the rest of the world's demand for the innovating country's goods shifts outward. The home country's imports become relatively cheaper, and some factors of production switch from producing goods that compete with imports and toward production of the novel good. The innovator's profits from foreign sales bring additional gains from trade to the home country.

The innovation, unless completely protected by patents, is likely to bestir imitators. If the innovation is first placed on the home market, domestic competitors are the first to feel the threat to their sales and, therefore, the first to take defensive action. When the innovation becomes an export item, imitation is also likely abroad. If foreign producers can also match the innovation, the shift of foreign demand for imports may be largely temporary. The home country's innovative gains disappear as successful imitation takes place abroad.

In this story innovation is only a one-shot disturbance to the circuits of international trade. However, some countries may regularly prove to be fertile sources of innovation. Their export lists would always contain new products that have not yet been successfully imitated elsewhere. We would have to explain their trade, then, not solely by their factor endowments or productivity advantages, but rather in part as "technological gap" exports. Do some countries enjoy special talents as innovators? For the United States, the answer may be yes. The argument goes as follows.

Innovation, whether by the tool-shed tinkerer or the corporate research laboratory, is the purposive activity of someone who perceives a "need" and finds a way to fill it. Needs are judged by the economic benefits from the innovation, which in turn govern the size of the potential profit awaiting the innovator. Most innovations seem to be labor-saving, as the forklift truck that reduces the labor involved in moving and stacking things. That is, most innovations seem to cut the quantity of labor used in a production process, relative to the quantity of capital. The biggest payout to labor-saving innovations, however, comes where labor is most expensive and where its price is expected to continue to rise. The United States, as the country with historically the highest labor cost, thus seems to offer the strongest incentive to the labor-saving innovation. In the nineteenth century, economic historians have argued, the scarcity and dearness of labor made the United States a fruitful source of mechanical inventions. Coupled with an abundance of labor skills (invention itself requires a high proportion of skilled labor) and congenial cultural traits, American inventive dominance has continued.

Thus a significant proportion of U.S. exports probably consists of "technological gap" trade. If U.S. inventiveness ever dried up and the cycle of imitation ran its course, the country's terms of trade would probably deteriorate and her level of income per capita fall relative to other countries.

The United States is, of course, far from being the only source of innovations. The role is also filled by countries with abundant skilled scientific labor, such as Great Britain, or by those afflicted with raw-material shortages and thus conscious of the usefulness of synthetic materials, such as Germany. The empirical evidence, however, is particularly clear for the United States. Industries making the strongest research effort (measured, for instance, by research and development expenditures as a percentage of sales) account for 72 percent of the country's exports of manufactured goods, but only 39 percent of the nation's total sales of manufactures.[16] Furthermore, one statistical study of 24 countries confirms the link between innovation and high labor costs. For each country an index of the "newness" of its manufactured exports was calculated. Innovation was found to be related to level of national income per capita, and high income per person is ordinarily associated with relatively costly labor.[17]

Consider the implications of the technological gap for world trade in a group of products like plastics or man-made fibers. Each group represents innovations, some new, some decades old. You would expect the highly industrialized countries, best suited and motivated to innovate, to enjoy the largest shares of world exports in new products belonging to such a group. As products age, however, their manufacture spreads to countries that are not themselves innovators, but that ultimately hold a comparative advantage. You would expect the United States to export a larger share of its production of new products not yet imitated abroad than of older products — except for goods so new that their use has not begun abroad. Finally, because many countries give heavy tariff protection to their domestic fiber and plastics industries, the proportion of a product's total world production entering into trade should fall as the product ages and as more imitators produce their domestic requirements behind tariff walls. G. C. Hufbauer's study of synthetic materials in international trade confirms each of these predictions.[18]

[16] W. Gruber, D. Mehta, and R. Vernon, "The R&D Factor in International Trade and International Investment of United States Industries," *Journal of Political Economy,* 75 (February 1967): 20–37.
[17] G. C. Hufbauer, "The Impact of National Characteristics and Technology on the Commodity Composition of Trade in Manufactured Goods," *The Technology Factor in International Trade,* ed. Raymond Vernon. New York: National Bureau of Economic Research, 1970, pp. 184–89.
[18] G. C. Hufbauer, *Synthetic Materials and the Theory of International Trade.* Cambridge, Mass.: Harvard University Press, 1966, chap. 6.

Product Cycle

The technological gap is a somewhat unsatisfactory explanation of dynamic trade patterns. Why is the gap so many years, no more, no less? The theory explains the elimination of the gap but not its persistence.

For a better performance in this role we can turn to a closely related model of the "product cycle." [19] The model of the product cycle suggests that changes occur in the input requirements of a new product as it becomes established in markets and standardized in production. These changes may shift the cost advantage from one country to another.

Someone has invented and marketed the radio. Again, we suppose that it cannot readily be imitated by producers in either the domestic or foreign markets. At the start its market success is uncertain. The new product does not automatically appeal to many customers. Its manufacture is on a small scale. Production techniques are likely to be novel and to require large inputs of skilled labor. "Mass production" is unsuitable because of both the small market and technological uncertainties. The good must be produced near its market, because the producer needs a quick feedback of information in order to improve its performance, reliability, and general appeal. Hence the innovator's home market will be the first served.

When the product is established at home, it will enter into international trade as the innovator tests foreign markets. Furthermore, the location of production may start to shift. Whereas production in the pilot stage may require much skilled labor, standardization and general consumer acceptance allow for mass production. This demands lesser labor skills, and yet may be no more capital-intensive. Furthermore, as the product grows standardized and its market becomes more competitive, the pull of cost advantages on the location of production grows stronger. While it remains a monopolized novelty, demand is likely to be price-inelastic. If it enjoys success, innovative profits can be earned even if production costs are not minimized in the short run. As the product matures and becomes standardized, imitative competition is likely to arise and make the demand facing the individual producer significantly more elastic. Costs start to tell. Unless the country where the innovation first becomes established has an ultimate comparative advantage, production will spread or shift to other countries as the product matures.

Once again, this model helps to explain changes in production and trade in new product lines, such as electronics. The United States has been a principal innovator, but production has also spread (with a lag)

[19] Raymond Vernon, "International Investment and International Trade in the Product Cycle," *Quarterly Journal of Economics,* 80 (May 1966): 190–207.

to countries such as the United Kingdom and Japan. Again, the export performance of American producers is better for new products than for those approaching maturity. Furthermore, for goods whose manufacture is spreading abroad we observe a shift from processes heavily dependent on skilled labor to automatic assembly processes using relatively more capital and unskilled labor.[20]

Technology and U.S. Trade Prospects

The concepts of technology gap and product cycle both point to an important source of gains from trade for the United States — the innovator's profits from being the first to make new products available to the rest of the world. Although Americans have come to take the nation's predominance in innovation for granted, some observers have recently come to fear that it is on the wane. Spending on research and development has declined as a percentage of gross national product in the United States. Although the U.S. ratio still exceeds most other industrial countries', many of theirs are increasing while the United States' R&D spending rate declines. Many influences may lie behind this trend. The product cycle may be speeding up. International transportation and communication have improved greatly since World War II, so the news about industrial innovations travels quickly around the globe. There is a fast-improving international market in proprietary technology, whereby new industrial knowledge is licensed between independent firms or transferred administratively within multinational companies. Developing countries are sometimes eager to establish high-technology industries even if those are not ideally suited to their production capabilities.

These and other major trends in the world economy suggest that the United States may be losing its industrial lead. That concern can be put to a test if we examine production trends in manufacturing industries around the world. In the United States outputs of the high-technology industries have been growing faster than other manufacturing sectors, as we expect. But what happens when we compare the growth rates of U.S. industries — high- and low-technology — to the growth rates of these same industries in the rest of the world? The higher is an industry in the technology scale (measured by research and development as a percentage of sales), the *slower* is U.S. output growing relative to output in the rest of the world. That pattern holds whether we compare the United States to the European Community countries, Japan, or various groups of developing nations.[21] Thus the U.S. gains from trade in innovative goods

---

[20] Seev Hirsch, *Location of Industry and International Competitiveness.* Oxford: Clarendon Press, 1967, chap. 4.

[21] Thomas A. Pugel, *The Changing Pattern of U.S. Industries in the Global Pattern of Industrial Production,* prepared for U.S. Congress, Joint Economic Committee, Special Study on Economic Change, 1979.

may be slipping. It is not clear whether U.S. policy can or should do anything about this slippage; it may be simply that "all good things come to an end."

8.5 SUMMARY

Economists have used models of production and trade to explain actual trade patterns of nations. W. W. Leontief, testing the hypothesis that American exports embody more capital per worker than American goods competing with imports (the Heckscher-Ohlin theorem), in fact reached the opposite conclusion. Among the forces that probably explain the "Leontief paradox" are: (1) highly skilled labor, abundant in the United States, is used intensively by export industries; (2) research and development are important sources of U.S. exports; (3) American imports run heavily to natural resources, and resource-intensive goods if produced at home would be quite capital-intensive; (4) American tariffs exclude labor-intensive imports, making it appear that labor-intensive industries are not especially import-competing; (5) factor-intensity reversals may cause the goods that are capital-intensive exports of the United States to compete with labor-intensive production in the importing countries.

The Heckscher-Ohlin theorem has also been called upon for guidance in explaining and predicting what lines of manufactured exports will be exported by the developing nations. The suggested answer is: those with low value added per worker. Such activities require relatively little physical and human capital relative to unskilled labor, and so they are suited to the factor endowments that seem typical of the developing countries. Indeed, we find that the poorer a country is, the farther down the scale of value added per worker do its exports typically come.

These models also help us to understand long-run changes and historical patterns in the international economy. The long-run changes in American trade have involved a shift of natural-resource-based products from export to the import lists; resources, once a relatively abundant factor in the United States, are now relatively scarce. Bilateral trade balances between countries or regions can be explained by relative factor abundance when we encompass three factors — capital, labor, and natural resources.

Changes in the structure of trade are often due to technological innovations that displace old products and introduce new ones. The "technological gap" model explains why the United States should be a prolific source of innovations, the production of which eventually is diffused to other countries. The "product cycle" explains how the speed of that diffusion is related to the changing input requirements of production processes and to the factor endowments of nations. U.S. research and development spending has been falling relative to that in other industrial countries, whose outputs of innovative goods have also been growing relative to those from American factories. Hence, this basis for America's gains from trade may be narrowing.

SUGGESTIONS FOR FURTHER READING

Baldwin, Robert E. "Determinants of the Commodity Structure of U.S. Trade," *American Economic Review,* 61 (March 1971): 126–46. Sophisticated summary and extension of evidence on the "Leontief paradox."

Baldwin, R. E., and J. D. Richardson, eds. *International Trade and Finance: Readings.* 2nd ed. Boston: Little, Brown, 1981. Part I contains important papers on models explaining the structure of international trade.

Hansson, Karl-Erik. "A General Theory of the System of Multilateral Trade," *American Economic Review,* 42 (March 1952): 58–68. Application of Heckscher-Ohlin model to bilateral trade patterns of major regions.

Hufbauer, G. C. "The Impact of National Characteristics and Technology on the Commodity Composition of Trade in Manufactured Goods," *The Technology Factor in International Trade.* New York: National Bureau of Economic Research, 1970, pp. 145–231. Extensive statistical test of theories explaining trade structure.

Johnson, Harry G. *Comparative Cost and Commercial Policy Theory for a Developing World Economy.* Stockholm: Almqvist and Wiksell, 1968. Theoretical extension of "technology gap" and "product cycle" concepts.

Leontief, W. W. "Domestic Production and Foreign Trade: The American Capital Position Re-examined," *Economia Internazionale,* 7 (February 1954): 3–32; reprinted in American Economic Association, *Readings in International Economics.* Homewood, Ill.: Richard D. Irwin, 1968, chap. 30. Original statement of the "Leontief paradox."

Vanek, Jaroslav. "The Natural Resource Content of Foreign Trade, 1870–1955, and the Relative Abundance of Natural Resources in the United States," *Review of Economics and Statistics,* 41 (May 1959): 146–53. Influence of natural resources on capital-labor intensity of U.S. trade.

9

Imperfect Competition in International Trade

Monopoly in international trade became marked as an urgent issue in 1973 when the Organization of Petroleum Exporting Countries attained the most lucrative monopoly in the world's history. Yet many other international markets are impurely competitive in less spectacular ways. We can use economic theory to explain the basic structure of the international economy most readily when we assume that markets are purely competitive. For many purposes that explanation is both clear and tolerably correct. But now we must face the impurities, which help to explain many facts about international trade as well as provide important conclusions about economic policy.

9.1 EXPORT CARTELS AND COMMODITY AGREEMENTS

A seller exercises monopoly power in international trade by charging a price in excess of his marginal cost. Since 1973 the price of crude oil has been far above its estimated marginal cost of production in the leading export countries, yielding the members an export surplus of $60 billion in 1974, and almost twice that in 1980 after another price increase. These riches result from the willingness of the OPEC-member countries to agree to charge a common high price. The oil price rise, of course, reduced the world's consumption of oil, not only because any price increase tends to cut the quantity demanded, but also because the disturbance reduced employment in the industrial economies and thus their demand for all imports, oil included. For the cartel to stick, its members had to accept a reduction in the quantities they produced and sold; the

161

four leading exporters made these cuts. Instances have turned up of sales by OPEC members for less than the cartel's price — for example, bilateral barter deals in which the oil seller lets the buyer "mark up" the prices of the goods shipped to pay for the oil — but these have been only minor. And in 1979 the effect worked the other way as some OPEC members took advantage of the restriction of Iran's output and leap-frogged over the cartel's agreed price.

Monopolizing a stock resource such as crude petroleum is not like mo-nopolizing the flow of some product or service. There is only so much crude petroleum in the earth's crust, to be used at one time or another, so the monopoly does not restrict the world's "lifetime supply." In order to maximize his wealth, the resource monopolist guesses when he will get the highest price for each unit of his stock resource and plans to schedule the barrels he extracts and sells among various future years so as to bring him the largest total wealth (in the sense of present value, with the profits of future sales discounted back to the present). But purely competitive owners of the fixed-stock resource (with the same time horizon and discount rate) would in general behave the same way, both as individuals and as a group. The stock-resource monopolist en-riches himself in a different way — exactly as OPEC did — by raising the price unexpectedly in the short run when a long lag is involved be-fore alternative sources of supply can swing into action. OPEC's enrich-ment from this source alone is impressive enough. Robert S. Pindyck estimates that, depending on the interest rate used to discount future revenues, the OPEC countries have increased their permanent wealth by 50 to 100 percent.[1]

Conditions for Successful Cartels

OPEC's success has stirred the envy of other primary exporters, partic-ularly the less-developed countries, and the fear of importers that they would be impoverished by a surge of monopolistic pricing. Indeed OPEC raises the question of what conditions are necessary to secure an effective monopoly in international trade. Cartels in primary products have previ-ously come and gone. What explains OPEC's success? What are the chances that other primary producers will emulate it? Economic analysis supplies a list of conditions necessary for a group of sellers to succeed in the joint exercise of monopoly power:

1. Is the price elasticity of demand low, so that the elevation of price is profitable? For the elasticity to be low the product must have no

[1] Robert S. Pindyck, "Gains to Producers from the Cartelization of Exhaustible Resources," *Review of Economics and Statistics*, 60 (May 1978): 238–51.

good substitutes. (Petroleum does face good substitute sources of energy, but it takes a long time to expand their supply and use.)

2. Are all important producers willing to join the agreement? Are there potential producers who will come into the market if the price is elevated?

3. Are the producers likely to sustain their agreement once the price is raised? The difficulty for them is that anybody would like to increase his production once price exceeds marginal cost, yet as a group they must cut back to make the price increase hold. Are they few in number? Are some members (at least) willing to make the necessary cuts? Does the group enjoy solidarity, which will help them stick together? Are there weak, or greedy, members who are likely to cheat? Is the product simple enough to preclude price concessions by rigging the ancillary terms of the transaction?

4. Are the buyers (countries or companies) incapable of organizing to apply counter-pressure? (The international oil companies have been complaisant, and the importing countries have not organized effectively.)

Various writers have surveyed the international producers of primary commodities to see where potential OPECs might be lurking.[2] Their conclusions are diverse, but most find relatively few products that offer the prospects of petroleum for a successful cartel.

Commodity Agreements

The recent flap over OPEC follows on a long history of attempts by countries or producer groups to manipulate their terms of trade. Primary-product cartels first became prominent after World War I. Largely the work of private exporters, they imitated the prewar trusts and mergers among industrial companies in the United States and other major nations. Most of them soon failed for reasons identified in our list: excluded sellers increased production, participants cheated on the price, and so on. In the 1930's, with unemployment rampant and primary-product prices especially depressed, governments often took a hand to promote international schemes to fix or stabilize prices and to compel the restriction of output or sales.

The arrangements of the 1930's often were aimed at stabilizing the price at a reasonable level rather than elevating it. Indeed, there may

---

[2] See the articles by Mikdashi, Krasner, and Bergsten in *Foreign Policy*, 14 (Spring 1974): 57–90. Pindyck concludes that the bauxite (aluminum ore) producers could enrich themselves proportionally even more than OPEC; copper producers have proportionally less to gain.

be real economic gains from building up buffer stocks to raise prices in periods of excess supply and selling them off to mitigate price increases when demand exceeds production. What is "stabilization" to the producer, however, can easily look like monopoly to the consumer. The plan prepared during World War II for the postwar era included a code of behavior to avoid disputes over international commodity agreements. They should be adopted only to preclude hardship for small producers. They should include consumer interests and give equitable treatment to all. Adequate supplies should be provided, and increases should come from efficient producers. These terms sound nice, but producers and consumers could not agree easily on what they mean in a particular case. A few commodity agreements — wheat, tin, sugar, coffee — have tried to follow these principles. They have often been blown off course by unexpected developments in the market.[3]

Through the United Nations Conference on Trade and Development (UNCTAD) the less-developed countries have demanded an international program of commodity agreements as the keystone of a "New International Economic Order." It would involve agreements covering eighteen commodities along with a Common Fund to finance the agreements and also to assist LDC exporters in diversifying their economies. The proposal seems to contemplate that the prices of primary commodities would be both raised and stabilized. It thus seeks elements of both monopoly and income stabilization for the primary producers.

An economist objects to the commodity-agreement proposal as a method of transferring income to the LDCs. Transferring income to producers by having them restrict supply and raise their selling price is an inefficient procedure: it costs more real resources than if the buyer simply hands over an equivalent transfer of real income. Thus any case for the monopoly element of the UNCTAD proposal must be political — that the industrial countries are more willing to give the LDCs foreign aid in the form of inflated commodity prices than as outright gifts, or that the recipients prefer the appearance of paying their way rather than receiving handouts. The evidence does suggest that there are real gains from running pure buffer-stock schemes with no element of monopoly. Even if their managers do not have perfect foresight in making their buying and selling plans, buffer stocks in many commodities could produce welfare gains exceeding the costs of operating them (the costs of storing the commodities and the interest on capital tied up in them).[4]

---

[3] A good survey of historical experience with commodity agreements is provided by J. W. F. Rowe, *Primary Commodities in International Trade.* Cambridge, England: Cambridge University Press, 1965, part IV.
[4] See David L. McNicol, *Commodity Agreements and Price Stabilization.* Lexington, Mass.: Lexington Books, 1978.

It is thus unfortunate that so much difficulty exists in untangling the monopoly and stabilization aspects of commodity agreements.

9.2 IMPERFECT NATIONAL MARKETS AND INTERNATIONAL TRADE

One justification for commodity cartels offered by the less-developed countries is that manufactured products are often sold at elevated prices under conditions of imperfect competition. Indeed, the evidence shows that price distortions are widespread if seldom so spectacular as OPEC's. In this section we shall consider some traits of national markets with competitive imperfections and show how they affect and are affected by international trade.

Introductory courses in economics usually present three models of market structures other than the purely competitive. A monopolist is the sole seller of a product that has no close substitutes. The model of monopolistic competition assumes a large number of sellers, none large enough to detect the influence of his pricing decision on the average price in the rest of the market. Nonetheless, each seller's product differs enough from products of his rivals that (unlike the pure competitor) he faces a downward-sloping demand curve. Finally, the sellers in situations of oligopoly are few enough that each takes some account of his rivals' possible responses to his actions. Although oligopoly is harder to describe in simple, deterministic, theoretical models, it is a common market structure in the industrial economy. Within the national economy, scale economies, product differentiation, and other forces conspire to permit markets to be dominated by a few sellers. They employ collusive behavior — not always successfully — to wrest from their market some of the excess profits it would yield to a pure monopolist.

These noncompetitive elements in national markets influence international trade in many important ways. They affect the international division of labor, making the bundle of goods and services that a country exports differ from what we might expect in purely competitive markets. They distort price relations from those that competitive markets would determine. In this section we shall consider in turn what economic theory and the available factual evidence reveal about these influences.

Important products are often produced by only a few sellers in a country. In the United States, the significant producers of automobiles, soap, or flat glass can all be counted on the fingers of one hand. One of the virtues of international exchange is that competition with foreign producers decreases the ability of domestic firms with potential monopoly power to cause misallocation of resources. A gain in economic welfare arises from putting a domestic monopolist into international competition.

Monopoly and Import Competition

One source of welfare gains from international competition can be illustrated in Figure 9.1. It shows not the monopolist's own demand and cost curves, but the effect of his behavior on resource allocation for the economy as a whole. If the economy were closed and both the clothing and food industries competitive, production and consumption would be at point C_1. We assume, however, that the food industry is monopolized. The monopolist maximizes his profits by producing less than the competitive output and charging a price higher than his marginal cost. In our two-good model of the economy, that means he restricts his output to some level such as F_M or F_M', causing too many factors of production to be shifted into the clothing industry. His monopoly price distorts the economy's relative prices to some value such as P_M or P_M'. (The diagram does not show exactly how the monopolist's profit-maximizing quantity is determined.)

FIGURE 9.1   Effect of Trade with
Import-Competing Monopolist (Food)

Without trade, monopolized food production at F_M or F_M' is below the closed-economy competitive level. When trade is opened, food's price falls from P_M or P_M' to $P_T C_2$; the welfare gain is greater than that from y_1 to y_2.

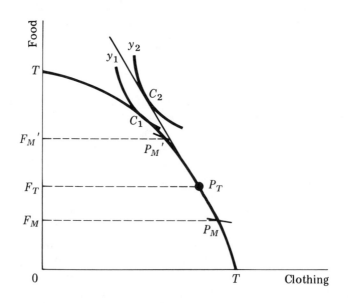

Suppose that the economy is now opened up to trade, and the monopolist finds himself facing much cheaper imports of food with a world market price shown by slope $P_T C_2$. Suppose further that the country is too small to influence world prices. We have now turned the monopolist into a pure competitor on the world market, because he can only sell whatever output is profitable at the given world price. He chooses output F_T, the same output that a purely competitive food industry would select. He might contract his output (from F_M') because of his cost disadvantage against the foreign producers of food. Or he might even expand output (from F_M) if his cost disadvantage is not too great, because it no longer pays him to restrict it in order to raise price.

The economy attains more gains from trade in this case than if food production had been competitive. Initially it was on a community indifference curve tangent to the price slope that intersects the production-possibilities curve at P_M or P_M'. This indifference curve (not shown) would lie below point C_1 and represent a lower level of welfare than community indifference curve y_1, which corresponds to a competitive economy without international trade. The overall welfare gain when trade is introduced can thus be decomposed into two parts: the movement from an indifference curve tangent at P_M (or P_M') to C_1 due to eliminating monopoly, and the gain from C_1 to C_2 due to the advantages of international specialization.

Monopoly and Export Opportunities

It may surprise you that the gains from exposing a monopolist to international trade are essentially the same if the monopolist becomes the exporter; export opportunities change his behavior toward the home market in the same way as the discipline of import competition. Figure 9.2 shows the effect of monopoly in the clothing industry (the food industry is now assumed competitive). In the absence of trade, output might be restricted to C_M or C_M', corresponding to relative prices P_M or P_M' higher than would prevail in the competitive closed economy (at C_1). Exposing the monopolist to world price ratio $P_T C_2$ induces him to expand his output greatly. Because we assume there is no restriction on imports of clothing at these same world prices, the monopolist can no longer exploit the downward-sloping domestic-demand curve. Instead he must sell on the foreign and domestic markets at the world price. Paradoxically, the actual domestic price of clothing could either rise or fall when the economy is opened to trade. It might rise if the nation's comparative advantage is very great, so that the monopolist's low costs cause him to maximize profits with a higher domestic price (P_M' is flatter than $P_T C_2$), but the force of international competition could also make him cut his price (P_M is steeper than $P_T C_2$). Once more, the economy's total

FIGURE 9.2   Effect of Trade with Exporting Monopolist (Clothing)

Without trade, monopolized clothing production at C_M or C_M' is below the closed-economy competitive level. When trade is opened at world prices $P_T C_2$, the monopolist must trade as a pure competitor on the world market and produces C_T. Domestic price of clothing can either rise (from P_M') or fall (from P_M).

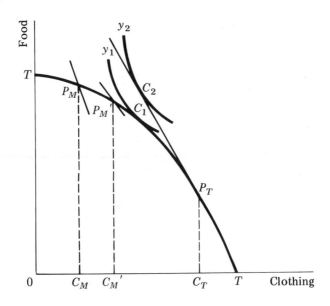

gain in welfare consists of the conventional gains from trade plus an extra gain due to eliminating the monopolistic distortion of production.

International Oligopoly and Restrictive Agreements

The preceding analysis illustrates the potential effect of international competition on monopoly in a sheltered domestic market, but it rests on the rather extreme assumption that there is only one seller in the home market but enough sellers for pure competition in the world at large. The fewness of sellers of a product results from traits of the product and of its production that do not vary much from country to country. If its sellers are few in one country, they are likely to be few in all regions. And if domestic sellers recognize the interdependence of their pricing decisions in the home market, they may recognize their interdependence in the world market. International oligopoly has many possible consequences. In this section we consider two of them: international industrial cartels and "dumping."

International cartels have existed among international producers in manufacturing industries, just as in primary production. Cartels can take various forms, but they have often consisted of agreements among firms to divide markets among themselves, fix prices, exclude would-be competitors, or otherwise try to increase joint monopoly profits. Such agreements can operate either within nations or across their boundaries. They have long been illegal under the antitrust laws of the United States, and since World War II their legality in the industrial nations of Europe has been circumscribed. Likewise, the operation of international cartels is best documented for the period between World Wars I and II, a fact that may reflect a subsequent decline in their strength and importance.[5] Most international cartels seem to have tried to divide markets among producing firms, to eliminate rivalry for customers. A common pattern was to allot each producer (or national group of producers) its home market and divide up the rest of the world — markets with no production, or production by nonmembers — among the parties. Industries such as those producing chemicals might divide the manufacture and sale of various individual products among themselves or agree to license patents on new discoveries only to each other. These arrangements, when successful, both raised prices around the world and made them differ from one national market to another.[6] Prices were sometimes rigid, because cartels' arrangements were not tight enough to permit continuous adjustment to keep a price at the monopolistic profit-maximizing level. And breakdowns of understanding sometimes led to the collapse of cartels into price warring and predatory practices.

In their effects on international trade, cartels apparently not only increased the degree of monopoly in domestic markets but also thwarted adjustments of production among countries in ways indicated by comparative advantage. A complete profit-maximizing cartel would rationally concentrate production in its most efficient units, sharing the total profit among its members. But this was seldom done internationally. Hence the probable effect of international cartels on the allocation of

---

[5] See George W. Stocking and Myron W. Watkins, *Cartels in Action.* New York: Twentieth Century Fund, 1946; idem, *Cartels or Competition?* New York: Twentieth Century Fund, 1948; especially chap. 4.

[6] For several years after 1928, tungsten carbide was sold by Krupp in Europe for about $50 a pound, by General Electric in the United States for a list price of $453 a pound. General Electric's manufacturing cost was quoted as $8 a pound. See Stocking, *Cartels or Competition?* pp. 132–33.

resources in the world economy has been to restrict the total quantity employed in the cartelized industry and also to distort the pattern of production among countries.

The international cartel is used by sellers in different countries to curb rivalry among themselves. Its use suggests that oligopolistic sellers may find collusion with their foreign rivals more difficult than with their domestic rivals. In domestic markets where sellers are few, competition often appears to be restricted by "tacit collusion." That is, through recurrent contact and experience sellers become adept at gauging each other's reactions and, without any formal collusion, can push the commitment of resources in their market toward that which a profit-maximizing monopolist would choose. For many reasons this tacit collusion will occur more easily within national markets than between sellers in different countries. Cultural differences and increased difficulties of communicating play an important part. The local markets served are likely to differ in many qualitative ways, and with them the general strategies sellers use in serving them. Transport costs and tariffs tend to make sellers less sensitive to the actions of their foreign than their domestic rivals.

Thus, oligopolists are likely to be more collusive with their domestic rivals and more competitive in dealing with foreign rivals. If we take this statement as a hypothesis about oligopoly markets, it explains several important patterns of business behavior affecting international trade. One is the failure of domestic oligopolists facing rising import competition to meet the lower price charged for the imports. If the imported product is a close substitute for their own and sells for a lower delivered price, this refusal, of course, costs them a significant share of the domestic market. They may suffer this erosion rather than cut prices because of the imperfect collusion among themselves. Every price change, especially one downward, raises the possibility that misunderstanding will occur and price warfare break out. For example, the steel industry in the United States has often been charged with maintaining list prices that are inflexible and insensitive to imports as well as to other competitive pressures. If "import discipline" affected the pricing behavior of domestic oligopolists, you would expect prices of domestic steel products to rise slowly where competing imports are large or where the prices of comparable foreign steel items rise slowly. But one statistical study of the prices of forty-six steel products in the mid-1950's found no such influence.[7] More recently the steel producers have responded to their foreign competition in a different fashion — demanding that the government curb imports by means of quantitative restrictions. Although im-

[7] Lawrence B. Krause, "Import Discipline: The Case of the United States Steel Industry," *Journal of Industrial Economics,* 11 (November 1962): 33–47.

port competition is generally a good antimonopoly device, oligopolies sometimes refuse to respond to its pressures.

Dumping

Another important result of oligopoly in international markets is dumping. Dumping occurs when producers sell abroad at prices that regularly yield them less net revenue (after payment of transportation costs, tariffs, etc.) than do sales of comparable goods in their home market. Note that this could not occur in a purely competitive market. A pure competitor sells his entire output at a price dictated to him by the market. If he can choose between two markets, one yielding higher returns per unit sold than the other, he will dispose of his whole output in the higher-price market. A profit-maximizing seller with some monopoly power, however, will not necessarily behave in this way. Consider the domestic monopolist illustrated in Figure 9.3. Demand in the home market is given by D, his marginal revenue by MR_d. If his marginal cost is MC, he maximizes profits at home by charging P_m, the sale price of the output for which $MC = MR_d$. The world price P_t is lower than P_m, but it still lies above MC over a substantial range of output, so the monopolist can profitably produce for export. Now suppose that different prices can be charged in the home and foreign markets, perhaps because a tariff protecting the home market keeps goods sold cheaply abroad from being reimported and undercutting the higher domestic price. A monopolist maximizes profits by setting a price that equates his marginal cost to the marginal revenue he can earn in each of his markets: If the marginal revenues were not equal, he should shift sales from the lower to the higher until they are equalized. In Figure 9.3 the marginal revenue from foreign sales is equal to the world price P_t, because that price is unaffected by the monopolist's level of exports. After he begins to export, the monopolist will sell in the domestic market at price P_d, which equates marginal revenue derived from the domestic market (MR_d) to that earned from foreign sales (MR_t). If his total production is OC, his marginal cost (MC) is equated to the common value of marginal revenue, and profits are maximized. Exports are BC, domestic sales OB. Notice that this discrimination between the domestic and foreign markets has caused a higher price to be charged in the domestic market than if no trade were occurring (P_d exceeds P_m).

We introduced the model of dumping in the context of oligopoly in domestic and international markets, yet explained it on the assumption of pure monopoly at home and pure competition abroad. These assumptions, however, merely push to the limit a difference between home and foreign markets that we suggested before — domestic oligopolists are likely to recognize their interdependence more fully than sellers based

FIGURE 9.3 "Dumping" and Discrimination
Between Domestic and Foreign Markets

Monopolist faces demand curve D at home and world price P_t. If he can charge separate prices at home and abroad, he sets P_d and P_t respectively, selling OB at home and BC abroad.

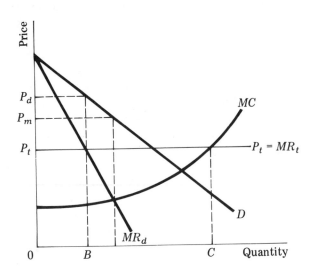

in different countries. This difference implies that the individual seller will view the demand curve he faces in the home market as less elastic than the demand he faces abroad: If he cuts prices he expects his domestic rivals to follow, but he assumes that sellers abroad are less likely to react. That difference in elasticities of demand in home and foreign markets predicts that sellers will prefer a higher price at home.[8]

The evidence seems to suggest that dumping occurs in many industries, and at the hands of producers in many countries. For instance, the disclosure that Japanese color television sets were being sold in the United States at prices much below those in Japan prompted a boycott by irate Japanese customers! A survey taken before World War II of pricing by seventy-six U.S. exporting firms found that forty-six of them received lower net prices on their foreign than their domestic sales, and

---

[8] Figure 9.3 is a special case of the model of discriminating monopoly because foreign demand is assumed perfectly elastic. For a treatment of the general case see Joan Robinson, *The Economics of Imperfect Competition.* London: Macmillan, 1933, chap. 15.

only nine got higher prices abroad.[9] Dumping appears to grow more prevalent when producers suffer a reduction in demand that leaves them with excess capacity. Then they will cut foreign prices, perhaps to levels that cover their marginal but not their average costs, while maintaining prices at home to avoid spoiling that market. As Figure 9.3 showed, excess capacity is not necessary for dumping, but it often provides an extra incentive.

Dumping presents an odd problem for economic policy. It favors the foreign consumer over the domestic one. You might expect governments, concerned with the welfare of their citizens, to try to keep their exporters from dumping. Yet the importing countries typically outlaw or discourage dumping. Their justification is that dumping is unfair to domestic producers, or that temporary dumping might be used to drive native firms out of business.

Product Differentiation

Another imperfection in actual markets is called product differentiation. The outputs of different producers of the same class of goods — brands of gasoline, typewriters, wristwatches, etc. — are similar in function and compete closely with each other. Nonetheless, consumers detect differences that make competing brands less than perfect substitutes. In their eyes brand *A* may differ from brand *B* in physical traits, images or attitudes created by advertising, and so on. Consumers hold diverse views on the relative merits of *A* and *B*, and a small cut in the price of *A* will not pull all the customers away from *B*. Differentiation can occur even when the number of sellers is large enough that no one is conscious of the effect of his actions on the other individuals. This market structure is described by the model of *monopolistic competition*. Differentiation can also occur, however, when sellers are few: *differentiated oligopoly*. In general, product differentiation reduces the sensitivity of sellers to each other's pricing decisions. The chances that a rival will react to one's own price reduction are reduced, because its impact on his share of the market will (ceteris paribus) be smaller when product differentiation is present. Differentiation also makes varying the product itself a competitive strategy: Rather than cut the price, one can offer a better product at the same price.

Not all rivals' products will be equally good substitutes for ones' own. A Lincoln may be a close substitute for a Cadillac, but a Volkswagen

---

[9] United States Temporary National Economic Committee, *Export Prices and Export Cartels,* Monograph No. 6. Washington: Government Printing Office, 1940, chaps. 5 and 6. For a general treatment of dumping and U.S. policy toward it, see William A. Wares, *The Theory of Dumping and American Commercial Policy.* Lexington, Mass.: Lexington Books, 1977.

may not. Often product varieties may be arranged in a chain of substitutes. Varieties *A* and *B* are good substitutes for each other, *B* and *C*, *C* and *D*, etc.; but products located far apart on the chain are not close substitutes. Now suppose that before international trade is permitted to occur, we observe in the home country such a chain of producers *A*, *B*, *C*, ... *N* of a product; and in the foreign country the same (general) product is produced by another chain of producers A^*, B^*, C^*, ... N^*. The two economies now are opened up to international trade.

If differentiation were not present, we would expect cost and demand conditions to produce a net flow of trade. If the home country were the net exporter, some producers abroad (the least efficient, presumably) would leave the industry and free their factors of production for other uses, while in the home industry new producers would enter, old ones expand, or both. With differentiation, however, we must ask how the two chains of substitutes will relate to each other after trade is opened. The chains may join end-on. That is, the home country's varieties *N*, *M*, *L*, ... may be relatively close substitutes for the foreign country's A^*, B^*, C^*, ..., but goods at the opposite ends of the two chains may be poor substitutes. For example, the ranking of the varieties in both countries may run from the relatively costly and high-quality (*A* and A^*) down to the relatively cheap and low-quality (*N* and N^*). But because levels of income per capita in the foreign country are lower than at home, the *absolute* quality level of the top-quality foreign varieties may about match that of the cheapest home varieties. If with the opening of trade the home country enjoys a cost advantage in the sense of comparative cost, the foreign producers competed out of business will be those at the head of the chain A^*, B^*, C^*, ...

An alternative possibility is that the two chains of substitutes, rather than joining at the ends, will overlap throughout. A^* proves to be a good substitute for *A* and *B*, B^* for *B* and *C*, etc. The effects of introducing trade in this case may differ dramatically from the previous one. Even if the home producers again enjoy a cost advantage, the prevalent downward-sloping demand curves may preclude their driving more than a few foreign producers from the market. More important, some foreign varieties will appeal to home consumers, so that some imports of the product will occur even if costs and demand conditions in general equilibrium favor the home producers enough that net exports occur. Thus, product differentiation can explain two-way flows of products in the same general class.[10] Furthermore, as the chain of substitutes becomes more tightly interlaced, each producer (in either country) finds himself facing closer rivals than before, implying a flatter demand curve for his

[10] *Can,* not *must.* In the previous instance of the chains of substitutes joining at their ends, no reason emerged for the occurrence of imports as well as exports.

product. He must behave more nearly like a pure competitor than before, and inefficiencies associated with prices in excess of marginal cost may be reduced,

A powerful test of the importance of product differentiation in international trade has been provided by the formation of the European Community, which has removed all tariffs among its member countries. When tariff protection is wiped out in purely competitive markets, one expects hitherto protected industries to be competed down. A country will find its net exports of a product group rising, if it enjoys a comparative advantage, or its net imports rising, if it is at a comparative disadvantage. Yet no such increases in net trade balances occurred. Instead, each Common Market country's exports to its partners rose in most product groups, rather than rising in some and falling in others. *Net* exports or imports changed little while gross exports rose all around, suggesting a large increase in the interpenetration of markets.[11]

This story is consistent with our second model of product differentiation, in which countries' product chains become interlinked. Indeed, evidence from other sources shows that this heterogeneity of products promotes two-way trade without any intermediary influence of tariff reduction. A good deal of two-way trade is found in manufactured goods. It suggests important sources of the gains from international trade not identified in traditional models: international trade provides buyers with a wider range of choices than they would otherwise have, and it ensures close competition for the national sellers of any given differentiated product.

Differentiation and Trade Patterns

Differentiation may affect the volume of trade between countries in other ways as well. For example, the tastes of citizens in different countries for a good, such as washing machines, may depend on their average level of income per capita. In rich countries, households may value their time highly and, therefore, be willing to pay for time-saving convenience in their home appliances. Among differentiated varieties of washers, then, they would prefer elaborate automatic equipment that requires little time or attention from its user. Consumers in lower-income countries, placing less value on household labor, would desire less elaborate and costly varieties that require more labor input from the user. Thus there would be broad physical similarities among the varieties preferred in all

---

[11] Bela Balassa, "Tariff Reductions and Trade in Manufactures," *American Economic Review,* 56 (June 1966): 466–73; Herbert G. Grubel, "Intra-Industry Specialization and the Pattern of Trade," *Canadian Journal of Economics and Political Science,* 33 (August 1967): 374–88.

high-income countries, other broad similarities among those chosen in middle income countries, and so forth.

Now consider the world distribution of the production of these differentiated varieties. The producer of differentiated consumer goods always enjoys an advantage over import competition in his home market because differentiation reflects the traits of the national culture and lifestyle. The domestic producer and his employees understand this background and use it to guide the "styling" of their product. The foreign producer either is guided by a different cultural heritage, or must incur costs or run risks in guessing what product traits will attract foreign consumers. The real costs of production may run against a local producer, of course, and "comparative disadvantage" might offset his advantages in supplying the differentiated variety of goods wanted by the home market. But the differentiated producer enjoys an advantage in serving the home market that is denied to the maker of undifferentiated goods.

Let us put together the propositions of the last two paragraphs. Producers of differentiated goods are likely to be strong in their home markets. The goods the home markets desire will depend on the citizens' level of income per capita. These propositions imply several predictions about international trade in differentiated goods. First, production is likely to be widespread among countries. International trade in these goods may occur, but the tendency for production to concentrate in the most efficient locations will be blunted — even without tariff protection. Second, home producers are likely to succeed in catering to "majority" tastes among their citizens; but foreign producers may find numerous pockets of "minority" tastes — odd sectors of the culture, outer reaches of the income distribution, and the like — attracted to their product varieties.[12] We often hear this proposition in everyday life, when people view imports (of differentiated goods) as "specialty" or "unusual" items. Third, countries with similar levels of income per capita and similar cultures may swap large volumes of differentiated goods with each other's consumers, and their chains of substitutes will tend to interlock in the pattern of A, A*, B, B*, etc, that was described above.[13]

---

[12] The United States appears to enjoy a comparative advantage in producing elaborate consumer durables, and countries like Japan and Italy have the advantage in simpler versions of the same products. See Louis T. Wells, Jr., "Test of a Product Cycle Model of International Trade: U.S. Exports of Consumer Durables," *Quarterly Journal of Economics,* 83 (February 1969): 152–62.

[13] For a somewhat similar argument see Staffan Burenstam Linder, *An Essay on Trade and Transformation.* Uppsala: Almqvist & Wiksell, 1961, chap. 3. Linder's hypothesis has found some empirical support. See J. W. Sailors, U. A. Qureshi, and E. M. Cross, "Empirical Verification of Linder's Trade Thesis," *Southern Economic Journal,* 40 (October 1973): 262–68.

9.3 SUMMARY

Certain conditions must prevail in the market for a primary product for its exporters to succeed in monopolizing it. Demand must not be too elastic. All producers must join and stick to the agreement once price is elevated. New producers must not enter the market. The Organization of Petroleum Exporting Countries has satisfied these requirements, but most cartels of primary producers organized in the past have failed. Cartels are somewhat similar to international commodity agreements, which may pursue objectives of monopolistic pricing but are primarily intended to stabilize the prices of primary commodities. Under some circumstances price stabilization can benefit buyers and sellers jointly; the use of commodity agreements to transfer income from buyers to sellers (through monopoly pricing) is economically inefficient but sometimes politically attractive.

When the domestic market is dominated by a monopolist, opening it to the competition of imports conveys greater benefits to the nation than when the domestic industry is competitively organized. The same is true when export opportunities are opened for the domestic industry: The gains are greater when domestic production is initially monopolized. If production of one good is highly concentrated in one country, it is likely to be in other countries as well. Oligopolies in different countries tend to form cartels, dividing markets among themselves and distorting the allocation of world production away from its most efficient pattern. Oligopolists find it harder to collude with their foreign than with their domestic rivals. This fact helps to explain "dumping" — selling abroad for net revenues per unit less than those obtained in the home market.

Product differentiation affects trade in diverse ways, depending on the interlinking of substitute varieties of a good produced at home and abroad. When products are differentiated, countries may both import and export the same goods. Furthermore, the domestic producer always enjoys an advantage from knowing the differentiated tastes of his home market, and so the extent of international specialization is less than it would be if differentiation were absent and costs alone controlled the location of production.

SUGGESTIONS FOR FURTHER READING

Baldwin, Robert E., and J. David Richardson, eds. *International Trade and Finance: Readings*. 2nd ed. Boston: Little, Brown and Company, 1981. No. 4 deals with two-way trade.

Caves, Richard E. "International Cartels and Monopolies in International

Trade," in Dornbusch, Rudiger and Jacob A. Frenkel, eds., *International Economic Policy: Theory and Evidence.* Baltimore: Johns Hopkins University Press, 1979. Chap. 2. Survey of theoretical models and evidence on this subject.

McLachlan, D. L., and D. Swann. *Competition Policy in the European Community.* London: Oxford University Press, 1967. Part 2 gives evidence on cartel behavior in recent years.

McNicol, David L. *Commodity Agreements and Price Stabilization.* Lexington, Mass.: Lexington Books, 1978. Good treatment of theoretical and welfare aspects.

Mikdashi, Z., S. Krasner, and C. F. Bergsten. *Foreign Policy,* 14 (Spring 1974): 57–90. Series of articles on OPEC and possibilities for cartels in other primary products.

Rowe, J. W. F. *Primary Commodities in International Trade.* Cambridge, England: Cambridge University Press, 1965. Survey of experience with commodity agreements.

Wares, William A. *The Theory of Dumping and American Commercial Policy.* Lexington, Mass.: Lexington Books, 1977. Theory and policy of international price discrimination.

10

International
Factor Movements
and Multinational
Companies

Our study so far has dealt with the international movement of goods and services. However, some of the most dramatic changes in the international economy have been brought about by international movements of factors of production. In the nineteenth century the countries of Europe sent forth their workers and capital in great quantities to develop nearly empty regions. Today the countries of northern Europe supplement their work forces with hoards of temporary migrants from southern Europe, and the multinational company carries on the international reallocation of capital. We shall first learn how international factor movements are related to trade and economic welfare, and then we shall explore the many policy issues relating to the multinational company.

10.1 FACTOR MOVEMENTS AND THE EFFICIENCY OF WORLD PRODUCTION

Gains from trade occur because goods move from where their relative prices are low (in the absence of trade) to where they are high. Economic welfare can also be increased when factors of production move to places where they are better paid. For either factors or goods, when we can assume that their prices equal their (marginal) values to society, the efficiency of the world economy is increased by a movement from a low-price location to a higher one.

But this similarity between movements of goods and factors does not capture the full story of their interrelation that emerges in the Heckscher-Ohlin model set forth in Chapter 7. In that model we proved that if both countries engage in free trade in commodities, and produce both commodities with the same technology, factor prices will be equalized between countries although factors are (in that model) completely immobile internationally. Free trade in commodities completely substituted for the international mobility of factors; with factor prices equalized internationally, no economic incentive remains for labor or capital to migrate even if barriers are removed. Note, furthermore, that if resources were transferred between countries, world outputs would not change. This finding supports our contention that gains in potential efficiency in production are signalled by a discrepancy between what a factor can earn in one region and another. A world of factor price equalization as a consequence of trade in commodities is a world in which factor mobility itself would be unnecessary in further expanding world output.

Given the stringent conditions needed for factor price equalization, these remarks hardly suggest the unimportance of international factor movements. Indeed, they indicate that factor mobility could be significant whenever commodity trade does not completely equalize factor returns internationally. Even if technology were identical throughout the world, the discussion of the many-commodity case in Chapter 7 revealed that countries with dissimilar factor endowments would generally be producing different sets of commodities. In such a case free trade would not equalize factor returns from one country to another. If capital, say, could migrate from the region in which returns were low to the country where capital earns higher returns, the efficiency of world production would be improved.

Figure 10.1 illustrates these points. Two transformation schedules are drawn — each showing the locus of maximum *world* outputs in a model in which each country has the same technology. The inner locus, TT, shows the possible world outputs of food and clothing if labor and capital in each country are efficiently utilized, and if free trade guarantees that producers everywhere face the same (world) commodity prices — but factors of production are not allowed to move from one country to another. The range AB corresponds to world outputs of the two goods where each country produces both food and clothing. The stretch northwest of A along TT has one country specialized in food, and the BT section of TT southeast of B has one country specialized in clothing production. Along both these stretches factor returns are not equalized between countries, so that once factors are free to migrate, world output will expand. The dashed curve, $T'T'$, shows possible world outputs when factors can move from one country to another.

FIGURE 10.1   The World Transformation Curve
with International Factor Mobility

The *TT* locus of production possibilities for the world assumes that factors
are immobile internationally. The expanded locus, *T'T'*, results if factors
can move across national boundaries in response to differential rewards.

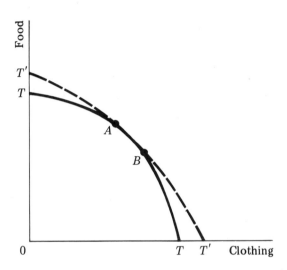

The gains to world production from international factor mobility can
considerably exceed those shown in Figure 10.1 if countries have different
technologies and if these differences are not rooted in the superiority of
the factors of production. This latter proviso is important. If, say, the
typical American worker is better trained and educated than the typical
Andorran, a higher American wage rate to attract the Andorran would
be the wrong signal. Only if differential returns to factors geographically
represent the contribution to efficiency of other factors or technology
will a migration of that factor yield increased output.

10.2 FACTOR MOVEMENTS AND INCOME DISTRIBUTION

Although factor movements can increase the efficiency of the world
economy, they are often restricted by governments serving what they
see as their national interest. Immigration of labor in particular is always under strict control. In this section we shall consider how factor

movements affect income distribution and efficiency within the receiving country.

We know from Chapters 6 and 7 that changing factor endowments alter the distribution of income in a way that depends on the nation's apparatus of production. The effect of an inflow of a factor from abroad is generally like that of a natural increase in its stock. Consider the model, developed in Chapter 6, in which capital and land are specific factors used only in the clothing and food industries (respectively) but labor is mobile between industries. A wave of immigration drives down wages, as we would expect, but it raises the rewards to both land and capital. An inflow of capital depresses the returns to capital and raises wages; but it also makes the landlords worse off, because labor is pulled from food production into clothing and the marginal product of land falls. We would expect the capitalists and landlords to join in favoring free immigration but restricted capital inflows, and the workers to take the opposite position. But what of the national income as a whole? Is there any gain from immigration that *could* be divided up to make all the native factors better off?

Some insight into this problem can be gained by considering a simple model in which all residents at home own the same bundle of two factors of production, say, labor and capital. Suppose, furthermore, that the country produces only one commodity, and does not exchange goods with other countries. The situation is illustrated in Figure 10.2. The original inhabitants possess the factor-endowment combination shown by point A, and the factor price ratio is given by the slope of line BB tangent to isoquant Q_1 through A. The community consumes what it produces, quantity Q_1. Suppose now that immigration is allowed, and that the new entrants bring with them, on the average, less capital per man than the original group possesses. The new aggregate capital-labor bundle is a point such as C, with the enlarged community producing quantity Q_2 and the capital-poor immigration reflected in the lower wage/rental ratio shown by the slope of the Q_2 isoquant at C. The question first raised concerns the fate of the original inhabitants. At the new factor prices the capital-labor bundle A, their endowment, is worth the same as bundle D. But D can produce quantity Q_3, which is greater than Q_1. In short, the original inhabitants can now consume more of the single commodity produced than they could before immigration.[1]

This argument is not new. It is a rehash of our account in Chapter 2 of the gains to be derived when a community can trade at prices different from those originally prevailing at home. The novel element is that there is only one commodity, and the new prices are factor prices. The original inhabitants, whose factor-endowment bundle is shown by point

---

[1] The foregoing argument was suggested by Harry G. Johnson in "Some Economic Aspects of Brain Drain," *Pakistan Development Review,* 7 (August 1967): 379–411.

FIGURE 10.2   Immigration Benefits Home Residents

The community owns the labor and capital shown by bundle *A*. Pre-immigration factor prices are given by the slope of line *BB*. Immigration alters factor prices, allowing owners of bundle *A* now to trade factor services to command output Q_3 at *D*, greater than initial Q_1.

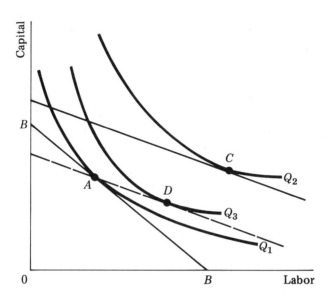

A in Figure 10.2, are viewed as trading *factor services* with an outside community at "terms of trade" for factors that would differ from those at home before immigration. As long as immigrants possess a different factor-endowment bundle from that of the original inhabitants, thus causing a change in the wage/rental ratio, the original community will gain. The major warning to be issued with this type of analysis is that it ignores possible effects of migration on a country's terms of trade. Should the country attract primarily those skills and resources used intensively in its export sectors, Chapter 4 has suggested how local incomes could be hurt.

10.3 DIRECT INVESTMENT AND THE MULTINATIONAL COMPANY

Direct investment is a distinctive form of international capital flow, because it affects both the nation's stock of productive factors and competitive conditions in its markets. Its distinctiveness lies in two traits.

1. Direct investment represents a capital movement, but the capital involved is entrepreneurial or risk-bearing. It does not merely finance the construction of plant and equipment. In its entrepreneurial role, direct investment is usually linked to the transfer of managerial skills and knowledge from one country to another. The corporation establishing or expanding a subsidiary abroad is the typical agent of direct investment.

2. It is strongly *industry-specific*. Its economically significant traits arise not so much from the transfer of capital from country *A* to country *B*, as from *A*'s *x* industry to *B*'s *x* industry. Specifically, direct investment flows along two industrial channels. *Horizontal* investment occurs when a firm producing a product in the source (lending) country establishes a subsidiary to produce the same good in the host country. *Vertical* investment occurs when it establishes a subsidiary to perform the next stage forward, or the next stage backward, in the fabrication and sale of its product. Many small foreign subsidiaries only distribute and sell the parent company's products in the host country; we shall largely ignore these cases of "forward" vertical integration. Much more important, in terms of the capital involved, are "backward" vertical integrations into the production of a raw material or input in the host country that can then be used by the parent company in the source country.

Because of these traits, an understanding of the causes and effects of direct investment is best gained by employing the concept of specific factors and by turning to models of individual industries and markets. The models of imperfect competition from Chapter 9 and the analysis of technological factors presented in Chapter 8 are especially useful here.

Causes of Direct Investment

Why should a firm invest in production facilities abroad? It does not know the language, the laws, the customs, the local markets. The foreign government may not be its friend. There must be a general explanation for profit-maximizing firms, at least in certain industries, establishing foreign subsidiaries in the face of these obstacles. The following explanation concentrates on horizontal investments.

We can start with a factual observation: Foreign investment is seldom undertaken by a company before it becomes an established, substantial seller in its domestic market. At this stage it has acquired managerial know-how, patents, trademarks, and other such intangible assets. These assets allow it to earn at least normal profits on its invested capital. Having been acquired while the firm built a position in the domestic market, they are now available for use elsewhere, if a profitable opportunity can be found.[2] At this point, foreign markets are apt to fall under its gaze.

Direct investment is sometimes an effective way to use these assets profitably abroad. Consider the company producing consumers' durable goods. It has discovered how to devise and modify features of its products to attract a significant share of those demanding such goods. Its products have attained a reputation for satisfactory durability and service. Its trademarks, patents, innovative and marketing skills, and (to a degree) its reputation with customers can be transplanted to foreign markets when it establishes production facilities abroad through direct investment. Furthermore, owning local production facilities aids it greatly in penetrating foreign markets. Such facilities make it easier to design products for the special requirements of foreign markets, and to modify the new product as information on consumer acceptance feeds back. Local servicing of such products may also lead to improved product performance.[3]

The firm described in this tale clearly does not sell in purely competitive markets. Indeed, the marketing assets that make its foreign investment profitable describe *product differentiation* as a characteristic of markets. We also described the firm as a large seller in its market. The marginally successful firm is not likely to have either the intangible assets or cash resources for profitable foreign investment; furthermore, gathering the information to start a foreign subsidiary is itself costly and likely to appeal only to a firm willing to stake a large investment abroad. Hence we deduce oligopoly as another trait likely to mark the industrial setting of firms making direct investments. If firms investing abroad must be both large and prominent in their home markets, their number in those markets must be few.

When we notice the industries drawing the most direct investment, the pattern strongly supports this analysis. American firms producing automobiles, other consumer durables, rubber, and pharmaceuticals are very likely to have subsidiaries abroad. Firms producing primary metals, paper, and textiles are not. The same holds in countries that have received large inflows of direct investment.

The causes of foreign investment are quite different for subsidiaries

[2] These forms of intangible capital consist of what economists call "public goods." When a technique or an idea is put to productive use in the United States, there is no less of it available for employment in Britain. The productive capacity of a machine obviously does not share this property. See Harry G. Johnson, "The Efficiency and Welfare Implications of the International Corporation," *The International Corporation*, ed. C. P. Kindleberger. Cambridge, Mass.: MIT Press, 1970, chap. 2.

[3] This account is closely related to the "product cycle" explored in section 8.4. For such an interpretation, see Raymond Vernon, *Sovereignty at Bay: The Multinational Spread of U.S. Enterprises*. New York: Basic Books, 1971, chap. 3.

supplying raw materials needed by their parents. The explanation of these investments at first seems obvious: how can a rubber company produce tires without crude rubber? The more interesting question, though, is why the raw material source is developed by a subsidiary of the company that will process it rather than by independent firms in the country where the raw material is found. The gain from this vertical direct investment seems to be the reduction of risk. Few companies in the world refine and fabricate copper. Important deposits of copper ore occur in only a few locations. If independent firms produced and refined the ore, both would be forced to commit funds to the construction of large fixed facilities without any guarantee about the bargain they could strike with the other party. What could the ore producer do if his smelter customer convincingly threatened to drop his business? What could the smelter do without an ore supply? "Vertical integration" in any industry reduces uncertainty. Because the firms extracting raw materials must be located where the resources are, and the firms processing and selling them where the markets are, foreign investment must be involved.

Direct Investment and Other Forces in the International Economy

Because of its distinctive character, direct investment interacts with other forces in the international economy in ways that differentiate it sharply from other types of capital flow. Let us consider some of these:

Exports and Absolute Costs. When the firm sees potential profits in markets abroad, exporting and direct investment often are alternative strategies for capturing them. They are not close alternatives always, or in all respects. Exporting may prove clearly superior when the firm's foreign sales are not yet large enough to utilize an overseas plant of efficient scale. Also, the firm that has established a producing subsidiary may continue to ship substantial exports to the same market, using its subsidiary as a marketing agent. However, we would always expect to find some companies close to the margin, with no clear preference for exporting or producing abroad.

This proposition implies an important contrast between direct investment and other capital movements: Its flow is sensitive to the exchange rate.[4] When the home currency depreciates (or is devalued), the foreign-currency cost of producing at home and exporting falls while the for-

---

[4] The contrast should not be drawn too sharply. We shall discover (Chapter 19) that securities lodged in individuals' portfolios may go through a one-shot readjustment when the exchange rate changes. And if asset holders expect the exchange rate to change in the future, they move their funds internationally in hopes of getting a capital gain (or avoiding a loss). But these flows of securities are not directly linked to differences in cost of production, as direct investment is.

eign-currency cost of producing abroad (via direct investment) stays unchanged. Hence direct investment should fall and exports expand. Variations in direct investment should be one source of elasticity in the demand for foreign exchange. When the outflow of direct investment from the United States was particularly heavy during the years 1958–65, with the dollar in external deficit, some argued that appropriate changes in exchange rates would help restore balance partly through cutting the flow of direct investment. There is some evidence that the cheapening of the U.S. dollar relative to other currencies since 1973 has made foreigners undertake more direct investment in the United States and led the United States to invest less abroad.

Tariffs in Host Countries. The choice between exporting and direct investment should reflect the producer's desire to serve a foreign market at the lowest cost. If the exchange rate potentially affects his choice, so should the level of tariffs surrounding the foreign market. Tariffs raise the cost of importing and tilt the decision toward direct investment. Surveys of foreign subsidiaries in host countries show that often they were founded when the parent had been serving the market by exports that were slapped with an increased tariff. Countries have often used tariffs to lure direct investment.

Net Versus Gross Flows. We expect capital to flow from the country where the profit rate is low to where it is high. The industry-specific character of direct investment clouds this simple prediction. The corporation invests abroad because no domestic use for its funds offers a higher expected return. But the firm does not consider investment in *every* other home industry as an active alternative to investing abroad. International differences in profits within an industry are more likely to be influential. Thus, direct investment could be flowing from, say, America to Britain in the automobile industry while moving from the British to the American petroleum industry. Indeed, such crosshauls could even occur in the same industry when firms use direct investment to invade each other's markets.[5] The multinational corporation is popularly thought to be an American invention, and American managerial techniques and research and developmental outlays are both bountiful sources of the intangible capital that is profitably used through direct investment. Yet foreign-based multinationals also span the globe and operate successfully in U.S. markets.

Competition in Product Markets. Direct investment occurs, we argued, in industries with market structures of differentiated oligopoly. This pattern should hold for both the source and the host country. Does

[5] See Edward M. Graham, "Transatlantic Investment by Multinational Firms: A Rivalistic Phenomenon?" *Journal of Post-Keynesian Economics,* 1 (Fall 1978): 82–99.

direct investment make them more competitive than they would be in its absence, or does it reduce competition? With oligopoly, the answer is almost always "anything can happen." Let us consider some of the possibilities. Sometimes a foreign subsidiary is started from scratch; sometimes the parent buys out a domestic firm in the host country. The former course surely is more likely to increase competition. Buying out a domestic firm means that direct investment does not raise the number of sellers in the host country's market. On the other hand, a newly founded subsidiary may increase the competitiveness of the domestic industry. Natural forces often inhibit the entry of new firms into oligopolistic industries, and the established foreign firm may be a valuable aid in keeping markets reasonably competitive. Many people in countries that host large inflows of direct investment worry deeply lest the international corporation prove too competitive and drive all its domestic rivals to the wall.

Benefits from Direct Investment and Their Distribution

The significance of direct investment for economic welfare is a matter of fierce controversy. On the one hand, its supporters laud it for transferring to the host countries not just capital but also technology and managerial skills. On the other, its critics charge it with exploiting the local market, impairing the nation's sovereignty, and frustrating its economic policies. Hence we shall carefully define the benefits of foreign investment and explore their division between the source and host countries.

The primary gain (if any) from relocating productive resources is measured by the net increase in the value of output. This increase in turn should be reflected in the extra reward they receive in the new location. The extra profits an enterprise earns on its foreign investment, over the best domestic alternative (with certain assumptions), measure the social benefit of the investment. The same goes for any rents accruing to its managerial talent or other assets utilized abroad. For intangible capital — patents, trademarks, know-how — the *gross* rewards measure gain, because its use abroad does not preclude use at home. Who gets this arbitrage gain? What other effects on welfare does foreign investment have? Let us examine the issues as seen in source countries (homes of multinationals) and host countries (homes of their subsidiaries) in turn.

Policy Issues in Source Countries

Taxation of Corporate Incomes. An important factor determining how the benefits are divided between source and host is the way countries levy the corporate profits tax. The profits of American multinationals provide the basic gain from foreign investment for the United States. Yet the U.S. government is a major loser because standard tax practices both divert profits on the foreign investments of U.S. companies to foreign treasuries and also induce the companies to shift their profits abroad (and thus into the foreign tax collector's hands). The general rule among countries is that the host country is the first to tax the subsidiary's profits, and the company's tax payments to the host country are then offset against its tax liability to the source country when those profits are repatriated. An example shows what is involved. Suppose that both source and host countries levy a corporate profits tax of 50 percent, and that a company earns a rate of profit (before tax) of 20 percent in the host country, whereas it could have earned only 16 percent had it invested the same funds at home. When the 20 percent is earned, the host country's tax authorities get 10 percent. The corporation keeps the remaining 10 percent; when it repatriates these profits, they become liable for taxation in the source country, but the credit for taxes paid to the host nation just offsets this. Had the direct investment not occurred, the corporation would have earned 8 percent after a tax payment of 8 percent to the source country. The real net return to the foreign investment of 4 percent $(20 - 16)$ exceeds the net gain to the corporation of 2 percent $(10 - 8)$. However, the host country gains more than the real net return (10 percent, compared to 4 percent), and the source country loses on the transaction; the corporation and the tax authorities together garner 16 percent from the domestic investment, but only 10 from the foreign. Thus corporation profits taxation not only guarantees the host country a cut of the primary gains, but can even award it more than the extra real product and thus leave the source country worse off.

U.S. tax law also creates an incentive for corporations to move profits onto their subsidiaries' books (e.g., by undercharging them for research or management services) whenever the host country's corporation tax rate is lower than that of the United States. This incentive arises because profits earned abroad are not subject to U.S. taxation until they are actually repatriated. A dollar of profit earned domestically cannot be reinvested before the tax collector takes his slice, but the whole of that same dollar earned abroad may be available for reinvestment.

Income Distribution. If capital is invested abroad, less remains at home to cooperate with labor in the source country. Unless relative factor prices are locked into place through their link to world product prices (see Chapter 7), wages are likely to fall just as the reward to capital rises. The process was described (for labor migration) in section 10.2. American labor has become highly conscious of this possibility and has pressed for legislation that would sharply restrict foreign investment "to protect American jobs." Although traditional economic theory says that labor is right, recent research in fact leans the other way. Foreign investment appears to an important degree complementary with U.S. exports; the subsidiary establishes distribution facilities and discovers markets abroad that actually encourage the parent's exports to that market and thereby increase its domestic output. Hence it is not clear that American labor in fact loses. Some studies have estimated rather large losses for U.S. labor, but they all neglect the link through product markets between American and foreign prices, which causes them to be seriously biased upward.[6]

Policy Issues in Host Countries

Just as profits from foreign investment are a major source of benefit to source countries, the taxes collected on these profits are also an important benefit to the hosts. In addition, hosts benefit substantially from any activities of foreign subsidiaries that incidentally raise the productivity of their own factor stocks. The subsidiary may show its local suppliers how to achieve better quality control, or its way of distributing its output may improve the general productivity of the distribution sector. Some of the knowledge comprising the intangible capital of the multinational corporation may leak out to its local competitors as they seek to emulate its success (or resist its competitive pressure).[7] The size of these gains — indeed, whether they are substantial at all — will vary from subsidiary to subsidiary and from host country to host country. Subsidiaries of manufacturing firms operating in developed countries like Australia and Great Britain have been found to extend significant productivity benefits of this sort. At the other extreme, a capital-intensive subsidiary operating in a less-developed country and making few transactions with local enterprises may have few secondary benefits.

Despite these benefits the prevailing attitude in host countries is one of hostility toward foreign investment. Even in the United States some members of Congress have expressed concern over the increasing number of foreign-owned enterprises! Let us examine some typical host-country issues.

High Profits. Subsidiaries' profits are "too high." There is no doubt that international corporations win high profits. This is hardly a surprise. They operate in industries where elements of oligopoly permit

[6] For a good discussion of these issues see C. Fred Bergsten, Thomas Horst, and Theodore H. Moran, *American Multinationals and American Interests.* Washington: The Brookings Institution, 1978, chaps. 2–3.

[7] For a survey of these effects in Australia, see Donald T. Brash, *American Investment in Australian Industry.* Canberra: Australian National University Press, 1966, chap. 8.

more than a competitive level of profits. Furthermore, the profit records that are observed and complained of naturally belong to subsidiaries that survive and prosper; the failures are ignored. Finally, within their industries the international corporations are the more efficient and hence the more profitable. Considering these explanatory factors, where does the complaint about high profits point? A good case can be made for procompetitive (or antitrust) policies bearing on subsidiaries and home-owned firms alike. Such a policy should be superior to one often proposed: tying the hands of subsidiaries and thereby awarding more monopoly power to their domestic rivals.

Resource Rents. The controversies over subsidiaries' profits are especially bitter when the subsidiaries extract natural resources. Their profits often derive not so much from market power as from rents from high-quality deposits of natural resources. Companies often secure concessions to develop these resources for relatively modest payments, simply because it is difficult to foretell their value. When large rents do materialize, the public grows irate at foreigners carrying off the wealth of their soil. As Professor Kindleberger remarks in his *American Business Abroad*, there is a little bit of the peasant in each of us. Subsidiaries extracting natural resources, traditionally a target for nationalization, are now often caught in "the obsolescing bargain." That is, they commit fixed investment to an extractive operation in a foreign land on some expected terms of local taxation. Once the investment is in place, however, the host government starts raising the tax bill. The government need leave the company only enough revenue to cover its out-of-pocket costs in order to keep the operation going. The company may therefore suffer a large loss on its investment. The threat of the obsolescing bargain has strongly encouraged multinationals to lend only their managerial skills to foreign operations and not their capital.[8]

Research and Development. Multinationals undertake most of their research in the source country and thus deny research and development activities to the host country. The multinationals usually centralize their basic research activities in their home country and undertake research in the host countries primarily to develop and adapt their products to local conditions more efficiently. Frequently, as in this instance, it is hard to grasp what alternative practices the complainers would prefer. Should the multinational corporation decentralize its research, perhaps losing some efficiency? It would still capture the profits from its discoveries (and incur the losses from its failures). A greater demand for host-country nationals in research jobs would be felt, but the reason for a nation's gains from research (as opposed to other skilled or professional activity) is not clear. People often treat science and re-

---

[8] Bergsten, Horst, and Moran, chap. 5.

search as "consumption goods," as if the nation's benefit depended on the number of its citizens wearing white coats and shaking test tubes, rather than upon its access to the fruits of research (wherever carried out). The ease with which research results travel across national boundaries suggests that this attitude is not rational.

Submission to Public Policy. Because of its international connections the subsidiary enjoys alternatives not open to home-owned firms, and it can often take successful evasive action when the screws of public policy are applied. For instance, confronted with new social legislation that raises production costs, it may channel any expansion of capacity to another country. Its ease of lending and borrowing internationally may frustrate the use of direct macroeconomic controls for internal or external balance. Does this freedom warrant restricting its activities? Here again the question of the alternative arises. A policy that causes a subsidiary to move its activities elsewhere might simply put a home-owned firm in the same straits out of business. A government whose policies fight market forces should ask whether it is using the most effective possible policies. The answer may be no. Even if its policies must clash with the market, it is hardly clear, as a general proposition, that reducing firms' sensitivities to market forces improves economic welfare overall.

Vulnerability to Foreign Government Pressure. The subsidiary is the servant of two political masters — the government of the country in which it dwells, and the government sovereign over its parent. Here lies a fundamental conflict of sovereignties, for which no easy remedy has been found. Efforts by the U.S. government to pressure foreign subsidiaries through their American parents have aroused more rancor than any purely profit-seeking actions by the subsidiaries themselves. A famous episode occurred in 1957 when the Ford Motor Company's Canadian subsidiary was exploring the possibility of a large sale of trucks to mainland China. At that time Canada's policy permitted and even encouraged an expansion of trade with China, while the United States sought to prohibit trade altogether. Washington voiced its displeasure, and parent Ford laid a restraining hand on its errant Canadian offspring, to the great displeasure of many Canadians.[9] Later interventions in Chile on behalf of IT&T are even more notorious. There is no doubt that the source-country government can get at the subsidiary through the parent; to a lesser degree, the host-country government can affect the parent through the subsidiary. No resolution exists short of an agreement of governments to keep hands off.

[9] See L. A. Litvak and C. J. Maule, "Conflict, Resolution, and Extraterritoriality," *Journal of Conflict Resolution,* 13 (September 1969): 306–15.

Structure of Political Forces. Business managers are an important interest group in any political system. Managers of foreign subsidiaries do not behave the same way politically as do domestic entrepreneurs. Some complaints about foreign investment simply assert a preference for a political system without foreign businessmen. In its usual form, this plaint stresses the possibility of foreign influence intruding on the national political scene and frustrating the sovereign will of the nation's own citizens. However, A. O. Hirschman has complained (from the perspective of Latin American politics) that foreign businesses are too timid; he would prefer assertive domestic entrepreneurs, as a counterweight to domestic political groups of whom he disapproves.[10]

These complaints about the foreign firm have been arranged to move from the purely economic to the purely political. To evaluate them broadly, they identify no systematic and severe economic costs of direct investment to the host country, although they certainly reveal offsets that must be chalked against the benefits conveyed. They do raise, however, the problem of national sovereignty pervading international economic policy. A nation would be most sovereign if it could mold its economic policy without heed to the economic or political reactions of the rest of the world. Yet perfect sovereignty is hardly conceivable without perfect isolation from the rest of the world. Hence, gaining the benefit of specialization and exchange means tolerating economic and political links to the rest of the world that create both constraints and opportunities for policy-making, but in any case cannot be prudently ignored. Economists are prone to urge policies designed to get the best of both worlds — to secure the benefits of international exchange and to use the leverage for policy provided by international sensitivities rather than fighting it. But this is not a complete answer to the nationalist who would rather ignore the existence of the rest of the world, even at some cost of real income to himself.

10.4 SUMMARY

The efficiency of the world economy can generally be increased if factors of production are mobile among countries. Commodity trade is a substitute for factor mobility, but generally an incomplete one. However, inflows of a factor to a country generally redistribute incomes among

---

[10] Albert O. Hirschman, *How to Divest in Latin America, and Why,* Essays in International Finance, no. 76. Princeton: International Finance Section, Princeton University, 1969.

factors already there, just as they raise real income overall. Immigration of labor reduces wages but raises the returns to capital. Inflows of a sector-specific factor would depress the rewards to that factor and to other specific factors but raise the wages of the general factor, labor.

Direct investment typically involves the creation of a subsidiary abroad by a corporation. It is thus sector-specific, and usually occurs in certain market structures. Some companies invest abroad to obtain sources of raw materials or other inputs (backward vertical integration); others acquire subsidiaries that produce the same product line as their parent (horizontal integration). Horizontal investment is an alternative to exporting, and thus direct investment should be sensitive to the exchange rate. It is also influenced by the host country's tariffs. Like other factor flows, foreign investment tends to create a real benefit by moving resources from less to more productive uses. The profit earned by the multinational company constitutes much of this benefit for the source country, but established conventions on corporate income taxation may cause much of the gain to be captured by the host country. The host also benefits from ways in which foreign investment raises the productivity of its own factor stock. Host countries often criticize multinationals for their high profits or rents from natural resources, their centralization of research and development in the parent, their access to alternative actions when squeezed by public policy, and their vulnerability to political meddling by the source country's government.

SUGGESTIONS FOR FURTHER READING

Baldwin, Robert E., and J. David Richardson, eds. *International Trade and Finance: Readings.* 2nd ed. Boston: Little, Brown and Co., 1981. Nos. 12 and 16–18 deal with multinational companies.

Bergsten, C. Fred, Thomas Horst, and Theodore H. Moran. *American Multinationals and American Interests.* Washington: The Brookings Institution, 1978. Treats many issues of behavior and public policy.

Brash, Donald T. *American Investment in Australian Industry.* Canberra: Australian National University Press, 1966. Survey of effects on one host country.

Caves, Richard E. "International Corporations: The Industrial Economics of Foreign Investment," *Economica,* 38 (February 1971): 1–27. Implications of "industry-specific" direct investment.

Hood, Neil, and Stephen Young. *The Economics of Multinational Enterprise.* London: Longman Group Ltd., 1979. Useful survey of the literature on multinational companies.

Johnson, Harry G. "Some Economic Aspects of Brain Drain," *Pakistan Development Review,* 7 (August 1967): 379–411. Treats some problems of international labor mobility.

Reuber, Grant L., et al. *Private Foreign Investment in Development.* Oxford: Clarendon Press, 1973. Behavior of multinational companies in less-developed countries.

Vernon, Raymond. *Sovereignty at Bay: The Multinational Spread of U.S. Enterprises.* New York and London: Basic Books, 1971. Survey of evidence on behavior of U.S. subsidiaries abroad.

III

THE THEORY
AND PRACTICE OF
COMMERCIAL POLICY

11

Tariffs and the National Welfare

Free trade brings benefits to all nations. This theme forms the foundation for any basic discussion of international trade. However, for centuries most countries have felt compelled to interfere with the smooth flow of commodities by erecting tariff barriers or other obstacles to trade. Part 3 of this book examines the nature of such impediments, asks how they may benefit special groups, and discusses attempts at cooperation in commercial policy both at the regional level (customs unions such as the European Common Market) and in larger groupings. The focus in the present chapter is on one weapon of commercial policy — the tariff — and its broad effects on national and international welfare.

11.1 THE TARIFF FOR A SMALL COUNTRY

A tariff is a tax on the importation of a commodity from abroad. If the country levying the tariff is small, the tariff has little effect on the world price of the commodity. Instead, the foreign commodity becomes more expensive at home behind the tariff wall both to producers of the commodity (who can be expected to support the tariff) and to local consumers (who will likely oppose the duty). In general, a tariff attracts resources to the protected sector and shifts demand away from foreign goods. On both counts a tariff reduces a small country's imports.[1]

---

[1] We shall always assume that the tariff rate is quoted on an *ad valorem* basis. This means that the domestic price of imports, say p_F, equals a multiple, $(1 + t)$, of the world price, p_F^*. The tariff rate is sometimes quoted as a percentage of the foreign price — e.g., $100t$ might be 28 percent. For an ad valorem tariff rate, t, the absolute

FIGURE 11.1   The Effect of a Tariff on Production

The initial free-trade prices are shown by line 1, production is at *A*, and national income, measured in units of food, is *OF*. A tariff on imports of food raises the domestic relative price of food as shown by line 2. Resources are shifted into food; production moves to point *B*. At world prices national income in food units has been reduced to *OD* (line 3 is parallel to line 1).

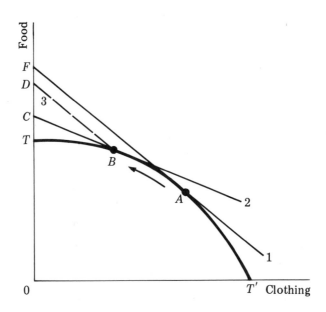

Tariffs and Production

Figures 11.1 and 11.2 are designed to highlight separately the impact of a tariff on production and on demand. Curve *TT'* in Figure 11.1 shows full-employment production possibilities for a small country initially producing food and clothing at point *A*, facing free-trade relative prices shown by the slope of line 1. Suppose the country imports food and proceeds to levy a tariff on food imports, thus raising the domestic

wedge separating home and foreign prices would rise if the foreign price rises. A different kind of tariff is the *specific* tariff — a rate quoted in absolute dollars per physical unit (e.g., \$2.10 a ton). If t' denotes this amount, p_F would equal $(p_F^* + t')$. An inflation of world prices would in such a case leave the absolute tariff wedge unchanged (and diminish its relative significance).

FIGURE 11.2   The Effect of a Tariff on Demand

Production remains at *A* on the right-angled *TAT'* transformation schedule.
A tariff raises the relative domestic price of food to line 2 (parallel to lines
3 and 4). Food consumption falls by the substitution effect (from *G* to *H*)
plus an income effect (from *H* to *J*). Distance *EC* measures the tariff
revenue in terms of food. The trade triangle shrinks from *GKA* to *JLA*.

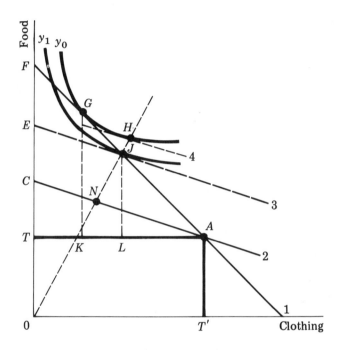

relative price of food by the amount of the tariff. The posttariff *domestic*
price ratio is shown by line 2, while the country's terms of trade are
still given by the slope of line 1. The tariff attracts resources to food,
driving up the opportunity cost in this sector until local costs reflect
the new higher domestic food price, at *B*.

In terms of domestic prices, production point *B* maximizes the value
of national production. And, yet, output evaluated at *world* prices has
fallen: Line 3 is parallel to line 1 so that national income in food units
at world prices is reduced from *OF* to *OD*. This is a signal that a small
country does itself harm by levying a tariff on imports.

Tariffs and Demand

The analysis of the impact of tariffs on demand is complicated by the fact that a tariff not only drives up the relative price of food imports to consumers, it also raises revenue. The assumption typically made about the tariff revenue is that it is redistributed back to the public. This may take the form of reductions in other taxes (say, income taxes) to balance the tariff revenue. In any case, we assume that the public's disposable income (and expenditure) consists now not only of produced income but also of the tariff revenue.[2] But this means that import demand depends partly on how much tariff revenue is raised, and the amount of tariff revenue raised depends on the quantity of imports demanded.

Figure 11.2 illustrates the effect of a tariff on import demand when we abstract from production changes. The production-possibilities schedule is the right-angled box TAT', serving to keep production fixed at point A. The initial free-trade terms of trade are shown by line 1, with the community's best consumption point at G. Distance GK represents the free-trade level of food imports, matched by clothing exports of amount KA.

A tariff raises the relative price of food imports to consumers and, as well, results in tariff revenues being collected and redistributed. The dotted line $ONJH$ in Figure 11.2 has been constructed to connect all possible consumption points consistent with the higher relative domestic price of food. (This *locus* is called an incomes-consumption line. For example, points N, J, and H are consumption bundles demanded at the new domestic prices and incomes shown by lines 2, 3, and 4 respectively.) Suppose posttariff prices are reflected in the slope of lines 2, 3, and 4 (all parallel). If consumers could stay on initial indifference curve y_0, the rise in food's price would evoke the substitution effect involved in moving from G to H. But income level y_0 cannot be maintained. The value of consumption at world prices must exactly match the value of production. Thus, point J is the consumption point chosen after the tariff is imposed because it is the only point on $ONJH$ that also lies on line 1 through production point A. All points on line 1 satisfy the requirement that quantities of clothing exported match demand for food as imports *at world prices*.

In terms of domestic prices, line 3 is the posttariff budget line. It is above a parallel line (2) through production point A. This reflects the fact that consumers' disposable income exceeds the value of production by the amount of the tariff revenue (EC in units of food). However, note

---

[2] An alternative procedure has the government keeping the tariff proceeds and spending them according to its own taste patterns, which may differ from those of the private sector. Our strategy of having the tariff proceeds redistributed allows us to consider a single set of preferences for the entire community.

that the tariff has harmed consumers — pushing them to consumption point J, which lies on a lower indifference curve than does G.

Tariffs and Imports

A nation's imports reflect both its demand for the importable commodity and its domestic production of that same commodity. Figure 11.1 was designed to show how a tariff encourages a greater production of importables. Production was kept fixed in Figure 11.2 in order to highlight the effect of a tariff in cutting demand for importables. These two strands are brought together in Figure 11.3. The free-trade equilibrium production and consumption points are represented by points A and G respectively, with the slope of line 1 indicating the fixed relative world price of clothing to food. A tariff on food raises the relative domestic price of food and encourages greater local production. This effect is shown by the move from A to B, where line 2 shows posttariff domestic prices. Line 4 is parallel to line 1, and shows combinations of clothing and food that have the same value at world prices as does the production point, B. The home country's consumption bundle after the tariff must lie somewhere along line 4; specifically it must rest at J where indifference curve y_1 has a slope equal to the *domestic* price ratio (line 3 is parallel to line 2). The home country's demand for imports has been reduced from GK to JL — a combination of greater production and lessened demand for food.

Tariffs and Welfare

In Figure 11.3 the tariff lowers real income from curve y_0 to curve y_1. At given world prices the tariff has lowered the aggregate value of production (compare OF with OD). Furthermore, point J is not even the best consumption point along line 4 because the tariff causes domestic prices (line 3) to be distorted away from world prices (shown by the slope of line 4).

This loss of real income may seem all the more noteworthy because with a tariff the home country receives tariff revenue, which, we assume, is passed on to consumers. Evaluated at the relative domestic price of food, the value of incomes earned in production after the tariff is distance OC in Figure 11.3. The tariff revenue is CE, and the budget line appropriate to domestic consumers is line 3, which lies *outside* the transformation curve (by the amount of the tariff revenue). However, the best point along line 3 (point J) is inferior to the best point (G) along the pretariff budget line 1, in which there was no tariff revenue.

Both domestic prices and world prices have a welfare significance that

FIGURE 11.3   The Effect of a Tariff on Imports

A tariff raises the domestic relative price of food (shown by lines 2 and 3) above the fixed world price (shown by lines 1 and 4). Domestic production of food rises from A to B. Domestic consumption of food falls from G to J. The trade triangle shrinks from GKA to JLB.

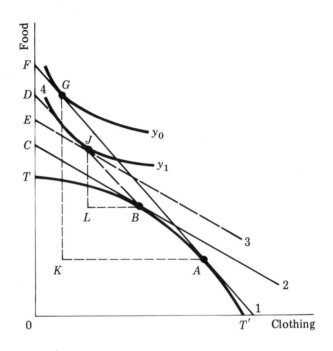

helps reveal why a tariff for a small country lowers national well-being. Domestic prices reflect the community's relative evaluation of commodities. (Marginal rates of substitution are equated to domestic price ratios.) World prices reflect costs of obtaining a commodity via trade. If a tariff is erected, the cost to the community of obtaining another unit of food imports (as measured by the required export of clothing at world prices) is *lower* than the value to the community of consuming another unit of food (as measured by the slope of indifference curves, or by the *domestic* price of food). This discrepancy between value and cost indicates that the purchase (at world prices) of another unit of food would yield more in satisfaction than would be sacrificed in cost. And yet the tariff has *reduced* imports instead and, thus, has lowered welfare. It has reduced imports both by reducing demand *and* by increasing local production. (In Figure 11.3 food imports have been reduced from *GK* to *JL*.)

11.2 THE IMPACT OF A TARIFF ON
WORLD AND DOMESTIC PRICES

We have shown that a tariff must reduce import demand and the sup-ply of exports at the initially prevailing world prices. If the tariff-levying country is not small in relation to world markets, its tariff will drive down the world relative price of imports or, equivalently, raise the rela-tive world price of its exports. The tariff can improve a country's terms of trade.

This point can be illustrated by the net home import demand curve, M, and foreign export supply curve, X^*, in Figure 11.4. The vertical axis measures the *world* relative price of food (hence the asterisks). In section 11.1 we showed that at any *given* terms of trade a tariff would cut back home demand for imports — from Q to A at the initial terms of trade in Figure 11.4. More generally, the home demand curve for imports, M, shifts to the left to M'.

The home country is not "small" in Figure 11.4. This is revealed by the fact that the new world trade equilibrium at Q' shows that the home country's tariff has lowered the relative price of imported food on world markets. That is, a country can use a tariff to improve its terms of trade. It acts like a seller of a commodity who finds himself with some monopoly power. By controlling supply, he can exercise some in-fluence over price. Just as a tariff reduces the home country's import demand at given world terms of trade, so does it reduce the quantity of exports supplied. Looked at in this way, a tariff is a means of forcing up the relative price of a country's exports on world markets. An improve-ment in the terms of trade means both a reduction in the world relative price of imports and an increase in the relative price of exports — they are the same thing. We should remember that although the government of the tariff-levying country can act like a monopolist, we still assume that private firms are numerous enough to act competitively.

If a tariff depresses the relative *world* price of imports, the *domestic* relative price of imports cannot rise by the full extent of the tariff. This relation points to a conflict in the motives lying behind the use of a tariff. Tariffs often aim to protect local import-competing industries, which wish to raise the domestic price of the commodities they produce. If the foreign supply curve is infinitely elastic, the domestic relative price of food rises by the full extent of the tariff. The foreign supply curve in Figure 11.4 does allow the tariff to depress the relative world price of food to some extent. If the foreign supply curve had been more

FIGURE 11.4   A Tariff Improves the Terms of Trade

The initial free-trade equilibrium is at Q, with the relative *world* price of food shown on the vertical axis at B. A tariff shifts the home import demand schedule leftward from M to M', and lowers the world relative price of food (to Q').

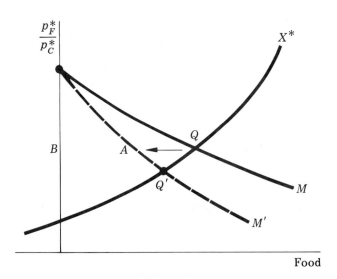

Food

inelastic, the world terms of trade would have improved by a greater amount.

There remains the curious possibility that a tariff might depress the relative world price of a country's import commodity to such an extent that the *domestic* price of imports falls as well.[3] In our example, the relative price of food could fall by a greater amount than the tariff itself. The important feature of such a possibility is that the tariff fails to protect the import-competing sector of the economy. Instead, it would drive resources toward the export sector. Yet this is just the case in which a tariff leads to a large gain in the world terms of trade.

The precise conditions required for a tariff to fail to protect need not concern us here. Needless to say, they require a low foreign elasticity of

[3] The argument that a tariff may fail to raise the price of the protected commodity behind the tariff wall is found in Lloyd Metzler, "Tariffs, the Terms of Trade, and the Distribution of National Incomes," *Journal of Political Economy*, 57 (February 1949): 1–29; reprinted in Caves and Johnson, eds., *Readings in International Economics*. Homewood, Ill.: Richard D. Irwin, 1968, chap. 2.

supply. Disturbances such as tariffs require large price adjustments when response to price changes (which is what elasticities measure) is low.

11.3 TARIFFS AND DOMESTIC WELFARE

If a country can improve its terms of trade by commercial policy, why is it not always beneficial to keep levying higher and higher tariffs to obtain ever better terms of trade? Our analysis of the small country case in section 11.1 should warn us that there is more to the argument than this: If a country cannot improve its terms of trade a tariff will actually harm welfare. There are two forces conflicting with each other in influencing the impact of a tariff on domestic welfare.

Figure 11.5 shows how welfare is linked to the height of the tariff for a country able to improve its terms of trade by trade restriction. We assume there is some rate of duty, t_1, large enough to choke off all trade. If such a tariff were applied, all gains from trade would be wiped out. Free trade (a zero tariff) is superior to no trade (with tariff equal to t_1 or

---

FIGURE 11.5   Domestic Welfare Depends on the Tariff Rate

Free trade leads to a level of real income indexed by *OA*. For a country with some influence on world prices, a tariff can improve its terms of trade and lead initially to a gain in real income. Rate t_0 is the optimum tariff. Higher rates of duty cost more in foregone opportunities to import than is gained by a lowering of import prices. Rate t_1 cuts off all imports, and leads to a level of real income identical to that of the no-trade state, which is lower than the free-trade level, *OA*.

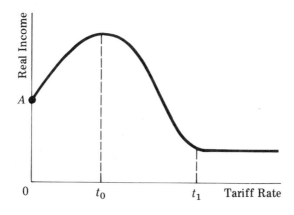

higher), so that the curve in Figure 11.5 is lower after t_1 than initially at A. Furthermore, the terms-of-trade improvement that would be brought about when a small tariff is first levied must improve welfare. There obviously must be some intermediate tariff rate, t_0, that is "optimal" in the sense of maximizing the level of domestic welfare.

Here we are not concerned with the value of the "optimal tariff." [4] Instead, it is important to understand the nature of the conflict between the two effects of a tariff on welfare. A tariff improves the terms of trade. By itself this raises welfare. But the terms-of-trade improvement has been deliberately engineered by having the tariff choke off local import demand. And any reduction in imports must serve to lower domestic welfare if the *cost* of obtaining these imports (as shown by *world* prices) is lower than their *value* at home (as shown by *domestic* prices). A tariff is a wedge that raises domestic prices above world prices. Too high a tariff rate causes a greater loss through foregone opportunities to import than that gained by the favorable price drop on remaining imports.

Throughout this discussion we have assumed that the foreign country passively allows the home country to pursue whatever commercial practices it pleases while it retains a policy of free trade. This assumption overlooks the very real possibility of retaliation by the foreign country in the form of its own tariff. Any foreign tariff worsens the terms of trade for the home country. If the foreign country does retaliate because of a tariff levied at home, it is no longer clear that the home country can benefit. Many outcomes of such a tariff war are possible. As we shall relate in Chapter 13, much of the tariff history of the major trading nations for the past forty years has been characterized by multilateral attempts to reduce tariff barriers, in full awareness of the dangers of escalation when a single country pursues an active commercial policy on its own.

11.4 TARIFFS AND WORLD WELFARE

Supporters of the free-trade doctrine point to the loss in *world* efficiency entailed by a tariff. Although the tariff-levying countries might gain, others stand to lose *more*. This argument focuses upon the dead-weight loss introduced by the *distortion* that a tariff creates between prices in one country and another. To probe further, we shall consider the argument in two stages: the effect of a tariff on world production, and the effect of a tariff on world consumption possibilities given the levels of production.

---

[4] This is computed in the supplement to Chapter 11 and illustrated by means of the offer-curve diagram in the appendix.

A tariff on food in the home country raises the relative price of food above its level in the foreign country. This higher price is reflected in a difference in the slopes of the two countries' transformation curves. Figure 11.6 superimposes the point showing production on the foreign transformation schedule — drawn upside down — on the point showing production at home. The production point is Q, and the tariff wedge separating relative prices at home and abroad causes price line 1 at home to be flatter than price line 2 abroad. The point 0^* shows posttariff world outputs of food and clothing relative to the axes through 0. If the tariff were removed, resources in each country would be shifted into the

---

FIGURE 11.6 A Tariff and World Production

Point Q represents production at home and abroad. The foreign transformation schedule, $T^*T^{*\prime}$, is upside down so that total world production is shown by O^*. The home country's tariff on food imports leads to a higher relative price of food at home (shown by line 1) than abroad (shown by line 2). If the tariff is removed, both countries would face the same price ratio; e.g., the common slope at A and B. If B is superimposed upon A, total world production expands from O^* to C.

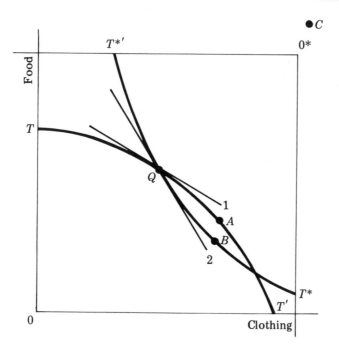

commodity in which that country possesses a comparative advantage — clothing at home and food abroad. Points A and B represent possible free-trade production points. The slope of TT' at A equals the slope of $T^*T^{*'}$ at B, and if B were to be superimposed upon A, total world outputs would expand from 0^* to C.

One consequence of a tariff, therefore, is a reduction of world outputs below the free-trade level. But from a world point of view this is not the only consequence. Recall from Chapter 2 our discussion of the box diagram and the contract curve (Figure 2.7). For convenience the box is reproduced as Figure 11.7.

The imposition of the tariff on food in the home country causes domestic prices (as shown by the slope of line 1) to differ from foreign prices (given by the slope of line 2). Therefore, the tariff leads to a consumption allocation *off* the contract curve (such as point A). Compared with free-trade point D (the forces making D the free-trade point are not shown), the home country is better off with a tariff at A and the foreign country is made worse off. But world welfare has been reduced in the sense that A is worse for *both* parties than some point on the contract curve, such as B.

11.5 SUMMARY

Tariff theory has both "positive" and "normative" aspects. The positive aspects are the effects of a tariff on prices, consumption, production, and trade. Proceeding first with a "small" country's tariff we found that resources are shifted into the import-competing sector of the economy and demand is drawn away from the imported commodity. On both counts the country's demand for imports falls at the given world terms of trade. If a country is large enough for its actions to influence world prices, the contraction in import demand induced by the tariff will lower the country's relative price of imports and thus improve its terms of trade. We had to settle for a more ambiguous result concerning the relative domestic price of imports. Typically a tariff is "protective," because it raises the local price of the dutiable item, but if foreign response to price changes is sufficiently inelastic, the relative world price of imports could fall by more than the tariff itself. In that case a tariff on food would, paradoxically, lower the relative price of food behind the tariff wall.

The "normative" aspects of a tariff deal with its effect on welfare at home and abroad. The foreign country is hurt by the tariff — its terms of trade deteriorate. For the home tariff-levying country, however, there is more to consider than the possible improvement in the terms of trade. Once the domestic price of imports is higher than the world price, any further tariff increases may reduce imports of a commodity for which

FIGURE 11.7   The Tariff Pulls Consumption off the Contract Curve

Initial free-trade equilibrium is on the contract curve at D. The home country's tariff improves home welfare (to y_0) and reduces foreign welfare (to y_0^*), but pulls the consumption point off the contract curve (at A). A point such as B would improve *both* countries' welfare compared with tariff point A.

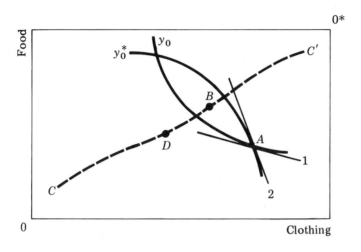

the cost of purchase abroad is less than the valuation at home (as measured by domestic prices). This loss in trade volume must be set against a terms-of-trade improvement in measuring the net benefits of a tariff. The extreme case of a tariff sufficiently high to choke off all trade shows that the optimal tariff must fall short of this. If the foreign country retaliates, the home country may end up with a lower level of real income than it obtained with free trade.

A tariff is an inferior way to redistribute income between countries. It introduces a distortion between domestic and world prices, and causes world outputs to settle at a suboptimal level while pushing consumption off the contract curve for any given levels of output. In this sense a tariff is a *second-best* instrument from a world point of view. Other means of redistributing income internationally — e.g., a direct gift from the foreign country to the home country — might allow both countries to emerge with a higher level of real income than with a distortionary tariff. This "second-best" concept has wider applicability to other arguments for tariffs, as we shall see in Chapter 12.

SUGGESTIONS FOR FURTHER READING

Jones, Ronald W. "Tariffs and Trade in General Equilibrium: Comment," *American Economic Review,* 59 (June 1969): 418–24. A brief analysis of basic tariff theory.

Metzler, Lloyd. "Tariffs, the Terms of Trade, and the Distribution of National Incomes," *Journal of Political Economy,* 57 (February 1949): 1–29. A more extensive account of tariff theory, concentrating on the effect of tariffs on domestic prices.

APPENDIX:
TARIFFS AND THE OFFER CURVE

The offer-curve construction described in the appendix to Chapter 3 is particularly useful in illustrating the impact of a tariff and the concept of the optimal tariff.

In pursuing the geometry we explicitly introduce a simplifying assumption: the home country is completely specialized in producing its export commodity, clothing. The constant level of clothing output is shown in Figure 11.A.1 by distance $O_T O_C$ (O_T refers to the *trading* origin and O_C to the *consumption* origin). The home offer curve, OR, intersects the foreign offer curve, OR^*, at point Q, establishing the slope of ray $O_T Q$ as the equilibrium terms of trade (the world relative price of clothing). That part of clothing production not exported is available for consumption at home, so that relative to the O_C origin any point in the diagram shows the home consumption bundle of food and clothing.

Two indifference curves have been drawn. The curve y_0 is tangent to ray $O_T Q$; this is why point Q was selected at those prices. Clearly other points on the foreign offer curve OR^* would represent more favorable trades for the home country. Point B lies on a higher indifference curve (not drawn). The curve tangent to the foreign offer curve, y_1, shows the maximal utility level possible for the home country to obtain.

How does the home country get to point A on curve y_1? By levying a tariff. As illustrated in the text, a tariff decreases the demand for imports and supply of exports at any given world terms of trade. That is, it shifts the offer curve in toward the origin. The *optimal tariff* rate is that which leads to the tariff-ridden offer curve $O_T R'$. Such a tariff has caused the relative *world* price of food, the commodity imported at home, to fall. This is shown by the greater slope of a ray from O_T through point A. The relative *domestic* price of food has slightly increased; the slope of indifference curve y_1 at its point of tangency with the foreign offer curve at A indicates the domestic relative price of clothing. The wedge between the two prices shows the optimal tariff rate. (A formula for this rate is provided in the supplement.)

Imagine the country achieving the optimal tariff in small stages — gradually shifting its offer curve in until point A is reached. For equilibrium points between Q and B on the foreign offer curve the home country is clearly being made better off as each tariff increase results in greater home consumption

FIGURE 11.A.1   The Optimal Tariff

A tariff that shifts home offer curve *OR* to *OR'* is optimal. Home real income at point A is greater than at any other point on the foreign offer curve, *OR**.

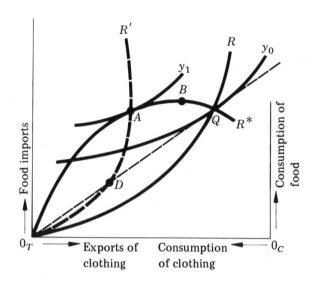

of *both* commodities; this is the result of the foreign country's offer curve being inelastic in this range. Past point *B* increases in the tariff rate improve the home country's terms of trade, but at a sacrifice of a lower volume of trade. Finally, at point *A*, the loss from a further reduction in import volume (where the cost of imports — the world price — is lower than the value of imports — the domestic price) matches at the margin the gain from still better terms of trade.

The spirit of this analysis is that the home country has the power to set world prices, subject only to the constraint that at these prices foreigners buy and sell the amounts shown on their offer curve. This may not be borne out in practice; the foreign country might well retaliate with tariffs of its own. As we see in Chapter 13, tariff rates most often reflect a process of multilateral tariff negotiations.

12

The Political Economy of Tariffs

It would be naive to suppose that nations levy tariffs only after carefully weighing the pros and cons for the entire community. Instead, special sections or groups often find that their interest can be served by interfering with free trade despite a loss to others in the economy. These special interests often *are* served because the political process frequently rewards a minority with strong convictions in the face of relatively mild losses to each member of a majority. In addition, special circumstances may seem to warrant restrictive trade policies when deeper analysis reveals that other weapons in a nation's fiscal armory are more effective or impose lower social costs. Tariffs are frequently "second-best" devices in achieving social goals.

The bulk of this chapter is devoted to a discussion of this array of arguments for trade restriction. At the end of the chapter we take notice of the fact that many items of commerce are not final consumer goods but raw materials and intermediate goods. Tariffs on intermediate goods make us distinguish between nominal tariffs on final consumer goods and the implied "effective" tariffs on their assembly within the nation's borders.

12.1 THE TARIFF AS A DEVICE FOR RAISING REVENUE

Long before the progressive income tax and other sophisticated instruments were devised to provide governments with necessary revenues, the

FIGURE 12.1   Tariff Revenue and Real Income

The curve showing tariff revenue reaches a peak at a higher rate of tariff than does the curve showing real income.

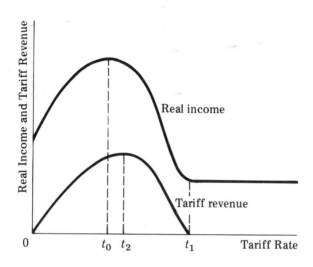

government agent at the port of entry typically extracted his toll on the inflow of merchandise from abroad. Any tariff rate that is not so high as to be prohibitive is a source of revenue. Although modern industrial states rarely rely on customs duties as a source of revenue, less developed regions often do.

The relationship between a tariff's impact on real income and on tariff revenue is expressed in Figure 12.1. A zero tariff yields no revenue. Tariff rate t_1 is assumed to be prohibitive, so that higher rates of duty as well yield no revenue. In the diagram we assume that revenues rise continuously, reaching a peak for rate t_2, and, as imports dwindle evermore, fall continuously to zero at rate t_1. The crucial point to notice is that the revenue-maximizing rate, t_2, exceeds the optimal tariff rate, t_0. An algebraic proof is provided in the supplement to this chapter. The geometric argument is provided in Figure 12.2.

Production in Figure 12.2 is assumed to be locked in at corner point A along the TAT' transformation curve. This simplifies the argument.[1]

---

[1] The argument is strengthened if production responds along a smoothly bowed-out transformation schedule.

FIGURE 12.2   The Maximum Revenue Tariff
Exceeds the Optimal Tariff

Tariff revenue is shown by distance CA. In the neighborhood of a tariff that maximizes revenue, a small increase in the tariff rate will not change tariff revenue. Consumption point D is on a lower indifference curve than point B and corresponds to a higher tariff.

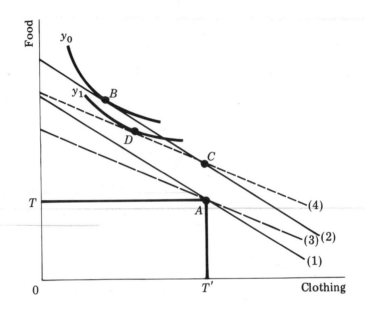

Consumption point B along indifference curve y_0 shows equilibrium with a tariff that has driven the domestic relative price of food imports to the height shown by lines (1) and (2).[2] Distance CA measures the tariff revenue in food units. Suppose the existing tariff rate maximizes tariff revenue, so that any further small rise in the tariff rate would leave tariff revenue unchanged (or slightly diminished). Thus in Figure 12.2 an increase in the tariff, which raises domestic food prices to the level shown by lines (3) and (4), leaves tariff revenue undisturbed at level CA. However, real income falls from y_0 to y_1 as consumption moves from B to D. This confirms Figure 12.1's illustration that the tariff rate, t_2, that maximizes tariff revenue exceeds the rate, t_0, that would maximize real income.

---

[2] The relative *world* price of clothing would be shown by the slope of a line connecting production point A with consumption point B.

That these two critical rates are not equivalent underscores the point that pursuing commercial policy for revenue purposes is not optimal strategy. Thus if at current tariff levels an increase in the rate of duty would lower tariff revenues, the current levels are too high for optimal welfare.

It is well at this point to recall that for a small country that cannot influence the world prices of what it buys and sells, the optimal tariff rate is zero. A tariff to raise revenue must then be rationalized by other arguments, e.g., the ease of collection on international commerce as compared with local sales or income taxes.

12.2 TARIFFS AND THE DISTRIBUTION OF INCOME

The American steel industry is one among many that feel threatened by foreign competition. What attitude toward tariffs or other protective devices would you expect from a steelworker especially trained in tasks that have little application outside the steel industry? Or from the owner of a specialized item of machinery that cannot be used for any other purpose than making steel? Productive factors that are tied to one industry or occupation are very much affected by trade and commercial policies. Special interests and specific factors employed in import-competing industries will usually favor trade restrictions.

If protection favors inputs specific to import-competing production, a counter-argument for free trade can be mounted by factors tied to the nation's export industries. The logic is there, but the argument is less obvious. We might not recognize that dismantling barriers to imports encourages prices and production in the export sectors.

The impact of relative price changes on the incomes of specific factors of production was analyzed in Chapter 6. But what of broad-based productive factors, such as relatively unskilled labor, which can move from one sector of the economy to another and which earn roughly the same wage in each? Our analysis in Chapter 6 suggested that such a factor is much less apt to be affected significantly by the price changes brought about by a tariff than are other factors (skilled labor, specific capital equipment) that are tied more closely to particular industries.

This conclusion tends to modify the "pauper labor" argument, which asserts that laborers in high-wage countries are hurt by competition from low-wage labor abroad. This argument tends to ignore that high wages reflect high productivity, made possible in part by ample supplies of cooperating productive factors (land, capital). Nonetheless, a germ of truth in the pauper labor argument is provided by the Heckscher-Ohlin model of production and trade, which we analyzed in Chapter 7. Suppose production in any sector requires only the services of two broad-based factors: capital and labor. Suppose, furthermore, that the high-wage country takes advantage of trading opportunities in order to import commodities that would be produced by labor-intensive techniques at home. A tariff that drives up the domestic price of these items serves as well to drive up the real wage. As we showed in the discussion in Chapter 7 of the Stolper-Samuelson result, a change in relative commodity prices gets transmitted into magnified changes in the returns to the two productive factors. One factor unambiguously gains from the tariff and the other factor loses. Such a strong result gets modified if there are more than two identifiable productive factors (such as in the specific factors case). Nonetheless, if a particular factor (say, labor) is intensively used in the production of import-competing goods, it may be expected to support a protectionist stance.

Can a factor of production whose wage is hurt by a tariff find sufficient relief in getting a cut of the tariff revenue? Once we consider the possibility of income redistribution through fiscal devices, logic demands that we ask how a tariff affects the community as a whole. This takes us back to the optimal tariff argument discussed in the previous chapter. For a "small" country (unable to affect world prices) free trade was optimal. For a country with some influence on world prices, some finite degree of protection seems attractive, but only if the danger of foreign retaliation is ignored.

However attractive the possibility of income redistribution through taxes and subsidies may appear in principle, the political facts of life suggest that such redistribution often fails to counteract the impact of commercial policy. There is no doubt that for many groups protectionist legislation helps support "artificially" high levels of income, and that such groups are not apt to be fobbed off with arguments about the welfare of the community as a whole.

12.3 THE TARIFF AS A "SECOND-BEST" DEVICE

Commercial policy can affect the economy in a variety of ways — by changing prices, outputs, employment, and incomes. But tariffs (and import quotas or other forms of trade restriction) are not the only weapons available to governments for influencing the economy. Taxes or subsidies on sales, production, consumption, or incomes of particular groups can also be employed. In many respects these taxes (or subsidies) are substitutes for commercial policy — but not perfect substitutes. Is a subsidy to production better or worse than a tariff? It depends very much on the objective of the policy interference. The tariff can often be used to help implement some social objective, but it proves frequently to be "second-best" to some alternative policy instrument. The following three cases suffice to make the general point.

1. *Production Goals*. Suppose that the free-trade level of production of some commodity is thought to be less than "desirable." Perhaps labor receives special valuable training in the production of this item. Or perhaps the community feels it should become more self-reliant on its own production in case foreign supplies are threatened in the future. (Witness the arguments about American dependence on foreign energy sources.) What is the optimal policy for encouraging greater domestic production?

Figure 12.3 illustrates the problem for the two-commodity case. Let food, the commodity being imported, represent the item that the community wishes to produce at levels exceeding the free-trade output. The latter is shown by point A along transformation schedule TT', with free-trade prices given by line 1, consumption by point B, and real income levels by indifference curve y_0. Let the desired higher quantity of food production be represented by distance OJ. To simplify matters, suppose that the country is so small that no change in its own policies can affect the world terms of trade.

A tariff on imports of food can shift resources into the import-competing sector to raise production from OI to OJ, the government's desired level of production of food. The domestic relative price of food rises, as shown by line 2. The new production point is at C and the consumption point is at E, with tariff revenue given by FG in units of the import commodity and the marginal rate of substitution along indifference curve y_1 at E reflecting the domestic price ratio. Trade has been restricted — imports of food, EK, are equal at world prices to exports, KC, of clothing. This illustration of the effect of a tariff exactly matches Figure 11.3.

Line HEC in Figure 12.3 has been drawn parallel to line 1 and therefore reflects the world terms of trade. Now suppose that instead of an import tariff the government had subsidized import-competing production, allowing resources to be shifted from the free-trade point, A, to point C on transformation curve TT'. The subsidy exactly offsets the higher costs of producing food at C compared with world prices. Consumers, however, are allowed to purchase commodities on the world market. Because line HEC, showing *world* prices, cuts indifference curve y_1 at E, consumers can reach the higher indifference curve, y_2, at H. If the government's goal has been to raise the production of food to OJ, it can achieve this goal by a tariff, but could also achieve it at a *smaller* sacrifice in welfare by a direct production subsidy. Using commercial (tariff) policy to achieve a production goal is inefficient compared with an approach directed expressly at producers without distort-

FIGURE 12.3 Tariffs vs. Production Subsidies
to Achieve a Production Goal

Free-trade production is at *A* and consumption at *B*. If *OJ* level of food
production must be undertaken, a tariff that raises food's relative price at
home to line 2 is sufficient. Consumption is then at *E*. A production subsidy could yield the same result for producers, but at a lower cost in welfare.
Consumption is at *H*.

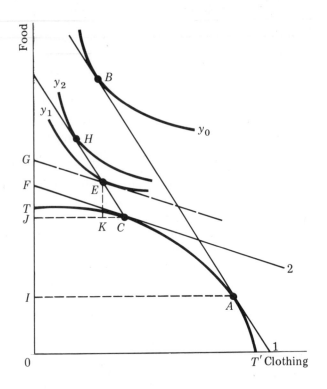

ing choices for consumers as well. Of course, the community as a whole
has still suffered the welfare loss in going from y_0 to y_2 in order to support production levels of food at *OJ*.[3] But presumably there is some
social gain attached to the achievement of the production goal.

2. *Consumption Goals.* Rather analogous remarks can be made about
the desire that some governments express to restrict consumption of

[3] This analysis can be found in W. M. Corden, "Tariffs, Subsidies, and the Terms
of Trade," *Economica*, N.S. 24 (August 1957): 235–42.

some items below the levels that the community would voluntarily choose in a free-trade situation. For example, the government may wish to restrict the private sector's consumption of imported automobiles or other items it deems to be unnecessary luxuries.

A tariff can accomplish the purpose; but so could a direct tax on consumption of the luxury item. These are different instruments, for a tax on consumption raises the price to consumers above the world level but leaves producers to face world competition at world prices. By contrast, a tariff would raise the domestic price to producers as well as consumers, and would encourage a transfer of domestic resources away from exportables and toward production of the luxury item. If the government's desire is solely to restrict *consumption*, needless losses are involved by using a tariff, for the production shift away from exportables causes the value of income produced at world prices to fall below its free-trade level.

Arguments for tariffs are often aimed at altering the production or consumption pattern of a free-trade regime. Heeding the pleas of special consumer or producer interests involves a loss in welfare to the nation as a whole. But the tariff affects both consumption and production; using it to alter either makes this loss larger than necessary. A more efficient instrument is a production tax or subsidy to change production or a consumption tax or subsidy if the government wishes to control consumption. In each case the instrument that works most directly on the objective should be used.[4]

3. *Domestic Distortions.* Market prices are not always perfect indicators of social costs and benefits. Occasionally elements of monopoly or of externalities in production or consumption distort market prices away from levels that represent social opportunity costs and values. For example, a commodity that enters a country's export lists may appear to have a low cost of production — and thus be exported — because no account is taken of pollution damage that is involved in the production process. (Firms may be dumping effluents into the country's streams and harbors at no cost to themselves but at considerable damage to the community.) In such cases it is possible to argue that levels of free trade are not optimal. Instead, those who would attempt to restrict exports (and imports) seem to find natural allies in ecologists and environmentalists. But once again we can show that trade restrictions offer

---

[4] Other examples and a more detailed discussion of the material in this section can be found in H. G. Johnson, "Optimal Trade Intervention in the Presence of Domestic Distortions," *Trade, Growth, and the Balance of Payments,* R. E. Baldwin et al. Chicago: Rand McNally, 1965. See also J. N. Bhagwati, "The Generalized Theory of Distortions and Welfare," *Trade, Balance of Payments, and Growth: Papers in International Economics in Honor of Charles P. Kindleberger,* eds. J. N. Bhagwati et al. Amsterdam: North-Holland, 1971, chap. 4.

only a "second-best" solution to a problem that is better met directly by consumption or production taxes that attempt to remedy the distortion.

If social and private costs differ, there is not only the danger that export levels, say, may be too high; it is also possible that the *pattern* of trade itself is distorted. To return to the pollution example, suppose that private marginal production costs excluding pollution costs fall short of costs in the rest of the world by less than the costs of pollution abatement. Then forcing producers to bear these costs would entail the industry shifting from being net exporters to becoming importers.

The reason why export taxes (or tariffs) are "second-best" devices in these examples is that it is either production or consumption levels that are distorted away from their socially optimal level, *not* trade levels. Commercial policy, by affecting *both* domestic consumption and production, is usually inefficient as a device for controlling either separately. Thus even though the achieved levels of trade may not be socially desirable (e.g., in the pollution case), trade policies designed to correct the situation involve unnecessary social costs.

12.4 COMMERCIAL POLICY AND ECONOMIC DEVELOPMENT

No survey of the reasons why countries have used tariffs and other restrictive devices is complete without a brief look at the special complaints often voiced by less-developed countries. Nations at early stages of development frequently view free trade as a set of arrangements that deliberately or unintentionally impedes their own industrialization efforts, notwithstanding the many counter-examples of trade serving as an "engine of growth" for many nations settled and developed during the nineteenth century.

One complaint about life in a trading world is that any nation — and especially a small, less-developed nation — to some extent loses control of its own destiny in being exposed to changes in world prices, demands, and supplies. This is an inevitable consequence of allowing production patterns to be based in large part not on local demands (over which the government presumably has some control) but on world tastes and the relative efficiency of local and foreign sources of supply. This introduces elements not only of "dependence" on foreigners but also of uncertainty as to the future course of the terms of trade. Such uncertainty can play havoc with tightly budgeted central planning.

Leaving uncertainty and "dependence" aside — features of trade that even wealthy, advanced countries cannot avoid (as learned by the United States and Western Europe during the recurring energy crises) — less-developed countries often argue that trade adversely affects the local structure of the economy in ways that can partly be avoided by judicious use of tariffs, quotas, and other devices that restrict and control trade. As we briefly survey these arguments you should note the "second-best" flavor of the case for trade restriction as compared with alternative development strategies.

1. *The Infant Industry Argument.* The term "infant" refers to young or not yet established industrial activities that are prevented from developing because local prices are kept too low by foreign competition. If only the "infant" could be allowed to develop, so the argument goes, the nation could establish a comparative advantage in these industries or, at the least, compete successfully at home given the natural protective umbrella of international transport costs. This is a time-honored argument — used, for example, by the American iron industry in the nineteenth century. But what guarantee is there that the "infant" will grow up even with tariff protection?

To probe further, note that it is not sufficient to argue that a protected, larger scale of output could result in driving down costs. Could protection ultimately be removed? Is the local protected market of sufficient size to provide the scale required to lower costs to foreign levels? Even if these questions can be answered in the affirmative, protection may not have been worthwhile for the community. Growing up takes time, and during this period consumers at home are paying more for goods than they would have done if resources had not been devoted to the protected sector. Any future gains must be discounted back to the present and set against these losses.

Suppose that even on such a calculation net gains may be had from developing the industry. Why won't this be apparent to private entrepreneurs? Business firms often make investments, the returns to which are spread out over future periods. That is, most investments involve a trade-off between present costs and future benefits, and if undertaken reflect an assessment that the present value of the benefits exceeds the costs. The argument for sheltering an industry during its growth is certainly weakened if prospective gains consist in economies of scale (average costs reduced with expansion of output) that are perceived by the firm.

The germ of truth in the infant-industry argument applies when the eventual gains from establishing the industry cannot all be recouped by those who have made the initial investments. Some form of externality must be present. To take an example, suppose workers gain by the skills learned during industrialization. These skills, deemed a gain to the community, can be transferred to other industries. That is, entrepreneurs in a particular sector may undergo costs of training the labor force that are subsequently lost to them if that labor moves to other occupations.[5] If so, it is maintained that protection should be given to offset these losses.

But is tariff protection the best way of supporting these industries? In the case just cited, where labor is improving its skills by on-the-job training, a direct production subsidy would not involve the consumption distortion imposed by the tariff. An even better device would aim at subsidizing the use of labor if indeed the externality involves primarily their skills.

2. _Growth, Protection, and Welfare._ If a country devotes newly available resources to its traditional export sectors, won't this encourage a drop in export prices? As we discussed in Chapter 4, in any country in which growth is biased toward exportables, that country's terms of trade will tend to worsen. Tariff policy can be used to encourage the local production of import-competing commodities, thus forestalling such a price deterioration in the export sector.

This kind of argument loses its force if the country under discussion is too small to affect world prices of its export commodity. Suppose this is the case, but that nonetheless the developing country has imposed tariffs on imports to support an import-competing industry over and above its free-trade level. We argued in the preceding chapter (see especially Figure 11.1) that such a diversion of resources entailed real income losses. But more can be said. As this country grows, its potential real income gains from growth are cut back the more it devotes its resources to the protected import-competing sector. In extreme cases, growth at home could even result in a loss of welfare.

Figure 12.4 illustrates these possibilities. Line 2 indicates world prices. The country has protected its import-competing sector, food, and so line 1, showing domestic prices behind the tariff wall, is flatter than line 2. At these protected prices the community's optimal production point along transformation schedule TT' is at tangency point A and consumption is at A'.

Now suppose that world prices remain unchanged and that the country's tariff structure is unaltered, but that the value of produced income at domestic prices rises by 25 percent. Points B, C, D, and E represent four possible alternative production points for which aggregate output at domestic prices would be 25 percent larger than at A. Point B is a point of balanced expansion relative to initial point A. For such a case, home consumption lies on a line through B with slope showing _world_ prices (i.e., parallel to line 2), point B'. Growth has increased real income. But suppose instead that only the import-competing sector had

---

[5] Note, however, that it is possible to argue that if laborers are aware of the value of skills learned in an industry, competition will drive wages in that industry below wage rates prevailing elsewhere in the economy.

FIGURE 12.4   Growth with Protection

With a tariff on food imports, line 1 showing domestic prices is flatter than line 2 showing world prices. *A'* is the initial consumption point corresponding to production along *TT'* at *A*. Growth to any of points *B*, *C*, *D*, and *E* shows a 25 percent increase in produced income at domestic prices. But corresponding consumption points *B'*, *C'*, *D'*, *E'* are not equivalent.

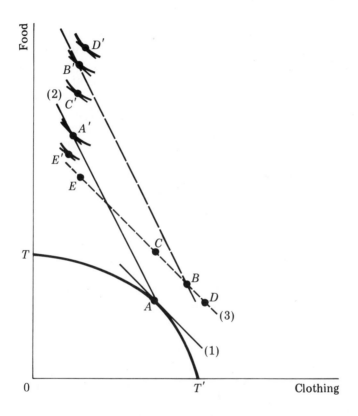

been allowed to grow (point *C* lies directly above point *A*). The real income gains would have been cut back, which is underlined by comparing the alternative of letting only the export sector expand (point *D* lies to the right of *A*). Consumption point *D'* is preferable to *B'* (which is preferable to *C'*).

Finally, consider the impact on welfare if resources are also actually forced away from exportables as a result of growth. Point *E* shows such a possible skewed growth point. Growth has been so biased in favor of the commodity (food) that is artificially high-priced at home that the seemingly higher-valued production point (compare E with A at domestic prices) represents an actual loss at world prices. This phenomenon could only occur if the import-competing sector is protected.[6]

The preceding argument is not meant conclusively to confirm a free-trade position. But it does point to the ongoing opportunity costs of protecting industries that compete with imports and distorting resources away from the export sector.

3. *Income Distribution and Domestic Saving.* Most developing countries are concerned with raising levels of investment, in part by borrowing overseas but also by encouraging domestic saving. We have seen that the distribution of income among productive factors can be radically affected by a policy of protection. Suppose that the factors differ in their propensities to save; owners of the factor used intensively in the import-competing sector save, say, 10 percent of any extra incomes, whereas the factor used intensively in exportables saves only 5 percent. A restriction of trade would then redistribute income toward the thriftier group and raise the average rate of saving. Many less-developed countries apparently believe that incomes earned by landowners from producing primary exports are not invested — or at least not invested in activities the government favors. If one makes that assumption, the most efficient policy is to tax landowner incomes directly. Export taxes, however, are often used as a second-best substitute.[7]

4. *Attracting Foreign Investment.* Another argument sometimes raised in favor of protection is that it may encourage foreign investment in home markets. A tariff can affect the pattern of investment. If a country is initially importing a commodity, a protective tariff wall forces foreign firms either to cut prices, lose sales, or, alternatively, try to produce the commodity directly in the home market and thus avoid the tariff. Such "tariff-factories" are not rare, as evidenced, for example, in the number of automobile assembly plants located in Argentina, Brazil, South Africa, and other countries that do not possess a comparative advantage in automobile production.

Studies of the multinational corporation show that a tariff often causes it to invest in a country. Previously it has exported to the market in question, investing in advertising and customer good will but not in physical production facilities. When its imports to the market are struck with a tariff, direct investment becomes more attractive than the only

[6] The possibility of welfare loss with growth, if an industry is protected, was pointed out by Harry G. Johnson, "The Possibility of Income Losses from Increased Efficiency or Factor Accumulation in the Presence of Tariffs," *Economic Journal,* 77 (March 1967): 151–54.

[7] Export taxes and import taxes are symmetrical in their tendency to restrict the level of trade.

alternative — writing off the firm's investment in good will and leaving the market entirely.

There is, however, something ironic about such a policy. Suppose a country is concerned to limit its dependence on foreign sources of supply by following a protectionist policy. It may also be anxious to diversify its productive structure by protecting its local industries against foreign competition. But keeping out foreign-made goods may just encourage the foreigner himself to come in. A country like Canada seems bedeviled both by a desire to protect a whole panoply of secondary industries and to limit the incursion of American direct investment, which such a protected market seems to attract.

12.5 TARIFFS, EMPLOYMENT, AND THE BALANCE OF PAYMENTS: A PRELIMINARY VIEW

Two widely quoted arguments favoring tariff protection can only be mentioned here, since the flexible-prices, full-employment assumptions that have characterized our discussion so far need to be altered to do these arguments justice. This will be done in Part 4 of this book.

The first argument states that tariffs (or other forms of protection) can save jobs or create jobs in those industries competing most directly with foreign goods. Even in our models this argument has validity: Protecting an industry does attract resources from other sectors. But this does not necessarily mean that overall employment will rise. What is left out of account is the question of employment in a nation's export industries. This problem becomes aggravated if foreign countries respond to the tariff by retaliating with barriers against home exports.

Although the argument for aggregate employment must be analyzed later (Part 4), a word should be mentioned about employment in each sector. Any change in world prices causes potential disturbances at home as the signal is given for some sectors to contract (and others expand). But output changes typically involve costs — relocation of labor from one industry to another and perhaps geographically as well. Frictions in readjustments could easily involve unemployment in some sectors, at least in the short run. If an industry is threatened by technical improvements or other forms of cost reductions abroad, it is understandable that a plea for protection should be registered for imperiled industries. Indeed, as the next chapter discusses, provisions involving such "peril points" are written into the American law. Most readjustments are costly and take time. Tariff protection might postpone the adjustment, but once again it must be judged "second-best" relative to direct retraining and relocation assistance.

The second argument is that a tariff can improve the balance of payments. Here our assumptions that prices clear markets and a community spends exactly the value of its produced income stand in the way of a proper appraisal of the argument. A balance-of-trade surplus represents an excess of exports over imports, and so it is tempting to argue that a tariff can create a surplus by restricting imports. But a trade surplus also indicates that the nation is producing more than it is spending, and we must await the analysis in Part 4 of macroeconomic relationships before asking how a tariff might create such an aggregate excess of output over spending.

12.6 EFFECTIVE PROTECTION

Actual production processes are rarely as simple as our theory has assumed. In particular, commodities at various stages of fabrication are outputs of some productive activities and inputs into others. Flour to make bread, spun yarn to make clothing, sheet steel to make automobiles — these are only a few examples of interindustry flows in what economists call "intermediate commodities." A large volume of international trade in these intermediate commodities has encouraged the development of a new concept in analyzing a country's commercial policy, that of the "effective rate of protection." It takes account of the fact that the "nominal" tariff applied to imports of a commodity does not by itself indicate the impact of protection for the domestic industry producing that commodity if it utilizes imported inputs that are subject to duty. The domestic industry "adds value" to the imported inputs, and the effect of protection on this "value added" is the key indicator of how protection affects resource allocation.

As an example, suppose the free-trade price of clothing on world markets is $1.00, and to produce a unit of clothing a country imports $.40 worth of spun yarn from abroad. The domestic industry then creates an additional $.60 worth of value added. Now suppose a 40 percent "nominal" tariff is levied on clothing imports, raising their domestic price to $1.40, and a 10 percent tariff is applied to imports of spun yarn, raising their cost to $.44 per unit of clothing behind the tariff wall. The domestic producer now receives as value added per unit of clothing $.96, the difference between $1.40 and the $.44 he spends as outlay on imported cloth. This difference represents an increase of 60 percent over the original value added, $(1.40 - .44)/.60$. The tariff structure has yielded a 60 percent "effective rate" of protection to domestic clothing producers, whereas the "nominal" rate on clothing imports was only 40 percent. This example illustrates the kind of "escalation" that can be built into a nation's tariff structure if commodities at a lower level of fabrication or processing (steel, yarn) are charged lower duties than more finished items (automobiles, clothing).

The ingredients in the effective tariff rate emerge from this example. The rate attempts to measure the percentage by which value added can increase over the free-trade level as a consequence of a tariff structure. Let the fixed free-trade price of imports of the *final* good be denoted by p_j^*. With a tariff at rate t_j on these imports, the domestic price becomes $(1 + t_j)p_j^*$. Suppose the productive process uses an imported intermediate good, i, with fixed world price, p_i^*. If a tariff at rate t_i is applied to imports of this intermediate good, its price behind the tariff wall is $(1 + t_i)p_i^*$. We also need to know how much of the intermediate good is required per unit of final output. Let this be denoted by a_{ij}, and assume it is fixed. Then at free-trade world prices the value added per unit of final output is

$$v_j^* = p_j^* - a_{ij}p_i^*.$$

Compare this with value added at domestic posttariff prices, v_j:

$$v_j = (1 + t_j)p_j^* - a_{ij}(1 + t_i)p_i^*.$$

The effective rate of protection by definition is

$$\frac{v_j - v_j^*}{v_j^*} = \frac{t_j p_j^* - t_i a_{ij} p_i^*}{p_j^* - a_{ij} p_i^*}.$$

Finally, divide both numerator and denominator by the world price of the final commodity, p_j^*, and let θ_{ij} denote the *share* of the intermediate commodity in a dollar's worth of final output at free-trade prices. That is, θ_{ij} is $a_{ij}p_i^*/p_j^*$. The effective rate of protection provided to the final commodity is thus:

$$\frac{t_j - \theta_{ij}t_i}{1 - \theta_{ij}}.$$

In our numerical example t_j was .40, $t_i = .10$, and θ_{ij} was .40. The effective tariff rate was 60 percent, although the nominal rate was only 40 percent.

In a recent study made for the World Bank, Bela Balassa computed the nominal and effective rates of duty for selected industry groups in seven developing countries. Some of the computations are rather startling. For example, in Chile in 1961 the nominal rate of duty on processed food was 82 percent.[8] This may sound high, but compare it with the calculated effective rate, 2,884 percent! Computations of effective rates

---

[8] These figures are from Balassa and associates, *The Structure of Protection in Developing Countries*. Baltimore: Johns Hopkins University Press, 1971, p. 54.

have been used in bargaining sessions when tariff schedules are negotiated. It is useful for all parties to know which local productive activities
receive especially favored rates of protection. The nominal rates are less
helpful than effective rates in providing this information.[9]

12.7 SUMMARY

The basic theory of tariffs set out in the preceding chapter focused on
the gain that a country may obtain if it has some monopoly power on
world markets and can improve its terms of trade by levying a tariff.
This gain provided the key valid argument for tariffs. In this chapter
we surveyed a number of other arguments for protection. These ranged
from the desire to redistribute incomes by protecting certain industries
and the factors used specifically or intensively by those industries or by
controlling production or consumption levels in certain industries to
encouraging "infant" industries to develop, sheltered in early years from
foreign competition.

In all the cases we studied we found that tariffs could help achieve
any of these aims. But in each case a superior set of policies could also
satisfy these objectives at a lower welfare cost. For example, if an industry seems to need a minimal home market, a tariff can be levied.
But levying a tariff involves a consumption loss represented by the distortion between world and domestic prices. A production subsidy can
achieve the same production goal and allow consumers to buy at world
prices. The basic point is that tariffs interfere with *trade*, whereas the
stipulated target or source of distortion often resides in production
alone or consumption alone.

In the final section we introduced the concept of the effective rate of
protection. This highlights the complexity in productive activity that
exists in the real world. Domestic productive processes often rely on
imported raw materials and intermediate products, and a tariff structure allocates resources more in line with the effective rates of protection
on these processes than with the nominal rates on the end products.

SUGGESTIONS FOR FURTHER READING

Black, John. "Arguments for Tariffs," *Oxford Economic Papers*, N.S. 11
    (June 1959): 191–208. A discussion of various arguments for protection.

[9] We have already remarked that effective rates of protection are higher than nominal rates for processes in which nominal tariffs on outputs are higher than tariffs
on intermediate good imports. Let e denote the effective rate. Then the formula
can be rewritten as $(1 - \theta_{ij})e + \theta_{ij}t_i = t_j$. This states that the nominal rate is a
weighted average of the effective rate and the tariff on inputs.

Corden, W. M. "Tariffs, Subsidies, and the Terms of Trade," *Economica,* N.S. 24 (August 1957): 235–42. A lucid treatment of alternative protective devices.

Grubel, H. G. "Effective Protection: A Non-Specialist Guide to the Theory, Policy Implications, and Controversies," in Grubel, H. G. and Harry G. Johnson, eds., *Effective Tariff Protection.* Geneva: General Agreement on Tariffs and Trade and Graduate Institute of International Studies, 1971. An introduction to the issues in effective protection.

Johnson, Harry G. "Optimal Trade Intervention in the Presence of Domestic Distortions," in R. E. Baldwin et al., *Trade, Growth and the Balance of Payments.* Chicago: Rand McNally, 1965. A general discussion of trade taxes and production and consumption subsidies, relying heavily on dia-grammatic analysis.

Stolper, Wolfgang, and Paul A. Samuelson. "Protection and Real Wages," *Review of Economic Studies,* 9 (November 1941): 58–73. The analysis of the effect of a tariff on wages and rents.

13

Tariff Policy and Trade Liberalization

Without doubt, tariffs and other governmental restraints on trade have curbed international specialization and reduced world economic welfare. We know, for example, that regions of the United States, trading freely with one another, attain far more specialization in production than do independent industrial nations of comparable size.[1] The persistence of widespread tariff protection proves difficult for economists to interpret, because it is seldom obvious that a nation's tariffs are advancing its own economic welfare, and they clearly reduce the welfare of the world as a whole. Despite the nearly universal presence of tariffs on international trade, countries do seem to recognize that their national interest in maintaining tariffs — whatever it may be — clashes with worldwide interests in freer trade. Their multilateral efforts to reduce tariff barriers are the subject of this chapter.

13.1 WORLD WELFARE AND TRADE WARFARE

A tariff reduces world welfare, as we saw in section 11.4, because it moves the trading equilibrium off the contract curve. Suppose that the home country (in a two-country trading world) imposes a tariff. What can the

---

[1] Bela Balassa, "Effects of Commercial Policy on International Trade, the Location of Production and Factor Movements," *The International Allocation of Economic Activity,* ed. B. Ohlin, P. Hesselborn, and P. M. Wijkman. London: Macmillan, 1977, chap. 7, especially pp. 242–48.

foreign country do? Should it follow its fighting instincts, and retaliate with a tariff of its own? Can it restore an efficient trading equilibrium, on the contract curve?

Historically, the fighting instincts have often prevailed, and we find many instances of retaliatory cycles of tariff elevation. Furthermore, it is quite possible for each country to raise its tariff in its own self-interest at each stage. That is, the home country raises its welfare with its initial increase, harming its foreign trading partner. The partner recoups some of this loss by raising its own tariff. The home country loses from that retaliation, but can then benefit from a further increase in its tariff. Yet each of these moves inflicts a loss on world economic welfare. There is a limit to how far the parties can continue to restrict trade with each gaining its short-run unilateral move. However, once that limit is reached, putting a stop to the deterioration of world welfare, there is no mechanism except international cooperation that can bring the parties back to the better situation of free trade. That is, neither can be certain to benefit if it reduces its tariff while the trading partner's tariff remains in place.[2] In the real-life world, with many countries trading together, the problem may be even worse, because the effects of one country's tariff increase may be diffused enough that it does not expect retaliation, or does not easily identify it. And a general treaty of tariff disarmament involves finding acceptable terms not for two but for many countries. When we study international efforts at trade liberalization, later in this chapter, we shall find ample evidence that countries do not expect to benefit by unilaterally removing their tariffs. Hence a concerted multilateral effort is necessary to move toward welfare-maximizing free trade.

Tariffs on Individual Products, Welfare, and Revenue

As we take up the story of international efforts at trade liberalization, we need a simple technique for showing the effects of changing the tariff on a single product on the economic welfare of producers and consumers and the government's tax revenue. This technique employs ordinary supply and demand curves, not to depict the forces of general equilibrium (as in previous chapters) but to concentrate on one market that we suppose to be a small part of the national economy.[3]

---

[2] For a more extensive analysis, see Tibor Scitovsky, "A Reconsideration of the Theory of Tariffs," *Review of Economic Studies,* 9, no. 2 (1942): 89–110; reprinted in American Economic Association, *Readings in the Theory of International Trade.* Philadelphia: Blakiston, 1950; and Harry G. Johnson, "Optimum Tariffs and Retaliation," *Review of Economic Studies,* 21, no. 2 (1954): 142–53.

[3] We call this type of analysis *partial equilibrium,* and it assumes that the market we are examining is small enough that changes in its ruling price do not perceptibly shift demand or supply curves anywhere else in the economy.

Figure 13.1 illustrates the method. The nation is a net importer of the product, and a small purchaser of it on the world market. Hence the world price is not affected by its purchases, and it can take any desired quantity at price P_w. The horizontal line extending from P_w is thus the supply curve for imports. The demand curve for the product is DD'. The supply curve, SS', shows the domestic output at various prices.

If no tariff is in force, price P_w prevails in the domestic market. Domestic producers supply quantity P_wK, and imports KL, of the total amount P_wL consumed. Suppose that a tariff is imposed at rate P_tP_w/P_wO. The world price cannot fall, and hence the domestic price (after payment of the tariff) must be elevated by the full amount of the duty to P_t (if any imports are still purchased). At this higher price, domestic supply is enlarged to P_tM, total consumption reduced to P_tN, and imports shrink to MN.

Because the world price is fixed, the nation as a whole must lose by imposing the tariff. Figure 13.1 shows how the effect is spread among consumers, domestic producers, and the government. The total welfare that consumers derive from any given commodity can be measured by what they would pay rather than do without the good entirely. For reasons explained in introductory texts on economics, this is approximated by the area under the demand curve and above the market price line. In Figure 13.1 this "consumers' surplus" under free trade is measured by the triangular area beneath the demand curve and above P_wL; when the tariff is imposed, it shrinks to the area above P_tN, and consumers lose an amount of welfare measured by the trapezoidal area P_wLNP_t.

A tariff likewise affects domestic producers' welfare. The area under the supply curve depicts the opportunity cost of factors of production (including normal profit to producers). Sometimes increases in output encounter diminishing returns, and as in Figure 13.1 the supply curve acquires an upward slope. Then some factors employed in the industry earn more than the opportunity cost of their services, and a "producers' surplus" results.[4] It is measured by the area above the supply curve. Thus, when free trade prevails and the ruling price is P_w, domestic producers enjoy the surplus triangular area SKP_w. When the tariff is imposed, the surplus rises to SMP_t. Thus domestic producers gain from the imposition of a tariff an amount measured by the area P_wKMP_t.

Before weighing these effects against one another, we must count one more: the tariff revenue collected by the government. After the tariff is imposed, the government gathers P_wP_t on each unit of imports. The

[4] The concept of producers' surplus is subject to serious qualifications. See E. J. Mishan, "What Is Producer's Surplus?" *American Economic Review,* 58 (December 1968): 1269–82.

FIGURE 13.1   Effects on Welfare and Government Revenue
of Tariff on Individual Product

Domestic demand is DD', domestic supply SS', world price P_w. Imposing
tariff $P_t P_w / P_w O$ leaves world price unchanged, raises domestic price to
P_t, and causes a welfare loss (net) measured by triangular areas 2 and 4.

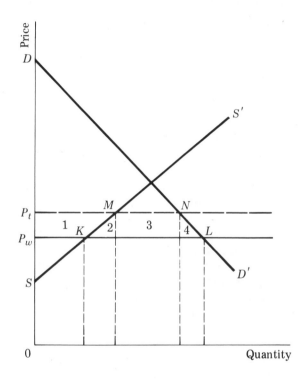

---

tariff yields total revenue of $P_w P_t \cdot MN$, the area labeled 3 in the diagram. What significance does it have for welfare? We can suppose either
that the government hands the revenue back to the consumers, or that
it provides public services just as valuable to them (at the margin) as is
their private consumption. Either way, government revenue is dollar for
dollar as good as surplus to the consumers. *(ie defere, learned etc)*.

Now we can summarize the welfare effects of a tariff on domestic interests. Consumers lose an amount equal to the sum of areas $1 + 2 +
3 + 4$. Producers' surplus increases by area 1. Government revenue grows
by area 3. Thus the net loss to the country from imposing the tariff is
areas $2 + 4$. Area 4 is often called the "deadweight loss" of consumers'

surplus due to the imposition of a tax. Area 2 depicts the excess real cost of securing output $P_tM - P_wK$ from domestic sources rather than from imports. This type of analysis suffers from neglecting the effects on other markets of this tariff through the terms of trade. However, it shows clearly (if roughly) the distribution of a tariff's welfare effects. We shall use these tools later in this chapter and in Chapter 14. First, the tariff policies of the United States provide background to international efforts to liberalize trade.

13.2 U.S. TARIFF POLICY AND THE RECIPROCAL TRADE AGREEMENTS PROGRAM

The United States' Trade Agreements Act of 1934 is to a large degree the cornerstone of international efforts to reduce tariffs. It also divides the tariff history of the United States, ending detailed control by Congress of America's tariff rates. The last gasp of congressional tariff-making was the Smoot-Hawley Act of 1930, which inflated rates so that the average dollar's worth of dutiable American imports paid a tariff of 53 cents. No wonder the U.S. share of world trade dropped from 16 to 11 percent in the next five years.[5] The world total also declined, as international trade shriveled in the face of the Great Depression of the 1930's.

The combined effect on U.S. exports of the depression and of retaliatory increases in other countries' tariffs prompted a major shift in trade policy in 1934. Congress authorized the President to negotiate agreements with foreign trading partners to lower tariffs hampering American exports. In return, U.S. tariffs would be cut on selected goods exported by the partner. The President could offer to cut the rates of duty set by the Smoot-Hawley Act up to 50 percent. By 1940 the United States had entered into bilateral trade agreements with twenty partners, thereby setting a ritual for these accords. Each country bargains for tariff reductions on tariffs constricting its exports. Nations judge the equivalence of their concessions by the value of *existing* trade to which they apply.

Trade Agreements and Welfare

Do these deals make much sense in terms of economic welfare? Not if the importing countries are small purchasers of the goods on which they grant tariff concessions. When a small country lowers a tariff on a com-

[5] On the origins of the trade-agreements program, see Don D. Humphrey, *American Imports*. New York: Twentieth Century Fund, 1955, chaps. 5, 6.

petitively produced import, the exporting countries get no benefit. They gain only if the world price rises, which requires that the importing country be large enough to influence the world price significantly. The small country cutting tariffs benefits only itself. Furthermore, as we saw in Chapter 11, its benefit depends on the amount of extra trade due to the lowered tariff (as well as on the size of the reduction), not on the quantity of imports that previously clambered over the barrier.

If the tariff-cutting importer is large enough to influence his terms of trade, or if he merely *thinks* he gives benefits to foreigners by reducing his tariff, the reciprocal trade agreements make some sense. A tariff reduction now raises the world price of the imported good, benefiting the exporter. The size of this benefit depends on the initial volume of trade (as well as on the size of the tariff concession). This terms-of-trade gain to the exporter is a loss to the importer unless his tariff was higher than optimal. The importer might not be a net gainer from cutting a single tariff (even though the world is). But the importer's terms-of-trade loss on one product can be offset by his gain as an exporter when a reciprocal agreement is signed. And these gains and losses are more likely to cancel if each party cuts tariffs on the same initial volume of trade.[6]

The United States and its trade-agreement partners tended to pick for liberalization goods for which each was the other's principal supplier. This choice was also consistent with tariff disarmament, because the reduced tariffs applied to imports from all sources, not just from the partner. Suppose the United States and Brazil grant each other tariff concessions on coffee and automobiles, respectively. Each is a large importer, and so their increased purchases raise the world prices of both goods. Both gain from lower trade barriers (see Figure 13.1). Because the prices (ex tariff) of each party's imports and exports move in the same direction, the change in their terms of trade should be small. The United States may also import coffee from Colombia, and Brazil may import some autos from Britain. Then the United States feels it has given away uncompensated benefits by paying a higher world price for Colombian coffee, Brazil by paying more for British autos. The United States and Brazil minimize these "spillover benefits" by cutting tariffs only on goods imported mainly from the partner country. Regrets over spillover benefits came to inhibit bilateral trade agreements and ultimately led

---

[6] Elements of monopoly and product differentiation in individual product markets, discussed in Chapter 9, probably contribute to causing the prices of a country's imports ex tariff to rise when the tariff is reduced. A study of U.S. tariff reductions in the 1950's found that nearly half of the price effects took the form of increased external prices, rather than reduced prices (including tariff) to domestic consumers. See M. E. Kreinin, "Effect of Tariff Changes on the Prices and Volume of Imports," *American Economic Review,* 51 (June 1961): 310–24.

countries to multilateral tariff bargaining, where these benefits could be taken into account.

Extent of Trade Liberalization

Congress has authorized the President to enter into tariff-cutting agreements only for limited periods. The authority was repeatedly renewed between 1934 and 1974, the last extension for a period of five years. In some of these renewals the executive gained additional authority to cut tariffs. Suppose that a tariff rate had been bargained down each time by the maximum permitted by law. The rate today would be only 3.4 percent of the Smoot-Hawley rate prevailing in 1934 after the effects of the most recent round of tariff reduction (the Tokyo Round, completed in 1979). Indeed, average U.S. tariff rates have fallen substantially. The average dollar's worth of dutiable imports paid around 50 cents in customs duties in 1934, but little more than 5 cents in recent years. A spurious force explains at least half of the decline, however. Many American tariff rates are defined by statute as *specific* rates — so many cents per pound, or dollars per bale. (Rates stated as a percentage of the foreign wholesale value of the article are called *ad valorem* rates.) The money prices of nearly all imported articles have risen substantially since the Great Depression, but the dollar values of the specific duties have remained the same (except, of course, for trade-agreement reductions); hence the incidence of most specific rates has declined by around three-quarters. Still, negotiated cuts in statutory rates have lowered trade barriers substantially, for both the United States and other industrial countries.

Since World War II, U.S. commercial policy has acquired many protectionist exceptions, letting some groups of import-competing producers win their freedom from foreign competition.[7] The exceptions divide into two types — those offering a general safety net for producers dislodged by import competition, and those designed to assist particular groups.

The most important general exemption has been the *escape clause*, which permits a domestic industry believing it has been injured by import competition due to a trade-agreement concession to petition the U.S. International Trade Commission (formerly the Tariff Commission) for relief. If it finds that injury occurred (and often it finds that the ills cannot be blamed on the tariff), it can recommend that the tariff be raised or that adjustment assistance be provided to retrain workers, aid businesses to increase their efficiency, or switch to other lines of pro-

---

[7] For further information, see L. B. Yeager and D. G. Tuerck, *Trade Policy and the Price System.* Scranton, Pa.: International Textbook Co., 1966; Sidney Ratner, *The Tariff in American History.* New York: D. Van Nostrand Co., 1972.

duction, and the like. Adjustment assistance is both fair and more efficient than restoring the tariff. Relocating factors of production after a tariff cut is costly, and indeed some factors may lose permanently from freer trade. The benefit goes to other factors and to consumers generally (in the form of enlarged consumers' surplus). Hence consumers — as taxpayers — should help the displaced factors to meet the cost of adjustment so the nation can enjoy a higher real income. Alas, adjustment assistance has not worked very well in practice.

Another general exception heavily used since the mid-1970's is the antidumping provision, which permits countervailing duties to be imposed when foreign exporters are found to be selling at a lower price in the United States than in their home market, and thereby injuring domestic industries. (Dumping was described in section 9.2.) Such important industries as steel have charged dumping in their request for relief from foreign competition. The political basis for the antidumping provision is rather obvious by its seeming fairness to domestic producers. An analysis of its effects, however, leads to somewhat different conclusions. To attain the most national economic welfare we want to secure imports as cheaply as possible (in terms of the exports exchanged for them). It matters not whether that cheapness is due to foreigners' low costs or their willingness to hand over their goods at low profit margins. The national interest requires no antidumping provision except to forestall the unlikely event that foreign oligopolists cut their export prices temporarily just to drive the American industry out of business. Yet world welfare may be increased by antidumping provisions, because the price discrimination that it involves is likely to reduce the allocative efficiency of the world as a whole.

Special protective provisions have also sheltered some sectors of the U.S. economy from import competition. An example is the National Security Amendment, which blocks action to decrease or eliminate any duty if the President determines that such actions "threaten to impair the national security." Preserving an industry essential for the national defense could surely justify interference with the market mechanism. As we saw in Chapter 12, however, the efficient way to maintain a socially needed level of output is to subsidize production rather than to restrict imports; a needless loss of consumers' surplus results from trade restrictions. Another important exemption from trade liberalization is given to agriculture. The United States, like most other countries, does not let supply and demand determine the prices of many domestic farm products. Imports have been kept out when necessary to hold these prices above world levels.

In recent years, special protectionist measures have often taken the form of import restrictions other than tariffs. We shall consider their significance in section 13.4.

13.3 GATT AND MULTILATERAL TRADE LIBERALIZATION

Since World II nations have agreed on tariff reductions largely through multilateral negotiations under the aegis of the General Agreement on Tariffs and Trade (GATT). GATT has fostered large tariff cuts and helped to settle serious disputes over commercial policy. In this section we shall review major provisions of the agreement and describe multilateral tariff bargaining within its framework.[8]

Provisions of GATT

GATT is a framework of rules for nations' management of their commercial policy. We shall consider its provisions in three areas — discriminatory trade controls, quantitative restrictions, and the settlement of disputes over trade policy.

GATT's most pervasive concern is that trade restrictions not discriminate between supplier countries. Any "advantage, favour, privilege, or immunity" granted in trade with one country "shall be accorded immediately and unconditionally" to like trade with all other GATT members. This provision is both economic and political. Economically, almost all forms of discrimination are inefficient: If A's preference lets B sell to her at a higher (net) price than does C, trade and production could be switched from B to C so that (when all adjustments are made) everybody in A is potentially better off. The political case for equal treatment rests on the likelihood that the victim of a discriminatory tariff will retaliate and raise a tariff against the offender. Discrimination is thus both a cause and an instrument of trade warfare and is likely to lead to higher restrictions on trade all around.

Another GATT rule is that domestic industry should be protected by tariffs rather than quantitative restrictions (QRs) or other devices controlling the quantity of trade directly, rather than the price at which it takes place. (We shall explore the rationale of this preference in section 13.4.) Like most sweeping provisions in international agreements, this one was hedged with important exceptions. One of these permits QRs to protect domestic agriculture.

A third function of GATT has been to provide an international forum to mediate disputes over commercial policy. Suppose that for a domestic reason a GATT member raises a tariff and thus harms another member's

---

[8] Two major studies of GATT are Gerard Curzon, *Multilateral Commercial Diplomacy: The General Agreement on Tariffs and Trade and Its Impact on National Commercial Policies and Techniques.* London: Michael Joseph, 1964; and Kenneth W. Dam, *The GATT: Law and International Economic Organization.* Chicago: University of Chicago Press, 1970.

interests. The plaintiff's complaint is circulated to all members, and any with an interest in the issue can join the subsequent discussions. A bilateral consultation takes place. If it yields an agreement, the decision is circulated to all members (lest third parties be injured). If not, a panel of conciliation is appointed to examine the complaint and make recommendations. The offender, for instance, may be urged to offer alternative tariff concessions. As a last resort the plaintiff may be authorized to retaliate, with the GATT members weighing the equivalence of the retaliation to the offense. The worth of this procedure is shown by the squalid tariff history of the 1920's when newly independent states boosted their tariffs, and each increase prompted a cycle of retaliation. The level and complexity of tariffs rose all around. Without GATT's surveillance, similar trade warfare could have occurred after World War II.

Multilateral Tariff Reduction Under GATT

GATT evolved from the U.S. trade-agreements program of the 1930's. It listed mutual tariff reduction as a major objective. The members of GATT devised a procedure for multilateral tariff bargaining designed to streamline the older bilateral procedure. Seven bargaining sessions have taken place since 1947, keyed to the U.S. President's successive renewals of authority to bargain for tariff concessions.[9] The first five sessions consisted of simultaneous batteries of bilateral negotiations. Each party could match the spillover benefits flowing from its own concessions against the incidental benefits gained as a third party from other negotiations. A net loser on spillovers could demand additional compensation. Hence each party could be sure of an equitable deal in both its bilateral negotiations and the incidence of spillover benefits. Thus GATT's bargaining procedure disposed of the inhibition that had threatened to strangle bilateral trade negotiations.

The procedure yielded broad and deep tariff cuts on the first try — at Geneva in 1947, but subsequent multilateral sessions produced diminishing returns. Many tariff rates in 1947 contained "surplus protection," elevating the price of imports more than enough to allow the competing domestic industry to operate profitably. Successive reductions peeled away the surplus and evoked protests from import-competing producers. Governments heeded the call and grew less willing to bargain. Some countries' tariffs had been whittled to low levels, so that foreign exporters would offer them little for further cuts. Some countries held back from further reductions for fear they would run out of trading stock.

---

[9] This linkage pays tribute less to the importance of the United States as a trading power than to the uniquely cumbersome character of America's fiscal machinery; other countries can bargain first and secure legislative approval afterward.

The Kennedy Round of multilateral tariff bargaining, completed in 1967, departed even further from bilateral bargaining between principal suppliers. The chief industrial countries agreed on the target of an across-the-board 50 percent cut in all tariff rates. They would forego balancing the reciprocal benefits stemming from this overall cut. Each country could propose to except some of its tariffs from the cut — presumably where unacceptable injury to domestic industries would result. Bargaining proceeded over the size of the exceptions lists, rather than over the 50 percent cut itself. The participants agreed to weighted-average tariff cuts of around 35 percent, making the Kennedy Round the most sweeping tariff reduction since the GATT went into effect.[10]

The most recent bargaining session, the Tokyo Round (1973–1979), continued the procedure of the Kennedy Round but also tackled the thorny problem of nontariff barriers to trade. In the tariff-cutting part of the agreement the industrial countries agreed to reduce their tariffs on average by another third over an eight-year period. Most of the major countries will reduce individual tariffs by a formula that shaves more off those tariffs that were higher initially. The practice should cause *effective* rates of protection (see section 12.6) to be lowered proportionally more than the average nominal rates. The Tokyo Round participants also agreed on a number of codes governing nontariff barriers; these are discussed below.

Gains from Trade Liberalization

After the Kennedy Round nominal tariff rates for the major industrial countries stood at relatively low levels. In 1973 United States tariffs on dutiable imports averaged 8.9 percent, those of the European Community countries 9.0 percent, Japan 11.2 percent, and Canada 14.2 percent.[11] Some observers have been skeptical that important welfare gains still remain to be achieved from further reduction of these moderate rates. The only way to answer such a question is to mobilize the data needed to measure the welfare gains identified in Figure 13.1. Before the Tokyo Round's completion an international research team developed a careful estimate of the industrial countries' gains from an outcome similar to, though somewhat more liberal than, that actually achieved by the negotiators (the actual outcome's benefits will probably be a bit smaller than these figures). The gains described in Figure 13.1 would amount to

---

[10] Two extensive studies of the Kennedy Round are Ernest H. Preeg, *Traders and Diplomats*. Washington. Brookings Institution, 1970; and John W. Evans, *The Kennedy Round in American Trade Policy: The Twilight of the GATT?* Cambridge: Harvard University Press, 1971.
[11] William R. Cline et al., *Trade Negotiations in the Tokyo Round: A Quantitative Assessment*. Washington: Brookings Institution, 1978, p. 10.

$1.7 billion annually. The investigators hold, though, that the experience of trade liberalization in the European Community (see Chapter 14) warrants inflating this figure substantially to allow for greater scale economies and innovative gains that go along with these static effects. A reasonable guess would quintuple the estimate of annual benefits to $8.5 billion. Furthermore, that is an annual gain, and it will go on affecting a larger volume of international trade each year. If trade grows at 5 percent a year following the Tokyo Round and future welfare gains are discounted at 10 percent annually, the present value of the Tokyo Round's reductions reaches an impressive 170 billion dollars.[12] The gains from tariff reduction would be proportionally higher still if the industrial countries could eliminate tariffs among themselves entirely. Tariff collection imposes substantial administrative costs and delays as well as uncertainties that depress the volume of international commerce.

Does the United States get its fair share of these gains? Would it gain from continued movement toward eliminating tariffs among the industrial countries? Economic theory suggests two issues to consider — the terms of trade and the distribution of income.

Because the United States is a large country, we might expect that tariffs affect America's terms of trade, which would deteriorate if the country reduced its tariffs unilaterally.[13] But that fact merely reminds us of the case for multilateral cuts in tariffs, which benefit consumers without moving the terms of trade much one way or the other.

Tariff removal by the United States could also redistribute income so as to harm some factors of production. We saw in Chapters 7 and 11 that, in a two-factor model, a tariff can benefit the factor used intensively in the import-competing industry even if it harms the nation as a whole. That factor would suffer if the tariff were eliminated and might deserve compensation from the benefits flowing to the rest of the economy. What are the distributive effects of the tariff? Table 13.1 shows tests of several hypotheses about its protective role after reductions negotiated in the Kennedy Round were completed. It covers only the manufacturing sector, rather than the whole economy, but gives some hints about the tariff's effect. For each industry the average levels of both nominal and effective rates of protection were measured (including nontariff barriers). Industries were ranked from the most protected to the least protected, and the list was divided into quarters. Then we averaged some traits of industries in these successive quarters:

1. Does the tariff protect labor-intensive industries? We saw (Chap-

---

[12] Cline et al., *Trade Negotiations in the Tokyo Round,* pp. 78–79 and chap. 8. "Dynamic" gains from scale economies and the like are discussed below in section 14.3.

[13] Giorgio Basevi, "The Restrictive Effect of the U.S. Tariff and Its Welfare Value," *American Economic Review,* 58 (September 1968): 840–52.

TABLE 13.1   Characteristics of Industries in Relation to
Levels of Protection Given by United States Tariffs,
Nominal and Effective, After Kennedy Round Reductions

Industry characteristics and tariff measure	Industries ranked by level of protection			
	Highest quarter	Second quarter	Third quarter	Lowest quarter
Labor-intensity (measured by payrolls as percentage of all factor payments)				
Nominal	46%	50%	53%	45%
Effective	47%	48%	52%	44%
Level of labor skill (measured by payroll per worker)				
Nominal	$6,000	$6,700	$7,200	$7,100
Effective	$6,000	$6,600	$7,500	$6,900
Size of manufacturing establishment (measured by value added per establishment in millions of dollars)				
Nominal	$1.8[a]	$1.4	$2.2	$3.6
Effective	$1.5[a]	$1.6	$3.2	$2.6

Source: Tariff rates—Robert E. Baldwin, *Nontariff Distortions of International Trade.* Washington: Brookings Institution, 1970, pp. 163–64; other data—United States Bureau of the Census, *1967 Census of Manufactures: Summary and Subject Statistics.* Washington: Government Printing Office, 1971, Table 3.
[a] The "ordnance and accessories" sector has been omitted from this class. The large establishments producing military wares hardly seem relevant to testing the effect of tariff protection.

ter 8) that one explanation for the "Leontief paradox" is that the American tariff systematically protects labor. We can measure the labor-intensity of industries roughly by the share that payrolls constitute of payments to all factors of production (the industry's value added). The top two lines of Table 13.1 show that the least protected industries are indeed the least labor-intensive. Beyond the bottom quarter, however, the hypothesis fails: The most heavily protected industries are not very labor-intensive.

2. Does the tariff protect low-skilled labor? Without sheltering labor-intensive industries generally, the U.S. tariff might nonetheless protect workers with low skills. Low skills command low rewards in the labor

market, and we would expect that annual payroll per worker would be small in industries requiring low levels of skill or education. The table shows that indeed the industries paying the lowest wages receive higher protection (both nominal and effective) than others. Freer trade might well harm the least-skilled segment of the labor force, and the nation should certainly consider more active policies to provide them with valuable skills.

3. Does the tariff protect small business? Industries containing many small plants or firms may enjoy high tariff protection, if only because they are seen by the public to deserve help. Table 13.1 shows that factor payments per establishment — an "input" measure of business size — are considerably lower for industries in the upper half of the tariff ranks than in the lower half. The tariff indeed seems to protect small businesses, and their adjustments problems would require attention if trade were freed.

These patterns show that the U.S. tariff probably changes the distribution of income so as to favor unskilled labor and factors of production employed in small businesses. The losers presumably are those who benefit from the earnings of physical and human capital. Thus, one cannot rule out the possibility that the tariff makes the U.S. income distribution more equal, and perhaps more equitable as a result. Yet the tariff is hardly a cheap way to redistribute income. The Council on Wage and Price Stability has provided estimates of the cost each year of preserving one job in each of several heavily protected industries: $81,000 for each protected job in the textile industry, $62,700 for each steel-industry job, $114,000 for each job in the shoe industry. There is surely a cheaper way to redistribute income.

The relation of the tariff to income distribution raises another question about the analysis of trade liberalization. The proximate reason for the structure of the U.S. tariff is "That's what a duly elected government chose." In order to explain tariff patterns and decisions about trade liberalization, one must ultimately model political and not economic behavior.[14] We have framed this chapter around the hypothesis that countries undertake multilateral trade liberalization because they can thereby raise world economic welfare in a way that probably insures each individual country against a terms-of-trade loss that would offset its share of this gain. But that purely economic hypothesis has not really been tested for its consistency with the motives behind these political decisions.

[14] But economists are not bashful about doing so. See Robert E. Baldwin, *The Political Economy of Postwar U.S. Tariff Policy,* Bulletin 1976–4, Graduate School of Business Administration, New York University, 1976.

13.4 NONTARIFF BARRIERS TO TRADE

Economists often believe tariffs to be less noxious than other trade restrictions. Despite GATT's opposition, many nontariff restrictions on
trade remain and new ones are being invented. Their removal has been
given high priority because they threaten to grow and undo the laborious
work of trade liberalization. The Congress has seriously considered legislation that would trigger quotas on many products if imports gained
significantly more of the American market. We shall first explore the
theoretical significance of nontariff barriers, and then survey some of the
major types in use.

Theory of Quantitative Restrictions

A nontariff barrier is a government regulation other than a tariff that
directly alters the volume or composition of international trade. Nontariff barriers are most easily understood by comparing them with tariffs.
We have picked quantitative restrictions for scrutiny.[15]

A quantitative restriction (QR) has basically the same effect as a
tariff, yet their incidental differences are important. The similarity is
shown in Figure 13.2. The supply and demand curves for an imported
product are shown by S and D; we omit domestic supply. A quantitative
restriction equal to OQ_0 per period of time is imposed. This is an effective restriction, because it is smaller than the free-trade flow of imports
(corresponding to point F). Imports are bought and sold on competitive
markets. Hence we know what prices must prevail inside and outside the
country's boundaries: P_t and P_w would clear the domestic and foreign
markets respectively, if OQ_0 imports are permitted. We know that a tariff
separates the domestic and foreign prices of an import, and that in equilibrium a tariff rate must equal the proportion by which it elevates the
internal above the external price. Hence a quota that produces a price
distortion of $P_t P_w / P_w O$ is equivalent in its *restrictive effect* to a tariff of
that percentage; we could depict the equivalent tariff by schedule S_t,
which lies uniformly above S by that percentage and indicates the domestic price (including tariff) that must be paid for a quantity of imports.

If a quota always has its tariff equivalent,[16] why do import-competing
producers often prefer protection by quotas over protection by tariffs?

---

[15] For general information on quotas and other nontariff barriers, see Robert E.
Baldwin, *Nontariff Distortions of International Trade*. Washington: Brookings In-
stitution, 1970; and G. and V. Curzon, *Hidden Barriers to International Trade*,
Thames Essays no. 1. London: Trade Policy Research Centre, 1970.

[16] This equivalence is subject to many limitations. See F. D. Holzman, "Comparison of Different Forms of Trade Barriers," *Reviews of Economics and Statistics*,
51 (May 1969): 159–65.

FIGURE 13.2   Comparison of Effects of Tariff and Quantitative Restriction

Demand and supply for imports are D and S respectively. Imposing a quota OQ_0 drives domestic price up to P_t, external price down to P_w. Effect is thus equivalent to a tariff of $P_t P_w / P_w O$.

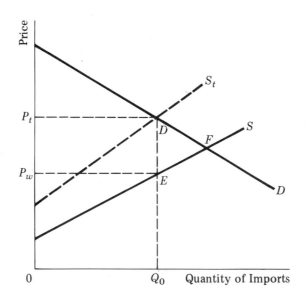

And why do economists often prefer the opposite? One difference is political: A producer group may be able to secure a quota corresponding, say, to a tariff of 150 percent; the general public might well consider such a high tariff too greedy and protest, whereas they cannot easily calculate the tariff equivalent of the quota.

Other differences are purely economic, however. When economic growth occurs, demand and supply schedules (as in Figure 13.2) shift steadily to the right. If the quota is constant, the tariff equivalent increases, although an ad valorem tariff would stay constant. A quota destroys the sensitivity of the market to any economic change that calls for more imports. If demand shifts toward this product (an upward shift in D), or productivity gains improve its supply (downward shift in S), the optimal quantity of imports increases; a tariff would permit some increase, but a quota does not. This defect supplies another reason that import-competing producers value quotas: They are protected against uncertainty about future economic changes that would increase the flow of competing imports.

Another difference has to do with the revenue representing that gap between the foreign and the domestic price. In Figure 13.2, a tariff of P_tP_w/P_wO would generate for the government revenue measured by the rectangle P_tDEP_w. When imports are limited by quota, no tariff is ordinarily collected. Yet the privilege of buying abroad at P_w and selling domestically at P_t is obviously valuable. The government might auction off licenses to import to the highest bidder. Competitive bidding by would-be importers would wipe out this potential profit and hand the government the same revenue as if it levied the tariff equivalent. On the other hand, the government might give away import licenses to the domestic importers, in which case they capture the proceeds P_tDEP_w. If it awards the licenses to foreign exporters, their country gains the scarcity rent. Note that the world welfare cost of the restriction, DEF, is the same in each case. The method of administering a quota only redistributes income.

U.S. Nontariff Barriers

The U.S. experience with its quotas on imports of sugar provides squalid evidence of the effects of dispensing quotas by methods other than auction. The sugar quotas have generally been worth about a quarter of a billion dollars to their recipients. When Cuba's sugar quota was canceled in 1960, a lobbying scramble began as other sugar-producing countries courted the favor of the Congress, especially its key committee members controlling the allocation among exporters. The allocation of sugar quotas among the producing nations is just capricious foreign aid; it does not concentrate output in the exporting country with the greatest comparative advantage.[17]

A close relative of quantitative restrictions is the so-called voluntary export agreement, whereby the importing country or countries solicit the cooperation of the exporters to restrict the flow of trade, using the threat of tariffs or quotas. An elaborate agreement for the restriction of trade in cotton yarn and textiles, involving twenty-nine countries, took effect in 1962. Under its terms some net importers employ quotas, and the exporting countries restrict shipments to the other importers. Export restrictions have been particularly popular in the United States, which has also pressed them upon foreign shippers of steel and noncotton textiles. This protectionist device is shot through with perversity. People

[17] D. Gale Johnson, *The Sugar Program: Large Costs and Small Benefits.* Washington: American Enterprise Institute, 1974.

think it is "nicer" for the importing country to secure voluntary control by exporters than to impose tariffs or quotas itself. Because exporter restriction is effectively identical to a QR with the quotas given to the exporters, this civility is costly to the importing country. The real income transferred from domestic consumers ($P_t DEP_w$ in Figure 13.2) goes not to the government or domestic importers, but to foreign exporters. Of course, the export quotas that cause this transfer may result simply from the exporting country's bargaining power. The privilege of exporting a dozen shirts to the United States has become a property right that is freely traded among businessmen in several Asian countries.

Nontariff Barriers in the Tokyo Round

These particular nontariff barriers sailed unscathed through the Tokyo Round, which represented the first broad multinational effort to reduce nontariff barriers. In the eyes of many observers it came none too soon: There has been a clear tendency for industrial countries to substitute nontariff barriers for the tariffs that were reduced in previous rounds of GATT bargaining. Whether the behavior codes agreed to in the Tokyo Round will put a stop to this trend remains to be seen. Nonetheless, they covered some major impediments to trade:

1. *Government procurement.* In the industrial countries governments nowadays buy a hefty share of the goods and services currently produced — usually on the order of one-fifth. Under the Buy American Act of 1933 a domestic producer's price is not considered unreasonably high by Uncle Sam if it lies no more than 6 percent above what a foreign supplier quotes; the margin rises to 12 percent if the domestic supplier is a small firm or located in a depressed area, and to 50 percent if the purchaser is the Department of Defense. Although more secretive about their preferences, other countries have been at least as dedicated patrons of local merchants. The Tokyo Round code seeks to bring this process out into the open, urging governments to publicize their procurement rules and give foreign suppliers a fair chance.

2. *Customs valuation.* Determination of the tariff on an import usually involves two steps — establishing the rate of duty and setting the valuation of the imported goods on which the ad valorem rate must be paid. Customs valuation practices can increase the incidence of tariffs by raising the value to which they are applied. A well-known feature of U.S. tariffs has been the valuation of certain imports not on the usual basis of their selling prices abroad but rather on the wholesale prices of competing goods produced in the United States. This is called the American Selling Price (ASP) system. Because the protected American producers charge higher prices than their foreign competitors, this practice increases the incidence of tariffs. The new Customs Valuation Code of

GATT defines a series of preferred methods of valuation, the ideal one being the actual value of the goods in the transaction at hand.

3. *Technical standards.* Another technical and administrative barrier to trade arises from the differing technical standards employed from country to country for electrical voltages, screw threads, chemical strengths, and other traits of manufactured commodities. These standards may not be designed to impede trade, but they can certainly do so when they force the exporter to redesign his product to foreign specifications before he can export it. The protective intent of technical standards surfaces when we witness industrial countries competing to get their national sets of standards adopted by developing countries, in order to give their exporters an advantage over foreign producers designing to different standards.[18] The Tokyo Round code seeks to keep standards from creating unnecessary obstacles to trade and brings standards codes into GATT's purview as a basis for complaints by governments whose commerce is injured by other countries' standards.

Other codes developed in the Tokyo Round seek to limit the red tape involved in import licensing procedures and to reduce the friction over government subsidies of exports and the countervailing duties imposed to combat them.

13.5 TRADE POLICY AND THE LESS-DEVELOPED COUNTRIES

The less-developed countries (LDCs) have stayed largely aloof from the trade-liberalization movement, preferring to restrict trade severely in order to further their economic development. They have tried to promote industry by using tariffs or other trade controls to raise the prices of imported manufactures. They hoped that factors of production could thereby be pulled into their import-competing manufacturing sectors out of subsistence agriculture, other low-productivity activities, or outright unemployment. LDCs' tariff rates on manufactures have therefore generally been very high. One study offers the following average figures for effective rates of tariff protection (as defined in section 12.6) in manufacturing industries: Brazil (1966), 79 percent; Chile (1961), 54 percent; Mexico (1960), 21 percent; Malaya (1965), 7 percent; Pakistan (1963–64), 92 percent; Philippines (1965), 34 percent.[19] Quantitative restrictions and exchange control as well as tariffs are commonly used,

---

[18] Robert F. Legget, *Standards in Canada.* Ottawa: Information Canada, 1970, chap. 15.

[19] Bela Balassa et al., *The Structure of Protection in Developing Countries.* Baltimore: Johns Hopkins University Press, 1971, Table 3.2.

and the local subsidiaries of multinational companies are required to replace imported components with domestically produced ones (these restrictions are called *domestic content requirements*).

In the 1970's the LDCs came to some disillusionment about the value of onerous trade restrictions. The import-substituting enterprise often turns out to be highly inefficient and to behave monopolistically in the domestic market. The infants receiving infant-industry protection are very slow to grow up. Furthermore, the opportunity costs of factors moved to import-competing manufactures can prove substantial. The trade balance may deteriorate sharply when sectors producing primary products for exports are heavily taxed to provide capital for government projects. LDCs' interest has, therefore, shifted visibly toward export-oriented industrialization and, by implication, lighter restrictions on trade.

LDC Exports and Tariff Preferences

This shift has had its effect in rapid growth of exports of labor-intensive manufactures from some LDCs in Asia and Latin America (see Chapter 8). A recent study by the Organization for Economic Cooperation and Development pointed out that a group of newly industrializing countries had expanded their share of world industrial exports from 2.5 percent in 1963 to more than 7 percent in 1977. The United States' percentage of manufactured imports bought from these countries rose from 5.9 percent in 1973 to no less than 20.0 percent in 1977.[20] Despite this success story the LDCs have been acutely conscious of the mountainous tariffs imposed on the kinds of goods they export by many industrial countries. We saw in section 13.3 that the U.S. tariff gives heavier protection to labor-intensive domestic industries, and the same seems to hold for other industrial countries. The LDCs urged successfully that they should be partially relieved of this tariff burden by a device that came to be known as the Generalized System of Preferences (GSP). Each industrial country would admit some quantity of imports from less-developed countries either free of tariff duties or at a lower rate than what other exporters pay. This privilege would allow LDCs profitably to expand any exports that they can manufacture at a cost lying between the world price and the industrial country's tariff-ridden domestic price. To provide them this benefit the industrial countries pay a price that can be identified in Figure 13.1. Suppose that tariff P_tP_w/P_wO

[20] Organization for Economic Cooperation and Development, *The Impact of the Newly Industrializing Countries on Production and Trade in Manufactures: Report by the Secretary-General.* Paris, 1979. The OECD study includes Spain, Portugal, Greece, and Yugoslavia as newly industrializing countries along with Brazil, Mexico, Hong Kong, Singapore, South Korea, and Taiwan.

is in effect, so that the country purchases MN imports from industrial nations. A quota arrangement now allows LDCs to sell one-half of MN without paying the tariff. The total quantity of imports and their domestic price P_t will remain unchanged. The sole welfare effect on the industrial country giving the preference is its loss of tariff revenue equal to half of area 3. Despite this cost, preferences have been granted to the LDCs by many industrial countries — including the United States in the Trade Reform Act of 1974.

As an income transfer and export stimulus the preferences have surely improved the welfare of those LDCs able to develop manufactured exports successfully. The preferences have been tightly hedged, however, as to the commodities covered and the size of the trade in any given commodity subject to preferences. One unfortunate by-product of the GSP was to make the LDCs hostile to generalized tariff reduction by the industrial countries in the Tokyo Round. As a glance at Figure 13.1 will show, the value of a preference is reduced in direct proportion by any cut in the tariff. But the across-the-board tariff reductions in the Tokyo Round also offered benefits to LDC exporters by cutting tariffs on products for which they did not enjoy preferences. One calculation suggests that they may gain more from the overall reduction than they lose through the erosion of their preference margins.[21]

Offshore Assembly Provisions

A feature of the United States tariff that has come to hold great importance for the LDCs is the provision for offshore assembly. The tariff collector's usual posture is that a good entering the country pays the standard tariff, even if it was originally made in that country and then exported. The provisions for offshore assembly waive this practice to allow goods exported from the United States and subjected to further processing abroad to pay duty only on the value added abroad and not the whole value of the commodity imported. By 1978 the total value of goods imported under the offshore assembly provision had reached $9.3 billion, 9.9 percent of the total value of manufactured imports (19.1 percent, in the case of manufactured imports from the LDCs). Of the $9.3 billion $7.0 billion was value added abroad, $2.3 billion value from U.S. production.

Although the offshore assembly provision is not restricted to the LDCs, it has held special importance for them. It allows American firms to sort out the various processes required to make a finished product, sending partially finished goods overseas to have labor-intensive processes

[21] R. E. Baldwin and T. Murray, "MFN Tariff Reductions and Developing Country Trade Benefits under the GSP," *Economic Journal,* 87 (March 1977): 30–46.

performed where they can be done more cheaply. Cut cloth is sewn into garments, wires are soldered onto electronic components. Of course, this maneuver works only if the goods are readily shipped and valuable relative to their weight; otherwise the two-way transportation costs swamp the savings from using lower-cost foreign labor. The LDCs benefiting most from these operations predictably have larger supplies of low-skilled but efficient labor, not much other basis for establishing a comparative advantage in their exports, and a political and economic infrastructure conducive to carrying out these operations reliably.[22]

13.6 SUMMARY

The theory of tariff welfare helps to explain international commercial diplomacy. Although free trade is optimal for the world as a whole, a large country can benefit by imposing its own tariff. Retaliation, however, is apt to leave everybody worse off. From such a situation, multilateral tariff disarmament is an attractive way to share the gains of moving to world free trade. These gains can be illustrated with simple partial-equilibrium demand and supply diagrams.

The United States' Reciprocal Trade Agreements program embodies such an effort at tariff disarmament. It was used from 1934 on in bilateral negotiations to lower duties set by the Smoot-Hawley Act of 1930. Eventually, concern with incidental terms-of-trade improvements given to third parties impeded these bilateral deals and encouraged the multilateral tariff reductions undertaken periodically since World War II. The United States has led the way with these, but American legislation has at times been hamstrung by protectionist features.

The General Agreement on Tariffs and Trade has been the vehicle for multilateral trade liberalization. The GATT tries to avoid discriminatory tariffs. It also encourages tariffs rather than quantitative restrictions when a domestic industry is to be protected. It has helped to keep commercial disputes between countries from escalating. Multilateral bargaining has secured large tariff reductions over the years, and industrial countries' nominal tariffs on manufactures now hover around 10 percent. The U.S. tariff protects low-skilled workers and small businesses.

Although we can calculate the tariff equivalent of a quantitative restriction, economists generally favor tariffs over QRs on principle. A

---

[22] Michael Sharpston, "International Sub-contracting," *Oxford Economic Papers,* 27 (March 1975): 94–135; J. Peter Jarrett, "Offshore Assembly and Production and the Internalization of International Trade Within the Multinational Corporation," Ph.D. dissertation, Harvard University, 1979. Chaps. 7, 8.

QR can hide a very high level of protection, and its incidence can rise over time. QRs are used when politically powerful producer groups desire heavy protection. "Voluntary" export agreements are a form of quota administered by foreign sellers, and are particularly costly in welfare for the importing country. In the Tokyo Round the members of GATT agreed on a series of codes that seek to limit important classes of nontariff barriers — those associated with government procurement, practices in valuing imports for determining the duty paid, technical standards of products, import licensing procedures, and methods of handling export subsidies and duties set to countervail them.

The developing countries have protected their domestic manufacturing sectors heavily in order to encourage economic development. However, they have grown somewhat disillusioned with the effects of heavy protection and now give more emphasis to promoting exports of suitable manufactured goods. Tariff preferences have been offered by the industrial countries to provide some market access for these goods. The offshore assembly provisions of the United States tariff also benefit the LDCs by promoting the export to them of unfinished goods that are further processed and then reimported to the United States. Many labor-intensive stages of production have thus been subcontracted to developing nations.

SUGGESTIONS FOR FURTHER READING

Amacher, Ryan C., Gottfried Haberler, and Thomas D. Willett, eds. *Challenges to a Liberal International Economic Order*. Washington: American Enterprise Institute, 1979. Contains papers on current issues in trade and related policies.

Baldwin, Robert E. *Nontariff Distortions of International Trade*. Washington: Brookings Institution, 1970. Analytical survey of U.S. nontariff barriers.

Baldwin, Robert E., and J. David Richardson, eds. *International Trade and Finance: Readings*. 2nd ed. Boston: Little, Brown and Company, 1981. Parts II and III contain papers on several aspects of trade liberalization.

Cline, William R. et al. *Trade Negotiations in the Tokyo Round: A Quantitative Assessment*. Washington: Brookings Institution, 1978. Measurement of the effects of liberalization.

Curzon, Gerard. *Multilateral Commercial Diplomacy*. London: Michael Joseph, 1964. Background and operation of the General Agreement on Tariffs and Trade.

Evans, John W. *The Kennedy Round in American Trade Policy: The Twilight of the GATT?* Cambridge: Harvard University Press, 1971. Detailed study of the Kennedy Round of tariff bargaining.

Ratner, Sidney. *The Tariff in American History*. New York: D. Van Nostrand, 1972. A useful short history.

Scitovsky, Tibor. "A Reconsideration of the Theory of Tariffs," *Review of Economic Studies*, 9, no. 2 (1942), 89–110; reprinted in American Economic Association, *Readings in the Theory of International Trade*. Philadelphia: Blakiston, 1950, chap. 16. Theory of tariff warfare and disarmament.

U.S. Commission on International Trade and Investment Policy. *United States International Economic Policy in an Interdependent World*. Washington: Government Printing Office, 1971. Volume 1 of papers submitted to the commission covers many aspects of trade policy.

14

Preferential Trading Arrangements

In the last chapter we explored the case for unrestricted trade from a world viewpoint and reviewed the mutual efforts of countries to remove impediments to trade. Campaigns for trade liberalization are not confined, however, to freeing trade around the world. Groups of nations often try to ease trade restrictions among themselves while leaving them intact against the outside world. In this chapter we shall deal with such efforts at partial liberalization.

Preferential trading arrangements now follow one after another. In 1957 six nations of Continental Europe formed the European Economic Community, prompting seven others to organize the European Free Trade Area. These two groups are now engaged in a slow and complex process of consolidation, with the European Community (EC), as it is now called, including nine full members. The EC's members are West Germany, France, Italy, Belgium, Luxembourg, the Netherlands, Denmark, the United Kingdom, and the Republic of Ireland. The less-developed countries, especially in Latin America and Africa, have gathered into similar if less far-reaching unions. Nor are preferences a recent discovery: Great Britain and her Commonwealth associates in 1931 agreed to levy lower tariff rates on goods imported from each other — Commonwealth Preference tariffs.

The economic effects of these arrangements, usually undertaken for both political and economic reasons, raise a number of important questions. Do the participants gain economically? If so, what factors control the size of the gain? Do the outsiders lose? If so, can the world as a whole become worse off? We shall explore the theory of regional trading arrangements in the first two sections of this chapter, then test some of its predictions against the experience of the EC. We shall also take up a related but distinctive regional group — the socialist block of countries, where trading arrangements are seasoned with the problems of organizing exchange among production ministries outside the market system.

14.1 FUNDAMENTAL EFFECTS OF TRADE PREFERENCES

A group of countries forms a preferential trading arrangement when they place lower restrictions on trade with each other than on trade with the outside world. The members need not be neighbors, but because they often are, we shall also call these "regional arrangements." Likewise, the preferences need not extend to all products traded, but we shall follow common practice in assuming that they generally do. Even assuming that preferences are given on all goods, we can imagine several different arrangements. The following terms for describing them have come into fairly standard usage:

Free-Trade Area. Members eliminate tariffs among themselves but keep their original tariffs against the outside world. The European Free Trade Area came honestly by its name.

Customs Union. Members not only eliminate all tariffs among themselves but also form a common tariff against the outside world.

Common Market. Members proceed beyond the requirements of a customs union to eliminate restrictions among themselves on international movements of factors of production. The European Community, often called "the Common Market," largely fits this definition.

Economic Union. Members proceed beyond the requirements of a common market to unify their fiscal, monetary, and socioeconomic policies. Belgium and Luxembourg formed an economic union in 1921, and the EC plans ultimately to go most of the distance to economic union.

These preferential arrangements are analytically interesting — and complex — because they both distort and liberalize trade. Trade is freed because some flows face lower restrictions than before. But trade is also distorted because goods coming into a member country pay different tariffs depending on their origin — the external tariff if from outside the group, a preferential or zero rate if from a partner. The distortion amounts to price discrimination — charging or (in this case) paying different prices for identical goods at a given market location. Because of this two-faced character of preferential arrangements, you would guess correctly that they can either improve or worsen the economic welfare of their members or of the world as a whole. In this section we shall analyze the effects of preferences in the simplest possible way, to show how they can either improve or worsen the allocation of resources. In the next section we shall push a short distance into the general-equilibrium analysis of preferential arrangements.

Trade Creation and Trade Diversion

Jacob Viner first showed that preferences could either improve or worsen allocation, in that they could lead either to *trade creation* or *trade diversion*.[1] Let us suppose that A and B form a customs union, leaving C (the rest of the world) outside. Previously, A produced part of its requirements of good x at home, inefficiently, behind its tariff wall. Partner B is the most efficient producer of x and the sole world exporter. When A abolishes tariffs against B (and all the necessary market adjustments have taken place), A's inefficient x industry is partly competed down, as A's imports from B expand. Trade has been *created*. The gains are the same as if A had eliminated its x tariff completely.

The effects are illustrated in Figure 14.1, which builds on a method of analysis set forth in section 13.1. A's demand and domestic supply curves for x are respectively shown as DD and SS. We suppose that x is produced in B under conditions of perfectly elastic supply, so that an unlimited quantity is available at price OP. A's external tariff is set at the rate PT/OP. Before the customs union was formed, the supply function for imports after payment of tariff was TT'; hence A produced amount OM of its consumption (ON) of x, importing MN from B. Elimination of the tariff against B now makes PP' the relevant import supply schedule and causes consumption to expand to ON', imports to M'N', and domestic production to shrink to OM'. The four numbered areas in the diagram measure the welfare gain. A's consumers of x enjoy a gain in surplus measured by the whole area 1 + 2 + 3 + 4, but not all of this is net gain to the country. Area 1 formerly was profit to A's protected producers of x, so this gain to consumers is offset by the loss of producers.[2] Likewise area 3 formerly represented tariff revenue collected by A's government that is now lost when the preference is given

---

[1] Jacob Viner, *The Customs Union Issue.* New York: Carnegie Endowment for International Peace, 1950, chap. 4. The exposition in this section draws heavily upon Harry G. Johnson, *Money, Trade, and Economic Growth.* London: Allen and Unwin, 1962, chap. 3.

[2] We ignore considerations bearing on the distribution of income in A, supposing that a dollar of income is equally good no matter who receives it. If x were consumed by the poor but deserving and produced by the rich and conniving, we might count the redistribution measured by area 1 as (to some extent) a net gain.

FIGURE 14.1 Welfare Effects of Trade Creation

PP' is the partner-country supply curve. Tariff removal cuts domestic price
from *OT* to *OP*, expands imports to *M'N'*, and raises welfare by areas 2 + 4,

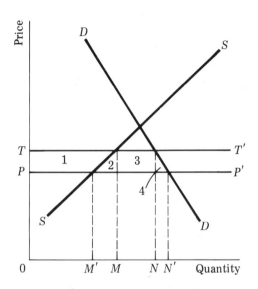

to *B*, If the government was spending its revenues on useful things —
parks and schools — there is no presumption that any net social benefit
derives from (in effect) giving the revenue measured by area 3 to the
consumers of *x*; therefore we assign it no net welfare significance. Two
triangles remain, both measuring net gains to *A*. Area 2 formerly represented part of the real cost of securing *OM* of domestic production; we
assume those resources are now put to other uses, so the extra surplus
measured by 2 is a net benefit. Likewise, area 4 represents a pure gain
in consumers' surplus not subject to any offset. The net benefit is areas
2 + 4.[3]

Trade diversion, on the other hand, would occur if *A*'s consumption
of *y* was formerly supplied by outsider *C*, the world's most efficient producer. *B* can also produce *y*, however. If *B* is not too inefficient, the
opportunity to sell in *A* without paying *A*'s tariff may let *B* undercut *C*,

---

[3] Notice that this benefit would be easily measurable in practice. We need to know
only the former tariff per unit — *PT* — and the increase in imports — *M'N'* minus
MN. The product of these multiplied by one-half approximates areas 2 + 4.

FIGURE 14.2   Welfare Effects of Trade Diversion

P_B indicates pretariff supply price in partner country, P_C pretariff supply price in rest of world. Tariff preference lowers internal price from T_C to P_B. Welfare loss occurs if area 5 exceeds area 4.

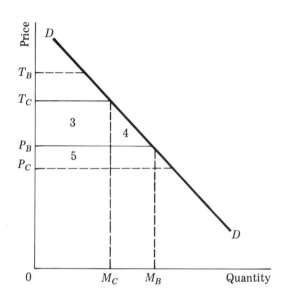

even though B is less efficient. This situation is shown in Figure 14.2, where A's demand curve for y appears as DD. We suppose that C can supply y at a domestic cost (and price) of P_C, and that this supply is perfectly elastic; likewise, B can supply y at the higher constant cost (and price) of P_B. Before the customs union is formed, A imposes an ad valorem tariff on imports of y equal to $P_C T_C/OP_C$ or $P_B T_B/OP_B$ — they are the same. A would buy from the least costly source after paying the tariff, and hence would import OM_C at price OT_C. Forming the customs union allows B's exports of y to enter duty-free, and A's consumption expands to OM_B. Areas in the diagram are labeled to illustrate the significant effects on welfare. Once again, lowering a tariff (even preferentially) allows a gain to A's consumers of y — areas 3 + 4. The meanings of these areas match their counterparts in Figure 14.1: area 3 shows tariff revenue formerly collected on imports from C, its loss offsetting the congruent gain in consumers' surplus; and area 4 depicts a pure gain in consumer's surplus not subject to any offset. A loss occurs, however, in the form of area 5. Formerly areas 3 + 5 measured the total tariff revenue collected on imports OM_C. But now this revenue is lost to A's government, and the part denoted by 5 instead paid by A's consumers to the higher-cost producers of y in B. It is pure social loss.[4] A *net* welfare loss from trade diversion occurs if area 5 is larger than area 4. It need not be, of course: The loss from switching to a less efficient source of supply could be more than offset by the gain from halting a restraint on consumers' spending.

Net Gains or Losses?

What can we say about the net influence of these forces? If A and B consume and trade many commodities, can we add up the net effect of all the instances of trade creation and diversion that will occur when they form a customs union or free-trade area? An accurate answer depends on the facts of each case. Nonetheless, some rough tests can suggest whether trade creation (which must raise welfare) is likely to prevail over trade diversion (which may or may not). For trade creation to predominate, the economies of A and B should be *actually competitive* (before the union) but *potentially complementary* (after it comes into effect). Trade creation requires protected production, initially, and hence the actual output patterns of the two economies must, due to protective tariffs against each other, look rather similar before they join in a customs union. Thus we stipulate that they should appear actually competitive. However, each member must also be the most efficient producer of goods protected and inefficiently produced by its partner — this condition guarantees trade creation rather than trade diversion.

Other simple tests for a union's welfare significance can also be used. Higher initial tariffs mean greater potential benefit. Higher initial tariffs enlarge areas 4 in Figures 14.1 and 14.2. If a common external tariff is formed (as in a customs union), the chances of benefit are enlarged if the new common tariff is lower than the previous individual ones — making trade diversion less likely, reducing the distance $P_C T_C$ (in Figure 14.2) and thus cutting the chance that P_B will fall within it. A larger preferential arrangement is more likely to be beneficial. This condition is obvious if we enlarge a hypothetical customs union until it includes nearly all the world's economic activity. With little production taking place outside, the union is almost sure to include the most efficient producer, and hence trade diversion is curtailed.

---

[4] No welfare gain for country B is involved, because the resources drawn into the production of y presumably were engaged in other activities where their value productivity was just as high.

14.2 DISTRIBUTION OF GAINS AND LOSSES FROM PREFERENCES

These techniques for measuring the welfare effects of trade creation and diversion assume that the country's terms of trade remain unchanged. This assumption underlies the perfectly elastic supply curves for imports employed in Figures 14.1 and 14.2. Were these curves positively sloped, the creation of preferences would worsen the home country's terms of trade with its partner, when that trade expands, or improve them with the outside world, when purchases are diverted to the partner country.

Countries seem to pick their partners for preferential arrangements primarily on political grounds, not from economic motives or calculations. Still, whether intended or not, a preferential arrangement is likely to change its members' terms of trade with the outside world and with each other. The possible results are diverse, but we can show some likely outcomes by considering preferential arrangements in the context of general equilibrium.

Let us start with a question that has a simple answer. Suppose that A and B decide to form a preferential arrangement, excluding C (the outside world). What tariff structure will maximize their joint gain from the venture? In the absence of any special market distortions, A and B should clearly adopt free trade with each other and levy the optimum tariff against the outside world. Even if each member's tariff was optimal before, from its own viewpoint, each gains from the expansion of previously restricted trade with the other. If their individual tariffs were not optimal, a further gain accrues from switching to the optimal tariff. Notice that their joint monopoly power in trade could well be greater than that of either separately. If they are sole exporters of a product and each previously calculated his optimal tariff taking the other's as given, further monopoly gains should accrue to them from setting their external tariff jointly. Should A and B form a free-trade area without changing their former external tariffs, the elimination of internal tariffs is still apt to improve their terms of trade with the outside world. The only requirement is the occurrence of some trade diversion. The switch of trade away from C, as A and B adopt preferences and increase their mutual trade, has the same effect on C as if A's and B's demand curves for imports from C were shifted inward. (Conversely, the preferential arrangement gains from trade creation with no corresponding loss for the outside world.)[5]

---

[5] This terms-of-trade improvement is analyzed and estimated for the EC by Howard C. Petith, "European Integration and the Terms of Trade," *Economic Journal*, 87 (June 1977): 262–72. He suggests that Germany's terms of trade may have improved as much as 7 percent, France's as much as 9 percent.

How are the gains from trade creation distributed between the members of a preferential arrangement? The respective sizes of the countries will be one determining force. Suppose that Canada and the United States were to form a free-trade area, with the United States being so much larger that its internal relative prices remain unchanged when the two tariff barriers fall and Canada's adjust fully to those in the United States. Reallocations of resources occur in both countries, but those in Canada are *proportionally* much larger. Canada gains from the chance to trade at U.S. internal prices without having to pay the U.S. tariff.

14.3 PREFERENTIAL ARRANGEMENTS IN PRACTICE

Customs unions and free-trade areas have been popular in the last two decades among both industrial and less-developed countries. The European Community was formed in 1957 by France, West Germany, Italy, the Netherlands, and Belgium-Luxembourg. The United Kingdom, Denmark, and the Republic of Ireland joined in 1973, and other countries are partial members. The community members moved to eliminate tariffs among themselves by staged reductions, finishing the job in 1968. The Common Market, in addition, has adopted a Common External Tariff, its rates set (with some exceptions) by averaging the rates for individual products that previously appeared in the member nations' tariff schedules.[6] Interest in such arrangements has also run high among the less-developed nations, although political difficulties have led to some frustration. For instance, eight South American nations plus Mexico have agreed to form a Latin American Free-Trade Area, and five Central American countries to create a Central American Common Market. In each case the union is propelled by political and economic objectives, with the latter including the real-income gains described in the preceding section and others, such as economic growth and economies of scale in production for small countries.

In this section we shall review some empirical evidence on the effects of preferential arrangements, in order to illustrate and give perspective to the theoretical concepts presented above.

Trade Creation and Diversion in the Common Market

We saw in section 14.1 that the welfare effects of a preferential arrangement are related to trade creation and diversion. Consider the effect of the Common Market on international trade in manufactures. We cannot

[6] For a description of the EC, see D. Swann, *The Economics of the Common Market*. Harmondsworth, England, and Baltimore: Penguin Books, 1970.

simply look at the size of trade flows — external and internal — before and after the EC was formed. They changed in response to forces other than tariff rates — the growth of national incomes, to take the most obvious. One reasonable way to estimate trade creation and diversion, however, is from changes in the sources of supply of manufactures to the Common Market countries, as Mordechai Kreinin has done.[7]

The reduction of internal tariffs resulted in trade creation that was reflected in a reduced share of each EC country's consumption of manufactures supplied by its domestic producers. Trade diversion is detected in the increased share of EC countries' imports coming from exporters in EC partner countries. Even without the EC, these shares would have changed due to movements in prices and incomes differing between the EC and the rest of the world. Kreinin experimented with various adjustments to control for these movements; finding none clearly superior to the others, he suggests taking an average of their results. He concludes that, as of 1969 and 1970, the EC had caused trade diversion of $1.1 billion but trade creation in the amount of $8.4 billion. Estimates by other investigators using somewhat different methods all yield the same general conclusion — trade creation exceeded trade diversion by a generous margin.[8]

To the static welfare analysis of customs unions set forth here and that of trade liberalization in Chapter 13, many students respond: "Is that all there is in it?" Are there no dynamic gains from greater scale economies, more vigorous competition, new incentives to invest and innovate? The economist's answer is: "If you believe that markets are competitive and always pretty much in equilibrium, yes, that's all there is." If that assumption fails to hold, however, the gains from tariff reduction — whether preferential or general — may be greatly enlarged. Consider these alternative assumptions, which hark back to our discussion of imperfect competition in Chapter 9:

1. Most producers (outside the primary sector) make goods that are specialized and differentiated, so that each faces a downward-sloping demand curve for his own output.
2. Elements of oligopoly may be present (especially in pre-EC Europe), so that producers' efforts to maintain and share out their collusive profits discourage them from making major plant expansions or otherwise getting an innovative jump on their rivals.
3. Business investment is subject to considerable uncertainty, so that

[7] Mordechai E. Kreinin, *Trade Relations of the EEC: An Empirical Investigation.* New York: Praeger, 1974, chap. 3.
[8] A survey is provided in Bela Balassa, ed., *European Economic Integration.* Amsterdam: North-Holland Publishing Co., 1975, chap. 3.

indications of an expanding market may increase the rate of capital spending that businesses desire to undertake.

Either of the first two assumptions suffices to predict that trade liberalization (preferential or general) will induce producers to make a dash for larger-scale and more efficient plants. Under the first assumption, each individual producer foresees the possibility of enlarged export markets that will absorb a substantially increased quantity of his output. Under the second assumption collusion gets harder to sustain when tariff barriers fall and foreign producers not in the cartel eagerly push their wares at more competitive prices; erstwhile loyalists of the cartel abandon that ship and try instead to make their activities as efficient as possible within a larger and more competitive market. Finally, the third assumption implies that these productivity-raising microeconomic adjustments not only change the qualitative character of investment but increase the rate of capital formation as well.

Although these effects should be large and seem easy to observe, it is in fact difficult to measure them with any accuracy. The first and second assumptions both imply that intraindustry trade (see Chapter 9) will be increasing, and that is certainly the case among the Common Market countries. There is some evidence that producers have rationalized their output lines, concentrating on what they make most efficiently, and that plant sizes run to more efficient scales. High and rising levels of domestic saving and investment are expected, and these have also been observed. Several observers conclude that these dynamic benefits "far outshadow" the static effects of tariff reduction measured above, but one cannot pretend to determine their sizes accurately.[9]

Preferential Arrangements Among Developing Nations

Preferential arrangements have been popular among the less-developed countries, where they are often seen as an adjunct to development planning. Development plans promote import-competing manufacturing industries behind massive walls of tariff protection. In the short run these industries are often clearly inefficient, because they lack a comparative advantage; governments believe, however, that in the long run their existence will further the country's growth. Now, one reason for the apparent inefficiency of these sheltered manufacturing industries is the small scale of markets for their products in less-developed countries. Empirical evidence suggests that scale economies can seriously hamper

[9] See Balassa's summary of this discussion, pp. 112–16; and also Tibor Scitovsky, *Economic Theory and Western European Integration*. London: George Allen and Unwin, 1958, chap. 3.

efficient production in the many less-developed countries with small populations and incomes per capita.

Rather than starting one small inefficient plant each in Colombia, Ecuador, and Paraguay to manufacture (or assemble) farm tractors, why not form a free-trade area and agree to put the tractor plant in one country, a maker of radios in a second, a tire factory in the third? Each country would gain its industrial sector, yet the disadvantages of small scale would be mitigated if each plant serves all three markets. Furthermore, the expansion of trade among them should be balanced. This goal has been an important motive for both the Latin American Free-Trade Area and the Central American Common Market (where national markets are hopelessly small). A study found that the nations of the Latin American Free-Trade Area, by locating plants of six important manufacturing industries at the most efficient sites, could save around 10 percent in production costs over a situation in which every member (or nearly every member) started its own protected production. Further gains would accrue in consumers' benefits (like area 4 in Figure 14.1).[10]

Actual effects of integration among the LDCs have been rather mixed. Each of the agreements has itself become stalled or reversed at times, and six members of the Latin American Free-Trade Area indeed formed their own more integrated Andean Common Market within the larger group. These preferential arrangements have achieved only partial freeing of their mutual trade, but they do show the expected pattern of expanding mutual trade during periods when internal tariffs were being cut. The attempt to farm out newly established industries among member countries has worked out rather badly in most cases. The allocations have usually been determined on a political rather than an economic basis, and have sometimes done little more than create or perpetuate regional monopolies. These LDC arrangements have not been showered with dynamic benefits.

14.4 TRADE PROBLEMS OF THE SOVIET BLOC

The theory of preferential arrangements can also be applied to the trade relations of the USSR and its Eastern European neighbors. These centrally planned economies trade heavily with each other, because of ideological preferences, restrictions on trade imposed for military and strategic reasons by the Western countries, and intrinsic problems in establishing trade relations between market and centrally planned economies. The Eastern bloc's principal trading association, the Council

[10] Martin Carnoy, "A Welfare Analysis of Latin American Economic Union: Six Industry Studies," *Journal of Political Economy*, 78 (July/August 1970): 626–54.

for Mutual Economic Assistance (CMEA), is not a preferential area in the same sense as the EC. Yet both East-West trade and trade among the CMEA nations raise enough problems related to the theory of preferential arrangements to justify reviewing them in its context. Furthermore, they allow us to consider the special problems of external trade in centrally planned economies.

Planning and trading in the CMEA countries are difficult to discuss because the institutions have been changing. From a situation in which the price system was not used for valuing alternatives and allocating resources, some members have moved over the past decade and a half to one in which the signals of a price system are increasingly heeded. These reforms have apparently not made great progress, however, and so our discussion will stress the problems they faced in allocating resources and planning trade without resorting to the price system.[11]

The managers of a socialist economy could in principle employ the price system to put resources to their best uses, even if they eschew private ownership of the means of production. Tell the manager of each production ministry or enterprise to expand output whenever its price exceeds marginal cost, contract it when price falls short of marginal cost. Tell the ministry in charge of prices to raise the price of any good, service, or factor of production when its demand exceeds supply, lower it when supply exceeds demand. Resources then would tend to be devoted to their best uses without any elaborate mechanism of central planning. Although the CMEA countries have moved toward using prices for rationing and signaling, they have depended primarily on detailed central planning to allocate scarce resources. In the USSR the mixture of outputs — consumer goods, producer goods, defense — has been chosen by the government, and the retail prices of consumer goods have been set to ration their arbitrary quantities in relation to consumers' demands and purchasing power. Wholesale prices have borne no relation to retail prices and served accounting purposes rather than guiding the mix of inputs and outputs chosen by production units. Those inputs and outputs instead have been set by "material balances": Enterprises submit lists of input requirements for the target outputs assigned to them; all inputs and outputs of a physical item are added up centrally, and the enterprises' plans sent back for revision in light of any excess supplies or demands thereby revealed.

International trade has generally been viewed not as an opportunity

---

[11] For a good short account, see F. D. Holzman, "Foreign Trade Behavior of Centrally Planned Economies," _Industrialization in Two Systems: Essays in Honor of Alexander Gerschenkron,_ ed. H. Rosovsky. New York: John Wiley, 1966, pp. 237–65. Recent changes are discussed by Mark Allen, "The Structure and Reform of the Exchange and Payments Systems of Some East European Countries," _IMF Staff Papers,_ 23 (November 1976): 718–39.

to benefit the CMEA countries through specialization but rather as a way to fill otherwise intractable excesses of requirements over supplies. Exports are merely the trading stock for securing imports — a piquant contrast to the mercantilistic habits of Western governments, which often treat exports as good per se and imports as a necessary evil. The task of securing these imports has fallen to foreign-trade organizations. They barter for the needed imports whatever domestic outputs are in short-run excess supply. National self-sufficiency has been viewed as a goal and trade as a source of potential disruption to planning. This posture is not wildly unrealistic for the vast and diversified Soviet Union, but it hardly made sense for the small countries of Eastern Europe when they copied the USSR's planning practices. It is no surprise that the foreign-trade turnover of the CMEA countries in 1955 was no more than one-third of expected Western market economies of comparable size and income levels.[12] The planners have been reluctant to invest resources (i.e., make a long-term commitment) in export production, and hence export trade has not seized ultimate comparative advantage, but rather has been a vent for temporary surpluses.

East-West Trade

The CMEA countries have undoubtedly diverted trade toward each other and away from the outside world. In 1948 no CMEA nation carried on more than 30 percent of its trade with other CMEA powers; now the figure is seldom less than two-thirds. This switch results from many forces, including discrimination by the West. Two sets of trade-restricting factors reflect the trading problems of planned economies and hence help to explain this shift.

One set of restrictive forces denies Western buyers the chance to "go shopping" in CMEA markets — obviously a deterrent to trade. Superficially, this restriction arises from the "inconvertibility" of CMEA currencies — meaning that they cannot legally be held by outsiders, and hence cannot be used freely to purchase within the Bloc. Yet this inconvertibility merely reflects the necessities of trade subject to CMEA planning procedures. Prices — the basis on which one shops — have not served (as in a market economy) to value alternatives among Bloc goods. If outsiders shopped on the basis of CMEA countries' internal prices, set for other internal purposes, the resulting trade could be quite inefficient. For instance, the USSR and other CMEA countries have preferred high prices for consumer goods and low prices for producer goods, neither reflecting opportunity costs in production.

[12] See Frederic L. Pryor, *The Communist Foreign Trade System*. Cambridge, Mass.: MIT Press, 1963, chap. 1.

The situation is described in Figure 14.3, where we show a transformation function for producer and consumer goods. We suppose that the planners allocate output between these two classes in the proportion given by line *OQ*, making no systematic use of international trade (except to meet temporary shortages or dispose of temporary surpluses). The relative prices in Western markets we suppose to be indicated by price slope P_w. It suggests that, by taking full advantage of international trade the CMEA country could export consumer goods, obtaining for final use the producer and consumer goods indicated by point *C*, superior to bundle *P* actually produced and used. On the other hand, the internal prices used by the CMEA countries, P_c, render producer goods cheaper. If Western traders were allowed to make offers at these internal prices, the CMEA country would export producer goods, and wind up at an inferior point somewhere along PP_c.

Apart from the irrational CMEA internal prices, Westerners could not be allowed to place orders ad lib without potentially spoiling the planned internal allocations, if planning via material balances allows no

---

FIGURE 14.3 Effect of CMEA Pricing Practices
on Potential Gains from Trade

Production takes place at *P*. With world prices P_w, the socialist economy would gain from producing consumer goods for export and trading to point *C*. Internal prices P_c, set to favor producer goods, cannot guide trade because they imply an inefficient specialization in producer goods.

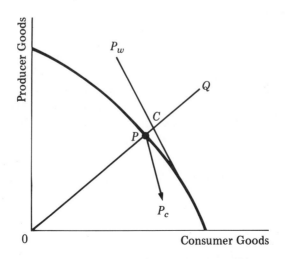

production for export in the long run. Hence East-West trade must be effected by the CMEA countries' foreign-trade organizations bargaining as best they can on Western markets, and at Western prices.[13] In the face of these difficulties it is surprising if East-West trade achieves any rationality in relation to the basic forces of comparative advantage. But the international trade of the USSR indeed does appear rational on the basis of the Heckscher-Ohlin theorem. Rosefielde found that the USSR imports relatively capital-intensive goods from countries endowed with more capital per worker and exports relatively labor-intensive goods to them. Similarly for its trade with countries less well endowed with capital: Soviet exports to them are relatively capital-intensive.[14]

In striking bargains with the West the CMEA foreign-trade organizations have suffered from many drawbacks. One is the lack of long-term supplies of potential exports designed to non-CMEA tastes and standards. CMEA managers, operating in a framework of quantitative production targets, have in effect lived in a seller's market and have not been guided by the salability of their goods. Hence CMEA goods (other than homogeneous raw materials) have commanded poorer terms of trade on Western markets than the terms among the CMEA countries themselves. Bargaining with the West has also been complicated by the CMEA's need to secure external balance and to meet periodic quotas on strategic imports. For instance, Western traders have been known to postpone negotiations with CMEA foreign-trade organizations until they knew the latter were under deadline pressures to fulfill their quotas — a timing hardly favorable to CMEA gains from trade. The CMEA countries also apparently hold very small reserves of foreign exchange, and because the Bloc currencies themselves are inconvertible trade must be balanced over the fairly short run.

Trade Among CMEA Nations

The CMEA countries seem to have diverted trade toward each other and away from the West. Have they also created a great deal of trade among themselves? On the one hand, you might suppose that integrated region-wide planning would allow these similar, centrally planned economies broad opportunities for exploiting cost advantages and scale economies in locating new productive capacity. On the other hand, arranging trade between sovereign centrally planned economies might be even more complex than arranging it between them and market economies.

Initially, the Eastern European countries copied the planning prac-

[13] This section, including Figure 14.3, draws heavily on Holzman, pp. 242–47.
[14] Steven Rosefielde, *Soviet International Trade in Heckscher-Ohlin Perspective: An Input-Output Study.* Lexington, Mass.: Lexington Books, 1973.

tices of the USSR, including its self-sufficiency and its emphasis on heavy industry. Even with the political dominance in the area of the USSR (hence references to the "Russian Embassy system of coordination"), only recently have the CMEA countries moved seriously toward coordinating their investment planning and abandoned a purely national approach. They have used numerous intermediate devices. Bilateral trade agreements have served to specify the intrabloc trade pattern in advance. But for a long time these trade agreements lacked integration with production planning. If they could not influence the placement of new productive resources, they could not advance the CMEA's division of labor. Production remained restricted to traditional patterns, and trade served only to vent short-run surpluses. The CMEA apparently promoted much technical cooperation among its members within some industries, and with this cooperation came *intraproduct specialization* in some outputs. But *interproduct specialization* that would give the CMEA nations significantly differing industrial structures came slowly. Only with the round of planning for 1966–70 was significant intrabloc coordination attempted in drawing up long-term plans, and rough trade and production balances struck for the region as a whole. By the 1976–80 cycle there was more coordination of sectoral plans across countries, so that they could be joined into a multilateral trading pattern. The CMEA countries still labor under difficulties in this coordination of their planning processes, however, because they lack any clear internal indicators of opportunity cost, and because the Western market prices that serve to value intra-CMEA trade are rather arbitrary bargaining chips among the CMEA members.

Because the prices used in intra-CMEA trade are bargained out among the members, Western observers have wondered who gets the better end of the bargain. Even if the CMEA gained from "trade diversion" away from the West — and it almost surely does not — the resulting benefits might be spread very unevenly. Hewett's calculations suggest that the USSR is actually the loser in intra-CMEA trade: that the USSR could shift the factors of production it now uses producing exports shipped to other CMEA members into producing goods to replace what it imports from them, and wind up with more goods overall.[15]

14.5 SUMMARY

Preferential arrangements among groups of countries — trading clubs, free-trade areas, customs unions, etc. — are now a popular way to cut

[15] Edward A. Hewett, *Foreign Trade Prices in the Council of Mutual Economic Assistance.* New York: Cambridge University Press, 1974.

tariffs. They can either raise or lower economic welfare, in that they both free trade (among their members) and distort trade (with the outside world). Beneficial trade creation results when protected production is competed down and trade expanded between members. The effects are like those of the nondiscriminatory removal of tariffs. Trade diversion occurs when a preference causes a country to switch its purchases from a more efficient to a less efficient supplier. That switch itself imposes a welfare cost, but it could be offset by a gain for consumers. A union is most likely to benefit the world when a lot of protected production is competed down, when very high tariffs are lowered, and when the union comprises a large proportion of the trading world.

A preferential arrangement is likely to shift the terms of trade of each party. The members would maximize their joint welfare by freeing trade among themselves and levying the optimal tariff against outsiders. A member who gives a preference to its partner loses (and the partner gains) if the member's terms of trade with the outside world fail to improve; if they improve, however, the member and the partner may both benefit. Speaking broadly, preferences seem likely to improve their members' terms of trade and welfare and to impose a cost on the outside world.

The European Community seems to have created a good deal of trade and diverted little. The modest diversion may be due to the way the common external tariff was formed by averaging members' previous tariffs. The EC has probably enjoyed dynamic gains much larger than its static effects. Dynamic gains are predicted if we suppose that many markets are imperfectly competitive. Among the less-developed countries an important potential benefit from preferences lies in exploiting scale economies in a larger market. Preferential arrangements formed in Latin America have achieved expansion of their mutual trade but have apparently not been very successful with planned international specialization.

The regional trading arrangements of the USSR and its neighbors do not take the form of a customs union, but preferences and efforts at trade creation are involved. Trade between planned and market economies is difficult when the former do not employ prices to measure the opportunity costs of outputs. The CMEA countries have secured essential imports from the West by barter, exporting temporary surpluses and not committing production in line with long-run comparative advantage. They have diverted trade heavily toward each other, but only recently have they begun to coordinate their planning machinery in order to pursue comparative advantage among themselves.

SUGGESTIONS FOR FURTHER READING

Balassa, Bela, *European Economic Integration*. Amsterdam: North-Holland Publishing Co., 1975. Papers measuring the effects of the European Community.

Grunwald, Joseph, M. S. Wionczek, and Martin Carnoy. *Latin American Integration and U.S. Policy*. Washington: Brookings Institution, 1972. Integration among less-developed countries and its effects.

Holzman, F. D. "Foreign Trade Behavior of Centrally Planned Economies," *Industrialization in Two Systems*, ed. Henry Rosovsky. New York: John Wiley, 1966, pp. 237–65. Analytical treatment of problems of foreign trade in a planned economy.

Johnson, Harry G. *Money, Trade and Economic Growth*. London: George Allen and Unwin, 1962. Chapter 3 contains a good simplified treatment of customs-union theory.

Krause, Lawrence B. *European Economic Integration and the United States*. Washington: Brookings Institution, 1968. Surveys effects of Common Market on various American interests.

Robson, P., ed. *International Economic Integration*. Harmondsworth, England, and Baltimore: Penguin, 1972. Papers on many aspects of economic integration.

Swann, D. *The Economics of the Common Market*. Harmondsworth, England, and Baltimore: Penguin, 1970. Describes institutions and rules of European Economic Community.

IV

INCOME, MONEY, AND THE BALANCE OF PAYMENTS

15

The Balance
of Payments and the
Foreign-Exchange Rate

In the preceding parts of this book we concentrated on the behavior of the "real variables" in the international economy — the quantities of goods produced, consumed, and traded. Prices were crucial in securing equilibrium, but only as the relative prices of goods (the terms of trade) or factors of production. Now we take up the behavior of monetary magnitudes — prices and values that are measured in currency units. These include nations' money price levels, the financial assets that they trade internationally, and — especially — the price at which currencies exchange for one another.

The analysis departs from the previous parts of this book in more ways than putting $ and £ price tags on all international transactions. It also relaxes certain key assumptions that underlay the position of market equilibrium described in Parts 1 and 2:

Cash balances. We assumed before that people exactly spend their incomes. Now we allow them to hold cash balances. They may decide to build up or run down those balances and as a result spend less or more than their current incomes.

Price flexibility. We assumed before that all money prices — and therefore relative prices — were flexible, rising when demand exceeds supply and falling when supply exceeds demand. Now we explore the consequences of prices that are sticky and resist downward pressure when supply exceeds demand. The result may be unemployment and unutilized capacity. The exchange rate is itself an adjustment device for bringing a country's international purchases and sales into equilibrium. In this chapter we introduce its role as a regulator of international transactions. We also present the balance-of-payments accounts, the statistical record that informs us how this adjustment process is proceeding.

15.1 THE FOREIGN-EXCHANGE RATE

The exchange rate is the link between nations' money price and cost structures. Is Paris an expensive place to visit? Are cameras cheap in Hong Kong? Are the Japanese low-cost producers of steel? These questions can be answered only by translating the local currency in which these goods are priced into our own — via the exchange rate. We shall define the exchange rate as the price of foreign currency. Suppose that we consider buying a suit in London priced at fifty pounds sterling (£50), and the exchange rate is $2 per pound. We multiply £50 by 2.0 to conclude that its cost in U.S. currency is $100. Or suppose that we budget $500 for a holiday in England; we divide $500 by the dollar price of sterling to calculate that we can spend £250.

The exchange rate is defined here as the dollar price of sterling, but we could just as well quote it as the sterling price of dollars, £1/$2 = £0.50. The choice is arbitrary, and indeed everyday practice varies widely. Americans usually quote the sterling exchange rate as the dollar price of sterling — the price of foreign exchange. But the British also quote this rate as the dollar price of sterling — for them the price of home currency. And Americans and Japanese both state the Japan–U.S. exchange rate as the yen price of the dollar. Although we always express the exchange rate in this book as the price of foreign currency, whenever you see a rate quoted elsewhere you must think about whether it is a dollar price of foreign exchange or a foreign price of the dollar.

International Exchange Expressed in Foreign Currency

People usually deal in monetary transactions — cash paid for things bought and cash received for things sold — and so the exchange rate is the monetary translator of the terms of trade for the purpose of individual transactions. Given the prices of each nation's goods and services in terms of domestic money, the exchange rate tells us whether we can profitably sell our goods abroad, and whether the goods (potential imports) offered by foreign countries are a better buy than import-competing goods available at home. Therefore, we can think of international exchange as regulated by the foreign-exchange rate, as a stand-in for the terms of trade. This is a partial view of the exchange rate's role, as we shall see in Chapter 19. That is because the exchange rate governs the terms of trade between different countries' goods and services only if we take price levels in national currency to be independent of the exchange rate; but in general they influence each other.

Therefore we proceed from the exchange of goods between nations, described in Part I of this book, to its financial counterpart in the flows of purchasing power. Assume that prices of all potential imports are given in foreign currency (pounds sterling), and all prices of exportable domestic goods and services given in domestic currency (dollars). The lower the exchange rate — the price of pounds sterling — the lower are the dollar prices of imports, and the more units of them we buy. We can think of these demands for importable goods and services as aggregated into a single demand curve for "pounds worth of imports," illustrated in Figure 15.1a, which resembles Figures 2.6 and 4.2 in the first part of this book. Suppose we buy a million pounds worth of imports at an exchange rate of $2.00. The exchange rate falls to $1.90 and we demand more of many or all types of goods we purchase abroad, the weighted average increase in our demands being 10 percent. Then the number of pounds worth of imports we purchase rises to £1.1 million.

Foreigners have demands for our exportable goods and services that depend on their dollar prices and the exchange rate. We could depict foreign demand by plotting the dollars worth of our exports demanded as a function of the foreign-currency price of dollars — the inverse of the exchange rate actually shown in Figure 15.1a. What we need, however, is to bring the foreign demand for our exportables together with our own demand for importables. To accomplish that, we simply recognize that foreigners who demand dollars worth of our exports are in the same breath offering to supply pounds in payment. With the pound prices of foreign goods given, that is the same as supplying pounds worth of foreign goods. Therefore we can transform the foreign demand for our dollar-priced exports into a foreign supply of pound-priced goods and services — the supply curve shown in Figure 15.1a.

An example may clarify this maneuver. At an exchange rate of $2.00 (or £0.50 per dollar) foreigners demand $2 million worth of our exports. Equivalently we can say that they supply £1 million pounds — or pounds worth of our importables. If the exchange rate falls to $1.90, that is equivalent to the pound price of dollars rising to £0.526. Foreigners might cut the dollars worth of our goods that they demand back to $1.75 million, equivalent to supplying £921,000 — less than before. These points would be consistent with the conventional-looking supply curve shown in Figure 15.1a. In this transformation the foreign demand for our exports has not slipped away; it has merely been expressed in a different form.

We have expressed the international exchange of goods and services in money terms — specifically with everything expressed in units of foreign currency. We could have carried the analysis through in terms of

FIGURE 15.1   Market for Exports and Imports Priced in
Foreign Exchange: Alternative Versions

U.S. citizens demand foreign exchange (sterling) in order to purchase
foreign goods and services. Foreigners supply sterling (i.e., demand dollars)
in order to purchase U.S. goods and services. The exchange rate of $2.00
is a stable equilibrium in part *a* of the diagram, an unstable equilibrium
(surrounded by stable ones) in part *b*.

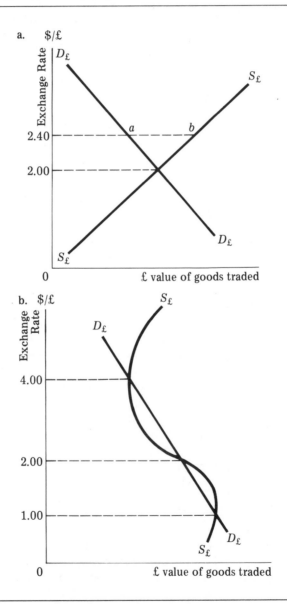

the market for traded goods and services priced in dollars. The exchange rate expressed in dollars per pound sterling is nothing but the reciprocal of the exchange rate expressed in pounds per dollar.

You may be concerned about one simplification we have made in describing both the terms of trade and the exchange rate. The terms of trade of concern to us are the relation between the prices of all things we sell to the rest of the world and the prices of all things we buy abroad. The terms of trade thus involve price indexes calculated over many goods and countries. But what about the market foreign exchange rate, which must be quoted as the price of a single foreign currency? In order to grasp what is happening to the dollar's value vis-à-vis the rest of the world (and thus to the U.S. terms of trade) we need, specifically, a price index of these bilateral foreign-exchange rates, a dollar price of all foreign currencies. Such a measure, called an *effective exchange rate*, has come to be frequently quoted. To construct an effective exchange rate we weight the bilateral exchange rate of the dollar against each foreign currency by the United States' proportion of trade with that country (or some such weight reflecting the country's importance in U.S. international transactions). Between 1971, when long-standing fixed exchange rates were abandoned, and the beginning of 1980, the effective price of foreign currency in terms of dollars (as calculated by the International Monetary Fund) rose by 27 percent.

Fixing the Exchange Rate

Governments often choose not to let the foreign-exchange rate be determined in the marketplace. Instead they fix or "peg" it at an official value. Figure 15.1a helps us to understand this process. An official exchange rate is only by accident the one that serves to equate the foreign-exchange values of traded goods demanded and supplied ($2.00 in Figure 15.1a). The rate that keeps trade in balance changes every time any disturbance strikes the trade flows themselves — that is, all the time. How can a government make the market exchange rate stay at or near a desired official value, if the rate left to its own devices shifts from moment to moment? The answer is that some government must stand ready to buy or sell foreign exchange at the desired price in order to make that price stick in the market. Suppose that $2.00 were the price at which the values of exports and imports are equal, as in Figure 15.1a, but that some government had chosen to make the higher price of $2.40 the official fixed value. Figure 15.1a shows that at that price there is an excess supply of sterling measured by *ab*. An exchange rate of $2.40 could prevail if *either* the U.S. government is willing to use dollars to buy up *ab* of sterling *or* the British government holds reserves of dollars that it will use for the same purpose. Any funds that the British government would hold for this purpose are called its *international reserves*.

From World War II to 1973 nearly all countries did peg their exchange rates in just this fashion under their commitment in the Articles of Agreement of the International Monetary Fund. These pegged rates were changed occasionally. Since 1973 the system of pegged exchange rates has been abandoned by the largest trading countries. The new system has been called the "managed float," meaning that countries broadly allow the market forces of supply and demand to determine their exchange rates, but sometimes use international reserves to intervene and modify the market rate (or the speed with which it is changing).

Stability of Exchange

Economists have devoted a great deal of attention to the stability of the foreign-exchange rate. These analyses are generally deficient because they neglect the connection between the exchange rate and the underlying general equilibrium of commodity markets. The stability of commodity markets was analyzed in Chapter 4 of this book. The theoretical question of whether a market equilibrium is stable, as we explained there, is not the same as the practical question of whether some particular market price stays put. The theoretical question is the following: If an equilibrium price (such as $2.00 in Figure 15.1a) is displaced slightly, will it tend to return to its original value? In Figure 15.1a an increase in the price of foreign exchange will create an excess of the value of foreign exchange offered to buy our exports over the foreign-exchange value of our own import purchases. With supply exceeding demand, in the absence of government intervention the price will be bid back down to $2.00. We found in Chapter 4, however, that consumption preferences could be such that certain prices represent market equilibria that are not stable: A small increase in price creates excess demand, not excess supply, and price gets bid up further. If those conditions prevailed in the underlying commodity markets, the supply curve in the market would look like the one shown in Figure 15.1b. There the $2.00 exchange rate is an equilibrium but it is not stable, because a slight increase generates an excess demand for foreign exchange, driving its price up until it reaches a stable equilibrium at $4.00. Similarly, a slight decrease in the exchange rate from the unstable equilibrium at $2.00 creates an excess of supply over demand and sends the equilibrium exchange rate coasting down to $1.00. That is, the unstable equilibrium must — under quite general assumptions — be surrounded by two stable ones. The problem of exchange stability is what we call a local one. It means that we do not expect to find the exchange rate at $2.00 (if that equilibrium is unstable), because any jiggle would drive it to a higher or a lower value. The economic issue created by unstable equilibria is really that they signal the possibility of alternative stable equilibria. We might have strong views about whether we preferred foreign exchange and thus foreign goods to be cheap or expensive, if either equilibrium value is a stable equilibrium. Is this possibility of unstable equilibria a curiosity, or does it have real practical importance? That depends (we show in the supplement to Chapter 4) on the size of a country's price-elasticity of demand for its imports and of the world's price-elasticity of demand for its exports. To assure a stable equilibrium these must on average exceed 0.50. The empirical evidence suggests that they usually do, although only in the long run, and not by a comfortable margin.[1]

We mentioned above that the theoretical problem of exchange stability is not the same as the practical question of whether a particular price tends to fluctuate a great deal. The price in Figure 15.1b could, of course, move around a lot, because small horizontal shifts of the supply or demand curve could change the values of the stable price equilibria by large amounts. However, a market price could also fluctuate simply because the determining curves shift about a great deal, even if they have but one stable equilibrium value at any given time. We shall consider below some of the forces that might make a country's exchange rate unstable in this popular sense, but we shall assume that the exchange rate is stable in the formal sense.

15.2 THE BALANCE-OF-PAYMENTS ACCOUNTS

A nation's balance-of-payments account is a statistical record of all transactions taking place between its residents and the rest of the world. This record is vital to understanding the disturbances and adjustments impinging on international transactions, and thus it is watched closely by policymakers. The payments accounts also provide the starting point for any serious study of international transactions.

The Accounting Framework

Broadly speaking, every transaction has two sides. We buy something, and pay for it. Or we sell something, and receive compensation. The ac-

---

[1] One survey of many statistical estimates of these elasticities placed the typical values between 0.50 and 1.50 for imports and between 0.50 and 2.00 for exports. (We omit the minus signs attached to these elasticities.) See Robert M. Stern, Jonathan Francis, and Bruce Schumacher, *Price Statistics in International Trade — An Annotated Bibliography*. London: Macmillan, 1976.

counting rules tell us how to classify and record every transaction. Here is the key rule:

> *Record as a credit* $(+)$ *any transaction resulting in a receipt from the rest of the world. Record as a debit* $(-)$ *any transaction resulting in a payment to the rest of the world.*

The receipt and the payment appear with signs opposite to those of the transactions giving rise to them; they are the "other sides."

Thus the sale of an export is classed as a credit, because the foreign buyer is obligated to make payment to us in some form. What might that form be? First, a U.S. export value at $5 might be compensated through barter by the shipment of an import also worth $5. Then the export is recorded as a $5 credit, the import — the compensation obtained for it — as a $5 debit. Second, an American export of merchandise valued at $10 might be shipped as a personal gift, say by an American of Italian origin to a relative in Italy. We record the export as a $10 credit in the U.S. accounts. In fact it gives rise to no receipt, other than the relative's gratitude. But to complete the double-entry system we must concoct a "debit" side to the transaction, and so we make up the category "unilateral transfers to foreigners," and enter the corresponding debit of $10. Third, and more typically, suppose that an export of $15, recorded as a credit, simply results in a transfer of $15 in U.S. funds from the Danish purchaser to the American exporter. The compensation takes the form of a drawing down of Danish holdings of U.S. currency and is recorded as a $15 debit. Fourth, suppose that an export valued at $20 to Great Britain again results in a cash payment, but that this time an American exporter decides to accept payment in British pounds sterling valued at $20. The compensating transaction this time is an increase in U.S. holdings of foreign currency, recorded as a $20 debit. The payments accounts after these four transactions have been recorded would appear as follows:

Debits $(-)$		Credits $(+)$	
Merchandise imports	$- 5$	Merchandise exports	$+50$
Unilateral transfers to foreigners	-10		
Reduction in foreign holdings of U.S. currency	-15		
Increase in U.S. holdings of foreign exchange	-20		
	-50		$+50$

We can construct a parallel series of transactions resulting in payments abroad. An American tourist's consumption of food and lodging in a foreign country is classed as a debit, because it results in a payment to the rest of the world. We call his purchases an import of tourist services and class it as a debit of, say, $10; if foreigners (temporarily, at least) accept dollars in payment, the corresponding credit item is an increase of $10 in foreign holdings of U.S. currency. An American investor purchases common shares worth $20 in a Japanese corporation; he pays by requesting his U.S. bank to draw down its holdings of Japanese yen by $20 worth, debiting his dollar checking account for the cost of the yen. These two transactions appear as follows:

Debits (−)		Credits (+)	
Imports of services	−10	Increase in foreign holdings of U.S. currency	+10
Imports of securities	−20	Reduction in U.S. holdings of foreign exchange	+20
	−30		+30

Now suppose that the examples we have mentioned are the only international transactions taking place between our country and the rest of the world during one period of time. What do they imply about the market for foreign exchange? In fact, U.S. holdings of foreign exchange are unaltered in total value: One transaction decreases our holdings by the equivalent of $20, and another increases them by the same amount. Foreign holdings of U.S. dollars, however, are decreased by $5, being raised $10 by one transaction but reduced $15 by another. This reduction *might* drive up the price of the dollar in the world's foreign-exchange markets. *The fact that every transaction has two sides in the accounting system in no way implies that demand and supply for foreign exchange will be equal.*

Some countries wish to keep their exchange rates fixed. If the commercial transactions already enumerated are driving up the foreign price of the dollar, some foreign government may decide to sell an equivalent amount of dollars to keep its own currency from depreciating. This sale itself does not enter into the U.S. balance of payments unless it is made to an American wishing to reduce his holdings of foreign currency. In that case it would appear as a reduction in U.S. holdings of foreign exchange (a credit), offset by a reduction in foreign holdings of dollars (a debit). If the sale is made by the foreign government to a foreign national, the transaction merely shifts U.S. liabilities from foreign official to foreign private holders.

Until August 15, 1971, a foreign government using the U.S. dollar as a reserve currency to stabilize its exchange rate could recoup its supply of dollars by selling gold to the United States Treasury. This transaction would enter the U.S. payments accounts with the import of monetary gold appearing as a debit (like any other commodity import). The increase in foreign holdings of U.S. currency represents the credit item.

These examples should supply a basic understanding of how the double-entry bookkeeping system works. Now we can see how these transactions are aggregated with the many other possible types into a summary of the nation's international transactions. Transactions are sorted not only into those resulting in receipts and those resulting in payments, but also into classes having different significance for the country's national income and national wealth.

The Current Account

The first important class of transactions is called the *current account*. It lumps together sales and purchases of currently produced goods and services and thus relates to the country's current national income. Specifically, it includes transactions that either yield national income or result from its expenditure. Its first major category includes exports and imports of merchandise: All movable goods sold, given away, or otherwise transferred between domestic and foreign ownership. Exports and imports of services also enter the current account. They involve current outputs and expenditures, but no movement of goods across national boundaries. Some of the important international service transactions are:

1. Transportation services include freight and insurance charges for the international movement of goods and also the expenditures of tourists on international travel to and from the country. When American imports arrive in foreign ships, or American tourists cross the Atlantic on a foreign airline, the transaction results in a payment and is recorded as a debit in the U.S. balance of payments.

2. Tourist services include all expenditures by a country's citizens when they are outside its borders (including those for travel once abroad). The expenditures of foreign tourists within the United States are classed as an export of tourist services and appear as a credit.

3. Business and professional services make up a diverse class of international transactions. International trade in the services of management consulting firms, engineering firms, and the like is brisk. A service import of the United States results when business firms ship statistical data abroad to Korea, Ireland, and elsewhere to be transcribed on tapes for electronic data processing back in the United States. This and other

purchases of business services are recorded as debits in the U.S. balance of payments.

4. An important class of international receipts results from the services produced abroad by U.S. capital stock. The interest or dividends earned by American capital abroad appear as credits. Conversely, earnings of foreign capital "working" in the United States are classed as debits. We must distinguish these payments for the *services* of capital, which appear in the current account, from international movements of the capital itself. The latter are considered below.

The current account finally includes unilateral transfers, gifts, and donations, public and private. As we saw before, these transactions are fictional, but useful and indeed vital to the double-entry system of book-keeping. The U.S. government offers economic and military aid to some countries abroad, and American citizens also on balance remit gifts and contributions to foreign countries. These donations naturally appear as debits. (The goods or funds given away constitute the corresponding credit.)

The balance on goods and services is the point of juncture between the international payments statistics and national-income accounts. Gross national product, the chief measure of a nation's economic output, consists of goods produced at home for consumption, investment, governmental use, and export. The statisticians measure these flows of goods, however, not as they are *produced* but as they are *purchased*. Hence the expenditure flows include all imports as they pass into these final uses, and the imports must then be subtracted to secure the desired measure of domestic production. The import total is ordinarily shown as a subtraction from exports, thus,

$$GNP = C + I + G + (X - M).$$

The term in parentheses, under current U.S. income definitions, is the balance of goods and services. In the national-income accounts it is called "net exports of goods and services."

The current-account balance in the payments statistics is closely related to the concept of "net foreign investment" appearing in the national accounts. After we subtract from the balance on goods and services the value of output donated abroad by governments and the private sector, we have in the current-account balance a measure of the net increase in U.S. claims on foreigners — that is, the net payments due the United States for goods and services sold abroad. These net claims — "net foreign investment" — appear in the national-income accounts as a component of gross investment of the United States.[2]

[2] See tables in the annual National Income Issue of the *Survey of Current Business,* appearing each July. The current-account balance and net foreign investment in fact differ by U.S. acquisition of Special Drawing Rights, a form of international-reserve asset to be discussed in Chapter 23.

The Capital Account

We just saw that a country's net sales abroad (after subtracting donations) must equal its increase in net claims on foreigners. The *capital
account* of the balance of payments displays the details of this change
in net claims or assets. It records the net trade between domestic and
foreign citizens in various financial claims. The balance of trade in these
financial claims then must equal the net change in U.S. claims on foreigners.

If we think of understanding balance-of-payments accounting as tra-
versing a golf course, the capital account has most of the sand traps.
The main one is semantic and relates to the nature of capital. For this
purpose and many others we think of capital as liquid purchasing power,
not embodied in machines or products. To export capital thus is to ship
purchasing power abroad, where it is put to use (and presumably earns
for the lender dividends or interest that will later appear in the current
account). The receipt for exported purchasing power is an imported bond
or share, representing a claim on that future income stream. We learned
how this transaction must appear in the accounts: The import of securities is a debit, giving rise to a payment, and is thus treated just like the
acquisition of an asset in the balance sheet of a firm. The transfer of balances into foreign hands represents the corresponding credit. But this
import of securities is called a *capital export*, because liquid purchasing
power is sent abroad. We face the seeming paradox that a commodity export appears as a credit, a capital export as a debit, in the international
accounts. But the paradox is not real, and you can keep the accounting
of capital flows straight if you remember that an export (import) of capital is an import (export) of securities, and that international flows of
securities and goods are accounted in directly similar ways.

The capital account contains three principal types of transaction:

1. *Direct investment* occurs when the residents of one country acquire
or increase control over a business enterprise in another country. When
IBM starts a new subsidiary in Europe, an outflow of direct investment
is recorded in the U.S. balance of payments equal to the value of the
equity that IBM acquires in the subsidiary (and, of course, to the outflow of equity capital involved in starting it). If an American buys shares
in a foreign company that do not give him control of it, however, the
flow is classed as one of portfolio rather than direct investment.

2. *Long-term portfolio investment* involves international transactions
in securities with an original term to maturity greater than one year. An
American purchase of the bonds of a Canadian provincial government,
giving rise to a payment, would count as a portfolio capital outflow.

3. *Short-term capital flows* involve securities with original terms to
maturity of less than a year. A foreign purchase of United States Trea-

sury bills is a capital inflow, giving rise to a receipt. We also include as short-term capital flows international shifts in the control of liquid funds. Thus, an increase in U.S. citizens' holdings of foreign exchange, giving rise to a payment, counts as a capital outflow. This statistical practice makes sense because of both the balance-of-payments accounting system and our concept of capital. British pound notes can be thought of as "securities," giving us a claim on United Kingdom goods and services, just as surely as British Treasury bills. And these bank notes can be acquired by spending our own dollar bills, a capital outflow giving foreigners a claim on the United States. (It is often useful to think of cash as a security that yields no interest except for its convenience in effecting transactions.)

In both the current and capital accounts we record "balances" as differences between corresponding subtotals of credits and subtotals of debits. By the accounting rule, a preponderance of credits (or receipts) makes the balance positive. A positive balance is also commonly referred to as "favorable" or "active." A balance with a preponderance of debits is negative by the accounting rule, and is called "unfavorable" or "passive." Notice the gravitational pull of the semantics! The receipts side owns all the good words, and has done so ever since the eighteenth-century mercantilists made a national virtue of "storing up treasure" and selling abroad more than one bought. Although economists from Adam Smith on have proclaimed that economic welfare depends on the goods available for the nation's use and not ultimately on the cash earned from selling output abroad, they have never conquered this linguistic outpost of mercantilism. We shall try to use terms that are as nearly neutral as possible.

Compiling and Presenting the Payments Accounts

When government statisticians assemble the record of a nation's international transactions, they of course do not observe directly the two sides of every transaction. Errors creep in for two reasons: Some transactions are valued incorrectly, so that the quantity recorded for one side of the transaction fails to equal that for its compensation, or a transaction is omitted entirely. An American professor may give a lecture in Canada, depositing his fee in his American bank. The fee turns up (initially, anyhow) as an increase in U.S. holdings of Canadian currency — a debit; but the statisticians do not ascertain that the professor has exported professional services, and this credit item goes unrecorded. Likewise, errors occur in the valuation of transactions. Bananas are auctioned only after they have passed the U.S. customs officer. When their entry is recorded, no one knows what their market value will be. A guess is put down. If it fails to equal the payment ultimately made for the bananas, an error will enter the payments statistics. The statistician measures each class of transactions as best he can. Because of these and other errors, his sums of credit and debit items will not be equal. He simply inscribes an item, "Errors and unrecorded transactions," equal to this difference.[3]

In Tables 15.1 and 15.2 we present condensed versions of the United States balance of payments for 1960–1972 and 1973–1979. The data in the tables are organized in quite different ways. They reflect respectively the format used by the United States in the 1960's and early 1970's (Table 15.1) and the new format adopted in 1976 as more responsive to the flexible exchange rates prevailing since 1973 (Table 15.2). We comment on these methods of presentation below. The two tables together show that a surplus of merchandise exports over imports declined in the 1960's and gave way to a deficit in the 1970's. Net exports of services moved in the opposite direction, with earnings from U.S. capital abroad rising to become a quarter of all sales abroad on current account. Private and government donations abroad are a large continuing outflow. The United States has been a substantial net exporter of long-term capital, particularly because of outflows of foreign direct investment. Net flows of other capital, particularly short-term funds, have been quite volatile, with large inflows from abroad in some years but considerable net outflows in the late 1970's. Various "balance" figures appear through the body of Tables 15.1 and as memorandum items at the bottom of Table 15.2. These balances are designed as interpretive aids, and we shall explain those not already mentioned in the context of surveying policies used toward the country's international transactions.

15.3 PAYMENTS ACCOUNTS AND POLICIES TOWARD NET INTERNATIONAL TRANSACTIONS

Under the Articles of Agreement of the International Monetary Fund (1946), the principal trading nations agreed that they would keep their exchange rates fixed at declared par values and change them only in the event of a "fundamental disequilibrium." Even since that commitment was abandoned in 1973, many countries have tried to hold their exchange rates at predetermined values. Yet, as we saw, an arbitrarily chosen rate need not clear the market for foreign exchange. A rate that does not clear the market necessarily leaves some disequilibrium.

The methods that countries use to deal with external imbalance are

[3] For a description of the compilation of the U.S. balance-of-payments statistics, see U.S. Bureau of the Budget, Review Committee for Balance of Payments Statistics, *The Balance of Payments Statistics of the United States: A Review and Appraisal,* Washington, 1965; and "Report of the Advisory Committee on the Presentation of Balance of Payments Statistics," *Survey of Current Business,* 56 (June 1976): 18–27.

closely bound up with the problems of measuring imbalance in the payments accounts. In this section we set forth the statistical measures of imbalance and their relation to the strategies available for dealing with imbalance in the exchange market.

Measuring Disequilibrium in International Payments

Return to Figure 15.1a and consider the imbalance that prevails if the United Kingdom and the United States desire to keep the exchange rate at $2.40. There is an excess supply of sterling of ab. Its counterpart is an excess demand for dollars of ab multiplied by $2.40. The primary method used by countries to preserve a fixed exchange rate in the short run is simply to stand ready to buy or sell foreign currency at the "official" price, thus satisfying excess demand or sopping up excess supply. Either the United States or the United Kingdom (or both acting in concert) could buy up the excess supply of pounds sterling, which is the same as providing the excess demand for dollars. If the United Kingdom performed the task, it would need to possess international reserves — assets that can be used directly to meet an excess demand for foreign exchange (dollars, to the United Kingdom). The United States could buy up sterling using its own currency, but, of course, would need reserves of foreign currency (sterling) if it ever expects to cope with an excess supply of dollars.

Balance of Official Reserve Transactions

The practice of using reserves to peg the exchange rate explains the most common approach to measuring imbalance in international payments. It depends upon the distinction between *autonomous* and *accommodating* transactions. Autonomous transactions are undertaken for ordinary commercial motives. They may frequently be influenced by the exchange rate, but they are not intended to affect the rate, or the state of international transactions. Accommodating transactions are undertaken to preserve or enforce a price of foreign exchange, and not ordinarily to pursue commercial profit. Broadly speaking, accommodating transactions are intended to keep the exchange rate at the official level. If we want our payments imbalance to indicate the size of international disequilibrium, we should shoot for a measure of accommodating transactions.

Suppose that the United States were to finance an international-payments surplus (ab in Figure 15.1a) by adding this amount of sterling to reserves held by the government. This accommodating change in her reserves would provide the United States with an exact measure of the balance. But what of the imbalance, in this same case, from Britain's point of view? The American surplus is exactly Britain's deficit. Yet,

TABLE 15.1 U.S. Balance of Payments, Selected Years, 1960–1972 (billions of dollars)[a]

Transaction	1960	1962	1964	1966	1967	1968	1969	1970	1971	1972
Merchandise trade balance	4.9	4.5	6.8	3.8	3.8	0.6	0.6	2.6	-2.3	6.4
Exports	19.6	20.8	25.5	29.3	30.7	33.6	36.4	42.5	43.3	49.4
Imports	-14.8	-16.3	-18.7	-25.5	-26.9	-33.0	-35.8	-39.9	-45.6	-55.8
Military transactions, net	-2.8	-2.4	-2.1	-2.9	-3.2	-3.1	-3.3	-3.4	-2.9	-3.6
Travel and transportation, net	-1.0	-1.2	-1.1	-1.3	-1.8	-1.5	-1.8	-2.0	-2.3	-3.0
Investment income, net	2.3	3.3	3.9	3.6	3.9	4.0	3.6	3.5	4.7	4.3
Other services, net	0.6	0.8	1.1	1.4	1.6	1.7	1.9	2.2	2.5	2.8
Balance on goods and services	4.1	5.1	8.5	4.6	4.4	1.6	1.0	3.0	-0.2	-5.9
Private remittances	-0.6	-0.7	-0.9	-1.0	-1.3	-1.2	-1.3	-1.5	-1.6	-1.6
U.S. government grants	-1.7	-1.9	-1.9	-1.9	-1.8	-1.7	-1.6	-1.7	-2.0	-2.2
Balance on current account	1.8	2.4	5.8	1.6	1.3	-1.3	-2.0	-0.3	-3.9	-9.7
U.S. government capital flows, net	-0.9	-0.9	-1.4	-1.5	-2.4	-2.2	-2.1	-2.0	-2.4	-1.3
Long-term private capital flows, net	-2.1	-2.6	-4.5	-2.8	-2.9	1.2	-0.0	-1.4	-4.4	-0.1
Balance on current account and long-term capital	-1.2	-1.0	-0.1	-2.6	-4.0	-2.3	-3.9	-3.8	-10.6	-11.1
Nonliquid short-term private capital flows, net	-1.4	-0.7	-1.6	-0.1	-0.5	0.2	-0.6	-0.5	-2.3	-1.5
Errors and omissions, net	-1.1	-1.2	-1.0	0.6	-0.2	0.4	-1.5	0.4[b]	-9.0[b]	-1.2[b]
Net liquidity balance	-3.7	-2.9	-2.7	-2.2	-4.7	-1.6	-6.1	-3.9	-22.0	-13.8
Liquid private capital flows, net	0.3	0.2	1.2	2.4	1.3	3.3	8.8	-6.0	-7.8	3.5
Official reserve transactions, net	-3.4	-2.6	-1.5	0.2	-3.4	1.6	2.7	-9.8	-29.8	-10.4

Source: U.S. Department of Commerce, Office of Business Economics, *Survey of Current Business,* 55 (June 1975): 26–27; 56 (March 1976): 39.

[a] Data for components may not add to totals or balances because of rounding errors.
[b] Includes allocation of Special Drawing Rights.

TABLE 15.2 U.S. Balance of Payments, 1973–1979 (billions of dollars)[a]

Transaction	1973	1974	1975	1976	1977	1978	1979[c]
Exports							
Goods and services	71.8	99.9	113.8	123.5	131.9	151.7	182.7
Goods under military grant	2.8	1.8	2.2	0.4	0.2	0.3	0.3
Income from U.S. assets	38.4	46.7	41.9	48.3	52.7	69.1	103.6
Imports							
Goods and services	−87.9	−123.9	−118.0	−145.7	−176.6	−203.9	−241.4
Income paid on foreign assets	−11.3	−13.4	−14.8	−16.4	−17.4	−25.8	−39.6
Grants and remittances							
U.S. military	−2.8	−1.8	−2.2	−0.4	−0.2	−0.3	−0.3
Other	−3.9	−7.2	−4.6	−5.0	−4.7	−5.1	−5.6
U.S. assets abroad (increase −)							
Official reserve assets	0.2	−1.5	−0.8	−2.6	−0.4	0.7	−1.1
Other government assets	−2.6	0.4	−3.5	−4.2	−3.7	−4.7	−3.8
Direct investment	−11.4	−9.1	−14.2	−11.9	−12.9	−16.7	−24.8
Other private investment	−8.9	−24.6	−21.2	−32.5	−18.8	−40.4	−33.8
Foreign assets in U.S. (increase +)							
Official reserve assets	6.0	10.5	6.8	17.6	36.7	33.8	−15.2
Direct investment	2.8	4.8	2.6	4.4	3.7	6.3	7.7
Other private investment	9.6	18.9	6.0	14.5	10.4	23.7	41.2
Statistical discrepancy	−2.7	−1.6	5.9	10.3	−0.9	11.1	29.8[d]
Balance on goods and services	11.0	9.3	22.9	9.6	−9.4	−8.8	5.3
Balance on current account	7.1	2.1	18.3	4.6	−14.1	−18.9	−0.3
Net transactions in reserve assets[b]	5.2	8.8	4.4	10.5	35.0	31.7	−15.6

Source: Survey of Current Business, 59 (June 1979): 33–34; 60 (March 1980): 54.
[a] Data for components may not add to totals or balances because of rounding errors.
[b] Comparable to "Official reserve transactions, net" (Table 15.1) with sign reversed.
[c] Preliminary.
[d] Includes allocation of Special Drawing Rights.

because we assumed that U.S. reserves finance the imbalance, Britain's reserves do not change. Something does change from the British viewpoint, however: Her short-term liabilities to foreign (i.e., United States) monetary authorities are increased. Thus the imbalance (deficit) from Britain's viewpoint is measured by the increase in her official liabilities, just as the American surplus is measured by the increase in U.S. official assets. A general lesson lies behind this example. The transactions that accommodate a country's external imbalance are measured not just by the change in its own reserves; we must also net out any change in stocks of its own currency held as international reserves by other countries.[4]

The principal measure of external balance that the United States has used is the balance of official reserve transactions, shown in Table 15.1. It indicates the net change in the country's international reserves, which consists of the net change in reserve assets of the United States and the net change in U.S. liabilities to foreign monetary authorities. The U.S. has traditionally held its reserve assets mostly in gold, but reserves of foreign currency and borrowing rights in the International Monetary Fund are also reflected. (The Fund's operations are discussed in Chapter 23.) U.S. liabilities to foreign monetary authorities include the dollars acquired by foreign governments in financing U.S. payments deficits (or paid out when the U.S. runs a surplus). The reserve-transactions balance thus seems to correspond quite well to the concept of accommodating transactions.[5]

Indeed, it did correspond quite well in practice, during the 1960's and early 1970's, the period covered in Table 15.1. However, from 1973 on, the rug was pulled from under the official reserve-transactions balance by two major developments. First, in early 1973 the major industrial countries abandoned the attempt to keep their exchange rates locked into fixed relations to one another. Strictly speaking, that meant no more accommodating transactions, hence an official-settlements balance of zero. In fact both the United States and other countries continued to intervene at times in the foreign-exchange market; the change from fixed exchange rates was one of degree, as we shall see in Chapter 24. That brings us, however, to the second reason why the reserve-transactions balance

---

[4] Another important conclusion of this argument is that it takes only one country to have a fixed exchange rate in a two-country world. If A's government stands ready to buy and sell unlimited quantities of B's at a poster price, B's exchange rate is fixed whether B approves or not. More generally, in a world of n countries fixed exchange rates will prevail if $n - 1$ of the countries actively peg the external values of their currencies. In practice, the United States served under the Bretton Woods system as the passive nth country, with most other countries stabilizing their currencies against the dollar.

[5] It also has the useful property of corresponding closely to the change in the monetary base of the United States associated with intervention in international payments.

went astray. There was a great increase in transactions that *looked* like accommodating payments and entered into the balance as calculated, but clearly had nothing to do with accommodating the U.S. balance of payments. The largest of these was due to the practice of Organization of Petroleum Exporting Countries (OPEC) of holding much of their new-found riches in the form of short-term claims on the United States.[6] OPEC holdings of U.S. Treasury bills were really commercial investments and not accommodating transactions. Other distortions — much smaller than those resulting from OPEC — crept in as other currencies joined the dollar for use as international reserves. Suppose that the U.S. balance of payments is in equilibrium, but foreign country A (holding its reserves in dollars) is running a surplus and gaining reserves while foreign country B (holding its reserves in another currency) is running a deficit and losing reserves. U.S. liabilities to foreign monetary authorities are increasing, but the flow has nothing to do with accommodating the U.S. balance of payments. By 1976 the partial irrelevance of the official-settlements balance and the distortions that blighted its measurement led to a decision that it should no longer be reported in official statistics (it can still be calculated by the user).[7]

New Form of Payments Accounts

Table 15.2 presents a condensed version of the form in which the United States now publishes its balance-of-payments statistics. The body of the table contains no "balance" figures whatsoever. Once burned, twice shy: the government grew fearful that *any* one balance figure would be mis-interpreted, and so all of them were expelled from the body of the table and told to live downstairs as "memorandum items" at the bottom of the table. The revised presentation also commendably sought to avoid any spurious welfare implications about "favorable" and "unfavorable" balances.

Table 15.2 differs from Table 15.1 in other ways associated with the interpretation of the statistical record. The 1960's-vintage presentation placed a great deal of emphasis on short-term capital movements, because it was thought that monetary policy could importantly influence net flows of short-term capital in defense of the fixed exchange rate.[8]

---

[6] These profits turned up not as the earnings of commercial companies but as government revenues held in the hands of the Saudi Arabian Monetary Authority and its counterparts in other oil-exporting nations.

[7] For discussion of this change see Robert M. Stern et al., *The Presentation of the U.S. Balance of Payments: A Symposium.* Essays in International Finance, no. 123. Princeton, N.J.: International Finance Section, Princeton University, 1977.

[8] This and other considerations lay behind the "net liquidity balance," shown in Table 15.1. That balance treated short-term liquid capital flows as accommodating transactions, along with official reserve transactions.

That proposition may be correct. However, no neat statistical separation identifies capital transactions that are and are not sensitive to monetary conditions. None can distinguish those that are volatile and speculative from those that are not.[9] The new presentation centers more neutrally on various foreign and domestic asset classes. In general the new presentation of Table 15.2 stresses total figures rather than balances, thus inviting the reader to think about the separate influences on the components of the balance.

Policy Toward Balance in International Transactions

Using or acquiring international reserves is just one way for a government to influence the balance of international payments. If at the going exchange rate a potential disequilibrium arises in international transactions, three sorts of events can head it off or correct it.

1. The government may change its official exchange rate, or let the market find a new rate such that equilibrium is restored. These choices are discussed in Chapters 18 and 19.
2. There are certain mechanisms of adjustment in the domestic economy that tend to restore equilibrium at the official exchange rate without government action. These adjustment processes are the subject of Chapters 16 and 17.
3. If the domestic adjustment mechanisms fail to restore full equilibrium and the exchange rate is not allowed to change, the government can still resort to a variety of policies to bring international transactions into balance. In this section we offer a preliminary survey of these policies.

The exchange rate is the link between the money price and cost structures of different countries. Excess demand in international transactions can be attacked by changing the exchange rate (and, thereby, the home-currency prices of foreign goods) or by changing the price level and leaving the exchange rate alone. To eliminate the disequilibrium in Figure 15.1a the United States government could allow its price level to be inflated, say by increasing its money supply, or the British monetary authorities could deflate the U.K. price level. In terms of Figure 15.2, the

---

[9] Another once-fashionable balance shown in Table 15.1 is the balance on current account and long-term capital (commonly called the "basic balance"). This was conceived not as distinguishing between autonomous and accommodating transactions but between those that reflect stable long-term forces (current account and long-term capital) and those that may be highly volatile (short-term capital). Persistent trends in commercial payments and receipts would allegedly be easier to detect in the basic balance once the noise from short-term capital movements is suppressed.

supply curve would tend to shift leftward to the dashed-line position ($S'_\pounds$) because American goods would become dearer abroad, inducing foreigners to offer a smaller value of sterling at any given exchange rate in order to buy them. And foreign goods grow cheaper to American purchasers, increasing the amount demanded and shifting the demand curve rightward to $D'_\pounds$.

The demand and supply shifts shown in Figure 15.2 can also be produced by actions of the nation's monetary authorities. The sterling value of American purchases from abroad of course includes foreign securities. Instruments of monetary policy might serve to remove the imbalance by lowering interest rates, thereby making U.S. securities less attractive to foreigners and foreign securities more attractive to Americans. Such a policy would restore equilibrium in international transactions by producing or enlarging a capital outflow — the same as a net inflow of securities. Such a policy would be a much more short-run matter than in-

---

FIGURE 15.2   Effect of Price-Level Change
on International Transactions

Inflating the domestic price level makes foreign goods cheaper, shifting foreign-exchange demand to the right. It makes home goods dearer to foreigners, shifting supply of exchange to the left.

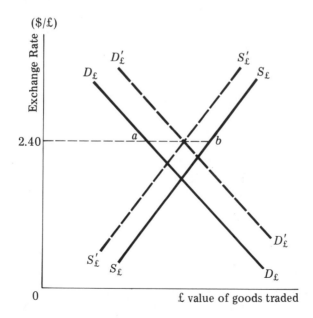

flating the general domestic price level. Also, the international movement of securities might amount largely to a one-shot rearrangement of portfolios rather than a sustained influence on international transactions year in and year out. This stock-adjustment aspect of capital-account transactions is discussed in subsequent chapters.

Another method of controlling the current-account balance is illustrated in Figure 15.3. Total spending on foreign goods and, therefore, the demand for foreign exchange depend on the level of employment at home. Perhaps the excess supply illustrated in Figure 15.1a came about because of a recession in the United States. Promoting fuller employment would therefore shift the demand for foreign exchange to the right and thus could improve the current-account balance and restore equilibrium in international exchange. (It might also reduce the flow of foreign exchange supplied by making American goods dearer abroad or increasing their delivery times; this effect is not shown in the diagram, but it can be important in practice.)

Finally, countries often try to deal with external imbalance by imposing controls on trade or long-term capital flows. These are not much help for ending a surplus, but are often put to use to combat a deficit. Thus the British government, facing the excess supply of sterling shown in Figure 15.1a, might impose exchange control. The government would then preempt foreign-exchange transactions, requiring its citizens to sell it their dollars earned abroad from the sale of goods, services, and so on. The available foreign exchange is then doled out to would-be buyers to whom the government gives highest priority. Those who would offer ab of sterling — the excess supply — are simply turned away and denied the opportunity to buy foreign exchange. To make exchange control work, the British government must compel its exporters to turn over all dollars earned, because frustrated buyers of foreign exchange would otherwise go behind the government's back, bidding more for the exporters' dollars and creating a "black market."

Of course, our knowledge of the equilibrium underlying the foreign-exchange market causes us to wonder whether exchange control will work. What happens if the planned expenditure of ab on British imports is diverted to domestic goods? It may serve to intercept domestic output that would otherwise have been available for export.

15.4 SUMMARY

Most countries create their own currency units, and most international transactions involve money. The foreign-exchange rate, the price of units of foreign currency in terms of domestic currency, is the link between national money prices. It is thus a crucial regulator of international

FIGURE 15.3   Effect of Increase in Employment
on International Transactions

When total spending is increased, part of the increase falls on imported
goods, shifting demand to the right.

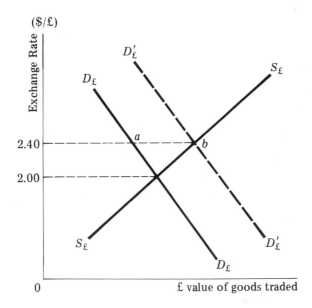

transactions. We illustrate disequilibrium and adjustment in international transactions by assuming that national price levels are given, then summarizing the demand for all foreign goods, services, and securities in terms of the foreign-currency units worth of them demanded each period of time. Foreigners' demand for domestic goods, services, and securities similarly gives rise to a supply of foreign exchange offered in order to implement these purchases. This is a "monetized" description of the underlying exchange. With all commodity (and bond) markets cleared and income equal to expenditure, the foreign-exchange values of international sales and purchases are equal as well. The formal problem of stability in this market really points to the proposition that there may be more than one stable foreign-exchange rate. We would naturally prefer an exchange rate corresponding to terms of trade more favorable to ourselves.

The balance-of-payments accounts provide our basis for understanding what is happening in the balance of international transactions. The tabulation rests on an accounting convention that records as a credit (+) any transaction resulting in a receipt from foreigners, and as a debit (−) any transaction resulting in a payment to the rest of the world. The receipt and the payment respectively give rise to the other side of the double entry. Although we identify two sides to each transaction the market demand and supply need not be equal.

International transactions are divided into the current account, covering transactions in currently produced goods and services, and the capital account, covering transactions in securities or claims on streams of future income. The current account includes merchandise trade, transportation services, tourist services, business and professional services, and donations (or unilateral transfers). The principal capital-account transactions are direct investment, long-term portfolio investment, and short-term capital flows. Statisticians can record most flows in the balance of payments with only approximate accuracy. The item "errors and unrecorded transactions" covers the net discrepancy in their measurements.

Conceptually, we should measure imbalance in international transactions from the net quantity of accommodating transactions undertaken to keep the exchange rate from changing (distinguished from autonomous transactions, not intended to affect the rate). This is basically the same as the change in a country's international reserves — if it deals with external imbalance solely by financing its deficit or surplus.

Countries can in principle choose other methods for causing a given exchange rate to be consistent with balance in international transactions:

1. Lowering the domestic price level cheapens home goods and services relative to those abroad and reduces excess net purchases abroad.
2. Easing monetary policy makes domestic securities less attractive relative to those abroad and increases net purchases abroad.
3. Expanding government expenditure increases the demand for imports and reduces excess net sales abroad.
4. Exchange control or other direct controls on purchases made abroad can reduce excessive net purchases abroad.

SUGGESTIONS FOR FURTHER READING

Cohen, B. J. *Balance-of-Payments Policy*. Harmondsworth, England, and Baltimore: Penguin, 1969. More detail on exchange markets and payments accounts.

Henning, Charles N. *International Finance*. New York: Harper, 1958. Includes information on methods and instruments used in actual financing of trade.

Meade, J. E. *The Balance of Payments.* London: Oxford University Press, 1951. Analytical basis for measuring "balance."

"Report of the Advisory Committee on the Presentation of Balance of Payments Statistics," *Survey of Current Business,* 56 (June 1976): 18–27. Latest changes in U.S. statistical presentation.

Stern, Robert M. et al. *The Presentation of the U.S. Balance of Payments: A Symposium,* Essays in International Finance, no. 123. Princeton: International Finance Section, Princeton University, 1977. Economists' comments on the current United States presentation.

United States Bureau of the Budget, Review Committee for Balance of Payments Statistics. *The Balance of Payments Statistics of the United States: A Review and Appraisal.* Washington: Government Printing Office, 1965. Last official appraisal.

16

National Income
and the Balance
of Payments

In Chapter 15 we learned that a country could find its balance of payments out of equilibrium (at least if it chose to fix its exchange rate at an official value). And we suggested that markets may be found out of equilibrium because money prices fail to adjust in commodity or factor markets, or because people's expenditure in the aggregate is larger or smaller than their income. In this chapter and Chapter 17 we bring these ideas together.

Here we take up the problem of sticky prices, which underlies the Keynesian model of the determinants of real income and employment. We shall find that disequilibria in the current account of the balance of payments affect employment and real income, and that domestic disturbances affecting employment and real income change the current-account balance as well. The nation's policies toward the balance of payments therefore change its level of employment, and its policies toward domestic aggregate demand alter the balance of payments.

In Chapter 15 we observed that an imbalance of international payments could persist only if the government stood ready to sell foreign exchange (to finance a deficit) or buy foreign exchange (to accommodate a surplus). That process is not important for the purposes of this chapter and Chapter 17. Therefore, to make the exposition simple, we brazenly assume that every country in the world uses the same currency — the dollar. When the United States runs a deficit in its official reserve transactions, the domestic money supply is simply reduced and the rest of the world's money supply increased by that many dollars.

16.1 INCOME DETERMINATION IN CLOSED AND OPEN ECONOMIES

The Keynesian model of national income determination was devised to explain how the economy could be in equilibrium with substantial unemployment, although its concepts are now used by economists to deal with a wide variety of macroeconomic problems. In this chapter we shall use it to address two questions: (1) How can we conveniently describe equilibrium of income and employment in the open economy? (2) How does that equilibrium relate to equilibrium in international exchange; and how do disturbances to domestic income affect international trade?

Equilibrium and Adjustment in the Closed Economy

Let us review the determination of income in the simple Keynesian model of the closed economy, with the aid of Figure 16.1. The upper part demonstrates how we find equilibrium in income and expenditure; it appears in most textbooks on introductory economics. For output and employment to remain unchanged, the total spending that people plan to undertake, when income is at a given level, must equal that flow of income. Some expenditure is independent of the level of income; call it *investment* (we neglect the role of the government). The balance of expenditure on *consumption* depends on the level of income. In Figure 16.1a we illustrate this dependence — the consumption function — with the line $C(Y)$. Thus, equilibrium requires that income (Y) equal planned expenditure on consumption (C) and investment (I), or

$$Y = C(Y) + I.$$

This is shown in Figure 16.1a by the intersection of the $C(Y) + I$ schedule with the 45° line. At lower levels of real income, planned expenditure would exceed income and income would rise. At income levels higher than equilibrium Y_0 planned expenditure would fall short of income and income would fall. Equilibrium income Y_0 does not need to equal full-employment income Y_F.

The lower half of Figure 16.1 is a different presentation of this equilibrium — one that we shall use later to illustrate equilibrium in the open economy. Suppose we rewrite our equilibrium condition as

$$Y - C(Y) = I.$$

The left-hand side is *saving* (S), the excess of income over consumption. Now move *investment* to the left-hand side as well,

$$S - I = 0,$$

and we have an equivalent condition for equilibrium in income. The $S - I$ function is in Figure 16.1b. It must slope upward. Investment, which enters with a minus sign, is a constant. Saving is negative at very low income levels, then becomes positive and rises to equal investment at Y_0 (where $S - I = 0$). At higher levels of income, saving exceeds investment.

We can also recall the effect on this equilibrium of a disturbance, such as a change in the flow of investment (generally, any exogenous component of expenditure). You have surely met this exercise in comparative statics in the guise of "the multiplier," which tells how a continuing in-

---

FIGURE 16.1   Keynesian Equilibrium in the Closed Economy

a. The conventional depiction of the equilibrium condition $Y = C(Y) + I$.
b. The equivalent condition $S = I$. Income equilibrium does not involve full employment.

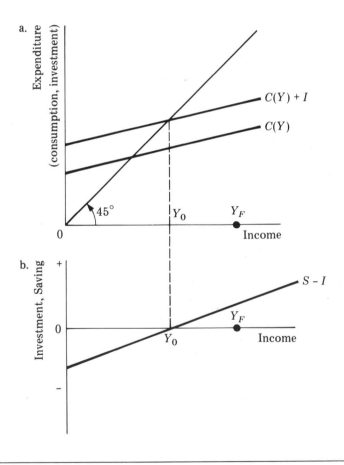

jection to expenditure raises income and employment until it is finally offset by increased leakages into saving. The induced increase in income due to this injection is given by the formula

$$\frac{1}{1 - \text{marginal propensity to consume}}.$$

We shall be developing multiplier expressions for the open economy. Hence, let us derive this expression from the equilibrium conditions given above. We noticed that saving must equal investment; i.e., that exogenous injections into the expenditure stream must equal the amount people plan to save — *not* to spend — out of the equilibrium level of income. But if this condition holds for each position of equilibrium, the *changes* in saving and investment between two equilibria must also be equal. Because the change in saving is endogenous and depends on the change in income, we can write

$$\Delta I = \Delta S = s\Delta Y.$$

The multiplier relates the induced change in income (ΔY) to the disturbance, the injection to investment (ΔI). Hence we can derive the multiplier directly as

$$\Delta Y/\Delta I = 1/s.$$

The coefficient s is the *marginal propensity to save* — one minus the marginal propensity to consume.

Equilibrium and Adjustment in a Small Open Economy

What happens to this analysis as we open the economy to trade? The answer is quite simple for the small open economy — too small for changes in its imports to affect total world expenditure on the small country's exports. We amend our condition for equilibrium in income flows, then derive multiplier expressions for income disturbances at home or abroad.

Take the version of the closed-economy equilibrium condition in which planned saving equals investment. The sense of this, we saw, was that it relates the exogenous injections into the income stream to the endogenous leakages out of it. Exports of goods and services (X) are exogenous like investment, because foreign spending on exports in the rigid-price economy is not influenced by income at home. (With rigid prices and excess capacity, foreign sales are not affected by the level of domestic purchases of exportable goods.) Likewise, spending on imports (M) puts income into foreign but not domestic pockets. It is a leakage out of the income circuit, like domestic saving. Hence, in the open economy, the

equilibrium condition relating injections and leakages in the income
stream is

$$I + X = S + M.$$

Notice that this condition does not require that the value of the imports we buy abroad equal the value of the exports we sell abroad. If we rearrange the terms of this equilibrium condition, it becomes

$$X - M = S - I,$$

i.e., the surplus in the trade balance (a net injection from abroad) must equal the excess of saving over domestic investment (a net domestic leakage).

From this condition for income equilibrium in the open economy, we can now derive the open-economy multiplier. The changes in injections to and leakages from the income stream, between two positions of equilibrium, must also be equal:

$$\Delta I + \Delta X = \Delta S + \Delta M. \tag{16.1}$$

To proceed farther we need a precise hypothesis about the effect on the foreign sector of any change in income. We have argued that exports in the rigid-price economy would be independent of income. Any category of domestic spending, however, could spill partly onto imports. To make the model as simple as possible, we assume that spending on imports varies, like the consumption of domestic goods, only with the level of income.[1] Hence we can relate imports to income in the same way as saving:

$$\Delta M = m\Delta Y,$$

where m denotes the *marginal propensity to import*.

We can then rewrite expression 16.1 as

$$\Delta I + \Delta X = (s + m)\ \Delta Y, \tag{16.2}$$

and the multiplier, when an exogenous change occurs in investment with exports constant, becomes

$$\frac{\Delta Y}{\Delta I} = \frac{1}{s + m}. \tag{16.3}$$

A change in exports, with investment held constant, has the same effect on income as an equal change in investment. The right-hand side of 16.3

---

[1] This assumption does not preclude imports from entering into investment, government expenditure, or even exports (as when raw materials are imported for processing and sale abroad). But it does rule out *changes* in imports when these exogenous spending categories change.

thus can be viewed either as the foreign-trade multiplier — the income change associated with an exogenous disturbance in exports — or simply as *the* multiplier in an open economy. We shall refer to it as the *open-economy multiplier*.

We stressed that the condition for income equilibrium from which we deduced this multiplier does not necessarily imply that exports equal imports. Suppose, nonetheless, that they are equal before an exogenous increase in exports occurs. Do imports increase by enough to restore the equality? Remembering that $\Delta M = m\Delta Y$,

$$\Delta M = m\Delta Y = m\,\frac{1}{s+m}\,\Delta X = \frac{m}{s+m}\,\Delta X. \qquad (16.4)$$

Because s and m are both positive fractions, the increase in imports has to be smaller than the increase in exports. The multiplier effects of an increase in exports thus cut into the initial improvement in the trade balance wrought by the rise in exports, but the extra imports fall short of the increase in exports so long as additional domestic saving is induced (that is, s exceeds zero). The trade balance is improved by the percentage that the leakage into domestic saving constitutes of all domestic leakages.[2]

Income adjustments help to restore equality between exports and imports when a disturbance strikes the foreign sector, but the income adjustments we have examined so far normally leave trade out of balance. By implication, we either earn more from our export sales abroad than we spend on imports or vice versa. Either way, we are left with two questions for attention below. First, where do the excess dollars come from (if $X > M$), or where do those spent in excess abroad go (when $X < M$)? We put that problem aside for now by means of our assumption that the whole world uses dollars, so that foreigners can readily produce them to buy excess exports or accept them for excess imports. The second question is what consequences this change in the domestic money supply may have for equilibrium in income.

We have touched on disturbances stemming from investment and from exports, but have not exhausted all the possibilities.[3] Exogenous distur-

---

[2] The improvement in the trade balance is $\Delta X - \Delta M$. By 16.4,

$$\Delta X - \Delta M = \Delta X - \frac{m}{s+m}\,\Delta X = \left(1 - \frac{m}{s+m}\right)\Delta X = \left(\frac{s}{s+m}\right)\Delta X.$$

[3] One omission is the government sector. Taxes on personal incomes, corporate profits, and even real estate are sensitive to the overall level of income. They constitute another endogenous leakage out of the system, like personal saving. (We can think of s in the multiplier formulae as including the tax leakage, which of course would raise its value.) Government expenditure is normally treated as exogenous, although it may depend in the short run on both total income and tax receipts.

bances can occur in the "endogenous" flows as well. For instance, consumers' tastes might shift toward imports, so that at a given (initial) income level expenditure is shifted toward imports and away from consumption of domestic goods, leaving personal saving unchanged. The reduction in spending on home goods affects the income circuit just like a reduction in investment.

We need a diagram of the open-economy multiplier, to help us with applications of the rigid-prices model. We can build one starting from the lower half of Figure 16.1, whose axes also serve for Figure 16.2. Again we measure income on the horizontal axis; Y_F would be full-employment income. The vertical axis displays (positive and negative values of) the leakages and injections in the income circuit. In Figure 16.1b we graphed the condition for equilibrium of income in the closed economy, $S - I = 0$. Now take the parallel condition for equilibrium in the open economy:

$$X - M = S - I.$$

The $X - M$ schedule in Figure 16.2 shows how the trade balance would change as income increases. Exports represent a constant exogenous flow of expenditure, which (for the small country) is independent of income; imports increase with income. Thus, when we subtract imports from exports we get a downward-sloping function. When income is less than Y_0 in Figure 16.2, imports are small and the trade balance ($X - M$) is positive; when income grows larger than Y_0, increased imports render it negative. The function $S - I$ was already constructed in similar fashion. Saving increases with income; investment, independent of income, is subtracted from it. When income is less than Y_0, saving is less than investment; it exceeds investment for income levels greater than Y_0.

In Figure 16.2, Y_0 is the equilibrium level of income at which $X - M = S - I$. The schedules intersect on the horizontal axis, indicating that $X = M$ and $S = I$. You know from the previous discussion that this is arbitrary, and not necessary for income to be in equilibrium. Suppose now that a disturbance increases exports by an amount Oc. We illustrate this by shifting the $X - M$ schedule upward by Oc, giving us the new schedule $X' - M$. Income, saving, and imports all rise. At income Y' we have $X' - M = S - I$. Notice that external equilibrium no longer exists; rather, there is a trade surplus of Ob, which is less than the initial improvement of Oc, because of the induced increase in imports of bc.

Income Determination in a Two-Country Model

In deriving the multiplier for an open economy, we have so far neglected the ramifications abroad of income and expenditure changes in one

FIGURE 16.2 Effect of Increase in Exports on
Income and Trade Balance

Income is in equilibrium at Y_0, which satisfies the equilibrium condition
$X - M = S - I$. Increase of exports by Oc raises income to Y' and leaves a
residual trade-balance surplus of Ob.

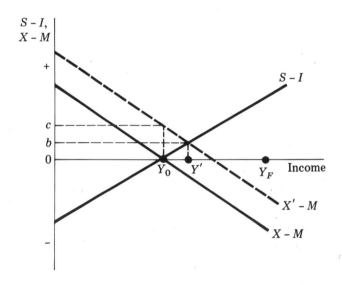

country. Yet, historically, such neglect would be a serious mistake.
During the Great Depression of the 1930's countries repeatedly used
policies to switch domestic expenditure away from imports and toward
home goods, in order to raise the utilization of home resources. These
switches of course reduced income and employment abroad: one country's reduced imports were another's reduced exports, and the term
"beggar-my-neighbor policies" was hung on such expenditure-switching
devices. These policies were not only unneighborly, but could fail to
raise incomes. At the very least, country A's diversion of expenditure
from imports would lower country B's income, and thus B's imports
from A. The *net* effect of the switch could be calculated only by subtracting from the multiplier-induced increase in A's income (due to the
switch of expenditure to home goods) the induced decrease that would
ensue from the fall in A's exports to B. (More likely, B would retaliate
against A's action by cutting imports from A by as much as the shrinkage of B's exports to A. In that case, neither country would gain employment, and both could lose some benefits from trade.)

Let us think of the world as having only two countries — the home and "the foreign country" (the rest of world). The conditions for equilibrium in income given earlier must now hold for each country. Using asterisks to denote the foreign nation, we now require equilibrium of income in each country:

$$I + X = S + M$$
$$I^* + X^* = S^* + M^*.$$

If we put a delta before each variable, we have the equations governing changes in the two countries' incomes. These relations are not independent, however. The home country's exports are the foreign country's imports, and depend on changes in its income. And the home country's income governs the foreign country's exports. Hence, we can rewrite these expressions:

$$\Delta I + m^* \Delta Y^* = s \Delta Y + m \Delta Y$$

(16.5)

$$\Delta I^* + m \Delta Y = s^* \Delta Y^* + m^* \Delta Y^*.$$

For equilibrium to prevail in both countries, both relations must be satisfied. Formally, to deduce the effects of any disturbance on income in either country, we must solve the equations numbered 16.5 simultaneously.

That procedure allows us to calculate a variety of multipliers, like expression 16.3 but taking account of repercussions abroad when a disturbance, domestic or foreign, causes domestic income to change. First, consider the effect of a change in domestic investment, $\Delta Y/\Delta I$. Expression 16.3 showed how the power of investment to "multiply" income is limited by leakages into domestic saving and imports. The import leakage now is not a total loss; it raises income abroad and leads to a *partial* reinjection to the domestic income stream from the increased foreign demand for our exports. Hence, the value of $\Delta Y/\Delta I$ when foreign repercussions are taken into account is higher than when they are not.[4]

Before, we could calculate a multiplier for $\Delta Y/\Delta X$ without regard to the source of the disturbance to exports. Because exports depend on income abroad, we must trace the disturbance to the foreign country's expenditure circuit. Expenditure abroad could change (so as to increase our exports) in two ways. A disturbance could increase total expenditure in the foreign country, or it could involve a switch of expenditure from

---

[4] We can solve the two equations in 16.5 simultaneously, setting $\Delta I^* = 0$, eliminating ΔY^*, to get

$$\frac{\Delta Y}{\Delta I} = \frac{1 + m^*/s^*}{s + m + m^* s/s^*} > \frac{1}{s + m}.$$

its home goods to its imports (our exports). If an increase of expenditure abroad should fall entirely on the home country's exports, the multiplier would be the same as for an increase in domestic investment. This exogenous increase in foreign spending on our exports affects both countries' incomes in the same way as an equal exogenous increase in domestic investment spending. If the increase in total spending abroad should fall initially on the foreign country's goods, however, the effect on the home country's income must be weaker, because a leakage into saving abroad occurs before the increase in expenditure begins to affect home-country exports.[5]

Suppose that the disturbance abroad involves no change in total foreign expenditure, but rather a switch from the foreign country's to the home country's output. Income in the home country will still increase, although the effect is less than for disturbances that raise foreign expenditure. Indeed, income abroad will be reduced.

16.2 MONETARY ADJUSTMENTS AND REAL EXPENDITURE

The Keynesian model in its simplest form analyzes the effects on income and employment when expenditure is not equal to income and the level of spending depends on the level of income. But many other economic forces can influence expenditure besides income. In this section we shall illustrate another determinant of spending by providing a role for monetary conditions and the interest rate in income adjustments. The appendix to this chapter provides an alternative treatment – more general than the one that follows, but also more difficult.

Recall a principal finding (from section 16.1) about the open-economy multiplier. A disturbance occurs in the form of a permanent increase in

---

[5] To compute the effect on domestic income of an increase in investment abroad, we again solve the two equations in 16.5, but with $\Delta I = 0$, to get

$$\frac{\Delta Y}{\Delta I^*} = \frac{m^*/s^*}{s + m + m^*s/s^*}.$$

If foreign expenditure is switched from foreign to home-country goods and does not increase overall, the multiplier becomes

$$\frac{\Delta Y}{\Delta X} = \frac{1}{s + m + m^*s/s^*}.$$

Notice that the sum of the two multipliers given in this footnote equals the multiplier in footnote 4. The increase in foreign purchases of our exports has the same effect as an increase in domestic investment. The equal decrease assumed in expenditure abroad is equivalent to a *negative* change in investment there. Hence, $\Delta Y/\Delta X = \Delta Y/\Delta I - \Delta Y/\Delta I^*$.

exports of amount ΔX. Income increases by this amount times the open-economy multiplier. Imports rise by less than exports:

$$\Delta M = \left(\frac{m}{s + m} \right) \Delta X < \Delta X.$$

The adjustment restores equilibrium in income but not in trade flows.

When exports exceed imports, the country is taking in more money than it spends on its international purchases. Its money supply is therefore increasing.[6] When the increase in exports first occurs, before any induced rise in imports has been felt, the money supply must be increasing at a rate of ΔX. As the income multiplier works itself out, induced increases in imports cut into this export surplus and constrict the injection of cash balances. But the multiplier mechanism itself, leaving a residual trade surplus, implies that this monetary injection will not be shut off entirely! After income flows have returned to equilibrium — when the multiplier process has worked itself out — the money supply continues to increase, with people's cash balances growing steadily in relation to their level of money expenditure.

Induced Investment

Are the expenditure levels of firms and households unaffected by these growing monetary hoards? Let us consider how Keynesian concepts of expenditure behavior can be used to trace the effects of growing cash balances on exports and imports. As the open-economy multiplier raises employment and real income, following the increase in exports, people hold more money to support their increased levels of money (and real) expenditure. Part of the inflow of cash balances is needed to fill the increased demand for transactions balances. But money expenditure stops rising when the multiplier effects have run their course, and at that stage the demand for transactions balances stops growing. But cash balances keep on increasing so long as export sales exceed import purchases. It is these excess cash balances that we expect to influence real expenditure.

In the Keynesian model consumption depends only on real income, not on cash balances. That is, households with excess cash are expected not to splurge on extra consumption but to put the unneeded balances into income yielding securities. Their purchases drive up the price of bonds, which is the same thing as lowering the rate of interest. Business

---

[6] One possibility is for the central bank to take action to offset this cash inflow. We assume for now that no offsetting ("sterilization," as it is called) takes place, and we show below that offsetting may be impossible even if the central bank tries to achieve it.

enterprises, noticing the reduced cost of funds, increase their borrowing (issue more bonds) and raise their planned levels of real capital formation. We now have another source of injection into the income stream. The initiating export injection not only raises income and expenditure directly, but it also injects cash balances (beyond the increased demand for transactions purposes), which drive down the interest rate and raise capital formation.

How large might this induced injection of domestic investment be? We can answer that question indirectly by first raising another question: by how much must income increase before monetary equilibrium is restored? Clearly, enough so that the injection of cash balances into the system ends, which requires the induced change in imports to equal the initiating change in exports:

$$\Delta M = \Delta X.$$

If imports are governed by a fixed marginal propensity to import (m), households become satisfied to purchase this level of imports only when income has risen by enough so that $\Delta M = m \cdot \Delta Y$. This condition reveals the increase in income necessary to restore monetary equilibrium:

$$\Delta Y = \frac{1}{m} \Delta M = \frac{1}{m} \Delta X. \tag{16.6}$$

Part of the increase results from the income multiplier analyzed above — let us call that part ΔY_k. The rest, ΔY_z, is due to the induced injection of domestic investment that occurs as the interest rate is driven down by households' efforts to rid themselves of excess cash balances. Because $\Delta Y = \Delta Y_k + \Delta Y_z$, we can secure an expression for ΔY_z by subtracting the old "open-economy multiplier" from our new expression for ΔY. Thus,

$$\Delta Y_z = \Delta Y - \Delta Y_k = \left[\frac{1}{m} - \frac{1}{s+m} \right] \Delta X = \frac{s/m}{s+m} \cdot \Delta X. \tag{16.7}$$

That is, the excess cash balances must induce enough extra domestic investment spending to raise income by $(s/m)/(s+m)$ times the initiating change in exports. Which part contributes more to the total increase in income? You can see that this depends on whether the domestic leakage into saving — the marginal propensity to save — is greater or less than the marginal propensity to import. In practice s could certainly exceed m, making the monetary adjustment more important than the conventional multiplier. Marginal propensities to import vary greatly from country to country, and in practice are apt to determine the relative sizes of these effects. In a small country, where the marginal propensity to import is usually high, the multiplier looks proportionally more important, even while the *total* change in income due to a given export disturbance $(\Delta Y = \Delta X/m)$ becomes smaller.

Induced Trade in Securities

Another development might occur to put a stop to that troubling monetary injection, the result of income reaching equilibrium with a positive trade balance. Suppose that bonds are freely traded internationally, and that all bonds bear identical risks and therefore all yield the same rate of interest, no matter what their country of origin. Now consider the implication of income equilibrium with a trade surplus, such that $S - I = X - M > 0$. If the country takes in $10 more each month from selling exports than it pays out for imports, it is also true that households are trying to buy $10 worth of bonds more than businesses are issuing. The price of bonds tends to be bid up, depressing the rate of interest. With bonds freely traded internationally, however, that cannot happen if our country is too small to affect world bond prices. Bonds are bought from foreigners to the tune of the whole of the savers' $10. The purchase of bonds abroad therefore puts a stop to the net monetary injection: We earn $10 more than we spend in international trade in goods and services, but we spend $10 more than we take in on international trade in bonds. The relevant multiplier formula remains just what it was in section 16.1.

Consider the difference between this case and the one just described, in which a monetary injection was extinguished by an induced expansion of domestic investment. The essential difference between the two cases lies in whether or not we assume bonds to be freely traded internationally. For the extra saving to drive up the price of bonds (depress the interest rate), these securities must be immobile internationally. Thus, these two outcomes — domestic investment expanded or more bonds imported — bracket the possible outcomes of an excess of exports over imports left after the Keynesian multiplier effect works itself out. If the income equilibrium involved an import surplus, of course the adjustment would involve either a reduction of domestic investment or an outflow of securities to other countries. In the following chapters we will often find that the results predicted by a model depend strongly on what we assume about international trade in securities.

16.3 THE OPEN-ECONOMY MULTIPLIER IN PRACTICE

Economists trying to predict the effects of actual income disturbances in the world economy have made heavy use of the concepts developed in section 16.1. Although the assumptions of the rigid-prices model are never completely satisfied, that model supplies reasonably accurate answers to some questions about economic behavior.

Measurement of the Open-Economy Multiplier

Estimates of the multiplier are usually made, not from simple formulas like those given above, but from elaborate statistical models of the economy. However, these models differ less in the way they depict the adjustment of income to disturbances than in the amount of detail they take into account. The leakage into saving, for instance, may be estimated separately for each class of income recipients, and the savings of businesses and governments are taken into account. Domestic investment is not completely exogenous, but responds somewhat to the growth of income and employment; inventories respond to short-term disturbances.

Table 16.1 presents the effects of an increase in exports as estimated by the Data Resources model of the United States economy, one of those currently used for economic forecasting. The calculations assume that exports of goods and services increased by $10 billion (about 3 percent) in 1980 and remained in each subsequent year $10 billion

TABLE 16.1 Predicted Effects of Increase in United States Exports on GNP and Other Variables, 1980–1990 (amounts in billions of dollars)

| | *Year* | | | | | |
Variable	1980	1981	1982	1983	1987	1990
Exports of goods and services	$10.0	10.0	10.0	10.0	10.0	10.0
Imports of goods and services	$ 1.5	3.5	3.2	2.7	4.7	6.3
Current-account balance	$ 8.5	6.6	6.8	7.3	5.3	3.7
Gross National Product	$14.9	19.3	17.1	17.4	26.9	35.8
Multiplier[a]	1.5	1.9	1.7	1.7	2.7	3.6
Investment	$ 3.0	5.5	2.1	0.3	4.1	8.1
Industrial production	0.9%	1.0	0.4	0.2	0.1	0.0
Capacity utilization	1.0%	1.0	0.2	−0.1	0.0	0.0

Source: Calculations from Data Resources model, courtesy of Professor Otto Eckstein, Harvard University. Copyright © 1980 by Otto Eckstein.
[a] Ratio in each period of predicted displacement of GNP to assumed change in exports.

higher than otherwise. The table shows the displacement of imports, gross national product, and other variables in subsequent years from the values the model would forecast in the absence of the disturbance. The line showing values of the open-economy multiplier indicates not an ultimate value, with all consequences of the disturbance having worked themselves out, but rather the cumulative effect of the disturbance up to the year in question. (In practice, we are much more concerned with predicting the effects of a disturbance over a few years than with its ultimate consequences.)

The table confirms our theoretical prediction that imports rise less than the initiating disturbance in exports, leaving a residual improvement in the current-account balance; after a decade, however, little of this improvement remains. The open-economy multiplier (calculated as the ratio of the predicted change in GNP to the change in exports) rises gradually to 3.6. The gain in GNP does not rise steadily in response to the export disturbance but rather fluctuates mildly around its upward trend. Some extra investment takes place, increasing the economy's industrial capacity. Industrial production rises by slightly more than one percent, but after six years the extra growth of capacity actually outruns the increase in production, and the proportion of utilized capacity falls.

International Transmission of Disturbances

Statistical models have also been used to measure the interdependence of nations' incomes that is highlighted by the Keynesian model. Suppose that U.S. GNP rises one percent because of an increase in U.S. government purchases of goods and services. U.S. imports are pulled up. Indeed, they may rise quite a bit, because some buyers turn quickly to foreign supplies if the demand increase occurs when U.S. industry is running close to capacity. (We describe that relation by the *income elasticity of demand* for imports, the resulting percentage change in imports divided by the initiating percentage change in income.[7]) U.S. imports are foreign countries' exports, and so their incomes rise and feed back into U.S. exports in the way described above. Large statistical models also take account of the tightening monetary conditions that coincide with rising GNP. Interest rates rise in the United States. They also rise in foreign

---

[7] Formally, we can express the income elasticity of demand for imports in various forms:

$$\frac{\Delta M/M}{\Delta Y/Y} = \frac{\Delta M}{\Delta Y} \cdot \frac{Y}{M} = \frac{\Delta M/\Delta Y}{M/Y}.$$

The last of these expressions reveals the income elasticity to be the marginal propensity to import divided by the average propensity to import.

countries, not only because of rising GNP levels abroad but also because of international capital movements (discussed in the following chapters).

Table 16.2 contains estimates of these induced changes, derived from a model developed by Professor Ray C. Fair of Yale University. Taking economic conditions as of the beginning of 1970, he first projected the changes in the variables shown without any "artificial" disturbance to U.S. GNP. Then he imposed the one-percent increase, mentioned above, and estimated by which percentage the variables shown would have changed after a year's time. U.S. GNP one year later is elevated 1.43 percent by the disturbance, and those of both Canada and Japan have increased appreciably (they are major trading partners of the United States — notice the large rise in their exports). Oddly enough, the GNPs of the three European countries have fallen a little despite small increases in their exports. That is because the dampening effect of higher interest rates, induced by tighter monetary conditions in the United States, more than offsets the positive effect on their GNPs stemming from exports and the open-economy multiplier. The large increases in their interest rates (compared to Japan's) reveal this mechanism at work. The change in imports for the United States is quite large, implying an income elasticity of import demand exceeding three. When we compare other countries' increases in GNP and in imports we notice that four of the six display income elasticities of import demand that are larger than unity.

The data in Table 16.2 thus illustrate the international linkages of national incomes and disturbances. But they also tip us off to an im-

TABLE 16.2   Predicted Effects of Exogenous Increase in U.S. GNP on Incomes and Trade Flows of Various Industrial Countries One Year Later (percentage change)

Country	Real GNP	Imports	Exports	Interest rate
United States	1.43	3.09	0.41	0.69
Canada	0.31	0.81	2.41	0.81
Japan	0.19	0.10	1.04	0.08
France	−0.09	−0.27	0.19	0.34
West Germany	−0.15	−0.42	0.25	0.39
United Kingdom	−0.05	−0.01	0.39	0.30

Source: Ray C. Fair, "A Multicountry Econometric Model," Cowles Foundation Discussion Paper no. 541, Yale University, 1979, Table 10.

portant role for international capital movements that will be explained later.

16.4 SUMMARY

In this chapter, we have dealt with the open economy in which money prices are rigid and the public's budget constraint need not always hold, that is, expenditure need not always be equal to income. To determine what happens when they are unequal, we need a hypothesis about what determines the level of expenditure. A Keynesian account of expenditure determinants in an open economy is set forth in this chapter.

The multiplier in the closed economy indicates the change in real income that follows a disturbance to expenditure. We estimate it as change in income necessary to restore equality between the injections into and leakages from the income circuit. In the open economy these leakages include imports as well as saving. Thus, the open-economy multiplier becomes $1/(s + m)$, in contrast to the value of $1/s$ in a closed economy. It predicts that an increase of exports will raise income and imports, although the increase of imports will fall short of the initiating rise in exports. The foreign repercussions of a change in domestic expenditure raise the value of the open-economy multiplier. The extra imports induced by our domestic expansion constitute a positive export disturbance abroad and rebound to raise our own exports.

When exports are not equal to imports, the economy's total purchases abroad are not equal to its sales, and its level of cash balances changes. An increase of exports not only raises domestic expenditure but also increases the money supply (unless monetary policy consciously prevents it). The monetary injection continues until imports rise to equal the higher level of exports. From this we deduce that the open-economy multiplier, allowing for the effect of cash balances on the level of expenditure, must equal $1/m$, which exceeds the value of $1/(s + m)$ that is associated with income adjustments alone.

The force that pulls imports up is expanded domestic investment, induced by lower interest rates. The interest rate may not fall, however, if bonds are freely traded internationally. Then the excess of saving over investment flows into purchases of bonds from abroad. Net spending on bonds bought abroad equals net earnings from the trade balance, and the monetary injection is offset.

Many empirical applications have been made of these relations between trade and real income. Multipliers can be estimated from complex statistical models of the economy. Such models also reveal the extent of interdependence of nations' income levels.

SUGGESTIONS FOR FURTHER READING

Dornbusch, Rudiger, and Stanley Fischer. *Macroeconomics.* New York: McGraw-Hill, 1978. Chapters 18 and 19 analyze macroeconomic adjustments using *IS-LM* analysis.

Duesenberry, J. S. et al., eds. *The Brookings Quarterly Econometric Model of the United States.* Chicago: Rand McNally, 1965. Chapter 11, by R. Rhomberg and L. Boissonneault, provides an elaborate statistical model of the international income linkages of the United States economy.

Fleming, J. M., and L. Boissonneault. "Money Supply and Imports," *IMF Staff Papers,* 8 (May 1961): 227–40. Tests effect of money-supply changes on imports.

Houthakker, H. S., and Stephen P. Magee. "Income and Price Elasticities in World Trade," *Review of Economics and Statistics,* 51 (May 1969): 111–25. Application of Keynesian income concepts to countries' trade balances.

Machlup, Fritz. *International Trade and the National Income Multiplier.* New York: Augustus M. Kelley, 1965. Classic work on open-economy multiplier, originally published in 1943.

Meade, J. E. *The Balance of Payments.* London: Oxford University Press, 1951. Part II provides a detailed treatment of income adjustments.

Robinson, Romney. "A Graphical Analysis of the Foreign Trade Multiplier," *Economic Journal,* 62 (September 1952): 546–64. Geometric treatment.

Tsiang, S. C. "Balance of Payments and Domestic Flow of Income and Expenditures," *IMF Staff Papers,* 1 (September 1950): 254–88. Enumerates ways in which a balance-of-payments change can disturb income.

APPENDIX:
THE IS–LM ANALYSIS OF THE OPEN ECONOMY

The relation between the trade balance and interest and money can be treated more generally than in section 16.2. Here we employ a rather sophisticated expository diagram that appears in most texts on macroeconomic theory, usually called the *IS–LM* analysis. It wraps up in a single diagram the relations among income, saving, investment, interest, money, and (for the open economy) the balance of international transactions. It proceeds by solving these simultaneous relations one part at a time, then putting the parts together.

Let us start with the nonmonetary parts of the Keynesian system, as they were developed in section 16.1. There we saw that the system is in equilibrium when the sum of the leakages equals the sum of the injections:

$$I + X = S + M.$$

In Figure 16.A.1 we show these two sums on the vertical axis. In the right-hand half of the diagram we show in the "leakage" schedule how saving and imports vary with income. Both increase when income increases, and so the function slopes upward. (The leakage schedule is the vertical sum of a

schedule showing imports as a function of income and one showing saving
as a function of income; only the latter is shown separately, and the former
is the vertical distance between it and the leakage schedule.) The left-hand
half of Figure 16.A.1 shows how the sum of investment and exports varies
with the interest rate, which is measured to the left from the origin. We
expect exports to be unaffected by the interest rate, but a lower interest rate
induces businesses to undertake a larger volume of investment projects. Thus
the slope of the "injection" schedule is due to the extra investment induced
by lower interest rates (this is often called the marginal-efficiency-of-invest-
ment schedule), and we can think of it as merely shifted upward by the
addition of the fixed quantity of exports $\overline{X}$.

Suppose that the interest rate is i_0. Businesses will carry out investment I_0,
corresponding to IX_0 of injections measured on the vertical axis. Income can
then be in equilibrium, with leakages (SM_0) equal to injections, only if
income is Y_0. Therefore we have found one pair of values of the interest rate
and income level that are consistent with equilibrium in income and investment. We could find many other pairs. If we lower the interest rate to i_1,
equilibrium of leakages and injections at IX_1, SM_1 requires that income be
Y_1. We can illustrate this in Figure 16.A.4 by the downward-sloping function

---

FIGURE 16.A.1   Equilibrium of Income Injections
and Leakages in Keynesian Model

Injections (investment plus exports) can be equal to leakages (saving plus
imports) at various combinations of the interest rate and income level,
such as i_0, Y_0 and i_1, Y_1. These different combinations lie on the IS schedule
shown in Figure 16.A.4.

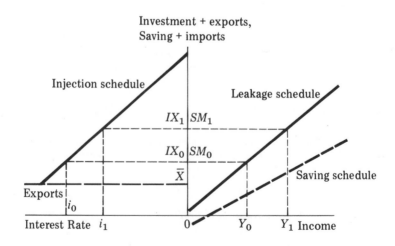

IS. It arrays all the combinations of interest rate and income that are consistent with equality between injections and leakages, although the injection and leakage components do not themselves appear in the diagram.

The equilibrium of saving and investment constitutes the nonmonetary part of the Keynesian system, and the *IS* function thus encompasses the same forces that we represented in section 16.1. People hold money for two distinct motives — transactions balances that are related to the level of income, and speculative balances related to the rate of interest. For financial markets to be in equilibrium, the demands for these two classes of cash balances must sum to the actual money supply. In Figure 16.A.2 we show the money supply on the vertical axis. Speculative balances are measured downward from the origin, transactions balances upward. The given total money supply we can think of as the thick, double-headed arrow — a fixed vertical distance, but one that can be moved back and forth to indicate various divisions of the money supply between speculative and transactions balances. The horizontal axis measures income (to the right) and the interest rate (to the left), as in Figure 16.A.1. In the lower-left corner of the diagram we show the speculative demand for money; the higher the interest rate, the more willing people are to forego the advantages of liquidity and put their funds into securities, and the smaller are speculative balances. The transactions demand for cash is shown in the upper-right quadrant of Figure 16.A.2. The higher the income, the larger are the transactions balances demanded by the public. Suppose that the interest rate is initially i_0. People hold speculative balances of S_0, leaving T_0 of the money supply to satisfy transactions balances. Amount T_0 will be demanded only if income is as large as Y_0. Therefore interest rate i_0 and income level Y_0 are consistent with equilibrium in the financial markets. If the interest rates were lower, i_1, speculative demand would expand to S_1, leaving only T_1 for transactions balances. The associated level of income consistent with financial equilibrium is only Y_1. A lower interest rate corresponds to a lower level of income, so long as financial-market equilibrium prevails. This relation is illustrated in Figure 16.A.4 by the upward-sloping function *LM*, which shows all combinations of interest rate and income level for which financial markets are in equilibrium.

Finally, we consider the country's international transactions. In section 16.1 we suggested that they could be in equilibrium only if exports were equal to imports. In fact, exports could exceed imports, and yet the country's total international receipts equal its payments, if we used the difference between exports and imports to buy securities from foreigners.[1] In Figure 16.A.3 we measure income to the right of the origin and the interest rate to the left, just as in Figures 16.A.1 and 16.A.2. The vertical axis shows the difference between exports and imports (which could be negative). It also measures the net flow of securities bought from abroad (*NFS*), which would be negative if on balance we are selling securities to the rest of the world. In the right-hand quadrant of the diagram we show the $X - M$ schedule, as in Figure 16.2. Let us call it the trade-balance schedule. On the left side of the diagram is a demand function for foreign securities. Given interest rates

---

[1] This possibility was suggested in Section 16.2.

FIGURE 16.A.2   Equilibrium of Money Supply
and Demand in Keynesian Model

Speculative demand for money plus transactions demand for money must
together equal the supply of money. Monetary equilibrium can prevail for
different combinations of the interest rate and income level i_0, Y_0 and
i_1, Y_1. These combinations lie on the LM schedule shown in Figure 16.A.4.

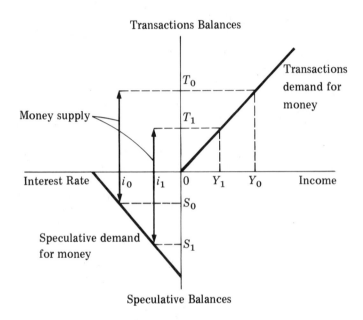

in the rest of the world, the lower is the interest rate at home the more
attractive are foreign securities, and the more are bought. Thus the *NFS*
schedule has a positive slope.

   Suppose that the domestic interest rate is initially i_0. At this high level
foreign securities are unattractive, and instead the country's own securities
are purchased by foreigners in amount NFS_0. For total international receipts
and payments to be equal in these circumstances, imports must exceed exports by an equal amount. That is possible only if income is as high as Y_0.
Had we picked the lower interest rate i_1, net purchases of foreign securities
would have been NFS_1, and equilibrium between total foreign receipts and
payments would have required an export surplus and income level Y_1. For
international payments to be in balance, a lower interest rate requires a lower
level of income. We show these combinations of income and interest consistent with equality between foreign receipts and payments as schedule *BB*
in Figure 16.A.4.

FIGURE 16.A.3   Equilibrium of International Receipts and Payments in Keynesian Model

For international receipts and payments to be equal, trade balance must equal net purchases of securities from abroad. Equality can prevail for different combinations of interest rate and income level i_0, Y_0 and i_1, Y_1. These combinations lie on the BB schedule shown in Figure 16.A.4.

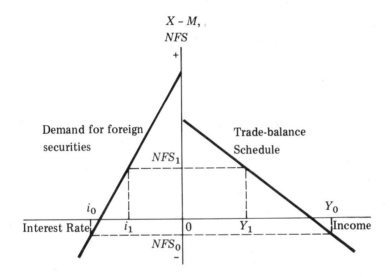

Figure 16.A.4 brings all these constructions together. At point K, where the three functions intersect, we have full equilibrium in the system. Injections into the income stream equal the leakages from it; international receipts and payments are equal, so that the money supply can remain unchanged; and the demand for money (speculative and transactions) equals the actual stock of it. This diagram allows us to follow the changes in all these variables when a shift occurs in the system. Let us suppose that domestic investment declines, shifting the IS curve leftward to $I'S'$. The intersection of LM and $I'S'$ at point E becomes a position of short-run equilibrium, but with international receipts and payments unequal (that is, we can be off the BB curve). But when they are unequal, as we explained in section 16.2, the money supply must be changing. At point E income is too low, or the interest rate too high, for international receipts and payments to be equal; receipts exceed payments, and the money supply is increasing. Now return to Figure 16.A.2 and consider what happens when the arrow describing the money supply is lengthened. A given interest rate is now consistent with a higher level of income, meaning that the LM curve shifts to the right. Indeed,

it must keep shifting until it passes through point F, whereupon the three schedules would once again intersect.

To summarize this adjustment process, the decline in domestic investment reduces income, creates a surplus in international payments, and depresses the interest rate. The induced monetary injection further depresses the interest rate and brings about some recovery of investment and income until the disequilibrium in international receipts and payments is extinguished. From this example you can see that Figure 16.A.4 is a complex but rich instrument for following all the changes that ensue when income equilibrium is disturbed in an open economy.

FIGURE 16.A.4   Equilibrium of Income and Interest Rate
in the Open Economy

Each function shows combinations of interest rate and income that equate part of the economy: the *IS* curve leakages from and injections into the income stream, the *LM* curve the demand and supply of money, and the *BB* curve the demand and supply of foreign exchange.

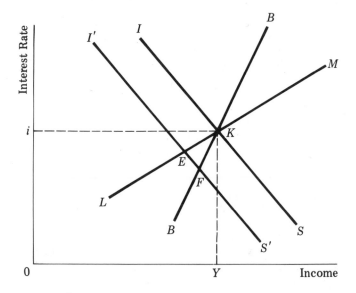

17

Money Supply
and the Price Level

The spiraling inflation rates of the 1970's caused serious social discontent within the industrial countries and hobbled their macroeconomic policies. Little could be done to curb unemployment, and foreign-exchange rates were tossed about like corks in the ocean. The economic forces determining the price level and the relation between a country's monetary conditions and its trade balance took on new importance.

In this chapter we shall develop a model to explain what determines the price level in an open economy. This model addresses many of the same questions as the Keynesian model of Chapter 16, and so we clarify at the start how it differs:

1. *Price flexibility*. Each money price is assumed to be flexible, rising when demand exceeds supply in the market in question, falling when supply exceeds demand. (In Chapter 16 prices were treated as inflexible downward, and we implicitly assumed that they would not rise until resources became fully employed.)

2. *Spending behavior*. People's decisions on how much to spend are influenced by the cash balances that they hold. They spend more of their incomes when they find these balances excessive and less when they become deficient. (In Chapter 16 consumption decisions were made to depend on income and we assumed that people used any excess cash to buy securities or sold securities when they needed to increase their cash balances.)

These two shifts in the assumptions that underlay Chapter 16 are independent of one another. We could, for instance, have modified our model of spending behavior without removing the assumption of downward price rigidity. To the first assumption — price flexibility — we will make one single exception. In this chapter we still assume the exchange rate to be pegged at an official value. We shall postpone until Chapter 18 the consequences of making the exchange rate flexible; we suppress the complication created by different national currencies by continuing to assume that all countries use the same currency — the dollar.

17.1 EQUILIBRIUM IN MONEY HOLDINGS AND THE PRICE LEVEL

As in Chapter 16 we shall start by examining the model's elements in a closed economy. You have probably encountered them before in an introductory course in economics as the "quantity theory of money," used to explain what determines the price level. Here we stress the model's ability to explain equilibrium in money income and expenditure and, thereby, the relation between monetary disturbances and the trade balance.

The model begins with a hypothesis about the demand for money: People desire to hold cash balances in proportion to their money expenditure. For convenience and safety, individuals and businesses hold some cash (or bank deposits) to tide them over the intervals between the receipt of income and its expenditure; these intervals and payment practices vary little over time. People do not let their cash balances get too small — they would risk being unable to make purchases when the need or wish arises. On the other hand, they avoid unduly large cash balances; spare cash can always be used to buy utility-yielding goods and services (we exclude bonds as an alternative asset), whereas cash balances (beyond some level) provide no extra utility in the form of added convenience in making transactions. Hence we suppose that for each household and firm — and thus for the economy as a whole — there exists a preferred ratio of cash balances to total money expenditure. This ratio may change; it fell when credit cards were introduced. It might also differ from country to country.

Now consider a closed economy with a given set of production possibilities. In Part 1 we saw how relative prices and the level of real income and expenditures are determined. With all money prices flexible, as we assume in this chapter, full employment prevails and all markets are in competitive equilibrium. Indeed, these variables are determined quite independently of money and the level of money prices. We take them as given when we consider the demand and supply of money. The country's preferred ratio of cash balances to money expenditure depends on the forces described in the preceding paragraph. Now if we know the money value of the total real expenditure — that is, if the price level is specified — we can calculate the quantity of money demanded. Furthermore, if that is the quantity of money *actually held* in the economy, we can say that cash holdings will be in equilibrium: People will have the cash balances they desire, given the level of money prices and total real expenditure. Note also that they must be spending just the value of their incomes; otherwise their cash balances would be either building up if they underspend or running down if they overspend. We can say that the domestic circuit of money expenditure thus is in equilibrium.

Now let us suppose there is some disturbance that makes people's cash balances overabundant. That could happen because they change their spending plans, for instance, deciding to get along with smaller cash balances in order to finance a boom in business investment. Cash balances could also be excessive if the government chose to create more money. For expository convenience we shall assume that the disturbance comes from an increase of 10 percent in the money supply.[1] Rather than hold extra cash balances, people temporarily increase their spending. But they cannot succeed in the aggregate. Income and expenditure are given in real terms, and there is no place for the extra cash to go except from hand to hand. What gives way, of course, is the price level. The 10 percent excess supply of money (at the initial price level) corresponds to an excess demand for goods, and their prices are bid up. The price level must rise until money expenditures again bear the desired relation to the supply of money that people hold. If that proportional relation stays fixed, the price level must rise by the same 10 percent as money supply. Note that in the new monetary equilibrium real incomes and *relative* prices should be the same as before; nothing has occurred that should alter them.

We can also examine the effects of other disturbances. An increase in productivity that raises the level of real income and expenditure would render cash balances deficient at the initial price level, and temporary hoarding would cause the price level to fall. An increase in the cash balances people wish to hold would also prompt them to underspend temporarily, and drive down the price level until it bore the new desired relation to the (fixed) money supply.

---

[1] We also assume that the increase occurs in certain ways. Gold is discovered, or money is printed to finance a government deficit, or the extra cash is "dropped out of an airplane." What we assume the government does not do is increase the money supply through open-market operations, buying up securities from the public. If people have more money but fewer securities we cannot be sure that they will increase their current spending on goods and services.

17.2 MONETARY ADJUSTMENT AND THE TRADE BALANCE IN THE OPEN ECONOMY

Now we shall extend this model to the international economy, proceeding in stages. The analysis comes across most clearly if we first take up the country too small to influence the world prices of the goods it exports and imports. To be explicit, we assume that the small country is completely specialized in the production of its export good (clothing); this assumption is not necessary for the results.

The Small Open Economy

Consider again the disturbance assumed in the preceding section — a 10 percent increase in the country's money supply, an extra $10 added to an initial $100. Starting from an initial equilibrium (which now includes equality between the values of imports and exports), this excess supply of money creates an excess demand for all goods — both domestically produced clothing and imported food. Let us suppose that one-half of the extra expenditure falls upon food imports, the other half on clothing. To buy the food the country simply spends $5 on the world food market. Being a small trader on the world market, it does not thereby affect the world price. And because we assume for the present that foreigners also use dollars as currency, this half of the $10 injection simply disappears into foreign pockets and out of the domestic monetary circulation.

What about the $5 of extra expenditure assumed to fall on home-produced clothing? You might suppose, following the reasoning of section 17.1, that it would drive up the domestic price level. Any tendency to bid up clothing's price, however, runs afoul of its status as the country's export good. Because clothing is sold abroad at a world price determined outside the country, the unit price that producers receive from export sales is independent of the amount they export. Because the clothing industry is competitive, any tendency for extra domestic demand to drive up the price simply diverts clothing from export into domestic channels without raising its price. The net impact of the half of the monetary injection expended on clothing is to divert that much clothing away from export markets. The country's exporters fail to receive $5 from abroad that they would otherwise earn, and that $5 is therefore a gross subtraction from the country's money balances.

Thus the $10 increase in the money supply is totally offset by the $5 paid to foreigners for food imports plus the repelled $5 that foreigners would otherwise have spent on clothing exports. The domestic money supply is back down to its original level of $100. And the domestic price level has not been affected at all (except possibly in transition, as when exportable clothing was being bid away from the regular foreign buyers). The foreigners' money supply is increased by $10, of course, but the force of our small-country assumption is to make that $10 such a small fractional increase in the rest of the world's money supply (say, $10/$10,000 = 0.1 percent) that its effect on world prices is imperceptible. Domestic citizens have enjoyed a one-shot increase in their level of consumption.

How is this story changed if we allow the small country to produce some domestic goods or services not entering into trade (haircuts)? The case of nontradables leads to no different result in the final equilibrium, although the price of nontraded haircuts can be expected to rise during the transition period as a fraction of the increased expenditure falls upon each commodity. The domestic prices of clothing and food are locked in place (as before), and real income stays unchanged. A rise in the money price of haircuts is, therefore, also a rise in their relative price, and that rise cannot persist indefinitely.

Let us see why that is so. Suppose that units of clothing, food, and haircuts all cost $1 each before the monetary injection occurs. The extra expenditure at first drives the price of haircuts up to $1.25. The quantity provided increases as some tailors become barbers to supply this increased demand. Two processes are at work, however, to undermine this temporary equilibrium of the haircut market at the $1.25 price. Every dollar of the monetary injection *not* spent on haircuts must be spent on food and clothing, and those dollars drain out of domestic circulation as we explained above. The external drain is in fact accelerated, because clothing output is somewhat reduced by the shift of factors of production into barber shops. With this erosion of the monetary injection, the temporarily inflated demand for haircuts shrinks, and the price retreats back toward $1. The monetary erosion through the trade deficit continues so long as cash balances are at all larger than before the initial injection. Eventually total money expenditure drops back to its old level. The economy's real income is unchanged, and so the demand for haircuts and hence their price must be back to its original level.

Finally, consider a disturbance imposed on the small country from outside, in the form of an increase of prices (and money supply) in the rest of the world by 10 percent. Given the assumption of a single world currency, and with all goods traded, domestic price of its exportable clothing must also be pulled up 10 percent. Consumers thus find the prices of home goods as well as imports (food) elevated 10 percent. The home-currency cost of their previous bundle of consumption goods increases by 10 percent, but their cash balances are unchanged. Because these cash balances are now inadequate, people temporarily depress their consumption in order to build them up to the desired higher level. The demand for imported food falls. Reduced demand for clothing frees more of it for sale abroad. Export earnings rise, import purchases fall, and the excess demand for domestic cash balances diverts the desired balances out of foreign pockets.

You might wish to compare this account of the monetary adjustment mechanism with that given by such classic writers as the philosopher David Hume.[2] He and many other writers supposed that the effect of an increase in a nation's money supply *initially* raises the prices of all home-produced goods in the same proportion. *Then* the dearness of the country's traded goods (relative to foreign goods) worsens the trade balance and drains off the extra money. But telling the tale in this form requires the assumption that identical traded goods — clothing produced at home and abroad — can sell at one price in one country, another price (converted into the home currency) in another. We have assumed instead that purely competitive commodity markets are continuously in equilibrium. (Which assumption is the more appropriate depends on factual evidence; we made Hume's assumption in discussing the price level as an instrument of policy toward the balance of payments — see Figure 15.2.)

A diagram may help to fix these ideas.[3] In Figure 17.1 the vertical axis shows the price level of domestically produced goods. We shall not define the measurement of that price level exactly except to say that it depends on the assortment of goods actually produced. The horizontal axis measures accumulation or hoarding of cash balances to the right of the origin, decumulation or dishoarding to the left. The horizontal axis also measures the trade surplus (to the right) or deficit (to the left). We can display both hoarding and trade surplus, or dishoarding and trade deficit, on the same axis because we showed above that hoarding must be equal to the trade surplus, or dishoarding to the trade deficit. In this space we show the upward-sloped hoarding function *HH*. *Given the quantity of money*, it shows for each price level how much hoarding or dishoarding people will undertake during each period of time in order to bring their cash balances into equilibrium with their expenditures. At price level *P* the public are satisfied with their cash balances and no hoarding takes place; at higher price levels they hoard to build up balances, and at lower price levels they dishoard. If this were a closed economy the equilibrium price level would always be *P*, the only one consistent with the given money supply. If the economy is open, however, that price level is also constrained by the level of money

[2] David Hume, "Of the Balance of Trade," reprinted in *International Finance: Selected Readings,* ed. Richard N. Cooper. Harmondsworth, England: Penguin Books, 1969, chap. 1.

[3] It is based on Rudiger Dornbusch, "Devaluation, Money and Nontraded Goods," *American Economic Review,* 63 (December 1973): 871–80.

FIGURE 17.1 Equilibrium in Price Level, Money
Supply, and Trade Balance

HH shows hoarding or dishoarding that occurs at various price levels, given
the money supply. *TT* shows level of domestic prices consistent with world
price level at the going exchange rate. An increased money supply shifts
the hoarding schedule to *H'H'*, creates deficit *CP*, and pulls the hoarding
schedule back toward *HH*.

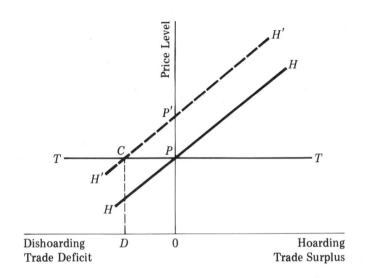

prices in the outside world and the (fixed) exchange rate. The horizontal
line *TT* is a trade-balance schedule; it declares that the only domestic
price level compatible with going world prices is *P*, no matter what
hoarding or dishoarding our small country might undertake. At *P* the
rest of the world will take up any excess supply of money (in exchange
for goods) or goods (in exchange for money) that our small country can
offer.

Suppose now that the domestic money supply is increased. This naturally shifts the hoarding schedule upward to *H'H'*; dishoarding will now
occur at the old price level *P*, and only the higher price level *P'* would
leave people satisfied with their increased monetary holdings. The price
level of traded goods, however, is locked at *P*, so the monetary injection
instead causes dishoarding and a deficit of *CP* (*OD*). This deficit drains
the money supply and shifts *H'H'* back down toward its original position.
Indeed, equilibrium is restored only when it returns to position *HH*.

Monetary Adjustment in the Two-Country World

Now we can explore the effects of monetary disturbances in the international economy when our economy is large enough to constitute a significant proportion of world economic activity. We saw previously that monetary disturbances at home lead to equal changes in money circulating in the rest of the world. Because it was assumed that the home country's money supply was a negligibly small fraction of the world's supply, the resultant change in the world's money supply could be ignored.

Once more, assume an increase of 10 percent ($10) in the money supply of the home country. The excess supply of domestic currency translates itself as before into an excess demand for traded goods. But now the increase in the demand for the imported good is big enough to drive up its world price. To see where the process ends, we turn to the equilibrium conditions that must hold when the increase in the home country's money supply has had its full impact. Real incomes and relative prices must wind up the same as before the disturbance, both at home and abroad, because nothing has occurred to change incomes or the relative demands and supplies for food and clothing. Therefore the *money* prices of both goods must have increased in the same proportion, for otherwise relative prices could not hold unchanged. If all money prices have risen in the same proportion (call it α), money expenditure must have risen by α percent in each country. Furthermore, each country could be satisfied with its cash balances only if these have also risen by α percent. The 10 percent rise in the home country's money supply thus must be equivalent to an α percent rise in the money supply of the world as a whole (when valued in terms of domestic currency).

How can we calculate α? This fraction must equal the ratio of the initiating increase in the home country's money supply to the initial money supply (valued in home currency) of the world as a whole. We will not prove the proposition formally, but it is easy to grasp intuitively. Forget national boundaries in our model. The money supply of the whole world is increased. In the new equilibrium prices of all the world's goods must be driven up in the same proportion.

A numerical example will confirm this and also bring out a few additional points. Make the home country's money supply initially $100, as before, and its national income $500. Because these are equilibrium values, the public's desired ratio of cash balances to expenditure must be 0.20. Now make the national income of the foreign country (the rest of the world) equal to the $1000, and its initial money supply $100 so that its ratio of desired cash balances is 0.10. As before, the home country's money supply increases by $10. By our assertion, the proportion by which world prices inflate must be equal to the proportion by which the world's money supply increases. The initial world money supply is $200, and so the increase is 5 percent. Let us see if this is consistent with restoration of the initial equilibrium. The home country's new level of money expenditure would be $525, the foreign country's $1050. Assuming the desired cash-balance ratios to be unchanged, their new desired money stocks would be $105 each; these add to $210, which is the new total world money supply. A point illustrated by this example is that our conclusion does not depend on all countries desiring the same ratio of cash balances to income levels.

Our small- and large-country cases taken together convey an important implication for international economic relations. A small country's monetary profligacy has no perceived effect on world prices, but that of a large country does. No wonder the world worries more about inflation in the United States than in Luxembourg.

17.3 MONEY AND FINANCIAL ASSETS IN INTERNATIONAL ADJUSTMENT

One purpose served by money in our model is to let people schedule their consumption differently from their income. An individual or a nation can draw down cash balances to acquire goods and services beyond what current income permits. Or consumption can be postponed by acquiring additional cash balances. But cash is only one of the financial assets that can serve this purpose. The person who would temporarily overspend his income can draw down his existing holdings of securities, or go into debt by issuing (selling off) his own promise to pay in the future. The person who underspends can build a portfolio of financial assets. In Chapter 16 we introduced the notion that individuals hold their financial wealth in some combination of money and bonds. That behavior is again assumed here. Money is riskless to hold but yields no interest payments; bonds pay interest but pose some risk of default. The risk-averse individual therefore holds some combination of the two assets. But a rise in the interest rate increases the opportunity cost of holding financial assets as cash and causes individuals to shift their assets toward bonds.

Relation Between Wealth and Expenditure

So far, this hypothetical description of the wealth-holding behavior of individuals does not differ from the Keynesian concepts of liquidity preference set forth in section 16.2. The difference comes in the assumption that we make about the relation between individuals' financial asset holdings (money or bonds) and their level of real expenditure. Bare-bones Keynesian models usually suppose that consumption expenditures are affected only by income, not by financial wealth. Monetarist model builders, however, like to suppose that real expenditure and wealth are closely connected. The crucial hypothesis is:

> *At a given interest rate, people try to keep the value of their bond holdings in some fixed proportion to their level of expenditure.*

A household is assumed on the average to hold, say, a year's income or expenditure in the form of financial wealth as a cushion against unemployment or a nest egg for retirement. Notice that this hypothesis about wealth holdings in general exactly parallels the monetarist hypothesis about cash balances: The household keeps on average half a month's income in cash for the convenience of managing transactions. With this assumption about the relation between wealth and expenditure we can develop the role of bonds in international adjustments. The same possibilities arise as in Chapter 16: Bonds might be marketed internationally and freely traded across national boundaries, or they might be immobile and traded strictly within the national market.

We take up the former case first, making bonds mobile across national boundaries. We also give all bonds the same risk characteristics, so that a bond promising a given stream of interest payments trades for the same price no matter what its national origin. The price of bonds and thus the rate of interest is the same everywhere. Now suppose the same initiating disturbance as before: Individuals find themselves holding 10 percent more of each financial asset than previously. When only cash assets were involved, we saw that expenditures would be temporarily stretched in order to dispose of the excess; because the small country could not affect world prices, it would simply run a trade deficit equal to the monetary injection. Now, however, the temporary overspending involves net sales of bonds as well as a depletion of cash balances. An excess supply of bonds might depress their domestic price (raise the interest rate). This cannot happen, however, because we assume their price to be set on the world market. Hence the excess supply of bonds is sold abroad, exchanged for a temporary increase in consumption. The adjustment thus occurs very much as if bonds were absent. The trade deficit is financed partly by a net outflow of securities, and only partly by a transfer of cash balances.

Adjustment with Bonds Immobile

Now make bonds immobile across national boundaries. They might be instruments such as a mortgage on Mr. Smith's house. However solid a citizen Smith may be about making his mortgage payments on time, lenders in faraway lands may have no convenient way to assess the risks to them, and so the debt instrument (bond) issued by Smith has only a local market. What we suppose is that such securities are traded freely on the national market (all carrying the same interest rate) but do not cross national frontiers.

Now introduce the same disturbance as before: Individuals determine that they are holding 10 percent more of each financial asset than is called for, given their desired relation between financial wealth and expenditure. Once again, they try to get rid of both money and bonds. But if everyone tries to dispose of bonds, and these cannot be sold outside the country, the price of bonds must fall. Individuals reduce the value of their holdings of bonds, relative to the money value of expenditure. But the reduction comes simply through a decline in unit values — a capital loss. The country does not enjoy a temporary bulge in consumption, as it does when bonds can be sold to foreigners.[4] In this case the trade deficit due to the monetary disturbance will be smaller than the reduction in the value of households' financial assets.

You should notice the parallel in procedure between this chapter and the preceding one. We constructed a model of the adjustment process without financial assets (bonds), then introduced bonds into the adjustment process. In both chapters we found the adjustment process to depend strongly on whether or not bonds are traded internationally. Real-life portfolios of wealth surely contain securities that vary between these two extremes in their international acceptability; bonds issued by major governments and stocks and bonds of well-known multinational corporations enjoy high international mobility, while the liabilities of less well known debtors are locked into national or local markets. Therefore we expect real-life adjustments involving the wealth-expenditure relation to operate as a blend of the full-mobility and no-mobility models set forth here. In what proportions are they blended? What fraction of a nation's portfolio of securities enjoys broad international markets? Some calculations by Tibor Scitovsky suggest that the proportion may run as low as 5 percent for the United States (a large country with a giant volume of internal investment and, hence, financial claims) and as high as 15 percent for the Netherlands (a small country and an active foreign lender).[5]

In this section we have developed one role for international capital movements in monetary adjustment — a role parallel to that of money in our flexible-prices model. Other roles will emerge in several later chapters of this book.

---

[4] For an account of the theoretical role of bonds in international adjustment, see Tibor Scitovsky, *Money and the Balance of Payments*. Chicago: Rand McNally and Co., 1969, chap. 8.

[5] Ibid., pp. 100–103.

17.4 THE GOLD STANDARD AND THE MONETARY MECHANISM OF ADJUSTMENT

In section 16.3 we illustrated the use of Keynesian concepts for analyzing changes in the open economy. We can similarly put the monetarist concepts to work to explain certain historical models of countries' methods of managing their international monetary affairs under the gold standard. Two properties of our monetarist model were that an exogenous change in the trade balance is associated with an equal change in the money supply, and that this relation is not affected by domestic monetary policy. The different variants of the gold standard can be described in terms of their adherence to (or departure from) either or both assumptions.

Gold Coin Standard

Gold continues to play some role in nations' international reserves, but one much reduced in importance. Before World War I gold was a firm link between the external transactions and internal monetary systems of countries on the "gold standard." Actual practices were quite diverse, so it is useful to look first at an unreal and simplified model, the gold coin standard. Suppose that all money in circulation consists of gold coin — no bank deposits or paper money. Each nation's mint stands ready to convert melted foreign coin — or newly mined gold — into national coin at a nominal cost. Thus, as a country defines the gold content of its national currency unit, it determines its exchange rate against other currencies. An importer faced with the need to make a payment abroad could then ship the appropriate weight of his own coin to be converted into coin of the realm where the debt was owed, if that were cheaper than buying foreign money directly. Suppose a quantity of gold could be converted into £1 worth of British coins or $2.00 of American coins. If the exchange rate (price of sterling) were more than $2.00, and if it cost almost nothing to ship gold between countries, it would be cheaper for the American importer to ship gold when making sterling payments. If it were less (i.e., dollars were more costly in sterling), the British importer would make his payments through gold shipments to the United States. Such movements of specie would keep currencies locked together at their "gold parity" exchange rates. As long as gold could be transferred legally and costlessly, no one would rationally buy foreign currency at any other price.

The operation of a gold coin standard would match both of our key assumptions about monetary adjustments. An excess of receipts over payments would lead to a gold inflow, an equal expansion of the money supply at home and contraction abroad. Furthermore, changes in the money stock would be linked automatically to imbalances in international payments; there is no room for discretionary action by the monetary authorities.

Gold Standard with Fractional Reserve Banking

This simplified gold coin standard has no exact counterpart in monetary history, although a number of countries once accepted the basic conditions for it — free convertibility between paper money and gold or gold coin, and no restriction on the international shipment of gold. These privileges prevailed widely during the heyday of the international gold standard, roughly from 1880 to World War I. But banking systems at this time were neither so simple nor so passive as this description implied. As the Industrial Revolution proceeded, financial systems emerged in which gold was not the principal medium of exchange but rather the reserve against which the banking sector issued a much larger quantity of other forms of money — paper (or fiduciary) currency and bank deposits. This form of "fractional reserve" banking carried two important implications for international monetary adjustments: a change in international reserves (the gold stock) could now cause a much larger change in money supply; and the banks' policy concerning interest rates could now affect the adjustment process. Both traits violate our key assumptions made above.

Under fractional reserve banking a change in the reserve base can cause a much larger change in the total money supply. Suppose that by law or custom banks must keep a reserve of one dollar against every ten of deposits held. If reserves of any one bank increased by one dollar, the system as a whole expands loans and deposits until the total money supply has expanded by ten dollars. This is the maximum expansion if the banking system is "fully loaned up"; if the price of bank credit — the rate of interest — is flexible, as other prices are assumed to be, cash balances like other resources should be fully employed.

Monetary Policy Under the Gold Standard

A banking system may make another difference to adjustments under the gold standard through the interest rate and international capital movements. Even before national monetary authorities emerged (such as the Federal Reserve System of the United States), banks were employing discretion to influence the monetary mechanism of adjustment. Suppose that the economy faces recurrent temporary imbalances. Sometimes (say, during a business boom) people try to overspend their incomes and reduce their money balances; at other times they underspend and build up their hoards. In a period of overspending the trade balance runs into deficit and the monetary authority loses gold. With fractional reserve banking, the natural consequence would be deflationary pressure on domestic prices. The banking system, viewing the trouble as temporary, might feel that the deflationary pressure serves no good purpose. It can be averted if the banks raise the interest rate they will pay to borrow from abroad. If capital is mobile internationally, a higher rate attracts loans from abroad. The capital inflow can offset the trade deficit, and no loss of reserves or monetary contraction need occur. This banking policy might be inappropriate if the disturbance is permanent (say, a shift of demand toward imported goods), but could usefully avoid needless adjustments if it is temporary. This behavior of the system may explain a fact that has greatly puzzled students of the gold standard's operation: Considering the theoretically central role of gold flows in regulating the system, surprisingly little gold actually did flow between countries. Trade deficits may typically have been financed by borrowing from abroad, rather than leading to an actual outflow of gold.

To what extent did banking policy avoid adjusting the domestic money supply to the changing international gold reserves between 1880 and 1914? If adjustments are to come about, an increase (decrease) in a country's monetary gold stock must be associated with an increase (decrease) in its money supply. If the banking system intervenes at all, it should raise its interest (or discount) rate when gold reserves decline, in order to prompt the contraction of the domestic money supply. Economic historians have found that European central banks did typically behave this way (especially in England, Germany, and the Netherlands). So far, so good for the gold standard. But one can put the central banks' behavior to a somewhat stricter test. When its gold reserves fell, a bank should not only have raised its discount rate, but also raised it *enough* to force the domestic money base to shrink as well. But this on the average did not happen! [6] Interest-rate policy may have protected the banks' international reserves through its effects on international capital flows, but it did not with any regularity force adjustments in the price level upon the domestic economies.

Modern Banking Systems

After World War I the major industrial countries tried hard to revive the prewar gold standard, and by the mid-1920's most countries had restored links between their gold (or foreign-exchange) reserves and their

[6] Arthur I. Bloomfield, *Monetary Policy under the International Gold Standard: 1880–1914*. New York: Federal Reserve Bank of New York, 1959. This study contains a good brief account of banking policy during the supposed heyday of the gold standard.

18

The Exchange Rate, Income, and the Trade Balance

What *causes* the equilibrium exchange rate to be what it is? What are the *consequences* of a change in the rate — stemming from some disturbance originating outside the country or from a decision by the government to set a new official pegged rate? This chapter and the two that follow attempt to sort out these complex relations. They are complex because:

1. Causation runs both ways. The exchange rate affects the equilibrium values of many variables in the domestic economy. The latter variables affect the equilibrium exchange rate.
2. International transactions include both goods (and services) and securities. Some models help us to understand the relation between the exchange rate and the current account of the balance of payments. Others help with the relation between the exchange rate and the capital account.

We lack a model that lets us grasp all these matters in a single unified framework and so proceed piecemeal. Here is our strategy. This chapter addresses the consequences of exchange-rate changes for income and the current account. The behavior of the capital account is mostly put aside; and we assume in most of the discussion that there are no international capital flows. In Chapter 19 we take up the causation running from incomes and money price levels to the exchange rate as well as the important role of financial asset markets in determining the exchange rate. Chapter 20 continues with the many links between the exchange rate and securities markets via the capital account of the balance of payments.

18.1 ADJUSTMENT WITH FLEXIBLE EXCHANGE RATES

One property of the flexible exchange rate is vital for the operation of domestic adjustment processes: when the exchange rate adjusts continuously to clear the market for traded goods, the value of commercial sales of foreign exchange is continuously equal to the value of commercial purchases. Both can go up and down together as various disturbances affect the system, but they are never unequal. Consider the traded-goods market shown in Figure 18.1, which depicts the purchasing-power flows that are counterparts to our country's international purchases and sales. Equilibrium was initially at point b, the intersection of demand and supply curves $D_{£}$ and $S_{£}$. When the demand for foreign goods shifts downward, the demand expressed in foreign exchange is reduced to $D'_{£}$. If the exchange rate is flexible, determined by the market, it falls from

---

FIGURE 18.1   Exchange-Rate Flexibility and Trade Balance

From equilibrium at b, demand for imported goods and services shifts to $D'_{£}$. If exchange rate is flexible, it falls from Of to Og; values of both exports and imports fall from $Ofbe$ to $Ogch$. If exchange rate is fixed at Of, the value of exports $(Ofbe)$ now exceeds the value of imports $(Ofad)$.

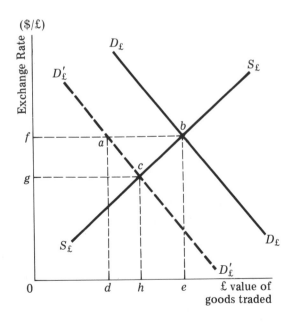

the initial equilibrium level *Of* to *Og*. If the exchange rate is kept fixed, it remains at *Of*, with the government keeping it there by buying up the excess supply of foreign exchange (*ab*) each period of time.

Now assume for simplicity that all international transactions are in goods and services (no private capital flows) and consider what happens to the value of exports and imports in these two cases. In the initial equilibrium, the total dollar value of foreign purchases is indicated by their foreign-exchange value (*Oe*) multiplied by the dollar price of foreign exchange (*Of*), namely the rectangle *Ofbe*. *Ofbe* is also the amount earned initially from the sale of exports. Exports and imports started out equal in domestic currency as well as foreign exchange. If the exchange rate is flexible and falls to *Og* after the demand for imports declines, the total values of exports and imports (domestic currency) must both fall to *Ogch*. But they remain equal to each other. If instead the exchange rate is pegged by the government at *Of*, the values of these trade flows become unequal after demand shifts to $D'_\pounds$. The demand for imports is valued at only *Od* in foreign exchange or *Ofad* in domestic currency, but export sales continue to bring in *Oe* foreign exchange (worth *Ofbe* in domestic currency). To avert the appreciation of domestic currency the government must buy up *ab* foreign exchange. The authority charged with stabilizing the exchange rate must pay out the equivalent of *dabe* in dollars each period to keep the exchange rate from sinking to *Og*. Thus, imports and exports can become unequal when the exchange rate is fixed, but not when it is flexible.

Keynesian Adjustments of Output and Employment

Our model of employment and output determination with rigid prices (Chapter 16) assumed that the exchange rate was fixed so that imports and exports could move independently of one another. If investment fell, the equilibrium level of income and employment declined and, with them, spending on all goods including imports. The effect on the traded goods market should be the shift from $D_\pounds$ to $D'_\pounds$ shown in Figure 18.1. The decreased demand depresses the exchange rate, and the falling price of foreign exchange — appreciation of the home currency — tends to depress the level of exports. In the Keynesian model, exports are an injection into the income stream, just as imports are a leakage from it. With the exchange rate flexible, any reduction in the import leakage induces an equal shrinkage in the export injection. There is no net external leakage from the income circuit, and *the open-economy multiplier becomes the same as that for the closed economy*. With a fixed rate, the multiplier's value for the (small) open economy was $1/(s + m)$; making the exchange rate flexible converts it to the larger value $1/s$, which is exactly the Keynesian multiplier for the closed economy. Any given change in autonomous domestic expenditure now has a larger effect on equilibrium income and employment.

The same insulation prevails when disturbances strike from abroad. With the exchange rate fixed, we saw that an increase in exports constitutes an injection to the domestic income circuit like domestic investment. A flexible exchange rate, however, responds to the increased foreign earnings due to the extra exports, and the declining price of foreign currency induces domestic buyers to substitute imports for home-produced goods. Indeed, the exchange rate can return to equilibrium only when that shift of domestic expenditure has gone far enough to offset the increased value of exports. There is no net injection to the domestic income circuit because the injection from abroad creates an equal leakage into imports.[1] The country's income circuit is insulated from disturbances originating abroad, although production is reallocated among industries.

The flexible exchange rate thus offers the advantage of protecting a country from the disturbances affecting the national incomes of its trading partners. But there is an offset to that advantage. Because the import leakage disappears from its own national-income multiplier, a country must suffer more destabilization from domestic disturbances to its own income stream. That is, a given set of exogenous disturbances to its domestic income circuit produces greater variations in income and employment when the exchange rate is flexible.[2]

In Figure 18.2 we illustrate these consequences of a flexible exchange rate. Its adjustment ensures that $X - M = 0$. This means that the $X - M$ schedule collapses to coincide with the horizontal axis of the diagram. External disturbances to X, therefore, cannot disturb the income level. When a domestic disturbance occurs, such as a decrease of investment from I to I', the $S - I$ schedule shifts upward. If the exchange rate is fixed, income declines from Y_0 to Y', and an external surplus of Ob appears. But if the rate is flexible, there is no such surplus, and income changes by the larger amount from Y_0 to Y''.

Monetarist Adjustments of Prices

Similar conclusions result if we shift to "monetarist" assumptions about the economy, making money prices flexible and letting expenditure and

[1] There is a theoretical qualification to this finding, because the changing exchange rate alters the country's terms of trade, and thus its real income and real level of saving. But this is probably not important in practice.

[2] Of course, domestic disturbances also induce variations in the exchange rate, and these may become unwelcome if they are large. The International Monetary Fund's research staff calculated that a one percent change in the level of manufacturing output in any of fourteen industrial countries demands an exchange-rate change of 5 to 15 percent in order to keep the country's trade in balance. See International Monetary Fund, *Annual Report 1978*, p. 42.

the demand for money vary with real income (as in Chapter 17). The open economy with flexible prices and a flexible exchange rate once again behaves just as if it were a closed economy.

Let us consider the disturbance of an increase in the domestic money supply. As before, we suppose that the public tries to dispose of excess cash balances by increased spending on goods, traded and nontraded. It seeks to secure extra imports and to intercept exportable goods destined for foreign shores. But with the exchange rate flexible, no actual deficit in the trade balance or excess demand for foreign exchange can occur. Instead, the price of foreign exchange is driven up (i.e., home currency depreciates). Without a trade deficit there is no way to vent the excess money supply abroad. Domestic prices must be driven up until they have risen in proportion to the increased level of cash balances. The domestic inflation affects both traded and nontraded goods. Of course, in the new equilibrium each traded good must sell at the same price in every national market. Therefore, the price of foreign exchange must rise in the same proportion as the domestic price level.

This proportional effect of money-supply disturbances on the domestic

---

FIGURE 18.2   Effect of Decreased Investment
Under Fixed and Flexible Exchange Rates

With the exchange rate flexible, the $X - M$ schedule coincides with the horizontal axis. A decrease of investment from I to I' moves income from Y_0 to Y'', whereas with a fixed exchange rate income only declines to Y'.

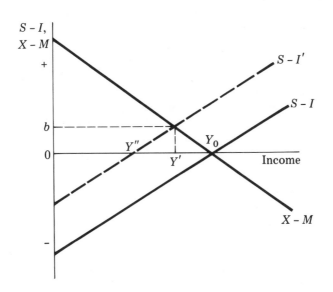

price level will hold whether the country is small or large in international commerce. And the money price level abroad also will be unaffected by the extent of the inflating country's international commerce. Thus, with a flexible exchange rate, a country must live with its own monetary disturbances. The rest of the world is left unaffected by them.

That same independence holds for disturbances originating abroad. Imagine, now, that all money prices abroad increase by 10 percent. A potential excess demand for the home currency now appears in the foreign-exchange market. But the excess demand can produce neither a trade surplus nor an injection into the domestic monetary circuit. Instead, the price of domestic currency is bid up. Indeed, it must rise in the same proportion as the increase in external prices — 10 percent — in order to keep the prices of traded goods the same at home and abroad. Just as the domestic economy must accept the undiluted consequences of its own monetary disturbances, so it is spared adjustment to monetary disturbances occurring abroad. Once again, the relative size of the domestic economy makes no difference to the result. But we must emphasize that the analysis depends on the assumption that nothing keeps the exchange rate from adjusting to hold imports and exports in continuous equality..

Implications and Qualifications

These similar conclusions from the Keynesian and monetarist models have some striking implications. Flexible exchange rates reduce the interdependence of countries' economic policies. According to the Keynesian model, A's higher unemployment no longer drags down employment in B; by the monetarist model the expansion of A's money supply no longer threatens price stability in B. Clearly the interdependence of countries' economic policies is reduced. A source of international dispute and disagreement is withdrawn, and with it the need for national administrative forces to be absorbed with the problems of coordinating policies internationally. Furthermore, a country is spared none of the consequences of its own actions. Monetary mismanagement, such as promiscuous inflation of the money supply, now brings about a large inflation of its own price level rather than a loss of international reserves and a small (or negligible) inflation of the whole world's price level. Mismanagement of employment policy, such as an inappropriate decline of capital formation, has a large adverse effect on the country's own employment, rather than some effect at home plus some "beggar-my-neighbor" unemployment abroad. Countries have a greater incentive to avoid the mismanagement of their own policies.

The implications of this analysis are rather striking, and it is important not to make too much of them. International capital flows, which we put aside until Chapter 20, are an important qualification. Even with the exchange rate flexible, the current account will not remain balanced in response to disturbances if changes in the exchange rate cause changes in international capital flows. Those flows are indeed likely to change so as to make the flexible exchange rate's insulating properties less than complete. Here we consider as special cases some ways in which capital flows might change when income disturbances take place.

Suppose that the fully integrated world capital market makes no distinction between domestic and foreign securities, so that a single rate of interest prevails throughout the world. Suppose that a boom occurs abroad, tending to pull up the interest rate there. With perfect capital markets interest rates cannot actually get out of line because investors in the home country hasten to acquire foreign securities. To do so, however, they must increase their demand for foreign exchange, bidding up the price and causing a depreciation of domestic currency. This in turn makes the home country's output relatively cheap to foreign buyers and promotes an export surplus for the home country, financed by the capital outflow. This export surplus becomes a multiplier injection, described by a rightward shift of the $X - M$ schedule in Figure 18.2, and domestic income is raised as well. The exchange rate is perfectly flexible, but some transmission of the income increase abroad nonetheless takes place.

We can identify other determinants of capital flows that make them accommodate a current-account imbalance, thereby causing the flexible exchange-rate system to mimic the behavior of a fixed exchange rate. Suppose that the disturbance is a recession at home that reduces the demand for imports. With our purchases from foreigners choked off, our currency tends to appreciate, squeezing our exporters out of markets abroad. Faced with poor markets at home and wishing to protect their positions in foreign markets against this temporary adversity, the domestic exporters may settle for thinner margins on exports and extend more trade credit to their foreign customers. This trade credit is a capital outflow that permits the home country to run a current-account surplus. That surplus both mitigates the recession at home and serves as an income depressant for foreign countries trading with us, because their exports fall but their imports do not. Once again, the insulating properties of the flexible exchange rate are limited (though not removed) by accommodating private capital flows.

18.2 EFFECTS OF CHANGES IN PEGGED EXCHANGE RATES

Completely flexible exchange rates have historically been the exception rather than the rule. From World War II to 1973 most market economies operated on the system of the "adjustable peg," using reserves to keep exchange rates normally locked at official values, changing them only when forced by large and prolonged disequilibria. Indeed, the reluctance of countries to change their official exchange rates was an important cause of the ultimate collapse of the so-called Bretton Woods system — the practices for managing exchange rates and international reserves that had prevailed since 1946, codified in the articles of agreement of the International Monetary Fund. Since 1973 many smaller countries have continued to peg their exchange rates to those of larger nations that are their principal trading partners. And while the larger trading countries have allowed market forces considerable play in determining their rates, they have also managed the market either openly or covertly to stabilize rates within certain ranges or occasionally to push them toward desired target values.

Because exchange rates have so often been fixed, or at least manipulated, we need to examine the effect on the domestic economy of substantial and sudden changes in the exchange rate — not the continuous adjustment of a market-determined flexible rate (analyzed above) but the policy-determined jumps of a rate subject to government management. To simplify the discussion, we shall deal with the case of a devaluation, or reduction in the foreign-currency price of the national currency. The analysis of revaluations (increases in this price) is symmetrical.[3]

Devaluation is difficult to analyze because its effects depend on so many things. What do we take as the appropriate model of a country's domestic economy, monetarist or Keynesian? What is the relation between its production structure and trade? What disturbance puts its balance of payments out of equilibrium in the first place? We shall deal with selected cases and emphasize how the effect of devaluation depends on what disturbance it seeks to rectify.[4]

Money Prices and Overvaluation

Devaluation could provide a straightforward remedy for a nation's external deficit if its money prices and costs have somehow gotten out of

[3] One unhappy consequence of our definition of the exchange rate as the price of foreign currency is that when a country *de*values its own currency the price of foreign exchange in terms of that currency *rises*.

[4] You may wonder how this analysis of adjustment to devaluation relates to the analysis of adjustment to disturbances with flexible exchange rates (section 18.1). Suppose any of the disturbances occur that we mentioned in that section. The exchange rate now is fixed, just as we assumed in Chapters 16 and 17. Domestic adjustment mechanisms respond, but may leave international transactions out of equilibrium (as we stressed in Chapter 16). That brings us to the starting point of this section: the exchange rate is left out of equilibrium, and the government increases it (devalues) to its equilibrium value. What we now examine is just this latter phase of the overall disturbance-adjustment sequence.

line with those in the rest of the world. Suppose that the goods it produces (exportables, import substitutes) are perfect substitutes for foreign goods in the long run but not in the short run. In the short run, a rise in their prices could cause some foreign and domestic purchasers to shift their buying toward foreign goods, thereby creating the deficit. A devaluation reverses the process, making domestic goods cheaper to foreigners and imports more expensive to domestic buyers; the domestic price level is thus restored to consistency with money prices abroad. It should improve the trade balance.

If all markets for goods and factors of production were competitive and money prices flexible, it is hard to see how devaluation would ever be a useful policy. Consider the small country that we analyzed in Chapter 17, with all its money prices flexible but locked into world prices by the going fixed exchange rate. If such a country devalued its currency — raised the price of foreign exchange — by 10 percent, it would simply raise its domestic price level by the same amount. If it improved its external balance (which should have been in equilibrium initially), the improvement could only be temporary. Indeed, we would expect even a temporary improvement only through the cash balance mechanism outlined in Chapter 17. Domestic transactors who face rising money prices because of devaluation find their cash balances inadequate to support their increased volume of money expenditures; they temporarily cut their consumption to restore the desired level, and that action causes a temporary improvement in the trade balance. But only a temporary improvement! This analysis of devaluation in the flexible-prices model provides a useful caution for an inflationary world. It shows that a possible outcome of devaluation — an unappetizing one — is the inflation of the domestic price level yet no permanent improvement in external balance.

The price effects of devaluation identified so far only have to do with general price levels, not with relative prices or the allocation of economic activity among the country's industries. However, one relative price, the price of nontraded goods relative to traded goods, is quite important in a country's adjustment to devaluation. A substantial proportion of most countries' economic activity consists of services (including government), construction, and some primary and secondary production activities that enter little, if at all, into international trade. For these outputs there is no international price link to the prices of their counterparts in other countries. A country may find itself in disequilibrium because the prices of nontraded goods have gotten out of line relative to tradables. Nontraded goods' prices might be pulled up by a domestic boom or a money-supply increase, for example, while tradables' prices are held down by international competition. In the appendix to this chapter we show how devaluation can provide a straightforward remedy to this distortion. It raises the domestic prices of tradables and thus can restore their equilibrium price relative to nontraded goods.

Devaluation, Income, and Expenditure

We shall now consider the relation between devaluation and income and expenditure. From the definition of national income and its components we know that the trade balance must equal the difference between income and expenditure. That is, since $Y = C + I + (X - M)$, it follows that $(X - M) = Y - (C + I)$. If devaluation is to improve the trade balance, it must also increase the difference between income and expenditure. Devaluation might have this effect simply because it corrects an inappropriately high level of domestic money prices that caused people to buy fewer of our exports, which provided us with less income than we were expecting. In this case, devaluation eliminates the trade deficit and raises income to the level of expenditure by correcting a situation in which actual income fell short of expected income and what was in fact spent.

But devaluation has important effects on the relation between income and expenditure that do not depend only on prices. The Keynesian analysis of Chapter 16 is helpful in bringing out these effects. Indeed, the condition for income equilibrium in the simple Keynesian model, $X - M = S - I$, is equivalent to the equation of the trade balance to the difference between income and expenditure when the latter are treated as planned magnitudes. Figure 18.3 illustrates the effect of devaluation on income and the trade balance by means of the same trade-balance $(X - M)$ and hoarding $(S - I)$ schedules used in Figure 18.2 and in Chapter 16. Intersection of these two schedules indicates an equilibrium level of income Y. This equilibrium corresponds, however, to a deficit of Of in the balance of trade. We have thus depicted a case of overspending, for by definition the excess of investment over saving equals the excess of total expenditure over income.

If the conditions for exchange stability are met, we know that a devaluation improves the balance of trade. Exports (valued in domestic currency) rise and imports tend to fall. Both changes raise the trade-balance schedule to a position such as $X' - M'$ in Figure 18.3, and the equilibrium level of income must rise. In fact, the diagram illustrates a devaluation correctly calculated to restore external balance *after* this induced increase in income. In the rigid-prices model of Chapter 16, devaluation leads to an exogenous injection into the income circuit of ef, the amount by which the trade balance would improve *if no income expansion took place*. The increase of income from Y to Y' displays the multiplier effect of this injection.

Notice the implication of Figure 18.3 for the size of the devaluation.

FIGURE 18.3   Effect of Devaluation on Income

Devaluation shifts trade-balance schedule to $X' - M'$, raising income from Y to Y'. Final improvement in the trade balance, Of, is less than the improvement that would have occurred without the expansion of income (ef).

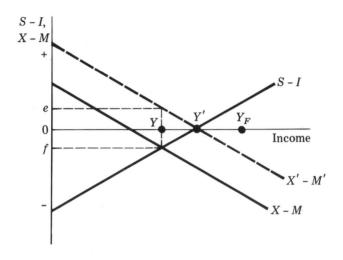

The change in the exchange rate was calculated to improve the trade balance by ef. That is larger than the devaluation indicated by the actual trade deficit, Of, because the higher level of income raises imports by Oe. But this increase of income raises saving by Of, and thus eliminates the overspending associated with the deficit. Another important feature of this new equilibrium at Y' is that the internal balance after devaluation does not entail full employment (Y_F). "Overspending" refers to the conditions for balance-of-payments equilibrium and *not* to the aggregate demand needed for full employment.

Devaluation can also affect the equilibrium level of real income because it changes the amount of total expenditure that will be made *out of any given income*. In terms of Figure 18.3, it shifts the hoarding function. If devaluation somehow caused people to spend more out of any given income, it would shift $S - I$ downward at the same time the $X - M$ schedule shifts upward, causing the new equilibrium point Y' to be located farther to the right. In this case devaluation would increase real income by a greater amount than before. On the other hand, if devaluation caused people to cut their spending from any given income, $S - I$ would shift upward and the expansion of income would be curtailed. We shall briefly consider three reasons why the hoarding schedule might be shifted.

Wealth and saving. Households' wealth may be adversely affected by devaluation. The prices of traded goods rise, but holdings of domestic currency and securities whose yields are valued in domestic prices suffer from reduced purchasing power. Feeling less wealthy, households may reduce their expenditure out of any given income in order to recoup their asset positions.

Investment incentives. More investment may be induced because of the dynamic pattern of price and cost changes that follows a devaluation. For a small country the domestic-currency prices of traded goods should rise promptly. The money costs of many inputs, however, should increase more slowly, because they are not directly determined in international markets. This lag applies to wages in particular, but also to any produced inputs (such as raw materials) that are nontraded goods. Because of the improving price-cost margin for traded goods, producers are tempted to increase their investment rate in the early aftermath of a devaluation.

Expectations. We have implicitly supposed that people always expect prevailing prices to continue into the foreseeable future. Before a devaluation, they do not expect the prices of traded goods to rise; afterward, they do not expect them to rise further. Yet expectations can affect expenditure levels in various ways when devaluation occurs or is expected. When people expect devaluation, they buy things whose prices may rise. Hence, when a country's payments deficit raises fears of a devaluation, savings may be reduced and real expenditure stepped up for speculative purchases of traded goods. The occurrence of devaluation removes this incentive and thus may reduce spending out of a given income. On the other hand, if a timorous government devalues by too little, it could conceivably fuel speculative fires and cause people to buy more traded goods in anticipation of the next devaluation.[5]

Empirical Evidence on Devaluation

The models we have reviewed give rather diverse predictions about the effects of devaluation. It is hard to gratify the wishes of a political decision maker for a yes-or-no answer to the question of whether a devaluation will improve the overall balance of payments (the "official settlements" concept of Chapter 15) or current-account balance of the

---

[5] Devaluation temporarily augments any inflation that is occurring, and in that way may contribute to the public's increasing expenditure out of a given income level. For historical evidence, see J. J. Polak and T. C. Chang, "Effect of Exchange Depreciation on a Country's Export Price Level," *IMF Staff Papers,* 1 (February 1950): 49–70.

devaluing country. Still, both the Keynesian and monetarist models imply a temporary improvement in the external balance, even if there is pessimism (especially among the monetarists) about how long the improvement will last. Therefore we shall glance at some evidence on the effects of actual exchange-rate changes to see what patterns appear.

Marc A. Miles examined the experience of fourteen countries that devalued one or more times between 1956 and 1972.[6] Starting from each year in which a devaluation occurred he examined the country's balance of trade and overall balance of payments in the three years before and after the year of the devaluation. He took account of the effects of the country's own fiscal and monetary policy, because those could reinforce the consequences of the devaluation or mask its consequences — depending on how they were managed. Controlling for these influences other than the devaluation allows Miles to tell whether a country's trade or payments balance was "better than normal" or "worse than normal" in any of the three years before or three years after the devaluation. The average pattern, taken over all fourteen countries' experience, suggests that the trade balance was fairly normal up until the actual year of the devaluation, whereas the official-settlements balance was slipping in the two years prior to the devaluation. In the first year after devaluation the trade balance bounced back sharply from its poor state in the year when the devaluation occurred, but the improvement only lasted a single year. The same pattern following the devaluation appears in the official-settlements balance. The latter actually shows the effects of devaluation somewhat more strongly than the balance of trade, suggesting an important role for capital flows — first moving in anticipation of devaluation and then reversing themselves after it occurs. Miles did not find a long-sustained improvement in either the trade or payments balance associated with the devaluation. His results seem generally consistent with the models set forth above, which suggest that a country best uses devaluation to bail itself out of some specific difficulty, and it should not expect the resulting improvement to be long-lived.

18.3 DEVALUATION AND OTHER POLICIES FOR EXTERNAL EQUILIBRIUM

Under the Bretton Woods system, countries tended to view changes in their exchange rates as a last resort of policy. First they would tinker

[6] Marc A. Miles, "The Effects of Devaluation on the Trade Balance and the Balance of Payments: Some New Results," *Journal of Political Economy,* 87 (June 1979): 600–20.

with an external deficit using a variety of subsidies to exports, taxes or quantitative restrictions on imports, and encouragements to capital inflows and discouragements to capital exports. Surplus countries have employed the same arsenal of policies, but leaning in the opposite direction. Each of these policies can potentially improve external balance. But they differ in three important ways.

1. *Effect on real income and employment.* We saw that devaluation could either increase or decrease the level of expenditure out of a given income. The stronger devaluation's tendency to raise expenditure, the more it increases income. The alternative policies to devaluation may differ in their effects on expenditure.

2. *Effect on economic efficiency.* In Part III of this book we explained the conditions under which controls on international trade distort the allocation of resources and thereby reduce real income. Devices used to secure external balance vary in the efficiency cost they extract. Some have no cost at all, whereas others can distort patterns of production, consumption, and trade.

3. *Cost of administration.* Some measures require detailed administrative controls and a costly bureaucratic apparatus for their application. Others can be applied with minimal cost of real resources.

We shall not attempt to rank these policies, or to mark one as always better or worse than the others. Indeed, the ranking is likely to depend on the economic circumstances. In Chapter 22 we shall take a broader view of the problem of choosing policies in situations where several economic problems must be dealt with.

Import Tariffs and Export Subsidies

We saw in Part III how tariffs that change the terms of trade affect the allocation of resources and the level of real income. A tariff's effect on expenditure, like that of devaluation, makes the taxed imports more expensive and switches expenditure toward home goods. Likewise, an export subsidy would shift the supply curve of our exports downward and, making them cheaper to foreigners, shift expenditures in foreign countries toward the goods that we produce. Thus, both export subsidies and import duties cause switches of expenditure resembling those due to a devaluation. They also act as expenditure-increasing policies in the home market. During the 1930's tariffs and related trade-control devices gained the epithet of "beggar-my-neighbor" policies when used to increase employment, rather than to curb imports or raise exports.

Nonetheless, tariffs and subsidies can, in principle, have the same effects as a devaluation on money prices. Suppose we wanted a 10 percent devaluation but were somehow forbidden to undertake it directly. A 10 percent devaluation would in the first instance mark up the domestic prices of all imported goods by 10 percent. Prices could be raised instead by a 10 percent ad valorem duty on all imports. Likewise, the devaluation would discount the foreign prices of all our exports by 10 percent. A 10 percent ad valorem subsidy on all of our exports would bring the same result.

> *Thus a devaluation of x percent is equivalent to an x percent tariff on all imports coupled with an x percent subsidy on all exports.*[7]

Furthermore, the tariff-cum-subsidy has no adverse effects on the allocation of resources.

Quantitative Restrictions on Imports

We saw in Chapter 13 that we can equate the static effect of a quantitative restriction on an imported good to that of a tariff large enough to induce the same cut in imports. The proposition also applies here, and it identifies quantitative restrictions as another expenditure-switching device that, like import duties, affects only domestic consumers of the goods subject to the restrictions. Quantitative restrictions (QRs) may affect domestic expenditure differently than tariffs, however. This difference is important, because the General Agreement on Tariffs and Trade registers a preference for quantitative restrictions over tariffs when one is needed to deal with external imbalance.[8] And governments seem to prefer QRs when caught with a sudden external deficit in conditions of full employment or inflation.

The difference is that import duties raise tariff revenue which, if the government does not immediately spend it, leaks out of the income circuit and reduces the money supply. Tariffs are thus an expenditure-switching policy with a heavy clout for expenditure reduction. An increase in government saving raises the hoarding function of Figure 18.3. QRs' effects may differ, however, if the quotas are doled out to domestic importers, or if imperfectly competitive foreign exporters will not raise their home-currency prices (for fear of long-run adverse effects on their sales). If the importers get the windfall profits permitted by the QRs, they presumably spend them and thus recycle the purchasing power into the domestic income circuit. If exporters simply fail to take advantage of the chance to shove up their prices, the windfalls are

---

[7] The parallel extends to the monetary effect of devaluation and tariff-cum-subsidy. If both changes together just restore external balance, the tariff revenues collected will exactly equal the export subsidy bill, so there is no net fiscal leakage or injection.

[8] The political reasoning behind this provision of Article XII was that tariffs once imposed on this pretext would become permanent, whereas a country would more readily dismantle emergency QRs. For further discussion of the General Agreement see section 13.3.

handed over to domestic consumers lucky enough to secure the rationed imports, and frustrated buyers presumably channel their purchasing power elsewhere in the domestic income circuit. QRs thus may perform an expenditure-switching function, but they are more likely to increase expenditure than are either import duties or devaluation. They are also more costly to administer.

Advance Deposits on Imports

A relatively new expenditure-switching device is the requirement that the importer make an advance deposit with the central bank of a sum related to the value of the good he wishes to import. Import-deposit requirements have been imposed by a number of less-developed countries, especially in Latin America, and have also been used in the industrial world. They are expenditure-switching devices with strong expenditure-reducing potential. The importer must leave his deposit with the central bank for a specific period, such as six months, and he receives no interest on it. The restrictive effect thus lies in the interest cost to the importer of having his funds tied up for this period. If all imports are subject to the same deposit requirement, the system acts as a uniform ad valorem special duty on imports. If the deposit were refunded only after six months, the deposit equal to the value of the imports, and the importer's cost of borrowing 10 percent per annum, the deposit requirement would be equivalent to a 5 percent surcharge on imports.

This device is interesting theoretically because its expenditure-reducing effect comes via monetary conditions. We have seen how the money supply is ordinarily contracted by the amount of the *net deficit* in the balance of payments. Import deposits, on the other hand, reduce the money supply by the *gross* value of imports entering the country during the period (e.g., six months) for which the deposits are held. That is, when the scheme goes into effect, money in the hands of the public (and the commercial banking system) is progressively siphoned off so long as importers place deposits with the central bank. When the first deposits are refunded, no more restriction takes place, but the money supply in circulation remains below what it would otherwise be as long as the scheme stays in effect. A deposit requirement thus reduces cash holdings, drives up interest rates, and reduces expenditure. A deposit scheme with expenditure-switching power equal to a 5 percent tariff would reduce expenditure significantly, rather than increase it.

Import deposits are particularly attractive to less-developed countries where inflation may be politically endemic and control of the money supply not well-developed institutionally. They are flexible administratively, because both the duration of the deposit and its size relative to the value of the goods imported can be varied freely. They can also be varied between products to achieve the effects of different rates of duty. In Chile at one time the ratio of the size of the deposit to the value of the goods varied from 5 percent to 5,000 percent, depending on the "essentiality" of the product. But like QRs they are costly to administer.[9]

Restrictions on Capital Exports

A highly popular balance-of-payments policy among the industrial countries has been to restrict capital exports when in external deficit or to restrict capital imports when in surplus. One major question about this policy is whether it is indeed effective for improving the balance of payments. Consider, for example, the Interest Equalization Tax used to restrict capital outflows from the United States in the 1960's. It unquestionably caused Americans to reduce their purchases of foreign securities, and to that extent improved the U.S. balance of payments. But this shrinkage in turn brought on other changes identified with the "transfer process" described in Chapter 4. Foreign borrowers, deprived of funds, are likely to reduce their investment spending, and with it their purchases of goods and services — including exports from the United States. And Americans now spend at home (whether for consumption or investment) at least part of the funds diverted from purchases of foreign securities. The extra domestic spending falls partly on imports. Thus the current account worsens as a result of the restriction of capital outflows, just as the capital account improves, and one cannot be certain that the tax brought a net improvement of the balance of payments.

Two-Tier Foreign-Exchange Market

Another device that has been used to control international capital flows is the two-tier foreign-exchange market. Suppose that Belgium is experiencing a substantial inflow of capital and upward pressure on the price of its currency. For some reason it is unwilling to accept the worsening of its trade balance that would follow if it revalues the Belgian franc. It therefore maintains its present fixed exchange rate for current-account transactions but requires parties who wish to make capital-account transactions to go to the competitive foreign-exchange market. There the exchange rate is left free to find its own level. Those

---

[9] For information on these controls see Jorge Marshall, "Advance Deposits on Imports," *IMF Staff Papers*, 6 (April 1958): 239–58; and E. A. Birnbaum and M. S. Qureshi, "Advance Deposit Requirements for Imports," *IMF Staff Papers*, 8 (November 1960): 115–25.

clamoring for Belgian francs to export capital to Belgium find the supply limited to the flow of currency made available by Belgians desiring to export capital to other countries. Capital exports and imports would be made equal to each other by the market-determined exchange rate for capital transactions, and no *net* international capital transfers could take place. The device could similarly be used to avert a devaluation when a country is experiencing capital outflows. The two-tier foreign-exchange market is difficult to administer because it requires elaborate controls. If the price of Belgian francs is higher in the competitive market for capital-account transactions, those wishing to export capital to Belgium have an incentive to gain access to its currency at the cheaper rate for current-account transactions. And Belgian importers who must buy foreign exchange at the (for them) less favorable current-account rate have an incentive to sell Belgian francs to buyers in the capital-account market. Controls must keep these parties apart, if the system is to work.

Capital controls tend to impair economic efficiency because they keep capital from moving from places where its expected return is low to where it is high. If that difference faced by the lender is also a difference in real social productivity, the control imposes a welfare cost. One cannot be dogmatic, though, about the welfare costs of capital controls because governments use the interest rate — the return to capital — extensively as a policy variable. When the central bank is influencing the price of credit, we can no longer be sure about the connection between the market price and social productivity of capital.

Devaluation and Other Policies in LDC Economies

The relation between devaluation and other policies is particularly important for LDCs, where devaluations often occur in an economy already laden with other controls. Studies have found that devaluations by LDCs often coincide with a relaxation and simplification of other controls, so that the effective net increase of the price of foreign exchange is much less than the nominal devaluation. For instance, the domestic price of an import that was elevated by a highly restrictive QR is now elevated — but not much more — by the devaluation as the QR is removed. This interrelation causes the effects expected of LDC devaluations to differ considerably from those of industrial countries' devaluations.

For example, we generally expect some inflation to follow devaluations: They raise the domestic prices of traded goods and tend to halt the drain of the money supply caused by a payments deficit. In LDC economies, however, they are much more likely to be deflationary. When devaluation replaces restrictive QRs, importers lose their windfall profits (the difference between the domestic and world prices of the imports), and these are in essence captured by the central bank. LDC governments depend heavily for tax revenue on ad valorem duties on imports, and collections of these rise following devaluation, reducing the government deficit. LDC devaluations are likely to redistribute income toward the producers of traditional primary-product exports, who in many LDCs tend to save more of their incomes than do other income recipients. The effects of devaluations by LDCs may be no more permanent than those of industrial countries, as we indicated above, but they can be quite different — and important — in the short run.[10]

18.4 SUMMARY

This chapter deals with the effect of the exchange rate on current-account transactions with net capital movements assumed away. A flexible exchange rate tends to isolate a country's trade balance from the effect of disturbances, whether they originate at home or abroad. Domestic expenditure tends to be unaffected by income or monetary disturbances abroad, but it is fully affected by disturbances at home because there is no leakage of expenditure or cash balances via the trade balance. These conclusions hold in quite similar fashion whether we employ a Keynesian or a monetarist framework of analysis. However, it is quite possible that capital flows will vary so as to make this isolation under flexible exchange rates incomplete.

Because the exchange rate is the link between national price levels, a devaluation can correct a deficit that has emerged because the money prices of the country's traded goods have risen. But a devaluation in the absence of price disequilibrium merely causes a proportional increase in the traded-goods prices of the devaluing country if it is small. Nontraded goods play an important role when a country devalues, because devaluation raises the relative prices of traded goods in terms of nontraded goods.

Devaluation increases expenditure, because in Keynesian terms it improves the trade balance and thereby promotes an increase in the level of income and employment. The income increase raises imports and partly offsets the effect of the devaluation. Another possible effect of devaluation on income circuits is a changed level of expenditure out of a given income; this can occur in various ways.

[10] See Anne O. Krueger, *Foreign Trade Regimes and Economic Development: Liberalization Attempts and Consequences.* Cambridge, Mass.: Ballinger Publishing Co., 1978; Richard N. Cooper, *Currency Devaluation in Developing Countries.* Essays in International Finance, no. 86. Princeton, N.J.: International Finance Section, Princeton University, 1971.

Devaluation switches expenditure (home and foreign) toward the goods of the devaluing country. Nations also employ other expenditure-switching policies, which can be compared to devaluation on the basis of their likelihood of raising income and employment. A uniform 10 percent export subsidy and import tariff would in fact have the same effect as devaluation on both external and internal balance. Quantitative restrictions having the same incidence would probably raise expenditure by a larger amount. Requiring that importers place no-interest deposits with the central bank, on the other hand, would be deflationary. (Any of these trade controls impose real costs on the economy if their incidence is not uniform on all goods.) Restrictions on capital exports may not improve overall external balance. If they succeed, they increase income and employment by less than a devaluation that also attains external balance. Devaluations by LDCs are often coupled with extensive changes in other controls.

SUGGESTIONS FOR FURTHER READING

Corden, W. M. *Inflation, Exchange Rates, and the World Economy: Lectures on International Monetary Economics.* Chicago: University of Chicago Press, 1977. Chapters 1–3 develop the analysis of exchange-rate changes in a small economy that produces both traded and nontraded goods.

Dornbusch, Rudiger, and Paul Krugman. "Flexible Exchange Rates in the Short Run," *Brookings Papers on Economic Activity,* 1976 (no. 3): 537–84. Investigates insulation properties of flexible exchange rates.

Fieleke, Norman S. *The Welfare Effects of Controls over Capital Exports from the United States.* Essays in International Finance, no. 82. Princeton: International Finance Section, Princeton University, 1971. Welfare costs vs. balance-of-payments gains in controlling capital flows.

Haberler, G. "The Market for Foreign Exchange and the Stability of the Balance of Payments: A Theoretical Analysis," in Richard N. Cooper, ed., *International Finance.* Harmondsworth, England, and Baltimore: Penguin, 1969, chap. 5. A partial-equilibrium approach to devaluation more traditional than that presented in this volume.

Johnson, Harry G. "Towards a General Theory of the Balance of Payments," chap. 11 in Richard N. Cooper, ed., *International Finance.* Presents a classification of policies similar to that used in this volume.

Miles, Marc A. "The Effects of Devaluation on the Trade Balance and the Balance of Payments: Some New Results," *Journal of Political Economy,* 87 (June 1979): 600–20. Investigates the effects of numerous actual devaluations.

Tew, Brian. "The Use of Restrictions to Suppress External Deficits," *Manchester School,* 28 (September 1960): 243–62. Problems with use of trade controls to suppress monetary imbalance.

APPENDIX:
DEVALUATION WITH NONTRADED GOODS

We can use a diagrammatic device like the transformation curve introduced in Chapter 3 to show how devaluation can rectify a disequilibrium
in the price of nontraded goods relative to tradables. We shall assume that
the economy produces both nontraded and traded goods; the latter can be
either exports or goods that compete directly with imports. We continue to
suppose that the country is too small to affect the world prices of any goods
that it trades internationally. We represent this situation in Figure 18.A.1.
With the relative price of exportables and importables unchanged, we can
lump together the total amounts of them produced, or the total amounts
consumed. Of course with changes in incomes and/or changes in the prices
of nontraded goods, the composition of "the" traded commodity can change.
For example, a rise in income may cause domestic consumption of importables to rise by more than exportables. But we can neglect these changes
and concentrate instead on the bundle of traded commodities, the relative
price of whose separate ingredients is locked by the given terms of trade.

Figure 18.A.1 illustrates a bowed-out transformation schedule, TT', between traded goods and nontraded goods.[1] It also illustrates a set of indifference curves for these two classes of commodities. The initial situation,
one of balanced trade and equilibrium in the foreign-exchange market, is
shown by point A, and the price of nontraded goods (relative to traded
goods) is shown by the slope of line 1. Quantity OE of the nontraded good
is produced and consumed. Distance AE represents both some mixture of
production and consumption of exportables and importables. These two mix-
tures are not the same — the bundle produced contains more exportables
than the bundle consumed. But the value of each (in units of one of the
traded goods) is equal to AE.

Suppose, now, that for some reason the price of nontraded goods should
rise, as shown by a steeper price line — line 2. These prices are *disequilibrium* prices: resources are shifted into nontraded goods and away from
traded goods, as shown by the movement from A to B. On the other hand,
consumers respond by shifting demand from the higher-priced nontraded
goods to tradables — the move from A to C. There is excess supply of the
nontraded good shown by FB. There is also a balance of trade *deficit*, shown
by CF. This deficit reflects the fact that with traded goods priced too low,
consumption (at C) exceeds production (at B).

A devaluation may well be a suitable remedy. If the price of nontraded
goods cannot be altered, the domestic-currency price of traded goods can be
raised by the appropriate devaluation because world prices of traded goods
are assumed to be unaffected by the country's actions. The budget line would
be flattened to the position of line 1, reducing demand for the now higher-

---

[1] The source of this diagram is W. E. G. Salter, "Internal and External Balance:
The Role of Price and Expenditure Effects," *Economic Record,* 35 (August 1959):
226–38. Recall the discussion of this type of diagram in a Ricardian model in
Figure 5.6.

FIGURE 18.A.1   Devaluation and Nontraded Goods

With the relative price of exports and imports unchanging, traded goods
can be lumped together on the vertical axis. External balance exists at *A*,
but a rise of nontraded-goods prices from 1 to 2 creates a trade deficit of
CF. If the money prices of nontraded goods cannot be reduced, equilibrium
can still be restored at *A* by devaluation.

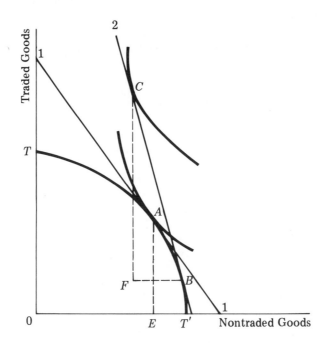

priced traded goods and shifting resources into exports and import-competing
goods. In this case, you can see that only nontraded goods were "overvalued,"
yet devaluation is still useful for restoring equilibrium in relative prices and
international trade. It is vital to recognize that the exchange rate here is not
directly connected to the terms of trade, as it was in Figure 18.1 and the
associated analysis. Now we are assuming that the home country's traded
goods have perfect substitutes abroad; before, we did not.

19

Factors Affecting the Foreign-Exchange Rate

Before 1973, when the exchange rates of the major industrial countries were pegged at official values, the determinants of the foreign-exchange rate were a preoccupation of government policymakers — but *only* of governments. In 1973 these countries greatly reduced their intervention in the foreign-exchange market and left exchange rates substantially to market forces. The general public suddenly found that exchange rates were moving in response to forces of demand and supply like other competitively determined prices. One had to understand (and, if possible, predict) what forces were pushing the Swiss franc up or the Canadian dollar down, in order to manage one's transactions to advantage.

In this chapter we take up the foreign-exchange market, the crossroads of forces determining the equilibrium value of a currency in terms of other currencies. Some general principles can be developed and placed beside the empirical evidence on the behavior of the major industrial countries' exchange rates since 1973. In Chapter 15 we introduced a simplified view of the influences determining the exchange rate. There we suggested that, with national price levels given, the exchange rate takes on the function of the terms of trade, equilibrating the exchange of goods and services between countries. Now we go beyond that partial view. Let us sketch the argument that will follow.

When somebody asks you what determines a price, "demand and supply" is usually a safe guess. For a financial asset "demand" depends on the rate of return that people expect to receive from holding that asset and the quantities of it they therefore desire to hold (at various prices). "Supply" in the short run may be a fixed stock, or there may be some mechanism that can change the short-run stock. Foreign exchange is simply money (cash or demand deposits) that has strayed off its national home base. Like money in the domestic economy, people hold foreign exchange in order to facilitate their transactions — in this case, international transactions with parties in other currency areas. Foreign exchange is a financial asset, and we expect that people decide about holding foreign exchange in the same way they decide about holding other financial assets. In this chapter we do three things:

1. Explore the actual market for foreign exchange and the financial institutions that take part in it.
2. Show the main influences on the demand and supply for foreign exchange that stem from current-account transactions.
3. Develop formally the process by which asset holders react to exchange-rate changes, so we can show how the capital account influences the equilibrium foreign-exchange rate.

These pieces together tell us what determines the exchange rate.

19.1 THE FOREIGN-EXCHANGE MARKET

We now consider briefly the institutions of actual foreign-exchange markets, in which people making international transactions buy and sell to adjust the balances of foreign currency they hold. The currencies of a number of leading countries are traded within and among financial centers (such as New York, London, Paris, Zurich). Many traders are active in each center, and the centers are in continuous touch with each other. Hence the market for any currency closely matches the economist's model of pure competition.

In New York the major banks deal in foreign exchange for their customers' convenience, buying exporters' proceeds and supplying the currencies needed by importers. They also deal "wholesale" in foreign exchange at two levels. First, they buy and sell among themselves through brokers who secure commissions for their services. A bank does not hold large inventories of currencies, and so it must go into the market to even out its position when demand and supply among its customers for a currency fail to balance. Finally, New York banks maintain trading relations and foreign-exchange balances with leading banks in other centers, and exchange is easily bought and sold across national boundaries through *cable transfers*, which cause a deposit lodged in a foreign bank to change hands.[1] Other traders are also present — the agencies of large foreign banks, specialized dealers in foreign bank notes,

---

[1] For a more detailed description, see Alan R. Holmes and Francis H. Schott, *The New York Foreign Exchange Market*. New York: Federal Reserve Bank of New York, 1965.

and out-of-town banks that manage their customers' exchange needs through the brokers or with their New York "correspondent" banks. Even a currency with an official fixed price is normally allowed to fluctuate within small limits, and so exchange rates in this market are in continuous motion.

Arbitrage

Exchange rates in different financial centers are kept nearly identical by *arbitrage*. Arbitrage is a general term in economics for buying something where it is cheap and selling where it is dear. If the price of Swiss francs in New York falls below that in London by more than the (small) cost of transaction, it pays to buy in New York and sell in London: This is foreign-exchange arbitrage. It tends to continue until the difference disappears. Arbitrage also keeps consistent exchange rates among the many traded currencies. Disregarding transactions costs, suppose that you buy $1000 worth of sterling in New York, sell it in Paris for German Deutschemarks (DM), then sell the DM for dollars in Frankfurt. If you wind up with either more or less than $1000, the exchange rates were not consistent. If a profit was made, you (and other arbitragers) will continue the transaction until the market rates are driven into consistency. If you made a loss, you went around the circuit the wrong way; the opposite series of purchases and sales would have yielded an arbitrage profit. Such transactions are called *triangular arbitrage*. Subject to the limits of transactions costs,[2] they maintain consistency among the bilateral "cross rates" connecting all the world's internationally traded currencies.

Vehicle Currencies

Arbitrage or no arbitrage, you might still wonder how the foreign-exchange market copes with the large number of independent currencies represented by the hundred-plus trading nations of the world. Is there an active market in every country for the currency of each nation with which it trades? The answer is no: In any center of foreign-exchange trading most of the business is done in only a few foreign currencies. This does not necessarily imply that the market is imperfect, or that it discriminates against the smaller trading countries. Rather, it demonstrates the convenience to all parties of picking a few leading

[2] The transaction cost of carrying out triangular arbitrage among the major currencies is very low, perhaps less than 0.1 percent. See Frank McCormick, "Covered Interest Arbitrage: Unexploited Profits? Comment," *Journal of Political Economy*, 87 (April 1979): 414.

currencies and using them as the basis for invoicing many international transactions. The U.S. dollar remains the world's principal *vehicle currency*, although a half-dozen others also play this role. The citizens of any country can readily manage most of their international transactions by conversions between their own currency and dollars. All currencies remain linked through the vehicle currencies. The number of exchange transactions, the size of currency inventories, and, thus, the cost of international transactions are thereby reduced.

Forward Exchange Markets

Trading in the foreign-exchange markets includes not only currencies for immediate delivery — *spot exchange* — but also *forward exchange*, currencies to be delivered on a specified date. Forward contracts generally mature in thirty, sixty, ninety, or more days from the date of execution. A market in forward exchange exists principally because persons committing themselves to future transactions involving foreign currencies want to know now what these commitments will be worth at maturity in their home currencies. Thus, a United States importer of British goods may be obliged to pay the shipper in sterling ninety days hence. If the price of sterling falls in the interim, say because the pound is devalued, his profits from the importing transaction are increased. But if the price of sterling rises, his profits are reduced or wiped out. He may wish to avoid taking his chances on either of these outcomes. A possible solution for him, of course, would be to purchase spot sterling now and hold it for ninety days. That would eliminate the exchange risk, but it would tie up his capital and perhaps cost him interest. A better solution, potentially, is to *hedge* his future payment by a forward purchase of sterling. That is, he enters a contract to pay a specified number of dollars ninety days hence in exchange for the sterling he will need. The dollar cost of his future payment is thus made certain. Other transactors in the forward market are those who expect to receive sums fixed in foreign currency, and who wish to avoid the risk of unexpected changes in the home-currency value of the proceeds. This group would include exporters who are taking deferred payment from their foreign customers, and the holders of foreign short-term securities, such as British Treasury bills.

The price of forward exchange is set by competition among these traders as well as by *speculators* in foreign exchange. The traders previously described take part in the forward market in order to cover their exchange commitments — i.e., so that their foreign-exchange payments and receipts will be equal at a future date. A speculator, by contrast, is willing to take an *open position*, committing himself to a future net sale or purchase of exchange. If he has sold forward, he must buy in the spot market on the agreed date in order to cover his commitment. He takes a chance on what will happen to the spot market by that time. Suppose that the price today of ninety-day forward sterling is $1.997. If the spot price ninety days hence is $2.012, the speculator earns $1\frac{1}{2}$ cents on each pound sterling that he buys forward. Like the importer whose obligation may be covered by the exchange he sells forward, he ties up no capital in the contract. On the day his contract matures, he simply pays $1.997 for each pound sterling he has purchased forward, and simultaneously sells it spot for $2.012.

The forward market thus allows people with differing expectations about future exchange rates and differing attitudes toward risk to improve their expected future positions. We shall consider its significance in detail in Chapter 20.

19.2 THE EXCHANGE RATE AND TRADE IN GOODS AND SERVICES

Some buyers come into the foreign-exchange market in order to facilitate their international transactions in goods and services. The American exporter must pay out dollars to cover his costs of production and probably wants his own profits in that form. The German importer to whom he sells receives Deutschemarks (DM) when he places the imports on the German market. At least one of these parties — or his banker — needs to hold balances of what is for him foreign currency — the American exporter if the transaction is invoiced in DM, the German importer if it is invoiced in dollars. These transactions balances, like balances of domestic money, are probably held in amounts related to the average volume of transactions and the unit price of each transaction — the quantity theory of money once again.

Suppose that initially trade between the United States and Great Britain is in balance, and people hold the volume of foreign exchange (pounds in the United States, dollars in Great Britain) that they desire. Over time the value of this trade doubles, with no change in payments practices or the currency of invoice. Transactions balances of each currency held as foreign exchange would probably double; growing at the same rate, they would exert no influence in the exchange rate — the relative price of one currency in terms of the other. If trade becomes unbalanced, however, with the United States buying more from Britain than it sells, the demand for sterling transactions balances should grow faster than the demand for dollar transactions balances. The market for foreign exchange is affected by the shift, which tends to drive up the dollar price of the pound. Thus we reach the straightforward conclusion that the adjustment of transactions balances is part of the process whereby an excess demand for foreign goods is likely to drive up the price of foreign currency. That conclusion brings us to a proposition widely used to assess the relation between trade flows and the exchange rate, the purchasing-power-parity hypothesis.

The Purchasing-Power-Parity Hypothesis

Economists' thinking about the relation between goods prices and exchange rates starts from a simple proposition about competitive commodity markets. With transportation costs neglected, a pound of copper that sells for $1.00 in one location should sell for $1.00 everywhere else. That proposition, the *Law of One Price*, merely asserts a central property of competitive market equilibrium. We assumed the Law of One Price (without giving it that name) in setting forth the monetarist model of Chapter 17. One can describe monetarist adjustment processes, however, without assuming that the law holds; indeed, that is the difference between the modern model and David Hume's account of monetary adjustments.[3] The Law of One Price has vital implications for what factors determine the equilibrium exchange rate. Suppose that many goods and services are produced and sold in the United States, and that we have defined the units of each good such that a unit costs $2.00 (5 pounds of potatoes, 1/4000 of an automobile, etc.). Suppose that in Great Britain each of these same commodity units is competitively produced and sold for £1.00. The market equilibrium price for a pound sterling must then be $2.00. Let it rise to $2.01 and all British goods look overpriced compared to their American substitutes; U.S. imports from Britain plunge. If British goods look dear to American purchasers, American goods similarly are a bargain for the British (for whom the cost of a dollar has fallen from £0.50 to £0.4975), and American exports boom. If the price of sterling were $1.99, the opposite changes would take place. Arbitrage of goods (like arbitrage of currencies, mentioned above) serves to lock together the prices of a given good sold in two separated markets. For the foreign-exchange market, this line of thinking suggests that the transactions demand for foreign exchange should be very elastic at the $2.00 price; the large shift in the trade balance caused by any deviation would similarly disturb the demand for transactions balances. This proposition about the influence of goods and services trade on the equilibrium exchange rate is called the *absolute* version of the purchasing-power-parity (hereafter PPP) hypothesis.

---

[3] The Keynesian model of Chapter 16 was explained on the assumption that the law does not hold — that the home country's output does not have perfect substitutes abroad. Without this assumption it is hard to justify assuming a stable marginal propensity to import, an important concept in that model.

The absolute version of the hypothesis should be distinguished from its *relative* version, which addresses changes in prices and exchange rates over time. Suppose that $2.00 is the equilibrium price of the pound sterling today. Some great disturbance causes the British price level to double, so that the goods that used to cost £1.00 per unit now cost £2.00. The relative version of the hypothesis asserts that the equilibrium price of sterling should now fall to $1.00. The general relation behind the numerical example is this: Calculate the ratio of the domestic (U.S.) price level today (after the disturbance) to its level yesterday (before the disturbance). Divide the result by the ratio of the foreign (U.K.) price level today to its value yesterday. Multiply yesterday's exchange rate by this fraction in order to predict today's exchange rate. Thus (1/2) $2.00 = $1.00. If the absolute version of the hypothesis holds at all times, or at least when "equilibrium" prevails, the relative version should hold as well.[4]

Why two versions of the hypothesis? There are both analytical and historical reasons. The analytical reason stems from the fact that the Law of One Price need not hold for every good and service, and hence the absolute version of PPP need not hold everywhere. Transportation costs obviously violate the Law of One Price, making a commodity cheaper near its point of production than at a distance. Some goods, such as bricks, incur transportation costs so heavy that they seldom move in international trade, and we call them nontraded goods. Personal services fall into this category. Nations create artificial transport costs in the form of tariffs and other trade restrictions that have this same effect. Some goods cannot be sold in a national market without heavy initial expenditures to provide a distribution network, service facilities, and advertisements or roving salespersons to inform potential buyers about them. Prices of these *differentiated* goods could differ a lot between countries in the short run, or differ somewhat for an extended period of time, without producers in the low-price market finding it profitable to invest in serving the high-price market. If the Law of One Price is suspended for some goods — perhaps for many goods — then the absolute version of PPP loses its foundation.

Even with the absolute version undermined, it has been suggested that the relative version might work reasonably well. If the structures of commodity markets stay more or less unchanged, the exported good that was cheaper at home than abroad last year is likely to be cheaper

---

[4] It *must* hold in our example, because all money prices are assumed to change in the same proportion. In an actual case, with prices changing by different amounts, the calculation could be thrown off because of structural changes occurring in the economy. See Lawrence H. Officer, "The Relationship between Absolute and Relative Purchasing Power Parity," *Review of Economics and Statistics,* 60 (November 1978): 562–68.

at home this year as well. If the equilibrium prices of nontraded goods (relative to traded ones) were high at home last year (compared to their relative price in foreign lands), why should the relation not hold this year? The relative version of the hypothesis thus gains force from the possibility that deviations from the Law of One Price may be rather stable over time. If the absolute version is always off by 10 percent in the same direction, then the relative one could still prove accurate. This analytical suggestion in fact squares with the historical origin of the relative version. During World War I many countries underwent massive inflations and suffered considerable disruption of their international trade. After the war how could equilibrium exchange rates be found? Some rough basis was needed for determining the neighborhood in which they might lie. The relative version was proposed as a method of estimating new equilibrium rates from information on the prewar rates and international differences in wartime inflation rates.[5]

Empirical Evidence

The many economic disturbances of the 1970's have posed in urgent if less spectacular form the same question that gave rise to the relative PPP hypothesis. In 1973 the fixed exchange rates abandoned by the leading industrial countries were in some cases far from their equilibrium levels, and traders (and governments) needed to guess what levels the market would find. Since then inflation rates have been both high and variable among countries, posing the question of how fully and rapidly exchange rates would change to adapt to them. As a result economists have undertaken many statistical investigations that shed light not only on PPP as a predictor of exchange rates but also on the adjustment processes that operate in international markets for goods and services.

The absolute version of PPP has been tested by checking its foundation, the Law of One Price. Do similar goods in fact sell at the same prices (given the prevailing exchange rates) in different countries at the same time? Irving Kravis and his associates made extensive comparisons among a diverse group of countries in 1970 — the end of a period of exchange-rate stability. They secured prices in each country for each item on a list of goods. Then they calculated a total local-currency price for the "basket" of goods on the list, converted it into dollars at the going exchange rate, and compared that dollar cost to the cost of the same basket in the United States. For the Western industrial countries the Law of One Price seems to hold reasonably well, but other countries'

[5] Gustav Cassel, *Money and Foreign Exchange after 1914.* New York: Macmillan, 1923.

prices fall on the low side of U.S. prices — somewhat low for Japan, decidedly low for the less-developed countries. They also extended the comparison to the relative prices of nontraded goods in these same countries. Nations' nontraded-goods prices are much farther out of line with United States prices than are their prices of traded goods. Competition in international markets thus has a lot of centripetal force pulling together the prices of goods in different national markets, even if that force is not irresistible.

A pattern apparent in this international comparison is for prices — especially of nontraded goods — to be lower the poorer is the country. Bela Balassa proposed an economic reason for this: A high-income country is more productive than a low-income one — that is, it obtains more goods and services from each unit of its stock of factors of production. However, the opportunities for achieving productivity advances vary from one good to another and may be much greater in manufacturing tractors, say, than in giving haircuts. On casual observation nontraded goods and services — especially services — seem to give fewer opportunities for productivity advances than do traded goods and services. Therefore nontraded goods should be expensive in rich countries and cheap in poor countries (relative to traded goods). The hypothesis is plausible as well as consistent with some data. Theoretical objections have been made to it, however, and it has not shown up too well in statistical tests.[6]

It is time to relate these price comparisons to the problem of predicting the equilibrium values of exchange rates. International competition counts for a lot in linking up the prices of internationally traded goods. But exchange rates do not always take exactly the values predicted by absolute PPP — especially as between industrialized and developing countries.

We suggested that relative PPP might work reasonably well even where absolute PPP does not. That is, the prices of "similar" goods might differ among countries for good economic reasons that we have simply failed to detect; changes over time in price levels and equilibrium exchange rates might still behave in the way predicted by relative PPP. On this question we also have a good deal of evidence. Kravis and Lipsey made the standard calculation of relative PPP for many pairs of industrial countries for various numbers of years within the period 1950–1970. That is, for each pair of countries and years for which they had data, they calculated the ratio of country B's price index to country A's and

[6] See Bela Balassa, "The Purchasing-Power-Parity Doctrine: A Reappraisal," *Journal of Political Economy,* 72 (December 1964): 584–96; Lawrence H. Officer, "The Productivity Bias in Purchasing Power Parity: An Econometric Investigation," *IMF Staff Papers,* 23 (November 1976): 545–79.

divided this result by an index of the exchange rate (price of B's currency in terms of A's). If relative PPP were dead accurate, this calculation would always yield the result of 1.0. Kravis and Lipsey found that relative PPP is quite accurate for short periods of time (two years, say), but misses by wider margins as the period of observation is lengthened.[7]

The fact that its predictions grow less accurate with the passage of time does not itself undermine the Law of One Price or the absolute version of PPP. Rather, it says that the structures of economies change over time, and with them countries' patterns of comparative advantage. The poor forecasting record of relative PPP in the longer run merely tells us that we lack a simple mechanism for anticipating accurately how exchange rates will change in response to changing relative prices and trade patterns. Still, the shaky short-run performance implies that the Law of One Price is not invincible for explaining how the prices of particular commodities move over time in different countries. Just as exchange-rate-adjusted price levels do not always move in parallel, the prices of particular goods have been found to move independently. For example, the prices of comparable pieces of machinery produced by the United States and West Germany expressed in U.S. dollars stayed quite closely in line with one another between 1953 and 1970 but swung wildly out of line between 1971 and 1975 as the Deutschemark (DM) appreciated against the dollar.[8]

The pattern noted in U.S. and German machinery prices for the Law of One Price to be violated when exchange rates are in motion is quite general and important. In a purely competitive industry DM prices of machinery in Germany would decline 10 percent following a 10 percent appreciation of the DM, and the decline would affect German-made and imported machinery alike. That would satisfy the Law of One Price. If the German and U.S. machinery industries were competitive but their products were different from one another, the DM price of U.S. machinery exports would fall 10 percent but the DM price of German-made machinery would fall by a smaller amount, or fall more slowly. Finally, if the U.S. machinery industry had elements of monopoly, DM prices of U.S. machinery would be lowered less than 10 percent, and perhaps left unchanged. Thus, imperfect competition in international traded-goods markets can account both for apparent failures of the

---

[7] Irving B. Kravis and Robert E. Lipsey, "Price Behavior in the Light of Balance of Payments Theories," *Journal of International Economics,* 8 (May 1978): 193–246. For more optimistic conclusions about relative PPP in the long run, see Henry J. Gailliot, "Purchasing Power Parity as an Explanation of Long-Term Changes in Exchange Rates," *Journal of Money, Credit and Banking,* 2 (August 1970): 348–57.

[8] Kravis and Lipsey, Table 11. Also see Peter Isard, "How Far Can We Push the Law of One Price?" *American Economic Review,* 67 (December 1977): 942–48.

Law of One Price and for some of the puzzling behavior of exchange rates in responding to forces affecting general price levels (the PPP hypothesis).

Purchasing-Power Parity and Causality

We began investigating the PPP hypothesis in order to equip ourselves to predict equilibrium foreign-exchange rates. Implicitly we have supposed that the causation runs from national money prices to exchange rates. If some exogenous force determined national price levels, that would indeed be the case — to the extent that the PPP mechanism actually operates. But theoretically the causality can run either way between a country's exchange rate and its price level. As the monetarist model of Chapter 17 suggested, a small country could revalue its exchange rate — cut the pegged price of foreign exchange in half, say — and its price level would adjust to the new fixed exchange rate. The depressed domestic-currency prices of foreign goods (pulled down by the Law of One Price) would render the country's cash balances excessive. The excess cash would be disposed of through a one-shot net intake of goods from abroad. The domestic prices of nontraded goods would be bid down, and the whole domestic money-price level would come to rest at one-half its former value.

The PPP hypothesis thus is really about *consistency* between exchange rates and price levels rather than about the *causality* between them. Ultimately we must think of the price level and the exchange rate being determined jointly: A simple model of this process emerges in the next section. Indeed, the theoretical models of fixed and flexible exchange rates together suggest that when the exchange rate and price level are inconsistent with each other the country can make a policy choice of whether it adjusts the exchange rate to the price level or the price level to the exchange rate.

In practical terms we see this interdependence of price levels and exchange rates in the pattern of adjustments following changes in exchange rates or other major disturbances. To appreciate the interdependence of prices and exchange rates and to assess the stability of the purchasing-power-parity relation we turn to Figure 19.1, which presents data for four countries over the period 1961–1978. Three indexes (1975 = 100) are shown for each country: the movement of its wholesale prices relative to those of its competitors; its effective exchange rate, defined as the price of its own currency in terms of a weighted average of its competitors'; and finally the purchasing-power-parity relation. The purchasing-power-parity relation is (just as we defined it above) the product of the relative wholesale price and the effective exchange rate indexes. (This PPP index is sometimes called a *real exchange rate*.) If the relative version of PPP held perfectly, the PPP relation would appear on the graph as a straight line. Let us see what conclusions are suggested by casual inspection of the figure:

1. *United States.* Because the United States is so large and relatively closed to trade, its price level should be more independent of disturbances abroad than any other industrial country. Its exchange rate should be caused by its price level, and not vice versa. That conjecture seems consistent with the figure. U.S. wholesale prices have shown little variation relative to those of America's competitors. However, after 1969 the

---

FIGURE 19.1. Relative Wholesale Prices, Effective Exchange Rates, and Purchasing-Power-Parity Relation for Four Countries, 1961–1978

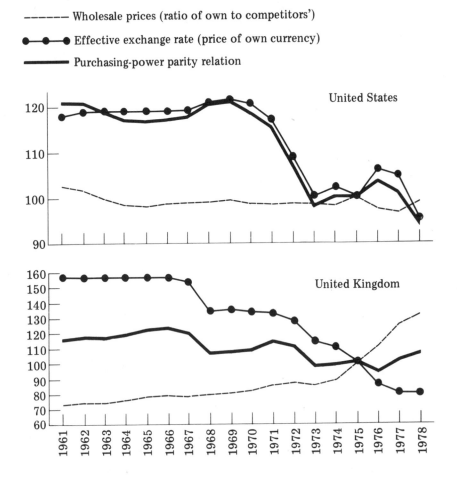

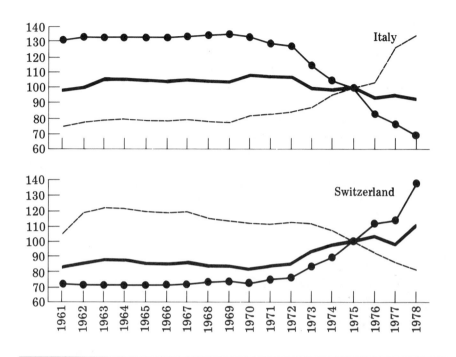

effective price of the dollar plunged, and the PPP relation followed it almost exactly. The falling PPP relation can be thought of as a worsening in the terms of trade of the United States. The only sign that exchange-rate movements affect U.S. prices comes at the end of the period, when the continued slide of the dollar's price after 1976 appears to precede a rise in the U.S. relative wholesale price.

2. *United Kingdom.* The United Kingdom, smaller and more open than the United States, shows a somewhat more complicated pattern. In 1967 the pound sterling was devalued about 15 percent. Britain's relative wholesale prices did not rise sharply in response but continued their modest upward trend relative to those of Britain's competitors. The Law of One Price did not promptly wipe out the price advantage that British producers gained against their foreign rivals. It was after the oil-price shock in 1973 that British wholesale prices took off, fueled by large injections into the money supply. The effective price of pounds sterling fell in mirror image. The PPP relation shows a long-term decline until the mid-1970's, when an upturn reflects Britain's newfound status as a petroleum exporter.

3. *Italy.* The inverse movement of relative wholesale prices and the effective price of the Italian lira dominates the pattern for Italy. Here the PPP hypothesis seems to show its most impressive performance, for

the PPP relation in the diagram varies little over the period. However, the diagram itself supplies few clues as to the weight of causation running between the exchange rate and the price level.

4. *Switzerland.* The Swiss case is interesting because we have an obvious hypothesis about the cause of the upward trend in the PPP relation during the 1970's. Switzerland's vaunted reputation as a safe (and tight-lipped) haven for nervous money has attracted massive capital inflows and driven up the price of the Swiss franc. We can be fairly sure that the fall in Switzerland's relative wholesale prices after 1973 reflects the force of capital flows elevating the Swiss franc. Thus, Switzerland is at the opposite pole from the United States — a small, open economy whose major economic disturbances come from the outside, and whose prices depend mostly on the exchange rate rather than the other way around.

19.3 THE EXCHANGE RATE AND INTERNATIONAL CAPITAL MOVEMENTS

These puzzles about PPP suggest that we may have so far omitted some important influences on foreign-exchange rates. The prime suspect, many economists now believe, is international capital flows. Why this should be so is a subtle matter and requires us to investigate the motives affecting people (and firms) who hold financial assets and move them from country to country.

Risk and Financial Portfolios

Capital might be expected to move internationally in response to differences in its real reward — its marginal product. If the marginal product of capital rises abroad, foreign entrepreneurs become willing to issue bonds and stocks that promise higher yields. American investors find these yields attractive and enlarge their demand for foreign exchange in order to purchase them. Initially, at least, a more attractive reward to capital abroad should increase the demand for and price of foreign exchange. True enough, but perhaps not helpful for the problem at hand. The marginal product of capital is not easy to conceive in the short run as having a single magnitude for a country, nor do we think of it as showing short-run fluctuations that might strongly influence the exchange rate.[9]

More important still, most of the financial assets in the world repre-

---

[9] There is also a subtle point that emerges from our discussion of international capital flows earlier in this book (Chapters 4 and 10). A net transfer of capital internationally involves changes in the demands for goods in both the lending and borrowing countries, and thus in the flows of exports and imports. What happens

sent debts incurred to finance expenditures made in the past, not current capital formation. The amount of outstanding securities is fixed in the short run as a legacy from past decisions about saving and investment. New investment opportunities — increases in a country's marginal product of capital — may cause more securities to be issued, but any year's proportional increase in the outstanding stock is usually tiny. If some event should cause persons holding this vast quantity of existing securities to try to reallocate their portfolios between securities of different nationalities, the resulting "stock adjustment" could produce a big change indeed in the demand or supply of foreign exchange. Therefore we must review some elements of the theory of financial portfolios, to see what it implies for international transactions in outstanding securities.

We assume that holders of financial wealth desire the largest possible return on their portfolios (interest, dividends, capital gains) but also wish to limit the risks to which they are exposed. No one wants a security with a low return and a high risk. But there are securities with high risks and high returns and securities with low risks and low returns, and the investor has to choose among them. The riskiness of the investor's whole portfolio, however, is not the same as the riskiness of the typical security that it holds. That is because the risks of different securities are at least somewhat independent of one another. If Ford falters, General Motors may be having a good year. If the Japanese yen declines, the German DM may rise. The portfolio holder therefore diversifies his risk by owning a number of securities. The riskiness of the whole portfolio becomes less than the riskiness of the typical security it contains. The less closely correlated are the fluctuating returns earned by different securities, the more is risk reduced through diversification.

International Diversification

Risk management in financial portfolios has important implications for international capital flows. Holding securities of differing national origins has at least two advantages:

1. If they are denominated in different currencies, they can reduce the risk to the holder's wealth from changes in exchange rates. Not all currencies can depreciate at the same time!

2. If they represent claims on the real assets located in different countries, risk will be reduced if disturbances that lower returns in one

---

to the exchange rate when capital movements change therefore depends ultimately on these associated changes in goods-and-services trade and their effects on the foreign-exchange market. Just as an increase in capital transfers need not affect a country's terms of trade one way or the other, it need not have a predictable effect on the exchange rate.

country do not coincide with changes that lower them in another. If Canada is having a recession, Belgium may be enjoying a boom. Therefore it is natural to expect financial portfolios to contain securities originating in diverse countries.[10] More important for the short-run behavior of exchange rates, any disturbance that makes asset holders rearrange their portfolios can cause potentially large shifts in the demand and supply of foreign exchange.

To see what portfolio adjustment implies for the exchange rate, suppose that only two long-term securities are available to asset holders — shares in domestic companies and shares in foreign companies. Any disturbance that occurs affects all foreign companies alike, and all domestic companies alike, but the two groups differently. The only way for the investor to spread risk is to own shares in both foreign and domestic enterprises. In equilibrium domestic investors will place some proportion of their wealth in foreign securities. Now suppose that some disturbance occurs that drives down the price of foreign exchange (causes domestic currency to appreciate) without changing the long-run profits that people expect to earn on securities denominated in either currency. If the public want to hold 20 percent of their wealth in foreign assets, and indeed did hold 20 percent before the depreciation, they will now be out of equilibrium because the home-currency value of foreign securities has declined, and so those securities now account for less than 20 percent of their wealth. Investors will demand more foreign exchange for the purpose of acquiring foreign securities.[11] Therefore the process of portfolio adjustment gives rise to some elasticity in the demand for foreign exchange. Specifically, the assumption we made (individuals desire a constant level of wealth and hold a constant proportion of their wealth in assets of each country) implies that a one percent fall in the price of foreign exchange would give rise to a one percent increase in the quantity demanded — unit elasticity. Note, however, that this demand curve is not your usual "flow" demand curve — so many widgets per period of time. Rather, it embodies a one-shot shift in the stock of foreign exchange that people want to hold, in connection with their international securities transactions. (By contrast, if the price of foreign exchange has fallen, they will tend to buy more foreign shoes in *every* future period of time.)

Consider the effect of another disturbance, something that raises the expected yield on all real assets located abroad and thus on all financial

---

[10] In Chapter 20 we note some evidence on international portfolio diversification.
[11] They will have suffered a capital loss on the foreign securities they held before. But that fact does not discourage restoring the original portfolio proportions unless this depreciation causes the public to expect that further depreciations will occur. We are assuming that the depreciation occurs once and for all; there is no such extrapolation of expectations about the exchange rate.

assets that lay claims to this yield. Even if the actual increase in returns comes some time in the future, expectations of those returns will cause people to try to raise the proportion of foreign securities in their portfolio. If this desire is not requited by capital gains on the foreign securities they already hold, the price of foreign exchange is bid up. The exchange rate has to stay elevated, even after the initial shift has occurred, to keep portfolios in balance given the rosy expectations concerning the yield on foreign securities.

These examples have an artificial air about them because they were rigged for consistency with the assumption that disturbances affect all foreign securities alike, and all domestic securities alike. Any "realistic" disturbance that affects individual firms and industries differently within a single economy brings about a more complex set of portfolio adjustments. The basic point remains, however, that any disturbance that *on balance* raises the proportion of their wealth that people desire to hold in foreign assets will bring about a portfolio shift that raises the demand for foreign exchange. It thus raises the exchange rate and keeps it elevated. Also, we have told the story as if all adjustments involved portfolios domiciled in the home country. There is no essential difference if foreign portfolios exist and are adjusted in the same way.[12]

Foreign Exchange in Financial Portfolios

The analysis of portfolio adjustment teaches another lesson about the determinants of exchange rates: *Foreign exchange is itself a financial asset.* We spoke of agents holding balances of foreign exchange to finance their international transactions, just as domestic cash balances are assumed held in proportion to domestic expenditures. The proportional relation between the cash balances and expenditures — foreign or domestic — should depend on the opportunity cost of holding these liquid assets. If cash balances pay no interest, the opportunity cost is the rate of interest that could be earned on interest-yielding investments. If the cash balances pay a low short-term interest rate, the opportunity cost is the extra interest yield on longer-term securities (the extra 2 percent on a 10 percent long-term bond over an 8 percent short-term deposit). In the case of foreign-exchange assets, however, another factor enters into determining the asset's yield — one's expectations about the future change in the exchange rate. Suppose that no interest can be earned on either domestic or foreign cash balances, and that foreign currency is expected to depreciate at 2 percent annually. That is the

---

[12] This analysis has been based on Penti J. K. Kouri, "Balance of Payments and the Foreign Exchange Market: A Dynamic Partial Equilibrium Model," Cowles Foundation Discussion Paper no. 510, Yale University, 1978.

equivalent of a *negative* 2 percent interest rate on the foreign exchange. People will not necessarily ditch their foreign-currency balances when they expect that loss, but they will certainly try to get along with the minimum foreign exchange for their transaction needs.

Consider what this behavior means for the exchange rate's response to any disturbances striking the system. A unit of foreign currency is a claim that can be exercised to buy foreign goods and services, rather like a foreign-currency bond or equity share. If some event leads people to expect an increase of the price level abroad, then the expected yield on their foreign-exchange holdings has dropped, and they will tend to shift their liquid assets away from foreign funds. That shift by itself depreciates foreign currency, in anticipation of the actual price-level increase.

The monetarist model of Chapter 17 provides an application of this financial-asset approach to the foreign-exchange market. Make the monetarist assumption that people hold cash balances in proportion to their rate of money expenditure. If each country's real income is given, its price level then is proportional to its money supply. Make the additional assumption that purchasing-power parity holds in its absolute version, so that the exchange rate depends directly on nothing but the relation between foreign and domestic price levels. Put these two relations together and you see that the exchange rate depends on the foreign and domestic money supplies. Other things equal, news in the morning paper that the domestic money supply is increasing faster than the money supply abroad will cause the price of foreign exchange to rise.[13]

This process by which exchange rates reflect shifts in asset-holders'

---

[13] We can express this argument formally. Assume that each country enjoys full employment, so that national income stays fixed at Y at home and Y^* abroad. Domestic and foreign price levels are P and P^*, nominal money supplies are M and M^*. For simplicity, suppose that the velocity of money (V and V^*) is given and does not depend on the interest rate. Then the home and foreign demands for money are respectively:

$$M = (1/V)PY \text{ and } M^* = (1/V^*)P^*Y^*.$$

Rearranging these expressions, the price levels are

$$P = V(M/Y) \text{ and } P^* = V^*(M^*/Y^*).$$

If E is the exchange rate (the price of foreign currency) and absolute PPP holds, then $P = EP^*$, or $E = P/P^*$. Substituting, we get:

$$E = \frac{M}{M^*} \cdot \frac{V}{V^*} \cdot \frac{Y^*}{Y}.$$

Home currency depreciates (that is, E rises) if the domestic money supply grows faster than that abroad, domestic real income grows more slowly than that abroad, or the domestic velocity coefficient increases relative to that abroad. For a lucid account of this approach see Rudiger Dornbusch, "Monetary Policy under Exchange-Rate Flexibility," in *Managed Exchange-Rate Flexibility: The Recent Experience*. Federal Reserve Bank of Boston, Conference Series no. 20 (Boston, 1978), pp. 90–122.

expectations has become vitally important for the external value of the United States dollar. That is because enormous holdings of highly liquid dollar assets (Treasury bills and near-money time deposits) are lodged in foreign hands. In the decline and fall of the Bretton Woods system (as we shall explain in Chapter 23) great quantities of dollar assets came into foreign hands, where they have remained in their short-term liquid form. Expectations of these holders about the yield on these dollar assets, relative to similar assets that might be held denominated in other leading currencies, can surely swamp any short-run effect on the dollar's exchange rate running through United States trade in goods and services.

Exchange Rates, Trade, and Portfolios: A Synthesis

We have shown that both the price levels of goods and expected yields on securities can determine the exchange rate's equilibrium value. How do we reconcile these competing explanations? After all, if PPP in its absolute version holds at all times, it suffices to determine the exchange rate. Today's price levels abroad and at home lock in today's exchange rate. Any rise in the price of foreign exchange caused by expectations about tomorrow's exchange rate would cheapen home goods relative to those abroad, produce an export surplus of avalanche proportions, and restore the exchange rate demanded by absolute PPP. On the other hand, large financial portfolios that are instantly reallocated in response to changes in expectations can also determine the exchange rate. If today's news induces portfolio changes that demand a depreciation of domestic currency, the shift in the foreign-exchange market can occur as fast as people can telephone their banks and brokers. The exchange rate then is dominated by the massive volume of transactions that can result from portfolio reallocations, and there is no room for PPP to influence the exchange rate.

To reconcile these conflicting models, a growing number of economists are inclined to accept a synthesis that runs along these lines: The financial markets can indeed carry out their stock-adjustment processes in short order, and they do anticipate future real adjustments. The Law of One Price can be grossly violated in the short run because of the time it takes to order goods abroad, get them produced and loaded on the boat, and so forth. Yet the law must ultimately prevail; we can hardly imagine the commodity markets running permanently out of equilibrium with unexploited opportunities to arbitrage goods from one country to another (limited, of course, by tariffs, transportation costs, and all that). Therefore we expect that financial forces will determine the exchange rate in the short run following any disturbance (from long-run equilibrium), but trade flows must dominate the long-run result. Does this scenario simply imply that the financial market anticipates the destination to which trade flows will ultimately take the exchange rate, and get there first? Not necessarily. The financial-asset mechanism can cause the exchange rate to overshoot its equilibrium value following a monetary disturbance, converging only in the long run on the equilibrium value dictated by PPP.[14] That long-run value will clear both commodity and asset markets.

This synthesis holds an important implication for our discussion in Chapter 18 of the relation between the exchange rate and the trade balance. Assume that the exchange rate is flexible and market-determined, and that a disturbance reduces employment and real income at home. Abstracting from international capital movements, we argued in Chapter 18 that the price of our currency would rise because of our reduced demand for imports. Exports would therefore decline and trade would become balanced at a smaller total volume. Now we see that the exchange-rate change itself will cause a change in international capital movements — an import of foreign securities, perhaps, to accomplish a stock adjustment in domestic and foreign portfolios. The current-account surplus resulting from the reduction of employment is then partly financed by a capital outflow. Restoration of a zero current-account balance is at least postponed. The exact story depends on the disturbance that we assume. But the general point is that exchange-rate changes bestir changes in international net capital flows, blunting the contrast that we drew in Chapter 18 between the effects of fixed and flexible exchange rates on trade flows.

---

[14] Rudiger Dornbusch suggests the following sequence. The domestic money supply is increased, lowering interest rates and leading to the expectation of a long-run depreciation of domestic currency. Both consequences reduce the attractiveness of holding domestic securities and bring about an immediate depreciation. That depreciation has to run beyond the long-run equilibrium level, however, because the interest rate on domestic assets has been forced down. People will not be willing to hold the stock of domestic securities in the new situation unless their expected yields are the same as those on foreign financial assets (the foreign interest rate is assumed to be determined on a large international capital market and hence is unchanged). The equalization of yields cannot occur unless domestic assets (and currency) are expected to appreciate relative to foreign assets, offsetting the excess of the foreign over the domestic interest rate. Therefore the short-run depreciation of domestic currency must overshoot the new long-run equilibrium exchange rate by enough to permit this subsequent equilibrating appreciation. See Rudiger Dornbusch, "Expectations and Exchange Rate Dynamics," *Journal of Political Economy,* 84 (December 1976): 1161–76. We have an empirical estimate of how large this overshoot would be. In his study of the U.S.–West Germany exchange rate Jeffrey A. Frankel estimated that a one percent increase in the United States money supply (not previously expected by the public) would lead to a short-run depreciation of the dollar by 1.23 percent, although the ultimate equilibrium depreciation would be just one percent. See his "On the Mark: A Theory of Floating Exchange Rates Based on Real Interest Differentials," *American Economic Review,* 69 (September 1979): 617.

19.4 SUMMARY

Foreign exchange is simply national money in the hands of nonresidents, and the foreign-exchange market is an adjunct of the markets for short-term financial assets generally. Foreign-exchange markets are competitive. Rates in different national markets are kept in line with one another by arbitrage. Traders cut the costs of currency conversion by using widely traded currencies, especially the dollar, as vehicles for transactions not involving either U.S. or British traders. The market for forward exchange allows relief from uncertainty about the future home-currency value of receipts or payments denominated in foreign exchange.

One motive for holding foreign exchange is closely analogous to the transactions demand for domestic money. The more purchase and sale transactions we make with people in another monetary area, the more foreign exchange are we likely to hold. This proposition links the demand for foreign exchange to the demand for foreign goods and explains one of the leading hypotheses about the forces that determine exchange rates. That is the purchasing-power-parity hypothesis. In its absolute version it declares that if $100 buys a given basket of goods in the United States, that sum converted into Deutschemarks should buy the same basket of goods in West Germany. It follows directly from the Law of One Price, the proposition that a perfectly competitive market causes a particular good to sell everywhere at the same price. Many market imperfections could cause absolute PPP to fail, yet the hypothesis might still hold in its relative version, which relates changes over time in equilibrium exchange rates to changes in countries' relative price levels. The empirical evidence on these relations between exchange rates and prices is mixed. The Law of One Price obviously exerts strong pulls on exchange rates, but it may do its work slowly and incompletely. The PPP hypothesis deals with a connection between prices and exchange rates but does not itself establish the direction of causation. Both theory and empirical evidence suggest that causality runs in both directions, with a force that varies predictably from country to country.

The adjustment of financial portfolios is another important determinant of exchange rates in the short run. Risk-averse asset holders include a variety of securities in their portfolios. Differences in the fates of the various national economies make the international diversification of portfolios a natural way to spread risks. This proposition holds for both long-term securities and short-term assets and foreign exchange. Because financial-asset markets can adjust very quickly, a development that changes the expected future equilibrium exchange rate causes asset holders to respond immediately (just as the stock market immediately discounts the effect of any news about a company's future prospects).

Financial markets can dominate the exchange rate in the short run because they adjust so much faster than markets for goods and services. However, the goods markets — the Law of One Price — must ultimately dominate. Hence, as a generalization, we expect that financial markets and international capital flows will dominate the determination of the exchange rate in the short run, and can readily cause it to overshoot its new long-run equilibrium value following a disturbance. But the influence of trade flows comes through eventually.

SUGGESTIONS FOR FURTHER READING

Aliber, Robert Z., ed. *The International Market for Foreign Exchange.* New York: Praeger, 1969. Chapters on markets in different countries.

Dornbusch, Rudiger. "Monetary Policy under Exchange-Rate Flexibility," *Managed Exchange-Rate Flexibility: The Recent Experience.* Federal Reserve Bank of Boston, Conference Series no. 20, (Boston, 1978), pp. 90–122. Reprinted in Robert E. Baldwin and J. David Richardson, eds., *International Trade and Finance: Readings,* 2nd ed. Boston: Little, Brown and Company, 1981. No. 26. Explains how money supplies determine both price level and exchange rate.

Genberg, Hans. *World Inflation and the Small Open Economy.* Economic Research Reports, no. 17. Stockholm: Swedish Industrial Publications, 1975. Chapter 2 offers an investigation of the closeness of countries' price-level movements during the period of fixed exchange rates.

Holmes, Alan R., and Francis H. Schott. *The New York Foreign Exchange Market.* New York: Federal Reserve Bank of New York, 1965. Describes institutions and traders.

Isard, Peter. *Exchange-Rate Determination: A Survey of Popular Views and Recent Models.* Princeton Studies in International Finance, no. 42. Princeton: International Finance Section, Princeton University, 1978. Useful guide to the literature.

Kravis, Irving B., and Robert E. Lipsey. "Price Behavior in the Light of Balance of Payments Theories," *Journal of International Economics,* 8 (May 1978): 193–246. Important investigation of international price relations and the Law of One Price.

Officer, Lawrence H. "The Purchasing-Power-Parity Theory of Exchange Rates: A Review Article," *IMF Staff Papers,* 23 (March 1976): 1–60. Thorough treatment of writings on this subject.

20

Capital Flows and Forward Exchange Markets

International capital flows, we saw in Chapter 19, can strongly influence the exchange rate in the short run. Chapter 22 will reveal their potent effect on the operation of domestic macroeconomic policy instruments. Therefore in this chapter we analyze some institutions and mechanisms important in the international transfer of capital. We need to understand the degree to which capital markets are internationalized and what these international flows imply for adjustment to disturbances in the international economy.

20.1 SHORT-TERM CAPITAL FLOWS AND FORWARD EXCHANGE RATES

The risks of foreign investment for the lender stem mainly from two sources. The borrower may default on the interest or principal that he owes. Or the currency in which the loan is denominated may decline in value before it is repaid. The international long-term lender generally must face these risks as a package: He estimates the range of possible rates of return on a foreign security after converting the payments of interest into his home currency, in the process allowing for the risks of both default and depreciation. The short-term lender faces a richer array of choices. He can lend abroad and insure the proceeds against changes in the exchange rate. Or he can include foreign currencies in his portfolio (hoping to reap the profits of an appreciation) without actually tying up any funds. The forward exchange market is the institution that makes these short-run portfolio positions possible. It allows the lender who does not wish to risk an exchange-rate change to "cover" the exchange risk and gain assurance at the outset about the domestic-currency proceeds of his short-term foreign loan. Such transactions are called "covered interest arbitrage" — arbitrage referring to any transaction involving a movement from a cheap market to a dear one. The forward exchange market also allows the asset holder to "speculate" by laying down a bet on the future foreign-exchange rate.

The forward exchange market deals in contracts for the future delivery of a currency. An American expects to receive a definite sum in British (sterling) currency three months hence. He feels confident about the sterling receipt, but he may also want assurance about its worth in U.S. dollars. That, however, will depend on the spot exchange rate three months hence. He can obtain that certainty, perhaps at a cost, by contracting now to sell his sterling proceeds on their receipt at a preagreed exchange rate for dollars. The seller of forward sterling might be an interest arbitrager who has bought a United Kingdom Treasury bill. Or he might be a U.S. exporter anticipating payment by his British customer. The buyer of the forward contract to deliver sterling might also be an arbitrager or a trader — one who expects to receive dollars three months hence and wants assurance about their value in sterling. (With only two currencies the buyer of forward sterling is necessarily a seller of forward dollars.) Or the buyer might be a speculator, willing to bet that the sterling that he contracts to buy can be resold on the spot for more than he paid for it. After examining each group of participants in detail, we return to their interaction in the forward exchange market.[1]

Covered Interest Arbitrage

Forward markets and covered interest arbitrage are not complex in principle, but their mechanics are hard to remember, involving as they do price ratios that can be stated in different ways. Hence we must carefully define our terms and examples. We shall concentrate on two countries, the United States and United Kingdom, and on capital flowing from the United States to the United Kingdom. We shall define the exchange rate as the dollar price of the pound sterling and give to the spot exchange rate the symbol rs. The forward rate rf is the price of sterling for future delivery. In practice forward markets exist for contracts of varying maturities, but we shall assume that all forward contracts call for delivery 90 days hence. Thus (once the forward market reaches equilibrium) only one forward rate exists. We noted in Chapter

[1] For simplicity we describe these transactors as separate groups of individuals. However, we do not expect the optimizing portfolio holder to think of himself *either* as a speculator *or* as a covered interest arbitrager; rather, he undertakes whatever package of activities offers the best risk-return combination at any given time.

15 that the spot and forward markets for dollars are the mirror image of those for sterling; the price of the dollar in these markets is $1/rs$ and $1/rf$ respectively. When the price of sterling for future delivery exceeds its spot price ($rf > rs$), we say that sterling trades at a forward premium; simultaneously, the dollar would be traded at a forward discount ($1/rf < 1/rs$).

The American interest-arbitrager is influenced by interest rates in the United States and United Kingdom, as well as by exchange rates. To show how they determine his profitable course of action, we express short-term interest rates not in percent per year, but percent per 90 days or quarter-year, the duration of the standard forward contract. We denote American and British rates respectively as iu and ik. Now, an American lender willing to accept the risk of a change in the exchange rate would invest in the United Kingdom if $ik > iu$. To avoid exchange risk, however, he must calculate the outcome of a more complex series of transactions. He could purchase a United States Treasury bill, which after 90 days would yield him dollar proceeds of its original cost plus interest, $1 + iu$. He chooses this transaction unless a higher dollar return is available through covered interest arbitrage. To make a covered investment in a United Kingdom Treasury bill, he first converts the same initial amount of dollars into sterling (at exchange rate $1/rs$), buys a United Kingdom bill in that amount, and simultaneously makes a forward sale of the sterling proceeds he will receive in 90 days; the proceeds are $1 + ik$ and would yield him $(1 + ik)rf$ when his forward contract is executed. For the covered interest arbitrage to be more profitable than a United States Treasury bill investment, it is necessary that

$$1 + iu < (rf/rs)(1 + ik). \qquad (20.1)$$

Another way to put the condition,

$$\frac{1 + ik}{1 + iu} > \frac{1/rf}{1/rs}, \qquad (20.2)$$

may be clearer because it can be given an easy verbal interpretation: Covered arbitrage is profitable if the (proportionally) higher interest yield on a sterling bill exceeds the (proportional) premium on the forward dollar.[2]

---

[2] You may find it helpful to work through a numerical example. Suppose that $rs = \$2.00$ and $rf = \$1.995$; thus, sterling is at a forward discount, and the dollar at a forward premium. Suppose that the American and British interest rates are respectively 6 and 8 percent on an *annual* basis, or 1.5 and 2.0 percent quarterly. Suppose (to make the arithmetic easy) a United States Treasury bill costs $200; 90 days later it will yield the investor $200(1.015) = \$203.00$. A United Kingdom Treasury bill would also cost an initial $200 in United States currency if its face value is £100, because £100 = $200(1/2.00)$. The proceeds of £102, when sold for-

Equation 20.1 or 20.2 reveals some important features of covered interest arbitrage. First, for short-term investments to be profitable abroad, the foreign interest rate does not have to exceed the domestic! Should the pound be traded at a forward premium (perhaps because speculators expect the dollar to depreciate), interest arbitragers might profit by exporting capital from the United States even when $ik < iu$. Second, if circumstances reverse the inequality in either equation, covered arbitrage from America to Britain will become unprofitable, but arbitrage from the United Kingdom to the United States would yield positive profits. Whenever market conditions fail to yield equality between the two sides of equation 20.1 or 20.2, short-term capital movements are profitable in one direction or the other — or would be, except for the small margin of transactions costs encountered in practice.[3]

Because we want to demonstrate below the determinants of the forward exchange rate we illustrate in Figure 20.1 the (excess) demand curve for forward exchange for covered interest arbitrage. To fix this demand curve we must take the other factors controlling the profitability of covered arbitrage as given. Once the interest rates and spot exchange rate are known, we can calculate (from equation 20.1) that value of the forward rate, rfa, which would render interest arbitrage unprofitable in either direction. The excess demand shown by curve AA thus is zero at this value. If the forward rate rises above this value, capital flows from the United States to the United Kingdom, attracted by the favorable terms of forward cover, and arbitragers offer a net supply of forward sterling; if $rf < rfa$, however, capital would flow the other way, and arbitragers selling forward dollars would demand forward pounds. Hence this schedule slopes downward.

Some economists have argued that this schedule would be highly elastic over a wide range, indeed elastic enough to lock rf at rfa rendering capital movements in either direction unprofitable. But other forces also impinge on the forward rate. There is no guarantee that the supply of funds available for interest arbitrage will be unlimited in the short run. Hence we have drawn the schedule AA in Figure 20.1 highly elastic only over a limited range.

---

ward at $1.995, would yield $(£102)(1.995) = 203.49$. Hence the covered interest arbitrage is profitable. We would reach the same conclusion by plugging these values into either formula given in the text, e.g.:

$$1 + 0.015 < (1.995)/(2.00)(1 + 0.02),$$

where the right-hand side of the inequality works out to be 1.01745.

[3] For movements between the United States and Britain or Canada, these transactions costs have been estimated at 0.18 percent per annum. See W. H. Branson, "The Minimum Covered Differential Needed for International Arbitrage Activity," *Journal of Political Economy*, 77 (November/December 1969): 1028–35.

FIGURE 20.1 Demand for Forward Exchange
by Interest Arbitragers

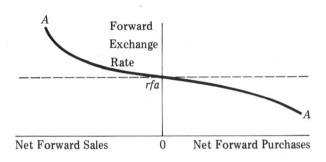

As a concluding exercise, let us notice how changes in the American
or British interest rate would influence the position of this curve. A
rise in *iu* reduces the attractiveness of covered arbitrage to the United
Kingdom, and a larger forward premium (or smaller discount) on the
pound would be necessary to offset it. Hence it would shift the curve in
Figure 20.1 upward, and tend to raise the price of forward sterling. A
rise in the British short-term rate, *ik*, would have the opposite effect;
the forward premium on sterling must fall if covered arbitrage to Britain
is not to become more attractive than before. Of course, the position
of the curve also depends on the spot exchange rate. If the spot price of
sterling falls, covered interest arbitrage becomes attractive unless the
forward rate also falls. A downward shift of the spot rate would therefore shift the arbitrage schedule downward.

Hedging by Exporters and Importers

Exporters and importers are a second group of traders who may take
part in the forward exchange market. Foreign-trade contracts often call
for payment months later, usually in the currency of one party. Either
the exporter or the importer thus faces an exchange risk. The exporter
receiving a known amount of (spot) foreign exchange at a future date
may want to hedge by selling it forward; if the transaction is in the
exporter's currency, the importer may buy forward exchange to cover
his future payment. To simplify, suppose the importer always faces the
exchange risk. The expense of forward cover is one of his business costs:
At the spot exchange rate when he arranges his transaction, a higher

forward rate for the currency he must buy means a greater total cost of the goods to him. Hence he will purchase a smaller quantity of imports — and of forward exchange. The demand for forward sterling by American importers will be negatively sloped.

Recall that a premium on the forward pound implies a discount on the forward dollar. If forward cover is expensive for American importers, it must be cheap for British importers. Their purchases of American exports may be encouraged, and their supply of pounds sterling to the forward market thus increased. The behavior of both trading groups together implies a downward-sloping excess demand curve for forward sterling.

To judge the importance of exporters and importers in the forward exchange market we need to know what proportion of them choose protection against exposure to the risk of exchange-rate changes. Apparently, those who trade in homogeneous, bulk commodities commonly seek forward-market protection. These commodities are often priced in vehicle currencies, so the transaction can involve foreign-exchange risk for both exporter and importer if neither home currency is the vehicle currency. Furthermore, world markets for these products often approximate pure competition, so that an exporter has no protection against disturbances through administrative control of the prices at which his goods sell (in whatever currency).

Contrast the exporter of differentiated manufactured goods to the trader in bulk commodities. The seller of manufactures may lack any significant long-run monopoly power in the world market, but he does control the price at which his goods are offered in the short run. The American manufacturer of electronic components who exports them to the United Kingdom can protect himself somewhat against an appreciation of the U.S. dollar (which cuts the dollar value of the sterling proceeds of his export sales) by raising the sterling price of his goods. Of course, that price increase will tend to decrease the number of units he sells. He becomes uncertain about the number of units sold to British buyers rather than the number of dollars earned per unit sold. Nonetheless, this control over prices seems to reduce his need to hedge the foreign-exchange proceeds he expects from sales abroad.[4]

---

[4] This analysis can be extended to the British importer who takes title to differentiated goods imported from the United States and holds inventories of them for sale in Britain. He faces a risk that the price of the dollar may rise before he comes to pay his U.S. supplier in dollars. However, any rise in the sterling cost of his dollar payment obligations tends to coincide with a capital gain (in sterling) in the value of his dollar-based imports. If he hedges his dollar payment obligation in the forward exchange market he throws away the hedge that is built into his business. See Ronald I. McKinnon, *Money in International Exchange: The Convertible Currency System.* New York: Oxford University Press, 1979. Chap. 4.

Speculation

The final group of transactors in the forward exchange market is the speculators. A speculator's profit depends wholly on the relation between the forward rate *rf* at which he buys or sells and the *future* value of the spot rate prevailing when his contract matures. He ties up no capital (except perhaps for margin requirements) because he buys and sells at the same instant. But he does carry the full risk of exchange-rate fluctuations, in part absorbing it from the arbitragers and traders desiring forward protection. How do speculators as a group conjecture about the future spot rate? The process must be subjective. Current and past values of the spot rate surely supply the basis for their prediction, but to cook them into a forecast each speculator must be his own chef.

Who are the speculators, and how large are the positions they can take in the forward exchange market? During the 1960's the impression grew that the potential volume of speculative transactions was of unlimited size. In those days, it probably was. Countries then not only pegged their exchange rates at official values (as we explained in Chapter 15) but also often clung to these official values even when all parties knew they lay far removed from market equilibrium levels. At such times the exchange rate had no place to go but down (or up, as the case may be), and speculation changed from being a sharp operator's game into a sure thing. In the 1970's, however, with official intervention in the exchange market irregular and often clandestine, the speculators lacked such easy pickings. How many gnomes can be found in Zurich under these conditions? McKinnon[5] suggests that the supply of speculative funds may not be all that large. Banks — the major foreign-exchange traders — are cautious about the size of speculative positions that they take, especially since 1974, when several major banks either failed or suffered serious losses when they made wrong bets in the forward market. Multinational companies are widely suspected of running busy speculative operations through the back door of the treasurer's office. However, the evidence we have suggests that they are mainly preoccupied with their nonfinancial activities and confine their exchange-market dealings to defensive positions designed one way or another to reduce their risk exposure. The limited evidence we have about the speculative positions taken by U.S. nonfinancial corporations suggests that they are only moderately good at predicting the relation between forward rates and future spot rates.[6]

[5] McKinnon, *Money in International Exchange,* chap. 8.
[6] Norman S. Fieleke, "Foreign-Exchange Speculation by U.S. Firms: Some New Evidence," *New England Economic Review,* March/April 1979, 5–17.

There has indeed been a long, general debate over whether we could depend on speculation to be stabilizing in the foreign-exchange market — forward or spot. The one basic proposition to emerge is that speculation should tend to stabilize the market if speculators are in fact successful and make money at their activities. Imagine a forward exchange market with its average equilibrium value constant in the long run but its actual value subject to periodic upward and downward disturbances. Would speculation amplify these disturbances? If so, the speculators would be buying when the price is high and selling when it is low. Their speculative activities would be unprofitable in the long run, and they would ultimately have to desist. Of course, this argument does not preclude speculators as a group guessing wrong and destabilizing a market in particular cases. It does not preclude a turnover of cannon-fodder speculators who notice a trend belatedly and get in at the top of the market (or out at the bottom). But it does establish that the best efforts of efficient speculators are not opposed to society's interest in stable markets.

Equilibrium in the Forward Exchange Market

The requirement for equilibrium in the forward exchange market is like that in any other market — demand must equal supply. In this market, however, each group of transactors we have described can be net demanders at some prices and net suppliers at others. Therefore, our equilibrium condition should be stated in a different but equivalent way: The sum of the groups' excess demands should equal zero. For example, if the arbitragers and traders are net forward sellers of sterling (perhaps because British interest rates are high and the British trade balance is in deficit), the speculators must be net buyers for an equilibrium price to be reached (the speculators may feel that the high interest rate, tending to depress the forward exchange rate, is purely temporary). Actual forward rates therefore reflect the interplay of the three groups of commercial traders. Can we say more than that?

1. Some economists have proposed that the arbitragers will dominate the determination of the forward exchange rate. After all, with the spot rate and national interest rates given, there is only one forward rate (rfa, above) that will eliminate the profitability of additional transactions in covered interest arbitrage. This arbitrage is very close to a sure thing — the securities themselves are nearly riskless, so investors cannot lose unless a government suddenly imposes massive controls on international payments. Why does covered interest arbitrage not continue until the forward rate is driven to the one value that makes additional flows unprofitable?

2. Other economists have proposed that the speculators will domi-

nate the forward exchange market. They reason this way: The speculator bets on the relation between the 90-day forward rate and the
actual spot exchange rate that will prevail 90 days hence. If the forward
rate does not *on average* turn out equal to the future spot rate, it implies that speculators are passing up opportunities for profit. That is,
if the forward price of sterling is typically less than the spot price when
the forward contract matures, you could regularly buy sterling forward,
turn around and resell it spot, and make a net profit. How can speculators be missing such opportunities?

In terms of Figure 20.1 these two propositions imply that both the
speculators and the arbitragers should have very elastic excess demands
for forward exchange. If the arbitragers will sell unlimited amounts
of sterling forward at $2.00 and the speculators will buy at $2.10,
where does the price settle down? Something has to give. Several
considerations might serve to reconcile these two allegedly irresistible
forces. The forward rate that eliminates profitable arbitrage depends
on the spot rate and national interest rates, but those variables — especially the interest rates — need not be independent of the amount of
covered interest arbitrage that is going on. Suppose that speculation
against the dollar has driven up the forward price of sterling (that is,
driven down the forward price of dollars). Forward dollars being cheap,
covered interest arbitrage toward Britain tends to become profitable.
If so, short-term capital pours into Britain. The flow tends to depress
the U.K. interest rate, drive up the interest rate in the United States,
and perhaps firm up the spot price of sterling. Any or all of these variables can change until covered interest arbitrage is no longer profitable
at the margin, all without any change in the forward rate. Therefore
the existence of unlimited funds ready and willing to engage in covered
interest arbitrage does not mean a perfectly elastic excess demand for
forward exchange, because these other prices can change to stem the
avalanche.

Nor need we accept the proposition that speculators will always drive
the forward rate into line with the expected future spot rate. Speculation is a risky activity, and risk-averse individuals limit the amount they
will bet on any economic outcome that is less than a sure thing. That
proposition is consistent with the model of portfolio adjustment by asset
holders, described in section 19.3. Therefore risk aversion suggests that
the speculators' excess demand curve will not be perfectly elastic, or
at least not perfectly elastic over an enormous range of risk-exposed
positions.

A reasonable if unspectacular conclusion is that nobody "dominates"
the determination of the forward exchange rate. When spot exchange
rates were generally pegged (before 1973), the evidence showed that
covered interest arbitrage dominated the forward rate except when spec-

ulative beliefs that the pegged spot rate might change swept through
the market. With the regime of managed floating, however, that generalization no longer applies.

Government Intervention in the Forward Market

The system of pegged exchange rates used up to 1971 committed governments to regulate their spot exchange rates, though not the forward
exchange rates for their currencies. Nonetheless, they sometimes chose
to operate in the forward market as well as, or instead of, the spot
market. Unless some group of transactors in the forward market has
a perfectly elastic excess demand (a horizontal line, in Figure 20.1),
government purchases or sales of forward exchange will raise or lower
its price.

Suppose the British government observes that sterling trades at a
discount in the forward market — the forward rate is below the spot
rate — and buys pounds forward to drive up their price. What can it accomplish? To understand its objective, we must recognize the interrelation between the forward and spot exchange rates. When the British
government buys forward sterling and drives up the price, it discourages some would-be buyers of forward sterling and encourages potential sellers. But these affected buyers and sellers, unless they are pure
speculators, can change their transactions in the spot market for sterling when the government's actions induce them to alter their forward
transactions:

1. When the government purchases forward sterling and drives up
its price, it encourages the net movement of short-term capital toward
Britain. This additional short-term lending involves more sales of forward pounds, but correspondingly additional purchases of spot pounds
(in order to make the initial investment). Hence the government supports the spot market for sterling indirectly, through the effect of its
purchases of forward pounds on the arbitragers' demand for spot pounds.

2. Intervention in the forward market sometimes can influence speculative transactions in the *spot* market. The speculator is always a
soothsayer, telling the future from signs that seem apt. One of the best
objective signs of the future level of a spot exchange rate is the currency's forward rate. The speculators are not the only group affecting
the forward rate. However, knowing nothing about the situation except that the forward rate lies below the spot, you would surmise that
speculators expect the spot rate to fall. That hunch could lead you to
sell pounds spot, or reduce your purchases, if such a speculative maneuver lies open to you. Conversely, if government purchases in the
forward market raise the rate and extinguish this signal of a possible
depreciation, speculative net demand for the spot pound would increase.

Hence, government intervention in the forward market also stabilizes the spot market, as speculators change their posture in the spot market on the basis of what is happening to the forward rate.

3. Governmental purchases in the forward market increase the cost of forward cover to American importers of British goods and lower its cost to British buyers of American goods. Hence the forward market intervention will worsen the British trade balance. This effect does not alter the conditions in the spot market *today*, however, because traders who hedge their future commitments do not use the spot exchange market. The higher price of forward pounds might cause an American importer to enter the spot market now, of course, to purchase sterling to cover his future obligations. But he would then take upon himself the role of speculator.

We conclude that government intervention in the forward market helps to support the spot market through its effect on arbitragers, and may also help through its effect on speculators.[7] Thus it gains a short-term advantage. The support entails no loss of reserves, until its forward contracts mature and the government must disgorge reserves of foreign currency in order to fulfill its commitments to purchase sterling.[8] One reason for intervening in the forward market, then, is to postpone the loss of reserves. This advantage may not be trivial for a country that is hard-pressed, because the market is apt to take a reported loss of reserves as a sign that the currency's value is likely to fall, and increase its speculative sales.

20.2 EURO-DOLLARS AND THE EFFICIENCY OF INTERNATIONAL CAPITAL MARKETS

International capital movements are induced by differences between countries in the yields expected on financial investments. If people are willing to make large enough changes in the composition of their portfolios when a difference in expected yields arises, that difference will be

[7] For a more extensive treatment see William H. L. Day, "The Advantages of Exclusive Forward Exchange Rate Support," *IMF Staff Papers,* 23 (March 1976): 137–63.

[8] A government willing to take its chances can risk an enormous commitment in the forward market because, if the spot price of its currency turns out to exceed the price at which it bought forward, it can unwind its commitments at a profit and lose no reserves at all. In 1966 Britain's forward commitments apparently reached a staggering magnitude, equal to all of the nation's owned reserves plus much of what she probably could have borrowed. Had devaluation occurred, the Bank of England would have suffered a substantial capital loss. See John Spraos, "Some Aspects of Sterling in the Decade 1957–66," *The International Market for Foreign Exchange,* ed. R. Z. Aliber. New York: Praeger, 1969, pp. 158–76; see also pp. 86–91.

competed away. The point applies not only to covered interest arbitrage but also to any international capital flow that is expected to be profitable — covered or not. Many observers feel that short-term capital has grown much more mobile internationally in the last three decades. This increased mobility and its consequences are important for both national macroeconomic policy and economic welfare, and so we consider an institution vitally associated with this increased mobility, the Euro-dollar market.

Operation of the Euro-Dollar Market

The Euro-dollar market deals in time deposits denominated in U.S. dollars but placed in banks located outside the United States. The banks (many of which are European branches of major American banks) accept these deposits and employ them to make short-term loans to borrowers who may be of any nationality. This market is like any other for bank deposits and bank loans except that the transaction is not denominated in the currency of the country in which it takes place. Euro-dollar banks in fact deal not just in dollars but in various leading currencies, and, indeed, the proportion of Euro-currency business done in dollars has been declining somewhat. The essence of transactions in the market is to sever the nationality of the bank from the nationality of the currency in which it deals — whatever that currency. Nonetheless, for expository convenience we shall speak of dollars as the typical Euro-currency. To complicate matters a bit more, the Euro-currency market is not just in Europe: The Asian currency market carries on essentially the same functions.

It is important to recognize the circumstances in which a Euro-dollar transaction involves an international capital movement. Because Euro-dollar banks stay fully "loaned-up," we need take account only of transactions between depositors and ultimate borrowers, intermediated by the banks. When a Euro-dollar deposit changes hands between citizens of different nationalities, the depositor's country experiences a short-term capital outflow to the borrower's country. When their citizenship is the same, no international flow occurs. The fact that the currency denominating the transaction may be foreign to one or both parties is not significant, although the depositor's hoard of dollars must reflect a net outflow from the United States in the past if he is not an American citizen.

Now let us consider the traders in this market. They include U.S. corporations who can earn a higher return on their liquid balances in the Euro-dollar market than at home. But they also include many non-Americans who acquire liquid dollar balances, or choose to hold their funds in dollars rather than another currency. Corporations abroad, including subsidiaries of American firms, often transact large amounts of business and hold their liquid balances largely in dollars. Central banks, likewise interested in maximum returns on their international reserves, have placed large amounts of dollar balances in this market. Indeed, among the most important early lenders in the Euro-dollar market were central banks of the Soviet Bloc countries, which hold dollar balances but were revolted at the prospect of placing them at short-term on Wall Street, that bastion of capitalism!

The prominence of non-American depositors in the Euro-dollar market vividly demonstrates the role of the dollar as a "vehicle currency" in international commerce. Even if traders try to maximize their profits (or income) only in terms of their national currencies, they will still hold balances of foreign exchange, particularly the most widely used foreign currencies. The convenience of transactors would be best served if only one currency existed in the world, ending the costs and risks of exchange conversion, just as communication would be eased if everyone spoke the same language. Lacking this utopia, traders as a group still benefit when a major currency comes into use for denominating trans-actions not even involving the country that sired the currency. The dollar and sterling have both played this role, and other currencies are taking it on.[9]

Borrowers in the Euro-dollar market can include anyone seeking large amounts of short-term funds. U.S. banks become heavy borrowers when credit conditions are tightened by the Federal Reserve System. It should be stressed, though, that the borrower in the Euro-dollar market is typically interested in short-term credit, and not in borrowing dollars per se. For instance, an important group of borrowers are local government units in Britain, which of course transact their business in sterling. When they borrow Euro-dollars, they (or their banks) "swap" the dollar proceeds into sterling for the duration of the loan. The "swap" involves only a simultaneous spot purchase and forward sale of sterling, to cover the borrowers against exchange risk. Thus, such a Euro-dollar borrowing represents the same covered interest arbitrage that we de-scribed in section 20.1, except that the switch of currencies is initiated by the borrower rather than the lender.

We thus see why an international market in short-term capital can be denominated in U.S. dollars (and other chief "vehicle currencies"). You may still wonder why this business should flow through non-Amer-

[9] Thus transactions in U.S. dollars constitute 47 percent of the business done in the French foreign exchange market, although only one-twelfth of France's trade is with the United States. This argument is developed in more detail by A. K. Swoboda, *The Euro-Dollar Market: An Interpretation.* Essays in International Finance, no. 64. Princeton, N.J.: International Finance Section, Princeton University, 1968.

ican banks, rather than through American banks, for which the dollar is native financial ground. The answer to that question shows how the Euro-dollar market helps to perfect international markets in short-term capital. First, foreign banks take Euro-dollar business because it is profitable. They face no significant exchange risk, because they can match the dollar assets and liabilities maturing at any date. And they can pay interest rates that attract lenders, yet charge rates that lure borrowers. They are thus taking business away from U.S. domestic banks. Perhaps they are more competitive than the U.S. banking system, in that the latter holds out for a higher margin of "price" over "cost" of short-term capital. The main reason, however, is surely the effect of U.S. government restrictions that widen the spread between the interest rates that U.S. banks can offer their depositors and the rates they ask for loans. One of these is the requirement that reserves be held against deposits; the Euro-banks, by close matching of the maturities of loans and time deposit liabilities, can nearly do without holding funds idle as reserves. Other restrictions, notably ceilings on interest paid on deposits, also hobble the U.S. banks as competitors. Euro-banks usually offer a smaller spread between deposit and loan interest rates than do U.S. banks, and naturally pull a lot of business away from them.[10] Of course, these same propositions about the unregulated and competitive Euro-dollar market hold for transactions in the other Euro-currencies in competition with the national banking systems that deal in those currencies.

Consequences of Euro-Dollar Market

The Euro-currency markets have had important consequences for the operation of the international monetary system. Some are rather obvious, others subtle. Some have been greeted with pleasure by policymakers, others with dismay.

1. *International mobility of capital.* For both depositors and borrowers the Euro-currency market provides a competitive alternative to domestic banking systems— one that can offer better terms at little or no increase in risk. The mobility of capital is increased between countries, not to mention between lenders and borrowers in the same country. This mobility is shown in the close relation of Euro-dollar interest rates to U.S. short-term interest rates and also to yields on covered interest arbitrage transactions emanating from other financial centers. That is, Euro-dollar loans or deposits compete closely with deposits in or loans from U.S. banks. They also compete with loans or deposits in

[10] See Gunter Dufey and Ian H. Giddy, *The International Money Market.* Englewood Cliffs, N.J.: Prentice-Hall, 1978. Chaps. 1 and 2.

other currencies, with the cost of forward-exchange cover taken into account. If national interest rates get out of line with Euro-currency rates, large capital flows take place to profit from the differential. National monetary authorities have not always been thrilled with the constraint that these flows impose on their ability to manipulate their national interest rates, as we shall see in Chapter 22.

2. *The U.S. balance of payments.* During the late 1960's the Euro-dollar market was growing apace while the United States ran an intractable balance-of-payments deficit. Not unnaturally, many suspected that the market's growth was swelling the deficit. However, close study has convinced most economists that the charge was false: There is simply little or no connection between the growth of the Euro-currency market and the balance-of-payments position of any particular country. Total Euro-dollar transactions can grow because Americans are clamoring for Euro-dollar loans (a capital inflow tending to produce a payments surplus for the U.S.) or because they are eager to place deposits with Euro-banks (an outflow and a deficit). Euro-dollar transactions among non-U.S. parties move deposits around on the books of U.S. banks, whose deposit liabilities are the fundamental assets passed around in Euro-dollar transactions, but they do not involve any significant capital outflow. To the extent that the United States ran a trade deficit, foreigners earned more dollars from selling goods and services to the United States than they spent buying from America. But they need not have retained the net outflow of funds as private dollar holdings, and if they retained them as dollars, those dollars need not have been placed on the Euro-dollar market. If anything, the U.S. deficit caused the Euro-dollar market's growth, rather than the other way around: The controls that U.S. authorities placed on foreign lending by U.S. banks encouraged parties to go to the unregulated Euro-dollar market.

3. *The world's money supply.* Total Euro-currency liabilities to non-bank depositors grew from a mere $7 billion to $9 billion in 1964 to something approaching half a *trillion* dollars at the start of the 1980's — an increase of around 30 percent annually. Some feared that the Euro-market was a Mad Money Machine run out of control, increasing the world's money supply while the world's central bankers wrung their hands in despair. This diagnosis requires close analysis. The Euro-currency market is a market in time deposits. Its transactions are very similar to those of savings banks in the United States. Both of them bid deposits away from U.S. commercial banks. These deposits then become claims of the Euro-banks (or domestic savings banks) on the U.S. commercial banks. The banks dealing in time deposits cannot themselves increase the U.S. money supply the way the commercial banks can (through the multiple expansion of bank credit), because

their liabilities are not a medium of exchange. But the Euro-banks do create time deposits that are part of no country's money supply. Suppose that a German firm (not a bank) receives a dollar payment and deposits it in a Euro-bank. The bank lends the funds to another nonbank, which deposits them in an American bank. The American money supply remains what it was before the chain of transactions began, but the German firm's deposit in the Euro-bank is additional money not part of any country's money stock. Probably more important than this explicit process of money creation is the general increase in liquidity that the market brings about.

4. *Effectiveness of monetary control.* Another concern of policymakers has been that the Euro-currency market is somehow out of control and provides liquidity to a nation's transactors in ways quite unrelated to the wishes of its national monetary authorities. Their specific fears (aside from the question of the market's effect on the world's money supply, just discussed) turn on two questions: Are banks running undue risks in their Euro-currency transactions, taking a chance on collapses that would impose costs beyond those to the immediate victim banks? Does the Euro-currency market provide a bottomless pool of funds to finance speculative attacks on particular currencies (those whose governments seek to enforce their own views about an "appropriate" exchange rate)? The concern voiced in the first question comes into perspective when we recognize that the Euro-currency market does not exist on some mythical desert isle: Euro-banks are simply large commercial banks, each domiciled in some country and subject to regulation by its monetary authority. Monetary authorities are increasingly prone to scrutinize the consolidated financial position of banks under their charge, including offshore Euro-business as well as domestic business. With regard to use of the market for financing of speculative positions, this is indeed easily done: A speculator betting on a decline in the value of a Euro-currency need only take out a loan in it, becoming "short" in that currency if he does not cover in the forward market. But the Euro-currency market is only one of many avenues for the determined speculator; it *intermediates* such transactions but does not *supply* funds available nowhere else.[11]

The constructive consequences of the Euro-currency network are probably best seen in its response to the financial consequences of the first great oil-price increase of 1973. In 1974 the oil-exporting countries (OPEC) took in oil revenues nearly $60 billion larger than their purchases of goods and services from abroad. That sum comprised an enormous transfer of purchasing power from the oil importers to the

[11] See Dufey and Giddy, chap. 4; and "Euro-Currency Market Controls," Morgan Guaranty Trust Company, *World Financial Markets,* March 1979, pp. 4–13.

exporters. In essence, the importers sold off securities to pay their oil bills. If the exporters had wished to hold just the securities that the importers sold, the transfer of wealth would not have disturbed the world's capital markets.

The trouble was that the exporters sought highly liquid, low-risk, short-term investments whereas the importers were dissaving from longer-term and riskier assets. Financial asset markets had to adjust the yields and the forms of securities they offered. Some help came from official arrangements to "recycle" this purchasing power (Chapter 23), but in fact private capital markets did most of the job. Euro-currency banks were under considerable strain to find borrowers who would take all the funds that the OPEC countries placed in short-term deposits. The system sometimes developed serious cracks. Some large banks were on the verge of declining further deposits. They found themselves exposed to great risks because their deposits had grown so rapidly while their equity capital remained unchanged. A few banks did fail as a result of unsuccessful forward exchange dealings, and indeed forward exchange markets grew thin for a time partly from doubts that Euro-currency banks could meet their obligations in forward exchange contracts. The system creaked, but the fact is that it hung together in the face of a massive disturbance.[12]

U.S. financial institutions also played an important role in this test of international capital markets. Short-term international liabilities and assets in the United States both increased massively, showing that the country was borrowing large amounts of oil money and relending it abroad. And forward exchange rates for most currencies (except Germany's) fell against the dollar, which is consistent with large flows of covered short-term capital to those countries from the United States.

20.3 PORTFOLIO ADJUSTMENTS AND INTERNATIONAL CAPITAL MOVEMENTS

In section 19.3 we described the process by which risk-averse investors can diversify their portfolios by holding a variety of assets. The returns to holders of financial wealth fluctuate over time, reflecting variations in the fate of the real investment projects whose earnings they claim. The more out of phase are the fluctuations for different securities, the more can the investor reduce the variability of his financial return by diversifying.

---

[12] Samuel I. Katz, *"Managed Floating" as an Interim International Exchange Rate Regime, 1973–1975, The Bulletin,* Center for the Study of Financial Institutions, Graduate School of Business Administration, New York University (No. 3, 1975), especially pp. 39–44.

International Diversification

1. One risk for the international lender is that of a change in the exchange rate between his currency and the one in which his assets are denominated. In order to curb the exchange risk to his portfolio, he would hold assets denominated in several currencies. The market-determined exchange rates of the 1970's increased the diversification gains from holding assets denominated in different currencies, even if they may have increased risks in other ways.[13]

2. The financial fates of companies (and, for that matter, local governments) within a country are often tied together. The nation's rate of growth, its ability to maintain full employment, its political stability, etc., affect the financial results of all its business firms in roughly the same way. That is, the levels and fluctuations of their profits, and the chances that they will meet payments schedules on their bonds, all move together. Because of this, the investor starting to diversify his portfolio gains less from adding new assets from the same country than from adding new assets from different countries. By "buying into" the growth and business cycle patterns of different national economies, he may cut his risks quite effectively.[14]

If lenders heed these considerations in building their portfolios, several interesting implications arise for the pattern of international flows of portfolio capital. Interest rates could differ between countries without causing capital flows; the risk characteristics of securities emanating from the high-yield country could make investors unwilling to add enough of its securities to their portfolios to eliminate the difference in interest rates. On the other hand, capital could flow between two countries even if their interest rates are the same. Differences in risk could make investors want to hold securities of both countries; their expected returns would stay constant when they diversify in this way, but the riskiness of their overall portfolio is diminished. Note that capital in this case would not flow only into or out of a country; securities would be swapped back and forth in both directions.

Finally, portfolio balancing tells us that differences in the sizes of

---

[13] Of course, borrowers may prefer to take the exchange risk upon themselves, issuing obligations in a foreign currency in order to secure a lower interest rate. The bulk of Canadian bonds issued in the United States are denominated in U.S. currency, so the Canadian borrower loses if the price of the Canadian dollar falls and gains if it rises. Borrowers in European capital markets have issued bonds payable in "packages" of currencies, or in alternative currencies at the option of the lender, in order to secure the best combination of exchange risk and capital cost for themselves. For examples, see J. O. M. van der Mensbrugghe, "Bond Issues in European Units of Account," *IMF Staff Papers*, 11 (November 1964): 446–55.

[14] Herbert G. Grubel, "Internationally Diversified Portfolios: Welfare Gains and Capital Flows," *American Economic Review*, 58 (December 1968): 1299–1314.

countries can affect the direction of capital flows between them. Suppose that the current market value of the total portfolios of financial assets in country *A* is ten times as large as that of country *B*. No capital flows have taken place between them in the past, but both *A*'s and *B*'s investors now become conscious of the potential gains from diversification. If most lenders wish to hold assets from both countries, the *net* capital flow would probably run from large country *A* to small country *B*. The value of *B* securities which citizens of *A* try to add to their giant (aggregate) portfolio will probably exceed the value of *A* securities sought in order to balance the relatively tiny *B* portfolio. The United States is a heavy net lender to Canada, and the sizes of their respective portfolios differ in at least a ratio of 10 to 1. Yet the proportion of U.S. securities held in Canadian portfolios appears to be larger than the proportion of Canadian securities held in U.S. portfolios. Perhaps portfolio balancing and the different sizes of these two nations help to explain this pattern of capital flows. Note, however, that it cannot be the *only* explanation, because Canadian interest rates have usually exceeded those in the United States.

Gains from Diversification

How large are the gains from international diversification? Economists have devised models that allow them to calculate an optimal portfolio of securities from information on the average returns to the various assets that might be included, the variability of those returns, and the degree to which the variations of different securities are out of phase with each other.[15] One such investigation covered the common stocks of twenty-eight countries. If you held a cross-section of United States equity stocks over the period covered by the study (1951–1967), you would have earned a 12.1 percent rate of return. If you had switched instead to the best diversified portfolio, your rate of return would have stayed the same, but its variability would have been cut by one-third. It is no surprise that the best countries' securities to combine in the portfolio are those of the "most different" countries — Austria, Japan, South Africa, and Venezuela are well represented in this optimal portfolio.[16]

[15] You may be surprised that there is one optimal portfolio for all investors, regardless of whether they may be individually risk-averse or willing to take big risks for high returns. The reason is the (assumed) existence of some risk-free liquid asset, such as Treasury bills. The best strategy for all investors, whatever their attitude toward risk, is to hold varying proportions of the optimal portfolio and the risk-free asset. Real gamblers can borrow and thus increase the effective riskiness of the optimal portfolio.

[16] These calculations are taken from Haim Levy and Marshall Sarnat, "International Diversification of Investment Portfolios," *American Economic Review*, 60 (September 1970): 668–75.

Extent of Diversification and Integration

Because economists have placed so much stress on portfolio adjustment and the gains from diversification, we naturally wonder how fully the financial portfolios of the real world have exhausted the gains available from international diversification. We are also concerned with the extent that international capital markets have performed their classical function of reallocating funds from locales where they would command a low rate of return to places where capital's marginal product is higher.

Table 20.1 shows a few key details of the international investment position of the United States at the end of 1978. For the private sector it includes not only stocks and bonds held by individuals and financial intermediaries but also the international loans and borrowings of U.S. banks and nonfinancial enterprises (trade credit and other loans extended by business firms and — most important — foreign direct in-

TABLE 20.1   International Investment Position of the United States, End of 1978 (billions of dollars)

Type of asset or liability	U.S. assets abroad	U.S. liabilities to foreigners
Private-sector assets and liabilities		
Direct investment	168.1	40.8
Portfolio investment:		
Corporate stocks	11.2	42.0
Corporate and other bonds	42.2	13.4
Assets and liabilities of U.S.		
nonbanking enterprises[a]	26.1	15.1
Assets and liabilities of U.S. banks[a]	129.6	86.9
Subtotal	377.2	198.2
Official reserves and other official assets		
International reserve assets[b]	14.2	—
Government securities and currencies	58.6	175.1
Subtotal	72.8	175.1
Total	450.0	373.3

Source: Survey of Current Business, 59 (August 1979): 56.
[a] These lines identify assets and liabilities by the kind of U.S. business enterprise reporting them rather than by the nature of the financial claim itself.
[b] This figure represents U.S. holdings of gold and claims on international organizations. Similar reserves held by foreign countries are not liabilities of the United States.

vestment). All of these claims should be considered when international investment behavior is investigated. Americans who want to diversify their portfolios internationally can choose between buying foreign bonds and stocks and buying shares in U.S. multinational companies that derive large proportions of their earnings from investments abroad.

That latter strategy is certainly the one followed by American investors. U.S. holdings of foreign corporate stocks are tiny compared to corporate bond holdings (let alone U.S. foreign direct investment), and make up hardly one percent of all U.S. firms' equities. The transaction costs for the individual investor clearly favor buying shares in American multinationals over buying equities in foreign countries, as do certain tax provisions. U.S. portfolios contain somewhat larger amounts of foreign bonds, and might hold more but for a prohibitive tax on bonds purchased from some countries during the period 1967–1974. However, these bonds offer little diversification value, because most of them originate in Canada and are denominated in U.S. dollars.

Evidence of somewhat more portfolio diversification appears in foreigners' investments in the United States. Foreign holdings of U.S. corporate stocks are rather large and volatile in the short run. European mutual-fund managers are said to consider it appropriate to hold 10 to 40 percent of their portfolio in U.S. equities. Only a few foreign countries are the homes of many large multinational companies, and so many investors abroad probably find investing in the stocks of large U.S. companies their best bet for international diversification.

Table 20.1 also reveals that the United States is a large net international investor only by virtue of U.S. multinational corporations. In earlier times large international capital flows took place through international sales of government and corporate bonds, to construct the railroads of the nineteenth century and the electric power stations of the twentieth. The classic role of the international financial center — London before World War I, New York in the 1920's — was to mobilize capital locally for export and acquire debt instruments to place in local portfolios. For a variety of reasons that model has given way. The Eurocurrency market (discussed in section 20.2) is now the leading center for new international bond issues, but it serves as a pure intermediary and draws on no specific local capital supply. The one conspicuous international transfer of capital to occur in recent years is the placement of OPEC's wealth abroad. In the 1970's at least half of foreign purchases of U.S. corporate stocks have been by OPEC.

Could it be that the United States is the exception rather than the rule, and that the smaller industrial countries are linked by fully mobile international flows of capital? Consider this test: If all the world were linked together in one liquid capital market, there would be little association between the level of saving in any one country and that country's level of investment. Savers would spread their funds around the world, wherever the highest yields could be obtained, and little would wind up as extra investment in their home country. On the other hand, if capital markets were quite fragmented by national boundaries, extra domestic saving would go mostly into domestic investment. The statistical evidence strongly favors the latter model. Between 1960 and 1974 the average industrial country exported or imported capital equal to only 5.2 percent of its gross (before depreciation) domestic saving. And changes in countries' saving rates were closely associated with changes in their own investment rates.[17]

We can safely draw the following conclusions about international capital flows. (1) Most savings are invested at home; large international movements of long-term capital have recently occurred only through the multinational company and through the placement of OPEC surpluses. (2) There is some evidence of international portfolio diversification, but it seems to be sharply limited by risks and transaction costs. (3) Short-term capital, protected by forward cover against exchange-rate changes, is highly mobile internationally, and the lengthening of maturities in Euro-currency credits means that the increased mobility of capital wrought by the expanding Euro-currency markets now extends out to rather long-term capital. The evidence on international portfolios shows that rather little of the world's stock of financial capital is footloose internationally, but enough is sensitive to give rise to large flows when expected yields change among the industrial countries. In Chapter 22 we shall see the implications for national economic policy of high international mobility of capital.

20.4 SUMMARY

Short-term capital exports are often covered by selling the expected proceeds in the forward exchange market. Interest arbitragers thus are one of the groups of transactors in the forward market, exporting capital and selling foreign exchange forward when its price is high enough to offset any differential between foreign and domestic short-term interest rates. Commercial traders (exporters and importers) also enter the forward market to avoid risks associated with future receipts or payments in foreign exchange. Finally, speculators enter the forward market, betting on the relation between the forward rate and the spot

---

[17] This section has drawn upon two unpublished papers from the National Bureau of Economic Research Program of Research on Capital Formation: David G. Hartman, "Long-Term International Capital Flows and the U.S. Economy"; and Martin S. Feldstein and Charles Horioka, "Domestic Saving and International Capital Flows."

rate that will prevail when their contracts mature. The equilibrium value of the forward exchange rate sets the net excess demand of these three groups equal to zero. The government may choose to intervene in the forward market, as a substitute method for influencing the level of its spot exchange rate.

Euro-currency markets are a major institutional part of the increasing international mobility of short-term funds. They comprise markets for bank deposits denominated in currencies of countries other than the one where the bank resides. The Euro-dollar market has increased the competitiveness of international financial markets but has also compounded the problems of countries whose policy objectives require the control of international capital movements. International capital markets coped successfully if not easily with the enormous transfer of wealth to the OPEC countries that followed the 1973 oil price increase. The Euro-currency markets may have inflated the world's money stock and they certainly increased its liquidity.

Asset holders who diversify internationally can avoid two types of risks: the many risks common to all investments in any one national economy, and the risk of exchange-rate changes for a single currency. The theory of international diversification predicts that international capital flows will move in all directions among countries, even if their interest rates are the same, and that small countries' securities might be in high demand if they offer good diversification value. However, United States asset holders' portfolios contain few foreign securities; American asset holders do most of their diversifying by owning shares in U.S. multinational companies. Foreign holdings of U.S. securities suggest somewhat more direct diversification of foreign portfolios. Most savings are invested in the saver's home country.

Overall, there is a high degree of international mobility of short-term capital, on the evidence of the Euro-currency market, enough to make a country's capital-account balance sensitive to domestic credit conditions. But the internationally mobile proportion of the world's capital remains quite small.

SUGGESTIONS FOR FURTHER READING

Baldwin, Robert E., and J. David Richardson, eds. *International Trade and Finance: Readings*, 2nd ed. Boston: Little, Brown and Company, 1981. No. 22 deals with speculators' performance in the forward exchange market, nos. 33 and 34 with the Euro-dollar market.

Cohen, B. J. *Balance-of-Payments Policy*. Baltimore: Penguin, 1969. In Chapter 2 Cohen summarizes the case for government intervention in the forward market.

Dufey, Gunter, and Ian H. Giddy. *The International Money Market*. Englewood Cliffs, N.J.: Prentice-Hall, 1978. Excellent treatment of the Eurocurrency markets.

Exchange Market Participants' Study Group. *The Foreign Exchange Markets Under Rates*. New York: Group of Thirty, 1980. Survey of actions of major exchange-market participants since 1973.

Grubel, Herbert G. "Internationally Diversified Portfolios: Welfare Gains and Capital Flows," *American Economic Review*, 58 (December 1968): 1299–1314. Theory of international portfolio diversification.

Hodjera, Zoran, "The Asian Currency Market: Singapore as a Regional Financial Center," *IMF Staff Papers*, 25 (June 1978): 221–53. Insight into institutional basis for offshore currency markets.

McKinnon, Ronald I. *Money in International Exchange: The Convertible Currency System*. New York: Oxford University Press, 1979. Good chapters on participants in the forward exchange market.

Morgan Guaranty Trust Co. "Constraints on International Bank Lending," *World Financial Markets* (December 1979): 6–13. Recent look at the prospects for recycling OPEC's wealth.

Stein, J. L. *The Nature and Efficiency of the Foreign Exchange Market*. Essays in International Finance, no. 40. Princeton: International Finance Section, Princeton University, 1962. Forward markets and speculative crises.

21

Inflation in
the World Economy

Inflation became a global problem in the 1970's. Consumer prices rose 135 percent for the world as a whole, doubling for the industrial countries and rising fourfold in the less-developed areas.[1] In this chapter we explore the international linkages among countries' inflation rates, to determine what the models and concepts set forth in Chapters 15 through 20 can tell us about the problem. We do not seek here to locate the ultimate causes or propose the appropriate remedies — would that we could! — but only show how to analyze the international aspects and consequences of inflation.

21.1 INTERNATIONAL TRANSMISSION OF INFLATION

At least until recently economists were prone to diagnose inflation without reference to international forces at all. "Cost push" or "demand pull" or increases in the country's money supply were the initiating forces. The course of inflation was discussed without heed to the economy's international linkages. This mode of thinking was shaken by the worldwide prevalence of inflation in the 1970's. Whatever the underlying causes, they are hardly likely to strike all countries independently at the same time. We now appreciate that inflation can be transmitted internationally, and not a few countries have suspected that their inflationary problems could be laid at the doors of their more profligate

[1] Data from International Monetary Fund, *IMF Survey*, November 12, 1979, p. 351, cover the period from 1970 through the first half of 1979.

neighbors. We first review our models of disturbance and adjustment in the international economy for the messages they convey about the international transmission of inflation.

Transmission Mechanisms

Let us first consider the transfer of inflation when exchange rates are fixed among all countries. In a sense that assumption makes the result obvious. The Law of One Price asserts that a given good must command the same price everywhere at any one time. It implies that prices at all locations must be going up at the same rate — or the fixed exchange rates must give way. However, we found (Chapter 19) that the law is widely violated in the short run. Both policymakers and the public have to struggle with inflation as a variable short-run matter, and with little certainty about what the morrow will bring. Therefore we consider the international transfer of inflation under fixed exchange rates in a short-run context, treating the Law of One Price as a possibility but not a certainty. When we apply the models developed in Chapters 16 and 17, we quickly discover that the commodity structure of trade strongly affects the transfer of inflationary disturbances. Consider these cases:

1. *The goods produced in our country are not close substitutes for foreign-produced goods*, either in our own consumption (importables compared to home-produced goods) or in foreigners' consumption (our exports compared to goods produced abroad). Prices can rise abroad without immediately spilling their full inflationary effect onto our economy via product markets. Demand both at home and abroad shifts toward home-produced goods, but the shift takes time, and so the direct effect of foreign inflation on supply-demand conditions in domestic product markets is a leisurely one. In these circumstances an improving current-account balance plays a central role in the process of transmitting inflation. The value of imports falls as domestic buyers pass up the more costly imported goods. The value of exports rises as foreigners order more of our relatively cheap exportables. The improved current-account balance is an injection into the Keynesian multiplier mechanism (Chapter 16), and the resulting increase in aggregate demand promotes inflation as soon as domestic industries bump into their short-run capacity limits.

2. *The traded goods produced and consumed in our country are perfect substitutes for those produced elsewhere.* In this case the Law of One Price should hold in the short run. With the exchange rate fixed, any inflation abroad is passed along directly to the domestic economy through competitive international product markets. Our country's trade balance plays no central role in transmitting the inflation. According to the monetarist model (Chapter 17), however, a current-account surplus

may *result* from the transmitted inflation. Higher commodity prices in domestic currency cause the public to find their cash balances inadequate, and an excess demand for money develops. If the central bank hesitates to meet this demand, people temporarily spend less than their incomes, and a trade surplus appears. The central bank can avert an appreciation of the country's currency only by buying up foreign exchange and paying out domestic money. It thereby creates the extra cash balances demanded by the public and "validates" the domestic inflation.

The channels for transmitting inflation identified in these two cases are alternatives to one another. If goods of differing national origin are close substitutes, inflation travels mainly through the microeconomic channels of individual product markets (the Law of One Price). If they are poor substitutes in the short run, the current-account surplus transmits most of the inflation.

To the extent that traded goods command the same prices everywhere — the Law of One Price holds — it in fact becomes difficult to tell in what country the inflationary disturbances arise. If we wish to find the culprit, the analysis of Chapter 17 suggests where to look for clues. The prices of nontraded goods and services in our economy are not locked to those of traded goods and hence respond directly to homemade inflationary disturbances. Suppose we observe that in country A the prices of nontraded goods have been rising faster than those of traded goods, while in country B the prices of local nontraded goods have been rising more slowly than traded goods. This pattern supplies strong circumstantial evidence that the bulk of the inflationary disturbance arises in country A, pulling up the world prices of traded goods and thereby the prices of B's nontraded goods.[2]

Other institutional features can also influence the specific processes of inflationary transfer. If factors of production are mobile internationally, their money prices become directly linked across national boundaries. In Switzerland, for example, more than one-quarter of the labor force are not Swiss nationals, and they presumably move freely between Switzerland and their native countries in response to wage differentials. Their movements would tend to align rates of money-wage increase in Switzerland to those abroad. Hence overall rates of inflation would be tied together.

Even without direct international links to foreign wages the labor market's institutions are likely to color the process of inflationary trans-

[2] Norman Fieleke's test of this model pins the blame on the United States for transmitting inflation during the period 1964–1970. See "The International Transmission of Inflation," *Managed Exchange-Rate Flexibility: The Recent Experience.* Federal Reserve Bank of Boston, Conference Series no. 20 (Boston, 1978), pp. 26–52.

fer. That is because the wage-setting process may be either sensitive or insensitive to inflation in the prices of traded goods. Suppose that in our country imports are included extensively in households' shopping baskets, so that consumer prices promptly reflect inflation abroad, and workers immediately notice the shriveled purchasing power of their pay envelopes. Suppose also that trade unions are powerful and can generally bargain wage settlements that at least hold their real wages constant. When the inflation lowers real wages, unions rise up and demand higher money wages throughout the economy. Domestic producers — not just those making traded goods — find their marginal costs elevated, and mark up their product prices accordingly.

However, traded-goods prices do not enter strongly or directly into some countries' consumer price indexes. And trade unions may be subject to "money illusion," paying attention to the number of dollars in their pay envelopes and not to the purchasing power of those dollars. Then inflation can (for a time, at least) lower the real wages (the money wage stays constant while product prices are affected by international inflation). Wages neither speed the transmission of inflation nor spread the infection to the economy's nontraded-goods sectors.[3]

As a summary exercise, we can ask what structural traits of an economy make it least vulnerable to importing inflation from abroad. The nation's traded-goods output should be distinctive, not close substitutes for tradable goods produced abroad. Its nontraded-goods sector, a slow receiver of inflation, should be large, so that the economy is relatively closed to trade. Its imports should not enter directly into personal consumption, and its trade unions should bargain on the basis of company profits rather than the cost of living (and thus real wages). The country should bulk large in the world economy; the greater its share of world economic activity, the less is it affected by any given proportional increase in the money supply abroad.

These traits seem to match the U.S. economy rather closely, and so it may enjoy a higher immunity to this contagion than any other industrial country. Indeed, the United States was surprised to discover in the

---

[3] During 1976 and 1977 a policy debate took place between the United States and other industrial countries, mainly Germany and Japan, over whether those countries should follow the lead of the United States and stimulate domestic aggregate demand more vigorously. The United States went ahead while Germany and Japan continued to resist. It has been argued, with some statistical support, that the countries' attitudes correctly reflect the way in which their wage levels respond to inflationary disturbances. Real wages are rigid in Germany and Japan, so that expansionary policies would immediately transmute themselves into inflation, whereas nominal wages in the United States are sticky, so the demand expansion posed less of an inflationary threat. See William H. Branson and Julio J. Rotemberg, "International Adjustment with Wage Rigidity," National Bureau of Economic Research, Working Paper no. 406, 1980.

1970's that it could suffer *any* inflation as a result of disturbances imported from abroad. Economists have offered various statistical estimates of the sensitivity of the U.S. price level to increases in import prices. Dornbusch estimated that domestic prices (consumer prices or the GNP deflator) are increased in the short run by about one-sixth of the rise of import prices, in the long run by about one-third.[4]

Exchange-Rate Changes

So far we have examined the channels of inflationary transfer on the assumption that exchange rates remain fixed, a condition obviously not consistent with sustained differences in national inflation rates. One could imagine a two-country world with country A inflating at 10 percent a year, country B inflating at 20 percent annually, the exchange rate (price of B's currency) falling 10 percent annually, and the "real" sides of both economies being in tranquil equilibrium. But how relevant is this case? The difficulty in practice is that inflation rates are never steady over time, nor are they accurately anticipated by the public. Therefore it is difficult to foretell exactly how a market-determined exchange rate will react to differing national rates of inflation, and to inflationary disturbances in general. We discuss some of the issues in the next two sections of this chapter.

21.2 INTERNATIONAL CAPITAL MOVEMENTS, INTEREST RATES, AND INFLATION

To relate international capital flows to inflation, it is helpful to expand on the admittedly unrealistic notion of inflation as a steady-state process in which everybody correctly anticipates what changes will occur and makes the best of the situation. That is because knowing whether people's expectations and plans are fully adjusted to inflation is vital to understanding its effects and those of policies to combat it. Suppose that everybody indeed expects the rate of inflation to cruise along at x percent annually, and has had time to adjust his plans to that expectation. If no other disturbances are striking the economy, the money prices of all goods and services should be adjusting upward at the same rate (so that relative prices stay unchanged).

---

[4] As we would expect, both fractions are higher than the actual share of imports in the total domestic absorption of goods and services. See Rudiger Dornbusch, "Monetary Policy under Exchange-Rate Flexibility," *Managed Exchange-Rate Flexibility*. Federal Reserve Bank of Boston, Conference Series no. 20 (Boston, 1978), pp. 114–15.

Interest Rates in Steady Inflation

Consider the way in which savers and investors adjust to these circumstances. Investors who borrow nominal dollars to build factories expect that the cash value of their factories' outputs will rise with the rate of inflation. Whatever the real productivity of their physical investments, they will be willing to borrow at any nominal interest rate up to the sum of the real (marginal) productivity of their investments plus the rate of inflation. Savers make a similar calculation in deciding whether to consume their incomes now or lend funds for real investment by the business sector. If their loans are denominated in nominal dollars, the real value of the nominal-dollar interest payments will shrink each period of time, as will the real value of the ultimate repayment they expect to receive. Therefore savers will raise the asking price for their loanable funds by the rate of inflation. The equilibrium interest rate therefore tends to be the "real" interest rate plus the rate of inflation.

Now we can consider the effects of fully anticipated inflation on international capital movements. If steady-state inflation rates differ among countries, exchange rates must be changing to offset the differences. Savers comparing the yields they expect on assets denominated in different currencies will demand an interest rate that compensates them for a currency's expected rate of depreciation. If the nominal interest rate at home is 10 percent and the price of foreign exchange is expected to fall 5 percent annually (because of faster inflation abroad), a foreign interest rate of 15 percent is needed to equilibrate international capital flows. In the case of covered interest arbitrage the forward exchange rate would similarly be discounted, and at any given time should lie 5 percent (on an annual basis) below the current spot rate. This argument suggests that capital-account equilibrium requires exchange rates to offset inflation differences, just as does current-account equilibrium.

Capital Flows and Expectations

How capital flows behave in the international economy depends quite strongly on whether people accurately anticipate the going rate of inflation or are not yet fully aware of the implications of a new inflationary disturbance. For example, we expect capital to flow from countries where the *real* interest rate is low to those where it is high. But in inflationary conditions, whether capital flows toward countries with high *nominal* interest rates depends on the state of expectations. We can see this process by following what happens as inflation intrudes on a noninflationary world economy and as the public comes to expect that it will continue. Suppose the United States has been experiencing generally stable prices, but now the Federal Reserve starts to increase the money supply at a more rapid rate. If the prices of goods and services are sticky and people's expectations about future prices do not change immediately, the monetary injection has a "Keynesian" effect of driving down the rate of interest. This disturbance tends to depress the dollar's value on the foreign-exchange market via two channels: The depressed interest rate encourages investment and other domestic spending, which in turn increases imports and worsens the trade balance; the lower interest rate also encourages a capital outflow (or reduces any inflow). Both of these adjustments increase the excess demand for foreign exchange and drive up its price. The fall in the U.S. interest rate is associated with an outflow of capital, just as we usually expect.

Now suppose that the monetary injections continue and the price level begins to respond. The American public comes to learn what will be the full consequences of each monetary injection and to anticipate them in the way described above: The interest rate and the price of foreign exchange are both marked up immediately to anticipate the inflation that people expect to result from any given monetary injection.[5] The effect of inflation on the price of foreign exchange does not await the shift in the trade balance, as it (to some extent) does when inflation is not anticipated. More dramatically, the domestic interest rate rises in response to a monetary injection when inflation is anticipated, whereas it falls when no inflation is expected. But this higher interest rate does not bestir any international capital inflow, nor indeed need it have any effect at all on international capital movements. The shift in nominal interest rates at home relative to those abroad in this case has no effect on the differential between real interest rates. And the relation between international capital movements and nominal interest differentials is entirely different from what we expect with unanticipated inflation.

Some Empirical Evidence

Some statistical evidence is at hand to confirm these contrasting patterns. Jeffrey Frankel analyzed the forces determining the dollar–Deutschemark exchange rate between 1974 and 1978, years when the inflation of the 1970's was getting rolling nicely. He did find that the rise in the price of the DM was speeded up by faster growth of the U.S. money supply relative to the German money supply. An indicator of the state of inflationary expectations had a similar effect. But Frankel found some evidence to suggest that the short-term interest differential between the two countries still played the role we expect when inflation is not fully

[5] We are assuming here, as we did in Chapter 19, that financial markets adjust immediately to the news of an inflationary disturbance but markets for real goods and services take somewhat longer.

anticipated. That is, an increase in the U.S. short-term interest rate could still pull in some capital from abroad and retard the dollar's depreciation.[6] Rather different results were reported by Jacob Frenkel in his investigation of the German hyperinflation of the 1920's. With prices rising explosively the public apparently came fully to anticipate the consequences of monetary injections, and the exchange rate responded without any intermediary forces.[7]

When inflation is not fully anticipated and prices adjust at different rates, resources can get misallocated in many different ways. Suppose that country A maintains a fixed exchange rate at the time it starts to inflate faster than its trading partners. The fixed exchange rate will eventually give way if the inflation continues, of course. But country A's central bank may fight a delaying action, using its reserves to stave off the inevitable depreciation. In the meantime A's nominal interest rate may be pushed up as domestic savers take note of the inflation that is under way. As long as the central bank can preserve the fixed exchange rate this increase in A's nominal interest rate is an increased real return to capital for foreign lenders. For a time A can go on receiving capital inflows for this reason, and not because capital's real productivity is higher in A than elsewhere.

21.3 VICIOUS CIRCLES AND ASYMMETRIES

In the turbulent 1970's several countries suffered difficulties that were described as "vicious circles." A typical tale of woe might go like this: Something causes the country's currency to depreciate. The prices of traded goods therefore rise in domestic currency. Trade unions observe that real wages have declined, and so they demand higher money wages, which push the domestic price level up even further. That inflation makes the exchange rate depreciate more still — the speculators having decided to bet against the currency — and the process goes on and on. This narrative is superficially plausible, but it troubles an economist. It leaves out important parts of the economic mechanism, notably the response of the demand and supply of money to these disturbances. And it fails to explain clearly how certain key markets for goods and for labor services are assumed to operate. We shall suggest that two conclusions emerge from a careful analysis:

[6] Jeffrey A. Frankel, "On the Mark: A Theory of Floating Exchange Rates Based on Real Interest Differentials," *American Economic Review,* 69 (September 1979): 610–22.
[7] Jacob Frenkel, "A Monetary Approach to the Exchange Rate: Doctrinal Aspects and Empirical Evidence," *Scandinavian Journal of Economics,* 78 (no. 2, 1976): 200–24.

1. It is difficult to concoct a "vicious circle" that continues without the connivance of the central bank increasing the money supply.

2. Certain patterns of wage and price determination can put central banks in a position where they are hard pressed to avoid inflation-promoting increases in the money supply.

Vicious Circles and Monetary Conditions

The "pop" account of a vicious circle set forth above leaves out the role of monetary adjustments. Suppose that our currency has depreciated because world demand has shifted away from our country's export goods. The resulting rise in the domestic prices of importable goods reduces the real value of the public's cash balances, because people hold the same nominal amount of money as before. The public should curb their spending in order to rebuild their real cash balances. True, if the rise in traded-goods prices causes people to expect more inflation, they have an incentive to swing in the other direction and increase their spending. But there surely is an ultimate limit to how far they can economize on real cash balances, so that real spending must eventually be cut back. That cutback depresses the prices of nontraded goods and services and tends to halt or reverse the depreciation of the currency. Of course, the central bank can change this story. Consider its response when the public starts to underspend in order to rebuild their cash balances. If the central bank is fearful that unemployment might result, it can expand the money supply and provide the extra cash that people wish to hold at the new price level. In that case the vicious circle is free to run. Thus, the public's demand for cash balances is itself a dampener of the inflationary effects of an exchange-rate disturbance. But the central bank can react in a way that keeps the ball rolling.[8]

The possibilities for vicious circles are increased by the likelihood of overshooting in exchange-rate adjustments. We saw in Chapter 19 that the swift response to disturbances of the foreign-exchange and financial-asset markets could readily produce an overshooting of exchange rates. When a disturbance strikes that must lower the external value of a country's currency in the long run, the immediate discounting of its prospects in the financial markets can make its value fall even more in the short run than it must in the long run. Add onto this sequence of events any "vicious-circle" conditions that force the central bank to

---

[8] Theoretical analyses of the vicious circle are provided by Giorgio Basevi and Paul De Grauwe, "Vicious and Virtuous Circles: A Theoretical Analysis and a Policy Proposal for Managing Exchange Rates," *European Economic Review,* 10 (December 1977): 277–301; and John F. O. Bilson, "The 'Vicious Circle' Hypothesis," *IMF Staff Papers,* 26 (March 1979): 1–37.

validate the price-level effects of depreciation, and you have an embarrassing richness of vicious-circle possibilities.

Some Empirical Cases

This amended version of the vicious-circle narrative matches all too well the consequences of the oil-price increase of 1973 (and the probable consequences of the 1979 increase). The OPEC countries raised the price of petroleum products as denominated in dollars. Petroleum enters as an input into many products, and its higher price affected the prices of other energy sources as well. At the same time the oil-price increase was deflationary in its effect on employment worldwide. That is because the OPEC countries, receiving this massive transfer of income and wealth from their oil customers, were quite leisurely about increasing their real expenditure. They displayed a very high propensity to save, in Keynesian terms. The oil importers would have spent much larger fractions of their incomes — had they retained them. Thus, spending by the OPEC countries expanded a good deal less than the amount by which it was cut back by the oil importers. That condition tended to reduce employment in the United States and other countries, and indeed did create a worldwide recession in 1974–75. Central banks, concerned with both full employment and price stability, found themselves facing the acute dilemma of a disturbance that increased both inflation and unemployment. They felt they must to some degree "validate" the increase in money prices due to OPEC. Great Britain's money supply, for example, increased 30 percent in 1974. As a result, international price disturbances coupled with endogenous money supplies were able to sustain or accelerate inflationary processes.

The last days of the Bretton Woods system in the 1960's supply another example of an alleged vicious circle that in fact depended on the policies of the countries in question. The United States was then running a substantial deficit in its balance of payments on the basis of official reserve transactions. That is, other countries were acquiring large amounts of dollars to keep their currencies from appreciating against the dollar. These reserve accumulations increased the monetary bases of the surplus countries and caught them up in "imported inflation." At the same time other countries such as the United Kingdom were also running payments deficits and being forced occasionally to devalue their currencies (in 1967, in Britain's case), and the increased domestic-currency prices of traded goods were a source of inflation. Thus, it was said, the Bretton Woods system inflicted inflation on both the deficit and surplus countries.

Once again, this interpretation neglects the central role of policy choices. Suppose the monetary authorities in all countries are increasing their money supplies at the same rate. Shifts in real demands and supplies in the international economy put some countries in surplus at the going fixed exchange rates and throw others into deficit. True, the surplus countries' money supplies are further expanded by their actions to prevent their currencies from appreciating. But the deficit countries' monetary bases are at the same time contracted by their deficits. The balance-of-payments positions of countries shift the incidence of inflationary disturbances around among them, but that does not amount to an inflationary bias for the system as a whole. A payments deficit helps to mitigate the potential inflationary effect of whatever monetary injection is coming from the central bank.[9]

Asymmetries in Market Responses

We have suggested that vicious-circle models turn out to have at their core some pattern of policy-making behavior. Indeed, economists of monetarist persuasion seem to feel that their work is done when they have sternly lectured central bankers on the folly of inflationary increases in the money supplies. But spendthrifts and profligates are not usually chosen to head central banks. Perhaps we should look further to market adjustment processes that may contribute to these apparent vicious circles.

Two asymmetries in market responses have been urged to explain the dilemma faced by those who make monetary policy. First, there is some evidence that the prices of differentiated manufactured goods are more flexible upward than downward — a possible if far from inevitable short-run pattern in imperfectly competitive industries. Suppose demand in world markets shifts away from British goods of this type and toward French goods, so that Britain experiences a tendency toward a trade deficit and a depreciation of the pound sterling. France faces the prospect of a trade surplus and appreciation of the franc. Now consider the policy options open to the British and French governments. The British

---

[9] A truer version of the 1960's story, many observers believe, centers on the fiscal and monetary policy of the United States. The United States sought to fight the Vietnam War and at the same time expanded domestic spending by the federal government without raising taxes. The resulting deficits greatly increased total expenditure and the money supply. Because of the Bretton Woods commitment to fixed exchange rates, other countries were forced to make massive accumulations of dollars, although by letting the dollar depreciate they could have "bottled up" the U.S. inflation and spared its effects on their own price levels. Thus, with exchange rates remaining fixed (until 1971), the effect of the U.S. policies was to produce a moderate amount of inflation for the world as a whole rather than a lot for itself and none for the rest of the world. See footnote 2 above.

face unemployment in their export industries. In order to avoid the unemployment they have an incentive to adopt expansionary macroeconomic policies, to allow the pound sterling to depreciate, or both. If any depreciation is allowed Britain can hardly avoid suffering some inflation. The French problem — rising prices of exportables and an export surplus — could be fought off by letting the franc appreciate, with anti-inflationary effects on the French price level. That appreciation would lower the franc prices of traded goods in France, however, and tend to create excess capacity outside the booming export sector if French producers resist cutting their prices to meet the lower prices of goods made abroad. If the French monetary authorities feel they cannot accept this outcome they avoid policies that would let the franc appreciate, and so the export boom translates itself into inflation in France. Thus, asymmetrical pricing responses in imperfectly competitive product markets combine with the natural reactions of policymakers to produce a vicious circle.[10]

If price responses may be asymmetrical in product markets, that asymmetry is surely a feature of the labor markets of the industrial countries. Money wages rise with (and perhaps without) any excess demand for labor, but they do not fall when labor is in excess supply and unemployment exists. The potential consequences for individual countries and the world as a whole are about the same as for asymmetrical responses in product markets. When world demand shifts from British to French goods, the failure of British wages to fall forces British authorities to allow a depreciation of sterling as an alternative to worsening the unemployment. They then have to worry about the degree to which they can successfully lower British workers' *real* wages through depreciation, when (by assumption) their *nominal* wages could not be bid down on the labor market.

In France, expansion in the export industries may provide an opportunity for unions to bargain higher wages, which may then spread to other sectors of the economy. In this climate allowing the franc to appreciate on the foreign-exchange market is unattractive because of the squeeze it would put on the profits of industries outside the export sector. Once again, with asymmetrical market adjustments and limited options open to policymakers, countries can easily find themselves in what appears to be a policy dilemma or a vicious circle.

---

[10] This model is a generalization to the international economy of the "demand-shift inflation" that Charles Schultze found in the United States in the 1950's. See his "Recent Inflation in the United States," *Materials Prepared in Connection with the Study of Employment, Growth, and Price Levels,* U.S. Congress, Joint Economic Committee, Study Paper no. 1. Washington: Government Printing Office, 1959. Chap. 2.

21.4 SUMMARY

If the exchange rate is pegged by the government, inflation can be transmitted from country to country by any of several channels: (1) If nations' goods are poor substitutes for one another, inflation abroad infects our country through an improving trade balance and rising aggregate demand, as both domestic and foreign buyers shift from foreign goods toward those produced at home. (2) If nations' goods are excellent substitutes so that the Law of One Price holds in the short run, the home-currency prices of our traded goods are pulled up directly by inflation abroad. (3) Wage-setting processes can speed the transfer of inflationary disturbances if labor is mobile internationally or if successful demands for wage increases are spurred by increases in the prices of internationally traded consumer goods. Having a large nontraded-goods sector slows a country's absorption of inflationary disturbances from abroad but does not ultimately protect it.

If inflation is fully anticipated by the public, real interest rates should be increased by the expected rate of inflation. Even with capital highly mobile internationally, nominal interest rates should differ between countries with different inflation rates, because international lenders take account of the depreciation expected in the purchasing power of their future interest payments and repayment of principal. Whether or not inflation is fully anticipated strongly affects the relation between international capital movements and differences in nominal interest rates.

Officials have expressed concern about the considerable changes in exchange rates occurring in the 1970's because they felt exchange-rate changes were involving their countries in vicious circles. Analysis of vicious-circle mechanisms suggests that cumulative spirals of inflation and exchange-rate depreciation cannot occur without accommodation by the monetary authorities. However, it is possible to see how the authorities get trapped into perpetuating a vicious circle. First, the fact that financial markets adjust to disturbances faster than goods markets can cause exchange rates to overshoot during an adjustment process, and the overshooting promotes vicious-circle responses. Second, asymmetries in the way goods and factor markets respond to disequilibria — prices rise with excess demand but do not fall with excess supply — readily put authorities in the position of having to choose between inflation and unemployment.

SUGGESTIONS FOR FURTHER READING

Baldwin, Robert E., and J. David Richardson, eds. *International Trade and Finance: Readings,* 2nd ed. Boston: Little, Brown and Company, 1981.

Nos. 31 and 32 deal with inflationary and other aspects of adjustment to the OPEC price disturbances.

Bilson, John F. O. "The 'Vicious Circle' Hypothesis," *IMF Staff Papers,* 26 (March 1979): 1–37. Theoretical analysis of this question.

Cleveland, Harold Van B., and W. H. Bruce Brittain. *The Great Inflation: A Monetarist View.* NPA Report no. 148. Washington: National Planning Association, 1976. Broad-brush empirical study of the early 1970's from the monetarist viewpoint.

Emminger, Otmar. *The D-Mark in the Conflict Between Internal and External Equilibrium, 1948–75.* Essays in International Finance, no. 122. Princeton: International Finance Section, Princeton University, 1977. Central banker's view of the problem of repelling imported inflation.

Fieleke, Norman S. "The International Transmission of Inflation," *Managed Exchange-Rate Flexibility: The Recent Experience.* Federal Reserve Bank of Boston, Conference Series no. 20 (Boston, 1978), pp. 26–52. Statistical evidence on processes of inflationary transfer.

Krause, Lawrence B., and Walter S. Salant. *Worldwide Inflation: Theory and Recent Experience.* Washington: Brookings Institution, 1977. Contains chapters on individual countries' experience as well as a good survey of international transmission processes.

V

ECONOMIC POLICY IN THE INTERNATIONAL ECONOMY

22

Policies for Internal and External Balance

The preceding part of this book dealt with adjustment processes in the open economy and with the effects of certain economic policies. Now we turn to the problem of choosing economic policies. Although each national government selects policies in pursuit of its own objectives, each one's choices affect the well-being of other countries as well. Conflicting and mutually frustrating choices should be avoided by periodic international coordination on a short-term basis. But needed even more for the efficient and harmonious management of policy is an international economic *system* — a framework of rules and institutions — that promotes desirable choices of policies. Chapters 23 and 24 will deal with our system of international economic policies.

22.1 MARKET ADJUSTMENT AND ECONOMIC POLICY

Economic courses often leave students puzzled about how to think about choosing economic policies. Models of adjustment processes (such as those presented in Chapters 16 and 17) explain how market forces act to bring the economy into equilibrium. Often, though not always, that equilibrium has some claim to being an ideal state of affairs. We concluded that on certain assumptions equilibrium in international payments is restored following a disturbance, whether domestic money prices are fixed or flexible. Does that mean no policy actions are ever needed, that we should sit and wait patiently for "equilibrium"? Or should we conclude, when the economy's operation poses a persistent problem, that our theory "is all right in theory, but it doesn't work in practice," and start wielding the nearest policy tool that is politically

acceptable? Neither posture is safe or prudent. The decision to implement or change a policy always rests on specific benefits and costs. Will
a policy assuredly get us to equilibrium faster than market forces? Does
it travel by a socially less costly route? Can it shift the economy's
structure to arrive at a *better* equilibrium (e.g., full-employment rather
than unemployment equilibrium)?

We need some new terms to signal the shift of our emphasis from the
market's quest for equilibrium to the policymakers' search for a desirable
state of the economy. By *internal balance* we mean their target level of
employment, aggregate demand, general price inflation, or some combination of these features of overall economic activity. They may be pursuing equilibrium at full employment in the Keynesian sense; we know
from Chapter 16 that other employment levels may also be consistent
with market equilibrium. By *external balance* we denote the policymakers' preferred state of international receipts and payments. Their
goal might be equilibrium in the foreign-exchange market, but it could
also entail a temporary disequilibrium designed to restore depleted international reserves.

Thinking About Policy Changes

With the aid of Figure 22.1 we can conceptualize the problem of choosing policies and relating them to market adjustments. At the top of the
diagram are shown some of the disturbances that can disrupt equilibrium in the foreign exchanges and domestic income circuits. Any disturbance that affects external equilibrium is likely to affect internal
equilibrium as well, as we discovered in Part 4. Therefore the arrows
run from each disturbance to both of the two boxes depicting adjustment mechanisms — those operating through the foreign-exchange market (associated with external balance) and through national income
circuits (internal balance). The mechanisms bring about adjustment to
each disturbance along a route and with a speed dependent on the
structure of the economy. Policymakers keep their eyes on certain target
variables. They might detect internal imbalance from unemployment,
inflation, rising order backlogs, and so forth; we condense these to "employment." Likewise external imbalance might be discerned from gains
or losses in reserves if the exchange rate is fixed, or movement of the
rate if it is flexible.

When one or both policy targets signals trouble the government has
available an arsenal of policy instruments that it can use. The instruments may be associated with particular targets, as the diagram suggests. We often think, say, of tax changes as a means to secure internal
balance, and governments often use them with a single problem in mind.
But in fact any macroeconomic policy tends to affect both internal and

external balance, whatever its user's intent. The interest rate is raised to combat inflationary pressure, and the policymakers express annoyance when it also attracts a large inflow of interest-sensitive capital that pushes the balance of payments into surplus. They blame multinational companies (or some other favored villain) for having taken advantage of the situation.

Yet, as we shall see, policies can be designed to turn these spillovers from unpleasant surprises to positive advantages. The trick is to take them into account at the start of the policy-making process.

22.2 ATTAINING INTERNAL AND EXTERNAL BALANCE

In this section we shall show how a government can set policies simultaneously to achieve internal and external balance. The process sounds

FIGURE 22.1 Relation Between Adjustment Mechanisms and Policy Instruments

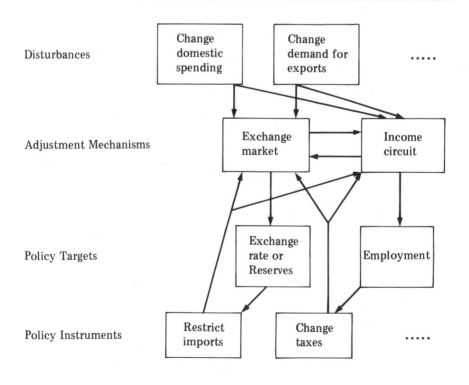

complicated, but in fact it demands no unusual information or exotic planning techniques. We pick two standard tools of policy, changes in the level of government spending, and changes in the exchange rate. (Monetary policy and the monetary mechanism of adjustment are taken up in section 22.3.) A change in either instrument affects both internal and external balance:

1. An increase in government expenditure raises aggregate demand and reduces unemployment; a decrease reduces overfull employment or potential inflationary pressure. Changes in government expenditure also affect external balance through the demand for imports: an increase in expenditure worsens the current-account balance; a reduction improves it.

2. A currency devaluation cheapens domestic goods relative to foreign goods, and thus improves the balance of trade in goods and services (henceforth the trade balance); a revaluation worsens it.[1] Through the trade balance, devaluation also alters total expenditure; the effect is the same as that of the exogenous export increases we studied in Chapter 16. An improvement in the balance (due to devaluation) reduces unemployment; a worsening (due to revaluation) reduces inflationary pressure.

These policy variables are measured on the axes of Figure 22.2, which allows us to show their joint effect on internal and external balance.[2] The vertical axis measures the exchange rate as the price of foreign currency, r. You must keep in mind that an *increase* in the price of foreign exchange (a movement up the axis) represents a *devaluation;* a cut in the price (movement down the axis) indicates a *revaluation.*

Assume that full employment prevails at a point such as K, corresponding to government expenditure (G_0, in this case) and the exchange rate r_0. Were we to lower the price of foreign currency (revalue), exports would fall relative to imports, and the contribution of the foreign balance to income would be reduced. Suppose now that the government wishes to raise public expenditure without upsetting internal balance, say, because more highways are needed. It does not wish to raise taxes (we assume them constant throughout). The increase in expenditure would be inflationary, but this effect can be curbed if the government cuts the price of foreign exchange. Revaluation discourages exports and,

---

[1] We shall assume that each nation specializes in its export good, or bundle of export goods. We can then avoid worrying about import-competing goods whose domestic prices change when the exchange rate changes.

[2] This diagram is based on one presented by T. W. Swan, "Longer-Run Problems of the Balance of Payments," *The Australian Economy: A Volume of Readings,* eds. H. W. Arndt and W. M. Corden. Melbourne: Cheshire Press, 1955, pp. 384–95. Reprinted in American Economic Association, *Readings in International Economics.* Homewood, Ill.: Richard D. Irwin, 1967.

FIGURE 22.2 Policies for Internal and External Balance

YY' shows combinations of the exchange rate and level of government spending that yield full employment. BB' shows combinations that yield balance-of-payments equilibrium. Combination K provides overall balance.

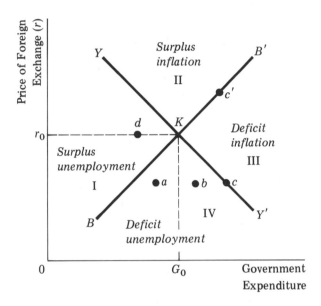

by making foreign goods cheaper at home, switches expenditure to imports. The trade balance (B, hereafter) becomes negative, and the government can raise G without disturbing full-employment income. A new combination of policies can thus be found, at a point like c, involving an increase of G and a reduction of r that will preserve internal balance. By this process we can find other combinations of the exchange rate and the government-controlled level of expenditure yielding full employment, and they will lie on a negatively sloped line in Figure 22.2, YY'. Any point on the line represents internal balance — we shall call it the "internal-balance schedule" — but every point indicates a different combination of the exchange rate and government expenditure. Any point to the right of YY' indicates too much government spending for the planned level of private expenditure, and thus potential inflationary pressure on the economy. Another way to interpret this balance is to say that, at the level of government spending, foreign exchange is too dear and therefore net sales abroad are too large. Every point to the left of YY', on the other hand, indicates a potential unemployment.[3]

External balance is affected by the price of foreign exchange, with B increasing when devaluation occurs (i.e., r increases). But B is also altered by policies that change the level of expenditure, because any policy-induced change in expenditure falls partly on imported goods and services. Assume again an increase in highway expenditure. It generates (through the multiplier) an increase in total income, which will be spent partly on foreign goods. The trade balance worsens. To preserve external balance the price of foreign currency must be raised. Exports will be encouraged, and consumers will retrench on imports. A new combination of G and r might give external balance at c'. Many combinations of exchange rate and government expenditure would be consistent with external balance. These will lie along a positively sloped line, BB' in Figure 22.2, that can be called the "external-balance schedule." Below this line, the exchange rate is too low for the current level of expenditure, and the external balance is in deficit. Above, the rate is too high, and an excess of exports over imports will appear.

By now we can see that only one combination of public expenditure and the exchange rate will yield external and internal balance at the same time, namely, the values corresponding to point K at the intersection of the YY' and BB' schedules. Any policy combination off the schedules indicates both external and internal imbalance; any point on one schedule but not at their intersection corresponds to one type of imbalance. We can go farther by identifying the exact economic ills indicated by points lying in the wedges between the YY' and BB' schedules — the "zones of imbalance" marked in Figure 22.2. They are:

Zone I: External surplus; internal unemployment
Zone II: External surplus; internal inflation
Zone III: External deficit; internal inflation
Zone IV: External deficit; internal unemployment

[3] In getting accustomed to Figure 22.2, you should note how sharply it differs from the diagrams usually employed in economic analysis. They ordinarily display the variable on one axis as a function of that on the other: quantity demanded as a function of price, or consumption as a function of income. Figure 22.2, however, is more complex. The dependent variables — the trade balance and aggregate demand — appear on neither axis. Each is a function of the policy variables shown on both axes. We graph values of government expenditure and the exchange rate that are consistent with desired levels of the trade balance and aggregate demand, but these levels cannot be illustrated on the axes. Analogies are found in Parts 1 and 2 of this book. Demand and supply curves show the response of output to changes in price. However, indifference curves (or isoquants) show combinations of commodities (or factors of production) that leave constant the level of income (or a firm's output, which is not illustrated directly on the axes).

Thus points *a* and *b* both indicate a deficit combined with unemployment; *c* involves an external deficit but full employment.

Selection of Policies

Figure 22.2 also shows us how policy should be employed to correct any imbalance. At point *c* the deficit calls for devaluation. Yet devaluation alone, which in the diagram would entail a movement vertically from *c* up to *c'* on *BB'*, would be inappropriate. Devaluation would restore external balance but throw the economy into inflation; the foreign balance improves and adds to private spending without public expenditure being reduced. A smaller devaluation, coupled with a cut in expenditure, is necessary to reach point *K*.

Now consider cases with neither internal nor external balance at the outset. At point *a*, for example, the deficit and unemployment clearly should be attacked by raising expenditure and devaluing the currency until internal and external balance are both reached at *K*. At point *b*, however, the same conditions call for devaluation combined with reduced expenditure. How can this be? As the rising price of foreign exchange improves the trade balance, the net foreign contribution to income rises. If public spending were not reduced, devaluation itself would move the economy vertically from *b* into Zone III, overshooting internal balance and unleashing inflationary pressures. The mix of policies appropriate for point *b* is thus qualitatively the same as for *c*; even if there is unemployment initially, expenditure reduction *may* be necessary to keep devaluation from throwing internal balance into inflation. Comparing cases *a* and *b*, we see that in Zone IV devaluation unambiguously helps the economy, but the appropriate direction of change for expenditure depends on whether public spending is initially above or below the level that would yield internal balance at *K*.

As you might suppose, the same sort of conclusion holds for each other zone of imbalance. In Zone I, for example, expanding government expenditure helps to combat both unemployment and trade surplus. Whether devaluation or revaluation is required, however, depends on the relative size of the two problems. Unlike the expenditure increase, which promotes improvement of both internal and external balance, any change in the exchange rate tends to move the economy toward one target but away from the other. Devaluation or revaluation must be used as a marginal corrective, applied with the appropriate increase of expenditure. Only in special cases like point *d* will one policy change — increasing expenditure — attain both internal and external balance. Despite the initial surplus no revaluation is needed.

Let us restate the main conclusions drawn from Figure 22.2: (1)

Many combinations of policy determining the level of public spending and the exchange rate will yield full employment, and many others will yield external balance, but only one will yield balance in both sectors. (2) Any policy instrument will generally change both internal and external balance. When one form of imbalance exists, one instrument is not enough. "If there is inflationary pressure, deflate!" may be good advice as far as it goes, but without revaluation it will create a new problem of external surplus if none existed before. (3) When there is imbalance in both sectors, one policy instrument can always be found that will move the economy toward both internal and external balance; only in special cases will it alone achieve balance in both. (4) When there is imbalance in both sectors, the appropriate direction of change in the other policy instrument is ambiguous, and cannot be calculated unless we know the correct value of that instrument in conditions of full balance.

We can say in passing that Figure 22.2 is an application of the general theory of economic policy. This theory assumes that all targets in the economy are interdependent, and that each policy instrument affects the attainment of all of the targets. One of its corollaries, illustrated above, is that one normally requires as many policy instruments as one has policy targets. With too few instruments at least one target will be missed, and the economy must usually settle for a "least bad" compromise. For instance, if the country were not free to change its exchange rate, and a rate lower than r_0 prevailed, expenditure would have to be set to yield the "least unpleasant" combination of external deficit and unemployment. Thus, in Figure 22.2 the points a, b, and c all lie on a horizontal line (not drawn) and thus correspond to an exchange rate lower than r_0. Expenditure could be set to preserve internal balance but with a large deficit (at c). Public spending could be cut to reduce the deficit slightly at the cost of some unemployment (at b), or cut heavily to remove much of the deficit at a heavy cost in unemployment (at a). Unless new alternatives can be found, the country must settle for a combination of evils.

22.3 BALANCE WITH FIXED EXCHANGE RATE

The analysis of Figure 22.2 tells us a good deal about organization of economic policy to attain both internal and external balance. We can demonstrate other aspects of this problem of economic policy by considering the following two questions: Will other combinations of policy instruments maintain internal and external balance? Can other important classes of international transactions, besides the trade balance, secure these policy targets?

In fact many instruments of policy can aid in bringing about internal and external balance. So far, only changes in the exchange rate have been used for their primary effect on international transactions. However, many other devices can accomplish the same purpose — namely, causing transactors in the home country, the rest of the world, or both, to switch their expenditures between home and foreign goods. We examined these alternatives in Chapter 18. Also, in referring to policies that change the level of expenditures we did not survey all policies that might do the job. The main candidates are fiscal and monetary policy. We shall now ask whether it makes any difference which of these is chosen for a role in stabilizing the economy. In the process we shall learn how to manage external balance through international capital flows.

The process of selecting policies described in section 22.2 supposes that nations are willing to change their exchange rates freely. That assumption generally fits the system of managed floating that has prevailed since 1973, under which the major industrial countries sometimes stabilize their exchange rates, sometimes nudge them to new levels (or let the exchange market do that job). But for a variety of reasons governments are often reluctant to change their exchange rates, and, indeed, under the Articles of Agreement of the International Monetary Fund they were committed to maintain fixed rates in the absence of "fundamental disequilibrium." Can they achieve both internal and external balance without changing the exchange rate?

Consider Figure 22.3. Its horizontal axis, identical to that of Figure 22.2, measures government expenditure. The vertical axis shows another variable that is subject to economic policy — the interest rate. (In practice many rates of interest persist in financial markets for loans or securities of varying riskiness and lifetime to maturity; we shall abstract from this diversity and suppose a single rate for a single type of security, such as bonds issued by "sound" corporations.) The interest rate can be influenced by the authorities through their control of the money supply, because a shrinkage leaves people feeling short of cash balances, and lowers the price of bonds and thereby raises the rate of interest. The interest rate in turn affects expenditure in the private sector of the economy, principally business investment. You should note that this formulation of the effect of monetary policy is a strictly Keynesian one, following from the model developed in Chapter 16. We implicitly assume that resources are underemployed and the price level stable, so that an increase in the money supply reduces the real interest rate and does not lead to expectations of inflation.

FIGURE 22.3   Effect of Fiscal and Monetary Policy
on Internal and External Balance

YY' and *BB'* schedules show combinations of fiscal and monetary policies
yielding internal and external balance. Policy combination *K* yields balance
overall.

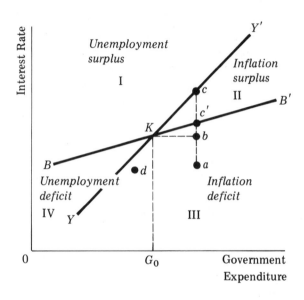

Internal balance, as before, depends on the right combination of the
two policy instruments.[4] But many "right combinations" can be found.
Starting from point *K* in Figure 22.3, where full employment is assumed to exist, suppose that the government desires to raise public
spending. Internal balance can be preserved by a rise in the interest
rate (reflecting a contraction of the money supply). The new internal
balance will lie northeast of *K*, at a point such as *c*, reflecting an easier
fiscal policy and a tighter monetary policy. All combinations of fiscal
and monetary policy yielding full employment fall on a line such as
YY', which has a positive slope.

---

[4] When we speak of a change in fiscal policy, alone, we assume that the interest
rate remains unchanged. A rise in government expenditure, and thus in total income, normally increases the demand for money for transactions. To keep the
interest rate from rising, monetary authorities would have to expand the money
supply to meet these transactions needs. Hence, when we speak of a change in
fiscal policy with monetary policy constant, we are holding the interest rate constant but not the money supply.

What about external balance? Suppose that point K represents initial external balance, and that the same policy changes as before are brought about, in order to observe their effect on external balance. An increase in public spending raises imports, because part of any increase in spending goes to buy goods and services from abroad. The offsetting contraction of monetary policy reduces private spending on both home and foreign goods. The right amount of monetary tightening offsets the worsening of the balance of trade caused by fiscal policy. A new point of external balance can be found northeast of K, and in general the external-balance schedule BB' will have a positive slope. Monetary contraction must be played against fiscal expansion in order to sustain external balance, just as to preserve internal balance.

YY' has been drawn steeper than BB'. This pattern reflects the role of international capital flows. In Section 19.3 we described how holders of financial wealth adjust their portfolios to changes in the yields on financial assets; by that process a rise in the home country's interest rate will cause domestic and foreign asset holders alike to shift their portfolios from foreign toward domestic securities. This increased export of securities is, of course, an inflow of capital and a positive change in the external balance. Thus, we generally expect a rise in a country's interest rate to improve external balance through the capital account.

Now return to the effects of a fiscal expansion offset by a monetary contraction. If the proportion of each dollar of expenditure devoted to imports is fixed, such offsetting shifts affect internal and external balance in the same proportions. Fiscal policy has no direct effect on international capital flows, so long as the interest rate remains constant. But a change in monetary policy does affect these flows. If monetary policy tightens, external balance improves in two ways. Not only are imports reduced, but receipts from abroad increase as capital is pulled into the country by the higher interest rate. The fiscal expansion worsens the balance of payments by increasing imports; a monetary contraction that would maintain internal balance makes an offsetting improvement in net external payments not only by causing an equal cut in import spending, but also by inducing a net improvement in the balance of capital flows. In Figure 22.3, the monetary contraction needed to restore *internal* balance, after an increase in government spending of Kb, is bc. But the monetary contraction needed to restore *external* balance is the smaller amount bc'. The external-balance schedule BB' is therefore flatter than the internal-balance schedule YY'. The two schedules intersect, and, as in Figure 22.2, only the combination of policies indicated by K will ensure simultaneous internal and external balance.[5]

[5] You should notice the differences between the external-balance schedule in Figure 22.3 and that in Figure 22.2. Each depicts policy combinations leading to zero

Policy Combinations

We can complete the analysis of Figure 22.3 by noticing the consequences of an inappropriate policy combination lying off the YY' and BB' schedules. Above YY' monetary policy is too tight for current fiscal policy, and unemployment occurs; below, monetary policy is too easy, and inflationary pressures are experienced. Above the external-balance schedule tight monetary policy both repels imports and attracts capital, provoking a payments surplus; conversely, points below BB' indicate a payments deficit. The four wedges converging on K once more indicate zones of imbalance, with differing combinations of internal and external imbalance. The Roman numerals identify them as in Figure 22.2; for example, Zone II again indicates external surplus and potential internal inflation.

Conclusions about the proper direction of change in the policy instruments also can be drawn from Figure 22.3 in the same way as from Figure 22.2. Point a lies in Zone III, and a deficit and inflationary pressure call for both a contraction of public spending and a rise in the rate of interest. The same problems at point b, however, would be solved by a contraction of fiscal policy alone; monetary policy is already tight enough to secure overall balance once the appropriate change in fiscal policy is made. At point c' external balance and inflationary pressure coexist. Fiscal policy must be tightened but monetary policy eased somewhat, in order to keep the fiscal contraction from throwing the balance of payments into surplus as inflationary pressures abate. Note that we can no longer neatly conclude, as we did from Figure 22.2, that in each zone of imbalance the direction of change for one policy instrument is unambiguous. In Zone III point a calls for fiscal contraction, as would any point lying between b and c'. At point d, however, a monetary contraction must be associated with fiscal expansion in order to secure a relatively large improvement in the balance of payments while removing only a relatively small amount of inflationary pressure. In Zone III, and in Zone I as well, the proper direction of change for both instruments depends on the relative sizes of the internal and external disequilibria. But, on the other hand, in Zones II and IV we can tell unambiguously the right direction of change for both instruments. In Zone IV unemployment and payments deficit are always fought by expansionary fiscal policy coupled with a tightening of monetary policy.

---

excess demand in the market for foreign exchange. In Figure 22.2 zero excess demand is secured by balance in the current account (with capital flows assumed nonexistent). In Figure 22.3 points on BB' generally involve an imbalance in the current account offset by an equal and opposite imbalance in the capital account.

The rising interest rate combats the restoration of full employment, but does less harm there than the good it does in eliminating the payments deficit; and the interest rate at any point in Zone IV is lower than it must be if balance is secured at point K. In the late 1950's and early 1960's, the United States suffered from unemployment combined with an external deficit (Zone IV); some economists urged on the basis of these theoretical considerations that fiscal policy should be eased and monetary policy tightened.[6]

Capital flows, if responsive to monetary policy, thus allow countries to secure overall balance without changing their exchange rates. The more mobile is capital, the less do interest rates change when monetary policy is used to secure overall balance. At the limit monetary policy can affect external balance without changing interest rates at all, and the BB' schedule becomes a horizontal line. At the same time changes in the money supply do not influence internal balance at all. Suppose that the central bank, neglecting this fact, applies its open-market policy and buys bonds, trying to place more cash in the hands of the public and to drive down the rate of interest (which is the same as driving up the price of bonds). Now, we expect that the public and the nation's financial institutions hold settled views on the money and bonds they wish to own, at any current rate of interest. After the central bank makes its purchase, they find themselves with more cash and less bonds than they prefer. They buy bonds, trying to restore their portfolios to the desired mix. Now, if capital were not mobile internationally, these efforts would drive down the rate of interest and accomplish the bank's goals. With capital internationally mobile, however, an unlimited supply of bonds can be bought abroad at the current price (interest rate). Hence the asset holders' efforts to restore their portfolios simply replace from abroad the bonds bought up by the central bank. The cash injected by the central bank's bond purchase is spent to buy bonds abroad. But the exchange rate is fixed, and this extra demand for foreign exchange requires the government to step into the exchange market, selling foreign exchange and taking up the excess supply of domestic currency. The central bank's cash injection winds up back in the government's pocket again! Neither the public's cash holdings nor the domestic interest rate have changed at all, and monetary policy only creates (or worsens) an external deficit.

Although we shall not develop the argument here, it can be shown that this frustration will not apply to fiscal policy. A cut in taxes or an

---

[6] Figure 22.3 and much of the analysis surrounding it is drawn from R. A. Mundell, "The Appropriate Use of Monetary and Fiscal Policy under Fixed Exchange Rates," *IMF Staff Papers,* 9 (March 1962): 70–77.

increase in government expenditure could stimulate total spending in the way described in the simple theory of fiscal policy.[7] Hence the government can stimulate employment at home if it picks the right policy.

Portfolio Adjustment — Some Qualifications

You may have noticed that this model paid no attention to the process of portfolio adjustment, developed in section 19.3, except for its most obvious implication that a rise in our country's real interest rate brings an inflow of capital. The model of portfolio adjustment implies two important qualifications to the analysis.

1. *Stock adjustment.* Consider the process by which holders of financial assets respond to a change in real interest rate differences between countries. They first shift some proportion of their total portfolio into securities carrying the higher interest rate. That shift of capital is in principle a one-shot stock adjustment and not a steady flow over time. Of course, the stock adjustment may be spread out over time. Not all investors readjust their portfolios every moment; some may wait for assurance that the higher interest rate will be sustained and warrants incurring the cost of the securities transactions. But the point remains that we should not think of the initial asset-stock response as a continuing steady flow. There is another effect of higher interest rates in a given country: In future years asset holders will choose to place more of their *new* savings in that country's securities than otherwise, and that change in behavior does represent an ongoing flow. But this change in the ongoing flow should be a good deal smaller than the initial adjustment of the outstanding stock, because the flow of new saving adds only a small proportion each year to the outstanding stock of securities.

In terms of Figure 22.3 these considerations imply that BB' describes the first shot of a stock-adjustment process whereas YY' represents an ongoing status of income flows. We cannot expect this figure to provide us with a policy combination that can be left in place to yield the same result period after period. In effect BB' is flat in the short run (when the

[7] In fact, capital mobility helps the application of fiscal policy. When the government tries to stimulate spending through fiscal measures, it increases its own deficit. It must sell bonds to finance this deficit, and the bond sales would ordinarily drive up the interest rate and partially offset the stimulus of the government deficit. With capital perfectly mobile, however, the extra government bonds face a perfectly elastic demand abroad, and can be sold without driving up the domestic interest rate or unleashing this offset. For a fuller account see R. A. Mundell, *International Economics*. New York: Macmillan, 1968, chap. 18; and R. I. McKinnon and W. E. Oates, *The Implications of International Economic Integration for Monetary, Fiscal, and Exchange-Rate Policy*. Princeton Studies in International Finance, no. 16. Princeton, N.J.: International Finance Section, Princeton University, 1966.

large stock adjustment occurs) and gets steeper in subsequent periods when the higher interest rate affects only the flow component of international capital movements.

2. *Interest payments.* When our country imports capital it must subsequently pay interest to foreign lenders, making the current-account balance in subsequent years more negative (less positive) than it would otherwise be. Each time it imports more capital, the interest bill goes up. This consideration also affects the interpretation we place on the BB' function. If capital is flowing in and the interest-payment obligation rising, it takes tighter fiscal policy, a higher interest rate, or both to maintain external balance in any given period of time. Thus we have a second reason for expecting the BB' schedule to shift each period of time.

22.4 THE STRATEGY OF INTERNATIONAL ECONOMIC POLICY

The major lesson emerging from our analysis is that each policy change affects both balances in the economy. The only sure way for a government to get them both right is to deal with both at once. To reach the real counterpart of the overall-balance point K in our diagram, authorities in charge of policy instruments need to know the exact size of the imbalances and what is being done with other instruments. They must also know the response of the economy to each change of policy. These requirements imply continual sessions in the cabinet room, so that the department or agency in charge of each policy instrument makes its decisions only with full knowledge of what the others are doing — and all of them working with accurate short-term forecasts of the economy's movements.

As the newspapers constantly remind us, national economic policy is not made so neatly. Monetary authorities may know what actions the fiscal policymakers are taking, but they may disagree or fail to coordinate their actions. They may differ on the proper targets for the economy: A treasury may be willing to accept a 10 percent rate of inflation, a central bank may not. The time they need to swing different policy instruments into action may vary, due to political constraints or other factors. Because of these limitations on policy-making, we would take comfort from a method of getting the economy to full equilibrium that is simpler than the simultaneous quest for balance. Is there an easier way to do it?

Policy Assignment

A candidate is at hand, known as *policy assignment.* Traditionally each policy instrument has been "assigned" to a target. The intelligent layman, asked why a country should devalue its currency, will answer: "To get rid of its international payments deficit." As we saw above, a better answer would be: "To get rid of its international payments deficit, unemployment, or both." Yet, as we contemplate the limits on the formation and coordination of policy, the layman may be right after all. Suppose that authorities setting each policy instrument are told to pursue a single target, ignoring the incidental effects of their actions on other targets. Following our example from section 22.3, we might assign the monetary authorities to maintain external balance, adjusting the interest rate only in regard to the current balance of payments, while the fiscal authorities change public spending only to correct internal imbalance. Figure 22.4, reproducing the principal features of Figure 22.3, shows how this practice would work.

Suppose the initial situation is that shown at point g, one of inflationary pressure and a potential payments surplus. The monetary authorities, observing the surplus, lower the rate of interest. If they do so by the appropriate amount the surplus is eliminated at point h on the external-balance schedule. Inflationary pressure remains, however, and the fiscal authorities now act, reducing expenditure to secure internal balance at i. This action restores the payments surplus in part, and the interest rate is again lowered by the monetary authorities to secure external balance at j. You can easily see that this process ultimately converges on full balance at K. Each authority's action re-creates a problem for the other, but the problem is smaller each time around.

What if the authorities had drawn different assignments, with the fiscal authorities changing expenditure to secure external balance and the monetary officials pursuing internal balance? Starting again from point g, the monetary authorities raise the interest rate to combat inflation, gaining internal balance at f. Fiscal policy next attacks the payments surplus by expansionary measures leading to point e. The inflationary pressure is now worse than it was at g, and the interest rate is again raised. This assignment, rather than stabilizing the economy, renders it unstable and forces the authorities to take larger and larger steps in pursuit of their respective targets! Clearly the assignments make a great deal of difference.

This conclusion is not affected by our arbitrary choice of point g (in Zone II) as a starting point. An initial situation of inflation and payments deficit at point g' would yield the same results. If the monetary authorities tried to eliminate the deficit, the interest rate would be raised to bring the system to point h, and the sequence would continue $i, j, \ldots$. But if they raised the interest rate to eliminate inflation, the system would come to f and continue on an unstable course. This demonstration does not depend on our assumption that the monetary authorities act

FIGURE 22.4 Effects of Assigning Fiscal and Monetary
Policy to Pursue Individual Policy Targets

Assigning monetary policy to external balance and fiscal policy to internal
balance produces stable adjustment path *ghij*. Opposite assignment produces
unstable path *gfe*. . . .

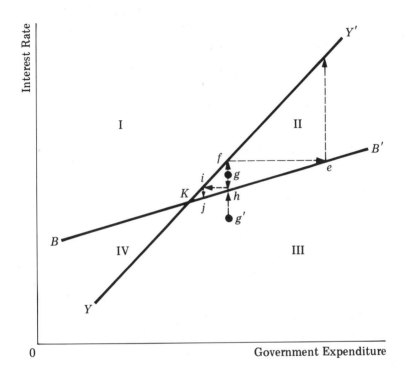

first. If this role falls to the fiscal authorities, the first adjustment is
horizontal from *g*. You should be able to show that the same conclusions
about stability will then follow.

These lessons about the importance of making the right assignment
can also be drawn from the policy system shown in Figure 22.2. Unless
the economy is very small and open, the exchange rate is likely to have
a particularly strong influence on external balance, fiscal policy on internal balance. Assigning the instruments in that way produces a stable
system, whereas the opposite assignment causes the policies to fight
against each other and create ever-widening disturbances.

22.5 POLICY PRACTICE IN THE 1970's

The policy models set forth in this chapter came under a cloud in the 1970's because their reliance on Keynesian mechanisms of adjustment left them ill-suited for dealing with inflationary conditions. Excessive aggregate demand in these models threatens *potential* inflation, averted by shifting to the right mix of policies. Actual inflation, however, spoils the game by bringing about continuous shifts in the YY' and BB' functions, especially BB'. Inflation in the country depicted in Figure 22.3, for example, not only shifts BB' by worsening the trade balance each period; it also undermines the analysis more fundamentally by raising the question of whether monetary policy can actually affect the real rate of interest, once people's expectations are fully attuned to the inflationary consequences of increases in the money supply.

Policy Coordination with Inflation

Let us see what happens to the analysis of policy coordination in an inflationary environment, using the model set forth in Figure 22.2 as our framework. The first problem is to define what is meant by internal balance. For a time economists placed their hopes on the concept of a *Phillips curve*, which embodied the hypothesis that there is a stable relation between the rate of unemployment and the rate of inflation. A country could achieve a higher level of employment if it accepted a higher rate of inflation. An unemployment rate of 6 percent might be consistent with 5 percent inflation, but lowering the rate to 5 percent might demand acceptance of 8 percent inflation, and so forth. Given this trade-off, the thinking went, a country had two choices. It could look for more policy instruments, such as "incomes policy" or plain unvarnished price and wage controls, that would reduce the inflation rate consistent with a given rate of unemployment. Or it could accept the trade-off for what it was and define "internal balance" as some best-attainable combination of inflation and unemployment. Such a stable combination may not be sustainable,[8] but let us suppose for the moment that it is. The internal balance schedule is redefined to encompass that preferred combination of inflation and unemployment. There is no assurance, though, that the inflation-unemployment trade-off chosen by

---

[8] A monetarist would insist that in the long run a country has no trade-off between inflation and unemployment. Once the public's expectations are fully attuned to the consequences of monetary expansion (either as a primary policy instrument, or to finance an expansionary fiscal policy), the whole adjustment comes in the price level while unemployment remains parked at its "natural level." If expansionary policies have temporarily coaxed the unemployment rate below this natural level, it will eventually drop back to the natural level as inflation becomes fully anticipated.

the economy at hand is the same as that chosen in the rest of the world. Suppose the country's preferred inflation rate is higher. Now consider Figure 22.5, which reproduces the essentials of Figure 22.2. We quickly recognize that overall balance at K cannot be sustained for long. If internal balance involves an annual increase in the price level and prices abroad remain (for instance) unchanged, the nation's goods in foreign prices grow steadily more expensive at the initial equilibrium exchange rate r_0. To maintain external balance with a higher home price level and the same government expenditure, the exchange rate must be increased to offset the deteriorating trade balance. This is true for any point on BB', not just for K; the whole external-balance schedule shifts upward. By the same token, at any level of government expenditure the export surplus grows smaller (or the deficit larger) as the price level rises, and a higher price of foreign exchange is needed to sustain internal balance. The internal-balance schedule also shifts upward. It is clear that a continual depreciation of the domestic currency is needed to sustain both internal and external balance.

Experience with Policy-Making

One is curious about the relation between the neat models of policy formation explained above and the policy-setting process actually followed by the industrial countries. Are internal and external balance pursued in these ways? If not, why not? The actual experience of policy-making is too diverse and hard to interpret to allow any detailed account here. But we can venture a few generalizations of the roughest sort.

The analysis of Figures 22.3 and 22.4 dates from the 1960's when the industrial countries were struggling to maintain fixed exchange rates that were departing farther and farther from their equilibrium values. When countries did not perceive external balance as a problem, they tended to use both their fiscal- and monetary-policy instruments for pursuit of internal balance. When a serious disequilibrium arose, however, there was a tendency to assign monetary policy to external balance, keeping fiscal policy for internal balance or leaving it passive. Also, additional controls would be drawn into play, such as the restrictions on capital outflow with which the United States nursed its external balance through the late 1960's. These extra controls can be understood in the context of policy assignment, but the whole package was not in the event sufficient to save the 1960's structure of exchange rates.

Because countries had in practice not found sufficient policy instruments to maintain internal and external balance with fixed exchange rates, the abandonment of fixed rates in 1973 was viewed as a boon for effective policy-making. It relieved the pursuit of internal balance from the constraint of the balance of payments, and indeed allowed the ex-

FIGURE 22.5   Internal and External Balance
with Inflation at Home

Inflation at home tends to shift both YY' and BB' upward. The equilibrium
exchange rate must rise.

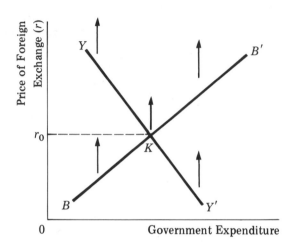

change rate to serve as a policy instrument (the analysis of Figure 22.2).
Studies of the major industrial countries' policy systems after 1973 confirmed this independence and the greater scope it allowed for using
policy instruments for pursuing domestic goals. They have also faulted
the wisdom with which the new-found independence was used. Exchange-
rate levels have been manipulated to serve many purposes — sometimes
to promote external balance but also to support internal-balance objectives, including the control of inflation. Exchange rates have been manipulated by means of many tools — controls on international capital flows
and domestic monetary-policy instruments as well as the use of foreign-
exchange reserves. There was again a tendency to assign monetary policy
to the pursuit of external balance, or at least divert it to that use when
a nation perceived a serious problem of external imbalance.[9] The management of floating exchange rates in the 1970's can also be seen in the
context of policy assignment. In 1979, with a second major oil-price

[9] A useful analysis of policy-making during the period 1973–1975 is provided by
Stanley W. Black, *Floating Exchange Rates and National Economic Policy*. New
Haven: Yale University Press, 1977. Chapters 3–5. Also see Otmar Emminger,
The D-Mark in the Conflict Between Internal and External Equilibrium, 1948–75.
Essays in International Finance, no. 122. Princeton: International Finance Sec-
tion, Princeton University, 1977.

increase upon them, several industrial countries sought to encourage the appreciation of their currencies (to avoid inflation) while using various fiscal measures to avoid too much reduction of domestic employment.

22.6 SUMMARY

Economic policy can aim at both internal balance (employment and price-stability targets) and external balance (equilibrium in international payments) if enough instruments are available. By setting both the exchange rate and government expenditure simultaneously at the right levels, internal and external balance can be obtained. Any departure entails imbalance in the form of deficit or surplus abroad, inflation or unemployment at home. One cannot jump to conclusions, by observing which of these ills prevail, about the right direction of change for each policy instrument. Each affects both internal and external balance, and before changing one you must observe its standing relative to the level that would produce full balance.

Even if the exchange rate cannot be varied, the adroit use of fiscal and monetary policy can secure both internal and external balance in the short run. This is the case if monetary policy affects external balance through changes in international capital flows as well as through the current account. Then a deficit coupled with unemployment is curable by tightening monetary policy while easing fiscal policy: Fiscal policy has relatively more leverage on employment and can bring about a net increase in income; the greater leverage of monetary policy on the foreign balance effects a net improvement in the flow of international payments. These conclusions are modified substantially when we recognize the process of portfolio adjustment.

This "pure theory" of economic policy requires a lot of information and coordination. A less ambitious approach is to instruct the authorities managing each policy instrument to pursue a single target. They then may approach full balance through a series of moves. Because each policy affects both targets, every time one policy lever is pulled it spoils the balance just achieved by the other policy-making agency. If the "assignment" is correct, however, these displacements will be smaller every time around. An incorrect assignment produces larger and larger displacements and destabilizes the economy. Correct assignment requires instructing each policymaker to pursue the target on which his instrument has the stronger leverage.

These models rest on Keynesian mechanisms of adjustment and fit rather poorly to circumstances in which inflation is under way. Even if a country can manage to select an internal-balance target that represents some combination of unemployment and inflation, it will have difficulty maintaining overall balance unless its chosen inflation rate should happen to match that of the rest of the world. The policy-making processes we actually observe do not resemble the models very well, because countries tend to set all policy instruments on domestic objectives and to address external imbalance only when it becomes insistent. The shift to flexible exchange rates in the 1970's therefore gave the industrial countries appreciable new freedom for dealing with their policy problems.

SUGGESTIONS FOR FURTHER READING

Black, Stanley W. *Floating Exchange Rates and National Economic Policy.* New Haven: Yale University Press, 1977. Studies actual patterns of policy choice in five countries.

Fellner, William et al. *Maintaining and Restoring Balance in International Payments.* Princeton: Princeton University Press, 1966. Chapters 2, 6, 7, 8, 10, and 13 deal with the choice among policy instruments for internal and external balance.

Meade, J. E. *The Balance of Payments.* London: Oxford University Press, 1951. Parts 3 and 4 provide a classic discussion of the theory of economic policy in an open economy.

Mundell, R. A. "The Appropriate Use of Monetary and Fiscal Policy under Fixed Exchange Rates," *IMF Staff Papers,* 9 (March 1962): 70–77. Pioneer analysis of internal and external balance without exchange-rate changes.

Swan, T. W. "Longer-Run Problems of the Balance of Payments," American Economic Association, *Readings in International Economics.* Homewood, Ill.: Richard D. Irwin, 1968. Chapter 27 demonstrates the joint use of exchange-rate changes and fiscal policy for internal and external balance.

Whitman, Marina v. N. *Policies for Internal and External Balance.* Special Papers in International Economics, no. 9. Princeton: International Finance Section, Princeton University, 1970. An advanced formal survey of the theory of internal and external balance.

23

International Reserves and Liquidity

Governments often choose to intervene in the market for foreign exchange, to keep the exchange rate from changing or hold it at a different level from what the market would choose. Under the Bretton Woods system, most countries accepted a formal obligation to peg their exchange rates at official values. Since 1973 many have shifted to a "managed float," sometimes placing a restraining hand on movements of their exchange rates, at other times allowing market forces free play.

We saw in Chapter 15 that a government can affect the price of foreign exchange in two ways. It can impose controls, taxes, and other policies that shift the commercial demand and supply curves. Or it can mop up excess demand or supply by using or acquiring international reserves. In this chapter we shall investigate the demand and supply of international reserves, and the effects of their creation and use.

23.1 THE DEMAND FOR INTERNATIONAL RESERVES

When the government intervenes to affect the price of foreign exchange, it makes the country's commercial purchases from the rest of the world differ from its commercial sales. When it spends reserves, purchases exceed sales; when it acquires them in the marketplace, sales exceed purchases. We can thus regard international reserves as a device to avert the continuous adjustment of a country's foreign purchases to its foreign sales. A country's demand for reserves somewhat resembles a household's demand for cash balances. The paycheck comes in at the end of the month, but the family's purchases are spaced out irregularly over the month. Hence it is both handy and prudent *on the average* to keep some cash balances, even though these may dwindle to nothing when the next paycheck is due. Countries likewise hold reserves to see them through alternating periods of surplus and deficit; we shall try to explain this long-term average level that they desire. It will depend on the *economic events* impinging on a country's foreign-exchange market, the *automatic adjustment mechanisms* responding to payments disturbances, and the *economic policies* used to bring the market into equilibrium.

The forces that determine each class of international transactions are apt to shift from time to time, pulling the demand-supply balance in the exchange market back and forth. Some of these disturbances may be regular or cyclical. A country that has a heavily seasonal tourist business may find its balance of payments regularly strong during the tourist season and weak in the off-season. Some of the forces affecting the balance are transitory shocks, while others represent a permanent new state of affairs. A crop failure creates a one-shot deficit in the balance of a country heavily dependent on this primary export; the development elsewhere of a cheaper synthetic substitute may cause a persistent deficit.

These forces combine to explain the historic pattern of disturbances in a country's exchange market and foretell the sizes of the shocks it can expect in the future. The reserves needed to finance the resulting deficits will depend, however, not just on these disturbances but also on the automatic adjustment mechanisms restoring equilibrium when external balance is upset. In Chapters 16 and 17 we saw that adjustment mechanisms involving cash balances, the price level, and real incomes theoretically will push a disturbed external balance back toward or to equilibrium. A deficit sets these mechanisms to work. Whenever the adjustment remains incomplete, however, reserves continue to flow out. Thus the more quickly these mechanisms work, the smaller is the total imbalance resulting from a disturbance, and the smaller the cumulative change in reserves needed to finance it. Hence we can say that the average reserves a country needs to hold will be smaller, if the corrections brought by automatic mechanisms of adjustment are speedier.

Furthermore, the demand for reserves depends on the policies chosen to eliminate an imbalance once it occurs. The government needs fewer reserves if it is willing to let its exchange rate change frequently. The faster and more freely it can and will apply policies to promote adjustment, the fewer reserves it needs. But countries are often unwilling to let the market determine their exchange rates and unable to apply other policies fast enough to avoid external imbalances. Policy instruments need time to take effect. A government often prefers to delay, in the face of some disturbance, before shifting its policies — perhaps from honest uncertainty about the permanence of the disturbance, perhaps from a natural tendency to procrastinate and hope that the winds of chance will turn favorable. Finally, there may be no effective policy for some transitory disturbances, and the best policy hence may be to "finance" the imbalance through a change in reserves rather than to shift policy to correct it.

Figure 23.1 suggests the combined effect of disturbances, adjustments, and policy actions on the demand for international reserves. Curve *A* shows the deficits and surpluses in a country's balance of payments caused by the disturbances striking it if no adjustment takes place. Curve *B* shows the residue of deficits and surpluses that might remain after automatic market adjustments and the best available eco-

FIGURE 23.1 Relation among Payments Disturbances, Automatic and Policy-induced Adjustments, and Changes in Reserves

Level of reserves rises during periods of surplus in "official settlements" balance, falls during periods of deficit.

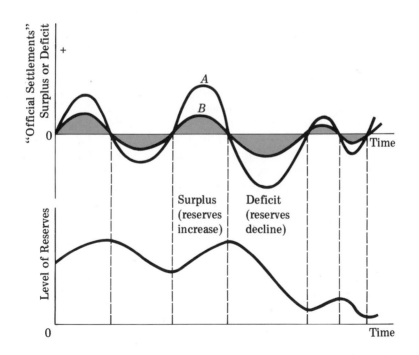

nomic policies have taken effect.[1] The areas between curve B and the base line show the cumulative gains in reserves associated with surplus (the hills) and the cumulative losses due to deficit (the valleys). The demand for reserves of a nation anticipating such a pattern would be related to the maximum drawdown that it expects. In the lower part of Figure 23.1 you see that we arbitrarily started the country out with barely enough reserves to finance its worst net payments deficit over the period of time shown.

Whatever average level of reserves a country holds, it faces some chance of running out during a string of bad years. The larger the cumulative losses it expects, and the smaller the chance it will take of going broke, the more reserves it must hold on the average.

Some other practical factors should also affect a country's demand for reserves. The amount demanded probably bears some relation to the size of its national economy — national income, or money supply — and of its foreign-trade sector.[2] Therefore, as a rough judgment, we expect the demand for reserves to grow with world income and trade. The opportunity cost of capital should also affect the country's demand for reserves. Reserves tie up purchasing power that could be invested in machines, foreign securities, or other income-yielding assets. These alternatives for a poor country may be valuable and urgent. Resources should be invested in reserves only up to the point where the worth of the last dollar of reserves in hand just equals the yield foregone on their best alternative use. The same rule should apply to the country's decision to use its reserves: It is dipping into capital, and should finance a deficit only if the net inflow of goods, services, or assets meets the opportunity cost of sacrificing the reserve asset.

Discussions of the demand for reserves sometimes distinguish between *transactions* and *precautionary* considerations. The government's guess at the average level of reserves it needs to keep from running out during bad times rests on an analysis of normal international transactions and their fluctuations. But a government aiming to peg its rate at a declared value must be able to stave off speculative attacks. The public, watching the level of reserves decline during a period of cumulative deficits, may fear an imminent devaluation and switch their assets into foreign cur-

---

[1] Notice that we give the government the benefit of the doubt by assuming that it always moves the balance in the right direction. Wrong measures, or wrongly timed ones, could make curve B lie outside A and increase the quantity of reserves needed.

[2] If most of the disturbances to its external balance arise from its domestic income circuit, it follows from the analysis of income changes presented in Chapter 16 that average reserves should increase with the ratio of imports to GNP. On the sources of disturbance, see E. Tower and M. M. Courtney, "Exchange-Rate Flexibility and Macroeconomic Stability," *Review of Economics and Statistics,* 56 (May 1974): 215–24.

rencies to avoid a capital loss. Precautionary reserves aim to avert such a speculative flight of capital, which inflates whatever underlying forces are responsible for the deficit and can force a country to devalue needlessly.

23.2 SUPPLY OF INTERNATIONAL RESERVES AND LIQUIDITY

We have examined the demand for international reserves without paying attention to the substance demanded, or the source of its supply. Reserves must consist of foreign currencies that can be used to defend the value of the holder's currency in the exchange market, or assets that can be converted into such currencies with no questions asked. And a country's international *liquidity* encompasses its opportunities to borrow reserves as well as the reserves in hand. We shall review the types of reserves and credit facilities and their historical origins.

Foreign Currencies

By far the largest proportion of international reserves are held in the form of national currencies, and the amount has increased greatly in the last few years, as is shown in Table 23.1. Countries whose currencies serve as reserve assets for other nations are called reserve-currency countries, and their balance-of-payments positions take on great importance for the growth of reserves. We saw in Chapter 15 that a country's net balance-of-payments position is measured (under the "official settlements" definition) by the change in its reserves position. That change consists of any increase in its own official reserves *minus* any increase in its currency held as official reserves by other countries. Thus, it follows from the accounting rule that an increase in foreign-currency reserves must be associated with a payments deficit of the reserve-currency country if no reserves are being created in other forms.

Throughout the 1970's about three-fourths of foreign-currency reserves were held in U.S. dollars (including Euro-dollars). The U.S. role as a major reserve-currency country evolved unconsciously after World War II. Immediately after the war, the United States was the only major industrial nation not to have suffered massive destruction of her productive capacity. The U.S. dollar hence was prized for its power to purchase the goods needed to keep consumption at a tolerable level in the European countries while they rebuilt their economies. Dollars were carefully conserved by European central banks, and their use closely controlled. From this experience the use of the dollar as a principal reserve medium was natural, because the success of European recovery

TABLE 23.1 Levels of International Reserves, Selected Years
1955–1979 (Billions of Special Drawing Rights)[a]

End of year	Gold [b]	Foreign exchange	Reserve positions in IMF	SDRs	Total reserves [c]
1955	35.4	18.5	1.9	0	55.8
1960	38.0	20.2	3.6	0	61.8
1965	41.8	25.2	5.4	0	72.4
1970	37.2	44.5	7.7	3.1	92.5
1975	121.6	136.9	12.6	8.8	279.9
1976	117.1	159.8	17.7	8.7	303.4
1977	137.4	200.1	18.1	8.1	363.7
1978	176.7	220.8	14.8	8.1	420.5
1979	360.0	245.3	11.8	12.5	629.6

Source: International Monetary Fund, *Annual Report of the Executive Directors for the Fiscal Year Ending April 30, 1975.* Washington, 1975, p. 34; International Monetary Fund, *International Financial Statistics,* 33 (April 1980).
[a] A Special Drawing Right's value was equal to one U.S. dollar until 1971 and rose afterward to about $1.30 in 1979.
[b] Gold is valued at its one-time official price of one SDR per ounce through 1970, at the London market price after 1970.
[c] Rows may not add to total reserves because of rounding errors.

was measured, during the 1950's, by the ability of countries to retain and augment their holdings of dollars. By the end of that decade, however, the realization dawned that many European countries were running substantial payments surpluses and the United States was running the counterpart deficit.

Throughout the 1960's the United States struggled with this deficit. Its conquest was inhibited partly by a political unwillingness to undertake decisive actions, but also by honest doubt whether eliminating the deficit would serve the interests of the trading world. No more deficits meant no more international reserves of any kind because (as Table 23.1 shows) other sources were growing slowly if at all. Yet too much deficit meant that foreign holders would become nervous about the possibility of the dollar's price declining in terms of other currencies. Was the U.S. deficit caused by the excess demand of other industrial nations for international reserves, or by an excess supply of dollars due to U.S. unwillingness to eliminate its deficit? Americans saw the Europeans as mercantilists who cherished their external surpluses; the Europeans countered that the United States was foisting unwanted dollars on them while American multinational corporations went about buying up the real assets of their domestic companies. There is no way to decide who was right, because it would have sufficed for *either* side to take action against the mutual imbalance. But the point remains that the size of that imbalance was entangled with the growth of international reserves, and there is no way to avoid that connection when national currencies serve as a chief reserves medium.

Gold

Gold has been the other major asset held as international reserves. Once it served as the sole form of international reserves and, indeed, as the base controlling the level of nations' money supplies under the gold standard (see Chapter 17). By 1970 it had shrunk to two-fifths of international reserves, and its share failed to expand until 1979, despite the explosion of its market price. It continued to play a vital role in the operation of the international monetary system until 1971. Recently countries agreed to phase gold out as an active international reserve, as we shall see, but it remains a glittering relic of monetary systems past. Gold's role was suggested by the name of the monetary system operating from World War II to 1971 — *the gold-exchange standard.* Countries were willing to hold much of their international reserves in foreign currency (dollars) because they had enough confidence that the dollar would both retain its value in terms of other currencies and remain convertible into gold, which by tradition they still viewed as the "ultimate" form of international reserves. The U.S. gold stock thus provided "backing" for the dollar, because the United States stood ready to exchange gold with foreign central banks at a price then fixed at $35 an ounce. Those banks could hold dollars in the form of United States Treasury bills, gaining a modest interest income while enjoying assurance that the dollar would not depreciate against gold.

The pyramid of the gold-exchange standard grew more unstable throughout the 1960's. The superstructure of dollar reserves kept growing, but the "base" of U.S. monetary gold began to shrink in 1959. The increasing leverage of the gold-exchange standard exacerbated the problem of the U.S. deficit and the quantity of dollars in official reserves. It shriveled the confidence of foreign holders of dollars — governments and private citizens alike — that the United States would remain able to convert its short-term liabilities into gold. Several forces retarded the growth of the world's monetary gold stock. Because gold's price stayed fixed while production costs rose, the supply of new gold failed to expand. Commercial demand continued to grow. And hoarders concerned with maintaining the value of their wealth increasingly bought gold as a speculative asset. The United States and other governments were caught in the middle: As the speculators' and hoarders' demands for gold came to outrun the new commercial supply, they actually lost gold from official reserves.

Because this loss clearly threatened to bring down the gold-exchange standard, the central banks agreed in 1968 to stop selling gold to private parties and to trade it only among themselves, still at $35 an ounce. This decision severed the private market for gold from the official market, and the commercial price quickly shot above $35 an ounce. The central banks would thereafter gain no more gold, but at least they could stop their losses.

Gold's status as the foundation of the international monetary system ended in August 1971 when the United States, faced with steadily eroding confidence that it could meet its foreign liabilities, refused to sell gold even to foreign central banks. This action cut the final linkage between the dollar and gold, leaving foreign countries to decide as they would how much their currencies' values would rise against the dollar. In order to avert appreciations of their currencies on the exchange markets, they had to buy up more dollars, now supplied by the United States on the basis of "no exchanges, no refunds." Between 1971 and 1973 surplus countries took in substantial flows of dollars in order to curb the appreciation of their own currencies. Then came the massive increase in oil prices, and currency reserves continued to rise rapidly, now falling into the hands of the oil-exporting countries.

Special Drawing Rights

The troubles with the gold-exchange standard in the 1960's led to widespread support for the creation of new reserve assets. If gold and dollars were not supplying all the reserves countries wished to hold, another asset could be added. And if the public's fear for the value of the dollar endangered the system's stability, the new asset could gradually displace the dollar as a reserves medium. Special Drawing Rights (SDRs) were therefore devised and accepted by members of the International Monetary Fund. Countries could use their SDRs under agreed rules to buy foreign currencies either from countries with balance-of-payments surpluses or from the International Monetary Fund. Between 1970 and 1972, $9 billion of SDRs were created. They constitute a small share of international reserves, but they hold promise for a larger role in the future.

Before 1971 an SDR was defined to have the same value as a U.S. dollar's worth of gold, so that a devaluation of the dollar against gold would also devalue it against SDRs. In 1974, however, with the values of most major currencies subject to the forces of the market, the method of valuing SDRs was changed. The SDR is now a "currency basket," valued as a weighted sum of certain widely traded national currencies. If one of those currencies depreciates, the value of an SDR falls by a small proportion in terms of every other currency and rises by a larger proportion against the depreciated one. The contents of the currency basket are reconsidered every five years under an agreed procedure, and currencies may shuffle into and out of the basket as changes occur in countries' importance in international trade and finance. Beginning in 1981 the Fund simplified the SDR's valuation, cutting the number of currencies from sixteen to five, the U.S. dollar (weight of 42 percent), the DM (19 percent), French franc, yen, and pound sterling (13 percent each). The change sought to broaden the SDR's use as a commercial unit of account.

Forms of International Credit

As most households discover, it is not necessary to keep cash on hand if credit is readily available. On the other hand, it is hard to secure easy credit unless one holds some cash. Both propositions also apply to international reserves. Various borrowing facilities have been devised for countries temporarily needing reserves, but they do not eliminate the need to own reserves.

The International Monetary Fund, born of the Bretton Woods Conference in 1944, began business in 1946 as an international organization to lend deficit countries additional reserves and to promote the removal of restrictions on international payments and the orderly adjustment of exchange rates. It held a pool of currencies and gold contributed by its members and made temporary loans of currencies to members needing more foreign-exchange reserves. The method by which members contribute resources and take out loans was changed in the 1970's, as we explain below. Each member of the Fund is assigned a quota based on its national income, international reserves, the level of imports, the variability of its exports, and the size of its exports relative to national income. The quota fills four functions: It determines the amount of the member's initial contribution of currency resources to the Fund, defines the size of the borrowings he can make from the Fund, sets the member's share of any SDRs created by the IMF and allocated to its members, and fixes the member's voting power in Fund decision-making. IMF quotas are subject to review every five years and have been increased several times. An increase of 32.5 percent took effect in 1978, and that same year the Board of Governors started the process that would bring another 50 percent increase (to a total of SDR 58.6 billion, around $76 billion in 1980 U.S. dollars).

The IMF got off to a slow start in the 1940's. Would-be borrowers just after World War II needed not short-term credit but long-term loans or gifts. These needs were filled in some measure by assistance from the United States under the Marshall Plan and other programs, and the Fund in essence sat out the period of postwar reconstruction. Borrowings from the IMF increased sharply around 1956, however, and the Fund has kept busy ever since, although with a shifting pattern of activities. Up to the early 1970's one could place a meaningful estimate on the total size of the credit facilities available in the IMF; at that time the Fund's unused credit facilities were about one-third of the total reserves listed in Table 23.1. Recently, however, the Fund has opened up many new "windows" through which members can borrow, under a dizzying array of terms. Also, it has been less rule-bound in handling loans. Hence there is no longer a meaningful total figure for the extra liquidity that the Fund can provide. The following list of special lending arrangements adopted by the Fund shows how it has responded to changing international monetary problems.[3]

1. *Stand-by arrangements.* A member anticipating the need to borrow from the Fund can work out a contingent stand-by arrangement in advance, saving delay — and the tactical disadvantage of giving notice to speculators — when a loan is actually needed.

2. *General arrangements to borrow.* In the early 1960's the Fund appeared short of currencies that borrowers could actually use in the market to stabilize their exchange rates. Its assets consisted of its members' contributions, with each one remitting the value of its quota 25 percent in gold, 75 percent in its own currency. The Fund's gold holdings were effectively immobile, and not all currencies were traded widely enough to prove useful on the exchange markets. In 1962 ten leading IMF members agreed to lend the Fund jointly a maximum of $6 billion of their currencies when needed by any of the ten.

3. *Compensatory financing of export fluctuations.* In 1963 the Fund added a special facility for lending to countries, usually less-developed, whose exports fluctuated in value. Such "compensatory financing" of temporary sags in exports, ordinarily limited to 50 percent of the member's quota, is additional to its regular borrowing privileges from the Fund. Because the export fluctuations of the developing countries do not tend strongly to coincide with one another, the facility for compensatory financing plays a useful function of pooling risks.[4]

4. *Oil facility.* In 1974 the Fund created a temporary lending facility to help less-developed members finance the initial impact of the increased cost of their oil imports, following the major price rise in 1973.

---

[3] A clear description of the Fund's many activities is provided in a special supplement (dated September 1979) to the *IMF Survey,* September 17, 1979.

[4] L. M. Goreux, "Compensatory Financing: the Cyclical Pattern of Export Shortfalls," *IMF Staff Papers,* 24 (November 1977): 613–41.

5. *Extended facility* and *supplementary financing facility*. Since the major industrial countries largely abandoned fixed exchange rates in 1973, they have been only occasional customers of the IMF. The Fund has accordingly shifted attention toward the needs of the developing countries. Among lending facilities designed for them, the extended facility provides longer-term finance (up to ten years, in 1980) for a country needing to deal with some basic structural maladjustment. The supplementary financing facility serves countries that have run into serious balance-of-payments problems that are large relative to their quotas.

The proportion of gross borrowings from the Fund between 1974 and 1979 that came from each of these facilities gives some impression of their relative importance. The Fund's original quota-based lending facility accounted for 53.5 percent of the total, the oil facility for 28.9 percent, the compensatory financing facility for 15.1 percent, the extended facility for 2.3 percent. A new buffer-stock account contributed 0.2 percent.

Some important credit facilities have existed outside the IMF. The most important of these are the bilateral "swap" arrangements worked out between central banks. They allow either partner, on short notice, to secure foreign currency by exchanging an equivalent amount of his own currency for that of the partner country. The swapped currency is guaranteed against exchange-rate changes. Swaps are normally repaid within three to twelve months. They were conceived in the 1960s, when major industrial countries often suffered large deficits due to short-term capital movements that would normally reverse themselves within a few months. They have continued under the managed float of the 1970's, however.

23.3 RESERVES DEMAND, SUPPLY, AND ADJUSTMENT

We discussed the demand for reserves from the viewpoint of the individual country, and then the institutional mechanisms that have provided international liquidity to the trading world as a whole. We need to bring demand and supply together to see how they interact and how demand/supply imbalances affect nations' policy choices and shed light on divergent national interests.

Two Positions from the 1960's

Some economists propose that the world price level adjusts to the quantity of international reserves in about the same way that the national price level adjusts to the quantity of domestic money according to the "quantity theory of money" (Chapter 17). Central banks are like households, they say. Give a central bank more reserves, and it will spend them by raising the money supply. If exchange rates are fixed, no matter in whose hands the extra reserves are placed, money supplies and thus the private sectors' levels of money expenditure will increase, and the world price level will be bid up. Raising the nominal quantity of international reserves therefore has no effect, they argue, because central banks are bent on holding only a certain target level of *real* reserves (i.e., dollars' worth of reserves relative to the national level of money expenditure). Nominal reserves are supply-determined, but their real value adjusts to holders' preferences through variations in the rate of inflation. This model interprets the complaint of surplus countries in the 1960's that reserve-currency countries like the United States could freely manufacture liquidity and force reserve accumulations and their inflationary consequences on their trading partners. And it sees a connection between the rapid growth of reserves between 1970 and 1973 and the initial outbreak of the 1970's decade's inflationary ills.

A contrary position placed great stress on the willingness of important surplus countries in the 1960's to go on accumulating reserves without apparent limit. Unwilling to revalue their currencies and hostile to any increases in domestic aggregate demand, they therefore continued to acquire masses of reserves, and some observers wondered if there was any practical limit to their demands for reserves.[5] Hence it was suggested that the quantity of nominal reserves was demand-determined, and that the U.S. deficit was a passive response to this gluttonous appetite for reserves. This view, needless to say, was popular in the United States. But there is no denying an asymmetry between the positions of deficit and surplus countries: A country losing reserves eventually has none, while one gaining reserves never reaches infinity!

The truth, as usual, lies somewhere between these two views. Both positions neglect the fact that countries always differ in their short-run situations, and some generally consider their reserves deficient while others find them excessive. Furthermore, the reserve-short and reserve-glutted countries may not react to their problems in symmetrical fashion. Countries short of reserves and unwilling to change their exchange rates often resort to controls that restrict payments made abroad. Countries in comfortable reserve positions may relax controls if they have them, and may let aggregate demand and employment run at somewhat higher levels than otherwise. But they may simply choose to enjoy the ac-

[5] Professor Fritz Machlup proposed, before women's liberation and somewhat in jest, the "Mrs. Machlup's wardrobe" theory of the demand for reserves. Mrs. Machlup does not really care how many costumes she has, but gains utility from adding one every now and then. Central bankers are not much concerned about the level of their reserves so long as small net increases are occurring.

cumulation of reserves and preclude (if they can) any expansionary effects of the inflow.

This eclectic view of countries' practices in managing their reserves carries some lessons for judging the adequacy of international reserves overall. "Enough reserves" are a compromise between too much and too little. Too little, and many countries impose controls and restrictions that are costly in economic welfare. Too much, and inflationary forces are promoted. The right quantity strikes the best balance between these costs — if we are wise enough to find it.

Reserves and the Managed Float

In any case the international debate over the adequacy of the world's quantity of reserves, framed between the positions just set forth, became rather muted in the 1970's as free resort to exchange-rate changes liberated countries from the need to worry seriously about their quantity of reserves. Indeed, in a pure regime of flexible exchange rates countries would logically need no reserves at all. And, some economists argue, if a need exists for smoothing out short-run fluctuations in the exchange rate, speculators in the foreign-exchange market should supply the necessary financing from their private wealth.

The proposition that flexible exchange rates obviate the need to hold reserves places a lot of faith in efficient private speculation. The end of fixed exchanged rates for the major countries left the general public much more uncertain about the levels of future exchange rates. The speculative funds supplied by risk-averse private parties may well have been curbed, leaving the central banks with a larger job of providing — or attempting to provide — stabilizing speculation in the foreign-exchange market (see section 20.1). Also we must recall the precautionary motive for holding reserves. Countries can easily contemplate that they might wish to peg the exchange rate again some day, or at least lend it a helping hand, even if it floats freely today.

The system of managed floating (considered more fully in Chapter 24), is a highly impure one, with some countries still pegging their exchange rates and others managing them occasionally behind the scenes. For this reason as well as the ones mentioned above, we cannot predict with confidence whether the demand for reserves actually declined in the 1970's. Statistical research does point to a decline that occurred as exchange rates became more variable, but the decline is a modest one. One study concentrated on the extent to which various countries use their international reserves, measured by the size of proportional short-run changes in reserves before and after 1973. The countries that have apparently let their exchange rates float most freely — the United States, Canada, West Germany — show an appreciable reduction in use, but other countries either reduced their reserves use modestly or increased it slightly. Similarly, a statistical study of the demand for stocks of reserves concludes that the industrial countries' demand for reserves was reduced between 1973 and 1976 but that the demand of the less-developed countries (most of which still peg their exchange rates) showed no decline.[6] The evidence thus broadly confirms our expectation that conditions in the 1970's have reduced the demand for reserves — and the urgency of questions about their total amount — without putting the issue of reserves adequacy completely to rest.

23.4 INTERNATIONAL MONETARY REFORM

We live amid the wreckage of the Bretton Woods system, including its international monetary institutions. Before the oil crisis of 1973, most countries agreed that the Bretton Woods system should be put back together again with minor amendments. But as "managed floating" became the only feasible policy toward exchange rates, and as the oil crisis transformed the problem of international reserves, the quest for a new system turned in a somewhat different direction. The Bretton Woods system now appears out of reach, undesirable, or both. Yet the time has not been ripe for a formal new monetary constitution. Instead, the members of the International Monetary Fund have been groping for agreement on certain general principles and transitional practices.

1978 Reforms

A bit of history provides necessary background to the analytical issues. In 1972 a committee of twenty IMF members was appointed to seek a comprehensive reform of international monetary arrangements. By 1974 the committee had agreed — not on what the reforms should be, only on what questions about the reforms needed to be resolved. The Committee of Twenty's agenda, the *Outline of Reform*, then served as the basis for further negotiations. By 1976 the negotiators had essentially given up on the long-run aspects of the *Outline of Reform*, which contemplated a return to fixed exchange rates, and concentrated on immediate concerns of making the managed float work better. That agreement, reached in Jamaica in 1976, led to an amendment to the IMF Articles of Agreement that came into force in 1978. Principal changes brought by this amendment included an expansion and liberalization of

[6] Esther C. Suss, "A Note on Reserves Use under Alternative Exchange Rate Regimes," *IMF Staff Papers,* 23 (July 1976): 387–94; H. Robert Heller and Mohsin S. Khan, "The Demand for International Reserves Under Fixed and Floating Exchange Rates," *IMF Staff Papers,* 25 (December 1978): 623–49.

the Fund's lending activities (the facilities described in section 23.2), surveillance over countries' management of their exchange rates (described in Chapter 24), and changes in the structure of international reserves designed to dethrone gold once and for all as a monetary asset and to promote the use of SDRs.

It is a paradox of the 1970's that the nations of the world finally gave up on the use of gold as a fundamental and stable store of value for public purposes, just as private wealth holders experienced a reborn faith in the metal that drove up its price almost twentyfold over the decade. The IMF reforms abolished the last vestige of an official price for gold in IMF transactions. The IMF returned part of its gold to the members who had originally contributed it as one-fourth of their quota subscriptions. The Fund has also been selling gold on the open market, impounding the proceeds in a special account to help the developing countries.

A change of greater potential long-run importance was the adoption of numerous measures to encourage the use of SDRs. Most of these are narrow and technical and involve only expanding the range of transactions between the IMF and its members for which SDRs could be used, promoting direct transactions in SDRs among IMF member governments (swaps, for example), and making the SDR the unit of account in IMF transactions. The real issue for SDRs, however, is one that lay outside the reach of the IMF negotiators: Can SDRs ever replace national currencies as the chief form of international reserves?

Reserve Asset Substitution

The logical case for the SDR's supremacy is airtight. It is fiduciary money that can be created by a process of deliberate planning. It costs nothing to produce — less than dollar bills, certainly less than gold. Its production is not entangled with the balance-of-payments position of any reserve currency country — the fatal flaw of the gold-exchange standard built into the Bretton Woods system. The problem is, how do we get there from here? That is, how are SDRs to replace the dollars and other currencies that now make up the bulk of international reserves (Table 23.1)? There are various problems to be solved.

The first difficulty is that the SDR is traded only among national authorities and thus cannot be used directly to intervene in the foreign-exchange market. To influence the dollar price of sterling you need dollars or sterling; SDRs are useful only after conversion into the needed currency. The new IMF rules improve the ease and certainty of that conversion, but they do not remove the need to hold balances of genuine foreign exchange. Unless SDRs are traded on a broad private market, monetary authorities will have to hold currencies as well as SDRs. That raises a portfolio problem for introducing SDRs into the system: central banks must find them attractive enough to hold alongside currencies (and gold), but they must not find the SDRs so attractive as to induce them to dump the accumulated currency balances (mostly dollars, and largely held as U.S. securities). It seems wise to regard the central banks as portfolio managers who pay attention to the economic risk and return of their portfolio of reserve assets (these things do, after all, affect the national income). Whether they hold dollars, shift from dollars to other currencies, or abandon currencies entirely for SDRs depends on the expected yields (in all senses) of these assets.

A behind-the-scenes battle has been periodically fought, both under Bretton Woods and in the 1970s, to keep central banks from dumping their dollar holdings and shifting into other currencies. Currency substitution has been discouraged — not so much from concern for the United States, which would suffer if central banks sell dollars for other currencies, but because of the turmoil that would result for the foreign-exchange markets and the lack of any other currency that can replace the masses of dollars outstanding in official reserves. During the period 1975 to 1979 the central banks' annual return on their dollars (adjusted for inflation) was −2.3 percent, when they could have at least broken even on other currencies and earned 2.3 percent on gold. The leading industrial countries, the largest holders of dollars, shunned the temptation of this incentive to substitute other assets for dollars, but many smaller countries are scurrying to diversify away from dollars.[7]

These ominous circumstances clearly make it desirable for central banks to replace most of their currency reserves with SDRs, but through some planned process where the displaced dollar assets are somehow penned up rather than being thrown on the market. Making the SDRs attractive enough is not itself the problem. Because the SDR is valued as a basket of currencies, it gives the central bank a diversified portfolio (although no hedge against worldwide inflation). The interest rates on SDRs, heretofore rather low, can be increased to put them in the neighborhood of national-currency assets. Somewhat more problematical are the detailed operations of the IMF Substitution Account that is proposed to hold the erstwhile dollar reserves, receive interest from the U.S. Treasury, pay interest on the SDR replacements for the dollars, and maintain the value of the SDR replacement assets. Would U.S. Treasury-bill interest rates cover the SDR interest costs? How can the Substitution Account break even if the dollar should on balance depreciate against the other "basket" currencies? Since the account must break

---

[7] Shifts in reserves holdings during the 1970's toward German marks, Swiss francs, and Japanese yen actually were mostly at the expense of the pound sterling; the dollar's share of world portfolios stayed quite stable. See "Reserve Diversification and the IMF Substitution Account," Morgan Guaranty Trust Company, *World Financial Markets* (September 1979): 5–14.

even, who agrees to make up its losses? For the United States that would make the deal more costly, perhaps much more costly, than the existing system of dollar reserves. But will other countries see that they have enough to gain from shouldering the burden of keeping the account solvent? Those are the issues that surround a clean-up of the outstanding structure of reserves.[8]

23.5 SUMMARY

A country with a fixed exchange rate holds reserves to tide it over fluctuations in its balance of payments. The size of the reserves it wishes to hold should depend on the size of the disturbances affecting its external payments, the speed and effectiveness of the automatic mechanisms that eliminate imbalances, and its willingness to use discretionary policy instruments (including exchange-rate changes) to restore equilibrium. These factors determine its transactions demand for reserves; in addition, it should hold a precautionary margin to convince speculators of its ability to defend its exchange rate.

Reserve assets take several forms. Foreign currencies must be held, at least as working balances, because the proximate function of reserves is to stabilize the external value of a country's currency. The dollar has been the most important reserve currency, and the U.S. status as a reserve-currency country has complicated the management of its own balance of payments. Gold played a fundamental role as a reserve asset in the gold-exchange standard that operated to 1971, but it was then dethroned as a fundamental reserve asset. Special Drawing Rights, an artificial reserve asset with many properties of gold, were first created during the period 1970 to 1972. Besides these assets that countries can hold in their reserves portfolios, they have access to various forms of credit: the basic lending facility of the International Monetary Fund as well as various supplementary and special-purpose funds.

Nations' demands for reserves interact with the available supply—if not like buyers and sellers in a conventional market. Some allege that increases in reserves merely cause central banks to go on spending sprees, causing inflation and depressing the real value of reserves to their preincrease level. Others assert that the growth of reserves has been demand-determined by the unlimited willingness of countries in external surplus to accumulate reserves. In practice, a judgment about the overall adequacy of reserves requires a balancing of the difficulties caused by too few reserves (controls, competitive devaluations) and too many reserves (inflation).

Nations' efforts to reform the international monetary system after the

[8] See *IMF Survey*, February 4, 1980, pp. 33, 42–44.

collapse of Bretton Woods first groped toward restoring fixed exchange rates, then retreated to making an orderly business out of the managed float. That regime, unlike a one of purely flexible exchange rates, has not much reduced nations' demands for international reserves. The resources and loan programs of the International Monetary Fund were expanded in 1978. Gold lost its last official function in the IMF system (although it remains an important reserve asset) and efforts were taken to promote greater use of Special Drawing Rights. The goal of making the SDR the main reserve asset requires some orderly way of retiring the large amount of national currencies—principally U.S. dollars—held as international reserves.

SUGGESTIONS FOR FURTHER READING

Baldwin, Robert E., and J. David Richardson, eds. *International Trade and Finance: Readings,* 2nd ed. Boston: Little, Brown and Company, 1981. No. 28 deals with reserve-asset substitution.

Heller, H. Robert, and Malcolm Knight. *Reserve-Currency Preferences of Central Banks.* Essays in International Finance, no. 131. Princeton: International Finance Section, Princeton University, 1978. Behavior behind shifting currency composition of reserves.

International Monetary Fund. *IMF Survey,* September 17, 1979. A special supplement to this issue provides a clear account of the IMF's many functions.

League of Nations. *International Currency Experience: Lessons of the Inter-War Period.* Geneva: League of Nations, 1944. Classic study by Ragnar Nurkse of international monetary relations in the interwar period.

Meier, Gerald M. *Problems of a World Monetary Order.* New York: Oxford University Press, 1974. Text and reprinted documents survey international monetary problems since World War II.

Murphy, J. Carter. *The International Monetary System: Beyond the First Stage of Reform.* Washington: American Enterprise Institute, 1979. Chapters 2 and 6 trace the 1970's reforms of the system.

Southard, Frank A., Jr. *The Evolution of the International Monetary Fund.* Essays in International Finance, no. 135. Princeton: International Finance Section, Princeton University, 1979. Account of the IMF's development as an operating organization.

Willett, Thomas D. *Floating Exchange Rates and International Monetary Reform.* Washington: American Enterprise Institute, 1977. The role of the IMF in a floating-rate world.

Williamson, J. "International Liquidity: A Survey," *Economic Journal,* 83 (September 1973): 685–746. Excellent advanced survey of economists' analyses of liquidity problems.

24

Flexible Exchange Rates and the International Policy System

Maintaining a fixed exchange rate is not a small chore. As we have shown in the preceding chapters, securing both external and internal balance — when the government cannot depend on automatic mechanisms of adjustment — requires accurate diagnosis of the nation's economic problems and the adroit use of multiple instruments of policy. With these requirements satisfied, the market for foreign exchange can clear at an arbitrarily chosen price. Why go to all this trouble when we could simply let the exchange rate fluctuate as needed to clear the market? The simplicity of that solution to the problem of external balance is the core of the case for flexible exchange rates. Yet there is surely an advantage to fixed exchange rates — an advantage we take for granted when we assume that a U.S. dollar earned in Massachusetts will always be worth exactly one U.S. dollar in Connecticut. In this chapter we shall explore the advantages and disadvantages of fixed exchange rates. As we shall see, this quest can become a search for the criteria of an "optimum currency area": How much economic activity should be linked by a single currency and hence subject to permanently fixed exchange rates?

24.1 FLEXIBLE EXCHANGE RATES: THEORY AND EXPERIENCE

There are two classic versions of the case for flexible exchange rates, relating respectively to the models of rigid and flexible prices developed in Chapters 16 and 17.

Flexible Domestic Prices

In a theoretical model in which all prices are flexible, automatic market adjustments can secure internal and external balance. As we saw in Chapter 17, full employment should prevail under a fixed exchange rate even without the active assistance of public policy. Following a disturbance, external balance is regained by net changes in the country's money supply that alter its price level and (temporarily) the level of real expenditure to restore equilibrium. If external balance could be obtained, in principle, with so little trouble when the exchange rate is fixed, why let it fluctuate? The answer suggested by Milton Friedman and others lies in finding the least costly way to bring about the necessary adjustments.[1]

A disturbance occurs — let us suppose a reduction in demand for the home country's export good. It causes an external deficit, and ultimately requires worsening our terms of trade to restore equilibrium in exchange. This adjustment could come about in either of two ways. With the exchange rate fixed, the monetary mechanism of adjustment could take its course, forcing down all money prices and factor payments within the country. Alternatively, the average level of domestic money prices could stay unchanged, and the adjustment could come about through a change in a single price — the exchange rate. Is it not simpler to change one price, rather than thousands of domestic money prices? The choice has been compared to the adoption of daylight saving time in the summer months. If we all wish to shift our activities one hour earlier in relation to the sun's daily cycle, why not set the clock forward an hour rather than reschedule every event to take place an hour earlier by the clock? The lower "transactions costs" of changing the clock correspond to the advantages of changing the exchange rate rather than all the domestic prices.

Rigid Domestic Prices

When domestic prices are rigid, or even sticky in the short run, we enter the world described in Chapters 16 and 22 where interventions of public policy are periodically necessary to maintain both internal and external balance. We saw that, in theory, these two objectives could be

[1] Milton Friedman, "The Case for Flexible Exchange Rates," *Essays in Positive Economics.* Chicago: University of Chicago Press, 1953; reprinted in *Readings in International Economics,* ed. R. E. Caves and H. G. Johnson. Homewood, Ill.: Richard D. Irwin, 1968, chap. 25. Also see Harry G. Johnson, "The Case for Flexible Exchange Rates, 1969," *Approaches to Greater Flexibility of Exchange Rates: The Bürgenstock Papers,* ed. G. N. Halm. Princeton, N.J.: Princeton University Press, 1970, chap. 8.

attained if the nation possesses two policy instruments — fiscal and monetary policy, fiscal policy and changes in the pegged exchange rate, etc. — which it can deploy freely. Owning the two instruments is not enough, of course. Perfect measurement and foresight are needed to use them correctly. There must be no constraints on the use of these instruments. No delays must occur while skeptical legislators are being convinced of the wisdom of the changes. Clearly our ideal prescription for attaining internal and external balance denies many of the realities of policy formation.

From this observation springs the second basic defense of flexible exchange rates, due to Professor James Meade.[2] Were the exchange rate not fixed, the market for foreign exchange (described in Chapter 19) would adjust to disturbances, continuously setting and revising the exchange rate to equate demand and supply. By fixing the price of foreign exchange we hamstring this market, and thereby take up the burden of a new policy target — external balance. Conversely, by switching from a fixed to a flexible rate the country reduces the tasks required of its available policy instruments. It potentially frees itself from the need to make unsatisfactory compromises that perpetuate internal imbalance as the cost of maintaining a tolerable state of external balance. The United States embraced this argument in the 1970's by espousing a policy of "benign neglect" toward the dollar's external value. This meant that proper policies should be set in regard to domestic targets in the expectation that market-determined exchange rates would then settle down at reasonable values.

This argument for flexible rates also draws force from our study of internal reserves and policy coordination among countries. A deficit financed by drawing down reserves transfers real resources to the deficit country from those in surplus, and the switch only accidentally moves them from less to more productive uses. A flexible rate removes the need for a government to spend its foreign-exchange reserves and thus to initiate such transfers. The government can occasionally spend or acquire reserves, if it chooses, without voiding the response of the exchange rate to market forces. The point about flexible rates is that such involuntary transfers of resources between countries are no longer a necessary part of the policy landscape. Fixed rates place a heavy burden on countries' capacities for the international coordination of financial policies. If flexible exchange rates were in general use, the need for international coordination of monetary policies might be reduced, and their enslavement to external balance ended.

[2] J. E. Meade, "The Case for Variable Exchange Rates," *Three Banks Review* (September 1955): 3–27.

Do Flexible Exchange Rates Work?

Many economists have favored flexible exchange rates against the opposition of practical men who manage international monetary affairs.
Indeed, partially flexible rates — the managed float — came into general use in 1973 not from official enthusiasm but from official inability
to reach and sustain a viable set of fixed rates. The long academic debate over fixed versus flexible exchange rates finally could be illuminated
by a major laboratory experiment. Evidence is now available on many
points that were once disputed on purely theoretical grounds. We draw
on evidence from the major currencies that have been subject to a
"managed float" since 1973, with a side glance at evidence on certain
earlier experiences with flexible exchange rates.[3]

1. *Have flexible exchange rates been highly unstable?* This question
is hard to answer meaningfully. How stable is stable? Should we blame
the foreign-exchange market for jitters when it had plenty to be jittery
about? Flexible exchange rates were introduced in 1973 against a background of massive disequilibria inherited from the 1960's, so the large
movements of exchange rates that followed may have been just a normal
market reaction. We can look, however, at the short-term variability of
exchange rates after they were initially set loose. If markets were func-
tioning well, the short-term fluctuations should have diminished with
time. Some evidence is presented in Table 24.1, which reports a measure
of short-term variation[4] for a few major currencies as well as an average
for eight industrial countries. The variability of exchange rates did decline between 1973 and 1975 but it has been irregular since then. New
sources of disturbance evidently cropped up in the late 1970's.

2. *Has speculation helped to stabilize exchange markets?* In Chapter
20 we raised the question of whether speculators act forcefully to stabilize foreign-exchange markets in the short run. Economists who study
speculative markets (such as markets for common stocks) put the question in the following way: Do the market participants make use of all
the information at hand on the future prospects of the financial asset,
when they plan today's transactions? If so, they will build into today's
price everything the world knows about the future economic yield on
that asset. This concept of an efficient market is a useful reference point
but, alas, there is no way to test it. One can measure how often people

---

[3] For a good brief summary of Canada's record, see A. F. W. Plumptre, *Exchange-
Rate Policy: Experience with Canada's Floating Rate.* Essays in International
Finance, no. 81. Princeton: International Finance Section, Princeton University,
1970; and also S. C. Tsiang, "Fluctuating Exchange Rates in Countries with Rela-
tively Stable Economies: Some European Experiences After World War I," *IMF
Staff Papers,* 7 (October 1959): 244–73.

[4] Technically, the measure is a standard deviation of monthly percentage changes
in the effective exchange rate, as calculated by the International Monetary Fund.

TABLE 24.1 Average Monthly Variability of Effective Exchange Rates for Selected Major Currencies, 1973–1979 (percent)

Currency	1973	1974	1975	1976	1977	1978	1979[a]
U.S. dollar	2.46	1.90	1.37	0.47	0.68	1.63	0.66
Pound sterling	1.68	0.77	0.95	2.41	0.96	1.52	1.29
Deutschemark	3.07	1.75	1.20	0.98	0.82	1.52	0.64
Japanese yen	2.58	1.93	1.01	0.99	1.55	3.38	1.41
Average of eight[b]	2.14	1.56	1.09	1.51	0.75	1.96	0.94

Source: International Monetary Fund, *Annual Report, 1979.* Washington, 1979. Table 10, p. 37.
[a] First half of the year.
[b] The four listed above plus the French franc, Italian lira, Canadian dollar, and Swiss franc.

proved wrong after the event — that they bid a currency up or down on what turned out to be unjustified grounds. But one cannot prove that they were wrong on the basis of what they knew at the time. Nonetheless, a good deal of research has been done attempting to test the efficiency of the foreign-exchange market. The most relevant research for our purposes addresses the degree to which forward exchange rates successfully predict subsequent spot exchange rates — as they will if speculators are abundant and well informed *and* dominate the forward market (see section 20.1). The forward markets improved their predictive accuracy for several years after 1973 but seemed to lose their touch in 1977 and 1978.[5] This pattern is identical to the one noted in the preceding section. The evidence on the Canadian dollar in the 1950's is somewhat kinder to the flexible rate. It was fairly clear that speculators bucked movements in the price of the Canadian dollar and pushed it back toward its average or trend value.[6]

3. *Have exchange rates moved so as to offset differing inflation rates?* The evidence is fairly convincing that exchange rates have tended to offset differences in countries' general rates of inflation.[7] This is consis-

[5] Richard M. Levich, "Further Results on the Efficiency of Markets for Foreign Exchange," *Managed Exchange-Rate Flexibility: The Recent Experience.* Conference Series no. 20, Federal Reserve Bank of Boston (Boston, 1978), pp. 58–80.
[6] Paul Wonnacott, *The Canadian Dollar, 1948–1962.* Toronto: University of Toronto Press, 1965, especially chap. 8.
[7] See the discussion in Isaiah Frank, Charles Pearson, and James Riedel, *The Implications of Managed Floating Exchange Rates for U.S. Trade Policy.* Monograph Series in Finance and Economics, 1979-1. New York: Graduate School of Business Administration, New York University, 1979. Pp. 26–29.

tent with the monetarists' prediction that the public will catch the news about the central bank's money-supply increases and promptly discount the exchange rate for the expected future inflation.

4. *Have exchange-rate movements pushed out-of-line trade balances in the right direction?* The evidence on this important question is difficult to assess. Because the relevant price-elasticities are very low in the short run we expect that a country's trade balance may worsen for a time following a fall in the price of its currency. (This pattern has been called the "J-curve effect," the time path of the trade balance resembling a J tilted to the right.) Price effects are expected eventually, however, to do their job. It is easy to find illustrations of correct response to exchange-rate changes in the 1970's, but the record is not a clean one. The trade deficit of the United States and surpluses of Germany and Japan have been made quite resistant to large exchange-rate movements. Some observers have suggested that behind these persistent balances lie built-in patterns of low saving (the United States) or high saving (Germany, Japan) and that capital markets have not succeeded in offsetting these habits through international capital flows. If so, exchange-rate movements may not suffice to cure what are fundamentally patterns of overspending or underspending rather than price disequilibria.

5. *Have exchange-rate movements blocked the international transmission of economic fluctuations?* In Chapter 18 we suggested that flexible exchange rates should bottle up income disturbances within the nations where they originated and protect their trading partners from infection. The immunity depends, however, on trade balances not showing any imprint of countries' income fluctuations; we noted that accommodating private international capital flows could easily block the insulation. The empirical evidence is quite clear that countries' business-cycle movements have not been more independent of one another since 1973. On the contrary they have been more closely synchronized.[8]

6. *Has the uncertainty of flexible exchange rates depressed international trade and investment?* There is evidence that the greater variability of exchange rates in the 1970's had its costs. Spreads between prices bid and asked in foreign-exchange transactions sometimes widened appreciably. Economists wondered whether international trade and long-term capital flows might have been depressed by the extra transaction costs and uncertainties. After all other influences are taken into account, was there a smaller flow of these international transactions in

[8] Duncan M. Ripley, "The Transmission of Fluctuations in Economic Activity: Some Recent Evidence," *Managed Exchange-Rate Flexibility,* pp. 1–22.

the open economy multiplier, which takes the value of $1/(s+m)$ for all disturbances when the exchange rate is fixed, falls to zero for foreign disturbances but rises to $1/s$ for domestic ones. A flexible exchange rate would therefore help to stabilize income for a country facing disturbances mainly from abroad, but it would reduce stability if a nation's income stream suffers from homemade perturbations. In practice this criterion probably favors a flexible rate for a small open economy, because foreign income disturbances are likely to bulk larger where exports are a larger share of national income.

The Domestic Instruments Available

A country's preferred system for managing its exchange rate would also be affected by any constraints on the policy instruments available for maintaining internal balance. Every student of introductory economics learns how fiscal and monetary policy can be used alternatively (in the closed economy) to secure full employment. Yet political constraints often limit a country's use of one tool or the other. In the United States, the need for agreement between the legislative and executive branches on any change in taxes or expenditures shackles fiscal policy; in the British parliamentary system, by contrast, major fiscal changes can be put into effect almost immediately. Some less-developed countries find monetary policy unusable because their domestic money markets are undeveloped, or because the money supply is tied by statute or convention to foreign-exchange reserves. If a country must count on only fiscal policy, or only monetary policy, to maintain full employment at home, it needs to know whether fixed or flexible exchange rates make its available policy instrument work better.

In section 24.1 we mentioned, as a basic argument for a flexible rate, that it relieves the country of the need to use scarce policy instruments to sustain external balance. On this ground a nation with an impaired supply of policy instruments would prefer flexible rates. The matter is not so simple, however, when capital is highly mobile internationally. We ordinarily think of monetary policy affecting aggregate demand and employment through a change in the rate of interest. If capital flows into or out of the country whenever the rate of interest rises or falls, one's hunch would be that the ability of monetary policy to affect employment is changed substantially. Indeed, when the exchange rate is flexible and capital highly mobile, monetary policy is an effective tool for altering aggregate demand, but fiscal policy is fettered. Hence, a nation blocked from using monetary policy for internal balance should think twice before adopting a flexible exchange rate in a world where capital is highly mobile. If fiscal policy is shackled, the argument reverses, and a flexible rate becomes particularly desirable.

Inflationary Pressures

One popular argument for fixed exchange rates holds that they are necessary (for some countries) to prevent runaway inflation. The competing claimants for the real income flow — workers, farmers, pensioners, shareholders, etc. — jointly demand more than 100 percent of the pie. A democratic government can keep their demands from leading to unreasonable inflationary pressures only by a political gambit: It must elevate the protection of its (fixed) exchange rate to top-priority status and justify curbing inflation by its adverse effects on the balance of payments. If one accepts the view that income demands can be quelled in no other way, this argument for a fixed exchange rate deserves some weight. But a government in this position adopting a flexible exchange rate does not obviously wield a weaker club. It can point to the "disgraceful" depreciation of a flexible exchange rate subject to inflationary pressures, to warrant attacking them.

Choice of Exchange-Rate Strategy

A glance at the exchange-rate systems chosen by various countries in the 1970's immediately suggests some systematic relations to their market structures. Large, industrialized, or diversified countries seem to choose flexible rates. Small, less-developed, or specialized ones seem to prefer fixed rates. Furthermore, the patterns appear to line up rather well with the bases just set forth for preferring fixed rates. In one investigation these patterns were tested statistically by comparing a sample of seventy-six countries.[12] The authors noted that with "managed floating," countries' exchange rates cannot be neatly classified as fixed or flexible. Therefore they devised a measure of each country's policy stance that is essentially a ratio of the extent to which its exchange rate changed to the extent to which its international reserves varied. They found that greater flexibility went with a less open economy (lower ratio of exports and imports to national income), a more diversified export sector, and a higher level of economic development (which they argued give the economy more flexibility in adapting to exchange-rate disturbances). They also found that countries had to resort to exchange-rate variation when their inflation rates were out of line with those of their trading partners. Thus, this investigation supports the conclusion that neither fixed nor flexible exchange rates hold absolute superiority; the choice depends on a country's situation.

Some countries have cast about for devices that might give them the

[12] Paul Holden, Merle Holden, and Esther C. Suss, "The Determinants of Exchange-Rate Flexibility: An Empirical Investigation," *Review of Economics and Statistics,* 61 (August 1979): 327–33.

best of both fixed-rate and flexible-rate worlds. Brazil and Israel, among others, have used a device called the "crawling peg" to stabilize their exchange rates while changing them as needed. Rather than making large, occasional changes, they alter their pegged rates by very small amounts but at frequent intervals. The chief aim of the crawling peg is to avert the pressure of speculative capital flows. When a rate changes overnight by 15 percent, a speculator correctly foreseeing the move can make a handsome profit. Suppose that a country in external deficit wishes to devalue its currency by a maximum of 3 percent a year via the crawling peg, and that the (short-term) interest rate prevailing in the rest of the world is 6 percent. If it announces its plan for a crawling devaluation and at the same time raises its interest rate to 9 percent, it destroys the incentive for speculators to move their funds outward. The 3 percent capital loss they can avoid by exporting their funds for a year is just offset by the 3 percent they would then forego in higher interest earnings at home.

A device of similar purpose that was used by various countries in 1971–73 is to maintain a pegged exchange rate but stabilize it only within a rather wide band; ±2¼ percent was used, but bands as large as ±5 percent have been urged. The band proposal aims to provide a measure of certainty to commercial traders without putting the government under the speculators' gun by committing it to continuous stabilization of the exchange rate.

24.3 ADJUSTMENT IN AN INTEGRATED MONETARY AREA

We have seen that countries in some situations might rationally prefer fixed exchange rates. These findings lead to a more basic question: How far can we extend the advantages of an integrated monetary area? How large is an "optimum currency area," a region united by a common currency unit so that exchange-rate changes become impossible? [13] Should all fifty United States employ the same currency unit, or would some regions benefit by declaring monetary independence? Should the members of the European Community proceed with their plans to establish a common currency and monetary area? To answer these questions, we need evidence on how adjustments take place among the regions of a single country. One hears no complaints about external imbalance from the state of Wyoming or the county of Durham. Do such imbal-

[13] The literature on this question is surveyed by T. D. Willett and E. Tower, *The Theory of Optimum Currency Areas and Exchange-Rate Flexibility*. Special Papers in International Economics, no. 11. Princeton, N.J.: International Finance Section, Princeton University, 1976.

ances occur? Are they automatically corrected? Or are they simply not noticed?

Regions do suffer from external imbalance, often very seriously. But they see the problem — quite reasonably — as one of adjusting to whatever *real* imbalance underlies the imbalance in net payments. A region by definition lacks control over its own money supply, and cannot bring external imbalance upon itself through unwarranted monetary policies. It may be subject to real disturbances, however, which leave it in external disequilibrium. A common source of regional payments disturbances is a change in the fate of a major regional industry. New England suffered an external deficit when manufacturers in the South discovered that they could produce textiles at lower cost than the Yankees, and expanded output. New England's textiles came into excess supply at the current terms of trade; the rest of the nation's goods came into excess demand. When the mountain states exhaust deposits of nonferrous metal ores (which they sell competitively at the world price), once again the area's factor services are in excess supply and the rest of the nation's goods in excess demand. The region is likely to spend more than the real income it can now command.

A region's adjustment problems do not appear to involve external imbalance partly because it holds no official "interregional reserves" to allow itself to run an exchange-market deficit. Thus there can be no ex post deficits measured in the way described in Chapter 15. But the many sources of internal disturbance to a region can easily provoke ex ante external imbalance, and one can often spot symptoms of adjustment to this imbalance even if no deficits become visible ex post. Let us explore some of the ways in which regional imbalances are financed in the short run, or corrected in the long run, within a national area such as the United States. We suppose that the country's demand shifts away from a major export of the region. At least in the short run, prices are sticky, so that resources become unemployed rather than permit a drop in their rates of pay.

Private Accommodating Capital Flows

If the adverse demand shift is permanent, the region must incur the adjustment costs of moving some of its factors to other activities where they can earn the highest reward now obtainable. And it may wish to consume more than its income, temporarily, to cushion the shock of shifting to a permanently lower level of real income and consumption. Hence adjustment is easier if the region's owners of factor services readily can borrow externally in order to finance these adjustments. The easier it is to borrow, the more fully the region is integrated into a national capital market.

Several traits of an integrated capital market make borrowing easier. Many securities held by individuals will be widely traded outside the region, so they can be sold to finance short-run overspending without any decline in their price. The region's banking system has access to an external wholesale market in short- and medium-term credit. Hence bank credit need not contract sharply when the external imbalance causes the region's banks to lose reserves — a likely manifestation of external imbalance. An integrated private capital market, by easing short-term transitional borrowing, thereby helps to mask external imbalance for a region. This private borrowing in a sense substitutes for the accommodating capital flows reflected by changes in the official reserves of a nation in external imbalance.[14]

Official Transfers in a Federal Fiscal System

Membership in a federal fiscal system can smooth a region's internal and external adjustments considerably. A region's citizens pay taxes into a central treasury, and public expenditures within the region are determined by a central authority. The outflow of tax payments from the region need not equal the inflow of expenditures from the federal treasury, in either the short or long run. Whatever the region's long-run status as a net donor or a net recipient of transfers, its position in the short run will shift with internal and external imbalances. We assumed that, because of price rigidities, the decline in demand causes regional unemployment and reduces incomes. Important taxes, especially personal and corporate income taxes, vary with the level of incomes, and regional tax payments fall when unemployment increases. In addition, some government expenditures are likely to rise — unemployment insurance and related welfare payments, any public works projects that are designed to combat unemployment, etc. The region's receipts from the central government rise and its payments fall; this net increase in inward transfer payments helps to finance the trade deficit that reflects the initial disturbance. Like the private borrowings described previously, it provides a transitional contribution to maintain expenditure levels and cover the costs of reallocation.

Factor Migration

When the demand for its export declines, a region faces only transitional difficulties if resources can be shifted to other regional industries paying

[14] For an interesting case study, see James C. Ingram, *Regional Payments Mechanism: The Case of Puerto Rico*. Chapel Hill: University of North Carolina Press, 1962. Especially pp. 113–33.

the same wages. For reasons set forth in Chapter 7, however, at least some factors of production are likely to be worse off after all readjustments have been made within the region. Rather than settle for lower rewards, they may instead migrate to other regions. The outward movement of labor, for instance, should relieve the region's external imbalance as well as the unemployment that reflects its internal imbalance. When a worker leaves, regional income goes down by the amount of his marginal product, and regional expenditure by the amount of his consumption. The region's trade balance (in the absence of capital flows or transfer payments) must equal the difference between output and expenditure, and changes when their difference alters. The unemployed worker's output is zero, whereas his consumption (sustained from personal savings, unemployment compensation, or borrowing) remains positive. Hence his departure should help to restore external balance. The same conclusion would follow even if he had not become unemployed, but the market value of his marginal product has sunk beneath his current level of consumption. Hence easy interregional movement of factors of production provides the region in an integrated national economy with another cushion for adjustment to external imbalance. However, this mobility may leave stranded any complementary factors of production that are immobile between regions. An important difficulty faced by "declining regions" is the burden placed on immobile resources; they cannot protect their real incomes, and they may fail to lower their money wages (either through price flexibility or a downward adjustment of the region's exchange rate) and thus forgo any remaining employment opportunities.[15]

These adjustments suggest the conditions needed for a country to benefit from permanently locking its exchange rate. Its factor markets should be integrated with those of other countries, so that private capital can assist in financing transitional difficulties, and labor and capital can migrate to avoid severe and prolonged adverse swings in their incomes. It would benefit greatly from membership in a fiscal union as well, to secure the cushioning benefits of transfers of federal funds. Fiscal unification is also needed to secure high factor mobility, because otherwise differing tax structures and regulations governing factor payments impede mobility. Finally, the region fixing its exchange rate must in effect abandon an independent monetary policy. Divergent movements of national price levels will ultimately be inconsistent with equilibrium at the initial exchange rate; and the imbalances resulting from

---

[15] In principle, the argument of this paragraph pertains to the long-run allocation of real capital as well as of labor. One must distinguish between the short-run advantages of a region in borrowing from outside in order to finance adjustments, and the best long-run alternative, which may be a permanent net export of capital from the region.

unequal rates of inflation grow larger as markets become more tightly integrated.

European Monetary System: An Application

A strategic site for testing these requirements for monetary unification is the European Community, whose members maintain a general commitment to full economic unification. They have made several specific steps toward monetary unification, most recently the European Monetary System. The system, begun in 1979, has these principal elements:

1. The exchange rates of the participating members are to be confined within a band, not to fluctuate outside a range of ±2.25 percent from declared par values. The group's rates can fluctuate jointly against other currencies, such as the dollar. This arrangement is known as the "snake," a metaphor that describes the Community currencies undulating with respect to other currencies but staying within a fixed distance of each other.

2. Members are to pool one-fifth of their international reserves, receiving in return claims on a new monetary unit, the European Currency Unit (ECU). The ECU, a sort of European SDR, is a purely theoretical currency unit, but the Europeans hope some day to make it a real transaction currency that could rival the U.S. dollar as a vehicle currency.

3. Eventually all of the European Community's international reserves are supposed to be centralized under the system, leading to a joint central bank.

The European Community's policies have over the years removed barriers to trade among its members and taken certain other steps toward unification of their markets. International factor mobility within the Community remains quite limited, and integration of fiscal and monetary policy does not extend beyond the consultation level. Hence the Community clearly cannot claim the requisites of regional integration. Outside observers, noting these facts, have usually concluded that the European Monetary System rests on wishful thinking, does not really command a high priority in the national policies of its members, and cannot withstand major economic disturbances. Defenders in the Community, however, have chosen to put cart and horse in the other order: Steps toward monetary unification would make apparent to all the need for unified policies and force this unity into being.[16] This idealistic position perhaps reads better as a political exhortation than as an economic prediction. Certainly, the economic analysis warns that

---

[16] See Philip H. Trezise, editor, *The European Monetary System: Its Promises and Prospects*. Washington: Brookings Institution, 1979.

the sledding is likely to be difficult. In any event the system in 1980 found itself buffeted by difficulties keeping some currencies within the snake and by widening differences in its members' inflation rates that foretold more troubles to come.

24.4 POLICY SYSTEMS AND INTERNATIONAL WELFARE

We have seen that benefits are promised by both the extremes of full exchange-rate flexibility and the full fixity of a common currency area. The valuation of these poles and the intermediate alternatives furthermore will differ from country to country. And the regime preferred by a given country is apt to vary from time to time with shifts in its perceived economic and political interests. One is tempted to let each country make its choice. If A wishes a flexible exchange rate, it simply eschews intervening in the exchange market. If B wants to peg its currency to A's, it need only hold reserves of A's currency. C and D can form a monetary union and handle their common external exchange rate as they will. Such a laissez-faire approach has its attractions, but it neglects the general interdependence among nations' policy choices.

We have stressed repeatedly that an economic disturbance in any open economy potentially affects the welfare of its trading partners — whether the disturbance is real or monetary, whether it stems from economic change or a shift of national policy. Because policies affect other countries they become points of contention in international relations. Just as there are gains to be shared from effective coordination, there are clashes to be averted through the avoidance of mutually inconsistent and harmful policies. Just as policies are interdependent in their effect, so are international negotiations over these policies politically interdependent. No country can resist the temptation to use its bargaining power on issue x to lever a concession on issue y — even where the issues are economically unconnected. Therefore the interdependence of issues would pervade international policy negotiations even if policies were not economically dependent in fact. Furthermore, the bargaining process has apparently grown more complex as the hegemonic powers, the United States and Soviet Russia, have lost some of their dominant roles in international affairs. A plural system of relations among countries surely appears more democratic, but it is not necessarily more stable or decisive.[17]

These features of the international process of policy coordination are

---

[17] C. F. Bergsten, R. O. Keohane, and J. S. Nye, Jr., "International Economics and Politics: A Framework for Analysis," *International Organization*, 29 (Winter 1975): 3–36.

important because different regimes of exchange rates (and international reserves) impose different requirements for international coordination. Let us take for examination four principal regimes for managing exchange rates:

1. *Complete flexibility.* No country intervenes in the exchange market.
2. *Managed float.* Countries intervene selectively, but exchange rates are basically market-determined. Some countries may peg to the currencies of their principal trading partners.
3. *Adjustable peg.* Some restored version of the Bretton Woods system; exchange rates are normally pegged at official values, but countries are obligated to adjust to eliminate fundamental disequilibrium.
4. *Monetary union* with a common currency or at least permanently fixed exchange rates.

The systems can be compared in their economic and political desirability on several criteria.[18]

Accommodating Local Diversity

A workable regime of international monetary relations must be able to accommodate important diversities among member nations. They may be diverse in their tolerance of inflation, their willingness and ability to use various types of controls (e.g., over capital movements), and their beliefs in the desirability of changes in exchange rates. The managed float and adjustable peg systems are evidently more attuned, by their very eclecticism, to diverse preferences among member countries. The managed float has notably allowed nations to peg or float their currencies in a variety of patterns.

Contributing to International Harmony

An effective system should contribute to harmonious international relations by providing some mechanism to resolve disputes arising from international economic relations or retarding the emergence of such disputes. The Bretton Woods system took the former tack of resolving economic disputes in an international forum. This was done through a combination of strategies — rules of behavior governing some practices (exchange control, managing a floating rate), international scrutiny of others (decisions to change exchange rates). The amendments to the International Monetary Fund agreement adopted in 1978 imposed a

---

[18] An extended analysis of this type is provided by Richard N. Cooper, "Prolegomena to the Choice of an International Monetary System," *International Organization,* 29 (Winter 1975): 63–97.

similar mechanism of surveillance over each member's management of its exchange rate in order to promote adherence to several principles: No one should manipulate exchange rates for "unfair competitive advantage" over other members; a member should intervene to counter disruptive short-run movements of its exchange rate; and respect should be given to the interests of other members, including those whose currencies are used for exchange-market intervention.[19] Of course, the proposals for monetary union envision a strong supranational government, either as a precondition for union or as a desideratum that would evolve from the very need for it revealed in the union's operation.

On the other hand, the managed float and purely flexible systems pursue an implicit strategy of reducing the economic spillovers (actual and perceived) of countries' policy decisions onto one another. If they entail few rules of the game and little coordinating machinery, they also tend to insulate countries somewhat from each others' decisions about rates of inflation and the like. Although it surely needs some rules to avoid clashes, the managed float performed surprisingly well in 1973 and 1974; no competitive depreciations of currencies occurred despite fears that nations would be tempted to this course in order to deal with massive trade deficits following the oil price increase. The pacific quality of the various exchange-rate regimes is thus in doubt, but the exacerbated disputes that marked the dying days of the Bretton Woods system hardly compare well to the resiliency of the managed float.

Attaining Economic Efficiency

The economic efficiency of the various regimes was discussed earlier in this chapter. Again, the case is not clear-cut. Monetary union puts forth strong claims for efficiency, but the efficiency is dependent on meeting its formidable requirements for centralized coordination of economic policy and in particular a supranational fiscal policy. The Bretton Woods system ultimately delivered little of the certainty in international transactions claimed for a fixed-rate system. It provided no mechanism for adjusting the massive disequilibria that emerged behind pegged exchange rates, and countries imposed batteries of ad hoc controls that entailed uncertainties arguably as large as those due to floating exchange rates. Managed or pure floating systems thus may do better at avoiding the use of inefficient controls — but we cannot be sure that they will retain this virtue in all weathers. And when the adjust-

[19] An interesting debate has proceeded over alternative methods for carrying out this surveillance. See Thomas D. Willett, "Alternative Approaches to International Surveillance of Exchange-Rate Policies," *Managed Exchange-Rate Flexibility,* pp. 148–72.

ment of pegged rates is delayed but ultimately proves necessary, in the interim investment decisions may be made that looked right at the "wrong" exchange rate but prove inefficient when it is belatedly changed. But a floating-rate system can also be faulted, because incorrect speculative expectations may sometimes push exchange rates to economically inappropriate levels and cause incorrect allocations and inefficient and perverse international capital movements.

Promoting Fair Distribution of Gains

An international economic system ought to distribute its benefits fairly among the participants. Because fairness, like beauty, exists in the eye of the beholder, it provides no solid criterion for grading alternative regimes. Monetary union ultimately exacerbates the problem of fairness. By its very ability to increase the international mobility of factors of production it tends to create depressed regions, from which the mobile factors have fled to greener pastures leaving the less mobile ones with reduced incomes and increased social overhead costs. Regimes dependent on pegged exchange rates must make adequate provision for international reserves, and their manufacture and use raise many questions about the distribution of seigniorage and other gains. But systems of floating rates can create their own problems of equity. A country can manage its floating rate in a way that seems to shift the terms of trade in its favor and against its trading partners, or it can manipulate the rate to export unemployment unfairly. And less-developed countries facing inelastic demands for specialized primary exports can suffer large swings in their exchange rates as real supply or demand disturbances affect their principal exports.

24.5 SUMMARY

Allowing the exchange rate to fluctuate freely in response to market forces has potential advantages that a country can view in two ways. When restoring exchange-market equilibrium requires changing the level of its prices relative to external prices, altering the exchange rate is easier and less costly than changing each domestic money price. Alternatively, letting the rate float removes external balance as a policy objective and allows use of the nation's scarce supply of policy instruments for other purposes. The flexible exchange rates of the industrial countries in the 1970's can be evaluated on numerous criteria of performance. The evidence is conflicting but on balance fairly favorable.

The case for fixed exchange rates is not a case for return to the adjustable peg of the Bretton Woods system, but rather for institutional arrangements that permanently remove the possibility of changes. The advantages of permanent fixity depend on the structure of the economy — its openness, the sources of disturbance that it faces, and the domestic policy instruments available. These considerations help to explain which countries have in fact continued to cling to fixed exchange rates.

The question of a fixed or a flexible rate can be generalized to the question of what constitutes an "optimum currency area," within which the rate is permanently fixed, and between which it floats. Adjustments taking place in regions of a single country reveal the conditions necessary for a nation to benefit from belonging to such a currency area. They include high levels of interregional (international) factor mobility, membership in an integrated federal fiscal system, and willingness to abandon an independent regional (national) monetary policy. It is difficult to see how a nation could gain from joining a larger currency area without at the same time subordinating itself to a federal government.

Although countries will differ in their preferences for pegging or floating their exchange rates, they share a common interest in the general system used for attaining external balance because of the comprehensive interdependence of their policy instruments. Viewed as an international system, the various regimes for managing the exchange rate can be appraised for accommodating local diversity, contributing to the avoidance of disputes, attaining economic efficiency, and promoting a fair distribution of benefits among participating nations.

SUGGESTIONS FOR FURTHER READING

Baldwin, Robert E., and J. David Richardson, eds. *International Trade and Finance: Readings,* 2nd ed. Boston: Little, Brown and Company, 1981. No. 19 updates the debate on fixed and flexible exchange rates, and nos. 29 and 30 appraise the European Monetary System.

Cooper, Richard N. *The Economics of Interdependence: Economic Policy in the Atlantic Community.* New York: McGraw-Hill, 1968. In Chapter 7 Cooper summarizes the evidence on the adjustment of interregional payments imbalances.

Dreyer, Jacob, Gottfried Haberler, and Thomas D. Willett, eds. *Exchange Rate Flexibility.* Washington: American Enterprise Institute, 1978. Papers on many aspects of exchange-rate flexibility.

Federal Reserve Bank of Boston. *Managed Exchange-Rate Flexibility: The Recent Experience.* Conference Series, no. 20. Boston, 1978. Contains papers useful for appraising the 1970's managed float.

Friedman, Milton. "The Case for Flexible Exchange Rates," American Economic Association, *Readings in International Economics.* Homewood, Ill.: Richard D. Irwin, 1968. Flexible rates are viewed as a device to improve performance of markets.

McKinnon, R. I. "Optimum Currency Areas," *American Economic Review,* 53 (September 1963): 717–24. Fixed rates are analyzed in terms of optimum currency areas.

Trezise, Philip H., ed. *The European Monetary System: Its Promise and Prospects.* Washington: Brookings Institution, 1979. Views of European and American economists.

SUPPLEMENTS

Supplement to Chapter 2:
The Equations of Exchange Equilibrium

This supplement introduces the reader to the notation and structure of the formal models that will be developed in subsequent supplements.

For notation, we shall use D to refer to demands and x to production. Thus D_F signifies the home country's demand for food, and x^*_C the foreign country's production of clothing. The asterisk is used, as in the text, to symbolize foreign variables. The price of commodity j is denoted by p_j if a monetary unit of account is used for the home country, or p^*_j if the foreign country uses a different unit of account or if the foreign price differs. In our two-commodity, food and clothing example, the home country's prices will be p_F and p_C. The relative price of food is p_F/p_C, and because this, the "terms of trade," is prominent in the real models of trade, we shall use the simple p (in the home country) and p^* (in the foreign country, if prices are different) to denote the terms of trade.

The use of equations in the text is not completely forsaken. For this reason a different numbering scheme is required for the supplements. Thus 2.S.4 refers to the fourth equation in the supplement to Chapter 2.

We shall start the account of the exchange model by stating prices in monetary units. The budget constraint for this model posits that for each country the value of aggregate demand must be restricted to, and equal to, the value of the endowment bundle. Thus:

$$p_C D_C + p_F D_F = p_C x_C + p_F x_F \qquad (2.S.1)$$

$$p^*_C D^*_C + p^*_F D^*_F = p^*_C x^*_C + p^*_F x^*_F. \qquad (2.S.2)$$

Assume that in a trading context the home country will import food. Then rewrite these two equations to highlight, on the left-hand side, the country's demand for imports and, on the right-hand side, the corresponding supply of exports:

$$p_F(D_F - x_F) = p_C(x_C - D_C) \qquad (2.S.3)$$

$$p^*_C(D^*_C - x^*_C) = p^*_F(x^*_F - D^*_F). \qquad (2.S.4)$$

The importance of *relative* prices is brought out by dividing 2.S.3 by p_C and 2.S.4 by p^*_C. Furthermore, in a free-trade equilibrium with no barriers to costless movement of commodities between countries, relative prices in the two countries are brought into line so that:

$$p(D_F - x_F) = (x_C - D_C) \qquad (2.S.5)$$

$$(D^*_C - x^*_C) = p(x^*_F - D^*_F). \qquad (2.S.6)$$

The symbol p is the relative price of food.

Suppose the terms of trade, p, clear the world market for food. That is, the home country's excess demand, $(D_F - x_F)$, equals the foreign country's excess supply, $(x^*_F - D^*_F)$. In such a case it is obvious from equations 2.S.5 and 2.S.6

that the world's clothing market must be cleared as well: $(D_C^* - x_C^*)$ will
equal $(x_C - D_C)$.

One consequence of this phenomenon is that free-trade market equilibrium
can be expressed either by the statement that world demand and supply are
equal for food (as in 2.S.7) or for clothing (as in 2.S.8):

$$D_F + D_F^* = x_F + x_F^* \tag{2.S.7}$$

$$D_C + D_C^* = x_C + x_C^*. \tag{2.S.8}$$

If the budget constraints in equations 2.S.5 and 2.S.6 are always satisfied,
2.S.7 implies 2.S.8 or vice versa. Oddly enough, neither market-clearing equation is typically used in the literature of the pure theory of trade. Rather,
they are replaced by the equivalent statement that in free-trade equilibrium
the value of the home country's imports equals the value of the foreign country's imports. This balance-of-payment equilibrium condition, in equation
2.S.9, follows from the two budget constraints 2.S.5 and 2.S.6 and either 2.S.7
or 2.S.8.

$$p(D_F - x_F) = (D_C^* - x_C^*) \tag{2.S.9}$$

This redundancy in stating equilibrium conditions is two-sided. On the one
hand it reveals that the model is more simple than a mere scanning of equations might reveal: There is only one market, and if the world demand for
clothing balances the world production at specified terms of trade, then the
food market must be cleared as well. Furthermore, the value of each country's
demand for imports would, at that market-clearing terms of trade, equal the
other country's demand for imports. On the other hand, it implies that there
are several ways to describe the same equilibrium: The food market is cleared,
the clothing market is cleared, or the home country's demand for imports
equals, in value, the foreign country's demand for imports. Saying the same
thing in three different ways can be confusing.[1]

Supplement to Chapter 3:
Real Incomes, Production, and Elasticities

We start by showing explicitly how to express changes in a community's level
of real income. This is followed by a breakdown of the impact of price changes
on demand into substitution and income effects. Production changes are also
considered and an expression developed for the elasticity of a country's demand for imports.

---

[1] That they are the same should be kept in mind when in Chapter 4 we describe
the conditions for market stability.

Changes in Real Incomes

Throughout we assume that a community's level of satisfaction or real income depends only on the bundle of commodities it consumes. For our two-commodity example we can state this formally as:

$$u = u(D_C, D_F).$$

The symbol u represents some arbitrary index used to measure utility or the level of welfare. Differentiate this expression to obtain:

$$du = \frac{\partial u}{\partial D_C} dD_C + \frac{\partial u}{\partial D_F} dD_F$$

which states that when the amounts consumed are altered, utility changes by an amount that depends on the marginal utility of a commodity (e.g., $\partial u/\partial D_F$ for food) multiplied by the change in the quantity of it consumed. The arbitrariness of the utility index can be removed by dividing both sides of this equation by the marginal utility of clothing:

$$\frac{du}{\partial u/\partial D_C} = dD_C + \frac{\partial u/\partial D_F}{\partial u/\partial D_C} dD_F.$$

The left-hand term is positive only if utility has increased. Furthermore, it is a measure of the change in utility expressed in units of clothing (the "utils" cancel out). Call this change in real income in clothing units "dy." The right-hand side can be simplified by noticing that the coefficient of "dD_F" is the *marginal rate of substitution,* the amount of clothing that must be added to compensate for a loss of one unit of food along an indifference curve. But in a market equilibrium this amount corresponds to the relative price of food, p. Thus, equation 3.S.1 can be derived as the basic expression for a change of real income:

$$dy = dD_C + pdD_F. \tag{3.S.1}$$

Equation 3.S.1 reveals that any change in the consumption bundle affects real incomes. The budget constraint, written here as equation 3.S.2,

$$D_C + pD_F = x_C + px_F \tag{3.S.2}$$

reveals that the *source* of any change in real income must reside either in a change in the endowment bundle or a change in the terms of trade. Differentiate equation 3.S.2 to obtain

$$dD_C + pdD_F + D_F dp = dx_C + pdx_F + x_F dp.$$

Subtract $D_F dp$ from both sides, and use expression 3.S.1 for dy to obtain equation 3.S.3:

$$dy = -(D_F - x_F)\, dp + (dx_C + pdx_F). \tag{3.S.3}$$

This basic expression for the change of real income in the home country provides the following breakdown:

1. The term $-(D_F - x_F)\,dp$ is the *terms-of-trade effect* encountered in Chapter 3. Assume the home country is a net importer of food and let M denote $(D_F - x_F)$. If the terms of trade deteriorate for the home country, dp is positive and real income at home falls by $M\,dp$, an amount proportional to the volume of imports.

2. The term $(dx_C + p\,dx_F)$, the price-weighted sum of any change in the home country's production bundle, enters directly into the measure of a change in real income.

This two-term breakdown of the influences on a nation's real income is absolutely basic for the applications to be considered in Chapter 4 and elsewhere in this book.

A Basic Production Relationship

The discussion of commodity exchange in Chapter 2 held constant the amount produced in each country as prices changed. This inflexibility in production response ensures that a change in prices results in a zero value for $\{dx_C + p\,dx_F\}$ in equation 3.S.3 for the change of real incomes, because dx_C and dx_F are each zero. If, instead, production possibilities are shown by a bowed-out transformation schedule (as in Figure 3.1), a rise in food's relative price (p) would encourage food production and discourage clothing output. Nonetheless, for output movements along the transformation schedule,

$$dx_C + p\,dx_F = 0. \qquad (3.S.4)$$

The reason is simple: At a competitive equilibrium (e.g., point B in Figure 3.1) the absolute value of the slope of the transformation schedule, $-(dx_F/dx_C)$, must equal clothing's relative price, $(1/p)$.

Substitution and Income Effects

The text of Chapter 3 suggested how any change in price has both a substitution and income effect on quantity demanded. The decomposition into these two effects can be expressed algebraically for small price changes, making use of equation 3.S.3's expression for the change in real income, which is simplified by 3.S.4's relationship among outputs.

The demand for any commodity depends on all prices and income. Alternatively, in a two-commodity model it depends on relative price (p) and real income (y).[1] For example, consider the home country's demand for food, written as in 3.S.5:

$$D_F = D_F(p, y). \qquad (3.S.5)$$

---

[1] The change in real income, dy, has been defined by 3.S.1. We are taking mathematical liberties in using the symbol y for real income itself. However, we only need the expression for dy as we only consider "small" changes in prices and demands.

Differentiate this with respect to food's relative price, p, to obtain:

$$\frac{dD_F}{dp} = \frac{\partial D_F}{\partial p} + \frac{\partial D_F}{\partial y} \cdot \frac{dy}{dp}.$$

The first term is the substitution effect of a price rise — as p rises food demand falls along an indifference curve. The second composite term shows the two aspects of the income effect we described in the text. The term dy/dp shows how real income at home has been affected by the rise in food's relative price. Equation 3.S.3 reveals that dy/dp is just $-(D_F - x_F)$, since any output response along the transformation curve has negligible impact on real incomes (by 3.S.4). If food is imported, dy/dp is negative. The other term, $\partial D_F/\partial y$, expresses the change in demand for food as a consequence of a unit rise in incomes with prices constant. This is not a pure number, since D_F is measured in food units and y in clothing units. Therefore, define a_F as $p \cdot (\partial D_F/\partial y)$, the home country's marginal propensity to consume food. This is a pure number, between zero and one if neither commodity is "inferior." Therefore equation 3.S.6 depicts the breakdown of dD_F/dp into substitution and income effects:

$$\frac{dD_F}{dp} = \frac{\partial D_F}{\partial p} - \frac{(D_F - x_F)}{p} \cdot a_F. \tag{3.S.6}$$

This breakdown of demand shows how important is the direction of trade. If food is imported at home, both income and substitution terms combine to reduce food demand as the relative price of food rises. However, if food were exported, the income effect of a rise in food's price would be positive, running counter to the substitution effect and, in some cases, resulting in more food being demanded locally.

The Hat Notation

It will often prove convenient to express the change in a variable, dx, as a fraction of the original value of that variable, x. We use a hat, " ^ ", to denote this relative change. Thus for any variable, x,

$$\hat{x} \equiv \frac{dx}{x}.$$

The Elasticity of Demand for Imports

This discussion of the components of demand behavior can be added to a consideration of production changes to investigate the *elasticity of demand for imports*, ϵ, defined as:

$$\epsilon = -\frac{\hat{M}}{\hat{p}}. \tag{3.S.7}$$

The minus sign is to make ϵ a positive number. M, of course, refers to home imports of food,

$$M = D_F - x_F,$$

so that

$$-\frac{\hat{M}}{\hat{p}} = -\frac{D_F}{M}\frac{\hat{D}_F}{\hat{p}} + \frac{x_F}{M}\frac{\hat{x}_F}{\hat{p}}.$$

The expression for

$$-\frac{D_F}{M}\frac{\hat{D}_F}{\hat{p}}$$

follows readily from 3.S.6. Let $\bar{\eta}$ represent the (negative of the) pure substitution term in demand,

$$\bar{\eta} \equiv -\frac{p}{M}\frac{\partial D_F}{\partial p}$$

and m the marginal propensity to import, which is the marginal propensity to consume the imported good (food) at home, a_F. Finally, define the elasticity of import-competing production, e, as:[2]

$$e \equiv \frac{p}{M} \cdot \frac{dx_F}{dp}.$$

Combining yields the final breakdown for the elasticity of demand for imports, ϵ:

$$\epsilon = \bar{\eta} + m + e. \qquad (3.S.8)$$

These are the three ingredients discussed in the text: a substitution term in demand ($\bar{\eta}$), an income effect (m), and a production response (e).

Supplement to Chapter 4:
Stability and Comparative Statics
in the Basic Trade Model

Stability in the two-commodity world trade model requires that an increase in the relative price of food reduces world excess demand for food. Conditions sufficient to guarantee stability can be derived and presented in two alternative, but equivalent, ways.

The Marshall-Lerner Stability Condition

This form of the condition concentrates upon the elasticity of each country's demand for imports. World excess demand for food is the difference between the home country's excess demand (M) and the foreign country's intended ex-

---

[2] An equivalent expression for e is $\dfrac{\hat{X}}{\widehat{(1/p)}}$ with demands constant, which could be termed the elasticity of export supply. (X represents $x_C - D_C$ for the home country.)

ports of food. These intended food exports have a value equivalent to foreign import demand (for clothing). This value is M^*/p. (The division by p is to change from clothing units to food units.) Therefore, stability requires an increase in p to lower $\{M - M^*/p\}$. That is, the condition for stability is:

$$\frac{dM}{dp} < \frac{d(M^*/p)}{dp}.$$

This inequality can be slightly modified by (1) dividing the denominators of both sides by p to highlight the *relative* price change, dp/p. We shall throughout use a circumflex ("hat") to denote relative changes: dp/p is written as $\hat{p}$. (2) Divide the numerator on the left-hand side by M and the numerator on the right-hand side by M^*/p (which equals M at the initial equilibrium). Making use of the hat notation for relative changes, the inequality becomes:

$$\frac{\hat{M}}{\hat{p}} < \frac{\widehat{(M^*/p)}}{\hat{p}}. \tag{4.S.1}$$

By definition, the elasticity of home demand for imports along the offer curve is $\epsilon \equiv -\hat{M}/\hat{p}$, while foreign ϵ^* is $-\hat{M}^*/\widehat{(1/p)}$, which is equivalent to $\hat{M}^*/\hat{p}$.[1] Since inequality 4.S.1 can be written as:

$$\frac{\hat{M}}{\hat{p}} < \frac{\hat{M}^* - \hat{p}}{\hat{p}},$$

substituting for ϵ and ϵ^* yields 4.S.2:

$$\epsilon + \epsilon^* > 1. \tag{4.S.2}$$

This is known as the *Marshall-Lerner condition for stability*. It suggests that in order for the market to be stable, offer curves cannot be too inelastic. The offer curves in Figure 3.A.1 intersected at stable equilibrium point Q. Note that at that point ϵ was less than one but ϵ^* exceeded unity, so that the Marshall-Lerner condition was obviously satisfied. To illustrate an unstable equilibrium, both offer curves must be inelastic. Instability requires the offer curves to cut each other in the opposite direction than shown in Figure 3.A.1 as at point Q in Figure 4.A.1.

An Alternative Stability Condition

Concentrate on the excess world demand curve for food. The condition for market stability is that the slope of this curve be negative, or

$$\frac{dD_F}{dp} + \frac{dD_F^*}{dp} - \frac{dx_F}{dp} - \frac{dx_F^*}{dp} < 0.$$

Multiply each term by $-p$, which also changes the direction of the inequality sign. Next, divide and multiply the first term by D_F, the second term by D_F^*,

[1] The relative change in a ratio, such as $\widehat{(x/y)}$, is the difference between the relative change in the numerator and denominator. Since "1" is a constant, $\widehat{(1/p)}$ equals $-\hat{p}$.

the third term by x_F, and the fourth by x_F^*. Finally, divide all terms by total world demand $(D_F + D_F^*)$ or by the equivalent (in the neighborhood of equilibrium) total world supply $(x_F + x_F^*)$. At this stage the condition for stability is:

$$\frac{D_F}{D_F + D_F^*}\left\{-\frac{p}{D_F}\frac{dD_F}{dp}\right\} + \frac{D_F^*}{D_F + D_F^*}\left\{-\frac{p}{D_F^*}\frac{dD_F^*}{dp}\right\}$$

$$+ \frac{x_F}{x_F + x_F^*}\left\{\frac{p}{x_F}\frac{dx_F}{dp}\right\} + \frac{x_F^*}{x_F + x_F^*}\left\{\frac{p}{x_F^*}\frac{dx_F^*}{dp}\right\} > 0. \quad (4.S.3)$$

The final step involves breaking down the demand elasticities into income and substitution terms and defining the appropriate supply elasticities. The breakdown of home food demand response to price was shown in Chapter 3's equation 3.S.6, repeated here as 4.S.4:

$$\frac{dD_F}{dp} = \frac{\partial D_F}{\partial p} - \frac{(D_F - x_F)}{p} \cdot a_F. \quad (4.S.4)$$

A similar expression holds for the foreign country. Multiply 4.S.4 by $-p/D_F$ and define the pure substitution term, $-\dfrac{p}{D_F}\dfrac{\partial D_F}{\partial p}$, as $\bar{\omega}_F$. This must be positive.[2] This yields equation 4.S.5:

$$-\frac{p}{D_F}\frac{dD_F}{dp} = \bar{\omega}_F + \frac{(D_F - x_F)}{D_F} \cdot a_F. \quad (4.S.5)$$

Similarly, define

$$\frac{p}{x_F}\frac{dx_F}{dp}$$

as e_F. This own-supply response to price must be positive, as must the corresponding e_F^* term. Finally, note that home imports of food, M, are $D_F - x_F$, while $(x_F^* - D_F^*)$ represents foreign exports (equal to M). Inequality 4.S.6 emerges as the alternative condition for market stability:

$$\left\{\frac{D_F}{D_F + D_F^*}\bar{\omega}_F + \frac{D_F^*}{D_F + D_F^*}\bar{\omega}_F^*\right\} + \left\{\frac{x_F}{x_F + x_F^*}e_F + \frac{x_F^*}{x_F + x_F^*}e_F^*\right\}$$

$$> \frac{M}{D_F + D_F^*}(a_F^* - a_F). \quad (4.S.6)$$

This form of the stability condition is in some ways more revealing than the equivalent Marshall-Lerner expression (4.S.2). Three sets of influences affect stability: (1) Substitution effects in demand. The first bracketed expression is a weighted average of each country's substitution term in demand. These are positive and each helps ensure stability. (2) Production response to price.

---

[2] Note that $\bar{\omega}_F$ is smaller than the *trade* substitution elasticity, $\bar{\eta}$, defined in the supplement to Chapter 3. Indeed, $\bar{\omega}_F$ is (M/D_F) times $\bar{\eta}$. They would be equal only if no food were produced at home.

The second bracketed expression is a weighted average (with each country's production share, instead of demand share, as weights) of production elasticities. These also contribute to stability. (3) The income effects. The expression on the right-hand side captures the *net* effect on the world's food market of the *redistribution* of real incomes inherent in a rise in food's relative price. The sign of $(a_F^* - a_F)$ is crucial. If the home marginal propensity to consume food (a_F) exceeds the comparable foreign propensity (a_F^*), the market must be stable (since the right-hand side of the inequality becomes negative). That is, a rise in p would cause home food demand (income effect only) to fall by more than foreign demand (income effect only) rises. Even if a_F^* exceeds a_F, the difference would be a fraction. Furthermore, the impact which any difference in the two countries' marginal propensities has on the market is modified by the fraction $M/(D_F + D_F^*)$. This shows the significance of trade (M) relative to total world demand or supply. If trade is not extensive, the market is likely to be stable.

Comparative Statics

The text of this chapter discussed several comparative statics exercises involving changes in tastes, the composition of outputs, growth, and international transfers. The basic equilibrium relationship for all these exercises (except transfers) is the balance of payments condition, 4.S.7 [see also condition 2.S.9]:

$$pM = M^*. \qquad (4.S.7)$$

The method of comparative statics involves seeing how a disturbance to the market causes prices to change so as to restore the equilibrium relationship shown by equation 4.S.7. That is, anything that causes imports in either country to change must bring about an equilibrating price response.

Proceed formally by differentiating 4.S.7, making use of our hat notation for relative changes:

$$\hat{p} + \hat{M} = \hat{M}^*. \qquad (4.S.8)$$

Imports in either country respond to a change in the terms of trade — this is what the offer curves describe. In addition, a disturbance may *shift* one or more offer curves. Let the relative change in imports at home that would take place at *constant terms of trade* be denoted by $\hat{M}|_{\bar{p}}$. This is the shift in the home offer curve. Similarly, $\hat{M}^*|_{\bar{p}}$ denotes the relative shift in the foreign offer curve. Putting these two sources of import change together,

$$\hat{M} = -\epsilon\hat{p} + \hat{M}|_{\bar{p}}$$
$$\hat{M}^* = \epsilon^*\hat{p} + \hat{M}^*|_{\bar{p}}. \qquad (4.S.9)$$

Substitute these into 4.S.8 and solve for the relative change in the terms of trade to get:

$$\hat{p} = \frac{\{\hat{M}|_p - \hat{M}^*|_p\}}{\Delta} \quad \text{where } \Delta \equiv \epsilon + \epsilon^* - 1. \qquad (4.S.10)$$

This is a basic, and readily understandable, result. From the Marshall-Lerner stability expression 4.S.2, the denominator, Δ, must be positive. What is directly shown is that the less sensitive are imports to price changes (small Δ), the more must price adjust to clear markets. Furthermore, the numerator of 4.S.10 has a ready interpretation. It shows the relative increase in world excess demand for the home country's import commodity (food) at the initial prices. In other words, 4.S.10 shows that the equilibrium relative price of food rises if the excess world demand curve for food shifts to the right and the market is stable.

In many applications of the basic trade model, we wish to analyze how real incomes at home and abroad are affected. The expression for real income changes at home was developed in the supplement to Chapter 3. A slight rewriting of 3.S.3 yields:

$$dy = -pM \cdot \hat{p} + \{dx_C + pdx_F\}. \qquad (4.S.11)$$

There is a terms-of-trade effect and a direct effect from production changes. Recall that for movements along the transformation curve, $\{dx_C + pdx_F\}$ equals zero. Therefore the second part of dy in 4.S.11 picks up the value of *shifts* in the transformation curve.

1. *A Change in the Composition of Home Outputs.* In this case assume that at constant prices food output rises by $dx_F (>0)$, clothing output falls by $dx_C (<0)$, but, at initial prices, there is no change in the value of aggregate production $(dx_C + pdx_F$ equals zero). This means that at the initial price there is no alteration in home demand for food importables (both price and income are constant at the initial price). But demand for imports falls as production rises: $dM = -dx_F$. Abroad no changes are posited at the initial prices. Substitution into 4.S.10 reveals that

$$\hat{p} = -\frac{1}{M \cdot \Delta} dx_F. \qquad (4.S.12)$$

With the terms of trade improving, so must real income at home. From 4.S.11 we obtain

$$dy = \frac{pdx_F}{\Delta}. \qquad (4.S.13)$$

The more inelastic are world demands and supplies, the more successful would be a policy of substituting import-competing production (x_F) for exportables (x_C). This is a theme picked up by the tariff literature.

2. *Export-Led Growth.* Suppose growth is biased so that at initial prices only the output of exportables at home expands: $dx_C > 0$ but, at constant prices, dx_F equals zero. No *shifts* in demand or supply take place abroad. At initial prices there is no change in production of food (importables), but because incomes expand (at *initial* prices), so does demand. That is, $dM = dD_F$ and $dD_F = (m/p)(dx_C)$. Demand for food rises by an amount determined by the marginal propensity to import food (m) and the increase in initial incomes in food units (dx_C/p). Substituting into 4.S.10 yields:

$$\hat{p} = \frac{m}{pM \cdot \Delta} dx_C. \qquad (4.S.14)$$

The terms of trade have deteriorated and, by 4.S.11, this deterioration offsets at least a part of the initial growth effect on real incomes:

$$dy = \left\{ \frac{\Delta - m}{\Delta} \right\} dx_C. \qquad (4.S.15)$$

The expression in brackets provides the condition for immiserizing growth. Stability insures that Δ is positive, but if elasticities are nonetheless low, Δ may not exceed the home marginal propensity to import. In such a case, real incomes at home would fall despite output growth.

3. *Balanced Growth.* The kind of growth just discussed was quite biased — at initial prices only the home country's export good expanded, which ensures a deterioration in its terms of trade. But what about balanced growth? Suppose the home country's transformation schedule shifts outward uniformly at rate μ — both dx_C/x_C and dx_F/x_F equal μ at initial prices. Assume also that demand for both goods expands in a balanced fashion at initial prices (as in Figure 4.5). Then imports (at initial prices) must also expand at rate μ ($\hat{M}|_{\bar{p}}$ equals μ). Substitute into 4.S.10 to show that neutral growth must cause a deterioration in the terms of trade (assuming no growth abroad):

$$\hat{p} = \frac{\mu}{\Delta} . \qquad (4.S.16)$$

It proves convenient to express the change in real income (given in 4.S.11) in relative terms. $\hat{y}$ is dy divided by initial income $(x_C + px_F)$. That is,

$$\hat{y} = -\theta_M \hat{p} + \mu$$

where θ_M represents the share of imports in the national income and μ, of course, is the growth rate at initial prices. This expression is perfectly general. Substituting the terms-of-trade change shown by 4.S.16 for the case of balanced growth yields:

$$\hat{y} = \left\{ \frac{\Delta - \theta_M}{\Delta} \right\} \mu. \qquad (4.S.17)$$

This result shows that even balanced growth can be immiserizing, for it does worsen the terms of trade. If elasticities are sufficiently low, their sum may not exceed unity by more than the share of imports in the national income. Expression 4.S.17 should be compared with 4.S.15. If we retain the assumption that at constant prices growth in demand is proportional, the marginal propensity to import (m) is the same as the fraction of total income spent on importables. Unless production of importables is nonexistent, this must exceed the share of income represented by total imports (θ_M). Export-led growth is more apt to worsen real incomes than is balanced growth.

4. *The Transfer Problem.* Discussion of the transfer problem requires a bit more preparation. The basic equilibrium relationship set out in equation 4.S.7 rests on the classical form of the budget constraint: In each country all earned income is spent. The transfer process has the home country spending less than its produced income by the amount of transfer (call it T in units of clothing), matched by an equal amount of excess spending (over earned in-

come) abroad. This implies that the value of spending on imports at home must as well be cut below the value of foreign imports by the amount of the transfer.[3] This is basic relationship of 4.S.18:

$$pM = M^* - T. \tag{4.S.18}$$

Assume that initially there is no transfer ($T = 0$ initially). Differentiation of 4.S.18 yields:

$$\hat{p} + \hat{M} = \hat{M}^* - \frac{dT}{pM}. \tag{4.S.19}$$

From this we may proceed as before (in the development of 4.S.10) to obtain:

$$\hat{p} = \frac{\left\{ \hat{M}|_{\bar{p}} - \hat{M}^*|_{\bar{p}} + \frac{dT}{pM} \right\}}{\Delta}. \tag{4.S.20}$$

With a transfer of purchasing power there are no production changes at the initial terms of trade.[4] But demand for imports falls at home and rises abroad. That is, $\hat{M}|_p = -m \, dT/pM$ and $\hat{M}^*|_p = m^* dT/pM$. In other words, the impact of the direct redistribution of income on the terms of trade is shown by $\hat{p}$ in 4.S.21:

$$\hat{p} = \frac{- \{m + m^* - 1\}}{\Delta} \frac{dT}{pM}. \tag{4.S.21}$$

This expression confirms the text's account that with transfer the terms of trade might go in either direction. Note that the numerator can also be written as $[(1 - m^*) - m]$ or, to use the terminology of 4.S.6, as $(a_F^* - a_F)$. Whether the real income transfer is a consequence of a change in the terms of trade (as in the stability expression 4.S.6) or of a direct transfer of purchasing power (as in 4.S.21), the same comparison between foreign (a_F^*) and home (a_F) marginal propensities to consume a particular commodity is required.

Finally, we confirm the text's argument that even if the terms of trade move in favor of the transferor, real income for the transferor cannot improve. The equivalent of 4.S.11 for the transfer problem is:[5]

$$dy = -pM\hat{p} - dT.$$

[3] The home budget constraint becomes: $D_C + pD_F = x_C + px_F - T$. Rewriting, $p(D_F - x_F) = (x_C - D_C) - T$. When markets clear, home intended exports equal foreign imports, M^*.

[4] Ignored here is the text's discussion of a possible transfer of real resources. A general treatment of the transfer problem, which includes possible supply reactions, is R. W. Jones, "Presumption and the Transfer Problem," *Journal of International Economics* (August 1975): 263–74, reprinted as chapter 10 in *International Trade: Essays in Theory*. Amsterdam: North-Holland, 1979.

[5] The interpretation of dy is the change in current real consumption. What is left out of account is the possibility that the transfer represents a loan, which will in future be repaid. Presumably this does not by itself lower "real income" for the transferor.

Direct substitution of $\hat{p}$ into this expression yields:

$$dy = -\left\{\frac{\epsilon + \epsilon^* - (m + m^*)}{\Delta}\right\} dT.$$

But the supplement to Chapter 3 decomposed the elasticity of import demand (ϵ, and, by analogy, ϵ^*) into a substitution term in consumption ($\bar{\eta}$ and $\bar{\eta}^*$), a positive elasticity in production (e and e^*), and the import propensity (m and m^*). Therefore with transfer the expression for dy can finally be given as in 4.S.22:

$$dy = -\frac{\{\bar{\eta} + \bar{\eta}^* + e + e^*\}}{\Delta} dT. \qquad (4.S.22)$$

Real income for the transferor must decline, as demonstrated in the text in Figure 4.6.

Supplement to Chapter 5:
Comparative Advantage and the Assignment Problem

Because the Ricardian trade model has such a simple production structure — each commodity produced only with labor at fixed coefficients — it is ideally suited to the analysis of production assignments in a world with many countries and commodities. The concept of the world transformation schedule, illustrated in Figure 5.4 for the two-country, two-commodity case, provides the focus for our discussion here of comparative advantage in the more general case.

It is useful to consider a concrete example. Suppose the world consists of three countries: A (America), B (Britain), and C (Continental Europe). Furthermore suppose only three commodities can be produced and consumed: corn (Co), linen (Lin), and cloth (Cl). Let the numbers in the following table show the invariant labor input-output coefficients in each country to produce a unit of each commodity:[1]

	A	*B*	*C*
Corn	10	10	10
Linen	5	7	3
Cloth	4	3	2

[1] This example, and much of the subsequent analysis, is found in R. W. Jones, "Comparative Advantage and the Theory of Tariffs: A Multi-Commodity, Multi-Country Model," *Review of Economic Studies,* June 1961, pp. 161–75, and reprinted as chapter 3 in *International Trade: Essays in Theory.* Amsterdam: North-Holland, 1979. See also ibid., chapter 18.

If only two commodities were to be produced, the techniques illustrated in Figure 5.4 for two countries could be easily extended to accommodate a third. For example, if only corn and linen are produced, Figure 5.S.1 would show that the relatively most efficient producer of corn is Britain, followed by America and, last, Continental Europe, despite the fact that all three countries have the same absolute costs. In drawing Figure 5.S.1 we have arbitrarily assumed all countries have the same size labor force, an assumption that does not interfere with our analysis of *patterns* of specialization in production.

Panel (b) in Figure 5.S.1 summarizes much of what the two-dimensional transformation schedule in panel (a) shows. All countries produce linen at the left-hand linen origin. The lettering reveals that country B is the first country to release labor to produce corn, since it has the greatest comparative advantage in producing corn *relative to linen*. Country A is next in the line

---

FIGURE 5.S.1   The World Transformation Schedule: Three Countries

The world transformation schedule in the three-country, two-commodity version is a three-segment linear schedule bowed out from the origin. Information as to the pattern of specialization for countries A, B, C in linen and corn can be summarized in the one-dimensional line in panel b.

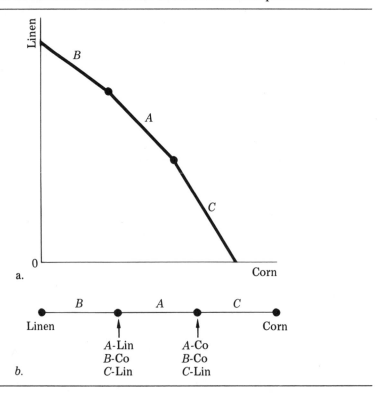

of comparative advantage so that two-thirds across to the corn origin countries A and B are completely specialized in corn and C in linen.

It is clear that adding one more country to a two-commodity analysis introduces no fresh difficulties. And a similar kind of ranking could display separately positions of comparative advantage in linen and cloth on the one hand and corn and cloth on the other. The information on bilateral cost ratios is computed from the table and summarized graphically in Figure 5.S.2. For example, if only cloth and linen are to be produced, and if two countries are to be assigned to produce linen and only one country to produce cloth, country B is selected as the cloth producer because its relative cost, $\frac{3}{7}$, is lower than either $\frac{2}{3}$ or $\frac{4}{5}$. Note that there are potentially three possible assignments that put one country in cloth and two in linen. Think of a *class* of assignments as a specification of the number of countries assigned to each commodity. In this example it was zero countries in corn, one in cloth, and two in linen. (There are five other classes of this type, e.g., zero countries in cloth, one in corn, and two in linen.) The doctrine of comparative advantage singles out the *efficient* assignment in each class.

But suppose all three commodities are to be produced. If each country were to be assigned a different commodity, which assignment pattern reflects comparative advantage? Turn back to the table of cost figures. If only corn and linen were to be produced and only countries A and B involved, clearly B has a comparative advantage in corn and A in linen. Now add country C and the new commodity, cloth. Country C is in absolute terms the lowest-cost cloth producer. Therefore, suppose we consider the assignment: A in linen, B in corn, and C in cloth. As just noted, A has a comparative advantage in linen relative to corn compared with country B. Likewise C has a comparative advantage in cloth relative to corn compared with B ($\frac{2}{10}$ is less than $\frac{3}{10}$). Finally, a bilateral comparison between countries A and C in linen and cloth shows that linen is produced relatively cheaply in A ($\frac{5}{4}$ is smaller than $\frac{3}{2}$). And yet this pattern of specialization is inefficient! There are six possible assignments in

---

FIGURE 5.S.2 Bilateral Cost Rankings

Patterns of comparative advantage taking two commodities at a time are summarized below as in Figure 5.S.1b.

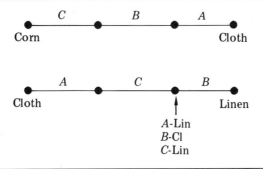

which all three commodities are produced and the efficient one has corn produced by country A, cloth by country B, and linen by country C.

To check out that this alternative assignment is indeed efficient, recall that the force of competition in world markets rules out inefficient production patterns. In a competitive equilibrium any commodity that is actively produced in a country must have unit labor costs equal to price so that profits are bid away. Furthermore, if a country does not produce a commodity, it must not be the case that unit labor costs are actually less than the world price of that commodity. As we now show, there is a range of world prices at which, simultaneously, country A can produce corn, country B cloth, and country C linen.

Since only relative prices matter, let us arbitrarily set the price of corn at unity. If country A is to produce corn, the wage rate in country A must equal $\frac{1}{10}$. This, in turn, reveals that *if* country A were to attempt to produce linen, unit costs would equal $\frac{1}{2}$. Therefore a competitive equilibrium in which country A does not produce linen must be one in which the world price of linen, p_{Lin}, is less than or equal to $\frac{1}{2}$. Figure 5.S.3 shows possible ranges for the world prices of linen and cloth (given our assumption that the price of corn is unity). Any value of p_{Lin} greater than $\frac{1}{2}$ is thus ruled out. Also, with a wage rate of $\frac{1}{10}$ the unit cost of producing cloth in A would be $\frac{2}{5}$, and this cannot fall short of the world price of cloth.

Now consider country B, which has been assigned to cloth production. The wage rate in country B depends on the price of cloth, and will equal one-third times p_{Cl}. Therefore, if B were to attempt to produce corn, the cost per unit would be 10 times the wage rate, which must not fall short of the price of corn (which equals unity by assumption). That is, $\frac{10}{3}p_{Cl}$ must be ≥ 1, which puts a lower bound on the price of cloth. Similarly, unit costs in B for linen production would equal $(\frac{7}{3})p_{Cl}$, which must be greater than or equal to the world price of linen. That is, any acceptable p_{Lin} must lie below the ray from the origin whose equation is $p_{Lin} = \frac{7}{3}p_{Cl}$. Finally, consider the required comparison in country C between the unit costs of corn and cloth and world prices. C is assigned to linen, so that the wage rate in C equals one-third the world price of linen. Its unit costs in corn would then be $\frac{10}{3}$ times the price of linen so that $\frac{10}{3}p_{Lin}$ must exceed unity to avoid C being a potentially profitable location for corn production. Finally, unit costs for cloth in C would be two times the wage rate in C or $\frac{2}{3}$ times the price of linen. This cost figure must not fall short of the price of cloth, which means p_{Lin} must exceed $\frac{3}{2}$ times the price of cloth.

The shaded area in Figure 5.S.3 shows combinations of prices of linen and cloth, relative to a unit price for corn, at which competition allows America to produce corn, Britain to produce cloth, and, simultaneously, Continental Europe to produce linen. Of the six assignments in the *class* for which each country produces a commodity distinct from the other two, this one is the only efficient one. There is *no* set of free-trade prices that would tolerate the others (e.g., A in linen, B in corn, and C in cloth as we originally suggested). This information is necessary in drawing the full world transformation surface. Such a surface would be three-dimensional, but a two-dimensional representation of the assignments can be made, just as panel (b) of Figure 5.S.1

FIGURE 5.S.3 Price Possibilities

If the price of corn is unity, any price combination for linen and cloth in the shaded area satisfies the competitive profit conditions when A produces corn, B cloth, and C linen.

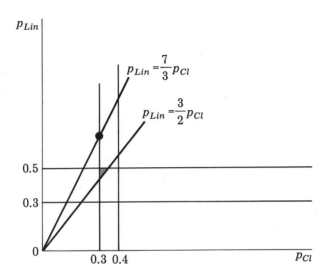

contained in one dimension the information about assignments captured in panel (a)'s transformation locus.

Figure 5.S.4 shows the efficient assignment pattern along the world transformation surface.[2] The bottom edge of the triangle corresponds to panel (b) of Figure 5.S.1, while the side edges replicate the assignment patterns in Figure 5.S.2. In constructing the shape of the surface it was necessary to go through our previous analysis in search of the efficient assignment for the interior point where all three commodities are produced and each country is specialized. Figure 5.S.4 suggests that the transformation surface is made up of planar elements, ridges, and points. Points correspond to positions in which all countries are completely specialized, and once the efficient assignment in each class of complete specialization is determined, the entire surface can be mapped out. Suppose we start at the linen corner, where all countries are producing linen. The cost figures suggest that country B has a strong comparative *dis*advantage in linen production, so that should the world wish to consume small amounts of either cloth or corn (or both), it is country B's labor that is

[2] The technique of reducing a three-dimensional surface to a two-dimensional pattern of assignments was pioneered by Lionel McKenzie in "Specialization and Efficiency in World Production," *Review of Economic Studies,* June 1954.

FIGURE 5.S.4 Assignments Along the World Transformation Surface

Along the ridges one country's labor force is being reallocated between two of the three commodities.

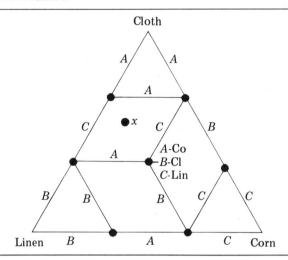

first freed up from its assignment to linen. Indeed, relative commodity prices in the lower left-hand triangle in Figure 5.S.4 are given solely by comparative labor costs in country B. Thus if the price of corn is unity, the price of linen would be $\frac{7}{10}$ and of cloth $\frac{3}{10}$. The lower left-hand triangle exactly replicates country B's planar transformation surface. At a point such as x, country B is completely specialized in cloth, while country A produces both linen and corn and country C produces linen and cloth. Thus country A's technology determines the linen/corn relative price $(\frac{1}{2})$ and country C's labor costs determine that the relative price of linen to cloth is $\frac{3}{2}$. Along a ridge just one country is incompletely specialized to two commodities, so that one relative price is fixed and the other free to vary (within bounds). At the interior point showing complete specializations, both relative prices are free to vary within the bounds set by the three adjacent planes; this corresponds to relative prices in the shaded area of Figure 5.S.3.

There is a simple general rule for locating the assignment that is efficient in its *class*. Reconsider the interior class in which each country is specialized completely to a different commodity. In the efficient specialization A was assigned corn, B cloth, and C linen so that in symbols,

$$w^A a^A_{Co} = p_{Co}$$

$$w^B a^B_{Cl} = p_{Cl}$$

$$w^C a^C_{Lin} = p_{Lin} \, ,$$

where w^i is country i's wage rate and a^i_j is country i's labor cost of producing a unit of commodity j. It is also the case that

$$w^A a^A_{Lin} \geq p_{Lin}$$

$$w^B a^B_{Co} \geq p_{Co}$$

$$w^C a^C_{Cl} \geq p_{Cl}$$

since otherwise some country would have an unexploited profitable production possibility. Multiply the three equalities to get:

$$w^A w^B w^C a^A_{Co} a^B_{Cl} a^C_{Lin} = p_{Co} p_{Cl} p_{Lin}.$$

Multiply the three inequalities to obtain:

$$w^A w^B w^C a^A_{Lin} a^B_{Co} a^C_{Cl} \geq p_{Co} p_{Cl} p_{Lin}.$$

A comparison now reveals that if the assignment *A-Co, B-Cl, C-Lin* was the efficient member of its class, the product $a^A_{Co} a^B_{Cl} a^C_{Lin}$ must not exceed $a^A_{Lin} a^B_{Co} a^C_{Cl}$. According to the table, the first product is 90 while the second is 100. The general rule is that the assignment pattern that *minimizes the product of labor coefficients* among all assignments in its class is the efficient optimal assignment. No other assignment patterns in that class can ever be supported in a free-trade equilibrium.[3] This is the generalization of the Ricardian law of comparative advantage that in the two-commodity, two-country case was cast in terms of cost ratios.[4]

As a final observation note that the doctrine of comparative advantage does not state what a country *will* produce. The actual production pattern depends largely upon demand. Instead, it points out production patterns that are *ruled out* by free trade. In our 3 × 3 numerical example there are 3^3 or 27 possible complete specialization assignments of countries to commodities. Of these 17 are inefficient and would never be observed in a free-trade world. The remaining 10 are the ones shown in Figure 5.S.4. The fraction of inefficient production patterns ruled out by the austere pressures of competition and free trade rises drastically as the number of countries and commodities expands.[5]

Supplement to Chapter 6:
The Specific-Factors Model of Production

This supplement provides a formal analytic treatment of the model of production described in Chapter 6. The community produces two commodities,

---

[3] Thus in Figure 5.4 in the text, the home country may produce food, e.g., at point *J*, or the foreign country may produce clothing, but with free trade it is impossible for *both* home food production and foreign clothing production to exist simultaneously.

[4] In equation (5.2) in the text, cross multiplying converts the comparative advantage criterion in terms of the minimum product of labor coefficients.

[5] For further discussion see R. W. Jones, *International Trade: Essays in Theory* (Amsterdam: North-Holland, 1979), chapter 18.

clothing and food. Labor (L) and capital (K) are combined to produce clothing. The input requirements *per unit* output of clothing are denoted by a_{LC} and a_{KC}. Labor is also used to produce food, in cooperation with land (T). Thus the per unit output requirements in the food sector are a_{LF} and a_{TF}. Capital and land are each used specifically only in one sector, whereas labor is mobile between sectors.

The Distribution of Income

Pure competition is assumed to prevail, and this assures that commodity prices (p_C and p_F) reflect unit costs of production. These costs, in turn, depend in part on the input mix used in production (the a_{ij}'s) and in part on factor prices. The wage rate is denoted by w, and the amount that must be paid per unit rental on capital is given by r_K and the rental on land by r_T. The competitive profit conditions are thus summarized in 6.S.1 and 6.S.2:

$$a_{LC}w + a_{KC}r_K = p_C \tag{6.S.1}$$

$$a_{LF}w + a_{TF}r_T = p_F. \tag{6.S.2}$$

Techniques of production are chosen so as to minimize the costs of producing a unit of output in the face of prevailing factor prices. To see what this entails consider the clothing sector. The assumption of constant returns to scale implies that the *unit isoquant* captures all there is to know about techniques of production. At the point of cost minimization, the iso-cost line (with slope given by [minus] the ratio of factor prices, $-w/r_K$), is tangent to the unit isoquant (with slope da_{KC}/da_{LC}). That is, cost minimization entails that

$$w\,da_{LC} + r_K\,da_{KC} = 0.$$

Once again it proves convenient to write these changes in *relative* terms (denoted by the "hat," "$\hat{\ }$"). Thus $\hat{a}_{LC}$ is da/a_{LC}. Also, write the factor *distributive shares* as θ_{LC} and θ_{KC} respectively, where, for example, θ_{LC} is wa_{LC}/p_C. Therefore, in the clothing sector cost minimization entails:

$$\theta_{LC}\hat{a}_{LC} + \theta_{KC}\hat{a}_{KC} = 0. \tag{6.S.3}$$

Similarly, in the food sector,

$$\theta_{LF}\hat{a}_{LF} + \theta_{TF}\hat{a}_{TF} = 0. \tag{6.S.4}$$

Each of these expressions states that if labor is used more intensively, less of the specific factor need be used along the unit isoquant. The left-hand side in 6.S.3 and 6.S.4 shows, for each industry, the relative change in unit costs involved in substituting one input for another. At a point of cost minimization this change must be zero: All cost reductions have already been taken at the minimum cost point.

We are now directly in a position to confirm Chapter 6's argument that each commodity price change is flanked by the changes in the returns to productive factors used in that industry. Differentiate 6.S.1 and 6.S.2, put into relative terms, and simplify by using 6.S.3 and 6.S.4 to obtain:

$$\theta_{LC}\hat{w} + \theta_{KC}\hat{r}_K = \hat{p}_C \tag{6.S.5}$$

$$\theta_{LF}\hat{w} + \theta_{TF}\hat{r}_T = \hat{p}_F. \tag{6.S.6}$$

Thus each commodity price change must be a weighted average of factor price changes, with the weights given by distributive shares — reflections of the importance of each factor in unit costs. Suppose now that commodity prices are disturbed, that clothing's price rises while the price of food remains unchanged. Conditions 6.S.5 and 6.S.6 then suggest that *some* factor's return will rise relatively by more than has p_C, while some other factor's return will absolutely fall (since $\hat{p}_F = 0$). As is easy to show, capitalists are the clear gainers and landlords the losers. We establish this by first showing that the wage rate must rise, but not as much, relatively, as the price of clothing.

The wage rate is determined by the condition that the labor force be fully employed. The clothing sector's demand for labor is written as $a_{LC}x_C$, where x_C shows the scale of output. But output is restricted by the availability of capital. If a_{KC} denotes the quantity of capital used per unit and if K units of capital are all the economy possesses, clothing output must be given by:

$$x_C = \frac{K}{a_{KC}}.$$

Therefore, the clothing sector's demand for labor can be written as $a_{LC}/a_{KC} \cdot K$. In similar fashion we see that the food sector's demand for labor is $a_{LF}/a_{TF} \cdot T$. Thus 6.S.7 is the statement that all the economy's labor force is fully employed:

$$\frac{a_{LC}}{a_{KC}} \cdot K + \frac{a_{LF}}{a_{TF}} \cdot T = L. \tag{6.S.7}$$

Differentiate this, assuming now that K and T remain constant but L may change, to obtain 6.S.8,

$$\lambda_{LC}(\hat{a}_{LC} - \hat{a}_{KC}) + \lambda_{LF}(\hat{a}_{LF} - \hat{a}_{TF}) = \hat{L} \tag{6.S.8}$$

where the λ's correspond to the fraction of the economy's labor force used in each sector.

To proceed, reconsider the relationship between the wage rate and the value of labor's marginal product in each sector. These must be equal (as equations 6.1 of the text state). Figure 6.S.1 illustrates how the quantity of labor used per unit of capital (a_{LC}/a_{KC}) depends inversely on the real wage in the clothing sector (w/p_C). The curve shows the marginal physical product of labor in clothing. Define the *elasticity* of labor's marginal product curve, γ_{LC}, as:

$$\gamma_{LC} \equiv -\frac{(\hat{a}_{LC} - \hat{a}_{KC})}{(\hat{w} - \hat{p}_C)}. \tag{6.S.9}$$

Similarly, in the food industry,

$$\gamma_{LF} \equiv -\frac{(\hat{a}_{LF} - \hat{a}_{TF})}{(\hat{w} - \hat{p}_F)}. \tag{6.S.10}$$

FIGURE 6.S.1   The Elasticity of Labor's Marginal Product

A drop in the real wage from OA to OB would encourage labor to be used more intensively — an increase in the labor-capital ratio from OA' to OB'. The elasticity of labor's marginal product in clothing, γ_{LC}, is defined as $-(\hat{a}_{LC} - \hat{a}_{KC})$ divided by $(\hat{w} - \hat{p}_C)$.

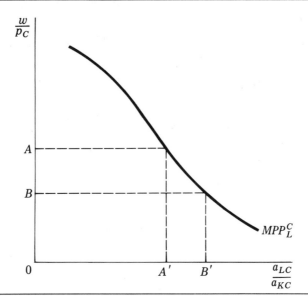

These concepts are crucial. Substitute the expressions for the elasticities, γ_{LC} and γ_{LF}, into equation 6.S.8 to obtain 6.S.11:

$$\lambda_{LC}\gamma_{LC}(\hat{w} - \hat{p}_C) + \lambda_{LF}\gamma_{LF}(\hat{w} - \hat{p}_F) = -\hat{L}. \qquad (6.S.11)$$

Or, solving explicitly for the change in the wage rate in terms of the commodity price changes and any change in the labor force,

$$\hat{w} = \beta_C\hat{p}_C + \beta_F\hat{p}_F - \frac{1}{\gamma}\hat{L} \qquad (6.S.12)$$

where

$$\beta_C \equiv \lambda_{LC}\frac{\gamma_{LC}}{\gamma}$$

$$\beta_F \equiv \lambda_{LF}\frac{\gamma_{LF}}{\gamma}$$

and

$$\gamma \equiv \lambda_{LC}\gamma_{LC} + \lambda_{LF}\gamma_{LF}.$$

γ_{LC} and γ_{LF} are the elasticities of labor's marginal product curve in each sector, and γ is the economy-wide weighted average of these two elasticities. γ directly provides the answer to the following question: If commodity prices are constant and the wage rate rises by 1 percent, by what percent will the entire economy's demand for labor fall? If γ is large, the answer is that the economy's demand for labor would be reduced by a relatively large amount. Conversely, equation 6.S.12 shows that a given increase in the labor force would, at constant commodity prices, reduce the wage rate, but not by very much if γ is large. The β coefficients, which add to unity, reveal the power of each commodity price separately to influence the wage rate. At constant overall factor endowments, the wage rate change is trapped between (i.e., is a positive weighted average of) the commodity price changes. Therefore, if clothing's relative price rises ($\hat{p}_C > \hat{p}_F$), this relationship, coupled with 6.S.5 and 6.S.6, establishes that:

$$\hat{r}_K > \hat{p}_C > \hat{w} > \hat{p}_F > \hat{r}_T.$$

The specific factors are most radically affected by price changes. The mobile factor (labor) finds its return rising in terms of one sector and falling in terms of the other.

Outputs, Prices, and Factor Endowments

Outputs respond to changes in relative prices along the transformation schedule. Outputs also respond to changes in factor endowments (at constant commodity prices). In the text we showed how an ample supply of capital lends a presumption that relatively much clothing is produced. By contrast, plentiful land encourages food production. Now we keep endowments of capital and land constant but explore the implication for outputs (and thus for positions of comparative advantage) of changes in labor abundance.

If, as we assume, the total capital stock is kept fixed, clothing output can expand only by using capital less intensively. Similarly, since x_F equals $\dfrac{T}{a_{TF}}$, food output can change only if a_{TF} is altered given that overall land is fixed in supply. Thus

$$\hat{x}_C - \hat{x}_F = \hat{a}_{TF} - \hat{a}_{KC}. \tag{6.S.13}$$

The ingredients are at hand to solve separately for $\hat{a}_{TF}$ and $\hat{a}_{KC}$. From 6.S.4 and 6.S.10,

$$\hat{a}_{TF} = \theta_{LF}\gamma_{LF}(\hat{w} - \hat{p}_F).$$

Similarly, 6.S.3 and 6.S.9 can be solved for $\hat{a}_{KC}$:

$$\hat{a}_{KC} = \theta_{LC}\gamma_{LC}(\hat{w} - \hat{p}_C).$$

The change in the wage rate is provided by expression 6.S.12, so that 6.S.13 can be rewritten as 6.S.14:

$$\hat{x}_C - \hat{x}_F = \sigma_S(\hat{p}_C - \hat{p}_F) + \frac{1}{\gamma}[\theta_{LC}\gamma_{LC} - \theta_{LF}\gamma_{LF}]\hat{L} \tag{6.S.14}$$

where

$$\sigma_S \equiv \theta_{LF}\gamma_{LF}\beta_C + \theta_{LC}\gamma_{LC}\beta_F > 0.$$

The effect of a change in relative commodity prices on relative outputs along the transformation schedule (i.e., for given factor endowments) is captured by the positive term σ_S, the elasticity of supply of relative outputs. This is generally larger the greater are the elasticities of labor's marginal product curves in the two sectors.[1] The coefficient of $\hat{L}$ reveals that *two* distinct features of the technology determine the composition of output. As the labor supply expands (at given terms of trade), clothing output will tend to expand more than does the food sector if the elasticity of labor's marginal product is higher in clothing (i.e., if $\gamma_{LC} > \gamma > \gamma_{LF}$). This is one feature. But the comparison of labor's distributive shares, θ_{LC} and θ_{LF}, is also important. The clothing sector tends to expand relative to food if θ_{LC} exceeds θ_{LF}. As the supplement to Chapter 7 reveals, this comparison of distributive shares is a comparison of *relative labor intensity* in the two sectors. In the Heckscher-Ohlin model of Chapter 7, these factor intensity comparisons assume critical importance.

Supplement to Chapter 7:
The Two-Sector Heckscher-Ohlin Model

The two-sector Heckscher-Ohlin model of production assumes each of two outputs (clothing, food) is produced in a constant-returns-to-scale competitive setting with the use of two primary inputs (labor, capital). The productive factors are each homogeneous and mobile between sectors. Prices are flexible and both inputs are fully employed:

$$a_{LC}x_C + a_{LF}x_F = L \tag{7.S.1}$$

$$a_{KC}x_C + a_{KF}x_F = K. \tag{7.S.2}$$

Furthermore, unit costs in each sector are, if output is positive, equated to the prevailing commodity price. Thus:

$$a_{LC}w + a_{KC}r = p_C \tag{7.S.3}$$

$$a_{LF}w + a_{KF}r = p_F. \tag{7.S.4}$$

Again, w refers to the wage rate, and now the common return to capital in the economy is denoted by r.

Equations of Change: Prices

As in the specific-factors model of Chapter 6, techniques of production are chosen so as to minimize unit costs. This condition implies 7.S.5 and 7.S.6: The distributive-share weighted average of changes in input-output coefficients

---

[1] In the supplement to Chapter 7 we compare this expression for σ_S with the comparable elasticity in the Heckscher-Ohlin model by making further simplifying assumptions.

along the unit isoquant in each industry must vanish near the cost-minimization point.[1] These relationships

$$\theta_{LC}\hat{a}_{LC} + \theta_{KC}\hat{a}_{KC} = 0 \qquad (7.S.5)$$

$$\theta_{LF}\hat{a}_{LF} + \theta_{KF}\hat{a}_{KF} = 0 \qquad (7.S.6)$$

are crucial, for they suggest that in differentiating 7.S.3 and 7.S.4 totally we obtain:

$$\theta_{LC}\hat{w} + \theta_{KC}\hat{r} = \hat{p}_C \qquad (7.S.7)$$

$$\theta_{LF}\hat{w} + \theta_{KF}\hat{r} = \hat{p}_F. \qquad (7.S.8)$$

These conditions state that in each industry the distributive-share weighted average of factor-price changes equals the relative commodity price change. They correspond to the pair 6.S.5 and 6.S.6 for the specific-factors model. But now more can be said: This pair of equations links the commodity price changes $(\hat{p}_C,\hat{p}_F)$ to the pair of factor-price changes $(\hat{w},\hat{r})$. Factor prices are determined *uniquely* by commodity prices as long as both commodities are produced, and assuming the techniques used in clothing and food differ.

This qualification about techniques refers to the capital/labor ratio employed in the two sectors. As in the text, assume that food always is produced with a higher capital/labor ratio than is clothing. This comparison must then be revealed in a ranking of distributive shares. Specifically, labor's distributive share in labor-intensive clothing (θ_{LC}) must exceed that in capital-intensive food (θ_{LF}). To see this, compute the determinant of coefficients in the pair of equations 7.S.7 and 7.S.8. Call this determinant $|\theta|$. By definition,

$$|\theta| \equiv \theta_{LC}\theta_{KF} - \theta_{LF}\theta_{KC}.$$

Substitute the formal definition of each distributive share (e.g., θ_{LC} is wa_{LC}/p_C) to obtain:

$$|\theta| = \frac{wr}{p_C p_F} (a_{LC}a_{KF} - a_{LF}a_{KC}).$$

Therefore, $|\theta|$ is positive if clothing is labor-intensive. But since distributive shares in any industry add to unity, θ_{KF} is just $1 - \theta_{LF}$ and θ_{KC} is $1 - \theta_{LC}$. Therefore $|\theta|$ can be rewritten as:

$$|\theta| = \theta_{LC} - \theta_{LF}.$$

The relationships shown by 7.S.7 and 7.S.8 underlie the shape of the curve in Figure 7.1. Subtract 7.S.8 from 7.S.7 to obtain:

$$|\theta| \cdot (\hat{w} - \hat{r}) = (\hat{p}_C - \hat{p}_F). \qquad (7.S.9)$$

Thus an increase in labor-intensive clothing's relative price must raise the wage/rent ratio by a magnified amount. And more can be said: If $\hat{p}_C$ is greater than $\hat{p}_F$ and clothing is labor-intensive,

$$\hat{w} > \hat{p}_C > \hat{p}_F > \hat{r}.$$

[1] This states that an iso-cost line is tangent to the unit isoquant. Details are provided in the supplement to Chapter 6.

The factor-price changes are magnified reflections of the commodity price changes. The *Stolper-Samuelson theorem* asserts that an increase in labor-intensive clothing's price (with food price constant) must unambiguously raise the *real wage*. This follows directly from this chain of inequalities.

If two countries share the same technology and produce both goods in common, free trade in commodities will not only equate commodity prices, it will also result in *factor price equalization*. Just treat the variables in 7.S.7 and 7.S.8 as relative differences between countries. Thus if $\hat{p}_C = \hat{p}_F = 0$ with free trade, so must $\hat{w}$ and $\hat{r}$ be zero.

Equations of Change: Outputs

The pair of full-employment equations suggests that outputs respond both to factor-endowment changes and to changes in intensive techniques. Differentiate 7.S.1 and 7.S.2 totally, and let λ_{ij} refer to the fraction of the total supply of factor i that is employed in commodity j. Thus

$$\lambda_{LC}\hat{x}_C + \lambda_{LF}\hat{x}_F = \hat{L} - \{\lambda_{LC}\hat{a}_{LC} + \lambda_{LF}\hat{a}_{LF}\} \qquad (7.S.10)$$

$$\lambda_{KC}\hat{x}_C + \lambda_{KF}\hat{x}_F = \hat{K} - \{\lambda_{KC}\hat{a}_{KC} + \lambda_{KF}\hat{a}_{KF}\}. \qquad (7.S.11)$$

Each equation points out the limitation on outputs provided by the overall endowment of the factor, as well as the intensity with which that factor is used. Consider the changed techniques in clothing: $\hat{a}_{LC}$ and $\hat{a}_{KC}$. Equation 7.S.5 provided one relationship between these two changes. Another follows from the *definition* of the *elasticity of substitution* between labor and capital in the clothing sector.[2]

$$\sigma_C \equiv \frac{\hat{a}_{KC} - \hat{a}_{LC}}{\hat{w} - \hat{r}} \qquad (7.S.12)$$

Solve 7.S.5 and 7.S.12 to obtain

$$\hat{a}_{LC} = -\theta_{KC}\sigma_C(\hat{w} - \hat{r})$$
$$\hat{a}_{KC} = \theta_{LC}\sigma_C(\hat{w} - \hat{r}). \qquad (7.S.13)$$

Comparable solutions are obtained for changes in the labor and capital coefficients in the food sector — merely replace C with F in the subscripts of 7.S.13.

With these solutions now in hand, reconsider expressions such as $\{\lambda_{LC}\hat{a}_{LC} + \lambda_{LF}\hat{a}_{LF}\}$, which shows for the economy as a whole how much of an increase or reduction in labor is required at unchanged outputs. Suppose the wage/rent ratio rises. Both industries will economize on labor. Thus 7.S.10 and 7.S.11 can be rewritten as:

---

[2] You may wonder how the elasticity of substitution, σ_C, is related to the elasticity of labor's marginal product in clothing, γ_{LC}, defined in 6.S.9. Since $(\hat{w} - \hat{p}_C)$ is equal to $\theta_{KC}(\hat{w} - \hat{r})$, from equation 7.S.7 or 6.S.5, γ_{LC} equals σ_C divided by θ_{KC}.

$$\lambda_{LC}\hat{x}_C + \lambda_{LF}\hat{x}_F = \hat{L} + \delta_L(\hat{w} - \hat{r}) \tag{7.S.14}$$

$$\lambda_{KC}\hat{x}_C + \lambda_{KF}\hat{x}_F = \hat{K} - \delta_K(\hat{w} - \hat{r}), \tag{7.S.15}$$

where

$$\delta_L \equiv \lambda_{LC}\theta_{KC}\sigma_C + \lambda_{LF}\theta_{KF}\sigma_F$$

$$\delta_K \equiv \lambda_{KC}\theta_{LC}\sigma_C + \lambda_{KF}\theta_{LF}\sigma_F.$$

Subtract 7.S.15 from 7.S.14 and let

$$|\lambda| \equiv \lambda_{LC} - \lambda_{KC}.$$

Then:

$$(\hat{x}_C - \hat{x}_F) = \frac{1}{|\lambda|}(\hat{L} - \hat{K}) + \frac{(\delta_L + \delta_K)}{|\lambda|}(\hat{w} - \hat{r}). \tag{7.S.16}$$

If clothing is labor intensive, $|\lambda|$ is a positive fraction.[3] Finally, substitute the link between factor and commodity prices provided by 7.S.9 to obtain:

$$(\hat{x}_C - \hat{x}_F) = \frac{1}{|\lambda|}(\hat{L} - \hat{K}) + \sigma_S(\hat{p}_C - \hat{p}_F) \tag{7.S.17}$$

where

$$\sigma_S \equiv \frac{\delta_L + \delta_K}{|\lambda||\theta|} > 0.$$

Several features of the two-sector production model are revealed by 7.S.17. First, note that σ_S must be positive since δ_L and δ_K are each positive and $|\lambda|$ and $|\theta|$ must have the same sign. If, as we have assumed, clothing is labor-intensive, both $|\lambda|$ and $|\theta|$ are positive. If clothing were capital-intensive each would be negative, making the product, $|\lambda||\theta|$, positive once again. σ_S denotes the elasticity of supply along the bowed-out transformation curve. Figure 7.2 in the text confirms the rising supply curve that reflects increasing opportunity costs of production — a positive σ_S. Second, note that at constant prices the coefficient of $(\hat{L} - \hat{K})$ in 7.S.17 reveals how the transformation schedule shifts as factor endowments change. It confirms that in Figure 7.2 the home country's relative supply of clothing lies to the right of the foreign country's curve if, as assumed, the home country is relatively labor abundant and clothing is labor intensive. Indeed, 7.S.17 confirms the magnification effect of uneven growth of factor endowments on outputs if the terms of trade are constant. If $\hat{L}$ exceeds $\hat{K}$,

$$\hat{x}_C > L > K > \hat{x}_F.$$

If only labor expands, one output must actually fall — the Rybczynski result.[4]

---

[3] You can see that $|\lambda|$ is the determinant of coefficients in 7.S.14 and 7.S.15. The argument is similar to the one used in discussing $|\theta|$.

[4] See the reference in footnote 10 of Chapter 7. This supplement is based on R. W. Jones, "The Structure of Simple General Equilibrium Models," *Journal of Political Economy,* 73 (December 1965): 557–72, reprinted in *International Trade: Essays in Theory.* Amsterdam: North-Holland, 1979.

Output Responses to Price Changes:
Sector-Specific and Heckscher-Ohlin Models

Outputs are more responsive to price signals in the Heckscher-Ohlin model than in the specific-factor model because all factors are mobile between sectors. This was a comparison that was discussed in the appendix to Chapter 7, and graphically revealed in the envelope property of the Heckscher-Ohlin TT curve in Figure 7.A.4. Here we probe more deeply into each model's expression for the elasticity of supply along the transformation curve, σ_S, to point out the basic similarity and the basic difference between models.[5]

In the Heckscher-Ohlin model the elasticity of supply with respect to prices was shown by σ_S in equation 7.S.17. δ_L and δ_K each contain a blend of information on the degree of factor substitutability in the two sectors, σ_C and σ_F. Thus σ_S can be rewritten as

$$\sigma_S = \frac{Q_C \sigma_C + Q_F \sigma_F}{|\lambda||\theta|} \tag{7.S.18}$$

where

$$Q_C \equiv \theta_{LC}\lambda_{KC} + \theta_{KC}\lambda_{LC}$$

$$Q_F \equiv \theta_{LF}\lambda_{KF} + \theta_{KF}\lambda_{LF}$$

Clearly this is larger the larger either sector's elasticity of factor substitution. To simplify, suppose $\sigma_C = \sigma_F = \sigma$. Furthermore, note that

$$Q_C + Q_F + |\lambda||\theta| = 1.$$

Therefore, in the Heckscher-Ohlin model the assumption of common degree of factor substitutability in each sector leads to 7.S.19 as the expression for σ_S:

$$\sigma_S = \frac{1 - |\lambda||\theta|}{|\lambda||\theta|} \sigma. \tag{7.S.19}$$

Two features of the model lead to elastic responses of outputs along the transformation schedule: first, a high degree of factor substitutability in each sector (σ), and second, fairly similar factor proportions, as shown by low values for $|\lambda||\theta|$. If factor proportions were identical, $|\lambda||\theta|$ would equal zero. If, by contrast, labor were used only in one sector and capital in the other, $|\lambda||\theta|$ would equal 1, and σ_S would be zero.

In the sector-specific model the expression for σ_S was given in equation 6.S.14. The elasticities of labor's marginal product curves, γ_{Lj}, are related to the elasticity of factor substitution.[6] Thus γ_{LC} equals σ_C/θ_{KC} and γ_{LF} equals σ_F/θ_{TF}. As in the Heckscher-Ohlin case simplify by assuming a common value for $\sigma = \sigma_C = \sigma_F$, since intersectoral differences between σ_C and σ_F do little to change the value of σ_S (in either model). Furthermore, simplify by equating labor shares between sectors. The rationale here is that the Heckscher-Ohlin model focuses upon the difference between factor intensities in the two sectors

---

[5] More details of this comparison are provided in chapter 7 of R. W. Jones, *International Trade: Essays in Theory*. Amsterdam: North-Holland, 1979.
[6] See footnote 2.

and assumes the *same* degree of factor mobility between sectors. (It assumes that labor and capital are each perfectly mobile between sectors.) By contrast, the sector-specific model focuses upon the different degree of factor mobility between sectors (labor perfectly mobile, capital — or land — completely immobile). It seems fair, therefore, to allow the same degree of labor intensity between the two sectors, as captured by θ_{LC} and θ_{LF}. Thus the share of the specific factor in each industry is the same. Let θ_S denote the common value of θ_{KC} and θ_{TF}.

These simplifications allow σ_S for the sector-specific model in equation 6.S.14 to be rewritten as:

$$\sigma_S = \frac{1 - \theta_S}{\theta_S} \sigma. \qquad (7.S.20)$$

A comparison with 7.S.19 for the Heckscher-Ohlin model reveals: first, the common role in the two models played by the elasticity of factor substitution, σ, and second, the focus in the sector-specific model on the importance of sector-specificity as captured by θ_S, the share in the national income of specific factors. A greater degree of factor specificity implies a lower value for σ_S, precisely as, in the Heckscher-Ohlin model, a greater disparity in factor proportions implies a low σ_S. Each model is designed to focus upon a different feature of the technology, with somewhat analogous results in terms of the response of outputs to prices.

Supplement to Chapter 11:
Real Incomes, Prices, and the Tariff

Real Incomes and the Optimum Tariff

Recall from the supplement to Chapter 3 the basic expression for the change in the home country's level of real income, dy, in terms of the domestic price-weighted sum of consumption changes. This equation was 3.S.1, reproduced here as 11.S.1:

$$dy = dD_C + pdD_F. \qquad (11.S.1)$$

This expression needs no modification in the case of tariffs, for it rests on the simple notion that real income depends only upon the quantities of each commodity consumed and the relative valuation at the margin of one commodity in terms of another, as reflected in the *domestic* relative price of food, p.

The home country's budget constraint informs us of the source of a change in real incomes. But with a tariff we can write the budget constraint in terms either of domestic or world prices. It is instructive to look at each in turn.

In terms of domestic prices, aggregate spending at home, $D_C + pD_F$, is limited to the value of income, which is derived both from income earned in producing commodities, $x_C + px_F$, and from the proceeds of the tariff revenue, which depends on the home country's quantity of food imports, M, the foreign relative price of imports, p^*, and the tariff rate, t, and is the product of these three terms. Thus:

$$D_C + pD_F = x_C + px_F + tp^*M. \tag{11.S.2}$$

Figure 11.3 illustrated this form of the budget constraint with all items measured in food units instead of clothing units. With posttariff consumption at J, the aggregate value of incomes at domestic prices was OE, the value of incomes earned in production was shown by OC, and CE was the tariff revenue.

Consider, now, a small change in the tariff rate. This change leads to changes in prices, the consumption bundle, and production so that:

$$dD_C + pdD_F + D_Fdp = dx_C + pdx_F + x_Fdp + d(tp^*M).$$

Shift D_Fdp to the right-hand side to obtain 11.S.3:

$$(dD_C + pdD_F) = -Mdp + (dx_C + pdx_F) + d(tp^*M). \tag{11.S.3}$$

Note that the left-hand side is, by the definition given in equation 11.S.1, the increase in the home country's real income, dy. Furthermore, the expression $dx_C + pdx_F$ on the right-hand side must vanish because the slope of the transformation schedule, dx_F/dx_C, must equal the negative of clothing's relative price, $1/p$.[1] Thus 11.S.3 can be simplified as 11.S.4:

$$dy = -Mdp + d(tp^*M). \tag{11.S.4}$$

That is, the sources of any real income gain to the home country are to be found in (1) a change in the domestic relative price of imports, dp, where any decrease in this price will raise real incomes at home by a factor given by the volume of imports, M; and (2) any increase in the tariff revenue, $d(tp^*M)$.

Expenditure and income are related by *world* prices. The domestic relative price of food, p, is given by $(1 + t)p^*$, and substituting this quantity into equation 11.S.2, noticing that M is given by excess food demand, $D_F - x_F$, results in equation 11.S.5:

$$D_C + p^*D_F = x_C + p^*x_F. \tag{11.S.5}$$

This equation states that at *world* prices the value of the home country's consumption bundle exactly equals the value of its production bundle. This equality was illustrated in Figure 11.3 by the fact that the posttariff consumption bundle, J, and production bundle, B, both lay on line 4 whose slope, $-(1/p^*)$, indicated the world terms of trade. Differentiate 11.S.5 to obtain:

$$dD_C + p^*dD_F = -Mdp^* + (dx_C + p^*dx_F).$$

Add and subtract pdD_F on the left-hand side and pdx_F on the right-hand side. This yields

$$(dD_C + pdD_F) + (p^* - p)dD_F = -Mdp^* + (dx_C + pdx_F) + (p^* - p)dx_F.$$

As already explained, $dD_C + pdD_F$ is the definition of the increase in real income at home, and $dx_C + pdx_F$ vanishes if resources are allocated at the

---

[1] See the supplement to Chapter 3 for a more complete account.

optimal point along the transformation schedule. Since the change in imports, dM, is equal to $dD_F - dx_F$, the entire expression reduces to 11.S.6:

$$dy = -Mdp^* + (p - p^*)dM. \tag{11.S.6}$$

It is difficult to overestimate the importance of the breakdown represented by equation 11.S.6 in understanding the welfare significance of tariffs. The first term, $-Mdp^*$, is the terms-of-trade effect, now stated in terms of world prices. Any policy that depresses the relative price at which the home country can purchase its imports in the world market will favorably affect welfare at home by an amount proportional to the volume of imports. But if trade is impeded, as it will be if a tariff exists, the second term, $(p - p^*)dM$, must also be taken into account. $p - p^*$ is the tariff wedge — it is the discrepancy (tp^*) between the relative domestic price of imports and the world price of imports. This second term indicates that any increase in the home country's level of imports must increase real income if the cost of obtaining imports in the world market (as shown by p^*) falls short of the relative value of imports in the local market (as shown by p). Any policy pursued by the home country that restricts imports entails a welfare loss if a tariff wedge has raised the domestic (relative) price of imports over the world level. This loss is directly proportional to the extent of the tariff rate.

The optimal tariff is found by setting dy equal to 0 in equation 11.S.6. (In Figure 11.5 $dy = 0$ at the optimal tariff rate t_0.) Replace $(p - p^*)$ by the equivalent expression, tp^*:

$$Mdp^* = tp^*dM.$$

Dividing both sides by p^*M, and recalling our use of the "hat" notation to express relative changes (e.g., $\hat{M}$ is defined as dM/M), we can express the optimal tariff as:

$$t = \frac{1}{\hat{M}/\hat{p}^*}. \tag{11.S.7}$$

The foreign offer curve remains stationary. Therefore if $\hat{M}$, the relative change in the home country's import demand, could be linked to $\hat{M}^*$, the relative change in foreign import demand, the expression for the optimal tariff given by equation 11.S.7 could be translated into an expression involving ϵ^*, the elasticity of import demand along the foreign offer curve.

The relationship between M and M^* is simple — it is given by the equilibrium condition 11.S.8 that states that at world prices the value of the home country's imports is equated to the value of foreign imports (or home country exports):

$$p^*M = M^*. \tag{11.S.8}$$

Taking relative changes in 11.S.8 yields equation 11.S.9:

$$\hat{p}^* + \hat{M} = \hat{M}^*. \tag{11.S.9}$$

Therefore $\hat{M}/\hat{p}^*$ equals $\hat{M}^*/\hat{p}^* - 1$. But $\hat{M}^*/\hat{p}^*$ is merely the definition of ϵ^*, the elasticity of the foreign country's demand for imports along its offer curve.[2] From this we see that the formula for the optimum tariff given in 11.S.7 can be rewritten as in 11.S.10:

$$t = \frac{1}{\epsilon^* - 1}. \qquad (11.S.10)$$

This formula needs to be interpreted carefully. It seems to state that if the foreign offer curve is inelastic, $(\epsilon^* < 1)$, the tariff should be negative. This interpretation of the relationships underlying the formula would be incorrect. Reconsider equation 11.S.6. If the foreign offer curve is inelastic, an increase in the tariff would cause home imports to rise. The terms of trade improve for the home country, and with ϵ^* less than one, foreigners offer more food for export. (See the discussion in the appendix to Chapter 11.) On both counts dy in 11.S.6 must be positive. The home country should raise its tariff until it reaches the elastic stretch of the foreign offer curve. Only then will a favorable movement in the terms of trade be countered by an unfavorable cutback in the volume of imports.

The Impact of Tariffs on World and Domestic Prices

Assume that the tariff level is initially at zero.[3] The expression for the sources of a real income change in equation 11.S.6 then reduces to the terms-of-trade effect:

$$dy = -Mdp^*.$$

Our first task is to derive a solution for the effect of a small increase in the tariff rate upon the world relative price of food, p^*. The basic equilibrium relationship in the market, equating at world prices the value of imports in the two countries, was given in 11.S.8. From this equation the equation in rates of change was developed in 11.S.9. The foreign offer curve related $\hat{M}^*$ to the change in the terms of trade, $\hat{p}^*$. Explicitly,

$$\hat{M}^* = \epsilon^* \hat{p}^*. \qquad (11.S.11)$$

The expression for $\hat{M}$ is more complicated. A change in the tariff rate shifts the home country's offer curve. Therefore $\hat{M}$ will exhibit a mixture of such a shift as well as a move *along* the home country's offer curve. Specifically, we may write $M = M(p^*, t)$ and decompose the rate of change as in 11.S.12:

$$\hat{M} = -\epsilon \hat{p}^* + \beta dt, \qquad (11.S.12)$$

where β, defined literally as $1/M \cdot \partial M/\partial t$, is the shift in the home country's offer curve at given world terms of trade. One of our primary objectives is to

[2] This elasticity formulation was introduced in Chapter 3. Because $1/p^*$ is the relative price of the foreign country's imports (clothing), ϵ^* is defined as *minus* $\hat{M}^*$ divided by $\hat{1/p^*}$, which is equivalent to *plus* $\hat{M}^*/\hat{p}^*$.
[3] A more general treatment is provided in R. W. Jones, "Tariffs and Trade in General Equilibrium: Comment," *American Economic Review,* 59 (June 1969): 418–24.

develop an explicit expression for β to guarantee that it is negative. In Figure 11.4 we argued that an increase in t would reduce imports at given world terms of trade.

Substituting 11.S.11 for $\hat{M}^*$ and 11.S.12 for $\hat{M}$ into 11.S.9 yields the following solution for the effect of a tariff on world terms of trade:

$$\hat{p}^* = \frac{1}{\Delta} \beta dt \qquad (11.S.13)$$

where

$$\Delta = \epsilon + \epsilon^* - 1.$$

The expression Δ captures the Marshall-Lerner condition for market stability discussed in the supplement to Chapter 4. If we assume the market to be stable, the sum of import-demand elasticities must exceed unity and Δ must therefore be positive.

Home prices are linked to foreign prices by the tariff rate: $p = (1 + t)p^*$. Taking relative changes in these terms and equating yields 11.S.14:

$$\hat{p} = \hat{p}^* + dt. \qquad (11.S.14)$$

With the solution for the terms-of-trade change, $\hat{p}^*$, given by 11.S.13 we may substitute to obtain the solution shown in 11.S.15 for the change in the relative domestic price of imports, $\hat{p}$:

$$\hat{p} = \frac{1}{\Delta}(\Delta + \beta)\,dt. \qquad (11.S.15)$$

Although Δ is positive, we have argued (and will subsequently prove) that β is negative. This argument underscores the doubts we expressed in the text that an increase in t must protect the import-competing industry.

To develop an explicit expression for β, the shift in the home country's offer curve as a result of a tariff, we shall examine more closely the determinants of the home country's demand for imports, M, which is the difference between its total demand for food, D_F, and local production of food, x_F. As discussed in Chapter 3, D_F depends on the *domestic* price ratio, p, and real income, y. Thus,

$$D_F = D_F(p,y).$$

Taking small changes we obtain:

$$dD_F = \frac{\partial D_F}{\partial p}\,dp + \frac{\partial D_F}{\partial y}\,dy.$$

The term $\partial D_F/\partial p$ refers to the substitution effect of an increase in food's domestic relative price on demand assuming real income is constant. We may put this into elasticity notation by defining $\bar{\eta}$ as:

$$\bar{\eta} \equiv -\frac{p}{M}\frac{\partial D_F}{\partial p}. \qquad (11.S.16)$$

Thus defined, $\bar{\eta}$ must be positive. The term $\partial D_F/\partial y$ is related to the marginal propensity to import, m. Adjusting for units,

$$m \equiv p \frac{\partial D_F}{\partial y}. \tag{11.S.17}$$

Introducing $\bar{\eta}$ and m into the breakdown of dD_F we obtain:

$$dD_F = M \left(-\bar{\eta}\hat{p} + \frac{m}{pM} dy \right). \tag{11.S.18}$$

The change in real income, dy, is linked to the change in the terms of trade; the relative change in the domestic price ratio, $\hat{p}$, is linked to the change in the terms of trade and the change in the tariff rate by 11.S.14. Thus the change in D_F can be rewritten as:

$$dD_F = -M[(\bar{\eta} + m)\hat{p}^* + \bar{\eta}dt]. \tag{11.S.19}$$

Turning to the supply side, the change in the production of importables, dx_F, is linked to the elasticity of import-competing production, e, by 11.S.20 (see the supplement to Chapter 3):

$$dx_F = Me\hat{p}. \tag{11.S.20}$$

Finally, substituting 11.S.14 for the change in domestic prices results in:

$$dx_F = M(e\hat{p}^* + edt). \tag{11.S.21}$$

We now have the ingredients for expressing the change in import demand as the difference between dD_F and dx_F. Thus,

$$\hat{M} = -[(\bar{\eta} + e + m)\hat{p}^* + (\bar{\eta} + e)dt]. \tag{11.S.22}$$

Compare this with 11.S.12 to prove that the breakdown of the elasticity of demand for imports along the offer curve is:

$$\epsilon = \bar{\eta} + e + m. \tag{11.S.23}$$

The expression for the *shift* in the offer curve, denoted by β in 11.S.12, is, by comparison with 11.S.22, revealed to be:

$$\beta = -(\bar{\eta} + e). \tag{11.S.24}$$

This confirms our argument that at constant world terms of trade an increase in the tariff constricts imports both by encouraging resource allocation toward the import-competing sector and by cutting back on demand for the imported commodity through the substitution effect.

We may now develop an explicit criterion for the paradoxical-sounding case in which a tariff so depresses the terms of trade that the relative domestic price of imports falls as well. Substitute the expression for β in 11.S.24 into the expression for $\hat{p}$ in 11.S.15 to obtain:

$$\hat{p} = \frac{1}{\Delta} \{\epsilon + \epsilon^* - 1 - \bar{\eta} - e\}dt.$$

This can be simplified by noting that the elasticity of the home country's offer curve (as shown by 11.S.23) consists of the two substitution terms, $\bar{\eta}$ and e, plus the home marginal propensity to import. Therefore the solution for $\hat{p}$ is:

$$\hat{p} = \frac{1}{\Delta} \{\epsilon^* + m - 1\} dt. \tag{11.S.25}$$

The verbal argument in Chapter 11 suggested that a tariff could fail to protect if the foreign import demand elasticity, ϵ^*, were sufficiently small. Equation 11.S.25 reveals that the critical value for this elasticity is $(1 - m)$ or, more simply, the country's propensity to consume its export commodity.

Supplement to Chapter 12:
Tariffs, Growth, and Welfare

This supplement continues the algebraic analysis of tariffs initiated in the supplement to Chapter 11. It provides a formal proof of the fact that the maximum-revenue tariff rate exceeds the optimal rate. For a given degree of protection, a criterion is developed relating growth to welfare changes. Finally, a broader analysis of the tariff, making use of matrix algebra, allows an easy overview of the question of gains from trade and commercial policy.

The Maximum-Revenue Tariff

In the supplement to Chapter 11 we expressed the home country's budget constraint in terms of domestic prices (see equation 11.S.2). When differentiated, this expression led to an expression for the change in real income, in terms of the change in the domestic price ratio and the tariff revenue. This equation was 11.S.4, which is reproduced below as equation 12.S.1.

$$dy = -M dp + d(tp^*M). \tag{12.S.1}$$

Consider this expression in conjunction with Figure 12.1. The optimal tariff rate is t_0, and we know from the optimal tariff formula (equation 11.S.10) that near t_0 the foreign offer curve must be elastic. This means that the tariff must be "protective" in the sense of raising p with a small further increase in t. Thus the $-M dp$ term in 12.S.1 is negative in the neighborhood of the optimum tariff, where dy equals zero. As a consequence, $d(tp^*M)$ must be positive. That is, at rate t_0 in Figure 12.1 the curve plotting the tariff revenue against the tariff rate must be positively sloped. Tariff revenue reaches a maximum at the higher rate, t_2.

Growth with Protection

The supplement to Chapter 4 analyzed the possibility of *immiserizing growth* — a situation in which expansion of a country's production of exportables during the growth process causes such a deterioration in the terms of trade that the community's welfare actually falls. Worries of worsening terms of trade have sometimes been cited in support of protection for import-competing commodities. Such protection tends to erode the potential welfare gains from growth for a small country.

Examine here the case of a country with fixed tariff rates and given world prices. For some reason (growth of resources, improvement in technology) the country's transformation schedule shifts outward so that at the fixed domestic prices (given world prices adjusted for fixed tariff rates) aggregate output expands. The budget constraint is shown in 12.S.2:

$$D_C + p^*D_F = x_C + p^*x_F. \tag{12.S.2}$$

(This repeats 11.S.5). Differentiation leads to 12.S.3:

$$dD_C + p^*dD_F = dx_C + p^*dx_F. \tag{12.S.3}$$

Note that there is no terms-of-trade effect because p^* is assumed constant. Add and subtract pdD_F on the left-hand side:

$$(dD_C + pdD_F) + (p^* - p)dD_F = (dx_C + p^*dx_F).$$

The first bracketed expression is, of course, the change in home real income, dy. The change in home consumption of food, dD_F, can only be explained by income effects since domestic prices are constant. That is, with the home country's marginal propensity to import food denoted by m,

$$dD_F = \frac{m}{p}\, dy.$$

The fraction $(p^* - p)/p$ is minus $t/(1 + t)$ so that:

$$\left(1 - m\frac{t}{1 + t}\right) dy = (dx_C + p^*dx_F). \tag{12.S.4}$$

This expression provides the criterion with which to judge growth in a protected economy. Real income gains are registered only if growth results in a greater aggregate production *evaluated at world prices*. This may sound paradoxical. The criterion for judging an increase in welfare is to measure consumption changes at *domestic* prices. And yet production changes should be evaluated at *world* prices because world prices measure the trade-off between production and consumption (see equation 12.S.2). Figure 12.4 illustrated how various possibilities of output expansion from point A — points D, B, C, or E, all showing a 25 percent gain in output at domestic prices — resulted in different real income gains. For point E the value of output actually fell at world prices.

Tariffs, Gains from Trade, and Welfare: A General Analysis

We wish to compare welfare or real income of an economy in two situations, in which prices, quantities traded, and trade restrictions may differ by more than "a small amount." There is no restriction on the number of commodities produced or consumed at home or abroad. For notation we use x as the *vector* of quantities produced at home, D as the *vector* of quantities demanded or consumed, p as the *vector* of prices ruling in the home country, and p^* as the *vector* of prices ruling abroad.[1] Not all commodities need be produced at home, so that in the vector $x = (x_1, x_2, \ldots, x_n)$ some entries may be zero. Similarly, not all commodities produced need be demanded locally, so that in the vector $D = (D_1, D_2, \ldots, D_n)$ some entries may also be zero. The two situations we wish to compare are denoted by a single prime and a double prime. Thus in the initial situation home prices are given by the vector $p' = (p'_1, p'_2, \ldots, p'_n)$. This vector may or may not represent a situation in which some international trade takes place. In the second situation prices have altered at home to $p'' = (p''_1, p''_2, \ldots, p''_n)$. Let the vector E represent the home country's set of *excess demands*. Thus,

$$E \equiv D - x.$$

An element E_i in the vector E is positive if commodity i is imported at home, is negative if i is exported, and is zero if high transport costs or tariffs result in no international exchange of the ith commodity.

The basic criterion with which welfare in the double-prime situation is contrasted to welfare in the single-prime situation involves a comparison of the value of aggregate demand in each, when the prices used for the evaluation are in both instances those of the double-prime situation. Thus welfare is deemed to have risen if

$$p''D'' - p''D' > 0. \tag{12.S.5}$$

This inequality states that if the initial bundle of goods consumed (D') could have been purchased in the double-prime situation, the community is assumed to have increased its real income.

This assumption is illustrated for the two-commodity case in Figure 12.S.1. The fact that the consumption bundle in the single-prime situation, D', lies below the line showing prices in the double-prime situation (and supporting demand, D'') is taken as a sufficient criterion for establishing that point D'' represents a higher level of welfare. Clearly if indifference curves do not intersect, point D' must lie on a lower indifference curve than point D''.

The vector of excess demands equals the vector of total demands minus the vector of production. Turn this equation around to state that demand equals excess demand *plus* production. Making this substitution for both the single-prime and the double-prime situations in the improvement in welfare criterion, 12.S.5, yields the inequality in 12.S.6 as an equivalent expression:

$$p''(E'' - E') + p''(x'' - x') > 0. \tag{12.S.6}$$

Prices at home in the double-prime situation will differ from prices abroad for any traded commodity that is subject to a tariff, an export tax, or a subsidy in the home country. Let the matrix T'' represent these taxes and/or trade subsidies. T'' is a *diagonal matrix*, all of whose elements are zero except the diagonal terms. What does the entry t''_i represent? This depends on whether commodity i is imported (E_i positive), in which case a positive t''_i represents a

---

[1] The analysis in this section rests heavily upon Michihiro Ohyama, "Trade and Welfare in General Equilibrium." *Keio Economic Studies,* 1972.

FIGURE 12.S.1   The Welfare Criterion for Two Commodities

Two alternative consumption bundles are illustrated: D' and D''. The prices
ruling when D'' is consumed are shown by line p''. The welfare criterion
whereby situation double-prime is superior to situation single-prime is shown
by the fact that D' lies below line p'', which means $p''D'' - p''D' > 0$.

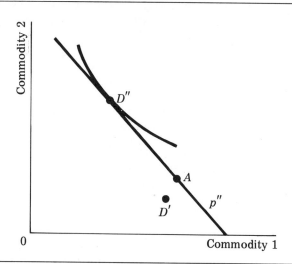

tariff and a negative t''_i an import subsidy, or exported (E_i negative), in which
case an export tax is a negative t''_i and an export subsidy a positive t''_i. In
short, $t''_i p^{*''}_i E''_i$ is positive if the government collects tax revenue and negative
if the government is subsidizing a trade flow. For any commodity, i,

$$p''_i = (1 + t''_i)p^{*''}_i,$$

where $p^{*''}_i$ is the world price of commodity i. This can be summarized in
matrix notation by making use of the identity matrix, I, whose off-diagonal
elements are all zero, and with "ones" all along the diagonal. Thus:

$$p'' = (I + T'')p^{*''}. \tag{12.S.7}$$

The home country's budget constraint states that the value at world prices
of aggregate excess demand is zero, both for the double-prime and single-
prime situations:

$$p^{*''}E'' = 0 \tag{12.S.8}$$

$$p^{*'}E' = 0. \tag{12.S.9}$$

Furthermore, if the single-prime situation refers to the pretrade situation at
home, each element of the vector E' would have to equal zero because in equilibrium local demand would have to be balanced by local sources of supply.
All the ingredients are now at hand to transform the welfare criterion,

12.S.6, into an explicit listing of the sources of an improvement in real incomes. To proceed we merely need to substitute the relationship shown in 12.S.7 between domestic and world prices into the first term in 12.S.6. Thus

$$p''(E'' - E') = (I + T'')p^{*''}(E'' - E').$$

This expression, in turn, equals

$$p^{*''}E'' - p^{*''}E' + T''p^{*''}(E'' - E').$$

But notice that by 12.S.8, $p^{*''}E''$ vanishes. This statement of the budget constraint at world prices applies as well to the single-prime situation (shown by equation 12.S.9), and thus allows us to add $p^{*'}E'$ (equal to zero) to the expression above. Thus rewritten it becomes

$$-(p^{*''} - p^{*'})E' + T''p^{*''}(E'' - E').$$

Substitute this expression for $p''(E'' - E')$ back into 12.S.6 to obtain 12.S.10 as the basic welfare criterion:

$$-(p^{*''} - p^{*'})E' + T''p^{*''}(E'' - E') + p''(x'' - x') > 0. \tag{12.S.10}$$

Each of the three terms in 12.S.10 should be familiar from our earlier discussion:

1. The term $-(p^{*''} - p^{*'})E'$ is the terms-of-trade effect. If the two primed situations represent different trading equilibria very close to each other, and if only one relative price (because only two commodities) exists, it is shown by the $-Mdp^*$ term in 11.S.6. Our general expression states that the community's welfare improves to the extent that the world price falls for any commodity imported ($E'_i > 0$), or rises for any commodity exported ($E'_i < 0$).

2. The term $T''p^{*''}(E'' - E')$ measures the change in the volume of trade for all commodities for which domestic prices, p'', differ from world prices, $p^{*''}$. The term $T''p^{*''}$ is the tariff wedge. Returning again to the case in which only two commodities are traded, and the two situations are very close to each other, this term reduces to the $(p - p^*)dM$ term in equation 11.S.6. It states in general that real income is improved if the level of imports rises for any commodity worth more at home (as indicated by p'') than it costs to obtain in world markets (as indicated by $p^{*''}$).

3. The term $p''(x'' - x')$ must in any case be greater than or equal to zero. It shows the change in real income attributable to the change in production. In the absence of distortions, x'' is the point on the transformation schedule that maximizes the value of output at domestic prices when these are given by p''. Therefore the value of any other production possibility, say x', at these prices p'' must be less. If the single-prime and double-prime situations are very close together in the two-commodity model, this term reduces to $dx_C + pdx_F$. As we argued in Chapter 3 and subsequently, this reduction approaches zero as an expression of the equality between the domestic price ratio and the slope of the transformation schedule.

This line of reasoning has been useful in comparing two states of trade, differing from each other in prices — perhaps as a result of changes in tariffs. It is also useful in comparing a state of trade (in the double-prime situation) with the pretrade situation. In such a case each element in the vector E' goes to zero. The welfare criterion, 12.S.10, then assumes the special form:

$$T''p^{*''}E'' + p''(x'' - x') > 0. \qquad (12.S.11)$$

Because the production term, $p''(x'' - x')$, must be non-negative, as we have just argued, this criterion yields a powerful result. Suppose that a complex mixture of tariffs and trade subsidies exists. Is the community better off than with no trade? The question needs to be raised because an export subsidy by itself can reduce welfare at home — this is akin to giving something away. The term $T''p^{*''}E''$ represents the *net* tariff-and-subsidy revenue to the home government. The criterion reveals that regardless of the pattern of subsidies, if this *net* revenue is positive, trade must be superior to no trade.[2] Note that it is *sufficient* for the double-prime situation to represent an improvement that the *net* revenue be positive. However, even if it is negative, it is possible for D'' to be preferred to D'.

Supplement to Chapter 21: Unifying Themes in Adjustment Processes

Two key assumptions distinguish the first three parts of this book, dealing with the pure theory and applications of international trade, from the discussion in Part 4 of adjustment processes in an open economy. The first of these is that all commodity and factor markets "clear" — that relative prices adjust in each and every market so that an equilibrium balance between supply and demand prevails. The second assumption characterizing earlier sections of the book is that all incomes earned in production are spent. With such a classical form of the budget constraint, quantities intended for export always balance intended import demand. Money, whether domestic currency or foreign exchange, serves merely as a convenient veil since no hoarding or running down of money or other assets is allowed. We begin this supplement by showing how a violation of either or both of these assumptions can lead to a balance-of-trade deficit or surplus.

Trade Deficits: Alternative Interpretations

Distinguish three categories of commodities: exportables (X), importables (M), and nontraded commodities (N). Let D_i represent demand, x_i production, p_i price. Then the community's overall excess (E) of spending over the value of currently produced income can be defined as in 21.S.1.

$$E \equiv p_x(D_X - x_X) + p_M(D_M - x_M) + p_N(D_N - x_N). \qquad (21.S.1)$$

Since demand for importables, D_M, exceeds the quantity locally produced, x_M,

---

[2] This result is attributable to Ohyama, "Trade and Welfare in General Equilibrium."

suppose that no inventories of importables are kept at home. That is, all local production is sold locally, and foreign sources provide any excess (call it M) between local demand (D_M) and supply (x_M). Exportables differ in that local demand (D_X) accounts for only a fraction of production (x_X). If world commodity markets clear, all intended exports, ($x_X - D_X$), are sold abroad and represent actual exports, X. Alternatively, the export market may *not* clear, in which case some inventory accumulation (positive I_X) or decumulation (negative I_X) takes place. That is, letting I_X denote the value of unintended inventory accumulation of exportables, and X represent actual quantity of exports, I_X is given by 21.S.2:

$$I_X \equiv p_X(x_X - D_X) - p_X X. \tag{21.S.2}$$

I_X is the value of the excess of produced exportables over sales, both locally and abroad.

A similar procedure can be used to define the value of unintended inventory accumulation or decumulation for nontradable commodities, except that with no foreign source or outlet available (by definition), I_N can be expressed as:

$$I_N \equiv p_N(x_N - D_N). \tag{21.S.3}$$

Finally, define the value of the trade *deficit* as B,

$$B \equiv p_M M - p_N X, \tag{21.S.4}$$

so that by substituting 21.S.2, 21.S.3, and the equality of M with excess demand for importables into 21.S.1, we emerge with the basic relationship between the trade deficit, aggregate overspending, and inventory accumulation shown by 21.S.5:[1]

$$B = E + \{I_X + I_N\}. \tag{21.S.5}$$

A trade deficit is a reflection of the community's spending more on all tradables than it produces. There are two "pure" sources for such a deficit. On the one hand the community could be planning to spend overall exactly the value of what it produces (i.e., E is zero), but not succeeding in selling all it plans at home or abroad so that the trade deficit (excess of spending on tradables) matches unintended lack of sales abroad (I_X) or of sales for the home market (I_N). The excess of spending on importables is reflected in the pileup of unsold commodities, $I_X + I_N$. In contrast to this case, suppose all relative prices are flexibly doing their duty, so that no unintended inventory changes occur. Then a trade deficit must reflect an *aggregate* spending level exceeding the value of produced income. For the first source of a deficit it is the *composition* of spending and production in various sectors that is out of line. For the second, the deficit reflects aggregate *overspending*. A deficit of the first type

---

[1] Compare with the basic national income relationship cited in Chapter 16, $X - M = S - I$. Break down investment, I, into intended accumulation of plant and equipment and unintended inventory accumulation. The excess of savings over intended investment is what we call minus E, while the $X - M$ in Chapter 16 is now our minus B.

FIGURE 21.S.1 The Income-Expenditure Relationship

The discrepancy between income and expenditure (hoarding) can be linked to a key variable u, which can be variously interpreted as national income, the interest rate, the price level, or the exchange rate.

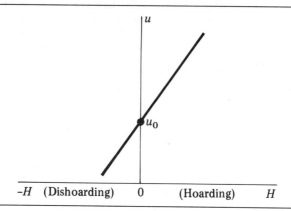

calls for remedial changes in relative prices. A deficit of the second type can be cured only by cutting back spending in relation to income.

The appropriateness of exchange-rate changes is often cited in cases in which domestic prices seem stuck at "too high" a level vis-à-vis foreign prices in the sense that exports are not selling as well as desired and, in general, sales of nontradables are not matching local production. (Alternatively phrased, importables are too cheap.) The exchange market pictured in Figure 15.1a illustrates that a deficit at some exchange rate (e.g., $1.80 per £) could be cured by raising the rate to a higher level (e.g., $2.00 per £). Such a view relies heavily on the underlying assumption that prices are sticky and markets are out of line. Furthermore, if prices *are* sticky, exchange-rate changes can in general only change prices of broad classes of importables in relation to exportables or nontradables.[2] We cannot rely on an exchange-rate change simultaneously to clear a myriad of individual markets with sticky prices. If prices are flexible, exchange-rate changes or other devices can alter the trade balance only by affecting E, the excess of aggregate spending over produced incomes.

Hoarding and the Adjustment Process

If all commodity markets clear, as we shall now assume, a country's balance of trade surplus is a reflection of its underspending, or excess of savings over planned investment, or what we shall call *hoarding, H*. To understand trade

[2] In the "small-country" case a devaluation can only serve to raise the prices of all tradables by the same relative amount. See Figure 18.A.1 and the appendix to Chapter 18 for an account of exchange-rate changes in this context.

balances it is useful to ask about the determinants of a nation's aggregate level of hoarding.[3]

Several alternative theories describing spending and hoarding behavior and the adjustment process in the balance of payments were elaborated in Part 4. These theories differed from each other in several respects. In some theories prices were sticky and unemployment prevailed. In others adjustment highlighted price changes or changes in exchange rates. However, several unifying themes ran through them all:

1. In each theory a key economic variable is singled out as the major determinant of the nation's hoarding behavior. In Keynesian models this variable is national income. Alternative models stress other variables: the price level, or interest rates, or the exchange rate. Whatever the model, denote this key variable by u. The assumption that hoarding depends upon u can be captured by equation 21.S.6 and by Figure 21.S.1.

$$H = H(u), \qquad \text{with } H'(u) > 0. \tag{21.S.6}$$

For high values of u the community earns more than it spends — hoarding is positive — whereas for low values of u the community dishoards.

2. In each theory a further relationship is required in order to establish the equilibrium value of u. For trading communities this extra relationship should contain information about foreign behavior, e.g., foreign demand for the home country's exports. In any event, in Figure 21.S.2 we show schematically a downward-sloping schedule, which intersects the hoarding schedule at point A, leading to the equilibrium value for u of OC. Distance AC shows the country's equilibrium level of hoarding, or excess of income over expenditures, which equals its export surplus (or balance on current account).

3. The existence of a trade deficit or surplus in a short-run equilibrium implies that the nation's level (and/or composition) of assets is changing through time. For example, a current account export surplus might be matched by an accumulation of reserves. These changes might be expected to shift one or both of the schedules shown in Figure 21.S.2 until a long-run equilibrium is established with balanced trade. (That is, the schedules shift until they intersect on the vertical axis.)

Consider how these simple themes are revealed in the various cases that were described in Chapters 15 through 21. Each case focused on a different interpretation for the key variable u.

National Income. Keynesian analysis stresses a positive relationship between a community's aggregate savings and the level of national income.

---

[3] Looking at the trade balance this way corresponds to Sidney Alexander's conception of the "absorption approach." See his "Effects of a Devaluation on a Trade Balance," *IMF Staff Papers* (April 1952), Vol. II: 263–78, reprinted in Caves, Johnson, eds., *Readings in International Economics*. Homewood, Ill.: Irwin, 1968, pp. 359–73. Note that even with sticky prices (Keynesian unemployment), commodity markets may clear — with production cut to match demand. Our use of the word "hoarding" differs from others in which hoarding refers to the net accumulation of money. In our discussion hoarding refers to the net accumulation of all assets other than planned real capital (investment). Thus it includes foreign bonds and stocks in addition to money.

FIGURE 21.S.2   Short-Run Equilibrium

The short-run equilibrium value of hoarding (or the trade surplus), CA, and
the value of key variable u, OC, is determined by the intersection of the
hoarding schedule, $H(u)$, and some other relationship between the trade
account and key variable u. This other relationship is described in subsequent
diagrams.

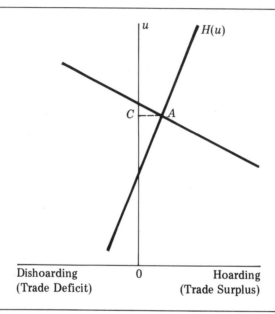

High-income communities save; low-income communities may attempt to dis-
save. A dollar increase in national income would flow partly into savings,
partly into consumption. In the simple version of the Keynesian model, investment is treated as autonomous, so that the positive slope of the H schedule reflects only savings behavior.

The basic statement of hoarding behavior in a Keynesian model suggests
that the higher a nation's income, the greater its excess of savings over investment and, therefore, the greater the trade surplus. However, a different interpretation is more frequently cited: higher income levels encourage higher
levels of import spending with no commensurate increase in exports (which
depend upon *foreign* income levels). That is, higher incomes lead to increased
trade deficits. The apparent contradiction in this pair of remarks is dissolved
once you notice that in a Keynesian model the value of national income is determined by the intersection of the $H(u)$ schedule (where u is national income, Y) with the trade balance schedule showing exports (X) minus imports
(M). As Figure 21.S.3 illustrates, equilibrium income level Y_0 balances the
trade surplus with the nation's excess of savings over investment. Higher
equilibrium levels than Y_0 can be achieved if either (1) the $X - M$ schedule
shifts to the right (greater foreign demand for the nation's exports or lower im-

FIGURE 21.S.3 Income Determination in a Keynesian Model

In a Keynesian model, national income is the key variable affecting hoarding. The equilibrium value of $u = Y =$ national income is determined by the intersection of the hoarding schedule and the trade balance schedule.

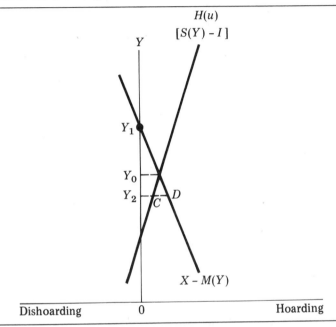

port demand at any income level), or (2) the $S - I$ schedule shifts to the left (less hoarding at any income level). In case (1) the trade surplus is indeed increased as hoarding rises along a given $H(Y)$ schedule. In case (2) the trade surplus deteriorates with growth as increased incomes increase imports along the given import schedule.[4]

In Chapter 16 we had occasion to observe that an equilibrium such as Y_0 in Figure 21.S.3 may only be temporary, as it reflects a trade surplus that would (let us assume) be balanced by an increase in the nation's foreign exchange reserves. One consequence of this increase in a nation's monetary base could, in a Keynesian model, be a lowering of interest rates, which encourages investment. According to this extension of our argument, the hoarding schedule would shift to the left (as I increases) as long as the trade surplus, and the

---

[4] Figure 21.S.3 corresponds to Figure 16.2 in the text. Note that if income is *not* at equilibrium level Y_0, the relationship among the trade surplus, hoarding, and unplanned inventory changes shown by equation 21.S.5 can be illustrated in Figure 21.S.3. For example, at income level Y_2 the trade surplus, Y_2D, exceeds the community's level of hoarding, Y_2C, by distance CD. CD represents the extent to which inventories are being run down at home in order to supply foreign demand for home goods.

resultant downward pressure on the interest rate, persists. In Figure 21.S.3 incomes would rise until the hoarding and trade balance schedules intersect at Y_1.

Interest Rates. A somewhat different set of circumstances allows the interest rate to assume key importance as the variable, u, determining hoarding. Suppose prices are flexible and the full-employment level of income is maintained. But now let savings (as well as investment) vary depending upon the rate of interest, i. Investment spending may be encouraged by a lowering of the interest rate and savings by a rise, so that the hoarding schedule is positively sloped as in Figure 21.S.1, with $u =$ interest rate.

In a world in which capital funds are highly mobile internationally, we can envisage a common world interest rate being determined by the balancing of one country's desire to hoard with other countries' desire to dishoard. Lump the rest of the world together and show by the $-H^*(i)$ schedule in Figure 21.S.4 the *dis*hoarding that foreigners would undertake at any given interest rate. At interest rate i_0, the home country's trade surplus represents a loan to the rest of the world to support their trade deficit (of amount OB^*). Two polar extremes could also be shown. The small-country case (with the home country small) is shown by a horizontal $-H^*$ schedule at prevailing world interest rates. The home country lends or borrows at this rate as befits its hoarding propensities. Toward the other extreme the home country becomes very large relative to the rest of the world as the $-H^*(i)$ schedule approaches the vertical axis. At the extreme in which the home country represents the entire world, its interest rate assumes its closed economy value, i_1.

FIGURE 21.S.4   The Interest Rate in a World Capital Market

The common interest rate in a world of international capital mobility could balance home hoarding (trade surplus) with foreign borrowing (foreign trade deficit, OB^*).

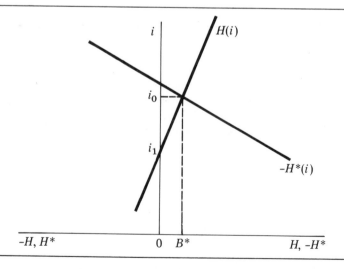

The short-run equilibrium with surplus OB^* in Figure 21.S.4 could not be expected to prevail indefinitely. As the home country accumulates foreign assets, its $H(i)$ schedule will shift to the left. Abroad, foreign attempts to borrow will be curtailed — the $-H^*(i)$ schedule would also shift to the left. If loans are repaid, the short-run equilibrium point would lie to the left of the i-axis, and the home country would be able to finance a trade deficit.

Price Levels. A more subtle theory describing hoarding behavior links the amount of underspending or overspending to the state of *disequilibrium* in a nation's asset markets. Consider here only the simple case in which money is the only asset. At any moment the nation has a given supply of money. Its demand for money is based, say, upon its level of planned expenditures or upon the money value of national income.[5] If this demand exceeds the existing supply, individuals will attempt to hoard — to abstain from spending all their income in order to accumulate funds and thus to raise the supply of money to the higher level demanded. Alternatively, an excess supply of funds can be "worked down" by an excess of spending over income. Individuals and communities may differ in the *rate* at which they wish to hoard or dishoard in an attempt to bring the money market back into equilibrium.[6]

Suppose, now, that prices are flexible, full employment is maintained, and the world's currencies are locked together by fixed exchange rates. From a position of initial equilibrium, a rise in the world price level would cause a community to hoard as the demand for money rises. That is, Figure 21.S.1 can now be interpreted as a schedule showing hoarding rising with increases in the price level assuming a given stock of money.

Figure 21.S.5 depicts the small-country case in which initial long-run equilibrium price level, P_0, is determined by the price level in the rest of the world. Now suppose a monetary expansion abroad raises this price level — this is shown by the upward shift in the horizontal schedule to level P_1. The local money market is thrown out of equilibrium; the higher price level encourages hoarding at home at rate P_1A. This implies a balance of trade surplus of the same amount. With money assumed to represent the only asset, reserves pile up at home and this serves to shift (over time) the hoarding schedule leftward until the surplus is eliminated (when $H(P)$ intersects the horizontal world price line at point P_1).

This small-country version represents one extreme. The other extreme

[5] Many writers have national income as the crucial variable determining the demand for money. For an argument supporting expenditure levels, instead, as the key variable in the money demand equation for an *open* economy see R. W. Jones, "Monetary and Fiscal Policy for an Economy with Fixed Exchange Rates," *Journal of Political Economy,* 76 (July/August 1968), part 2: 921–43.

[6] This simple account deliberately ignores the complexities introduced by the existence of bonds and other assets. In a more complex world hoarding can still be linked to the desire to accumulate wealth (over and above real capital equipment). The new dimension that is added to the analysis is the concern with the *composition* of asset holdings. For further remarks see, for example, R. Dornbusch, "A Portfolio Balance Model of the Open Economy," *Journal of Monetary Economics* (January 1975), or R. W. Jones, "Portfolio Balance and International Payments Adjustment: Comment," in Mundell, Swoboda, eds., *Monetary Problems of the International Economy.* Chicago: University of Chicago Press, 1969, pp. 251–56.

FIGURE 21.S.5   Hoarding and the Price Level

From initial equilibrium in asset markets at P_0 (with zero hoarding), suppose
the world price level rises to P_1. The community cuts its spending below
income levels to accumulate extra monetary reserves. As money flows in, the
$H(P)$ schedule shifts leftward until it intersects the P axis at P_1.

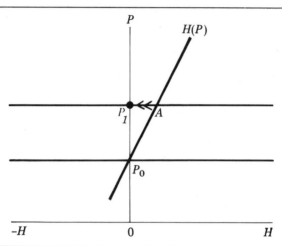

shows the home country in isolation — cut off from trade with the rest of the
world. In such a case, the country's price level, P, is shown by the intersection
of its hoarding schedule, $H(P)$, with the *vertical* P-axis. A country in isolation cannot balance its excess of production over spending by exports to other
countries. The "large-country" case, in which the country is engaged in trade
and has some influence on the price level, was discussed in Chapter 17. As
suggested there, the world price level is determined by the intersection of the
home country's positively sloped $H(P)$ schedule and the rest of the world's
negatively sloped dishoarding schedule. (The diagram would resemble Figure
21.S.4 except with the price level replacing the interest rate as the key variable, u, determining hoarding.) The existence of a trade surplus or deficit
would then cause a reallocation of the world's monetary reserves, so that
the schedules would shift until long-run equilibrium is established along the
P-axis.[7]

Exchange Rates. A variation of this theory allows a nation's exchange rate
to change in a world in which, for simplicity, foreign prices of traded commodities are assumed fixed. In this small-country case a devaluation of the

[7] The basic diagrams are found in R. Dornbusch, "Devaluation, Money, and Nontraded Goods," *American Economic Review*, December 1973 (LXIII, 5): 871–80.
Note that both in this case and in the Keynesian case the crucial variable, u,
could be considered the money value of the national income, Y. In the Keynesian
case the price level was fixed, so Y would rise only if real output and employment
rise. If full employment is maintained, an increase in Y is matched by (caused by)
a proportional increase in the price level, P.

exchange rate causes a rise in the price level at home. Using the same argument as previously, let key variable u in Figure 21.S.1 now represent the exchange rate. Devaluation from rate u_0 and a rise in the price level leads to initial positive hoarding. The consequent trade surplus causes local reserves to be built up, shifting the hoarding schedule leftward until eventually equilibrium (at the higher exchange rate) is reestablished.

We turn now to a pair of examples that combine monetary and real influences. The first of these involves a more elaborate description of exchange-rate changes for a small country producing tradables and nontradables.

Monetary and Real Factors Combined: Devaluation

The monetary approach to exchange-rate adjustments, described above, can easily be extended to introduce the real influence on demands and resource allocation of a change in relative prices. We start with the small-country case, in which world prices of all tradable commodities are given and not subject to influence by the small country's policies. Initial equilibrium is shown at point A in Figure 21.S.6, at which local demand and production for nontradables is in balance and, as well, the aggregate value of production of all tradables equals the consumption of all tradables. This implies that exports and imports

---

FIGURE 21.S.6 Devaluation and Relative Prices

Initial balanced trade equilibrium at A is disturbed by the small country's devaluation. Reduced value of cash balances shifts the spending line inward and lowers the relative price of nontradables. Devaluation creates a (temporary) trade surplus of amount BC.

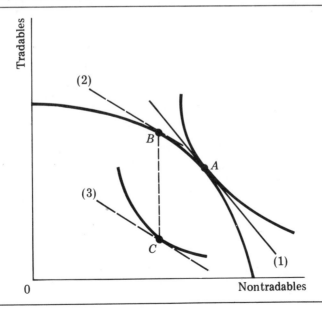

FIGURE 21.S.7   Devaluation and the Market for Nontradables

The devaluation shifts the demand curve to the left as the rise in the price
level encourages hoarding. The relative price of nontradables must fall to
clear the market.

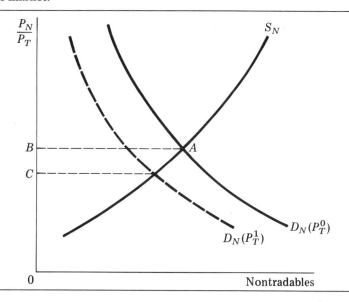

have the same value.[8] The price of nontradables relative to tradables is shown
by the slope of line 1.

When the small country devalues its exchange rate, the absolute prices of
all tradables rise in the same proportion. But what happens to the price of
nontradables? It may either rise or fall, but the monetary theory of devaluation ensures that the *relative* price of nontradables falls. Figure 21.S.7 will
confirm this. But first note the impact of the devaluation on spending, production, and the trade balance in Figure 21.S.6. The rise in the relative price of
tradables encourages a release of resources toward both importables and exportables — the move from A to B. The monetary argument, whereby the
higher price level associated with the devaluation encourages temporary hoarding, shifts the spending line inward to line 3. Lines 2 and 3 are parallel —
both indicating the new lower relative price of nontradables that is required
to match demand and supply for nontradables: Production (at B) and consumption (at C) are equal. But the devaluation has created a temporary
trade surplus of amount BC.

Figure 21.S.7 focuses on price determination in the market for nontradables.
Assuming full employment is maintained, the upward-sloping supply curve,
S_N, is derived from the transformation curve in Figure 21.S.6: Greater pro-

---

[8] The use of transformation curves and indifference curves to illustrate equilibrium
with nontraded goods was discussed in Chapters 5 and 18. See especially Figure
18.A.1.

duction is called forth at higher relative prices. Devaluation does not alter the supply relationship. But a rise in the exchange rate does shift the demand curve. This is the monetary effect of a rise in the price of tradable goods (from P_T^0 to P_T^1). At any given relative price (e.g., initial OB) the higher price level reduces demand for all commodities. Thus the D_N curve shifts leftward. The market for nontradables clears at price OC, which corresponds to the slope of lines 2 and 3 in Figure 21.S.6. As monetary reserves are built up through the trade surplus, the D_N curve shifts back toward its initial position. In the long run, devaluation raises the price of nontradables by the same proportional amount as the devaluation.[9]

The large-country case is more complicated because the prices of tradables may not rise by the full extent of the devaluation and the terms of trade may change. This invalidates the use in Figure 21.S.6 of a composite traded commodity. Nonetheless, the preceding analysis for the small-country case sets the stage in asking how the home country's reduction in demands for exportables and importables at initial terms of trade matches the foreign country's rise in demands as their spending is allowed to increase with the increased real value of their cash balances. The problem is that of a *transfer* of spending from one country to another. The simple lines of analysis were discussed in Chapter 4.[10]

Monetary and Real Factors Combined: The Oil Crisis

A simple monetary account of a country's reaction to a deterioration in the terms of trade — such as that encountered by most countries when the price of oil quadrupled in the early 1970's — might at first glance seem surprising. Suppose we take the small-country case and let the price of exportables remain constant. The rise in the price of importables raises the price level, and encourages hoarding. The story seems similar to that of devaluation — hoarding leads to a trade surplus. But the outcome sounds odd: Countries hit by the rise in oil prices running trade surpluses!

This account is unfair to the monetary approach because it neglects a crucial difference between a terms-of-trade deterioration and a devaluation for a small country. The terms-of-trade deterioration causes local real incomes to fall, and according to the monetary view a fall in real incomes induces a de-

---

[9] The absolute price of nontradables may or may not fall in the short run. More details are provided in R. Dornbusch, op. cit. For an account of devaluation with rigidities in prices, see R. W. Jones and W. M. Corden, "Devaluation, Non-flexible Prices, and the Trade Balance for a Small Country," *Canadian Journal of Economics,* February 1976: 150–61. An analysis of devaluation when there is temporary sluggishness in wage response, thus introducing unemployment possibilities, is found in K. Noman and R. W. Jones, "A Model of Trade and Unemployment," in J. Green and J. Scheinkman, eds., *General Equilibrium, Growth, and Trade.* New York: Academic Press, 1979, 297–322.

[10] Nontraded goods complicate the analysis. A general discussion of transfer with nontraded goods is found in R. W. Jones, "Presumption and the Transfer Problem." *Journal of International Economics,* August 1975, (5, 3): 263–74, reprinted as chapter 10 in *International Trade: Essays in Theory.* Amsterdam: North-Holland, 1979.

cline in monetary demand. This effect works counter to the price level effect.

These two effects can be combined if we assume the demand for money, Z, is proportional to the money value of incomes. This latter figure is a composite of the price level, P, and the level of *real income*, y. Thus,

$$Z = k \cdot P \cdot y. \tag{21.S.7}$$

Taking relative changes,

$$\hat{Z} = \hat{P} + \hat{y}. \tag{21.S.8}$$

The change in real income depends on the terms of trade.[11]

$$\hat{y} = -\frac{p_M M}{Y} \cdot \hat{p}_M. \tag{21.S.9}$$

If the price of imports rises by 50 percent and imports represent 10 percent of the national income, real incomes are reduced by 5 percent. The change in the price level depends on the changes in prices of importables ($\hat{p}_M$), exportables (which we assume do not change in price) and nontradables (which we neglect). Thus,

$$\hat{P} = \frac{p_M D_M}{Y} \hat{p}_M. \tag{21.S.10}$$

If the price of importables rises by 50 percent and consumption of importables constitutes 20 percent of total spending (or incomes), the price level rises by 10 percent. Combine 21.S.10 for $\hat{P}$ and 21.S.9 for $\hat{y}$ to obtain:

$$\hat{Z} = \frac{p_M x_M}{Y} \hat{p}_M. \tag{21.S.11}$$

If the nation produces any oil (or whatever the importable is that has gone up in price), the terms-of-trade deterioration serves to *raise* the demand for money. It still seems to be the case that the oil importers should meet the price rise by running surpluses on the trade account!

Two further comments can serve to turn this result around to square more readily with observed trade deficits run by oil-importing countries. First, many countries responded with increases in their local money supplies. If the money supply is raised in excess of 21.S.11's rise in money demand, the monetary approach predicts a trade deficit. Viewed in somewhat different terms, many countries hit by the deterioration in their terms of trade refused to allow the reduction in real incomes to be translated immediately into reduced real spending. That is, they overspent — relying on borrowing and reserve losses to resist the cuts in real spending suggested by the rise in import prices.

The second comment is more intricate. The analysis leading up to 21.S.11 suggested a (somewhat paradoxical) surplus for oil-importing countries since the impact of the higher price level in increasing monetary demands outweighed the effect of the real income loss in reducing the demand for money. But what about oil-exporting nations? Their real incomes have risen. Both the price level effect and the real income effect point in the same direction —

---

[11] See the supplement to Chapter 4.

toward an increase in the demand for money. That is, this logic suggests that they *also* would run trade surpluses. But not all countries can be in surplus!

The difficulty is that if the world's supply of money is really kept constant (which it most definitely was not in the early 1970's), the world's price level could not rise. The increase in oil prices would have to be matched by reductions in other prices.[12] This suggests our asking what the monetary theory would predict if the price of oil went up and other prices fell so as to keep the world price level constant but nonetheless retain the terms-of-trade effects that were so evident during the oil crisis. Now a plausible scenario emerges from the monetary theory. With reference to 21.S.8's relationship with the world price *level* now constant, the demand for money would fall in those countries that are net importers of oil, because real incomes would fall. These countries would thus tend to overspend — running trade deficits to match the trade surpluses created in oil-exporting countries. Note how the monetary theory thus describes how the real income redistribution among nations called forth by changes in terms of trade gets *moderated* in its impact on current real expenditure levels. The losers run temporary deficits and the gainers surpluses.[13]

Concluding Remarks: Stocks, Flows, and Exchange Rates

The preceding discussion of balance-of-trade deficits and the income-expenditure relationship has emphasized the *flow* dimensions of the adjustment mechanisms. Imports, exports, incomes, and expenditures are each measured by values per unit of time. For example, it is suggested that if a country decides to spend more than its income, and if no special provisions are made for foreign loans in anticipation of this, pressure would develop to depreciate that country's currency. But, as Chapter 19 has emphasized, a nation's exchange rate is determined in a stock market. Overnight a speculative switch out of dollars into deutsche marks or Swiss francs can bring considerable pressure on the exchange market. (German banks, leaning against the winds in 1973, learned this to their horror, and capital loss, as they tried to support the deutsche mark against a revaluation.) Shifts like this may not even be picked up by a country's balance-of-payments statistics: French businesses dumping Euro-dollars on exchange markets (picked up, say, by Swiss banks) can alter the dollar/franc ratio even though no entry is made in the U.S. balance of payments.

These remarks also serve to emphasize the usefulness of trade and adjustment models in which each country holds more than one asset. Switches out of bonds into money, or out of one currency into another, have potentials for size and speed not adequately captured by the slower process of asset accumulation and decumulation over time.

[12] Alternatively, real output declines could serve as well to reduce some countries' demands for money balances.
[13] This account is based on R. W. Jones, "Terms of Trade and Transfers: The Relevance of the Literature," in *The International Monetary System and the Developing Nations*. AID, Department of State, 1976, reprinted as chapter 11 in *International Trade: Essays in Theory*. Amsterdam: North-Holland, 1979.

Index